Denis O'Driscoll

A HISTORY OF EDUCATION

A Social Interpretation

JAMES MULHERN
PROFESSOR OF EDUCATION
UNIVERSITY OF PENNSYLVANIA

Second Edition

THE RONALD PRESS COMPANY · NEW YORK

7MP

Library of Congress Catalog Card Number: 59–6107

PRINTED IN THE UNITED STATES OF AMERICA

Preface

This book is the outcome of courses in the history of education, comparative education, and philosophy of education taught at the University of Pennsylvania for the past thirty years. It aims to present in concise form the historical foundations of modern education, with a view to meeting the needs of students enrolled in courses in the history of education.

It does not view education as embracing only pedagogical theories and practices, isolated from their social setting. It views it, rather, as an aspect of the total cultural scene in the societies and historical periods with which it deals. Formal education is examined as a product of the economic, social, political, religious, moral, and intellectual factors which determined its forms from society to society and from period to period. And, in recording events, the relation of social evolution to educational change, both theoretical and practical, is always kept in mind.

In examining education as a cultural phenomenon, three clearly differentiated types of society—primitive, Oriental, and Western—are discussed. While Westerners have viewed Minerva as a Western deity, the wisdom of the Orient and of preliterate peoples should, in the changing modern world, be accorded respect. Wisdom has never been either societal or geographical. The West has not had a monopoly of it.

While we may question the practice of ignoring, in teacher-education courses, minds and ways other than our own, the largest portion of this book, in keeping with current thought and demand, is devoted to Western society and Western education. However, much more than the usual amount of space is given to primitive and Oriental societies. Where the time allotted to courses in the history of education is limited, the teacher may omit the earlier chapters and use that larger part of the book which deals with Western social and educational history.

In reconstructing our educational past, an attempt has been made to strike a balance between formal educational practices and the informal education which is derived from life and cultural conditioning. It is impossible to reconstruct in detail, within the limited scope of a single volume, the cultural scene and the ways of life of a variety of societies over a long sweep of history. It is hoped, however, that what is presented will reveal the significance of informal education in the building and preservation of societies and in shaping the world of today. To acquire a broader knowledge both of formal and informal education, wide reading is essential. In the footnotes, and in the list of selected readings appended to each chapter, the student will find some valuable sources of that broader knowledge.

There are offered, throughout this book, sometimes implicitly and sometimes explicitly, interpretations and evaluations of ideals and institutions. This has not been done in a spirit of finality. Meanings in history, as in other sciences, are difficult to discover. Those suggested here are designed to challenge the reader's thinking, not to determine it. It is better to be wrong in our quest for meanings than not to seek meanings at all.

Among the many new features of this Second Edition are a fuller treatment of Graeco-Roman culture and education; a new and more comprehensive treatment of mediaeval society and its educational practices; a more extensive examination of educational theory and practice in Europe and America in post-Renaissance and post-Reformation times; a new chapter on the history of American education, of special importance for students; and an account of recent educational developments in Europe and in the Soviet Union.

I am under a heavy debt to many writers and associates. I have profited by the labors and scholarship of many specialists in history and its related fields, whose ideas and, perhaps, phrases have become part of my own thinking and expression. Many of these persons must remain nameless, since the sources of one's own thoughts are often forgotten. My indebtedness to some of the unforgotten ones is acknowledged in footnotes and elsewhere.

Among the specialists in the history of education to whose writings I am indebted are Arrowood, Boyd, Brubacher, Butts, Cremin, Cubberley, Drake, Eby, Edwards, Good, Graves, Kandel, Knight, Meyer, Monroe, Noble, Reisner, Richey, Ulich, Wilds, and Woody. To the last, Thomas Woody, my teacher and long-time colleague, I owe a debt which can never be adequately acknowledged.

Miss Jeannette Weiss patiently checked and rechecked all footnotes and references and typed and retyped the manuscript. The uniform orderliness of the documentation and organization is due in large measure to her patience and her care.

Lastly, I am deeply indebted to my wife, Maud, for her constant encouragement during long periods of work, and for her tireless assistance in reading proofs and preparing the index.

James Mulhern

Philadelphia, Pennsylvania
March, 1959

Contents

Contents

Part I

INTRODUCTION

1 The Point of View

History is the story of man's achievements since he first began to keep written records, a period of about 7,000 years. With the millennia which preceded the period of recorded events, the historian, as such, does not deal. The events of the prehistoric period fall within the scope of archaeology, anthropology, and their allied fields. The historian, however, uses the findings of these disciplines.

It has been customary for historians to divide the whole historical period in the West into ancient, mediaeval, and modern. Such a division, while convenient, has no adequate basis in the facts of history. There is no exact date which marks the end of the ancient world and the beginning of the so-called mediaeval period; nor is there any exact date which marks the end of the Middle Ages and the beginning of modern times. No "law" of history is so well established as the law of unbroken continuity.

Education and Social Change

The present volume deals with the relation of education to evolving society from primitive to modern times. Ignoring the customary divisions, however useful they may be for purposes of general history, the present volume will deal with the culturally differentiated societies usually referred to as primitive, Oriental, and Western. Each one of these has its own distinctive social and educational characteristics, and each of them, although changed by the hand of time, still survives. Change, sometimes rapid, sometimes slow, has been a mark of them all.

The story of man has been one of struggle, a struggle against the world and against men. At any stage in the struggle the final outcome has never been certain, and seldom perhaps foreseen. Indeed, the most significant results of men's acts have often been the opposite of those that were intended. A war, for instance, fought "to make the world safe for democracy" hastened, if it did not produce, the totalitarian systems of our own time. The world as it is today in its economic, social, political, religious, moral, intellectual, and educational aspects is the result of the struggles of the past. And the struggles still go on. By all of them education has been affected. Everywhere, its chief function has been that of preserver of existing institutions, institutions sometimes static and sometimes progressive, but formal education did not usually perform that function well.

Origin and Nature of Institutions

Embodied in every social institution there is an ideology, a conception of values, a fear, a thirst for power or some other spiritual element. Some of these are biological in origin, but most of them have their roots in the physical and cultural environment. In different environments men's ideas, attitudes, and sense of values differ. The chief differences between men and their modes of behavior are rooted in culture rather than in human nature, for human nature is essentially the same everywhere. These spiritual possessions which, for convenience, we may call mind, are often the product not of the present environment, but are an inheritance from the past, the memory of which has sometimes been lost in the mists of hoary antiquity. The past is not dead. The social past lives in modern societies, just as an ancestral past lives in every individual. In man's environment, immediate and remote, originated his mind and his institutions, and each society adorns the minds of its children, as it adorns their bodies, after the traditional pattern, and in keeping with real or supposed needs.

Factors Influencing Education

In the immediate environment there have been operating since primitive times certain basic factors, or forces, which have shaped man's ideas and his institutions. Of these factors, the most important have been: (1) the economic, (2) the religious, (3) the social, and (4) the political.

The weight of the influence of each of these has varied from time to time, but economic conditions have been generally the most potent of all in determining thought. Our primary needs are physical. While, for instance, it is true, regarding the spiritual and intellectual life, that man does not live by bread alone, it is just as true that he cannot live either physically or spiritually without it. Unless and until man's basic physical wants are supplied, there can be no living of the better and fuller life, for death is the arch-destroyer of would-be creators of art, poetry, religion, and philosophy. From another viewpoint, the economic factor, as a property system, is seen reflected in other social institutions. Agrarianism, for instance, is reflected in feudal government, and capitalism in republican government. But the economic factor has not been the sole determinant of the ways of man.

It would seem that in far-off primitive times the religious force, which has had a profound influence on our thought-life and institutions, originated in man's economic needs. Without knowledge of the natural causes of most of the ordinary phenomena of nature, and fearful of forces which he did not understand and which he wished to control, primitive man adopted animism as, first of all, an explanation of these forces, to him mysterious and at times dangerous, and, secondly, as a means of controlling them. While at times religious thought may have transcended the material and physical world, evidence of the close relationship between man's religious beliefs and his physical wants exists abundantly even in more advanced religious systems. The Egyptian heaven, for instance, was described by Egyptian priests as a field of beans where the corn grew many cubits high, and in the Christian Scriptures heaven is described as a place where man never suffers the pangs of hunger and thirst. It is difficult for men to think except in terms of their environment. This religious force, however we may choose to explain its origin, had, from primitive times until today, a pronounced influence upon education.

In its widest connotation the word *social* may be used to designate all aspects of life in any society. It may be used so broadly that it will include the economic, political, and religious aspects of communal life. In the more restricted sense in which we shall generally use it, the word shall be understood to refer to the organization or structure of society, and the interrelationship of the various parts of the structure. There is, moreover, a bond of unification within the structure of society which has its roots in the gregarious urge in man, whether that urge be native or acquired, and this bond is in its nature *social* as distinguished from such bonds as the economic, religious, or political. Just as many religious practices had their origin in the economic needs of man, so, too, many forms of social organization and custom had, doubtless, a similar beginning. Yet regardless of origin, the social force seems to have operated, at times, as an independent force. Many ancient and, indeed, many quite recent social systems were erected upon a foundation of slavery. Class differentiation within societies has, to a greater or less degree, been an almost universal characteristic of social systems. Each sex, also, usually held a position of its own in the social edifice. The condition of women varied in different societies, but generally throughout the historical period they held a social position inferior to that of men. All such plans of social organization and forms of social structure were reflected in the educational practices of the past.

Forms of government have existed in society since primitive times. With their rise there emerged that influence or force which we call political. When primitive groups passed from the nomadic to the agricultural mode of life and settled in a territory to which they established their right of ownership, tribal government began to assume more definite form, and chieftains, who wielded considerable power, ruled over the territory, the right to rule often becoming hereditary. The political force gathered momentum as smaller tribes became welded together into greater and greater group unities, this process of unification culminating in the rise of great political states in Oriental and Western civilizations. These great states have been ruled by governments differing widely in form, some of them absolute despotisms, others democratic in varying degrees. But whether autocratic or democratic, established governments tend to perpetuate themselves. The nature of governmental systems has exerted a most significant influence upon education since the rise of Oriental despotisms.

Out of these forces grew the thoughts, ideas, attitudes, and philosophies of men, and to preserve and perpetuate these spiritual possessions men established institutions. Among these institutions is the school. In some form or another, the school has existed among all peoples and on every social level. More than any other institution, it has reflected the conditions of life and the attitudes of the people who established it, for in the school all cultural forces converge. In a very real sense the school has been the embodiment of those spiritual realities which we generally call ideals. To understand any institution, one must understand the ideals embodied in it, and this calls for a study of the forces out of which ideals spring. Ideals are not themselves primary forces in the moulding of institutions or in the changing of the world, as the ideological determinists hold. The environment produced them; the process has not evolved the other way.

Social Evolution

In the plan of organization followed in this text there is not implied an acceptance of the theory of a linear evolution of modern civilization. Many leading scientists, philosophers, sociologists, and historians of the eighteenth and nineteenth centuries saw in history a process of gradual social change at work. The English classical economists, the Hegelian political philosophers, many socialists and many pre-Darwinian biologists helped to shape the concept of a linear social evolution. Hegel, Comte, Spencer, and Marx did much to spread that theory. Lewis Henry Morgan, in his *Ancient Society* (1877), championed the linear theory and traced the steps from savagery to civilization. Marx and Engels acclaimed his work. The reaction against Morgan's thesis was led by such men as Franz Boas and Robert Lowie.

Today the concept of gradual, progressive, linear social evolution has been rejected very generally by social scientists as illogical and contrary to factual evidence. The rejection is, in part, due to a general distrust of theory by empiricists now apparently lost in the woods of data, woods growing ever larger and denser, so that the world of the social scientists is threatened by the malady of data neurosis, for which there is no cure but the sunlight and open spaces of theory. Laufer, writing in the *American Anthropologist* in 1930 (XXXII, 162), said: "I must confess that I am in a state of mind where I would no longer give a dime for a new theory, but I am always enthusiastic about new facts." The linear theory is, no doubt, untenable in the light of our present limited evidence, but better an unsound theory than no theory at all, provided we use our researches to test it and provided the scientist reposes no blind faith in it. There is evidence that a reaction has now set in against the arid empiricism of Boas and the idea that facts speak for themselves. L. A. White, writing in the *American Anthropologist* in 1947 (XLIX, 406-407), remarked: "Facts as facts lie inert and meaningless until they are quickened into life and meaning by the creative power of intelligence. . . . The consequences of this anti-imaginative, anti-theoretical outlook were much what one might expect: a mass of facts that did not mean much or make much sense. . . ." The debate still goes on. That there has been a social evolution, albeit not linear or even gradual, seems to be borne out by the records. The steps in the process and the factors producing them are, however, still matters of speculation. Indeed, the evidence we now have on any phase of the problem is not sufficient to warrant a final conclusion.

Education and Culture

The word *culture* is very frequently used to designate the polished manners, refinement, and artistic skill of individuals. But the word *culture* has another meaning. Many anthropologists and sociologists use the word to designate all the spiritual, as distinct from material, possessions of a people. Thus interpreted, a civilization, in its material aspects, is dead. A sphinx, a pyramid, a Parthenon, a skyscraper, or a battleship may mark the character of a civilization, but these are in the category of the dead. A civilization, however, has in it a living principle, a soul, a culture, a something which of its nature is indestructible. A civilization in its material aspects may perish, but the animating principle of that civilization, its culture, lives on, usually with some modifications, in the civilization that succeeds it. Men may destroy their pyramids, their temples, or their battleships, but they cannot destroy the ideas embodied in them. An idea cannot be destroyed by any instrument of destruction which man has created.

Cultures, not civilizations, are transmitted and inherited. When we speak of our cultural inheritance we have in mind, or ought to have in mind, all those spiritual things which have been transmitted to us as the fruit of the spiritual experiences of mankind, or of that part of mankind with which we are linked by the living bond of cultural relationship. It is true that culture, as we have described it, has its roots in the material environment. It is true that many of our beliefs and feelings center around material things such as tools, domesticated animals, or the Nordic race, but these feelings themselves are distinct from the material objects in which they have come to be embodied. While some modern writers disagree regarding the emphasis that ought to be placed upon the spiritual or material elements, the following statement of Wissler on the meaning of culture may be accepted as authoritative:

> As we shall see over and over again, it *is* a core of ideas and beliefs, actuating a people and in a large measure controlling their career, that forms the backbone, or at least the unifying element, in the culture-complex: but our experience with the peoples of the world indicates that whenever we find sharp contrasts in such homely and outward affairs as housing and feeding, we are certain to find equal, if not even sharper contrasts in beliefs, social ways, ideals, ethics, and in fact all mental attitudes toward things of whatever sort. Without pausing then to consider the significance of this simple fact . . . we may take it for granted that wherever there are sharp differences in peoples as to such fundamental necessities as housing, clothing, and feeding, there will likewise exist differences in belief and ideals, so great and having so much originality of form, that the whole life complexes of these peoples must be taken as distinct cultures.[1]

Culture is, therefore, not an individual attainment, but the sum total of the spiritual life of a whole society or an entire people.

[1] C. Wissler, *Man and Culture* (New York: The Thomas Crowell Co., 1923), p. 3.

Each primitive tribe, for instance, had its culture, which acted as a unifying force within the tribe and as a divisive force with regard to all other tribes. Each individual tribesman bore the marks of that culture. Just as tribes put their physical marks on the bodies of their members so they marked their souls as well. Outside of his tribe there was no refuge, no life, for the savage. Expulsion from his tribe usually meant death. Ideals, feelings, and beliefs have been more effective in establishing and maintaining divisions among men than the wide expanse of oceans and the most impregnable military fortifications. Looking back to the cultural beginnings of the race, it appears that cultures have always been significantly racial, group, particular, or national in character. Enlightened men there have been who have dreamt happy dreams of a universal culture, and some notable attempts have been made to make these dreams realities. Krishna, Lao-tze, Buddha, Zoroaster, Jesus, Mohammed, Akhenaton, and Asoka were among those who caught a glimpse, in one degree or another, of a universal, world-embracing culture. From the East, the idea of a universal culture passed into the thought-streams of the West. We find the idea of universalism embodied in the Macedonian and Roman empires. We find it in the religious empire of Christendom. This Eastern dream, however, made some headway, for a time, against the force of particular cultures in the West, but modern nationalism is a negation of that dream.

The force of culture is the most conservative and persistent of all forces. By education, formal and informal, conscious and unconscious, the culture of the group is imposed upon the growing child. Accepted by the group and transmitted by education, culture becomes a most effective barrier against new ideas and against progress. With regard to this conservative aspect of culture, Wissler remarks:

> For one thing, new ideas that fail are said to be untimely. What is meant is that the idea in question does not readily fit into the culture-complex of the group and, in consequence, does not become a part of culture. It seems to matter not at all as to the merit of the new idea; it may be one of the basic conceptions of the next great advance in culture, and yet unless the tribal setting is favorable, humanity must wait. It seems strange indeed that there should be so much waste in the making of culture and the tribe be blind to the potentialities of its own best minds, or that man with all his power of thought should proceed by a kind of trial and error method in the working out of his own salvation. No doubt many times in the life history of each tribal culture comes a grand opportunity, which if seized upon with enthusiasm would make it the leader of the world. So it is that the tragedy of tragedies is the birth of a genius before his time.[2]

[2] *Ibid.*, pp. 183–84.

Of all the means by which culture has been preserved and transmitted, the language and literature of peoples have been the most significant. Language and literature have thus played an important rôle in the culture-life of peoples. Through the native speech, a people maintains its continuity with the past and, for a conquered people, the last and greatest tragedy comes when the conqueror robs them of this vital spiritual link with the past. Through language and literature have been preserved and transmitted the best, as well as the worst, ideals of mankind. Humanity suffers whenever we destroy any treasure-house of ideas, for some of the noblest spiritual conceptions of men may thus pass from remembrance. Music, various forms of art, and symbolism in its many aspects have supplemented oral and written expression in the preservation and transmission of culture.

This phenomenon of culture finds its practical expression in the customs, behavior, or in what is generally known as the folkways of people. And education has been the means whereby these behavior patterns, these folkways, have been impressed upon rising generations since the beginning of organized society.

Folkways and Progress

ON THE PRIMITIVE LEVEL. Progress is the adaptation of man to his changing environment. There are implied in the concept three essential elements: (1) that of environmental change, which is something external to man himself, (2) that of a spiritual or non-material change, which takes place internally in man and which is largely conditioned by a changing economic, social, political, or religious world, and (3) that radical changes in our thought-life have generally, if not always, been preceded by changes in our external world. Man is not, however, a mere creature of his environment, for by his nature he has the will and the capacity to create. The world of culture, which he created, reflects his nature and his needs. But material changes take place much more rapidly than spiritual changes. There has been something in the culture-life of groups since primitive times which has acted as a most conservative force and has constantly struggled against change, particularly against change in our beliefs, attitudes, and organized social life. As a result of this spiritual conservatism of men, there has always appeared, as a group phenomenon during periods of changing material conditions, what anthropologists call a culture-lag. As a result of this lag, serious social maladjustments develop. The machine, for instance, has brought a fundamental, revolutionary change into the external environment of Western peoples in the past hundred and fifty years, but no corresponding revolutionary change has occurred in our social, ethical, or political conceptions. There is much truth in the charge that while we now travel at a speed of many hundreds of miles an hour, our thoughts and philosophy of life are still essentially the same as they were in the horse-and-buggy days.

Men, as a rule, have always been fearful of change, for change has been a threat to the material security, the power, or the privileges of some, as well as a threat to the spiritual tranquillity of many. Primitive peoples, living in a natural environment whose operations they did not understand, and in an imaginary environment which they themselves created, and, fearful of these real and imaginary enemies, opposed all material and spiritual changes. In their folkways, customs, and rules and practices of everyday action, which were supported by the powerful sanction of the group, primitive peoples found repose from all doubts and uncertainties.

Man, because he fears the unknown, the uncharted seas, has, ever since his primitive beginnings, struggled against the forces that demanded changes in his intellectual, spiritual, and social mode of life. The generality of men today, as always, want certainties. In established customs, folkways, dogmas, and intellectual and spiritual acceptances, men have found those certainties which, during periods of time, allayed their fears. But few, if any, of these certainties have stood the test of time, and idol after idol has been cast aside to be replaced by newer ones. The history of man's quest for certainty reveals that what men have sought most ardently they have never found. For, strictly speaking, there is nothing certain except change; nothing certain except uncertainty. And what this visible world could not supply, men, since primitive times, have found in an invisible world which they themselves created. Rocked in the cradle of an ever-changing deep, where the demon of fear breathes terror into restless souls, man has sought for himself a spiritual tranquillity and has found it in the realm of the absolute. And that absolute, which is discernible only to the "mind's eye," men have tried, but always in vain, to embody in their earthly institutions, their monarchies, their empires, or their churches. This struggle to bring the absolute to earth appeared, theoretically at least, in such modern political experiments as the recent Italian Fascist state. But the absolute is today where it has always been, in the realm of dreams, in the world of ideals unrealized.

Primitive peoples found in their folkways, their culture, their traditional modes of life those certainties which they desired. Social and individual habits of life grew, through long periods of time, out of primitive modes of action. A way of right living and conduct had been found. Thus developed fixity of social custom and action. Digression on the part of individuals from the beaten path of conduct was opposed and thwarted by group custom and the group mind. Then, as now, the "genius before his time," who caught a glimpse of a newer and better way of life and action, lived in vain. We might describe him, as Matthew Arnold described Shelley, as "a beautiful but ineffectual angel beating in the void its luminous wings in vain." But, into primitive life and society change came, usually, it seems, after long periods of fixity. Had that change not come, all of us who today call ourselves civilized would still be savages. Change came in social life with every great crisis. Earthquakes, plagues, destructive wars, floods, exhaustion of the food supply, and all such catastrophic occurrences so changed the primitive environment that the savage was forced to abandon many of the old folkways and adapt himself to new conditions. Peaceful trade relations between tribes must, also, have played some part in progress among primitives, in much the same way that intertribal or international commerce has always produced change in the cultural life and folkways of all trading peoples, a phenomenon readily apparent in our own day. But environmental change does not explain all happenings. Most tribes have remained on the preliterate level, although presumably their environment must have changed. The Germano-Romanic tribes of Europe began only after the eighth century to build a high civilization, and this without any notable change in their environment. The causes of the rise and fall of civilizations, while interestingly examined by men like Toynbee, Sorokin, and Spengler, remain in doubt.

ON THE ORIENTAL LEVEL. Thus, driven upward probably in the main by a changing environment, men found, eventually, a new mode of social life, new certainties and new security in the larger social unities of Oriental nations. Over long ages, the process of the blending of cultures had gone on, and with this blending went the growth of larger societies. Whole tribes and their cultures became parts of larger wholes by the process of assimilation, the sword, no doubt, playing a part in the process. A settled agricultural existence contributed to the softening of cultural barriers. The change from primitive to Oriental social forms must have required untold millennia of time. The blending of tribes of 50 or 500 families into an empire of 400,000,000 souls, such as the Chinese empire, was not accomplished in a few centuries. Whenever or however the change to the Oriental social level first occurred, the dawn of history finds that man has definitely passed far beyond his primitive social beginnings. But on the Oriental plane of society men are still held together by their folkways, their culture, although these are now strongly supplemented by despotic political and ecclesiastical machines of social control. Still further, we find on this level that man has discovered a new means of communicating his thoughts, his ideas, to his fellows. Now man has a written literature. Primitive peoples used a variety of methods, other than the voice, of communicating their thoughts to others, but the voice was by far the most important. A primitive hunter knew how to indicate, by marks on trees, in what particular direction he had gone; carved sticks and other objects on which signs were engraved were often used to transmit the messages of chiefs within the tribal territory and beyond it. But while writing may be said to have originated in these tribal practices, long ages passed before man learned to preserve for all times the thoughts, ideas, and experiences of the past through the agency of literature.

Not until Oriental times do we find man in possession of this storehouse of past experiences, this cultural fortification, literature. Its invention not only made it possible for men to rise above the level of savagery, but its possession placed the Oriental in a position far more favorable to his effective control of the present and future environment than was his primitive forebear. And this advantage was due to his more complete knowledge of the past than the primitive possessed. The past has always been, and it continues to be today, a living, active, dynamic force. Indeed we might say that it, more than anything else, is the "divinity that shapes our ends, rough-hew them how we will." Every present has been, and every present will be, a culmination of its past. Man's dependence upon the past is complete. In our language, our laws, our morals, our folkways, our knowledge, and our several institutions, we live not in the present but in the past. We cannot think or act rationally except upon the basis of our memory of the past. The individual man is so completely dependent upon his recall of experience by memory that, without such recall, he is as helpless in solving the most ordinary problems of his everyday life as the baby in its cradle. A man whose memory has been destroyed knows not whence he came nor in which direction his destination lies. Without an ability to recall the past, life would be a veritable chaos. The more fully we know and understand the past, the more certain we become of correct procedures in the present and the future. All of our failures to solve the problems of today and tomorrow are due, in large measure, to our lack of knowledge of the past. The more distant that past, the more uncertain, as a rule, is our knowledge of it; and many of our modern attitudes, ideas, and institutions are not of recent but of very remote origin. The great universe of nature and man that lies behind us is still almost entirely unexplored.

Our heritage from that past is both good and bad. In its bad aspects, it is a reactionary force which all too frequently and effectively impedes the march of progress. And thus it is that all the beliefs, practices, and commonplaces that we take for granted as indispensable are the very acceptances that need most to be questioned, and these are usually those of longest duration—those whose roots run farthest back into the life and thoughts of mankind. Some of these reactionary beliefs and practices are educational or pedagogical in character, and all of them, no matter what their form, have been transmitted and perpetuated by education in its formal or informal, conscious or unconscious, aspects. Tradition is one of the strongest of social forces.

It is because of the importance of this past for today and tomorrow that literature, the chief repository of culture and the strongest link between the past and the present, has been such a vital factor in the evolution of society. Small primitive societies, and they were all small, were easily held together by a feeling of blood relationship or a strong territorial attachment, but simple bonds like these are inadequate for the unification of the people of great empires. But a literature, largely religious in character, was invented by the priests and prophets of the Orient. This literature established that cultural bond of unity which was indispensable for the social stability and unification of groups now scattered over a wide expanse of territory. On the Bibles of the Hindus, Persians, Babylonians, Egyptians, Hebrew-Christians, and Mohammedans great civilizations were built. In some degree, all of this ancient religious literature claimed to be divine in origin. The best wisdom of the wisest men of a distant past was preserved in that literature. In it men found the answer to all baffling questions regarding the mysterious unknown as well as regarding the modes of conduct which will guarantee one's individual well-being in this and in an after-life. And it bore the seal of the great ones of a distant past whose wisdom came, in time, and under the influence of priestly indoctrination, to be looked upon as divine and authoritative. The authority of these books, within the various civilizations, became final. While only a few, as a rule, outside of the circle of an hereditary priestly caste could read this literature, the basic dogmas, ideas, and philosophy of life embodied in it were effectively imposed upon the masses of the people. The masses of the people in any great society can be held together, over a long period of time, by the method of keeping them in fear and ignorance as well as by the modern method of enlightenment, or what passes in much of our present-day world for enlightenment.

It was through this literature, through this culture, that the living hand of an ancient ancestral past weighed heavily upon Oriental civilizations. And we still, perhaps, worship our social and our educational ancestors, at times, not wisely but too well.

Again, on the Oriental level, as on the primitive, social habits became fixed, thought became uniform, and men believing. This fixity was attained through the influence of religious and political despots who made literature their chief tool. Men now, again, have another culture, other folkways, other certainties. Here men lived by that philosophy which teaches that "as it was in the beginning, is now, and ever shall be, world without end." They lived by the philosophy of "whatever is, is best." They lived by the philosophy that that is true which has been clearly and indubitably transmitted by the past. As in primitive, so again in Oriental times the folkways were passed on from generation to generation by education in one form or another, but on this latter level the process, in its formal aspects at least, was, unlike that of the primitives, a clearly conscious one, directed generally by a privileged priestly class, which was the strong right arm of a political despot who was regarded and worshiped as a god. But again crises arose to destroy the folkways and the certainties of men.

Another culture, other folkways, remained to be found, for on the Oriental level men had not yet invented that way of life the core of which is individual freedom, political liberty, democracy, and fearless spiritual and intellectual independence.

No doubt many factors contributed to the development of the new crises, but commercial and military contacts, first between one Oriental nation and another and then between the Oriental and Hellenic, or Greek, peoples, were the chief causes of that spiritual disturbance which preceded the rise of a new social order in Greece and the West. Peoples exchange their ideas with their merchandise, and war has always been one of the transformers of material and cultural idols.

There came, then, to the nations of the Near East a period of contact and conflict, a period in which the process of culture-blending went on apace, a period of crisis for the souls of men, a period of new uncertainties, when men were forced to learn the rules of the game of life anew. But those who learned the new rules best, and who profited most by them, were not the Orientals themselves but their spiritual progeny, the Greeks. All the peoples of the Near Orient—Cretans, Babylonians, Assyrians, Egyptians, Phoenicians, Hittites, Aramaeans, Persians, Chaldeans, Medes, and Hebrews—are the spiritual forefathers of the Greeks, and in many ways of all modern peoples of the West. That much generally is known about our indebtedness to the Orient, but archaeological and historical research has not yet revealed the exact place where Western civilization originated. It has been established, however, beyond all reasonable doubt, that our civilization originated in the valley of the Nile or in that between the Tigris and Euphrates. But, wherever it originated, the West added a new and important element to its Oriental inheritance, the element of liberty.

Oriental peoples accepted despotisms of the most tyrannical sort, whose forms became static, and unchanging; their intellectual life was devoid of that curiosity which is essential to discovery, their religious interest in the stars producing, however, some rudimentary knowledge of astronomy and mathematics; their tyrannical religious systems forced upon their submissive minds the acceptance of the most inconceivable superstitions and traditions; their art, lacking entirely the spirit of moderation characteristic of Greek art, took delight in temples, tombs, palaces, and other creations impressive not by their beauty but by their colossal size and strength; and their mythology was extravagant and unreal, like the stories of ancestors who turned night into day, or who lived for many hundreds of years before their hair turned gray. Here every aspect of life was marked by uniformity, a uniformity imposed upon men, and accepted by them submissively. The very opposite of this way of social life was discovered by the Greeks.

ON THE WESTERN LEVEL. The Greeks, and in a very special way the Athenians—for Athens is the cradle of European liberty in most, if not all, of its aspects—invented a new way of life, characterized by variety, originality, freedom, and faith in the capacity of human reason and intelligence to solve the problems of a changing society. Of all the gifts of Mediterranean culture to Europe, the greatest by far are liberty and faith in intelligence. Before Greece, the world knew no liberty, except the liberty of despots to destroy liberty. Instead, tradition, custom, and the folkways took the place of intelligence in the solution of social problems and the direction of human destinies. The new age of liberty, reason, and intelligence reached its height in Athens in the Periclean Age, 461-429 B.C. This was an age when the old Athenian folkways had completely broken down beyond any hope of their restoration. There were many reasons for the breakdown of the old principles and habits of social life. First of all, the Greeks never had a religious literature, a holy book, whose teachings all men were required to accept, nor had they an hereditary priesthood which spoke with final authority on questions pertaining to truth and man's beliefs and conduct. The Greek mind was thus from the beginning a much freer mind than was the Oriental mind. This freedom made possible that free inquiry into the nature of the physical universe and social problems which characterized Greek intellectual and social developments.

Since the seventh century B.C., when the Ionian physicists were exploring, in a very free and critical way, the mysteries of the physical universe, Greek knowledge of nature and of natural causes increased very rapidly. By the dawn of the Periclean Age, the old myths regarding creation and the nature of the universe had been definitely abandoned not only by the intelligentsia but by a rapidly increasing number of the populace, especially in Athens. Soon men who had learned to look at the universe with critical minds were to turn that same critical faculty upon the structure of society. And social myths, the old folkways, fell as did the ancient cosmic myths. To this final disillusionment, in which a critical philosophy of the universe and an increasing knowledge of natural forces played an important part, a great increase in wealth and power in Athens, in the years following the wars with Persia, and the success of a long struggle for political democracy in Athens itself, made a most significant contribution. The final outcome, which some social conservatives tried vainly to check, was the disruption of the old standards of social life. The Periclean Age was an age of almost universal disregard for traditions, an age of social unrest and disbelief, an age of moral laxity.

It is significant that this great period of human intellectual and artistic achievement was an age of the greatest moral revolt and disregard of traditional forms of behavior, and an age when the individual enjoyed greater freedom from social control than during any other period in history, with the possible exception of the Augustan Age in Rome, which is as notorious for its disregard of traditional morals as it is famous for its achievements in literature and thought. The Romans, however, were largely imitators of the Greeks, while the Athenians were creators. Francis Galton, in his famous book *Hereditary Genius,* in which he expounded the theory that genius is hereditary, called attention to the fact that, between 530 and 430 B.C., Athens produced fourteen illustrious men whose achievements have seldom, if ever, been equaled and never surpassed. Galton, however, ignored the influence of environment upon the development of genius. Whatever may be the importance of the individual's native endowments, it is a well-established fact that genius can come to the fullness of blossom only in a favorable environment. Of every country churchyard we may say, with Gray:

> Some mute, inglorious Milton here may rest,
> Some Cromwell guiltless of his country's blood.

Primitive and Oriental environments, over many thousands of years, produced few notable geniuses, and indeed the greatest geniuses of Athens were the products of slightly more than half a century. During this short period, the racial stock of Athens remained essentially unchanged, the environment in its economic, political, social, and intellectual aspects being the changing factor. Professor W. W. Hyde, in an article which appeared in the *General Magazine and Historical Chronicle of the University of Pennsylvania* (No. 1, 1935), has this to say about the greatness of Athenian achievement in the period 461-429 B.C.: "But in the short period Athens, never having over 250,000 inhabitants including slaves, literally produced more men of genius than all the world together has produced since in any similar lapse of time, and masterpieces rarely equalled and in some cases never excelled." This age of greatness continued, but with diminishing vigor, until Athenian and Greek liberty was destroyed by the Macedonians in 338 B.C. It is, indeed, more than probable that the new social crisis which resulted in the breakdown of the restrictions imposed by the old folkways on individual liberty produced that thoughtful and intelligent approach to the problem of social reconstruction which appears, for the first time in history, in such social and political theories as those of Socrates, Plato, and Aristotle. Back of that crisis lay an increase in power, wealth, freedom, and knowledge, which had been accumulating over a period of two centuries and which, in the fifth century B.C., produced a veritable social explosion. In the explosion, the individual broke loose from his old social moorings, from the old habits of individual and social conduct, from the old folkways, and set out to find a better or a best way of life.

Thus began in the social world of the West the reign of intelligence in the ordering of society; thus began the spirit of hankering after the ideal society which is still a characteristic of Western culture; thus began among men an age of enlightenment characterized by a critical attitude toward the past, by doubt, inquiry, and remarkable discovery, and by a struggle for freedom which, in spite of lapses into various forms of servitude, has brought remarkable advances in many phases of life, and which still continues, although here and there among our Western nations the spirit of despotism recently raised its monstrous head. But the blessings of liberty, having been discovered, men will not readily relinquish. Byron, in *The Giaour*, gave eloquent expression to that faith of man in the value of liberty:

> For Freedom's battle once begun,
> Bequeath'd by bleeding Sire to Son,
> Though baffled oft is ever won.
> Bear witness, Greece, thy living page,
> Attest it many a deathless age!
> While kings in dusty darkness hid,
> Have left a nameless pyramid.

The education which will prepare men for life in a society of ever-changing folkways, in a society established on the principle of liberty, must be different from that in the societies of fixed folkways on the primitive and Oriental levels. But, while Athenian society had undergone a revolutionary change, and democracy had succeeded autocracy, the old educational practices of the autocratic régime of earlier days continued, for the force of institutionalized educational tradition is strong. But youth demanded, and eventually teachers provided, a new education, designed to free the human mind, and to develop that critical attitude toward life and social practices which is essential to the preservation and improvement of liberal, democratic institutions. This new education has been called liberal, for it was designed to meet the needs of men who were politically free as well as to liberate the human mind from those forces which in the past had enslaved it. Many centuries of struggle, however, had still to elapse in the West before women and slaves were accorded that freedom which is implied in the idea of democracy, as we interpret it today. Thus, as our idea and our practice of democracy have expanded since the days of the Athenian struggle, so our conception of a liberal education has also changed, and today our progressive educational philosophers interpret a liberal education not only in terms of the political and spiritual freedom of the individual but also in terms of his interests, vocational needs, and aptitudes.

Thus men have been emancipated, but not yet completely, from the tyranny of fixed social custom and habit. Thus men have turned, but not yet completely, from the way of uncritical acceptance of the folkways, to the way of intelligent, critical, thoughtful questioning of tradition and of deliberate striving for better things. And faith in the new way of life finds unquestionable justification in the fact that, in a few centuries (about six in all) of critical outlook and of comparative freedom, Western peoples have accomplished more than was accomplished in all the other centuries, both historic and prehistoric, during which the spirit of man was enslaved by social custom and the deadening reactionary hand of unreasonable and arbitrary authority.

The Individual, Society, and Progress

It follows from what has already been said that the freedom of the individual is an important condition of discovery and indispensable to the well-being of democratic societies. The greatness of any society will depend, in the long run, upon the greatness of the individuals who compose it. As John Stuart Mill in his essay *On Liberty* remarked: "A state which dwarfs its men, in order that they may be more docile instruments in its hands even for beneficial purposes, will find that with small men no great thing can really be accomplished." In most primitive societies, only an occasional individual, usually one whose warlike exploits were of the most extraordinary character, enjoyed a measure of personal liberty. Often such a one became a tribal chief. In Oriental societies, only the political and religious aristocracy—and these were but a small fraction of the entire population—enjoyed a form of liberty, but even these were not spiritually free, for traditional beliefs and fears of the supernatural and unknown, as well as the force of age-old custom, set definite and narrow limits to the circle within which they might enjoy freedom. The minds even of the priests of the ancient Orient were uncritical and submissive.

The West discovered the value of individual liberty, individual intelligence, and individual initiative, and on these foundations our modern democracies have been established. They will continue only so long as they provide for the fullness of growth of the individuals who compose them; only so long as they continue to provide an education which will develop in their citizens a critical, forward-looking, vigilant attitude. "Eternal vigilance is the price of liberty," and in thoughtful, intelligent planning for the future lies the promise of a better world tomorrow.

In this building of the better world, the teachers of the future will take a prominent part. While thinking forward, they must constantly look back to the course of social and educational evolution in the past, so that they may not lose a sense of direction. What the direction has been, history reveals. What it will be tomorrow, the historian ought to be able to predict.

Selected Readings

Marvin, F. S. *The Living Past.* London: Clarendon Press, 1920.
Mulhern, J. "Significance of the History of Education in the Education of Teachers." *Educational Outlook,* X (March 1936), 167–81.
Reisner, E., *et al.* "New Emphasis in History of Education in Response to War and Postwar Demands." *XXIX Yearbook of the National Society of College Teachers of Education* (1944), 14–35. Ann Arbor, Mich.: Ann Arbor Books.
Robinson, J. H. *The New History.* New York: The Macmillan Co., 1912.
Sorokin, P. A. *Social Philosophies of an Age of Crisis.* Boston: Beacon Press, Inc., 1950.
Spengler, O. *The Decline of the West.* 2 vols. (Trans. C. F. Atkinson.) New York: Alfred A. Knopf, Inc., 1929.
Sumner, W. G. *Folkways.* Boston: Ginn & Co., 1907.
Toynbee, A. J. *Civilization on Trial.* New York: Oxford University Press, 1948.
Wissler, C. *Man and Culture.* New York: The Thomas Crowell Co., 1923.
Woody, T. "Clio and the Teacher." *School and Society,* XXXIX (March 17, 1934), 321–30.
———. *Liberal Education for Free Men.* Philadelphia: University of Pennsylvania Press, 1951.

Part II

SOCIETY AND EDUCATION IN THE PRE-RENAISSANCE WORLD

2 The Education of Pre-literate Peoples

It has been asserted that the invention of the phonetic alphabet was man's first step from savagery to civilization. Such an assertion is based upon a very narrow concept of civilization, which indeed ought to involve all forms of human activity and achievement. Nevertheless, the alphabet and literature are a very important aspect of the boundary between primitive and Oriental societies. Pre-literate peoples, usually referred to as primitives or savages, have their own peculiar social and educational institutions. The word "primitive" must not be interpreted literally, for we know nothing about society in its first and completely primitive stage. The inference, however, that societies have evolved from a gregarious ancestry is indisputable. Anthropologists apply the term primitive to those people, clearly human in every basic respect, who live today in a pre-literate, arrested stage of civilization. These people, still found in many parts of the world, are the primitives with whose social and educational practices we are here concerned.

The Primitive Environment

ECONOMIC ASPECTS. Men have always lived not in one but in three environments: (a) that of the physical and animal world—the physical environment, (b) that of social relationships—the social environment, and (c) that of ghosts or mysterious forces—the "imaginary environment." Underlying these three environments, or these aspects of the general environment, and related to them all, have been certain basic forces, the most influential being the economic force. Man's primary needs, those for food, clothing, and shelter, had a profound influence upon his mode of physical and cultural life. The mode of satisfying physical wants differed under different geographical and cultural conditions, but the wants of the body had, everywhere, to be supplied. Anthropologists generally agree that hunger and sex are the basic forces motivating society, and that of these the food urge is the most compelling motive in the life of an individual and a community. While the food quest is the most important activity both of individuals and of communities on the primitive social level, many aspects of primitive life cannot be explained in terms of economic needs. There are many primitive practices that do not harmonize with the doctrine of economic determinism, proposed by some anthropologists and historians as explanatory of all human activities. A primitive may, for instance, grow more yams than he can possibly eat, his motive being to attract attention to his wealth and to enhance his prestige in the community. And history supplies many examples of men who have submitted to martyrdom for political, social, or religious ideals, the economic motive for accepting death being difficult, if not impossible, to establish in many such cases.

In primitive society the food quest is the chief activity of the people, and the most important institutions and practices have to do with the acquisition, ownership, and distribution of food. Indeed, one of the strongest bonds of social unification among primitives is the nutritive bond. Commensalism is often a custom of savages and it seems to create a feeling of good fellowship. Sex is largely a disruptive force which primitives have to restrain by such devices as taboos, but the food quest calls for co-operation which is encouraged in many ways by tribal custom. The primitive family is essentially economic in character, the need for food being the chief bond of attachment between the child and its parents. The primitive child is indeed sometimes inhumanly treated and often put to death when food is scarce.[1] The supply of food is meager, and primitive man does not live far from the starvation level. Successful food-getters, therefore, stand high in social esteem, and their personal qualities and skills are greatly admired. Primitives, too, believe that success in the food quest is impossible without the help of supernatural agencies, and a whole system of magic surrounds the various economic activities of the tribe, special magicians often performing the crude and weird rites thought to be necessary if success in the economic struggle is to be assured. Food prohibitions are numerous. Many of the restrictions are connected with the worship of totems and applied to all members of the tribe, although food conservation and respect for the authority and palates of the tribal elders, who often eat the delicacies forbidden to the younger

[1] A. J. Todd, *The Primitive Family as an Educational Agency* (New York: G. P. Putnam's Sons, Inc., 1913); E. S. Hartland, *Primitive Law* (London: Methuen & Co., Ltd., 1924), pp. 73–74.

generation, are evidently important purposes of many prohibitions.[2] These tribal food regulations are an important part of the education of tribal youth.

Economic activities are everywhere divided between males and females, and in certain tribes there is another division of labor on the basis of age, males, in this case, being organized into "age-grades" each having its own economic duties to perform. The usual duties of men are fighting, hunting, and protection of their families, while those of women are housekeeping, the care of the children, gardening, and carrying burdens, for primitive women are the beasts of burden, as many women in societies on higher social levels continued to be until modern times. The successful exploitation of the environment makes necessary the co-operation of all members of the tribe. To this end labor was divided and, by the most stringent tribal and totemic sanctions and taboos, the traditional division of labor was continued through the long ages of tribal existence, apparently with little, if any, modification. Some of the food procured by this labor is recognized as the property of the individual or his family, but much of it belongs to a wider kinship group. Tribal custom frequently compels the hunter to apportion the flesh of the animal he captures among a wide circle of kinsmen, while it permits him to keep a mere morsel of the worst meat for himself.

The social aspect of food is, then, apparent among many primitive tribes. Yet communism in property is exceptional on the primitive level, although tribal overright to tribal territory and the hunting-grounds is usually recognized and, in the case of hunting, established in practice. Family exclusiveness and well-defined family rights in regard to children, personal belongings, and portions of tribal lands in agricultural tribes are the tradition and practice among most primitive peoples.[3]

In addition to the problem of food-getting, primitive peoples are also concerned with the economic problems of securing clothing and shelter. Methods of clothing the body and of providing shelter differ with different tribes and are determined by climatic conditions and the folkways.

Connected with the economic activities of primitives, a variety of industries, arts, and crafts developed. The hunter, the fisherman,

[2] S. Porteus, *The Psychology of a Primitive People* (New York: Longmans, Green & Co., Inc., 1931), pp. 255–69.

[3] B. Malinowski, *The Family among Australian Aborigines* (London: University of London Press, 1913), pp. 149–65; Hartland, *op. cit.*, pp. 85 ff.; N. Miller, *The Child in Primitive Society* (New York: Brentano, 1928), pp. 220–40; R. H. Lowie, *Primitive Society* (New York: Liveright Publishing Corp., 1920), pp. 205–56.

the gardener, the artisan, or the warrior needed his tools or his weapons, and many technical skills were essential to the satisfaction of basic economic needs. All the arts and crafts and technical abilities of primitives are relative to their environment, but everywhere the excellence with which they perform the activities necessary to supply their economic wants is remarkable. Snares, traps, bows, arrows, spears, and nets, for instance, are needed by hunters and fishermen; gardening implements are needed by gardeners; many household utensils are needed by the women. Primitives are adept in making these tools, but specialization in the arts and crafts is decidedly rare, although a few men and women, in an occasional tribe, specialize in a few crafts, and their children pursue the same occupations as their parents.[4] Changes or improvements in these tools, weapons, and utensils were rarely introduced, for the primitive became spiritually attached, by the bond of culture, to the implements of his economic life.[5]

The ways in which primitives use these implements and the methods they employ in their various economic activities are also of considerable interest and significance. The primitive hunter, for instance, baits, allures, stalks, and snares his prey with remarkable skill. The primitive fisherman and the primitive agriculturist follow the traditional methods of the tribe which, while they are crude, are on the whole remarkably successful and always skillfully used. With all of these methods some form of magic came to be associated, and thus they became traditional and fixed. As the implements of primitive economic life almost never changed, so the methods of using them likewise remained unaltered over long periods of time.

All of these skills in the arts and crafts and all of these methods of economic activity are transmitted from generation to generation by apprenticing, as it were, the boys and girls of the tribe to their parents and elders, whose activities they learn to imitate. Much of the education of the primitive youth has to do with the economic aspect of his life, but this particular phase of his education is informal and sometimes unconscious, being determined by the basic physical wants of the tribal group and its individual members and taking the form of spontaneous reaction to environmental conditions.

SOCIAL ASPECTS. (1) GENERAL CHARACTERISTICS. Economic needs and conditions underlie many primitive social practices. While generalizations about tribal institutions are dangerous, few

[4] R. Thurnwald, *Economics in Primitive Communities* (New York: Oxford University Press, 1932), pp. 33–72; Miller, *op. cit.*, pp. 241–48.

[5] Thurnwald, *op. cit.*, pp. 41 ff.

exceptions will be found to the assertion that the family is the most universal and persistent of primitive social institutions. While it has a variety of forms, it appears everywhere as a group which comprises a married couple and their children. The reasons for it, probably, are economic and biological rather than sociological.[6]

Above the family comes the clan, which is essentially an extended family and which is based generally on actual blood relationship of the individuals who compose it. It is an aggregation of families leading an orderly and stabilized social life. Very definite laws, customs, and rules, hoary with antiquity, govern the relationships of individuals within a clan, and of one clan and its members to another clan and its members. Such rites frequently arise out of considerations having to do with property rights which are zealously guarded by the clansfolk.

Above the clan stands the tribe, which is a group of clans speaking a similar language, having similar institutions, and using similar weapons, tools, and techniques. The tribe is essentially a cultural unit, other aspects of its organization being of secondary importance. Its existence, however, provides a cultural basis of unity in its territory, and makes the exchange of goods and commerce between the clans freer and more effective.[7]

An important characteristic of the primitive social group, which we shall call the tribe, is its very limited size or population. Another important characteristic of this group is its solidarity and like-mindedness. There are many ties that bind the tribal members together. The necessity for food, clothing, and shelter demands a common struggle and creates a food or nutritive bond of great cohesive force. The actual or imaginary bond of blood-kinship, and the territorial bond which results from long-continued life on the ancestral lands of the tribe are unifying forces of great importance. The good earth to which tribes have been long attached takes on a sacred significance, and profound emotions grow out of that attachment. Tribes fight to death for their territory. When some tribes are forced to wander they take earth from the old territory with them, for with that earth have long been linked the spirits of their ancestors, and earth spirits. Related to this territorial bond of unity is that cohesive force which grows out of long-continued propinquity or contiguity.

[6] F. W. Blackmar, *History of Human Society* (New York: Charles Scribner's Sons, 1926), pp. 109–20; Lowie, *op. cit.*, pp. 63–74; E. Westermarck, *A Short History of Marriage* (New York: The Macmillan Co., 1926), pp. 23–24.

[7] Thurnwald, *op. cit.*, pp. vii–ix; Blackmar, *op. cit.*, pp. 109–12; Lowie, *op. cit.*, pp. 17–38, 40–74.

(2) Primitive Social Equality. Within the tribe social distinctions and inequalities are generally unobtrusive. Where these exist they are usually distinctions of rank, which come with meritorious achievements of individuals, rather than with birth. While it is dangerous to generalize, it can be safely stated that primitive youths generally begin life on a basis of equality, an equality which is seldom seriously disturbed. Even when distinctions based on wealth arise, the poor man usually enjoys the privilege of entering the home, or sitting at the table, of his wealthy neighbor as an equal. Here and there among primitives an hereditary caste system has developed. While students of primitive society stress, as a rule, the apparent practice of the subordination of the individual by his group, there is a degree of individualism possible for the primitive man which makes him something better than a mere cog in the social wheel.[8]

Where centralized government, under the control of a powerful chief, has not developed, or developed only in an imperfect way, much authority is vested in the elders of the tribe, and they enjoy many privileges which are denied to the younger generation. In societies in which the males are graded into groups according to age, the old men enjoy a great prestige. Women never appear to be graded in this way in primitive society.[9]

In some primitive groups, secret societies exist, and those admitted to them have a social standing of exceptional character, but membership in such societies is not hereditary. These supplement the family and the tribe as a force making for tribal cohesion, their secret character inspiring outsiders with awe and curiosity. They act as further agencies of social control in tribes which have no strong chiefs, and their members are carefully selected and enjoy special privileges.[10]

Medicine men, or shamans, occupy a somewhat unique social position. They rose to prominence chiefly because of their reputed success in dealing with the ghosts of the imaginary environment, and their position became hereditary in many tribes. Primitives believe that the medicine man is able to control all forces of evil, and he is thus reverenced with awe and respect. He is physician, clairvoyant, spiritualist, diviner, prophet, necromancer, and a variety of other weird things, at one and the same time. He is the

[8] R. H. Lowie, *Primitive Religion* (New York: Liveright Publishing Corp., 1924), pp. 3, 76–81; Thurnwald, *op. cit.*, pp. 79–83.

[9] Porteus, *op. cit.*, pp. 255–69; R. Dixon, *The Building of Cultures* (New York: Charles Scribner's Sons, 1928), p. 210.

[10] W. I. Thomas, *Source Book for Social Origins* (Chicago: University of Chicago Press, 1909), pp. 792 ff.

intermediary between man and the supposed mysterious powers with which unenlightened men fill their world. The institution of shamanism acts as a conservative social force which aids the tribal government in preserving unchanged the beliefs and usages of the group. The medicine man is exempted from the hard labor of the ordinary tribesman, a fact which gives rise to the question as to how much the desire to escape from irksome duties had to do with the rise of many of our professions.

In addition to medicine men, many tribes have their story-tellers or tribal historians whose duty it is to learn and transmit the lore of the tribe. These experts in the folklore of the tribe are not priests, an office in society first held by the shamans. To this special group of story-tellers ought to be added also the professional dancers and musicians of the tribe. Medicine men, the primitive priests, contributed little, if anything, to the origin of music and dancing, although they indulge in a religious dance which is peculiarly their own. There is little evidence of a conclusive character to support the claim that history and art, in all its forms, had a priestly origin.[11]

(3) SEX AS BASIS OF SOCIAL DIFFERENTIATION. It has been noted that labor in primitive society is divided mainly on the basis of sex, although the medicine man, among all primitive peoples, and an occasional individual possessed of some special knowledge or skill, in scattered tribes, represent the beginnings of vocational specialization. These practices are, however, exceptional, and it is the lack of specialization that is the conspicuous characteristic of primitive economic ways of life. Males and females, however, always occupy distinctly separate spheres in the tribal social and economic organization. The status of women and social customs regulating their place and duties in primitive societies differ widely as we pass from one tribe to another. There are groups in which descent is traced from the mother, and groups in which it is traced from the father, these latter being the more numerous. In matrilineal groups the mother's brother exercises considerable authority over his sister's property and children, and in patrilineal groups husbands are not infrequently "henpecked." Spinsters and widows are rare among primitives, for social custom frowns upon the single status of either male or female adults. Marriage, too, brings economic advantages to men and women alike, the men generally having the greater advantage.

The primitive woman is valued mainly as an economic asset. Her chief duties are cooking, providing shelter, gardening, and

[11] *Ibid.*, pp. 281–303; J. L. Maddox, *The Medicine Man* (New York: The Macmillan Co., 1923), pp. 1, 7, 91 ff., 132, 150, 240, 289; Lowie, *Primitive Religion*, p. 3.

bearing children. Frequently she is purchased by her husband from her parents and, should she be childless, her parents are often required to provide another daughter to take her place. While in exceptional tribes the position of women is not one of marked inferiority, primitive women generally hold a position decidedly less favorable than that of their male counterparts. A woman is prized generally as a laborer and a bearer of children, and children in turn are sought and prized chiefly for the economic contribution they can make to the family and the tribe. It has been computed that the percentage of tribes in which women hold a decidedly inferior position is 73 in the case of agricultural, and 87.5 in the case of pastoral, groups.[12]

Tribal custom assigns to men and women separate and exclusive duties, and this separation is preserved by a variety of sanctions sometimes so sacred in character that a violation of the traditional practices results in very serious penalties for the transgressor. To have the labors imposed on them by tribal custom lessened, the women in many tribes encourage polygamy, because in this way they can have many helpers.

Women and men, then, in primitive society are clearly differentiated both as members of society and as laborers. Among some groups the sexes are so segregated that both are required to speak different languages on certain special occasions. Women are the household drudges, and men are the warriors and the hunters. And each sex is educated for its own exclusive duties. Girls learn the duties of women by assisting their mothers; and boys, the duties of men by assisting their fathers. In this field of informal primitive education there operated, in a very real sense, that activity school of which our modern educators speak so frequently and enthusiastically.

(4) Social Control and the Group Mind. Since primitive times each separate social, racial, religious, and political group has been characterized by a mind, or an ideology, peculiar to itself. One can say that there is a Chinese mind and a Hindu mind; a Christian mind and a pagan mind; an authoritarian mind and a liberal mind. This phenomenon of mind is a result of the formal and informal educational influences of each separate environment. Every child who is not an idiot has a capacity for acquiring the culture of his group. The primitive child, as it grows, assimilates the traditional ideology peculiar to his tribe. Each tribe has its own peculiar ideas and attitudes regarding such things as food, clothing, shelter, marriage and sex relationships, the economic activities of

[12] Lowie, *Primitive Society,* p. 193.

men and women, respect for elders, and the relationship of tribal members to totems and the world of spirits, etc. The sum total of these tribal ideas is the culture of the tribe. The tribal modes of activity, or the customary methods of doing things which embody these ideas, are the folkways. Each tribe has its own culture and folkways which are uniquely its own, and which mark an individual as a member of his particular tribe. Marriage laws and prohibitions, for instance, have been adopted by many groups in the course of human history to preserve and solidify such groups. Food laws and prohibitions have similarly been adopted for the purpose of marking off one group from another. And such practices have been so emotionalized by a variety of devices that the mere mention of forbidden food, for instance, is sometimes enough to produce violent gastronomic disturbance in the devotee of a culture which forbids the use of that food. Economic necessity, no doubt, gave rise originally to all such practices and feelings connected with food, but the feelings and the practices continued long after the necessity that produced them had disappeared. They continued because a social, and often a religious, motive had been used to enforce the economic regulation, such motives becoming in time a part of the group culture, and culture, as we have seen, is a very conservative and persistent force.

While the individual in some tribes enjoys a certain degree of freedom in respect to a few aspects of his behavior, primitive man is not the unfettered being that Rousseau thought him to be. Unlike us, he has little privacy in his life, and anything unusual in his conduct is reproved by his fellows. The beliefs and customs of his people restrict his liberty on every side and he becomes a veritable slave to social tradition and religious terrorism. There is scarcely an action which he performs with which is not associated some religious or other form of belief.

Some customs are so sacred that they are enforced by what is known as taboos. Any violation of such customs, which are sanctioned by taboos, stirs up the wrath of the whole community against the offender, and primitives make no distinction between voluntary and involuntary violations. Brutal floggings, mutilation, and execution are often inflicted upon the transgressor of tribal custom. In a society founded on kinship, no punishment is worse than exile, because among savages the alien is despised and permitted to starve, if he is not actually killed. And banishment from the tribe is sometimes inflicted for a violation of tribal custom. In tribes in which slavery has developed, offenders for certain crimes are reduced to servitude. Primitives, too, use the weapon of scorn and ridicule to punish a criminal. This publicly voiced contempt is very effective because it is universal, and wherever the offender turns jeers and invectives are hurled at him.[13]

The control of the savage by his tribe is thus nearly complete. This is particularly true of the actions of the individual. While each tribe has its own way of thinking, to which the individual usually conforms, an occasional skeptic, or heretic, does arise, for restraints are placed not so much on thought as on conduct. And this freedom of thought is possible because the primitive, says Professor Radin, believes that thought is concerned only with the realities of the natural and social environments which he accepts as fixed and unchangeable. Indeed, the primitive probably enjoyed greater freedom of thought and verbal expression than Orientals for whom the written word and thought became themselves ultimate realities and the cause of visible things. By Orientals, the visible word was conceived as an expression of a creator's thought. The primitive "word" confirmed the existence of realities, but the Oriental "word" was something existing "in the beginning" and was itself the first and most enduring reality. In Oriental societies human thought was shackled by "words," and lost a freedom which it enjoyed on the primitive level.[14]

All of the social ways of life and conduct, the folkways, and all of the beliefs of the group regarding the social, religious, and physical world become by education, both formal and informal, conscious and unconscious, the ways of life and beliefs of each individual. From the acquisition of these ways of thought and life the primitive child cannot escape, because by the very fact of living in his group he acquires these thoughts and these ways.

RELIGIOUS ASPECTS. (1) ANIMISM. The word "religion" means that which binds. Viewed from a sociological and historical standpoint, religion has been a force binding individuals together and giving their group stability. It has played a prominent rôle in the moulding of the minds of people, and in the regulation of behavior, by producing the customary emotional reactions to the demands of different environments. The question has often been asked as to whether or not religion has existed at all times and among all peoples. The answer to that question will depend upon our definition of religion. Should we define it in terms of monothe-

[13] G. Brown, *Melanesians and Polynesians* (London: Macmillan & Co., Ltd., 1910), pp. 451–61; Malinowski, *op. cit.*, pp. 372–458; Hartland, *op. cit.*, pp. 6–8, 138–41.

[14] P. Radin, *Primitive Man as a Philosopher* (New York: Appleton-Century-Crofts, Inc., 1927), pp. 41–61.

ism and an organized priesthood, its universality must be denied. If we say it is "a belief in Spiritual Beings," as E. B. Tylor defined it in his *Primitive Culture* (1871), then its universality must be admitted. This latter definition, almost universally accepted by ethnologists and anthropologists, will include all primitive groups among the religious peoples of the past.[15]

While some writers have denied the evolutionary character of religion and have argued for the existence of primitive monotheism, the preponderating opinion of students of the question is opposed to such a view.[16] The most elementary and universal conception in primitive religious thought is *animism,* or the belief that animate forces determine and control the actions of all things in the world, whether of men and living things or of inanimate things, such as rocks or water. The primitive, then, believes in the presence in everything of an *anima,* or a "double" of itself, and that this "double" is the cause of nearly all the activities of man and natural things. To the savage everything is, like himself, a living thing. Some writers distinguish between *naturism* as a form of thought which addresses itself to the phenomena of nature, as apart from man and animated beings, and a co-existing animism which is concerned with all conscious and living beings. Other writers hold that naturism was the earliest form of thought and prevailed when man did not distinguish between himself and the objective, external world. Animism, according to this latter view, replaced naturism when man became conscious of his own subjective existence as distinct from the external world.[17] Levy-Bruhl questions the validity of certain aspects of the long and almost universally accepted animistic theory, but in this, as in some of his other views, he stands practically alone.[18] G. Elliot Smith holds that animism was an Egyptian product and was transmitted to primitive peoples in the period following 2600 B.C., a view with which few scholars, if any, are in accord.[19] Thus we shall accept the traditional view, which has not yet been seriously challenged, that animism is the religion of all primitive peoples at a particular stage of their development, and that, with accidental variations, it is common to all primitives today

[15] J. Deniker, *The Races of Men* (New York: Charles Scribner's Sons, 1912), p. 214; Thomas, *op. cit.,* p. 698.

[16] Radin, *op. cit.,* pp. 342–74; J. A. Montgomery, *Religions of the Past and Present* (Philadelphia: J. B. Lippincott Co., 1918); Lowie, *Primitive Religion,* pp. 99–134.

[17] Montgomery, *op. cit.,* pp. 16–18; E. Clodd, *Animism, the Seed of Religion* (London: Constable & Co., Ltd., 1905), p. 26.

[18] L. Levy-Bruhl, *How Natives Think* (New York: Alfred A. Knopf, Inc., n.d.), pp. 15–31, 38–68.

[19] Lowie, *Primitive Religion,* pp. 99 ff.

who have not been in close touch with civilization and Christian missionaries for any length of time.

In the midst of a world filled with strange forces and strange phenomena, some of them of dangerous and fearful import, primitive man was forced, by fear of physical want and destruction, and by fear of strange forces which he did not understand, to inquire into the causes of things in order to control his environment. He feared the falling trees and rocks, lightning, earthquakes, and storms because of their capacity for evil, and to such happenings as these he gave an animistic explanation. The causes of many of the most ordinary natural occurrences he did not know. This ignorance made him dread particularly all those invisible agencies, or forces, which operated everywhere throughout his environment. Thomas Hobbes, in his *Leviathan,*[20] says that the fear of the invisible was the seed of religion. Every unknown thing or force was a source of dread to the savage. His religion, animism, which was the direct result of that fear, was the first religion, the first philosophy. Animism endows everything, whether natural or made by the hands of the savage himself, with a spirit or "double." His dreams, for instance, convince him of the existence within himself of a more subtle being, a "double," which temporarily separates itself from his body and, of itself, engages in all the activities of the wakeful man. Death, he believes, occurs when the double leaves the body and loses its way or forgets to return. His experience with shadows, reflections, and echoes strengthened his convictions. Echoes are thought to be the voices of the "doubles" of men and animals. Night, indeed, for the savage is caused by the "doubles" of all things, which during the hours of darkness take control of the world; and primitives feared the night and its ghostly sounds and apparitions.

Unable to grasp the idea of natural causes, primitives attribute most occurrences to the operation of supernatural agencies. The number of spirits in the savage world is infinite. To the primitive, this supernatural or imaginary world exists side by side with the natural world and is equally real. Nay more, some supernatural agency is looked upon as the cause of disease, death, fortune or misfortune, etc. Dogs, cattle, crops, fish, arrows, spears, human beings, and the whole infinite variety of things have their "doubles," their genii, their guardian angels toward which men must know how to act properly if they will live correctly and successfully.

Some spirits or "doubles" are considered benevolent and others malevolent, and man must know how to act toward all of them. In societies far more advanced than those of savages, animism con-

[20] II. 1.

tinues under many forms. The veneration of trees, holy wells and water, stones, bells, and many other objects is a survival from primitive days. Savages use bells to drive away evil spirits. The "doubles" of the dead returned to savages in their dreams, and thus animism led to ancestor worship, the grave becoming our first altar and our first temple; and many churches and altars have been erected over the graves or relics of saints. In the Far East ancestor worship has been almost universal. Egyptian civilization was built upon the tomb, and the deification of holy men in India and their canonization in Christendom have been a common practice. The survival of primitive ideas and culture in later societies, and even to the present day, is attested by an evidence so convincing in quality and quantity that its significance cannot reasonably be questioned. Just as our bodies retain vestiges of our descent from lower forms of animal life, so our minds to this day bear unmistakable and still active vestiges of our primitive origin.[21]

(2) Totemism. Totemism is the cult of some animal, bird, plant, or, much more rarely, some man-made object because of its supposed kinship with the group. While totemism has a very wide distribution among primitives in Australia, America, Africa, Melanesia, and parts of Asia, it is not universal, as animism is. Frequently the totem group believes that it is descended from the totem. Among some groups the totem is thought of as a most sacred thing. Totemic groups have developed a strong sense of blood relationship, and frequently bear the names of their totems. The forms of totemism differ widely from tribe to tribe. Among some tribes, for instance, the totem animal may not be eaten, while among others no such restriction exists; and exogamy may or may not be coupled with totemism. Certain characteristics, however, belong to totemism wherever it exists: first, the magical bond which unites the human group with the animal group, or other form of totem group, and, second, the strong feeling of friendship produced by the totem cult within the human group itself.

Totemism has a marked influence upon the social character of every member of the group. Being frequently associated with tribal origin and descent, it links the present with the past and creates a feeling of religious brotherhood which is probably stronger than that of blood relationship. The savage's dread of, and reverence for, the totem is an outgrowth of his belief that the totem is related to the ancestral spirits of the tribe. Indeed, some primitives, ignorant of the biological relationship of father and child,

[21] Clodd, *op. cit.;* Montgomery, *op. cit.*, pp. 10 ff.; Lowie, *Primitive Religion*, pp. xiv–xvi, 99 ff.; Brown, *op. cit.*, pp. 190–95, 218–24; Maddox, *op. cit.*, pp. 5–6, 20.

believe that the spirit of some totem is the father of each child born into the group, just as Satan was thought by many a few centuries ago, and by some even today, to be the parent of many children born to witches in Europe.[22]

(3) MAGIC. Magic is the pretended power and art of controlling events and of producing extraordinary results by compelling spiritual agencies to bring into operation some hidden powers of nature. Among primitives, religion and magic co-exist, magic, indeed, being a religious practice. As embodying an attempt to control the forces of nature, magic is the forerunner of science. Magic, however, cannot be called primitive science because primitives have much definite factual knowledge which they discovered by the methods of trial and error and observation.

The primitive turns to magic when he enters the realm of the unknown. Some phases of his economic activities, for instance, of hunting and planting, are to him mysterious, and here he turns to magic. He knows, let us say, how to build a strong boat and how to sow grain, but strange forces destroy his boat and his crops sometimes fail, and so he launches his boat with magical rites, as we still do, and he sows his crops and cultivates them, supplementing his labors by the performance of magical ceremonies, and by praying occasionally for rain or drought, as we ourselves sometimes do still. Since the savage's knowledge of the natural world is, unlike ours, very rudimentary and limited, he turns to magic in connection with nearly every event of his everyday life. Birth, sickness, death, marriage, agriculture, commerce, and an infinite variety of events are linked to the operation of good or evil unseen agencies which he does not understand but which he knows he must control.

To control primitive man's unknown world the savage turns for aid to the magician, the medicine man, the sorcerer. To these, however, he appeals only when he is unable to direct his ends. There are certain common forms of magic which each individual performs, but there are other forms which only the expert magician can use successfully. In all cases the exact practices and the exact words must be used. Magic, too, may be either black, which is illegal and anti-social, or white, which is legal, social, and publicly approved. Witches, or users of black magic, are feared and often killed. To the magicians the tribesmen go for the medicine or charm necessary to produce the desired results. A wizard can sell a thief a medicine which is supposed to put a whole village to sleep,

[22] M. Summers, *History of Witchcraft and Demonology* (New York: Alfred A. Knopf, Inc., 1926); Montgomery, *op. cit.*, pp. 19–20; Miller, *op. cit.*, pp. 15–16; Lowie, *Primitive Society*, pp. 137–45; Lowie, *Primitive Religion*, pp. 158–59.

and honest people will go to white magicians for drugs which are supposed to counteract the spell of the black magician's medicine. This dread of black magic creates a respect for good social forces and, thus, indirectly black magic contributes to group solidarity.

There are magicians who specialize in weather control, or in thunder control, or in control of the prices of merchandise. In connection with magic, fetishism flourishes, and primitives have always with them a variety of objects which are supposed to exert an influence on the good or evil powers that affect men's lives. Primitive fetishism has survived in the belief of some moderns in the efficacy of rabbits' feet, lucky stones, and a variety of other similar objects.[23]

There is a very intimate connection between the savage's religious and magical beliefs and practices and his economic life. Primitives put themselves into the proper religious relationships with all those animals, plants, and objects which have a bearing upon the satisfaction of their physical wants. The tribal spirits are worshiped and placated during crises in the economic life of the tribe and individuals. Gratitude is publicly expressed to the spirits for victory in war, for rain, for abundance of crops and herds, for freedom from disease and the ravages of wild animals. A definite ritual has grown up around the use of food; and sacrifice, as a rite binding men together and uniting them with the spirit world, is almost universal among primitives. Cannibalism, which no doubt had an economic origin, continued as a religious function even after the original cause for it had disappeared, and its relation to the practice of sacrifice, which has survived in many cultures, is very close.

(4) Religious, Formal, and Mental Education. It was chiefly out of these religious beliefs and practices that the formal education of primitive peoples arose. The instruction of primitive youths in the practical skills necessary to acquire food, clothing, and shelter was informal in character, as we have noted. But in regard to one's relation to the imaginary environment and its spirits, education of an extremely formal character developed. The savage's practical education was acquired informally; his formal, cultural education was acquired through the most formal rites of tribal initiation which, as we shall see, began at the age of puberty, and were the entry to tribal membership. Primitive man's interpretation of the invisible world and its powers and activities furnished the content of his intellectual education, the only formal education which he received. As compared with the more elaborate interpre-

[23] Porteus, *op. cit.*, pp. 49–234; Lowie, *Primitive Religion*, pp. 33, 54, 136–46; Maddox, *op. cit.;* Montgomery, *op. cit.*, pp. 20–21; Brown, *op. cit.*, pp. 176, 236–44.

tations of the great literate civilizations of the Orient and the West, his was simple and unprofound. But, in common with other intellectual systems, it was rooted in his desire to control his environment. As compared with the informal and practical education of primitive youth, this mental education occupied far less time than it did among the literate people of advanced civilizations, where physical and practical education suffered a decline among the privileged classes, probably to the detriment of these civilizations. The physical and practical activities of nature peoples, as primitives are appropriately described, were permeated and determined very largely by their explanations of the invisible world. Indeed, primitive man's intellectual life was far less separated from everyday realities than was that of the great literate civilizations. While formal education was concerned with primitive man's explanations of his world, his whole culture and folkways created for these explanations an emotional foundation of great force. In literate civilizations, rational interpretations of the world often sought and found emotional support from religion and theology. However, many philosophical or rational explanations of life and the universe did not seek such support. Nor does the scientist seek to emotionalize his findings and his interpretations of them. But for tribal unity, primitive man's explanations of the invisible, woven into the fabric of his religious beliefs, were most effective instruments.

POLITICAL ASPECTS. Among savages, the political organization is at best poorly developed, although there are no groups in which one cannot discern the exercise of legislative, judicial, and executive functions by some form of authority. Australian tribal life, for instance, is dominated by the older men, and women are rigidly excluded from the exercise of anything approaching political activity. Among some Australian tribes an assembly of elders functions as a secret agency of government, whose proceedings are never divulged. The Arunta peoples of Australia have no such assemblies, nor is there among them anyone who can be called a tribal chief. The Aruntas, however, have a headsman of each totem group whose position is hereditary, and a group of such headsmen form a tribal governing board, which concerns itself chiefly with the regulation of ceremonials. Elsewhere in the primitive world one finds a variety of practices. Indeed, one sometimes finds a chief who rules by divine right and who is thought to be an incarnation of the greatest spirit of the tribe, a belief that survived through Oriental into modern times. A variety of forms of government exists among savages, so much so, indeed, that one cannot say that any particular form of government is peculiar to men closest to nature.

Primitive Culture

In the sense in which we are using the term "culture," all primitive peoples have a culture. It is the sum total of their ideas and beliefs regarding the physical, social, religious, and political world in which they live. And these beliefs have to do with such things as food, clothing, shelter, tools, arts, industries, marriage, social groupings, government, customs, the spirit world, and totems. These ideas find outward expression in a variety of activities, practices, customs, and traditional modes of behavior which we call the folkways. Born into this cultural environment, the child acquires, as he grows up, the traditional ideas of his people, by a process of education that is in the main unconscious. During the formal initiatory rites by which adolescent boys and girls are admitted to tribal membership, the great secrets of tribal history and of tribal duties to the spirit world are communicated to the young by a process which is, in some of its aspects at least, the embodiment of a conscious purpose. And the folkways, which embody these ideas and beliefs, the growing youth acquires by imitating the activities and customs of his people and, with this group way of life, custom and powerful tribal sanctions force the individual to conform. Primitive education is, then, in a very important sense, cultural in character.[24]

So conservative is this force of primitive culture and these folkways (and culture and folkways are highly conservative still) that primitive peoples are blind to the potentialities of their often very rich environments. Their culture renders them unable to seize upon better ways of exploiting their environment and of satisfying their wants. Travelers tell us that savages are unable to grasp the superiority of, for instance, the civilized man's more useful tools, unless the superiority is demonstrated to them in the most laborious and painstaking fashion, and that even then they may reject them in favor of their own crude implements. This attitude of aversion to the new, even though it is decidedly better than the old, is not due to any inferior mentality in savages but to the nature of their cultural heritage.

Primitive Educational Practices

To illustrate the educational practices of primitives generally, we shall examine those peculiar to the Arunta tribe of Central Aus-

[24] Dixon, *op. cit.*, pp. 3–31, 33–71; E. B. Tylor, *Researches into the Early History of Mankind* (London: John Murray, 1878), pp. 121–23, 182–91; Deniker, *op. cit.*, pp. 201–13; Miller, *op. cit.*, pp. 3 ff.; Thomas, *op. cit.*, pp. 20–26, 593–664; Blackmar, *op. cit.*, pp. 129–37.

tralia, basing our account upon the studies of Spencer and Gillen, *The Native Tribes of Central Australia* (1899) and *Across Australia* (1912). Spencer and Gillen lived among the Aruntas for nearly a generation, learned their language, and observed them closely. While one may question their interpretations of what they observed (since cultural differences always impede understanding of thoughts, feelings, and motives), no one can reasonably question the accuracy of their observed facts. It is doubtful that the techniques of observation used by modern so-called dynamic anthropologists reveal the soul of primitive cultures better than those used by Spencer and Gillen. It should be noted, however, that the practices of no two tribes are exactly alike. This much can be said: All primitives socialize their children by education. Arunta practices provide a good illustration of the education of primitive children. No doubt, their ways have been changed in recent years by contact with white civilization.

The Arunta tribe occupies a territory of considerable extent, and is divided into small clans. The number of individuals in a clan runs from about twenty-five to a hundred. Each clan occupies its own division of the tribal territory, has its own dialect and its own totems. Exogamy is the rule of these people; that is, the individual must marry one who belongs to another clan. The Arunta people have not yet reached the agricultural stage, and live on wild berries, wild vegetables, and various species of animals and living things.

Arunta mothers kill their newborn children when food is scarce or when they are already burdened with too many children. They believe, however, that the child's spirit will return again in some other child, for it is thought to be an ancestral or totem spirit which never dies. The parents are kind to the children whom they permit to live. In camp, the children laugh and play through the greater part of the day.

INFORMAL EDUCATION. (1) PRACTICAL. Boys and girls under the age of twelve or thirteen live in the women's part of the camp and accompany their mothers into the scrub where, with their toy digging sticks, they mimic the operations of the women as they dig for roots and small animals. The children help the women to carry back to camp a collection of lizards, rats, frogs, etc., as well as grass-seed which the women bake into flat cakes. Thus, while civilized children are in school getting many of their experiences from books, the savage child is reading the book of nature and learning by actually doing in play the things which will later become a serious life activity.

At about the age of twelve, boys pass into the charge of the men, whom henceforth they live with and accompany on hunting expeditions. The boy now makes and carries his mimic weapons as, indeed, he did even while he was still in charge of the women. With these mimic weapons he performs all the actions of the hunter, but as yet only by way of play. By this method of playful imitation of the activities of their elders, Arunta boys and girls acquire those skills upon the perfection of which their physical life depends. Not until boys have passed through some of the ceremonies of tribal initiation, at about the age of fifteen, are they permitted to carry and use real spears, boomerangs, and shields, for the possession and use of these are privileges of men. While Spencer and Gillen do not give a detailed description of the games of Arunta children, one can always infer from their remarks that the games are intimately related to life needs and that the children take an intense delight in playing them.

(2) Physical Education. The body of the primitive child is thus developed by a variety of physical activities which in youth assume the character of play, but which in later life become the serious work of every man and woman. The physique of the Arunta man is excellent and his carriage is remarkably graceful. The same is true of women under the age of twenty-five. Probably because she is a beast of burden who pursues her work with a child on her back, while she carries other heavier burdens at the same time, all of which deprives her body of that freedom of motion which men enjoy, the Arunta woman ages rapidly after she has passed her twenty-fifth year, loses soon all her grace of body, and seldom lives beyond the age of fifty. Dancing, which holds a prominent place in many social and religious functions, must be considered an important aspect of physical education. Women often have a part in the dances.

(3) Social and Religious Education. Just as the Arunta child is educated by living and acting in his physical environment, so is he educated socially and religiously in the same informal and unconscious way by actual participation in the social and religious life of his people. He acquires the language of his people, a language which embodies the various ideas or culture of his group. In that language there are no terms for father, mother, uncle, aunt, husband, or wife, but there are group names by which all members of certain groups or subgroups are known. The child will soon observe that with these terms, or names, certain intergroup or extragroup relationships are associated, and that all his elders observe

certain rules of behavior in regard to these relationships, the behavior differing with the relationship. A particular form of conduct comes to be associated with the group name, and thus the name takes on a deep significance for the child, which becomes even deeper as the relationship and behavior which it suggests are emotionalized for him by the invariable and uniform practice of his people as well as by the habits of action which he has acquired by imitating the actions of his elders. The Arunta child, for instance, learns by living with his people that those bearing a particular group name always and invariably marry those who bear the name of a different and special group, and he comes to feel, as his elders do, that any other scheme of marriage is unthinkable. Such feelings are developed by rules that, for instance, forbid males and females of certain groups to address each other except at a distance of from 40 to 100 yards as the case may be. Thus, unconsciously and informally the Arunta youth learns the modes of tribal relationships and of the behavior proper to his group. When his clan pays a visit to a neighboring clan, as it often does, the youth learns how to behave toward his neighboring tribesfolk, for, on all such occasions, there are the traditional usages which all observe.

By listening to his people and observing and imitating their conduct, he comes into possession, also, of the religious experiences of his group. Every newborn child is considered a reincarnation of one of the old ancestors and it is given, at birth, the proper totem name and becomes henceforth a member of its ancestral totemic group. The very name a boy or girl bears is a constant reminder of his or her relationship to the ancestral and totemic spirits and of the behavior proper to all members of the totem group in their relationships to the physical, social, and religious worlds. Children of the Aruntas come to know, too, that there are certain religious objects in the possession of the elders that are most sacred, and that these *Churinga*, as they are called, may not even be looked at by women or uninitiated boys.

Life, too, in the group is one of almost constant religious ceremonials from which women and children are barred, a fact which makes their mysterious nature all the more impressive for those excluded. The youths belonging to the kangaroo totem learn that kangaroo people are responsible for the supply of kangaroos; those of the witchetty grub totem learn that their group is responsible for the supply of witchetty grub; and so on for all of the other totems, an economic duty being thus emotionalized for all members of a totem group by elaborate religious ceremonial.

A significant practice of the Aruntas, which is social rather than religious in character, is the corrobboree. This is a sort of festival characterized by singing, dancing, and the most unrestrained hilarity. A corrobboree lasts usually for about two weeks, and recurs frequently. All members of the group, including women and children, attend the celebration, although the men are the performers, the women and children being the audience. The men who perform paint and decorate their bodies in a most elaborate fashion, and during the dance gesticulate wildly. Their shouts, in which the women join, can be heard for miles. The corrobboree is by far the most popular social function of the Aruntas and relieves, for a time at least, the dreadful monotony of savage life. Whatever may be its purposes, it serves to enhance the prestige of the men in the minds of women and children, and it brings a measure of joy into the usually drab lives of the people.

Thus, by informal association with his mother, his kinsfolk, and his childhood companions, the primitive child learns the ways of life of his people. By actual participation in the various activities of men and women, boys and girls become proficient in the performance of their own life duties. The whole atmosphere, too, in which the people live is one of almost continuous ceremonial. While women and children are excluded from many parts of these ceremonies, men during their entire lives engage in them, and thus the rites provide a form of life-long education for those who take part in them as well as for those who are forbidden for religious reasons to witness the sacred performances.

FORMAL EDUCATION. (1) INITIATION CEREMONIES FOR BOYS. Every Arunta boy must pass through certain formal ceremonies before he is admitted to full tribal membership. There are four major ceremonies, the first of which is performed when the boy is about twelve years of age, and the last of which is sometimes postponed to the age of twenty-five or thirty. These ceremonies are:

1. Painting and *Alkirakiwuma,* or hurling the boy into the air
2. *Lartna*—circumcision
3. *Arilta*—subincision
4. *Engwura*—fire ordeal

They are performed by men who stand in some special relationship to the boy. Women witness the first ceremony and dance while it is being performed. The painting of the boy embodies some form of totemic symbolism. While it is being done, the boy is told that this first ceremony will hasten his growth to manhood, and that henceforth he must not play with women or girls but must live in the company of men. His nose is now bored and he begins to wear the nose bone. When this ceremony is over, the boy, who previously was known by the name *Ambaquerka,* a name applied to all pre-initiates, is given a new name. He is now called *Ulpmerka,* a name which he retains until after the ceremony of *Lartna.*

When the boy has reached the stage of puberty, he is subjected to the second ceremony, that of circumcision. His elders make elaborate ceremonial preparations for this rite without letting the boy know anything about what is going to happen. At the proper time, the boy is seized by three young men who shout wildly and, while he struggles to escape, is carried away bodily to the initiation grounds which have been prepared in the customary way for the ceremony. On the grounds he finds himself surrounded by men and women, the latter performing a shield dance.

It ought to be noted here, and in connection with all the remaining ceremonies, that the chief events in the supposed history of the group are re-enacted and dramatized during the process of initiation, and the most solemn occasions in tribal history and the most sacred secrets of the group are communicated to the initiates at the proper time and in a most impressive ceremonial way.

The preliminary rites having been enacted, the boy is placed alone behind a specially built brake from which he is occasionally taken to witness certain performances and to submit to certain ceremonies. A council of elders directs the proceedings. In the course of the ceremony he is told that he is no longer *Ulpmerka* but has a new name, *Wurtja,* and that he must obey, without question, every command of his elders who have charge of his initiation. Above all, he is admonished that he must never reveal any of the proceedings to women or children under pain of death to himself and his nearest relatives. From the surrounding bush the weird sounds produced by the bull-roarers break occasionally on his ears. He has never heard them before, and he is told that they are the voice of the great spirit.

The boy himself is occasionally called upon to perform an act or guard a certain object given to him, under pain of destruction by some spirit. For nearly four days he must live in partial seclusion to remind him that he is about to join the ranks of men and to enter a new form of life, as well as to impress upon him the necessity of compliance with tribal rules and of respecting the dignity and authority of his elders. On the night of the fourth day, the men sing the song of the totem ancestor who first introduced the stone knife at circumcision, and then yell aloud the words and notes of the *Lartna* song.

These totemic ceremonies continue for a few additional days.

Never before had the boy heard the totemic and ancestral secrets of his people, secrets descending from a supposedly great historic past, and now impressed upon him by a weird and elaborate dramatization of the events in the lives of the tribal ancestors of an ancient mythical antiquity. At various intervals the women enter the initiation grounds and dance, while some of them perform other minor parts in the ceremonial; and from the bush comes the steady sound of the bull-roarers.

On about the tenth day from the beginning of the ceremony, the youth is circumcised with elaborate rites, and thereafter he bears a new name, *Arakurta,* a name which he retains until the rite of *Arilta* is performed some six weeks later. The ceremony of *Lartna* has been painful but the boy had to bear it courageously, and that of *Arilta* is even more painful. From the rite of *Arilta* women are excluded.

In connection with the rites of *Lartna* and *Arilta* the new initiate is permitted to see and handle for the first time the most sacred *Churinga,* and to learn the great secrets regarding their origin and nature. By this time many of the great tribal mysteries have been revealed to him. At the close of the ceremonies he is elaborately decorated and is led into the presence of the women who greet him with dancing and singing, in which some of the men join, and which are continued all through the night.

The last and greatest ceremony of initiation is that of *Engwura,* after which the initiate is called *Urliara.* The natives believe it gives strength to all who have been subjected to it. It is not a clan ceremony, but one in which men and women from all sections of the tribe take a part. Only members of the immediate clan, and probably a few invited neighbors, participate in the *Lartna* and *Arilta* rites, but the *Engwura* is an occasion for a general assembling of all the tribal elders. Through it, young men are made to feel their subordination to the elders; through it, the virtues of courage and self-restraint are taught them; and, through it, the last of the great secrets of the group are revealed to them. A veritable multitude of ceremonies follow one another—corrobborees, preparing the ceremonial grounds on which one sacred drama after another is enacted, the complete separation of the sexes for a period of six weeks, and the final elevation of the young men to the rank of *Urliara,* many young men from the whole tribe being now initiated at one time.

In the actual ceremonies, the sacred *Churinga* are given elaborate ritualistic veneration, as are also the totems of the various local groups. The elders call upon the owners of the various ceremonials to perform them, and only that is done which the elders decree. On this occasion one might say that the history not only of a clan but of the whole tribe is re-enacted in a dramatic way by those best versed in tribal lore. Multitudinous formalities in dress, decoration, and ceremonial performance are observed with the most scrupulous exactness. All the world has now, indeed, become a stage and every man an actor, each one gravely performing many parts. Every night during the six weeks the men indulge in wild, boisterous singing which resounds through the hills. As among all primitives, dancing has a prominent part in the entire *Engwura* ceremonial. Most noteworthy is the reverent silence of all present when they are in the presence of the *Churinga*, and the respectful attention which the young men pay to the old man who has been chosen, because of the accuracy of his knowledge, to instruct them in regard to these objects and the history of the tribe. This old man, revered for his learning, is known as an *Oknirabata*, or great teacher, and his rôle in the ceremonials is very prominent.

The whole ceremonial ends with the ordeal of the fire test to which all initiates are required to submit. A great fire is built for the purpose and, when it is burning bright, it is covered with green bushes and leaves. On the top of this burning pile, and protected only by a thin covering of green wood and leaves, each initiate is required to lie for about five minutes. The temperature at the time when Spencer and Gillen witnessed the ceremony was 110.5° F. in the shade and 156° F. in the sun. On top of the burning pile on such a day the heat is stifling and the smoke from the burning timber and leaves is suffocating. Moreover, the boys are required to undergo this fire ordeal twice on the same day. The *Engwura* rites end with a fire ceremony in the women's camp to which the men now return with much ritualistic display. Women and children, however, are forbidden under pain of dread penalties, to visit the *Engwura* grounds for many months.

To the young men who pass through this greatest of Arunta ceremonies a new name is given, that of *Urliara*. They are now full-fledged members of the tribe to whom all the sacred traditions and secrets of their people have been revealed. And those secrets have been revealed to them in a most impressive way. The secrets, indeed, are few and might have been communicated to them orally in a few hours. But primitives use a more effective method of teaching. The whole performance, from the *Alkirakiwuma* to the *Engwura*, is marked by a ceremonialism so elaborately formal and awe-inspiring and so surrounded by solemnity and secrecy that an indelible impression is made upon the souls of the youths who pass through its mysteries and trials. These youths have thus been made heirs of tribal culture, obligated to transmit to posterity the wisdom, ideas, and beliefs of their people.

(2) FORMAL EDUCATION OF GIRLS. Girls who have arrived at the age of puberty are, among the Aruntas, subjected to the operation of *Atna-arilta-kuma,* which corresponds to the *Arilta* ceremony for boys. The operation is performed by men. There is no elaborate ceremonial connected with it. The girl is, however, painted and decorated after it has been performed, and she becomes immediately the wife of a man to whom she has been betrothed since her birth. In the case of a girl, then, formal instruction with regard to the world of spirits is conspicuously lacking. Her duties to that world she learns by informal association with her people, particularly with the older women with whom she was permitted to witness certain parts of totemic ceremonies which men perform. Formal mental education is not her portion in the cultural climate of the Arunta people.

EDUCATIONAL PURPOSE. It is not certain that the Arunta people, or indeed other primitives, have a conscious purpose in such education as has been described here. Indeed, all of their educational practices may be but an unconscious reaction to the physical, social, and imaginary environments in which they live.

Arunta tribesmen teach their youth, and the youth learn, largely without the use of reason, and in this same irrational fashion culture has been, in the main, transmitted even to our own day. But while many post-primitive educational systems and practices have embodied a conscious purpose, primitive processes seem to be devoid of deliberate and conscious planning. Dominated, as they are, by tribal custom and tradition, the Arunta elders educate their boys in the traditional way because that way is traditional.

But, whether conscious or unconscious, Arunta education meets the practical and cultural needs of the tribe, and its goal can thus be called practical, in respect to those aspects which have to do with the satisfaction of physical wants, and cultural, in respect to those other aspects which are concerned with social relationships and man's dealings with the spirit world. To preserve the tribe and its culture unchanged may be said to be its basic purpose. Not a thought is given to the need for change or improvement. It achieved, however, the socialization of the child, which is the basic goal of modern education.

CURRICULUM. The subject matter of Arunta instruction, as indeed of that of all primitives, is the experiences of the tribe. This material of instruction grows out of the immediate environment, real or imaginary. All the knowledge, habits, and skills necessary for the satisfaction of one's physical wants form a prominent part of the curriculum, and are acquired by youth informally through participation in the daily economic activities of the older men and women of the tribe. Differentiation on the basis of sex characterizes this and other aspects of the curriculum, because labor has been divided on that basis, and the sexes have different social and religious activities to perform. In addition to practical experiences, the Arunta curriculum comprises a wide variety of social experiences, which have to do with all the traditional modes of behavior governing all social relationships.

Then, there are those experiences, in a wide variety, which have to do with the relation of men and women to their totems and to the whole spirit world, some of which are communicated by the informal associations of tribal life, but most of which are provided for in the very formal ceremonies of initiation and of totem worship. The physical education of the primitive grows out of these activities and takes the form of play, games, hunting, throwing the spear and boomerang, dancing and work in its many aspects. Dancing, games and sports had generally a religious significance in addition to an economic and social one.

The Aruntas are neither a trading nor a warfaring people. Living in complete economic and cultural isolation, nothing finds its way into their curriculum which is unrelated to their own immediate environment. It is a curriculum which, in its social and cultural aspects, is loaded with symbolism, for primitives, like ourselves, control the individual by symbols rather than by force. Feelings are aroused, attitudes are developed, ideas are conveyed, and actions are determined by symbols. National and religious groups have such symbols as a flag or cross, which stand for something groups consider valuable. The Arunta people, and all primitives, have their gestures, their sounds, their dancing, their music, their ritual, their language, and a variety of material objects, all of which are, for them, symbols of spiritual treasures.

The value of symbols in education is apparent. Language, for instance, comprises a variety of sound symbols, which make communication easy. Without language, teachers would have to carry pupils bodily to many classroom exercises. As it is, the teacher need but mumble a few sounds and pupils proceed to their appointed tasks. Much of primitive culture, as of our own, is embodied in symbols, and the primitive, like us, is almost as unconscious of its operation as he is of the air he breathes. The only differentiation that enters into the curriculum is that based upon the traditional differentiation of the duties and activities of the sexes. As yet, no obtrusive class distinctions exist; nor is there a caste system, which, on higher levels of civilization, introduced educational differences and inequalities.

In the midst of the many conflicts and cross currents of the modern world the question of "what shall we teach" gives rise to heated debates and controversies, particularly in the area of the social sciences, "the new fundamentals" as they are sometimes called. In a rapidly changing culture the problem of the curriculum is a disturbing one, but it is not so in the fixed, static culture of primitive tribes. Authoritarian modern states tolerate no controversies, but liberal states do, for they thrive on disagreement. The fear of communism, perhaps more than communism itself, threatens to rob us of the freedom to disagree.

METHOD. To be effective, methods of instruction must conform with the character of particular social systems. In static, despotic, and authoritarian systems, the method used must be such as to produce submissive and uncritical minds, if despotism and authoritarianism are to endure. In free, democratic societies, the method to be used must be such as to free the human mind from those forces and agencies that threaten its independence, and to develop in the individual that critical attitude which is essential to the preservation of democratic institutions. Indeed, the method of instruction is one of the most distinguishing differences between the educational process of authoritarian and liberal states.

The educational method of the Arunta people is essentially imitation. The tribal elders, in performing the initiatory and other ceremonies, imitate their dead fathers. Children imitate the activities of their elders. In all physical, social, and religious activities, each new generation learns by imitating the ways of the older generation. Perfection in these ways comes by repeated imitation. By trials and effort, whether in play or work, youths become masters of those physical skills essential to the preservation of life; and by simply living with their people and imitating their social and religious ways they acquire their culture and habits. Thus are habits of life and action formed. In this way the individual is robbed of the freedom, if not of the capacity, to depart from the folkways of his people. In connection with tribal lore, songs, and ritual, an element of memorization enters into primitive method but, since primitives have no literature, the memoriter method is with them of minor importance.

This activity method was approved by Plato, among the Greeks, for vocational groups, and it has been enthusiastically advocated by educational theorists in the West for over three centuries. Primitive education is, indeed, life, and primitives learn by living. In the initiatory rites, however, boys are but passive witnesses of the various ceremonies and passive recipients of tribal secrets communicated to them in a soul-stirring way.

While there is little doubt about the use and effect of imitation in the over-all picture of primitive method, it is worthy of note that, among some savages, the child enjoys great independence, and that youths are often permitted the luxury of rebellion against authority. Perhaps youth has always been rebellious and the progressive element in society. But the rebellious spirit of the primitive child is gradually subdued by the culture of his people, a culture that has withstood such rebellion and has learned to tolerate it.

SCHOOLS. The family and the tribe are the schools of savages. One might consider that the education received by boys and girls prior to tribal initiation is elementary. This stage of education is, in the main, organized within the family. In this school youths are, as it were, apprentices, who learn the rules of the game of life by actually doing the things that life itself demands. The clan and tribe, through their elders, provide the formal school of initiation, with which the family has practically nothing to do and which may be considered the secondary education of primitive youth, for all primitives, like the Aruntas, have such a school.

TEACHERS. Among the Arunta people, there is no special teaching profession. Parents have particular charge of the practical education of their children, and tribal elders are the teachers in the formal school of initiation. In the ceremony of *Engwura,* one man who is specially versed in tribal lore and who is regarded as the great teacher plays a prominent part, but he is but one of the many elders who participate in the ceremony. All participants in the *Engwura* are chosen for their various parts by the council of elders. The chief difference here between primitive practices and those of great literate civilizations is that, in the latter, a special class, a priesthood, acquired the privilege of exploring the invisible world and of explaining its mysteries to youth. While tribal elders, shamans, and tribal historians, because of their age and experience, performed special teaching functions among primitives, they did not constitute a special teaching class or profession.

PUPILS. All of the Arunta boys, without exception, receive the same education, informal and formal, and all girls are educated alike. There are no distinctions except those based upon sex.

CONTROL. Control of education is vested in the family and in the tribe. All that formal education which is essential to an individual's promotion to tribal membership, or citizenship, is controlled by the tribal elders, members of a boy's immediate family having little or no part in the proceedings. So essential is this cultural education to tribal solidarity and the perpetuity of its customs that it is entirely a group function. The claim, sometimes made, of the historical priority of family rights in moulding the minds of children is not supported by the evidence we now have. Primitive society, not the parents, assumed the responsibility for explaining the invisible environment to youth. If parents had any so-called natural rights in the matter, society did not respect these rights. The culture, not any law of nature, was the determining factor.

RESULTS. Arunta education achieves what obviously is its chief end, the preservation of the tribe, but it makes no provision for the improvement of tribal life, no provision for change or progress. Arunta women and girls continue to dig for worms and rats in the old traditional way and with the old traditional digging sticks, and men hunt with the same weapons and use the same hunting techniques that their forefathers are thought to have used since the origin of the tribe in the mythical happenings of a mythical long-ago. Nor do they desire to change these ways. Strangely enough the ways of civilization, when adopted, have led to disaster. Since their contact with the whites, the Aruntas have adopted some civilized modes of dress, with the result that pulmonary and other diseases have wreaked havoc among them, and the tribe seems to be slowly passing to its "happy hunting ground." Contact with civilization has brought a great crisis for the Arunta people.

That crisis has its physical and social aspects. The physical crisis, some few will survive, but the Arunta social system, with its beliefs and customs, is doomed to disintegration. By that crisis they are being forced to progress beyond the stage of fixed, unalterable custom, and those who survive the crisis will do so by their individual capacity for adaptation to a changing environment both in its physical and cultural aspects. The culture of the survivors will be a blend of native and civilized cultures, the product being about 90 per cent native and 10 per cent civilized. When we engraft a new culture upon an old stem the product is always a blend of the old and the new. Thus, for instance, have many pagan elements survived in Christianity, many primitive African elements in the Christianity of American Negroes, and many Confucian elements in the religion of those Chinese whom our missionaries have converted to Christianity in our own day.

While the practices of the Arunta tribe furnish a good example of primitive educational procedures, it must be noted that, among primitive peoples generally, a great variety of practices exists. Generalizations about such practices are as hazardous as those about their culture and folkways. There is now available an abundance of works upon the educational practices of most of our primitive groups, some of which ought to have a place in the library of every teacher-training institution. In the appended list of selected readings will be found some of those which, in the author's opinion, will have great significance for the student in the field of education.

Selected Readings

Benedict, R. *Patterns of Culture.* Boston: Houghton Mifflin Co., 1934.

Hambly, W. D., and Hose, C. *Origins of Education among Primitive Peoples.* London: Macmillan & Co., Ltd., 1926.

Kidd, D. *Savage Childhood.* London: A. & C. Black, Ltd., 1906.

Lowie, R. H. *Primitive Society.* New York: Liveright Publishing Corp., 1920.

Mead, M. *Coming of Age in Samoa.* New York: The New American Library of World Literature, Inc., 1949.

Miller, N. *The Child in Primitive Society.* New York: Brentano, 1928.

Radin, P. *Primitive Man as a Philosopher.* New York: Appleton-Century-Crofts, Inc., 1927.

Raum, O. F. *Chaga Childhood.* London: Oxford University Press, 1940.

Spencer, B., and Gillen, F. J. *The Native Tribes of Central Australia.* London: Macmillan & Co., Ltd., 1899.

Spencer, F. C. *Education of the Pueblo Child.* New York: The Macmillan Co., 1899.

Todd, A. J. *The Primitive Family as an Educational Agency.* New York: G. P. Putnam's Sons, 1913.

Wissler, C. *Man and Culture.* New York: The Thomas Crowell Co., 1923.

3 Egyptian Society and Education

Of the ancient Oriental peoples who built great civilizations, the Chinese, Hindus, Egyptians, Babylonians, Assyrians, Persians, and Hebrews have been significantly great in their achievements. The student of social and educational problems will find it extremely profitable to study the social and educational systems of ancient China and India, for these are excellent examples of Oriental systems generally. Moreover, Western civilization and culture are indebted, directly or indirectly, to the peoples of the Far East, our borrowings from India being particularly notable.[1] Our greater indebtedness, however, to the nations of the Near East is attested by an abundance of evidence which any interested person may find discussed in the works of archaeological specialists and of historians. Since all Oriental civilizations have much in common, we shall examine only two of them, that of Egypt and that of India. Both are typically Oriental. To both of them our Western culture is indebted in varying degrees. It is now fairly certain that the cradle of Western civilization is either the valley of the Nile or that of the Tigris and Euphrates, but more probably that of the Nile.

Egyptian Society

RISE AND FALL OF EGYPTIAN CIVILIZATION. Egypt is smaller than Belgium, being but 12,500 square miles in area. A long narrow valley, fertilized by the annual inundations of the Nile, it extends from the Delta in the north to the mountains of Ethiopia in the south, a distance of about 700 miles. The first human occupation of the Nile region dates, according to Breasted, from about 18,000 B.C.[2] From eighty feet below the modern surface, the remains of

[1] J. A. Montgomery, *Religions of the Past and Present* (Philadelphia: J. B. Lippincott Co., 1918), p. 114 *passim*.

[2] *The Cambridge Ancient History (C.A.H.)* (12 vols.; New York: The Macmillan Co., 1923–39), I, 86.

successive civilizations have been discovered in the alluvial deposit. From these remains, archaeologists have built up the story of the prehistoric civilization of the Nile Valley.

The historical period, or the period of written records, dates from approximately 5000 B.C. With the original inhabitants, who were probably of the Hamitic race, other races mingled as time went on. A conquering people from Syria, of a different race, established, about 8000 B.C., the northern kingdom. From their coming dates the great development of Egyptian culture. But, while foreign races came and conquered, there is no doubt that the original inhabitants were the base of the population far into historical times and that their descendants are to be found in more isolated communities even to the present day.[3] In spite, however, of this occasional infiltration of strange races, Egypt was peculiarly free from invasion because she was protected by desert on one side, and by sea and desert on the other. Such happy circumstances permitted this great Eastern civilization to develop in comparative peace and, for a long period, in apparently comparative isolation. In the historical period, however, she came into closer and closer contact with her Eastern and Western neighbors.

The political unification of Egypt was the work of the Syrian invaders, already referred to. They set up two separate kingdoms on the Nile, one in the north, another in the south. It seems probable that these two separate civilized communities were in existence as early as 4300 B.C.,[4] and their unification dates from about 3500 B.C. The Nile civilization was so advanced in 4241 B.C., that, in that year, the calendar, according to some authorities, was instituted[5] and the length of the solar year was determined with almost perfect accuracy. By the will of the king, this calendar was henceforth established and accepted throughout the state. Without a directing state organization and authority this establishment would have been impossible. Until about 1650 B.C., Egypt was free from the rule of foreigners. About that year, however, sovereignty passed into the hands of the Hyksos kings, of the Semitic race and akin to the Hebrews.[6]

Another thousand years elapsed before foreigners again invaded Egypt, laid waste her land and treasures, and desecrated her shrines. In the eighth century B.C., an Ethiopian ruled Egypt. Then came the Assyrian invasion (675-663 B.C.), a second Hyksos conquest.

[3] *Ibid.*, pp. 33–34, 244, 264–66.

[4] *Ibid.*, p. 265.

[5] *Ibid.*, pp. 173, 248–49.

[6] *Ibid.*, p. 173.

This event marks the end of Egyptian independence, except for a brief period in the sixth century B.C. In 525 B.C., Egypt fell under the sway of Persia. Then, in 332 B.C., Alexander the Great made Egypt a part of his great Greek empire of the Near East. After the Greeks, there came in turn, as her masters, the Romans, Arabs, Turks, and British.

ECONOMIC LIFE. (1) AGRICULTURAL ACTIVITIES. It was the extraordinary fertility of the Nile Valley which made Egypt so important. That fertility was the gift of the Nile, which annually overflowed its banks and, on receding, left behind it, over the whole length of the country, a loam which made the valley one of the richest agricultural sections of the world. Here prehistoric man soon passed from the pastoral to the agricultural stage of civilization, and here he learned to store away, in canals and reservoirs, a supply of water sufficient for irrigation purposes during the long yearly drought. These irrigation systems probably had much to do with the unification of river communities, all of which had to contend with the same economic problems. The success of the Egyptians in solving this problem of irrigation made it possible to feed a great population and to build probably the greatest civilization of the ancient world.

Some philosophers of history attach the greatest importance to the factor of race in human progress, while others stress such factors as a challenging geographic environment, individual genius, creative minorities, cultural freedom, cultural cross-fertilization, and luck, or a combination of these. Whatever may be the importance of biological and cultural factors in the building of civilizations, it seems to be fairly certain from the evidence we have that a favorable climatic and geographic environment is a condition *sine qua non* of the rise of great civilizations. The physical environment must be favorable or, at least, not unfavorable. There is much debate and uncertainty regarding the racial origin and relations of the Egyptians, but the physical and cultural environment in which they lived and worked is well known. It would appear from the history of Egypt that the environmental factors were the determining ones. However, conditions which are conducive to rapid development at one stage of civilization may hamper its growth at another stage. Indeed, the natural protection which Egypt enjoyed by her isolation in her own fertile habitat led in earlier times to a precocious growth, but actually cramped the further progress of civilization in later days.[7]

[7] F. W. Blackmar, *History of Human Society* (New York: Charles Scribner's Sons, 1926), pp. 142–49; R. Thurnwald, *Economics in Primitive Communities*

In addition to contributing heavily to the political unification of people and the development of their culture, the Nile made the Egyptians an industrious people. They had to keep its water within its banks, divert it into canals, distribute it over the land by irrigating devices before a single morsel of vegetable food could be secured. This demanded ceaseless labor on dykes and canals, and in plowing, and planting and watering crops. Agriculture was the basic "business" of the Egyptians, and they raised a great variety of vegetables and fruit. Very early, we find them using the ox-drawn hoe, forerunner of the plow, instead of the primitive digging-stick, a change which represents a great advance in man's way of life. Cattle-breeding and agriculture became closely connected when men harnessed oxen to their plows, as was the practice in Egypt. Goats, sheep, cattle, donkeys, geese, and ducks were raised from prehistoric times on. From the same ancient times large houseboats were used to navigate the river. The Nile as a channel of trade thus laid a basis of early social unification.

(2) ARTS AND INDUSTRY. As a result of the demands of economic life and the superabundant gifts of nature, Egypt bristled with activity. Arts and crafts flourished and multiplied from early prehistoric times, and very many specialized vocations developed. Even the primitive Egyptian was a skillful artisan who has left behind him many examples of his arts, particularly vases of great beauty. This prehistoric man invented a drill capable of cutting the hardest stone. Brick, pottery, glass, leather, and wood industries developed and flourished from very early times.[8]

By the beginning of the first dynasty (*c.* 3500 B.C.), artists in ivory, wood, metal, stone, jewelry, beads, and textiles were numerous and were encouraged by the wealthy court of the Pharaohs. Many arts and crafts developed also in connection with the temples and with the religious and funeral rites of the people. Indeed, the mummification and burying of the bodies of the dead became a flourishing business, gave employment to hosts of laborers, and increased the wealth of the priests and the temples. The need for storing away the water of the Nile led to great activity in the field of engineering. A veritable network of dykes, reservoirs, and canals extended along the river from the mountains to the sea.

(New York: Oxford University Press, 1932), pp. 93–98; J. Davis, *Readings in Sociology* (Boston: D. C. Heath & Co., 1927), pp. 68–69; P. A. Sorokin, *Social Philosophies of an Age of Crisis* (Boston: Beacon Press, Inc., 1950).

[8] *C. A. H.*, I, 242–43; J. Breasted, *Ancient Times* (Boston: Ginn & Co., 1916), pp. 38 ff.

The Pharaohs, the political despots of Egypt, have left a record of their glory and their shame in art, painting, sculpture, architecture, obelisks, sphinxes, and lastly in the pyramids which are the tombs of the kings and the most stupendous buildings of the ancient world. In the construction of these pyramids millions of laborers spent their lives. The largest pyramid is 480 feet in height, and its base covers thirteen acres. Herodotus says that 120,000 men were employed for twenty years in constructing this colossal structure. Sixty-seven such architectural monstrosities were erected along the edge of the desert. They furnish mute but still eloquent testimony to the despotism, the shame, as well as the wealth, the glory, and the culture of Egypt at the height of her greatness.

The monstrous grandeur of the pyramids was rivaled by the extravagant palaces of the Pharaohs and the temples of the gods, in the construction of which other millions of artisans, laborers, and slaves were employed from age to age and from century to century. And the bountiful valley of the Nile supplied the superabundant food which fed these miserable millions who were the physical and spiritual slaves of political and ecclesiastical despots and of a wealthy feudal nobility.

(3) Commerce. In addition to all such internal economic activities, the Egyptians carried on a profitable trade with their Oriental neighbors, with Crete and the Aegean, and later with the Greeks. Cretan and Phoenician traders were frequent visitors to the ports of the Nile, and from the Delta to the cataracts of the Nile were gathered ships bearing freight from all the world. Trade was conducted over land routes through the Isthmus of Suez as well as over the shipping routes of the Mediterranean. Egyptian products were in use in the palaces of the sea-kings of the Aegean and throughout the Near East, and with this merchandise of Egypt went the culture of Egypt. The early Cretans learned the glazing of pottery from the Egyptians, and pottery made by the Minoans of Crete, from about 2500 B.C., has been found in abundance in Egypt. Egyptian cities were filled with traders from Eastern and Western lands, traders who imported the wonders and culture of other peoples to Egypt and carried back to their own countries the products, the culture, and the stories of the wonders of the people of the Nile.

Agriculture, industries, and foreign trade brought great wealth to the land of the Pharaohs, but it was a wealth that became concentrated in the hands of rulers, priests, and an official or feudal nobility. Side by side with great wealth developed great poverty, and a graded society based upon wealth and power arose and perpetuated itself through the long centuries of social evolution along the Nile. The great material conquest of the Egyptians was followed by an impressive growth of social, political, and religious institutions.[9]

SOCIAL CONDITIONS. (1) SOCIAL CLASSES. There was no hereditary caste system in Egypt as there was in India, but in practice a system of social stratification grew up and hardened. At the top of the social edifice stood the deified Pharaoh, the members of his immediate family, and the great officials of the royal court. The priests and a few nobles occupied the second place in the system and were the social and intellectual aristocracy of the land. The priests were free from taxes and were greatly respected because of their learning and religious functions. The feudal nobility of older days merged with the army as the imperialistic ambitions of succeeding Pharaohs raised the military men to a position of greater and greater importance. A class of warriors thus arose and stood just below the priesthood in social rank. They too were tax exempt in addition to other privileges. Many soldiers were recruited from the laboring classes and war captives.

With the development of a great political and administrative machine, a new official class, whose lower ranks were recruited from the old middle class of merchants and craftsmen, grew up from about 1600 B.C. Local districts were administered by a whole army of these functionaries of the crown, political administration thus opening up numerous political careers for members of the middle class. The most lucrative official positions in local and central administration passed into the hands of the earlier feudal nobility who, deprived of great landed estates which they once possessed, became the royal favorites and either held high official positions at home, or acted as generals of the Pharaoh's armies during military expeditions abroad. These greater officials and army generals became the nobles of the empire. Below these privileged groups came artisans, shepherds, farmers, and slaves. These classes owned no land, the farmers being renters of the land they tilled. The duty of these classes was to labor, pay taxes and support the ruling classes.

The underprivileged portion of the population was so large that casual visitors sometimes refer only to this group and the priests. These unfortunate masses have passed into the "field of beans" without leaving much direct trace of their sojourn, but the privileged official class has left us, in their tombs especially, and in sculpture,

[9] Blackmar, *op. cit.*, pp. 159–64, 171–81; Davis, *op. cit.*, pp. 68–69; Thurnwald, *op. cit.*, pp. 93–98; A. H. Sayce, *The Religion of Ancient Egypt* (2d ed.; Edinburgh: Clark, 1913), pp. 30–36.

relief-work, and paintings, the evidence by which it has been possible to reconstruct the life and customs of their day. Egyptian society thus rose from the broad base of serfdom through farmers, shepherds, merchants, artisans, lower and higher political and military officials, and a very numerous priestly class to the great officials of the Pharaoh's court, the royal family and the divine king himself, who was worshiped and feared by his people as a despot and a god.

In time the priests became very numerous, and were organized into one great national organization. The priests formed a perfect hierarchy running from high priest through several grades of subordinates. Indeed, one-fourth of those buried in the great cemetery of Abydos during this period were priests.[10]

The degradation of the laboring classes was appalling. During periods of famine—for Egypt had such periods—the poor were forced to sell themselves into slavery in return for food from the king. In the thirteenth century B.C., the temples possessed 107,000 slaves, or about one person in every sixty to seventy of the population of the country. The total population at this time was probably between 6,500,000 and 7,500,000.[11]

A wide gap, then, separated the serf from the nobility. The nobility and fine ladies dressed elaborately, but the poor were as raggedly clad as they were inadequately fed. The rich, enjoying leisure, found an outlet for their physical energies in a variety of sports; the poor, in slavish and laborious toil. The rich feasted, and enjoyed music and dancing, while servants waited upon them at every turn, and doctors and dentists looked after their health.[12]

The whole social system was linked to professional and vocational specialization, for Oriental society was highly complex and labor was now highly specialized. It also reflected the concentration of property in the hands of the upper classes. Over a long period of time, changes in social rank did occur. The old feudal nobility, for instance, passed over into the class of political officials. The fundamental character and inequalities, however, remained practically the same. While it was possible for youths of the lower classes to ascend in the social scale, in practice this seldom happened, for sons, as a general rule, followed the occupations of their parents. As far as the fellah, or common man, is concerned, Egypt was the most unchanging country in the world with the possible exception of India.[13]

10 *C. A. H.*, II, 49.

11 Blackmar, *op. cit.*, pp. 157–59; *C. A. H.*, II, 40–104, 164–95.

12 Blackmar, *op. cit.*, pp. 175 ff.

13 *C. A. H.*, I, 279, 280, 287, 323; III, 12; Blackmar, *op. cit.*, pp. 157–64.

(2) STATUS OF WOMEN. Women held an important position in Egyptian society. The early society was matriarchal, and thus the practice of placing property in women's possession continued until the fall of Egypt. Women were even permitted to hold the position of the Pharaohs, but few of them ever did. The priesthood was open to them. Generally speaking, women stood in a position of equality with the men of the social class to which they belonged. Egypt had her district goddesses, as well as district gods. In civilizations dominated by men the gods have generally possessed only male attributes. The religious literature of Egypt contains many admonitions to husbands to be kind to their wives, and sets high ideals of marital virtue. Egyptian morals, however, were loose, and many women lived a life of degradation. The Pharaohs, in addition to their queens, had numerous concubines. One hundred and fifty children of Rameses II are known to us. One of the Pharaohs even forced his own daughter into a life of prostitution. Even to the time of the Caesars, daughters of the Theban nobility were licensed to a life of immorality at the temple of the god Amon. But, on the whole, women were held in high esteem. Their duties were, chiefly, those of housekeeping and marketing. Men sometimes did the weaving.[14]

(3) MORALS. From the theory found in Egyptian literature, one might too readily conclude that moral standards were high and were observed. This literature is filled with moral admonitions and advice. Here, religion was a religion of deeds, and *The Book of the Dead* was a moral code. Whether practice conformed with theory is difficult to determine. Of the advices and maxims, this can be said: utilitarianism and convenience, rather than any pure ideals of right and wrong, were made the basis of one's dealings with relatives, equals, inferiors, and superiors, while one's relation to the gods was put on the purely business basis of "give and take." The moral wisdom of the Egyptians was a canny, worldly wisdom, devoid of sentiment or idealism, for the Egyptian lived by facts and realities, not by principles and ideals.[15] It is doubtful that moral codes and theories, as such, have ever had much influence upon moral behavior.

[14] *C. A. H.*, I, 289; A. Erman, *Life in Ancient Egypt* (London: Macmillan & Co., Ltd., 1894), pp. 115 ff.; Sayce, *op. cit.*, p. 143; W. M. F. Petrie, *Religion and Conscience in Ancient Egypt* (London: Methuen, 1898), pp. 131–35; A. Heilborn, *The Opposite Sexes* (London: Methuen & Co, Ltd., 1927), pp. 99–106; G. Maspero, *History of Egypt, Chaldea, Syria, Babylonia, and Assyria* (9 vols.; New York: Grolier Society, Inc., n.d.).

[15] Petrie, *op. cit.*, pp. 86–93, 110–30, 139–56, 160–62.

RELIGIOUS SYSTEMS. (1) GODS AND BELIEFS. Egyptian religion is another step beyond the primitive in the evolution of religious thought and practice. Traces of animism, totemism, and nature worship abound here. Flinders Petrie finds 438 gods, spirits, and other sacred creatures in the Egyptian system.[16] Devils and evil genii, with vicious designs upon men, never rested from their diabolical pursuits, but the good genii combatted the vicious band. As the centuries passed, there is some evidence in priestly thought of a drift toward a monotheistic conception of one god in three persons, but the religion of the masses was influenced but little by the thought of the priests of the temples, and the popular religion always remained animistic and polytheistic. A cultural cleavage thus separated the masses from the intellectual aristocracy, as it has continued to do in most societies ever since. The religion of the priests and the temples was the cultural inheritance of a powerful social élite. The gods of the rich were not the gods of the poor, though the poor probably shared in some aristocratic beliefs.[17]

The Pharaoh was head of all temples and their different worships. Of the gods in the Egyptian pantheon only a few can be referred to here. Nine-tenths of the Egyptian gods were cosmic. Râ was the sun-god; Géb, the earth-god; Nun, the ocean-god; and Hapi, the Nile-god. In addition to cosmic gods, there were animal and human gods worshiped in Egypt. The sacred bull held a prominent place among the divinities, and came in time to be looked upon as an incarnation of Râ or of Osiris. But the most prominent of all the gods was the human god Osiris, the dead king, long associated with the blessings of the Nile and the development of the arts and crafts, and who became the judge of the dead. By a process of identification and amalgamation, greater gods evolved from the local and lesser ones, with the result that one or another god came to be considered the supreme god of the pantheon.

Osiris, the dead king and judge of the dead, evolved indubitably from primitive animism and ghost worship. During his lifetime, every Pharaoh was a god, and all men became gods after their death. Out of man's desire to find a resting-place for his *anima* or "double," the belief in the immortality of the soul probably arose, and it was one of the most important of Egyptian beliefs. With it was linked the one indispensable dogma of the Egyptians, the judg-

[16] *Ibid.*, pp. 69–71; Montgomery, *op. cit.*, pp. 37–38; G. Allen, *Evolution of the Idea of God* (New York: Henry Holt & Co., Inc., 1897), pp. 91–126; Maspero, *op. cit.*, I, 214–15.

[17] Sayce, *op. cit.*, pp. 204–28; Petrie, *op. cit.*, pp. 28–47.

ment of the dead. A favorable judgment made the dead person one with Osiris. The nature of the punishment inflicted on sinners who did not pass the test of Osiris is not clear from Egyptian records. One of the requisites for a favorable judgment was the ability of the deceased to recite the lengthy *Negative Confession before Osiris*, which is the moral code of Egypt and remarkably like the Hebrew Decalogue, which it antedates. It was, indeed, the magic formula which forced Osiris to pass a favorable decree. There were other formulas which had to be memorized if one were to find his way safely on the perilous journey to the heaven of Osiris. All of these, through the voice of a priest or relative, could be memorized after death by one's double, and this was the usual way, since few Egyptians could read.[18]

But apparently only the priestly, intellectual, and official classes had the opportunity to read and memorize those formulas during life. For the poor who had no opportunity to memorize the formulas there was no place in the heaven of Osiris, except probably as slaves of their old masters. Egyptian religious practices became magical, formulistic, and burdened with ceremonialism. A magical gesture with the hand, or the repetition of some meaningless formula, was sufficient to determine the decrees of the gods. Indeed, one who knew the magical procedure might, in purely religious matters, live and act without fear of heaven's wrath.

The idea of death became the central idea in the culture of Egypt, and the Nile Valley became a veritable tomb. Mummification of bodies, the building of tombs, and the performance of funeral rites were matters of most serious import to rich and poor alike.

The entire religious system was mainly a reflection of primitive traditions and of economic needs. Thus the Nile and the sun were worshiped because of their relation to the fertility of the soil and to full stomachs; and the world of Osiris, as depicted in tombs, was but an idealized Egyptian world in an idealized valley of the Nile, except that a strange gloom and uncertainty mingled with this idealism.

Out of this religion of death developed the doctrine of the *Ka* or spiritual "double" which every living individual was said to possess and which left him at death. In a peculiar sense, it was man's individuality. In its origin, this belief is related to primitive animism, but later this *Ka* became identified with one's inner mental states and with pure thought, as distinct from purely material things, and from the body. Yet the *Ka* of a dead man was provided with food offerings. The image of such an offering was thought to

18 Maspero, *op. cit.*, I, 262–63.

be as good as the thing itself. There is, indeed, little difference between the Egyptian concept of the *Ka* and that of the soul in Greek and Christian thought. Sayce says that Plato's doctrine of Ideas was a development from that of the *Ka*.[19]

In painting, sculpture, drawings, etc., the *Ka* was depicted side by side with the body it occupied, for the Egyptians reduced all abstractions to concrete form. The *Ka* was thought to hover around the mummy but, should the mummy perish, the statue of the dead one would eventually become the abode of the *Ka*. It was believed that the *Ka* would eventually return to the body and restore it to life, a doctrine akin to that of the Resurrection. All these beliefs regarding the *Ka* were connected with the cult of Osiris. Some of this thought of Egypt was partly amalgamated with Greek thought, and, in its Hellenized form, it affected the thought of Alexandrian Christians and, through them, of later Europeans. The Greeks regarded the Egyptians as their teachers in religion, and it was from them that they got their glimpse of immortality, a day of judgment and of rewards and punishments after death. And Egyptian gods and religious ideas became popular in Rome in spite of state opposition. We are, indeed, still under the influence of the thought of ancient Egypt, for culture does not die.[20]

(2) Priesthood and Literature. The culture of Egypt was controlled by an all-powerful and wealthy priesthood which became in practice very largely hereditary. That priestly class, as already described, created and controlled nearly all of the literature of the country, a literature predominantly religious. Some of it is more ancient than the pyramids. As early as 3500 B.C. the priests were passing from the use of the hieroglyphic, or pictographic, script to a cursive script. The earliest writing was pictorial. At the next stage, the picture of an object became an ideograph, or symbol of an idea. Later a phonetic value was given to the picture or ideograph, and alphabetical signs were invented to describe it.[21] Thus, at an early date, the Egyptians actually had an alphabet, but they failed to profit by the discovery, for they continued to use the older picture-signs, and the consonantal group-signs, side by side with the alphabetical signs. Tradition and priestly conservatism hung heavily over this civilization. The period of greatest literary activity

[19] Sayce, *op. cit.*, p. 49.

[20] *Ibid.*, pp. 12 ff., 82–99, 101–22, 127–51, 153–80; *C. A. H.*, I, 284, 326–55; Petrie, *Religion and Conscience in Ancient Egypt*, pp. 48–52, 69–71; Petrie, *Personal Religion in Egypt before Christianity* (New York: Harper & Bros., 1909), pp. 107–37; Montgomery, *op. cit.*, pp. 33–49.

[21] S. Rappoport, *History of Egypt* (New York: Grolier Society, Inc., 1904), III, 291 ff.

dates from about 2800 B.C., and much of the literature was produced in the centuries immediately following that date, and is prophetic or Messianic in character.[22]

To this was added a group of writings of an ethical or didactic character, bearing such titles as "Teachings" or "Instructions." Connected with the Osiris cult, a moral literature, of which the *Negative Confession* is the basic part, grew up and became important during the period of the Middle Kingdom (2375-1580 B.C.). The *Negative Confession* is Chapter CXXV of the *Book of the Dead*, a collection of hymns, recitations, selections, spells, and incantations which comprise a great part of the religious literature of Egypt, some of which date back to the fourth millennium B.C. The *Am Duat* or *Book of the Other World* was a rival of the *Book of the Dead*. It dealt with the god Râ, while the *Book of the Dead* dealt chiefly with the god Osiris.[23]

Thus, by a process of slow growth, the Egyptian religious literature developed, a literature closely comparable to the bibles of other nations. The wisdom of Egypt was preserved in these books, and the priests held the key to this knowledge, for they were the learned class. Knowledge created a gulf between the laity and the priests, but especially between the lower and higher social classes. The poor were held in subservience by fear, superstition, ignorance, and ecclesiastical and political tyranny. The state was a theocratic state. The priests, custodians of culture, were the bulwarks of the political system, who, by their control of education and the written word, established a tyranny over the minds of the people which ended only with the fall of their civilization, and then only in part. Some changes in the social system and in thought did occur but these were few; nor did they represent any fundamental change in the despotism which the court and the priests exercised over the minds and bodies of the people whom they ruled. Egyptian civilization and its culture were static to a very marked degree. Here individual liberty was rare or unknown. Indeed, the change to Christianity and later to Islam altered only the forms of prayers and beliefs on the Nile, and the tyranny of the ancient culture still casts an ominous shadow over the children of Râ and Osiris.[24]

(3) SPREAD OF EGYPTIAN CULTURE. The influence of Egyptian culture upon Hebrew and other Eastern thought systems and upon

[22] *C. A. H.*, I, 345–47.

[23] Sayce, *op. cit.*, pp. 181–203.

[24] W. J. Perry, *Gods and Men* (London: John Lane, The Bodley Head, Ltd., 1927), pp. 67–74; *C. A. H.*, I, 189, 245, 272, 317, 326–55; II, 196–209; III, 417–25; Sayce, *op. cit.*, pp. 30–36, 181–203; Rappoport, *op. cit.*, II.

the thought of Greece and of Christendom was very marked and is supported by an abundance of reliable evidence.[25]

POLITICAL CONDITIONS. The Eastern conception of the state from ancient until modern times was the very antithesis of the conception which the Greeks and Romans gave to the world. The Oriental conception is based on the assumption that it is by the will of the monarch alone that the whole machinery of state is set and kept in motion. This was the Egyptian philosophy, and here everything was done for the glory of the Pharaoh. Wars were waged, great buildings erected, and slaves toiled for his honor and fame. The Pharaohs were great monarchs who succeeded one another in impressive array. They were represented as the benefactors of their subjects and of the gods. Gods, indeed, they themselves were, and as gods their subjects worshiped them. Thus they exercised their despotism not merely by the might of a military machine but by issuing commands which their people accepted as an expression of the will of heaven. Nowhere in the world was the idea of the theocratic state so firmly established as in Egypt, and nowhere else did the social structure resist change more effectively. An alliance between church and state, between religion and politics, resulted in one of the most complete despotisms in the history of human society. Here religion was national, and when Akhenaton (*c.* 1380-1362) attempted to create a world religion, embodying the idea of a universal culture based upon the cult of a one and only sun-god, he met, as do most reformers, with such violent opposition that his attempt failed completely.[26]

Formal Education

Because of the complexity of Egyptian life and society, it became necessary for the Egyptians to advance beyond the simple, unorganized, or loosely organized, educational procedures of primitive society. It was no longer possible, because of this complexity, to acquire, by the imitation of elders, the necessary experiences to sustain society and prepare the individual for his rôle in life. Therefore the formal school and a special teaching profession appeared, and day by day, and year by year, youths attended these formal schools for the purpose of acquiring that cultural and technical knowledge necessary for the highly specialized pursuits of a highly

[25] Sayce, *op. cit.*, pp. 82–99, 229–50; *C. A. H.*, II, 345–51; IV, 87–111; VI, 164–66; Petrie, *Religion and Conscience in Ancient Egypt*, p. 21; Montgomery, *op. cit.*, pp. 48–49; Petrie, *Personal Religion in Egypt before Christianity*, pp. 107–37.

[26] *C. A. H.*, I, 213–14, 276–79, 285; II, 40–104, 109–30, 157–62; Erman, *op. cit.*, p. 53; Sayce, *op. cit.*, pp. 22, 37–45.

developed and complex cultural and industrial civilization. The formal school of Egypt was essentially cultural; that is, its primary purpose was to teach the language, literature, and ideas of the nation. Because of the essential relationship between this culture and the arts, crafts, sciences, and professional activities of the country, these technical subjects were under the influence of the priests even though they were not taught in the formal schools, for painting, sculpture, architecture, law, medicine, engineering, etc., are ways of expressing the culture of a people just as is the written word and literature.

Vocational pursuits in ancient Egypt were thus, by custom and religious requirement, linked to the cultural framework of the entire nation, and their forms and techniques were controlled by the culture-custodians of the nation, the priests of the temples and the temple colleges. In every activity that touched the cultural life of the people, the idealism and the form had to conform closely to traditional thought or artistic pattern. To vary from these traditions would be highly revolutionary and irreligious. That is why Egyptian literature, thought, art, architecture, medicine, etc., are marked, even over extremely long periods of time, by an evident and persistent uniformity. There was some variation, some growth, but it was slight. That variety and diversity of thought and creation which are the result of individual freedom and initiative are impressively lacking in the life and achievements of Egypt.

EDUCATIONAL PURPOSE. The purpose of Egyptian education, as provided in the formal schools of the country, was (a) cultural and (b) vocational. There were many specialized arts and crafts, but they were mostly in the hands of those on the middle and lower levels of the priestly class. In the building and decoration of pyramids, temples, tombs, and palaces artisans were in great demand. All of these buildings were filled with works of art. In time something like craft gilds arose, and various objects necessary for burials were made in factories and in quantities. Price lists were published.[27] With the development of trade there arose a great foreign demand for Egyptian manufactures. Out of this domestic and foreign demand grew vocational education. Skilled artisans stood at about the middle of the social scale. The great multitude below them engaged only in laborious and unskilled tasks. In Egypt, as has been noted, these vocations had a very important cultural significance.

[27] G. A. Reisner, *The Egyptian Conception of Immortality* (Boston: Houghton Mifflin Co., 1912), pp. 14 ff.

In addition to these artisan activities, there were also professional groups who ranked above the artisans. Priests, who performed religious rites, and who guarded, taught, and wrote commentaries on the scriptures, comprised one profession. Medical practice was largely in the hands of special priests, who formed a medical profession. Although there was no class of lawyers, every important official of high administrative rank was versed in the law and acted as judge. These high administrators of the Pharaoh formed the legal class.[28] The just administration of law was considered a duty to the gods. There was also a great multitude of scribes whose duty it was to keep the records of the state and the temples and carry on domestic and foreign correspondence.

Educational purpose was, thus, in a marked degree practical or vocational, and students were attracted by the rewards of learning, but the most fundamental purpose was that of preserving Egyptian civilization by preserving its traditional culture. And this purpose was conscious and deliberate, for Oriental education was a planned education through which men were consciously working toward consciously determined goals.

CURRICULUM. (1) READING AND WRITING. The curriculum was determined by the needs of the civilization and was in harmony with Egyptian educational purposes. It included the reading and writing of the scripts, the development of which we have noted earlier. Egyptians believed that their writing was invented by the god Thoth who taught it to the early people of the valley, a belief which had a very conservative influence. The development of the written language did not keep pace with that of the spoken or popular language. Egypt, thus, came to have two languages far apart in their forms: the language of books and of written records, and the spoken language. This condition is somewhat similar to that of mediaeval Europe where Latin was the language of written records, while vernaculars, or vulgar tongues, were the spoken languages. Egyptian schoolboys began their formal schooling with a study of the three scripts. While the later forms of script came, in time, to be commonly used for everyday affairs, the religious texts were always copied in the ancient hieroglyphs, though these were not reserved solely for religious records. This is an excellent example of political and religious conservatism. Partly, to prevent any change in ideology some modern religious groups still preserve their culture in dead languages. Tradition, no doubt, has had much to do with that practice.

[28] *C. A. H.*, II, 46–47.

Writing was the only gateway to lucrative employment, to social privilege and a life of ease in Egypt. The scribe, the most typical figure of ancient Egypt, was exempted from manual labor and was supplied with food gratis by the royal storekeepers. The profession of scribe was the first step to official positions. One father advising his son to become a scribe said: "I have never seen the smith as an ambassador nor the goldsmith as a messenger. But I have seen the smith at his work at the mouth of his furnace, his fingers like the crocodiles . . . and he stank more than eggs or fish." [29] Royal scribes had brilliant careers, and the temple libraries were filled with the scribes of the gods, while poorly paid simple scribes kept the records of the tombs. Most scribes occupied a lowly social position, for anyone who could read, write and cipher was a scribe, and there was apparently always employment for him in government offices, temples or in the palaces of the nobility. He was usually the tax collector. It was, however, because the rewards were sometimes great that the Egyptians revered learning and held learned men in high respect. Only the learned man enjoyed any degree of personal freedom.

As intercourse with the other countries of the East developed, the Egyptian scribe studied the Babylonian cuneiform script which was widely used throughout the Mesopotamian region. With the expansion of the Egyptian empire, knowledge of foreign scripts became increasingly necessary for those scribes engaged in foreign service. Thus the curriculum prepared boys to read and write native and foreign languages and to keep records of the state, temples, cemeteries, and commerce. Letter-writing had a very prominent place in the education of the scribe. Some such letters, still preserved, show that some scribes were possessed of notable epistolary skill. Records were kept on papyrus, a paper made of reed, but occasionally a substitute for papyrus was used. Scribes wrote with reed pens. There is no evidence that the Egyptians studied grammar or used a dictionary.

(2) LITERATURE. Many Egyptian schoolbooks have been discovered. In them are fairy tales, accounts of travelers, and wildly extravagant stories about the deeds of fabulous men of the past. More important than these, because more generally used, were books of proverbs, moral instruction, admonition, and good manners. These were designed to point the way to a happy life. They warn boys to love their books so that they may escape the miseries of military and agricultural life.

[29] *Ibid.*, p. 222. (By permission.)

Famous among such books of "Instructions" were the sayings (2883-2855 B.C.) of Ptahhotep. This old seer bewailed old age as the greatest of all evils, but remarked that cleverness was the sole antidote against this evil. His wisdom was naïvely worldly. His philosophy recommended the doing of good lest worse befall. He admonished men to be kind to their wives because, he said, women are moved more effectively by persuasion than by violence. He recommended proper and polite behavior at table.

Students copying such instructions learned the art of writing and the rules of behavior at the same time. In point of time, the "Teachings of Dwauf" and the "Maxims of Ani" succeeded those of Ptahhotep. In these later proverbs the profession of literature is exalted.[30] In addition to such reading material, schoolboys read and sang the ballads and songs of Egypt, and these, too, were usually moral or religious in purpose. Schoolboys sang to the accompaniment of the pipe, the lyre, and the harp and were probably taught to play these instruments.[31]

Above such literature as this was the purely religious literature which was the chief study of the priesthood, a study pursued in the temple colleges rather than in the schools of the scribes. On this literature the priests wrote commentaries and, in the temple colleges, students studied the meaning of the texts. While, in theory, these sacred books were to be touched only by the gods, scribes copied them and, thus, changes in the text were introduced. The priests were too busy explaining the books to guard them against the carelessness or wilfulness of temple scribes.

(3) SCIENCES. In addition to such literary studies, the priests, and probably some privileged laymen, studied certain sciences. Some progress was made in astronomy. Time was divided according to the course of the sun and of the moon, these discoveries becoming the basis of our own calendar. The purpose of such studies was the practical one of computing the time of the recurrence of the Nile's overflow or of religious festivals. Superstition and magic, however, retarded the development of these sciences. In fact, every branch of intellectual activity, except mathematics, was checked in its growth by magic and superstition. In the fields of geometry and arithmetic something was accomplished, but nothing of much significance because there was no practical need for advanced mathematical knowledge, the Egyptians being concerned here only with the problems of everyday life. Apparently, they could multiply numbers only by 2; they seem to have had no method of division;

30 *Ibid.*, pp. 223–25.

31 Erman, *op. cit.*, pp. 256, 384 ff.

and their knowledge and use of fractions was very elementary.[32] Their arithmetical results were accurate, but their methods were cumbersome. They used geometry in measuring land and other surfaces, in mensuration, but they fell into many errors here. The Nile, often effacing boundaries, created a need for surveying. On the whole the Egyptians must be considered good practical mechanics and geometricians rather than scientists in the Greek sense. They contributed, however, to the growth of that experience and practical skill out of which the Greeks later rose to the realm of science, to the formulation of principles and laws.[33]

To these practical sciences ought to be added those of architecture and engineering in which the Egyptians displayed great practical skill. While their work in these fields was based on a knowledge that was purely empirical, the results fill even modern engineers with astonishment. That these sciences formed a part of the systematic work of the priestly colleges is not quite clear, but that their study and application were in the hands chiefly of the priestly class may reasonably be inferred from the dominance of the priests in Egyptian life, their greater leisure, and the importance for religious and official purposes of such sciences and skills.

One other science, medicine, remains to be mentioned. There was a chief physician attached to the court apparently as early as 3000 B.C.[34] Medicine was designated the "difficult science" at that early date. Medical science, however, was permeated by superstition and magic. Its origin was attributed to the gods. Diseases were attributed to demons or to some other supernatural beings which entered the patient, and which had to be expelled before medical remedies could take effect. Some doctors used exorcism alone. Physicians were generally members of the priesthood.

Because of the practice of opening bodies for mummification, the Egyptians knew something about the location of the larger organs, but, on the whole, their opportunities for anatomical knowledge did not result in any significant discovery. The blood vessels were well known to them, but not the circulation of the blood. Religious scruples were connected with embalming, and it was never performed by doctors.

In treating common ills, the physicians prescribed some remedies of value. Castor-oil, vinegar, ointment, honey, acacia, alum, and such like, were used in prescriptions. The Egyptians extracted many drugs from plants and used them in treating diseases. Poul-

[32] *C. A. H.*, II, 215–18.
[33] *Ibid.*
[34] *Ibid.*, I, 173; II, 219.

tices were applied to external sores. Some medicines were considered panaceas, but usually specific remedies for specific ills were used. The drugs were often crude, as the excreta of dogs, the blood of bats, or dung of crocodiles. In European pharmacopoeias of the seventeenth century some of these medicines were still listed, and others as crude had been added to them during the intervening centuries.[35] Egyptian doctors were exterminators of lice, rats, and all vermin. They were asked to prevent and cure mosquito bites. They had remedies for baldness, and cosmetics for beautifying the skin.[36] There was a special medical profession in Egypt from very early times, but many of the most famous doctors were priests, and medical practice was probably controlled by the sacerdotal class.[37] Dentistry, too, had its practitioners, and the teeth of Egyptian nobles were filled with gold then as now.[38]

METHOD AND DISCIPLINE. Throughout the whole educational process, the Egyptian pupil learned by imitation of traditional forms of writing and of thought. Drill and memorization characterized the method used. The beginning student wrote with a stylus upon wood, limestone, or broken pottery. When he had acquired some skill he was permitted to use papyrus. More advanced students in the writing schools learned by spending a part of the day doing the actual work of the profession for which they were preparing. This work was done in some government or other office. It was, indeed, the method of learning to do by doing. Literature was learned by the method of memorization, whole portions of the sacred books and many magical formulas being committed to memory in the exact form in which they were thought to have been originally written.

Free discussion of the meaning of this literature was a privilege and a practice of the higher priests of the temples, but probably of these only. But, in spite of this freedom which came to be embodied in written commentaries, the words and forms of the original literature were considered sacred. The exact words, for instance, of magical rituals and formulas by which men could determine the decrees of the gods were considered essential for the attainment of the ends which men sought. While the errors of scribes occasionally brought minor changes into this literature, and while scribes were apparently free to omit portions of the text or to modify the original expression,[39] the belief that it must be preserved in its original form

[35] V. Robinson, *The Story of Medicine* (New York: Liveright Publishing Corp., 1931), pp. 13–14.
[36] *C. A. H.*, II, 219–21.
[37] Erman, *op. cit.*, p. 357.
[38] Blackmar, *op. cit.*, p. 176; Maspero, *op. cit.*, I, 303–14.
[39] Rappoport, *op. cit.*, p. 317.

was at least widespread, and in that supposed original form it was memorized. No better methods exist than those of Egyptian imitation and memorization for insuring the fixity and stagnation of human thought and society. The Egyptian mind was enslaved by its worship of words and by its fear of tampering with these words lest the wrath of the gods should be turned against men. Schoolboys wrote essays on many magical beliefs and superstitions, this practice serving the purpose of perpetuating them.

Discipline in the schools was severe. Flogging was a universal practice. For some violations of rules, or neglect of duty, boys were bound in shackles and sentenced to the temple or school prison for as long as three months, for the Egyptians believed, as did the Hebrews after them, that a boy must be trained and broken as are horses or donkeys, a belief that continued in Western thought until our own day. Friendly advice, however, was frequently substituted for torture by Egyptian teachers and seers.

ORGANIZATION. (1) CHILDHOOD TRAINING AND EDUCATION OF SCRIBES. Mothers nursed their children for three years. In their early years, boys and girls went nude, and some boys remained naked even after their formal schooling had begun. The home was the school of childhood, where children learned the first rules of life by contact with their parents and playmates. Egyptian girls had their dolls, and boys had their toy crocodiles.

At the beginning of the fifth year boys entered school. Some were admitted as boarders but, apparently, most of them were day students.[40] This school was the school for scribes, and was sometimes conducted by a government department and sometimes by the city temple. In this school, boys remained until they reached the age of sixteen or seventeen. Here they studied for one or other of the professions, but changing from one professional course to another was apparently a common practice. When boys reached the age of thirteen or fourteen, they were employed for a part of each day in the department or office for which they were being trained. Many boys, including the sons of the Pharaoh, had private tutors, while many others learned their letters and writing exclusively as apprentices in some office, a practice very common in Roman Egypt. Many school exercise books, with the masters' corrections, have been discovered.

Should a boy desire to enter the priesthood, he went, at the age of seventeen, to the temple college to pursue a course of study the length of which depended upon the particular priestly office he

[40] Erman, *op. cit.*, p. 163.

chose as a life activity. We have noted that many professional or vocational activities had come into the hands of the priestly class.

(2) Apprenticeship Training for Trades. Artisans and craftsmen learned by acting as apprentices to those skilled in the many trades that had developed. Practical training in these fields was provided for outside of the formal schools of the government departments and of the temples.

TEACHERS. In the writing schools attached to governmental departments, the head official of the department was the principal teacher.[41] These officials were evidently laymen, who taught writing and the copying of records as the needs of their departments required. All formal instruction higher than that in writing and copying seems to have been in the hands of the priests, who had charge of all instruction in religious literature of which they were the national custodians. The teaching of the sciences and mathematics, also, was probably in their hands exclusively. Their control of the higher education of the upper classes seems to have been complete. The enslaved masses, who were held in subjection by force and fear, had a culture of their own of which their masters did not rob them, for the higher gods of the Egyptian pantheon did not destroy the cruder gods of the unenlightened populace. Control of formal cultural learning gave the priests dominion over the minds of Egyptians. By priests and government, united for a common purpose, the culture of the nation was preserved unchanged, and perpetuated.

STUDENTS AND STUDENT LIFE. Formal schooling in Egypt was a boy's prerogative. Probably 95 per cent of all boys were excluded from school because of social and economic inequalities. In the schools, instruction was either free or inexpensive, the length of the course, however, creating an obstacle for poorer students. Those of the upper classes mingled in the same schools regardless of differences in rank. The masses were controlled by the method of keeping them in fear and ignorance, and in slavish subjection to their masters. Some students indulged in riotous living and immoderate beer and wine drinking,[42] to the regret and alarm of their teachers. Girls were excluded from these schools, but those of high social rank might apparently receive the same instruction as boys, but from private tutors.

CONTROL AND SUPPORT. Political or ecclesiastical officials had control of all formal schooling of boys, for the right to instruct youth

[41] *Ibid.*, p. 329.
[42] *Ibid.*, p. 256.

for official or professional life was, by custom if not by law, the privilege of these officials. The control of these over the apprenticeship training of artisans was exercised indirectly, since the forms of arts and crafts were determined by the demand which, in Egypt, was mostly political and religious in character.

The fees, if indeed any were charged, in the departmental schools of the government and in the temple colleges, must have been small. Instruction in writing in governmental schools was probably considered one of the ordinary duties of the department officials. Parents supplied their sons with food,[43] until the boys were admitted to the profession of scribes, when they received their food gratis from the royal store. The temple colleges, as parts of the temples, were extremely rich, and the privileged few who attended these colleges in preparation for the priestly profession were probably supported largely by the temple endowments.

PHYSICAL EDUCATION. (1) MANUAL SKILLS. Apprenticeship in the various manual arts and engagement in the trades and agriculture provided physical training for manual laborers.

(2) MILITARY TRAINING. There were more foreign mercenaries than native Egyptian soldiers in the later imperial army. In peacetime, the native soldiers performed farm labor to keep fit for active service. There were also systematic military exercises and games employed to harden the bodies of soldiers and develop a warlike spirit in them. They were trained in the use of weapons. Running, jumping, wrestling, boxing, leaping, war-dancing and mimic battles were among the exercises of the soldier. The cavalry, who fought from chariots, received special training in archery, while the infantry were divided into divisions, each one specially trained in the use of some special weapon. The importance of mental, in addition to military, training for the officer class was recognized.

(3) SPORTS AND ATHLETICS. The Egyptians engaged in many sports, games, and gymnastic activities related to soldiering. The sport of hunting became a duty because of the destructiveness of certain wild beasts, while it was also a good preparation for battle. The laboring class fished and, at times, hunted, but perhaps seldom for sport. Fishermen were sometimes boatmen also. The Egyptians were skillful in making and using the weapons and utensils used in these activities.

Among the gymnastic practices, we find wrestling, lifting weights, fighting with the stick and longpole, and ball-playing. There were professional wrestlers, and these received special en-

[43] *Ibid.*, p. 330.

couragement in Greek Egypt. Swimming in the Nile and in the private pools of the nobility became a common practice. Women sometimes participated in ball-playing and archery. Whether the Egyptians knew the relationship between physical exercises and health is not clear, but the upper classes gave much attention to cleanliness and bathing. Children were well supplied with toys, many types of which are still being used by the children of the modern world.

Dancing was common among the masses, but the upper class deemed it unbecoming. The nobility, however, were entertained by professional male and female dancers and musicians, beloved by gods and men alike. The dancing was both religious and profane. Slaves as well as free Egyptians entered the dancing profession. There were female dancers attached to the temples. It is unlikely that there were any schools to train these performers, and the apprenticeship plan was most probably used.

Informal Education

Life on the Nile was itself educational. Men and women assimilated the culture of their nation or their social class here as elsewhere by informal association with their fellows and by participating in the activities of the home, the temple or other agency of worship, the political life of the nation, the commerce, arts, crafts, military activities, sports, music, and dancing, or, generally, in the folkways of the people. Society here, as everywhere, was itself a great school.

In regard to vocational training, as distinct from the cultural, the apprenticeship system of training was generally in use. Scribes, as we have noted, spent part of their time on the actual job, while they studied writing in school under a writing teacher, or as apprentices to master scribes. Physicians, engineers, artisans, boatmen, farmers, soldiers, etc., learned most of the tricks of their trade by the apprenticeship method.

Educational Results

The education of Egypt accomplished what it set out to accomplish, but no more than that. It gave youths that vocational or professional instruction necessary for the discharge of the duties of the professions that had now emerged. Beyond this, it helped to preserve unchanged, over long periods of time, the civilization of which it was a part, by transmitting the traditional culture to each new generation. Here, indeed, the school was in a very significant way the watch-dog of national culture. The achievements of Egypt, notable in many respects, were connected with the emergence of a leisure class of officials and priests. Formal education was in their hands. That greater achievements did not result from the leisure and social privileges which they enjoyed was due to the tyranny of a political system and of a thought system, both of which came to be accepted by all as divine. The human mind was thus enslaved by an official and a religious orthodoxy which had its roots in tradition, in very limited knowledge, in fear of the unknown and of change, in the selfishness of the ruling classes, or generally, we might say, in the culture of Egypt. Education was the instrument for the perpetuation of that orthodoxy. Men thought of their Egyptian society as the creation of the gods, and therefore the best possible society. That man should tamper with this creation was apparently inconceivable for them, for the attempt of the Pharaoh, Akhenaton, to introduce monotheism failed completely. The world had to wait for other men and other times to face the reality of the inevitability of change, and to recognize men's right and duty to discuss social and intellectual problems freely with a view to building a better society than the traditional one.

Egyptian civilization was built upon the written word, a book, which was the repository of national culture. That culture was guarded by priest and king, for its source was thought to be divine. To the written word the Egyptians became slaves. It served, however, a vital purpose in that, without such a device, a great populous society could not have been established and held in unity. Its invention marks the transit from tribal to national culture and greater social unities. But the germ of universal culture, while it appeared, had but a short-lived existence. The idea of a universal culture built upon the conception of the fatherhood of one God and the brotherhood of all men kept on appearing in Eastern thought, and, eventually, through Hebrew-Christian and Graeco-Roman channels, passed into the culture stream of Europe, where it has since been competing, now strongly and again feebly, with local, racial and national ideals.

Selected Readings

Breasted, J. H. *History of Egypt.* 2d ed.; New York: Charles Scribner's Sons, 1911.

Bury, J. B., *et al. Cambridge Ancient History. (C.A.H.).* 12 vols.; New York: The Macmillan Co., 1923–39.

Erman, A. *Life in Ancient Egypt.* London: Macmillan & Co., Ltd., 1894.

Leeder, S. *Modern Sons of the Pharaohs.* London: Hodder & Stoughton, Ltd., 1918.

Maspero, G. *History of Egypt, Chaldea, Syria, Babylonia, and Assyria.* 9 vols.; New York: Grolier Society, Inc., n.d.

Montgomery, J. A. *Religions of the Past and Present.* Philadelphia: J. B. Lippincott Co., 1918.

Moret, A. *The Nile and Egyptian Civilization.* New York: Alfred A. Knopf, Inc., 1927.

Petrie, W. M. F. *Personal Religion in Egypt before Christianity.* London: Harper & Bros., 1909.

———. *Social Life in Ancient Egypt.* Boston: Houghton Mifflin Co., 1923.

Sayce, A. H. *The Religion of Ancient Egypt.* 2d ed.; Edinburgh: Clark, 1913.

Wilkinson, J. G. *The Manners and Customs of the Ancient Egyptians.* 3 vols.; Boston: Cassino, 1883.

Woody, T. *Life and Education in Early Societies.* New York: The Macmillan Co., 1949.

4 Ancient Indian Society and Education

Ancient India, as ancient Egypt, stands as a good example of those theocratic, priest-dominated societies of the ancient Orient, where secular interests and activities were subordinated to the religious. In India, until recent times, the priests "stood at the gates of knowledge with flaming swords," as Charles Beard said of the colonial American educational scene. Secular needs there were which had to be served in this ancient society of Brahmins, but religion determined the mode of that service. The relation of education, whether formal or informal, to any society is well reflected in the ways of this ancient civilization.

The Development of Indian Society

THE ARYAN CONQUEST. While the Aryans (cultivators of the soil?) may have been indigenous to India, it is more probable that they were outsiders who overran the country in the period *c.* 2000-1500 B.C. Their earliest literature, the *Rig-Veda,* shows them engaged in a bitter struggle with the Dasyus, presumably the aborigines of the country, and of whom little is yet known. It is certain that the Aryans belonged to the Indo-European cultural family which spread over much of Europe and parts of Asia in the third and second centuries B.C. By 500 B.C. their military and cultural conquest of India had been completed, though from the struggle their own ancient culture did not emerge unimpaired.

INDO-EUROPEAN CULTURE. Nineteenth-century philologists discovered the Indo-European family of languages: the Aryan (including Indian and Iranian), Greek, Italic, Keltic, Teutonic, Balto-Slavic, Armenian, and Albanian. That discovery revealed these languages as variations of an original Indo-European language. Witness, for instance, the equivalents of the English "mother" in them: *mātár* (Sanskrit); *mātar* (Iranian); *mater* (Greek); *mater* (Latin); *mathir* (Irish); and *mair* (Armenian). Some time between

3000 and 2000 B.C. the people who spoke the Indo-European mother tongue separated and, in time, cultural differences appeared among the dispersed groups. Yet, they long retained in common much of their original culture. Among their many common ancient customs were the following: the patriarchal joint-family; destruction of female infants; early marriage of girls; the suicide of widows; ancestor worship; and the worship of nature forces as gods. The sky-god, Father Sky, was worshiped under the names *Dyāús-Pitár*, in India; *Zeus-Pater,* in Greece; and *Ju-piter,* in Rome. Christianity was one of the greater forces making for cultural change in the western branches of the Indo-European family.

THE NON-ARYANS OF INDIA. (1) DRAVIDIANS. Because the conquered people of India, the Dasyus, most probably spoke Dravidian tongues, they are usually called Dravidians. They differed from the Aryans in color, speech, and culture. The *Rig-Veda* speaks of their dusky skin, flat noses, "fiendish" voices and godlessness. It is noteworthy that phallic worship, the most probable root of Aryan contempt for their religion, was, in time, given a prominent place in the religion of the conquerors themselves. For the rise of the caste system there is some significance in the fact that the Sanskrit word *varna,* which the Aryans used to designate large social classes, one of which was the Dasyu group, means color.

(2) THE INDUS VALLEY PEOPLE. Before 3000 B.C. there lived along the Indus and Ravi rivers the "Indus Valley People," a literate people, whose culture spread apparently as far east as the Ganges. Very recent excavations at Harappa and Mohenjo-daro show that these people built elaborate brick cities, were far advanced in industries and arts, and traded with Mesopotamia, Egypt, Crete, and probably Greece, as well as with much of India. And beneath their cities lie the unexplored remains of earlier cities built by earlier unknown people. The skeletons found at Mohenjo-daro reveal the presence of four different races in the ancient city.

The Indus Valley People worshiped, among other objects, phallic symbols, and many animals, birds, and trees which are worshiped in India still. Shiva, later a leading Hindu deity, was apparently one of their gods, as was also, apparently, the great Mother Goddess widely worshiped in the ancient Near and Middle East, and, in modern India, by the lower classes, even to the present day. The swastika and the Greek cross, in widespread use in the very ancient world, appear on seal-amulets of Mohenjo-daro.

The Indus Valley People probably borrowed many of their gods and symbols from the earlier primitive inhabitants, presumably the Dasyus. Many elements of more primitive cultures found a place in theirs, and the Brahmin priests of India are still trying to destroy this ancient cultural residue by identifying it with supposed Aryan religious traditions. As archaeological research progresses, new light will, no doubt, be thrown upon the still largely unknown history of earliest India.[1]

PERIODS IN THE HISTORY OF ANCIENT INDIA. While Indian history falls into periods, each with its own rather definite characteristics, the limitations of space forbid here all but the most general reference to periodically labeled changes in the culture and institutions of the country. The student will find such a systematized handling of the subject in works dealing exclusively with Indian history.[2]

The periods, in the order of time, are usually designated the Vedic, Epic, Rationalistic, Buddhist, and Puranic, the names being derived from the literary and religious developments which mark the several epochs. The present brief account is concerned with the Indian scene only until the Mohammedan conquest in 1194, when the Puranic Period was well advanced. Wherever reference is made to the present-day scene, that is done chiefly to illuminate the past, though it also reveals the static character of Indian society since the Brahmins came to dominate it.

HINDUISM. Hinduism, to which we shall at times refer, includes every kind of creed, and is a congeries of many cults, united in a common culture and directed toward a common ideal-goal. It is more than a faith. It is a way of life and a social system. Though it has the emotional marks of creeds, it is a culture rather than a cult. It has a place for every belief, including atheism, which can be reconciled with its social and ethical ideals. As a religion, it claims to be the only universal one, since it recognizes them all as true, and seekers of truth, though none may ever find it. A Hindu may be a Christian, Jew, Muslim, or anything else, if he accepts the social system, and observes the ritual of Indian culture. Modern Hinduism is the end-product of an age-old evolutionary process. Economic, social, political, religious, and intellectual factors have shaped its growth and character.

THE ENVIRONMENT

ECONOMIC ASPECTS. (1) GENERAL. Indian geographical and climatic conditions favored the growth of a great civilization. On

[1] E. Mackay, *The Indus Civilization* (London: Lovat Dickson & Thompson, 1935).

[2] For a fairly full and, on the whole, a good account, see R. C. Dutt, *A History of Civilization in Ancient India* (Rev. ed., 2 vols.; London: Kegan Paul, Trench, Trubner & Co., Ltd., 1893).

the east, south and west, the land is bounded by the ocean; on the north, by the snow-covered Himalayas, in which great rivers, which flow down to the sea, have their rise. Generally, the land is fertile; the climate, torrid; and nature, bounteous in its gifts of food. Drought was, however, an enemy of the ancient Aryans, as it still is of their descendants. In this land of rivers, frequently flooded in dry seasons by mountain rains, the ancient Aryans built reservoirs and irrigation systems, and were apparently successful in their struggle with nature, as they were in their struggle with men, in which they were aided by mountains as well as rivers. Ancient India was also a land of forests, great reservoirs of water, of which nature made the tiger custodian. Many of those forests have been laid bare by the axe of well-armed, thoughtless, and sometimes greedy men, with the result that once fertile areas, of great size, have become vast, parched wastes.

The phenomena of mountain, river, storm, drought, etc., furnished the Vedic singers of the once warlike and vigorous Aryans with imagery in describing the drama of the doings of both gods and men. Thus the great god Indra, of the *Rig-Veda*, is a war-god, a storm-god, and a god of fertility, who controls the waters of heaven and earth, and wages celestial wars against his celestial enemies. The *Rig-Veda* reveals the early Aryans as agricultural warriors, waging, as a united people without noticeable social inequalities, a struggle against nature and the Dasyus. A sense of security, resulting from their conquest of the Dasyus, and an enervation, due mainly to the climate, robbed in time this once vigorous people of the spirit which brought them victory over nature and men. Their later literature reveals them as an effete, ceremonious, lifeless people advanced in learning but decayed in vigor.

The Aryan masses permitted their once-honored manual activities to become despised, and themselves reduced in time to the status of the Dasyus, by an indolent, parasitical priestly class, and by a military nobility, enervated by luxury and increasing inactivity, whom the gods of history were to hurl in time from their earlier position of pre-eminence in the social system. Shut away with the Dasyus in a peculiarly Indian environment, in centuries-old isolation from western Indo-Europeans, the Aryans built their own unique Arya-Dravidian civilization.

The rivers had a not insignificant influence upon the developing civilization. In addition to their military and agricultural uses, they became trade routes between river communities. Along them since ancient Vedic times many of the famed holy places and temples of India arose, to which many millions every year still make pilgrimages. Many rivers became holy and were believed to possess the power of washing away sins. As holy rivers and shrines increased, the priests became more numerous, more wealthy, and more powerful until, about 500 B.C., they stood at the top of the social hierarchy.

The economy of Aryan India was basically agricultural. The industries necessary in peace and war developed from the earliest times in the families and villages. Occupational specialization grew with the civilization. There were priests, soldiers, farmers, traders, etc., and a growing array of artisans. Work in wood, stone, and the various metals was done by men; weaving, by women. Many ornamental objects were made. The chief development in architecture and sculpture began with the Buddhist period. India is dotted with ancient temples, shrines, and palaces which testify to the physical endurance, the patience in executing endless details in ornamentation, and the skill of the workers who created them. Indian temples are enormous.

Much of the art of India came to maturity as an expression of the religious ideals of priests and people, both Aryan and Dravidian, and it is largely native in design. The equipment of great armies of ancient kings called for skill in making weapons and armor. Farmers, shepherds, and artisans, in time, were exempted from military service. War and sports gradually became the exclusive activities of the military nobility and of millions of professional soldiers, who in time of peace led a life of idleness. Government was in the hands of the military nobility.

While Phoenicians, Greeks, and others traded at times with India; while invaders frequently made attacks upon the country; and while inquiring travelers from China, Greece, and elsewhere came occasionally to see the country, the ancient Hindus, with their religious prejudices against travel, lived in almost complete isolation from the rest of the world. They were not traders; nor did they desire commerce with other peoples.

(2) THE GILD SYSTEM. Occupational gilds existed before 600 B.C. and reached their final form by A.D. 300.[3] Plowmen, merchants, artisans, etc., were thus organized, and their rules and customs were approved by priests and kings. The merchant gilds became very powerful. All the gilds trained apprentices, almost exactly as did mediaeval European gilds. The master was required to treat his apprentice as a son, and the apprentice to respect the person and knowledge of his master. Said an ancient document: "Science is

[3] E. W. Hopkins, *India Old and New* (New York: Charles Scribner's Sons, 1901), pp. 169 ff.

like a river, ever advancing downward to a humbler level."[4] Until the close of the Buddhist period (*c.* A.D. 500), caste did not strictly determine one's occupation, and youths had much freedom in choosing a vocation.

Though changed by centuries of growth, these old gilds still survive. They have become interwoven with caste, village, town, and city life into the strange and interesting fabric of modern Indian society. The gild apprenticeship system of education has now almost disappeared. The idea of an inherited trade still persists, but few take it seriously. Where occupation and caste are identical, caste members are, *ipso facto*, gild members. Because of the public importance of certain trades some artisans belonged to the privileged Vaisya caste. Membership in a gild, once acquired, becomes a family inheritance. Prices and wages are still often fixed by these gilds. Factory owners, however, reject such regulations. Everywhere in this ancient land, old ideas and practices struggle with the new.

(3) THE LAND SYSTEM. The earliest Aryans gradually passed from a semi-nomadic and pastoral to an agricultural mode of life. In early Vedic times priests, warriors, and the Aryan masses engaged in agriculture, but had seemingly only use of the land for which they paid rent to the king, who had sole ownership of it. In time the priests abandoned agriculture lest they injure worms, and they later branded it, with other manual occupations, impure. Finally, only the Aryan masses, and perhaps a rare Dasyu, engaged in such work. Transfer of ownership of land from kings to people began with gifts of land to friends and priests. Similar gifts were made later to village communities, though here overright remained with the kings, described in literature as the "protectors" and "devourers" of their people. Only priests' land was exempted from royal overright. In Manu's time (*c.* 300 B.C.), the priests arrogated to themselves, in theory, the earlier royal prerogative of the supreme ownership of everything, though kings in practice retained ownership. By A.D. 500, the peasant had become absolute owner of his fields, but the king legally remained his preserver and devourer.

The peasant, however, lived in one of two types of village community, each with its own system of land ownership: (a) the severalty village, with its headman, in which the holdings, always apparently separate as regards use, were distributed periodically among individual villagers, each of whom paid his own taxes; and (b) the joint village, without a headman, in which individual

[4] *Ibid.*, pp. 174–75.

holdings were inherited parts of a single estate, and for which the community paid the taxes. Strictly speaking, communism in land has not existed at any time in India, although the joint village plan has many elements of communism in it. These ancient villages are still there and seem to have been changed but little by the hand of time.

SOCIAL ASPECTS. (1) FAMILY. The family has been the most closely knit unit in Indian society, and it has existed since very early times, as it still does, in two forms: (a) the joint-family, and (b) its outgrowth, the separate family. Members of the former live together and hold their property in common; those of the latter live separately and own their property separately. The joint-family has been the general type. The ancient Hindus believed, as do most modern ones, that hell awaits the man who leaves no son to perform religious rites for him and the family ancestors. Only male descendants of ancestral males belonged, strictly speaking, to the joint-family, for marriage breaks the family ties of girls, who must worship the ancestral idols of their husbands. Women and girls do not own family property. The family includes sometimes hundreds of individuals, all living in or around the ancestral home where the family idol is worshiped; and it includes all dead members back to the first prehistoric father of them all. It was India's most important agency of informal education which, among other things, checked the growth of the feeling of independence and selfishness in children.

(2) VILLAGE. India's social life has always appeared in a village setting. Today, nine-tenths of the total population live in some 700,000 small, largely self-supporting villages of great antiquity. There are: (a) joint villages which may be either joint-family communities, or clan communities composed of two or more supposedly related families, and (b) severalty villages, composed of unrelated families.

The village is the unit in Indian communal life. From it the peasant goes out to till his fields in the great open spaces which separate the villages. There are very few separate homesteads on India's countryside. Each village was economically independent, and employed, and paid out of village funds, its own craftsmen, personal servants, and lowly street sweepers. Like the family, the village provided informal education of great moral and practical significance.

(3) CASTE SYSTEM. In the caste system there are, when we include the Outcastes, five major castes, which are subdivided into

over two thousand sub-castes. These sub-castes are the real castes. The five major castes are: (a) Brahmins, (b) Kshatriyas, (c) Vaisyas, (d) Sudras, and (e) Panchamas (Outcastes). The first three are supposed to be pure-blooded Aryans, and are called the "twice-born" castes because they alone may wear the sacred thread and enjoy the privilege of formal cultural education. The Sudras are supposedly Dasyus who were received into the Hindu community. And the Panchamas, who are theoretically outside of society, are presumably the progeny of mixed marriages, or Dasyus who, for some now unknown reason, were branded "unclean." While there are marked differences between North and South India in the numerical standing of sub-Brahmin castes, the Brahmins everywhere dominate the system as they have done for nearly fifteen hundred years.

The upper four major castes have had since ancient times their special occupational fields: for Brahmins, the priesthood; for Kshatriyas, government and soldiering; for Vaisyas, business and farming; and for Sudras, servant activities. A Brahmin in distress was permitted to engage in certain occupations of Kshatriyas and Vaisyas. The Panchamas were never assigned a field of occupation, and were forced to live in degraded, isolated groups. Stealing is the only activity permitted for some lowest Outcastes, whose chief commandment is "Thou shalt not be caught."

The caste system is very old and uniquely Indian. Lacking the experience in legal orderliness which centralized government and even cities provide, India grew under the rule of customs which, varying with localities, was always directed by the Brahmins who, favored by Indian conditions, were able to impose their will upon society. In its present form, it has existed since about A.D. 750, though that form had been slowly shaped during the preceding millennia.

Every Hindu belongs to some sub-caste, which hereafter we shall call a caste. Membership in one's caste is hereditary, and in it one remains until death. But death does not end the drama which for each one is eternally re-enacted according to the almost universal Hindu belief in metempsychosis, first proclaimed by India's God in the *Upanishads*.

It is thus believed that, by divine, inexorable, cosmic law, called Karma, the tragedy of life is unendingly repeated, and at each rebirth one is placed in that caste of men, animals, or insects, to which his deeds in earlier lives entitle him. A man reaps what he sows. His place in the caste system is an index of his moral worth as determined by the moral law of the universe. It is that law's decree that only by ever faithful observance of the rules of one's caste during a series of lifetimes can one rise in the caste system. Here, each man, by heaven's decree, has his duties eternally fixed for him. It is a most significant psychological fact that billions of Hindus have believed the myth of the divine institution of a system which has condemned most of them to a life of toil, and some of them to degradation and misery. Ability did not count here. Heredity fixed one's lot on earth and in heaven. A few general caste practices of ancient origin will suggest the broader picture.

One must not marry outside of his sub-caste. He may eat only specified food which must be cooked by specified people. He may never eat, drink, or smoke with a lower-caste man. He may not cross the ocean. To touch an Outcaste (an Untouchable) brings defilement from which he must be ceremonially purified. Even the shadow of an Outcaste defiles a Brahmin. Some Untouchables are so low that they defile a Brahmin should they come within thirty yards of him. They may not live in the same village with Hindus. There are some 70,000,000 of these miserables in this supposedly God-made society of India. Untouchability is officially repudiated under the new government, but laws alone cannot change ancient customs. A Hindu may be a moral vagabond or an atheist and retain his caste status, but he will lose it if he accepts a drink of water from a social inferior and remains unrepentant and unpurified. All other castes and even his own family join in the persecution of an impenitent rebel against caste rules.

The caste system has a most interesting history of which we can suggest but the most meager outline here. Among the Aryans of 2000 B.C. there were, as among nearly all ancients, three classes—nobles, priests, and common people—but these were not castes. The caste system was so firmly established during Buddha's lifetime (*c.* 560-477 B.C.) that he accepted it as a necessary social scheme, and attacked not it but Brahmin tyranny. The religious equality of all castes was, however, a Buddhist ideal. A further hardening of caste practices occurred after Buddha's time. When all available facts have been collected and weighed, one is compelled to conclude that the caste system has been the product of many forces: In it survive some practices of the ancient Aryan tribal and family systems. Race, class and occupational prejudices, and sacerdotal power and ambition, all operating under favorable conditions of climate, geographical and cultural isolation, of governmental weakness, and of village and family corporate life, gradually moulded old tribal social traditions into the caste system of historical times. The system furnished a solid basis for the class hierarchy, which the Brahmins, the selfish makers of caste rules, came to dominate. It was they who moulded the religious scruples which permeate it. The Dasyus were eventually caught in the social net of their masters. Mixed breeds were condemned to a lowly place. Sub-castes were multiplied in accordance with a scheme of racial and occupational impurity. Thus was born gradually in ancient times the caste system. The rôle of the priests in the drama of its birth may be seen from a few extracts from the *Code of Manu* (*c.* 300 B.C.):

In order to protect his universe He, the most resplendent one, assigned separate (duties and) occupations to those who sprang from his mouth, arms, thighs, and feet.

To the Brahmanas he assigned teaching and studying (the Veda), sacrificing for their own benefit and for others, giving and accepting (of alms).

The Kshatriya he commanded to protect the people, to bestow gifts, to offer sacrifice, to study (the Veda), and to abstain from attaching himself to sensual pleasure.

The Vaisya to tend cattle, to bestow gifts, to offer sacrifice, to study (the Veda), to trade, to lend money, and to cultivate land.

One occupation only the lord prescribed for the Sudra, to serve meekly even these (other) three castes. . . .

Of created beings the most excellent are said to be those which are animated; of the animated, those which subsist by intelligence; of the intelligent, mankind; and of men, the Brahmanas. . . .

The very birth of a Brahmana is an eternal incarnation of the sacred law; for he is born to fulfill sacred law, and becomes one with Brahman. . . .

Whatever exists in the world is the property of the Brahmana; on account of the excellence of his origin the Brahmana is, indeed, entitled to it all.[5]

The *Code of Manu,* one of the sacred writings of India, is a lengthy justification of Brahmin ascendancy. The Hindu was taught to accept it as a body of truths approved by God. It confirmed the Brahmins' long-standing, exclusive custodianship of sacred literature, and made them its sole interpreters and teachers. The blind, priest-directed faith of Hindus in the myth of the divine origin of the caste system is but one of many examples of the viciousness of at least some forms of indoctrination. The *Code* pronounced the *Vedas* to be the repository of all knowledge:

The four castes, the three worlds, the four orders, the past, the present, and the future are all severally known by means of the Veda.

Sound, touch, color, taste, and filthy smell are known through the Veda alone. . . .

Even that which one Brahmana versed in the Veda declares to be law, must be considered (to have) supreme legal (force, but) not that which is proclaimed by myriads of ignorant men.[6]

[5] G. Buehler's translation, in O. J. Thatcher (ed.), *The Library of Original Sources* (Milwaukee: University Research Extension Co., 1907), I, 201–2.

[6] *Ibid.,* pp. 215, 217.

The influence of such authoritative pronouncements still predominates in India.

(4) STATUS OF WOMEN. By eternal social and moral law, of which caste rules are an expression, women have been assigned their place and duties in Indian society. Down the centuries the sacred books echo and re-echo the old idea:

> A woman is not independent, the males are her masters. . . .
>
> Their fathers protect them in childhood, their husbands protect them in youth, and their sons protect them in age; a woman is never fit for independence.[7]

In Hindu thought and practice women are treated as men's inferiors. The inspired book, *Bhagavad Gita,* implies that to be a woman is evidence of sin in a former life. Karma determines one's sex as it does everything else. Because only sons could perform the essential religious family rites, female infants were unwelcome and often destroyed. Religious disabilities, their exclusion from the study of the *Vedas,* God-required marriage of pre-adolescent girls, widows' religious duty not to remarry, the custom of *sati,* or widow-burning, polygamy (common only in the higher castes), and the *purdah* (curtain) system contributed, each its share, to the subjection of women. With the exception of the last, these practices are ancient, and some of them have had a fluctuating history. The purdah system required women to seclude themselves in their own rooms while at home, and hide their faces behind veils or curtains while outside of their homes.

In the early Vedic Period women were nearly men's equals in dignity and status. They studied the *Vedas,* and sometimes taught them. For their social fall, the Brahmin priesthood seems to have been chiefly responsible. The sacred book, *Satapatha Brahmana,* as did all later law books, forbids a man to eat with his wife. Women were forbidden to hear the *Vedas* read even by their husbands in family rites. By 700 B.C. most of their ancient privileges had vanished. Marriage was now a required sacrament and almost the only career of women. Child marriage soon became a general practice. Mass marriages of boys of eight and girls of six years of age became common, and still continue in parts of India. The treatment of lower-caste widows was more humane than of those of the higher castes. High-caste widows, who did not commit *sati,* had to go into perpetual mourning and, generally, keep their hair cut off, avoid family festivities, eat but once a day, and abstain from all food and

[7] F. M. Müller, *The Sacred Books of the East* (London: Oxford University Press, 1882), XIV, Part II, 31.

drink during two days each month—all this because their sins in a former life were believed to have caused their husbands' deaths. To these few of the many tragic practices ought to be added the exclusion of women from ownership of family property. Hindu husbands often forced them to surrender their personal property under threat of a second wife.

In spite of tyrannous rules and customs, and occasional manifestations of male inhumanity, India has been, in the large, a land of beautiful family life, of devoted fathers and husbands, of faithful wives, and of dutiful children. Man-made laws are often too weak to change human nature. In the variegated cultural scene of India it was possible for individual women to become saints, scholars, artists, teachers, and social servants, but only by renouncing the Brahmin decrees that marriage and parenthood are a universal duty and that widows should withdraw from the world. Unwarranted conclusions about practices seem to have been drawn from the priest-made ideals of the scriptures such as those for wives. Says the *Mahabharata* of the ideal wife:

> She should be beautiful and gentle, considering her husband as her god and serving him as such in fortune and misfortune, health and sickness, obedient even if commanded to unrighteous deeds or acts that may lead to her own destruction. She should rise early, serving the gods, always keeping her house clean . . . eating only after the needs of gods and guests and servants have been satisfied, devoted to her father and mother and the father and mother of her husband.[8]

Says the *Code of Manu:* "Though destitute of virtue, . . . a husband must be constantly worshipped as a god by a faithful wife."[9]

With our Western cultural prejudices we are likely to err in evaluating Hindu ideals and practices, not only as they affect women but also as they affect every individual and the whole society of India. Indian and, indeed, all Eastern philosophers argue just as convincingly for their ideals and practices as our philosophers do for ours.[10]

(5) Some Merits and Defects of the Caste System. Theoretically, the caste system has much to recommend it. The Brahmins defended it upon the grounds that it provides for wide variations in ability, aptitude, and character among individuals; that one's place in society ought to be determined by his ability and moral worth; that the good society ought to be ruled by wise, intel-

[8] Cited by A. Coomaraswamy, *The Dance of Siva* (New York: The Sunwise Turn, 1918), p. 22.

[9] *Ibid.*

[10] K. Shridharani, *My India, My America* (New York: Duell, Sloan & Pearce, Inc., 1941); Coomaraswamy, *op. cit.*

lectual, and spiritual aristocrats, having the economic security and leisure necessary for their work; that responsibility for one's acts and punishments for offences should rise with the intelligence and social position of individuals; and that the lower one's social status is the greater should be his personal liberty.

In its practices it has been defended on the grounds that (1) it is a co-operative, not a competitive system; (2) it recognizes the identity of the basic interests of all men; (3) the castes, all of which are self-governing, are democratic, each one providing equality of opportunity for its members; and (4) each caste, while stressing collective responsibility, has promoted the growth of character and occupational proficiency in its individual members, and ensured orderliness and stability in society as a whole.[11]

Some historical facts are noteworthy here: The caste policy of segregating the aborigines, now apparently the Indian middle class, and of Aryanizing them was better than that of destroying them. Aided by the Hindu family, the caste system protected the ancient culture against invaders, whom it eventually absorbed, as it still protects it against Western influences. It promoted learning and vocational skills by making them the special duties of groups. It developed in every man a strong feeling of belonging to a group and of pride in his ancestral and caste heritage. Its socially divisive tendencies have been softened by the widespread awe and respect for the Brahmins, which the priests imposed upon the credulous masses. Against such possible or probable merits, the system has, for Western eyes, glaring defects.

The Hindu has been perhaps the most changeless of social systems. New castes were created from time to time, but basically the system never changed. The Brahmin overlords have not always been the best and wisest Indians, and the great natural talent of numerous lower-caste men for leadership was wasted while the priests ruled by divine right. To knowledge and spiritual progress some Brahmins have made very great contributions. Others of them have been morally corrupt, religious impostors, who preyed upon a superstitious people, and commercialized holiness.[12] The subjection of women and the degradation of the Untouchables are defects which we have examined. Women in Western democracies, however, have emerged but recently from a form of social bondage, while they lost ground in their struggle for freedom in Nazi-Fascist

[11] R. K. Mookerji, *Ancient Indian Education* (London: Macmillan & Co., Ltd., 1947), pp. xx–xxi.

[12] J. B. Pratt, *India and Its Faiths* (Boston: Houghton Mifflin Co., 1915), chap. viii.

states. And it is worth realizing that we have our own Untouchables in the West.

RELIGIOUS ASPECTS. (1) RELIGIOUS LITERATURE. The changing religious scene appears in a voluminous literature, of which only the basic books can be mentioned here. The *Rig-Veda,* put into writing probably about 350 B.C., after centuries of growth and oral transmission, is probably the earliest book. The three other *Vedas* have much in common with this religious textbook. The four *Vedas* were enlarged by (1) priestly commentaries or rituals of sacrifice (*Brahmanas*) to which were added mystical sections (*Aranyakas*) to be studied by seers in the forests, (2) their philosophical appendices (*Upanishads*), and by (3) the *Sutras,* which reduced to simple instructional form the wisdom and teaching of the basic literature, particularly of the *Brahmanas.* This literature was regarded either as revealed, or "enounced" by inspired men, and, in earlier times, so holy that it might not be written. In time the lower castes and women were forbidden to read it, or hear it read.

Less sacred than these, but still sacred and authoritative, were (1) the *Code of Manu;* (2) the Epics, called *Mahabharata* and *Ramayana;* (3) the *Puranas,* the sectarian scriptures of modern Hinduism; (4) the sectarian ritualistic manuals, frequently called *Tantras;* and (5) the *Bhagavad Gita,* the bible of Krishnaism. The last became the crown of Hindu religious-philosophical literature. Most of these post-Vedic books were written at various times between 500 B.C. and A.D. 700. It is probable that writing was not used for literary purposes until about 350 B.C. Until that time literature was mnemonic, and many compositions were probably lost. For more than a thousand years preceding 500 B.C. Indian literature was exclusively religious in content or in purpose.[13]

(2) THE GODS. The early Aryans worshiped friendly, personified nature gods, such as Heaven, Earth, Storm, and, above these, the seven highest gods, sons of the great mother goddess, Eternity, who are viewed as powers directing the acts of the lower gods. Of these the warrior god, Indra, came to be deemed the creator and preserver of all things. Most of these gods had economic roots; the Vedic heaven, physical delights. Besides holy gods, there were many malevolent demons against whom the gods warred. And there were female gods and female demons. The demons were evil-eyed and cloven-hoofed. Life in heaven and hell was a reflection of life in society, the gods, however, being immortal.

Out of the vaguely trinitarian conception of the Vedic god Agni

[13] Mookerji, *op. cit.,* p. xxi.

(Fire), post-Vedic Brahmin priests created a trinity, with Brahma as the creator, Shiva as the destroyer, and Vishnu as the preserver. The new God, Brahma, is but the "word" or potent sacred formula of the *Rig-Veda* now identified by philosophical speculation with reality, or "the soul of the universe." In this post-Vedic, monotheistic pantheism the many Vedic gods were absorbed, chiefly by identification, by the new deities. Incarnation myths grew. Thus the men, Krishna, the Christ of India, and Rama were worshiped as incarnations of Vishnu, as they still are. In spite of absorption and identification of deities, the gods grew in number to at least a million, of which all except the great gods (Brahma, Vishnu, Shiva, Krishna, Rama, and Kali) are mere local godlings, such as spirits of trees, streams, etc.

Most Indian gods had wives who, except Kali, were modestly submissive to their husbands. The sometimes gentle, sometimes terrible Divine Universal Mother, Kali, the wife of Shiva, was worshiped as a symbol of female energy, regarded as nature's active force, which, among other things, hid the Absolute from the eyes of men.

These partly personal, partly cosmic gods, growing dreamy like the climate of India, were indifferent to moral issues. While they were bringers of good and evil, they were beyond good and evil. Moral law resides in the universe, but the gods are not subject to it.

Finally there appeared in the *Upanishads,* as the crown of religious thought, the theological-philosophical concept of Brahman—the one god, the single power back of all things and powers. Brahman is the essence, totality, and inner unity of all things, the Absolute of Absolutes, in which all things have their source. Brahman is a neuter, actionless, impersonal force with which, while it is not the universe, the universe is identified. Brahman is not merely the sum total of all laws and things. It is the purely spiritual essence of all things, and unknowable through material things, though the material world, made worthless by the concept, can be known only through "It." This concept reduced all gods to one, with which the world was identified; "the one" and the world being, in turn, identified with "the Self" of the universe and the individual. As "the Self," Brahman is an intelligent, conscious being, and the only being which is free, for, being actionless and without desires, he is not subject to Karma. Thus Hindu thinkers climbed from the "word" of the *Rig-Veda* to the zenith of philosophical idealism. Says the *Upanishads:*

> He who dwells in all beings . . . whose body all beings are, and who pulls (rules) all beings within, he is thy Self, the puller (ruler) within the immortal. . . .
>
> He who dwells in the mind, . . . whom the mind does not know, whose body the mind is, and who pulls (rules) the mind within, he is thy Self, the puller (ruler) within the immortal. . . .
>
> That Self is to be described as No, No. He is incomprehensible . . . ; he is imperishable.[14]

God is thus significantly defined as "*Neti, neti, neti, neti*—meaning not this, not that, not even that, and not that either." [15] But the concept is not, as we have seen, merely negative.

The *Bhagavad Gita* presents a purely theistic conception of God, and identifies Brahman with Vishnu, whom it incarnates in Krishna. Similarly, Shiva is often conceived as a one, only, personal God, often represented as dancing to symbolize the joy he finds in his cosmic acts. Many Hindus for centuries have seen in such conceptions but different names for the one only God, whom they have preferred to see as a personal being.

(3) SECTS. There are as many sects as there are gods and godlings. The Brahmins, perhaps cleverly, did not attempt to rob the masses of their numerous caste, local, and ancestral primitive deities, which they still worship. To the learned Brahmin, all these are but the one God manifesting Himself in different forms to men of different mentality and moral worth. The Outcaste worshiper of some crude image is deemed mentally incapable of grasping a sublime, spiritual idea of the one God. The villager knows the gods of the temples, but he reduces them to the size and form of his local deity. The great sects comprise the devotees of the great gods. Buddha, once widely worshiped, was, after A.D. 500, hurled by a triumphant Brahminism from the Indian pantheon, an act not in keeping with the ideals of Hinduism.

(4) SOME BASIC RELIGIOUS IDEAS. Religion, ethics, and philosophy became in India almost inextricably intertwined. In the endless web of Hinduism, here are some important threads, largely religious: (1) there is one unknowable God who is the only reality; (2) there are numerous other gods which men ought to respect; (3) revealed literature, as interpreted by Brahmins, is the final religious authority; (4) divine moral law, Karma, operates through the caste system to reward and punish men; (5) men can stop the operation of Karma by avoiding action and by austere self-denial and world-renunciation; (6) the material world is an illusion; only

[14] Thatcher, *op. cit.*, I, 135, 158–60.

[15] Shridharani, *op. cit.*, p. 251.

the spiritual is real; and (7) the soul is the divine self, reality, residing in each person.

The idea of the immortal soul, the knowing, divine self within each individual is the center of Hindu belief, and the point of beginning and end of all inquiry. The goal of religion for each one is the knowledge of this God within him. Few Hindus question this doctrine of the soul, for their education has not led to doubting. Eventually, it has been believed, this soul will be freed from Karma and united with God eternally. Even the atheist has accepted the doctrine of Karma and its counterpart, the immortality of the soul. Hindus have always lived in eternity.

Linked to the doctrine of the soul is that of Karma and transmigration of souls. Karma explains all things and occurrences in the visible and invisible worlds. It explains, for instance, a man's character, wealth, conduct, etc. The god Brahman is, by essence, free from Karma and rebirth. On Karma rest all ethical doctrines. Many Hindu philosophies taught that men could escape from it by knowledge, intellectual and moral discipline, and monastic renunciation of the world. Buddhist monks and laymen saw escape from it in the eradication of all desires. Under Hinduism proper, relief from it was promised to him who, without desire for reward, discharged his almost endless duties faithfully.

(5) Ecclesiastical Domination. Since the overthrow of Buddhism, the Brahmins have held social ascendancy. The increase of priestly power was largely due to the growth of an ecclesiastical monopoly in the fields of learning and religious culture. After Vedic times, a meaningless, highly ceremonious ritual, and an involved, philosophical theology grew up under the direction of "divinely appointed" custodians, the priests. Warrior intellectuals challenged for a time the priestly monopoly of learning and teaching. The *Upanishads* resulted from these lay activities. The Buddhist movement, while it received many Brahmin converts, was an attempt chiefly of the warrior class to modify Brahminism, but it failed, although nearly one-half of all Hindus once accepted that faith. The Brahmins, with their accumulation of privileges and wealth, and their traditional reputation for learning and holiness, had become firmly entrenched. Particularly because learning became, in the course of time, their monopoly, they came to be regarded by the masses as superior to ordinary men. Prior to A.D. 500, kings and their warrior nobles kept a check upon priestly power. During India's Dark Ages (A.D. 750-950), the old royal houses fell, and the feudal barons, the Rajputs, who succeeded them, persecuted the Buddhists, upheld Brahminism, and permitted the priests to

dominate the social and cultural system, as they still do. Though priestly functions have been exclusively theirs, many Brahmins have engaged in other activities, some of them more profitable. As a class they have been wealthy. Some of the priests proper are endowed, hereditary, temple office-holders; others engage in religious service outside of the temples, and live by the gifts of the faithful, whose sins they make white as snow—for a price.[16]

(6) BUDDHISM. Though crushed in India, Buddhism became the religion of one-third of mankind. Buddha's teachings were new in India not in their ideals but in their points of emphasis. Highest among the ideals which he called upon men to aim at were self-mastery and universal love. The destruction of suffering was the ultimate goal at which he aimed. The essence of his teaching appears in "The Four Noble Truths":

1. Existence is suffering.
2. The desire to exist is the root of suffering.
3. To destroy this desire is to destroy suffering.
4. The destruction of suffering results from following "The Noble Eight-fold Path" which consists of Right Faith, Right Intention, Right Speech, Right Action, Right Conduct, Right Effort, Right Thought, and Right Meditation.

Holiness, asceticism, and a love of all feeling things, not the formal acceptance of dogmas, are the marks of the good life. While Buddha said that he came not to teach philosophy but to save the world, his teachings gave rise to a philosophy among his devotees. On all metaphysical questions he was himself an agnostic; in religion, an atheist. Yet he asked men to be guided in their lives by the doctrines of Karma and rebirth. The virtuous, as distinct from the learned man, by observing Buddhist precepts, could earn extinction (*nirvana*) of desire in life, and a high and happy rebirth. To the learned, who were also virtuous, Buddha offered escape from rebirth and a final *nirvana* (*parinirvana*), a complete extinction apparently of the individual by his absorption into the impersonal, actionless World Soul.

It was as a religion of social reform that Buddhism was most significant. Buddha, born a Kshatriya, taught that conduct, not birth, should determine one's caste. As did Christianity, Buddhism appealed to the lowly, who suffered from caste injustice. Caste distinction was abolished in its monasteries, although some prejudices seem to have continued there. Its greatest triumph came when the emperor Asoka (*c.* 250 B.C.) dedicated his life to the

[16] See Pratt, *op. cit.*, p. 145.

spread of its gospel throughout India and the world. That gospel reached Egypt, Syria, and Palestine and had, no doubt, some influence upon Christianity. In India, its monasteries became in time rich, and its monks another idle, parasitical priesthood who substituted ceremonials for social service. After A.D. 500 it was uprooted by a revitalized Brahminism.

(7) ETHICS. The basic virtues enjoined upon Hindus by their moralists were honesty, truthfulness, piety, charity, and respect for the life of all feeling things. Ethics and religion in India have always been closely knit together, and religious observances have been moral duties. The worst of all sins has been that of injury to any living creature, even to a biting insect. Flowers and trees were also protected by this principle of non-injury. Killing birds and animals for sport, as Westerners sometimes do in India, has not increased Hindu respect for us. The Golden Rule, for which Hindus seem to have more respect than Westerners, appears in their *Mahabharata* as follows:

> This is the sum of all true righteousness—
> Treat others as thou wouldst thyself be treated.
> Do nothing to thy neighbor which hereafter
> Thou wouldst not have thy neighbor do to thee.[17]

British officials, while not careful observers, have noted the scrupulous adherence of Hindus generally to their moral code. Perhaps the West has something to learn from them. Many of India's noble, ethical ideals cannot, however, be logically reconciled with caste injustices. Here, as with us, ideals and practices are often far apart. The good and the bad in India are rooted in the social heritage, whose survival has been one of the cultural and educational phenomena of the world.

POLITICAL ASPECTS. Ancient Aryan India was divided into separate kingdoms, and was never firmly welded into a united nation. At times some of the kings, by successful military exploits, became divisional emperors, as did Asoka in the third century B.C. The nearest approach to national unity came under the Andhras emperors, and their successors, the Gupta and later dynasties in the period 26 B.C.-A.D. 740. This was the period of India's greatest philosophical and scientific achievements, when learned men pursued their studies at imperial seats and under imperial protection. From the second century B.C. until the fifth century A.D., India was periodically invaded by foreigners beginning with the Bactrian

[17] *Ibid.*, p. 98.

Greeks and ending with the Huns. The invaders who remained in India adopted the Buddhist faith, and finally lost their identity in the cultural panorama of their new environment.

During India's Dark Ages (A.D. 750-950) a curtain fell over the nation's history. At their close, the Rajputs, of unknown origin, but probably foreigners converted to Hinduism, had risen to power as feudal overlords. These in turn fell before the might of the Muslims and, since 1194, have enjoyed a sort of independence in isolated strongholds. That date marks the end of Indian national independence. The spirit of Western nationalism, of recent origin here, brought to India, China, and other Eastern lands, a demand for independence and for the right of each people to determine its own destiny. The Far East, under the leadership of China and India, promises to write the next great chapter in the history of mankind.

The caste, family, and village systems of social organization had a disintegrating effect upon the nation, which industrialism and urbanization have now begun to offset. With the fall from power of the kings and warrior class, the Brahmins became the unchallenged controllers of culture and formal education. Religious knowledge and formal education, once the right of all Aryans, were now made an exclusive Brahmin privilege. For a thousand years following this Brahmin triumph, approximately 97 per cent of the people lived and died illiterate. Theocracies have shown a great capacity to thrive on the ignorance and superstition of the masses.

INTELLECTUAL ASPECTS. (1) PHILOSOPHY. A strong claim could be made for ancient India's pre-eminence in philosophy. Here, developing thought on such questions as the nature of being, reality, knowledge, man, etc., parallels very closely that of Greece and the Christian West.

There were six great orthodox, or Vedic, philosophies in India. The philosophy of the sects which rejected Brahmin and Vedic authority remained outside of these orthodox systems. The period 750 B.C.-A.D. 750 was the chief era of philosophical speculation. The agnostic spirit, a root of wisdom, then wove out of Vedic mythology systematized philosophies. The six systems, though disagreeing on many questions, showed themselves to be reconcilable with the *Vedas*, and received Brahmin approval. Inquiring, among other things, into the what and how of knowledge, Hindu philosophers invented a system of logic, which has much in common with that of the Greeks, and a method of inquiry which combined both the deductive and inductive procedures. Out of their inquiry came also psychologies answering questions about the nature of the knowing organism, its various parts and their functions, and the various aspects of the psychological process involved in acquiring knowledge.

The orthodox philosophers professed to believe that the highest truths could be found only in the *Vedas,* and they regarded reason as subservient to faith in arriving at a knowledge of such truths. The function of reason was the discovery of real meanings through a reconciliation of apparently conflicting Vedic thoughts. It could discover no new truths. In addition to faith and reason, sense perception, human authority, and other means were recognized as subordinate sources of knowledge by some, and as primary sources of knowledge by others.

The orthodox schools were opposed by heretical philosophers who denied the infallibility of the *Vedas.* There were many of these heretics, particularly from Buddha's time onward. The agreement of all the schools on certain basic points is remarkable. The materialist Carvaka school stands alone in rejecting the following theories which, except as indicated, are accepted even by the Buddhists and Jainas:

1. The theory of Karma and rebirth
2. The theory of Mukti, or Emancipation, which teaches that, by acquiring true knowledge and eradicating desires, one will become eventually free from joys and sorrows, including rebirth, thus reaching by a short route the final goal of the cosmic moral process, whether we call it *nirvana* or give it another name
3. The theory of a permanent soul, in nature pure, but tarnished by its surroundings, a theory rejected by the Buddhists alone
4. The theory that life is sorrow; that pleasure increases sorrow; and that this sorrow can be ended only by ascetical moral discipline, and by true knowledge of the universe and the soul, and of its ultimate victory over Karma
5. The theory that certain specified moral practices, which include noninjury to living things, are essential to salvation

The doctrine of Mukti has a special educational significance. It proclaims that supreme happiness is attainable only through a life of asceticism, and of intellectual effort leading to a knowledge of the identity of one's own self and the Soul of the Universe. For the ignorant man transmigration can never cease. True knowledge of true realities makes man infinite, immortal and forever free. Indeed, such knowledge is emancipation, which is the realization of the true nature of man. True knowledge is always knowledge of one's Self. Such knowledge blots out feelings of joy and sorrow and ends all change, even death, because, with its attainment, man enters the Endless Sea of unchanging reality.[18]

It is both socially and educationally significant that the only philosophies which survived well in India were those, whether orthodox or heterodox, which denied the existence of the Absolute, a concept perhaps too abstract for the generality of men. Its abstractness does not tell the whole story of its fall. The warrior philosophers, who made Brahman, the Absolute, their central idea, regarded the traditional Hindu gods as inferior to learned men. This Brahman idea tended to spread among the masses and threatened Brahmin ascendancy by destroying respect for the old pantheon and the sacrificial religion of the *Vedas.* To tame the new thought, the Brahmins made it the last and highest study in their schools, and reconciled it with the sacrificial Vedic system, the study of which continued to hold a large place in the curriculum. Philosophy was thus removed from the streets and forests, and subjected to caste rules governing learning and teaching. Democracy was not to enter India by the back door of lay intellectualism and popular enlightenment.

(2) THE SCIENCES. The *Rig-Veda* recognized the existence of immutable cosmic laws of which the Creator is the preserver.[19] There was nothing apparently in the Brahmin religion to stifle the spirit of scientific inquiry. The ancient Hindus made large contributions to scientific knowledge. They invented the decimal and so-called Arabian systems of notation. They also invented zero, saw its reality, and made it the dividing point between positive and negative quantities. The Arabs but refined the Indian systems of arithmetic and algebra, and transmitted them to Europe.

By 1000 B.C., astronomy, long evolving, had become a distinct science, but the Hindus used this knowledge merely to fix the dates of religious festivals. The lunar-zodiac scheme of astronomical calculation was a native invention of the period preceding 1000 B.C. Between A.D. 500 and 1200, Hindu astronomers stated as theory, based upon careful observation of facts, the actual causes of lunar and solar eclipses, and the basic ideas back of Newton's law of gravitation. Astronomy remained, however, a servant of ancient religious myths.

In mathematics we see their achievement at its best. The Hindus invented algebraic calculus, and were the first scientists to apply algebra to astronomical and geometrical problems. In 1202, Leonardo of Pisa in his *Book of the Abacus,* based upon Arabic

[18] Mookerji, *op. cit.,* p. xxiv.

[19] Pratt, *op. cit.,* pp. 49–50.

works, first made this algebra and the zero concept known to Europeans. In trigonometry and arithmetic the Hindus were also pioneers at many points. Hindu geometry, dating from the eighth century B.C., was developed in connection with the building of altars. After construction rules had become fixed, the Hindus neglected geometry in favor of algebra.

In geography, natural history, medicine, chemistry, and surgery, the Hindus made notable progress between 800 B.C. and A.D. 600. Some authorities say that Hippocrates borrowed his *Materia Medica* from the Hindus.[20] The *Atharvaveda* is to a large extent a medical treatise and lists the herbs which cure a long list of diseases and injuries. In time special medical schools arose, and the University of Taksasila became especially famous for its work in medical botany and surgery.

In other fields than science, however, India's greatness lay. Her claim to pre-eminence among ancient peoples in the fields of language, grammar, logic, psychology, philosophy, religion, and ethics cannot be successfully contested. Only in the richness and variety of literature, in sculpture, architecture, and the social and physical sciences did Greece surpass her. The Hindu vision of scientific phenomena was, however, dwarfed by a fixed religious horizon.

To science, as to philosophy, the Brahmins contributed less than did men of lower social rank. Caste laws, from those of Manu onward, placed even physicians and astronomers upon the level of menial castes, and declared their work impure. Priestly contempt for all non-Brahmin activities eventually degraded almost the entire field of useful activities.

ASCETICISM. India has been a land of moral and religious ascetics ever since triumphant Aryan civilization reached its religio-moral seed stage. While the two have many things in common, we can distinguish between worldly and otherworldly asceticism, the former looking to a material reward, the latter, to a religious reward. Since primitive times some have practised austerities in order to gain such things as wealth or power. In time, the power sought came to be magic power, and worldly then began to become otherworldly asceticism. Indian asceticism passed through those stages of development and, by 700 B.C., otherworldly ascetics were numerous there. The four orders of men, as recognized by the sacred laws, were those of the student, householder, hermit, and ascetic, the last two differing from each other only in the forms of torture prescribed for them. *The Laws of Vasishtha*, for instance, read in part:

[20] Dutt, *op. cit.* (People's ed.; Bombay, 1891), pp. 728–29.

(Let the ascetic) shave (his head); let him have no property and no home. . . .

Let him wear a single garment. . . .

Let him sleep on the bare ground. . . .

Let him (constantly) seek in his heart the knowledge (of the universal soul).

(An ascetic) who lives constantly in the forest shall not wander about within sight of village cattle.

Freedom from future births is certain for him who constantly dwells in the forest, who has subdued his organs of sensation and action, who has renounced all sensual gratification, whose mind is fixed in meditation on the Supreme Spirit, and who is (wholly) indifferent (to pleasure and pain). . . .

Let him, though not mad, appear like one out of his mind.[21]

To gain miraculous powers these early hermits organized a system of physical and mental exercises designed to bring the body, the senses, and the mind under the yoke (*yoga*). Generally they were celibates. They retained caste distinctions. Silence, endurance of extremes of temperature, eating disgusting foods, covering their vermin-infested bodies with unspeakable filth, and maintaining excruciating bodily postures, sometimes for years, were among their ascetical practices. They are said to have devised 8,400,000 painful bodily postures.[22] It is probable that some of these practices antedate the Karma doctrine.

The Karma-believing ascetic renounced the worship of gods, his caste, family, property, and all forms of activity, except begging, because he deemed these to hold man world-bound. Such asceticism spread among all the great sects. In his yellow robe, his loin cloth, or completely naked, the monk of India has pursued his solitary, contemplative life. Because the ascetics accepted in time some philosophy which promised emancipation from Karma, they, though remaining solitaries, came to be recognized as members of religious orders.

In addition to the hermitage, communities of monks, vowed to ascetical practices, arose. The Buddhist movement, for instance, came to center in monasteries, and was ascetical, although some bodily comforts were provided for the monks.

Through a thousand channels, asceticism eventually permeated Hindu society and left its mark upon educational ideals and practices. Today, the old otherworldly asceticism is giving way to a worldly form of which the life of Gandhi furnishes a well-known example.

21 Müller, *op. cit.*, XIV, Part II, 46–47.

22 F. M. Müller, *The Six Systems of Indian Philosophy* (New York: Longmans, Green & Co., Inc., 1899), p. 457.

Brahmin Education

TYPES OF FORMAL EDUCATION. From the viewpoint of purpose there were two types of formal education in ancient India, the religio-cultural and the aristocratic-vocational. From the viewpoint of the group which generally provided it, there were two types of schools, the Brahmin and the Buddhist. The student who seeks an account of Muslim education will find a chapter on that subject in F. E. Keay's *Ancient Indian Education*,[23] and a detailed and scholarly account in Part II of R. K. Mookerji's *Ancient Indian Education*. The vocational training of manual workers was provided through the apprenticeship system, and much of it was under the supervision of the gilds. The religio-cultural type of education, in a long view of the Indian scene, was a special privilege of the priestly class, for whom it had also a vocational significance. The aristocratic-vocational was designed to meet the special cultural and vocational needs of Kshatriyas and Vaisyas. Sometime before 500 B.C., the education of these latter classes (earlier, it would seem, provided generally by their own lay teachers) began to be supplied by Brahmin schools. If that be true (though the evidence leaves the matter doubtful), then earlier Brahmin schools were attended mainly by Brahmins, though the legal right of all pure-blooded Aryan boys to Vedic learning was doubtless recognized.

PURPOSES AND IDEALS. While stated here and there in books, the purposes appear perhaps more clearly as an integral, though implicit, aspect of the cultural scene than as systematically stated ideals. As religio-philosophical and educational thought developed, the emphasis came to be placed upon the attainment of a far-away goal in an otherworldly tomorrow, in which, indeed, the contemplative Hindu felt himself to be always living. For him, the individual, caste, the cosmic order, etc., are all one great unity; and the past, present and future are but inseparable aspects of the eternal Now. Education was thus viewed as inseparably intertwined with every other phase of the eternal scheme. In practice, the individual, caste, etc., were treated as separate, and the individual was assigned a subordinate place in the divine social order. That the Hindu did not lose sight of practical, national realities may be gathered from the sacred books, as the following patriotic prayer from the *Vajasaneyi Samhita* reveals:

> Oh Brahman! May in this Kingdom be born the Brahmana who is radiant with supreme knowledge. . . ! May here be born the Kshatriya who is a true hero, a good marksman, a skilful shot, and an accomplished chari-

[23] London: Oxford University Press, 1918.

oteer. . . ! Also cows which yield plenty of milk, oxen that can draw well, the swift horse, and the good housewife! . . . May we get rain according to our needs and our plants yield good fruit and crops! May there be happiness and prosperity for all! [24]

The basic purpose of education was to enlighten the individual about the divine social order and his place in it through a study of the *Veda,* which means knowledge. That purpose, evident in the life of the home, caste, temple, school, etc., was cultural. Immediately, it was social, and the ideal of duty (*Dharma*) was stressed by all leaders. A man's first duty was to the social order. Compliance with that was the core of religious life. The *Sutras* of the post-Vedic age reduced knowledge and men's duties to concise and memorizable form, without any innovation in traditional content, and became the school texts of the new period. Yet, the Hindu looked beyond the social goal to the attainment of spiritual harmony between the individual, society, and the divine cosmic order. To say that the individual was the chief concern of education, as Mookerji does, is to take a too narrow view of the practices.[25]

What Hindus discovered during their metaphysical flights into the Infinite was usually far removed from life's realities, though their dreams had many practical, social results, either good or bad according to one's concept of values. Men need, however, other food than metaphysics. The mystics of India needed that other food for their celestial flights and, while despising manual laborers and labor, had their physical needs supplied. Because they could not escape from worldly realities, a vocational purpose came to be embodied in formal education, and was frequently stated by writers on education. Indeed, the immediate purpose was to train priests, princes, merchants, etc., for their practical pursuits. The law books have much to say about the knowledge and skills needed in these vocational fields. Enough Vedic learning was to be provided for laymen to inspire and guide their work. The devout Hindu, however, always deemed practical training subordinate to the education of the soul.

Education, then, was not concerned primarily with the acquisition of objective knowledge. Though the universe is composed of individual objects, man, it was held, cannot know it through a knowledge of its parts. He must seek to know directly the source of the whole and its parts. To do this the mind must withdraw itself from the material world of objects. The supreme aim of education was thus to train the mind as an instrument of knowledge,

[24] Keay, *op. cit.,* p. 65.

[25] Mookerji, *op. cit.,* pp. xxv ff.

not to furnish it with objective information. The method of education (*yoga*, or discipline) was, therefore, more important than its content.[26]

CURRICULUM. (1) LITERARY STUDIES. The formal education of India was built almost entirely upon books. While some education came from life then as now, much of it came from books, the records of past experience, as it still does among literate peoples, each new generation of which, because of those records, is able to begin life at the point reached by the preceding generation. Animals can learn only by life and experience.

The ancient Aryans deemed the *Vedas* and the learning they contained as sacred, and the whole Brahmin caste became their preserver. In the sacred laws we read: "Sacred learning approached a Brahmana (and said to him), 'Preserve me, I am thy treasure, reveal me not to a scorner, nor to a wicked man, nor to one of uncontrolled passions: so (preserved) I shall be strong.'"[27]

The literary studies developed gradually in the course of centuries. The Indian alphabet, of uncertain origin, was but little used, except perhaps for commercial purposes, before Asoka published his rock edicts (*c.* 242 B.C.). Previously, the literature of the schools was mnemonic, and was memorized and transmitted orally, as have been the ballads and folklore of many peoples even to our own day.

The early speech of the *Rig-Veda* was a local vernacular, called Vedic. Sanskrit is Vedic speech as shaped by learned assemblies and systematized by the grammarian, Panini, about 350 B.C. It became the language of the learned, of official documents, and of orthodox Hindu culture. Nonconformist scriptures have usually been written in other languages. After the tenth century A.D., Sanskrit works were translated into Indian vernaculars, some of which became local media of instruction. Yet, Sanskrit remained the official vehicle of Hindu culture, although, for the masses, it has been largely a dead language ever since writing came into use. Though dead, it long remained the only language of books and schools, which thus only the learned understood. The mark of caste was stamped upon it as learning became more and more a priestly privilege. By controlling this grammatically perfect instrument, the priests have exerted a most conservative influence upon Hindu culture.

Even the most ancient Aryans, motivated perhaps by race hatred, considered their speech God-made, and insisted upon linguistic

[26] *Ibid.*, pp. xxii ff.

[27] Müller, *The Sacred Books of the East,* XIV, Part II, 10.

purity in members of the Aryan family. Such an attitude made easy the acceptance of the fixed grammatical forms which Panini gave to Vedic speech, changed by centuries of growth, as it was, but which, when Sanskritized, was destined to change no more.

In Brahmin schools great stress was placed, especially for Brahmin students, upon the study of words. The god Brahman was identified with the word, and was the thing denoted by every word. Word study and grammar thus came to be the essence of philosophy, the heart of the curriculum, and the way to emancipation from Karma. Grammar, broadly considered, was the science of sciences, the stairway to heaven, the light guiding priests, warriors, and merchants to the proper discharge of their several duties.

The earliest curriculum consisted of the study of one *Veda,* and related subjects, taught by a priest whose family specialized in it. In time, all the *Vedas* were taught in each school. Even in Vedic times, the Brahmins recognized six subjects as essential to an understanding of the *Vedas* and their ritualistic use. These were called *Vedangas* (*Angas*), or members of the *Veda.* They were phonetics, metrics, grammar, etymology, astronomy, and religious ceremonies. Music and singing came to hold an important place in the education of priests. Out of these, many later priestly studies grew. Of the later studies, philosophy was the most important.

To maintain their social supremacy, the Brahmins introduced philosophy into their schools, and made it the queen of studies, perhaps in order to tame it and keep it tamed. Sankara, the leading Vedantist philosopher, held that the *Vedas,* science, history, etc., referred only to the "unreal" phenomenal world, and that it is only through *Vedanta,* the basis of true knowledge, that one could be freed from Karma. The *Vedas,* he said, teach how Brahman is to be worshiped, not how "it" is to be known. Many such philosophers viewed the traditional curriculum as an obstacle to the attainment of a true knowledge of reality. The Brahmin schools faced the challenge of this rationalism, and made philosophy serve "useful" ends. In Brahmin hands, it became the "destroyer of ignorance," gave "meaning to life," and taught men how to attain the "goal of existence." By the early Christian era it seems to have risen to the leading place in the curriculum for the priestly class.

(2) Non-Literary and Vocational Studies. When the education of Kshatriyas and Vaisyas was brought directly under Brahmin control, about 500 B.C., the earlier curriculum was enlarged to meet the needs of this wider school clientele. A list in one of the *Upanishads,* for about the year 100 B.C., has, in addition to the old subjects, such new ones as logic, ethics, augury, military tactics,

arithmetic, astronomy, the study of serpents and poisons, dancing, singing, playing, and the making of perfumes. At about the same date, some schools were teaching also sacred dramatics, history, aesthetics, and the eighteen vernacular scripts of India.[28] Many of those subjects were evidently designed to meet the needs of others than Brahmins. In the long view of the Indian scene, the *Vedas* and *Vedangas* constituted the priestly curriculum.

By A.D. 200, a clear distinction was being drawn between the "sciences" and the "arts." The former were viewed as subjects of study; the latter, as training for practical activities. The sciences included literature, grammar, phonetics, elocution, economics, arithmetic, astronomy, astrology, anatomy, physiology, theory and practice of medicine, and history with stress upon its economic, social, and moral aspects, as reflected in the acts of governments. For priests, the emphasis was placed upon the sciences; for laymen, upon the arts.

Among the studies of princes, at this time, we find the *Vedas*, religious ritual, grammar, rhetoric, elocution, arithmetic, astronomy, economics, education, medicine (including anatomy and surgery), eugenics, augury, the art of love, singing, music, chess, dice, tricks, sculpture, arrangement of flowers, study of precious stones and clothing materials, weaving, sewing, wax-work, animal training, dancing, archery, military tactics, and other physical exercises.[29] It was also customary to have princes travel at home and abroad to study foreign customs and the needs of their own people. On their travels at home they were to study irrigation, local government, interest rates, and basic economic problems, including production and distribution of goods, weights, wages, taxes, etc., and the treatment of widows and orphans. A system of chivalry, with lofty ideals, and similar to mediaeval chivalry, developed among the military nobility.

The educational theorist Kautilya (*c.* 250 B.C.) recommended that princes, having learned the rudiments, should study the *Vedas*, logic, philosophy, ethics, economics, political science, and physical and military activities. His economics included agriculture, cattle-breeding, and business practices.

The *Code of Manu* required the Vaisyas to know all merchandising and the laws governing its practice, weights and measures, soil and animal husbandry, foreign countries and people, treatment of servants, and vernacular languages.[30]

[28] S. V. Venkateswara, *Indian Culture through the Ages* (New York: Longmans, Green & Co., Inc., 1928), I, 171 ff.

[29] *Ibid.*, pp. 166 ff., 194 ff.

[30] Mookerji, *op. cit.*, pp. 54 ff.

This changing curriculum reflected the growing culture of India, and was designed to meet both cultural and vocational needs. The Chinese visitor Hiuen Tsang found the following studies being taught in the schools, in the period A.D. 629-645: (1) the science of words, (2) the science of arts, (3) medicine, (4) philosophy, and (5) religion. The content of these studies remains a matter for conjecture. At that time education began with a study of the forty-nine letters and the ten thousand compound letters of the alphabet. Then came the reading of a primer, and writing. At the age of eight, pupils began to study grammar, "the science of words," and sometimes spent twelve years on that subject. The choice of post-elementary studies seems to have been determined by the students' future needs.

(3) PHYSICAL EDUCATION. Systematic physical education was provided only for princes and soldiers, and its basic purpose was military. The *Ramayana* and *Mahabharata* describe the content of military training dictated, no doubt, largely by the divisions of the army—horse, foot, elephant, and chariot. Running, mounting, throwing weapons, marching, driving the chariot, use of armor, swimming, etc. were among the exercises. Apparently but a small part of this education came under Brahmin supervision. Yet, the story of Indian education would be inadequate without some reference to India's provision for the needs of the body.

Hindu worshipers often engaged in religious bathing, swimming, and dancing. The baths of ancient Mohenjo-daro were probably used for religious purposes. The devotees of the dancing-god, Shiva, danced in frantic delight in his honor, generally unaware, however, of the cosmic and physical significance of the divine art. The morning bath has been a traditional religious duty of the twice-born castes, the pure body symbolizing the purity of the soul. The sacred books sometimes prohibit the use of food deemed injurious to health, and recommend fasting as a cure for disease. Asceticism, however, lessened Hindu concern for bodily health. Says an *Upanishad:* "In this evil-smelling, substantial body, shuffled together out of bones, skin, sinews, marrow, flesh, seed, blood, mucus, tears, eye-gum, dung, urine, gall, and phlegm, how can we enjoy pleasure?" [31]

The military from earliest times had their own formal training. The army had four divisions: (1) infantry, (2) cavalry, (3) chariots, and (4) elephants. Officers and soldiers were trained for all of these branches. Spears, bows, swords, sabres, battle-axes, lances,

[31] Cited in J. N. Farquhar, *The Crown of Hinduism* (London: Oxford University Press, 1915), p. 261.

long javelins, and slings were the chief weapons of war. War activities became in peacetime the sports of the nobility. Prior to 1000 B.C., some Brahmins became famous for their military skill and taught princes the art of defense. Women seem to have received military training at times.[32] Archery, fencing, club contests, and lassoing animals were the most popular sports of princes. On hunting expeditions, in earlier times, the noblemen were accompanied by armed women riding in chariots.

In the Brahmin schools, the Kshatriyas were instructed in military science, usually, it would seem, by laymen under Brahmin supervision. Most of their military training, however, was probably provided outside of such schools.

For the masses, physical education came through their daily toil in vocational activities and through religious ceremonies which demanded physical action.

METHOD AND DISCIPLINE. Traditionally, rote learning, facilitated by music and the singing of the *Vedas,* characterized learning and teaching in the Brahmin schools. Familiarity with the mere sound of the *Vedas* was deemed by many of greater educational value than an understanding of their meaning. The *Rig-Veda* reminded teachers that there are three grades of mental ability—high, medium and low—which they must keep in mind in instructing youth. Before written literature began, students memorized the longest texts without knowing their meaning. Later, the written books continued to be memorized, but the *Sutras* made the task easier. A study of the meaning of the books, however, followed their memorization from the earliest times, and the teacher encouraged his students to ask questions.

Yet, this spirit of inquiry seems not to have led to doubts about the doctrine of the divine origin and infallibility of the *Vedas.* Where inquiry must keep within the bounds of unquestionable assumptions and "first principles," with which all answers must be reconciled, freedom to question is but a most effective instrument to strengthen the chains that enslave the human mind. Learning by hearing the *Veda* rather than by reading was the usual practice. The *Mahabharata* would punish with hell-fire those who wrote the *Veda,* and Kumarila (*c.* eighth century A.D.) deemed the practice a sacrilege. While writing came into use as an aid to memory, the emphasis was placed upon hearing and oral instruction. At the highest stage of education, the method was that of conference and discussion.

32 *Ibid.,* p. 245.

Brahmin education was an intellectual and moral discipline. It was the privilege only of the twice-born castes, who were born again into the pure Aryan family by the ceremony of initiation, which marked the beginning of discipline. New names were given to the initiated who, henceforth, had to carry and wear the symbols of their different castes. The sacred laws fixed the eighth, eleventh, and twelfth year after conception as the proper age for the initiation of a Brahmin, a Kshatriya, and a Vaisya, respectively. The sixteenth, twenty-second, and twenty-fourth years, respectively, were the latest permitted for initiation. The uninitiated became Outcastes unless they performed ceremonial penances.

With initiation, the period of studentship began. The student led an austere life. Chastity, mental purity, self-control, and a contemplative spirit were deemed essential to learning, and he had usually to prove his fitness in these respects before his teacher accepted him as a student of the *Vedas*. Thereafter, he had to serve his teacher meekly, subdue his passions, and avoid all occasions of temptation. Teachers of the Vedanta philosophy, reputedly freed from Karma through their knowledge of Brahman, were worshiped by their students as gods, and a similar respect was extended to other teachers later. Rules for students were prescribed by sacred law. Though differing in minor details from book to book, their spirit is always the same. The *Laws of Vasishtha*, similar to those of Manu, read in part:

> A professed student shall serve his teacher until death. . . .
>
> A student . . . shall bridle his tongue.
>
> He shall eat in the fourth, sixth, or eighth hour of the day.
>
> He shall go out in order to beg.
>
> He shall obey his teacher.
>
> He either (may wear all his hair) tied in a knot, or (keep merely) a lock on the crown of his head tied in a knot (shaving the other parts of the head).
>
> If the teacher walks, he shall attend him walking after him; if the teacher is seated, standing; if the teacher lies down, seated.
>
> He shall study after having been called (by the teacher), and not request the latter to begin the lesson. . . .
>
> (While reciting his prayers) he shall stand in the daytime and sit down at night.
>
> Let him bathe three times a day. . . .[33]

The *Laws of Baudhayana* have such rules for students as these:

> Let him avoid dancing, singing, playing musical instruments, the use of perfumes, garlands, shoes. . . .
>
> Let him take hold (of his teacher's) right (foot) with the right (hand), and of the left (foot) with the left hand. . . .

[33] Müller, *The Sacred Books of the East,* XIV, Part II, 40 ff.

(Let him embrace his teacher's leg) below the knee down to the feet. . . .
(The pupil) must assist his teacher in making his toilet, shampoo him, attend him while bathing, eat his leavings, and so forth. . . .[34]

In India, as in China, the behavior of individuals was minutely regulated, and little was left to one's choice. The life of the student and all important aspects of pupil-teacher relationship were thus regulated.

Brahmin education was a disciplining of the mind, will, and body. The body was disciplined by ascetic postures and breathing exercises, prescribed for the various hours of the day and for various functions. Such discipline was deemed necessary for fruitful study and the control of passions. But, discipline was an end of education, not a means to an end. Study and instruction were but means through which habits of thought, feeling, body control, and behavior were to be acquired. Austerity (*tapas*), a practice of the gods, was the guiding ideal in education. The Karma doctrine, somewhat like that of original sin, lent support to the disciplinary practices of the schools.

After 500 B.C., corporal punishment, earlier unusual, became a common school practice. Manu approved the flogging of students with a bamboo or a rope, and later lawgivers approved his wisdom. Teachers, however, discovered that such punishment was not appropriate for students above the age of sixteen. Its use indicates that some schoolboys were not always in spiritual accord with the divine moral order and the asceticism of the schools.

Viewed in the large, the method was that of *yoga*, or the development of the self by discipline and meditation. *Yoga* means the yoking or control of the senses in order to unite the individual with the spiritual universe. It also means the integration of the mental processes. As an educational practice, it means the separating of desires from their natural objects in the external world in order to attain spiritual perfection. That there is a perception which is extra-sensory is a doctrine of *yoga* psychology, for *yoga* is a psychology of learning, associated with a theory of knowledge and a philosophy of life. The phenomenon of extra-sensory perception has been a subject of scientific inquiry in recent years by Dr. J. B. Rhine of Duke University, Durham, North Carolina. In India its acceptance as a theory and its practice in education date from early Vedic times.

ORGANIZATION AND SCHOOLS. The earliest schooling was provided by *Rishis* or seers who taught their sons and other boys the

[34] *Ibid.*, pp. 152–54.

hymns of the *Rig-Veda.* Each *Rishi* had thus his own family school. Formal schooling customarily began after the boy had received the sacred thread of initiation. In his childhood, an Aryan boy received moral and religious training from his mother, a practice approved by Manu. Some boys, prior to initiation, studied the rudiments under a private teacher.

In Vedic and early post-Vedic times (2500-1000 B.C.), Brahmin teachers specialized in teaching different *Vedas,* and boys apparently chose the school and the *Veda* most closely associated with their family tradition. Twelve years were required to complete the course in one *Veda.* In this early period, attendance at four schools, each one for twelve years, was essential for a mastery of the four *Vedas.* Few students, no doubt, stayed in school for the entire forty-eight years. Even after the *Sutras* had appeared, the length of the usual course continued to be twelve years. Since, in earlier times, boys married usually at the age of twenty, the course for Kshatriyas and Vaisyas, when these began to attend Vedic schools, was probably an abbreviated course. Being excluded from the performance of the sacrificial ritual, these lay boys required less religious instruction than did Brahmins, who, it is noteworthy, were deemed intellectually superior to them.

In the over-all picture, primary instruction consisted in the memorization of oral or written texts by groups of pupils; secondary, in the individual, supervised study of the truth and meaning of the texts, the student subjecting himself to *yoga* and solitary meditation; and higher, in the work of assemblies or academies of advanced students and learned men meeting, as it were, in seminars, to discuss profound and intricate questions of a metaphysical nature. Those mentally and spiritually unfit for higher learning were weeded out of the schools at the end of the secondary stage. In the course of the centuries, Brahmin schools of different types appeared and disappeared, of which the following deserve special recognition.

SCHOOLS OF THE PRIVATE GURUS. From the earliest times a special caste of priests had teaching as their occupation. Their usually one-teacher schools came to exist everywhere in India. They were private schools established by individual *gurus.* Some of these *gurus,* because of a large student body, used advanced students as assistant teachers, and thus originated the monitorial system, which England borrowed from India in the early nineteenth century, and which enjoyed great popularity for a time in the United States. The private *guru* followed closely the Vedic educational tradition, and his school remained through the centuries the chief bulwark of the ancient cultural heritage. These private schools sometimes acquired names based upon the particular text of a particular *Veda* or *Brahmana* in which the teacher or teachers specialized. Thus, for instance, arose such names as *Sakhas, Charanas,* and *Brahmana-Charanas.* But whatever the name, they, as well as other Brahmin schools, existed to preserve and transmit to posterity the wisdom of Vedic literature.

As compared with the private, the corporational type of school has played perhaps a less important cultural rôle in India.

PARISHADS. A *Parishad* was an assembly of learned Brahmins who acted as advisers on religious and philosophical questions and sometimes as ministers in the courts of princes. These assemblies, of ancient origin, became numerous and were permanently located in various centers. A legally constituted *Parishad* was required to have specialists in the *Vedas* and *Angas* among its members. Most of the members were teachers, and students came to these centers to study under them. And it is most likely that Brahmin universities were an outgrowth of *Parishads.*

TOLS. In very many places there arose schools called *Tols.* In famous religious and political centers many *Tols* existed side by side. The *Tol* was a one-room, one-teacher school, surrounded by a group of mud huts in which the students lived. These schools, while offering many studies, became famous chiefly for their work in law and logic. The enrollment in a *Tol* seldom exceeded twenty-five students. It was a free school supported by the gifts of patrons, which were often sufficient to provide even free food and clothing for the students. Where many *Tols* existed at one center, they took on at least the appearance of a university. Originating before the Muslim conquest, the *Tol* has survived to the present day.

FOREST COLLEGES. These were schools which, for quiet and seclusion, were established in forests. Their buildings were mud huts. A water pot and a sleeping mat seem to have been the only furnishings of the dwelling huts of students and teachers. The fame of these colleges led to their endowment by kings, princes, and people. They became centers of philosophical speculation and of advanced literary study.

COURT SCHOOLS. Before India's Dark Ages, kings and emperors often surrounded themselves with scholars and master artisans. In royal courts, learned men discussed questions of religion, philosophy, grammar and literature, science, and art. While they endured, these court schools were pre-eminent in intellectual brilliance, and attracted the most learned teachers of India. In them philosophy seems to have held the place of highest distinction.

TEMPLE COLLEGES. These schools came into prominence after A.D. 500, were taught by the temple priests, and were supported by temple funds. Where these funds were not sufficient to provide free food and clothing for students, rich farmers and merchants usually supplied the deficiency. In some cases, the temples paid students for attending their schools, a privilege, no doubt, reserved for Brahmins. Brahmin-approved literature and philosophy, particularly the Vedanta, were the most honored subjects in the course. In the largest of these colleges, the enrollment sometimes reached three hundred.

GHATIKAS AND AGRAHARAS. In the early Christian era, there arose a few schools of local character called *Ghatikas,* where most learned Brahmins met to explore the most profound teachings of the *Vedas.* They were attended by both undergraduate and post-graduate students, but the emphasis in them was upon the most advanced theological and philosophical study. The *Agrahara* was a large, richly endowed settlement of learned Brahmins engaged in study and teaching.

MATHAS AND VIDYAPITHAS. Brahmin monasteries, called *Mathas,* arose after A.D. 600 and undertook the promotion of Vedic learning and orthodox Hinduism when Buddhism was in the last stage of its decline. The study of grammar, literature, logic, and Vedanta philosophy was stressed in them. Their purpose was the preservation of Brahmin orthodoxy and Hinduism. With their spread, the more liberal view of culture disappeared from Brahmin schools. They were endowed by kings and other rich patrons, and in them tuition and maintenance were free.

The *Vidyapithas,* of which only six were established, arose in the period which gave rise to the *Mathas.* While they had a similar purpose, they were less intolerant than the *Mathas.* Grammar, literature, logic, and Vedanta philosophy were their basic subjects.

Neither the *Mathas* nor the *Vidyapithas* gave much attention to the study of religious ritual. Both aimed rather at establishing an intellectual basis of orthodoxy, and their speculations remained, with great consistency, within the bounds of Vedic dogmas.

After the Muslim conquest the *Mathas* and the *Tols* became the regular types of Brahmin schools, the latter eventually predominating in number and influence.

SPECIAL SCHOOLS. From about 500 B.C. onward, schools specializing in various subjects arose, because of an increase in knowledge which made it impossible for students to master all subjects Among these were schools of (a) grammar, (b) law, (c) astronomy, (d) sacrificial ritual, (e) logic, and (f) philosophy. The *Code of Manu* was compiled in such a law school. Schools of this type have survived into modern times.

UNIVERSITIES. Because of their very advanced studies, a few great centers of learning, established under both Brahmin and Buddhist auspices, may appropriately be called universities. From about 1000 B.C. until today great Brahmin scholars met in philosophical conventions to debate publicly intellectual questions of the most profound nature. These conferences might be called public universities. The most famous formal Brahmin universities were those at Taksasila, Benares, and Nadia. The curriculum of these universities was most probably similar to that of Buddhist universities. Only for the latter is there now any definite information. Religion, philosophy, logic, literature, and the science of words, mathematics, astronomy, and medicine received, no doubt, the chief emphasis. Certain practical studies taught in Buddhist universities, with their middle-class clientele, were probably neglected in Brahmin institutions.

STUDENTS. The "orders" of student and householder were recognized in the most ancient times. However, only a student of the *Vedas* and related subjects was officially regarded as a student. The rules of studentship were laid down in one of the *Vedas*, the *Atharvaveda*, and remained unchanged in the Brahmin system until today. The curriculum, but not the method of teaching and discipline, underwent change. From the day of his religious initiation (*upanayana*) as a student until the completion of his studies the student was governed by the laws of the sacred book. A study of conflicting claims and evidence points to the conclusion that, as a general practice, the initiation and formal studentship, under Brahmin control, of Kshatriyas and Vaisyas dates from about 500 B.C. There is little doubt that all Brahmin boys, from the earliest times, studied the *Vedas*. For the other two classes, until that date, instruction was generally confined to vocational pursuits, and was provided by their fathers. From domestic chaplains the sons of the lay nobility, no doubt, received some Vedic instruction in earlier times. Being excluded from priestly occupations, they received, with probably a few exceptions, even after the Brahmin schools admitted them, less religious, philosophical, and literary instruction than did Brahmin students.

The Brahmins, probably, did less to attract Vaisyas than Kshatriyas to their schools, for the curriculum shows less concern for their needs.[35] When Brahmin ascendancy became at last secure in post-Buddhist times, both of these classes were again excluded from the schools. Alberuni, a Muslim (*c.* A.D. 1000), says that a Vaisya who then dared to study the *Vedas,* and was so accused by a Brahmin, had his tongue cut out, if he were found guilty. Soon thereafter, the Kshatriyas were similarly deprived of their educational privileges. In the broad sweep of Indian history, the interest of these lay classes in Brahmin education was a weak one. Except during the period of lay enlightenment (*c.* 500 B.C.-A.D. 650), the Kshatriyas and Vaisyas largely rejected the privilege which was their birthright.

In early Vedic times, the Sudras seem to have had access to Vedic learning, but soon they, in common with women and Untouchables, were excluded from it.[36]

There is but little conclusive evidence regarding the rate of literacy in India prior to modern times. There is some indirect evidence in the ancient literature which indicates that even not all Brahmin boys attended school in early post-Vedic days. Since, in those same times, the Kshatriyas and Vaisyas seldom received formal literary training, only a small portion of the population was then literate. The compulsory education requirement for the upper three castes was not well observed.

The period 500 B.C.-A.D. 650 was marked by increased lay interest in learning, due mainly to Buddhism. The Oxford historian, Vincent Smith, is of the opinion that the rate of literacy among the total population reached 60 per cent at the close of that period.[37] That figure seems to be too high when we consider the prevailing attitude toward women and the lower castes. The facts, however, warrant our according to India a place of unique leadership in mass education in the ancient world. In the early nineteenth century, only about 5 per cent of Indian children were enrolled in schools, and the census of 1931 showed only 3 per cent of the depressed castes, and 8 per cent of the total population, to be literate.

TEACHERS. In early Vedic days, Kshatriyas were permitted to teach the *Vedas,* but later only Brahmins could legally teach them, and they could not be studied without a teacher. In the field of religious and philosophical teaching the Brahmins came to acquire an almost complete monopoly. For a time, laymen challenged their pre-eminence in philosophy and, no doubt, lectured on that

[35] See Mookerji, *op. cit.,* pp. 151–54.
[36] *Ibid.,* pp. 52–53.
[37] K. Shridharani, "Indian Nationalism and Education," *Schoolmen's Week Proceedings* (1943), p. 60, published by the University of Pennsylvania.

subject. There were wandering lay teachers even in Vedic times, some of whom taught nonconformist doctrines, and thus foreshadowed the coming of Buddha.

In such practical, secular fields as political administration, commerce, etc., laymen were usually the teachers, and that practice had the approval of Kautilya and even of Manu. Since these practical pursuits were regulated by Vedic laws, the lay teacher had to know these laws, and his teaching thus, probably, came to be supervised by Brahmins. In the village vernacular, commercial schools of modern times, the origin of which is obscure, the teachers have been generally laymen of the scribe caste, and Brahmins have not supervised their work.

For over 2000 years, Vedic knowledge was carried in the heads of learned men, not in books, and could not become the property of every seeker. It was spread at the will of its possessors, and upon their terms, to students selected according to rigid standards of ability and character. The teacher was completely independent in his choice and retention of students. Thus was a literary education preserved and transmitted without the aid of books. Each of the millions of teachers was a living library which could not be destroyed by war, vandalism, or autocrats. Indian culture has thus been preserved and transmitted by an unbroken line of teachers rather than by libraries. Central libraries were unknown in India. Max Müller has said that if all the manuscripts of the *Vedas* were destroyed, they could be completely recovered from the memory of modern Brahmin teachers. The obligation to preserve their ancient culture they discharged with seriousness and solemnity.[38]

From early Vedic times the qualifications and conduct of Brahmin teachers were regulated minutely by sacred law. Before teaching, a Brahmin must have performed all student duties, and have studied the subjects which he was to teach. As a teacher, he must make students observe all the rules of studentship, and accept no remuneration for his services other than gifts and the proceeds of his students' begging. Some teachers acquired valuable property through the gift system.[39]

The *Code of Manu* describes the ideal teacher as one of gentle speech, who, even when offended, never offends by word; who never injures another by thought or deed; and who never, under penalty of losing heaven, makes others afraid of him by word or act. Yet, Manu approved corporal punishment. The lawgivers, gen-

[38] Mookerji, *op. cit.*, pp. 214 ff.
[39] *Ibid.*, pp. 202–4.

erally, conceived the ideal teacher as learned, chaste, cheerful, kindly, correct in his speech, exemplary in his life, firm in his beliefs, content to live by begging and by his students' begging, and willing to reveal all his knowledge to zealous students. The teacher of old was apparently held in great respect. That ancient spirit of esteem had departed from the scribe-taught, village vernacular schools of nineteenth-century India, according to the testimony of British officials. Yet one who is still entitled to the name *guru* is held in great respect.

SUPPORT AND CONTROL. Most of the schools being of the private type, gifts of students and philanthropists and the proceeds of student begging were the chief sources of support. Schools of the corporational type derived much of their support from endowments secured in various ways. Royal grants of land to Brahmins often carried a provision for free education. Kings sometimes granted village revenues to Brahmins. Thus one group of 30,000 Brahmins, in 1091, were living by the revenues of 144 villages. Such grants usually required the recipients to teach, a duty which they learned to ignore, except in so far as preaching fulfilled it.

The general education of ancient India was free. The sacred books forbade teachers' fees as unworthy of priestly calling and offensive to heaven. India, however, rewarded in other ways the Brahmin custodians of her culture, while she did not neglect their material needs. Some teachers of special subjects charged fees, but their specializations were outside the field of general education, as interpreted in India.

As regards control, the private character of Indian education is significant. Political authorities seem to have exercised no control over the education even of political and military officials. Nor was there any organized central agency of Brahmin control. The priests were, however, powerful, and intolerant of unorthodox teachers. Yet the unorthodox enjoyed great liberty until Brahminism triumphed over Buddhism. Such later schools as the *Gathas* reflected the spirit of triumphant intolerance, though priestly control over them remained unorganized. The Brahmin teacher, however, like many other teachers in other lands and times, was effectively controlled by his cultural heritage, his class interests, his training, and by written and unwritten laws. The centuries-old stability of the culture which he guarded is eloquent testimony to the effectiveness of such instruments of control.

Buddhist Education

Since the general plan and spirit of Buddhist education was similar to that of the Brahmins, a detailed account of it would result in unnecessary repetition. With the exception of differences in religious and social ideology, in types of schools, and in the provision made for girls' education, Buddhist and Brahmin educational practices are strikingly similar. In the scale of values, the Buddhists, as did the Brahmins, placed their moral and religious ideals at the top. Buddhist education, like the Brahmin, was basically a religious, moral, and intellectual discipline. In it, indeed, less attention was paid to practical needs than in the Brahmin system.

Because Buddhism was a revolt against the Brahmins, it negated Brahmin claims to exclusive rights in teaching and sacrificing. Rejecting the idea of an infallible authority, either of men or a book, Buddha put knowledge in the place of belief, and demanded mathematical certainty for everything. Yet, he was not able to reject the idea of Karma. His teaching was a strange blend of ideals of social reform and of a disregard by the individual of everything except his own escape into the blessedness of *nirvana*. His followers, however, took great liberties with his teachings, many of which were obscure in meaning.

While included in the curriculum, the *Vedas* were not the basis of Buddhist education. Buddhist literature, though not deemed infallible, replaced them as the source of wisdom and morality. Sanskrit, however, remained as a study in the new schools, but vernaculars replaced it as the language of instruction. Its prestige increased, however, as Buddhism declined. The entire curriculum was largely borrowed from the Brahmins. As in Graeco-Roman and mediaeval Christian civilizations, Indian grammar included the study of much literature. The Buddhist student began his study at the age of six and completed it at about the age of twenty. Then he began the higher studies of prose and verse composition, logic, philosophy, metaphysics, medicine, etc. On the completion of these higher studies he might enter a Buddhist university, if he passed the difficult entrance examination.

On all instructional levels, the texts and treatises, many of them lengthy, had to be memorized. Then followed discussions and debates on their meaning. The life and behavior of students were regulated by stringent rules similar to those governing the conduct of Brahmin students. Teacher-worship and menial service on the part of the student marked teacher-student relationships.

While the hermit life was regarded by them as the ideal, Buddhist monks generally lived in monasteries, of which there were about 5,000 in India at the height of the movement. Poverty, chastity, and obedience were required of all monks. While the Brahmin system was almost wholly one of individual teachers and schools, large corporations of students and teachers marked the Buddhist system. Every monastery had its school, and many of them became famous seats of learning. These schools were open not only to interns (called "children") but also to externs (called "students"). The former were the novices who had dedicated themselves to monastic life with its ascetical requirements. Each novice had to choose a monk as a special teacher. He was promoted to the status of monk by a series of ceremonies beginning when he was eight years old and ending when he was twenty. During those probationary years, he had to engage in manual labor. As a fully ordained monk, he spent his life in further study, meditation, teaching, and preaching.

Buddhist schools and monastic life were open to all castes, but, apparently, only a minority of Buddhist youths were attracted to them. The monks and nuns constituted, at any time, but a small fraction of the total Buddhist population, though they seem to have numbered millions at the height of the movement. Indian monasticism was Buddhist, although the *Mathas* and a few Brahmin religious orders were partly monastic in character.

We have no conclusive evidence that the Buddhists had any other schools than those of the monasteries. It appears certain that these provided all formal education, from elementary to higher, for the students who attended them. They were most noted for their work in logic and medicine. Six of them grew into schools of university rank, that of Nalanda being the most famous.

The University of Nalanda originated about A.D. 400 near the site (Rajgir) where Buddha convened his first religious assembly. It consisted of six richly endowed colleges. To it came students from all over India, and from all over the Near and Far East. The Chinese traveler Hiuen Tsang, in the seventh century, says that it numbered 10,000, of whom 1,510 were teachers. As in other Buddhist universities, tuition, board, and lodging were free, but only the most brilliant students were admitted. At each of the four gates, a dean of admissions maintained his office. This learned official gave each applicant a searching examination. Tradition has it that no one who failed that test, even though he were the son of a king, was ever admitted as a student. Tsang tells us that 70 per cent of the applicants failed to pass the entrance examinations. Nalanda closed around A.D. 850. Its magnificent ruins still stand as a reminder of the glory that once was India.

The studies for which Nalanda was most noted were grammar, literature, logic, philosophy, metaphysics, "human life," astronomy, geography, architecture, arts and crafts, medicine, divination, and music. Law and, apparently, mathematics received less attention in Buddhist than in Brahmin schools.

The learned monks of Nalanda, says Tsang, engaged in discussion of profound questions all day long. Here came students and learned men, who were not students, to settle their doubts, and to gather wisdom which they were to communicate to the outside world, not always, however, for purely unselfish ends. Of all ancient Indian schools, Nalanda acquired the greatest and most widespread renown.

While Buddhism, with its socially liberal ideals and practices, flourished, it enlarged very notably the educational opportunities of Indian youth of the sub-Brahmin castes, particularly of those excluded from Brahmin schools. Lay Buddhists who did not enter the monasteries received their religious education from Buddhist traveling preachers, but had to find their secular education in non-Buddhist schools, for the monasteries did not admit day scholars until late in Buddhist history. The high degree of literacy, of which we have spoken earlier, was made possible by Buddhist liberalism and by the growth of Buddhist monasteries and nunneries. Tuition, board and lodging were free in all these schools, but students, generally, were required to work and beg in order to support themselves and the monks, who, like the Christian monks of the West, came to devote themselves more to prayer than to labor. The overthrow of Buddhism, coupled with the destruction produced by invasions since A.D. 1000, brought a great decline in learning, and a neglect of all practical concerns by the schools that survived the crisis.

PHYSICAL EDUCATION. The demands of the body were not neglected in Buddhist monasteries, and the monks engaged in a variety of sports and games, including dancing, hop-skip-and-jump, tossing balls, tumbling, chariot racing, archery, riding horses and elephants, wrestling, boxing, and fencing. In addition to these, there were many games of chance and skill which provided some spiritual relaxation for them. The study of medicine, for which their universities were famous, contributed, no doubt, to this interest in physical activities.[40]

[40] *Ibid.*, pp. 447–48.

Education of Women

UNDER HINDUISM. In earlier Vedic times the wives of Brahmin priests and of some noblemen were permitted to study the *Vedas*. After about 500 B.C. the only education permitted them was informal training in domestic pursuits, morality, and good manners. The women who acquired a literary training in later times were so few that, in the tradition of India, they have become one of the marvels of the universe. The laws assigned to women the duties of rearing children, housekeeping (which included milking the cows), and the safeguarding of their husbands' property, activities for which a literary education was not necessary. In some minor religious rites they were given a part to perform, and for that duty they were instructed, as girls, by their parents. While husbands were regarded as the natural teachers of their wives, most of the instruction of girls and young wives was entrusted to mothers and mothers-in-law.

One group of women, the temple prostitutes, received a formal education, which included some literary instruction. These women were taught music, singing, dancing, acting and reciting as a training for their part in temple ceremonies. Mind-reading, fortune-telling, manufacture of perfumes, beauty-culture, and detecting criminals and spies were among their activities. It is probable that the temple priests were their teachers in most of these arts.

UNDER BUDDHISM. While some minor heretical sects, such as the Jainas, accorded women literary privileges, only the Buddhists, in practice, provided extensive formal educational opportunities for them. Buddha, with some grave misgivings, approved the admission of nuns to monastic communities. The nunneries which were organized were much fewer than the monasteries for men, and they were placed under complete control of the monks. Novices were admitted to the nunneries by the monks, and the nuns always held a subordinate and separate position in the system.

What provision was made for the education of girls in these nunneries remains a matter of doubt. Domestic arts, religion, and morality were certainly taught. It is almost certain that the novices were also instructed in reading and writing. All nuns were instructed by monks twice each month. Whether or not the nunnery schools were open to externs, as were the monastery schools, is not now known. Even though the mass of girls were excluded, the nunneries, when we consider the large number of girls who chose the community life, enlarged significantly the educational opportunities of Indian women.

Vocational Education

Indian Aryans, like their Graeco-Roman kinsmen, acquired a contempt for manual labor, and made it the lot of the aborigines and of those of hybrid or doubtful origin. These lowly folk preserved and transmitted the arts and crafts since ancient times. As we have seen, training in these skilled manual occupations was under the control of the gilds, and it was provided by the apprenticeship system. The rules governing apprenticeship were laid down in the law books.[41] Craft techniques were believed to be of divine origin, and remained largely unchanged throughout the centuries. Only those who knew the divine techniques, as described in the sacred books, could, as an almost universal rule, engage in the skilled occupations. The apprentice, in addition to hand training, committed to memory the prescribed rules of his craft, as found in the sacred books and as transmitted orally by master craftsmen, who were illiterate and had never seen even the alphabet. The craftsman's workshop was the vocational school of India, and craft interests were protected by the various gilds which functioned as supervisors of craft training. There were sixty-four arts and crafts mentioned in literature. This is the general picture, but it is not entirely complete.

Kings bestowed signal honors upon famous craftsmen, and gave employment to many of them. Shipbuilders, armor-makers, and image-makers worked for kings only. From such royal monopolies, the kings collected revenues. The king's craftsmen, however, learned the trades by the apprenticeship plan. In such respect were these men held that even occasional princes became apprentices to them.

For the vocational needs of the military nobility, public administrators, merchants, and agriculturalists, all of whom belonged to the twice-born castes, some provision was made in both Brahmin and Buddhist schools from 500 B.C. onward, but, at best, it was very inadequate. The Brahmins were more concerned about the laws regulating such pursuits than about the efficiency with which they were performed. What formal instruction was provided in these fields was largely of the bookish variety, and the men engaged in these pursuits learned chiefly by practical experience how to perform them. In the curriculum of some higher schools and universities, a study of the "arts and crafts" sometimes appears, but it is most improbable that such a subject could, especially in Brahmin schools, mean much more than a study of laws governing these ac-

[41] *Ibid.*, pp. 349–51.

tivities. The study of medicine appears frequently in the curriculum of Brahmin and Buddhist schools, but practically nothing is known about the content and plan of medical instruction.

The Buddhists gave special attention to the commercial education of princes. They called this study *Rupa.* It is probable that it included a study of coinage and exchange, commercial arithmetic and bookkeeping. Catering chiefly to the middle and lower classes, the Buddhists probably gave more attention to vocational studies than did the Brahmins, but detailed information about this aspect of their work is lacking. The silence of the records is not proof that they neglected the vocational needs of their students.

Lay Vernacular Village Schools

In our scheme of classification of Indian schools and educational practices no entirely logical place exists for a description of village vernacular schools. Their significance, however, would, in any scheme, call for special treatment.

A British report on education in Bengal (1835-1838), and later reports for other provinces show that there were, in larger villages, Hindu vernacular schools, called in Bengal *Pathsalas.* The date of their origin is uncertain. While they existed in the seventeenth century, and may have arisen in imitation of Muslim vernacular schools, it is probable that they originated in attempts in ancient times to meet the special needs of the merchant class. Their vocational purpose is readily apparent. The reader's attention is called to the similarity between the *Pathsala* and the city vernacular school of later mediaeval Europe.

The British reports show that the enrollment in a *Pathsala* seldom exceeded twenty pupils, and that the teachers, while occasionally Brahmins, were usually of the despised writer caste. The curriculum consisted of reading, writing, arithmetic and bookkeeping, the teaching of which was traditionally considered a degrading occupation by the twice-born castes. The pupils generally belonged to the Brahmin and writer castes. It is, however, noteworthy that some *Pathsalas* admitted Untouchables, caste ceremonial being, no doubt, carefully observed. The students were from six to sixteen years of age, and were taught individually. The monitorial plan of instruction, of ancient origin, as we have seen, was in use in these village schools.

The Bengal *Pathsalas* and their equivalents, with different names, in other provinces were vernacular, not Sanskrit, schools, designed to meet the business needs of the commercial class. They were outside of the traditional Brahmin school system.

It is probable that merchants, political administrators, and farmers, both Brahmin and Buddhist, provided vernacular schools of the 3R's for vocational purposes before the sacred books were put into writing. With the degradation of the scribe (*c.* A.D. 1) everything connected with his occupation became degrading. Although the sacred books were eventually translated into Indian vernaculars, these vulgar tongues never enjoyed the high respect bestowed upon Sanskrit. An odium thus came to attach to the teaching of occupational pursuits which demanded instruction in the vernaculars, but the need for such instruction remained. The merchant class, particularly, must always have made some provision for it, and the village vernacular schools of modern times, in no way a result of British influence, are probably a survival of an ancient practice which long ago attained its present institutional form.

The *Pathsala* has been a product of village life, and India has been a land of villages. It has been, and is, the people's school. While the British reports show that many of the 700,000 villages had *Pathsalas,* there were, in the early nineteenth century, less than 1,200 Sanskrit schools of the old type in India, of which the *Tols* were the most numerous. The British investigators found vernacular schools of the following types: (1) temple schools, (2) schools supported by village magnates, (3) private-venture village schools, and (4) family tutorial schools of individual merchants. However, probably less than 10 per cent of Hindu boys were then receiving formal elementary education.

India and the World of Tomorrow

The world of today is a patchwork of cultures and institutions, back of which lie long histories. The struggles and turmoils of our time cannot be fully understood without that perspective which history alone can provide. The civilization of India, still but little changed by the hand of time, furnishes an excellent example of the force of tradition and of the influence of education, formal and informal, upon the outlook of men and societies. Industrialization and contact with the West have begun to have their effect upon this ancient civilization, which still clings as far as possible to many of its ancient ways, although some Hindus have become advocates of almost complete Westernization. Untouchability has been made illegal by the Indian government, but it remains a national habit of mind. Government positions, schools, scholarships, and temples are now open to the outcastes. But the minds of orthodox Hindus in the villages have not yet been much touched by the official enlightenment. The new educational opportunities for the Untouchables hold the chief promise for the ultimate success of the reforms. All attempts at reform since Buddha's time, and there have been many, failed. Such prejudices are hard to uproot, and they are a threat to national security wherever they exist. Western interests and example have been forcing India and China, as indeed other peoples, to adopt our ways of industrialization and nationalism. Resentment to Western imperialism, and to the doctrine of white supremacy, has increased among the people of both lands. While motives of justice and honesty ought to determine our attitudes and acts toward our Eastern neighbors, that of self-interest seems to offer the chief promise of an enlightened policy in our dealings with them. The whites constitute less than one-third of the total population of the world. Someone has remarked that unless we develop good relations with our yellow, brown, and black neighbors we may find ourselves, in some not very distant day, riding in the Jim Crow seats.

One most important step toward desirable relations with our Eastern neighbors is the development in our youth of respect for their culture and achievements. Our schools in the past have been too much occupied with our own Western cultural heritage. We still, for instance, continue to think of a liberal education in terms of our Graeco-Roman-Christian tradition. In practice our "humanities" have very largely excluded the great contributions in such fields as religion, literature, philosophy, and art of Eastern peoples. If we are to teach religion in American public schools, perhaps we ought to have our pupils study all the great religious movements of the world. If we are to teach appreciation of art, why should we exclude from the picture the art, let us say, of India and China? Our man-made music of the West is not superior to the man-made music of the East. There are no "natural" laws of music. The music of Persia, with its eight basic scales, and the music of East India, with its six hundred basic scales, are as worthy of study and appreciation as our own, with its two basic scales. If we want international understanding and peace, we must aim, among things more basic (such as economic justice), at the moulding of good cultural relationships with our neighbors. The world of tomorrow must find ways for that cultural exchange which is indispensable to peace.

Indian society and education are now undergoing important changes. In the future, it would seem, there will be less emphasis in Hindu schools upon ancient literature and metaphysics, and more upon the realities of modern life. From the myths of the past India is being forced to turn to scientifically ascertained facts—facts about life, about her own society, and about the world.

From the political, religious, social, and intellectual despotisms of the ancient East, which Egypt and India typify, we shall now turn to examine the rise and progress of a secular civilization and an education based upon respect for personal liberty and upon the principle that the individual stands first in the scale of values.

Selected Readings

COOMARASWAMY, A. *The Dance of Siva.* New York: The Sunwise Turn, 1918.

DASGUPTA, S. *A History of Indian Philosophy.* London: Cambridge University Press, 1922, Vol. 1.

DUTT, R. C. *A History of Civilization in Ancient India.* Rev. ed., 2 vols.; London: Kegan Paul, Trench, Trubner & Co., Ltd., 1893.

FARQUHAR, J. N. *The Crown of Hinduism.* London: Oxford University Press, 1915.

GRISWOLD, H. D. *The Religion of the Rigveda.* London: Oxford University Press, 1923.

HOPKINS, E. W. *Ethics of India.* New Haven: Yale University Press, 1924.

———. *India Old and New.* New York: Charles Scribner's Sons, 1901.

India Speaking. The Annals of the American Academy of Political and Social Science (May 1944), CCXXXIII. Philadelphia, 1944.

KABIR, H. *Education in New India.* New York: Harper & Bros., 1957.

MOOKERJI, R. K. *Ancient Indian Education.* London: Macmillan & Co., Ltd., 1947.

MUEHL, J. F. *Interview with India.* New York: John Day Co., Inc., 1950.

MÜLLER, F. M. *The Six Systems of Indian Philosophy.* New York: Longmans, Green & Co., Inc., 1899.

NURULLAH, S., and NAIK, J. P. *History of Education in India during the British Period.* 2d ed.; London: Macmillan & Co., Ltd., 1951.

O'MALLEY, L. S. S. *India's Social Heritage.* Oxford: The Clarendon Press, 1934.

PRASADA–ISVARI. *History of Mediaeval India from 647 A.D. to the Mughal Conquest.* Allahabad: Indian Press, 1925.

PRATT, J. B. *India and Its Faiths.* Boston: Houghton Mifflin Co., 1915.

SÉNART, É. *Caste in India.* (Trans. E. D. Ross.) London: Methuen, 1930.

VENKATESWARA, S. V. *Indian Culture through the Ages.* New York: Longmans, Green & Co., Inc., 1928, Vol. 1.

WOODY, T. *Life and Education in Early Societies.* New York: The Macmillan Co., 1949.

5 Graeco-Roman Society and Education

In the Mediterranean area, Greece is the land where the West begins. For thousands of years, the people of ancient Greece had been in commercial, military, and cultural contact with the civilizations of the Near East, as well as with those of their Mediterranean neighbors to the west. Greece was, in a very special way, the point where Eastern and Western cultures met and, to a degree, blended, as well as the point of origin of many of our Western ideals and institutions.[1]

In Greece there arose an array of independent city-states, which for many reasons—one of them the Greek spirit of liberty and independence—never became united into one national state, until, conquered by the power of Macedon in 338 B.C. and then by that of Rome in 146 B.C., they were forced into a unity as a subject people. The Roman empire was in a very real sense the culmination of an age-old striving for Grecian unity which was never realized by the Greeks themselves. In the things of the spirit—art, science, philosophy, literature, etc.—Greece was strong, but in organizing and moulding material institutions she was weak. The Romans, on the contrary, displayed an unparalleled practical genius for organization and the building of institutions. The Roman empire was one of many attempts, some of them old when Rome was still a city on its seven hills, to build a world culture and a world empire. To that end, Rome assimilated Greek culture in as far as it could be reconciled with utilitarianism and, when a further cultural element was needed, she made Christianity the servant of the empire in the days of Constantine the Great. The Roman attempt at a world empire finally failed, but the dream of universalism survived in the Chris-

[1] H. R. James, *Our Hellenic Heritage* (New York: The Macmillan Co., 1927), I, 3–14, 17–24; *The Cambridge Ancient History (C.A.H.)* (New York: The Macmillan Co., 1923–39), III, 248–50; VI, 398–400, 418–20, 423, 429, 431–37, 532–33.

tian system, until the time of the Reformation, and in the nebulous Holy Roman empire, until the dream was further shattered by Napoleon I.

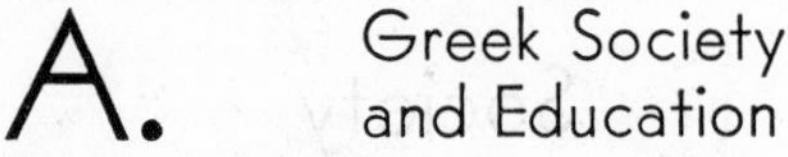

The Greek People

The Greek people were a blend of many populations. First there were the Aegeo-Cretans, an indigenous Mediterranean stock, whose presence in the region can be traced back to about 20,000 B.C. These had their own culture, and built up a remarkable civilization in Crete, on other Aegean islands, and on the Greek mainland.[2] This Minoan civilization flourished in the period 6000-1200 B.C., attained its Golden Age in the period 1700-1400 B.C., and then rapidly declined as a result of internal and external causes. From about 1600 B.C., Aryan tribes, the Nordics of ethnology, came into Greece in a series of migrations and settled among the earlier people. These migrations ceased about 1000 B.C. In later times, these Aryan conquerors called themselves Hellenes because of their supposed common descent from a mythical ancestor named Hellen. Of the Hellenes, the last to invade the peninsula were the Dorians who came in a steady intrusion from about 1100 B.C., and dominated a great part of the country. Many of the earlier settlers, whom the Dorians dispossessed, found a refuge at Athens, and others swarmed across the Aegean, settling on the islands and on the Ionian coast. These people are usually called Achaeans. The Dorian conquest ended the Heroic Age, of which Homer sang, and ushered in a dark age which continued until the eighth century B.C., when another age of splendor began. Of the Doric states, Sparta was the greatest and, of the non-Doric, Athens is by far the most famous.

General Aspects of Greek Life

The civilization of Greece was in the making for thousands of years before the dawn of history, and much is known today of the earlier steps in the development of Greece and its education. In a brief treatise, such as this, little can be said of the educational practices of Greece prior to the Doric conquest. It must be noted gen-

[2] *C.A.H.*, I, 589–90.

erally, however, that Hellenic Greece inherited the culture, the ways of life, the arts, crafts, and educational traditions of the ancient Aegeo-Cretan-Mycenaean-Achaean civilizations. This inheritance plus certain borrowings from the Orient blended with the Hellenic contribution to produce what we know as Greek civilization and culture. Hellenic Greece was composed of hundreds of little independent city-states, and a man was a citizen of his city (*polis*), not of Hellas as a whole. Many of these states were very small. The largest and most powerful were the Dorian state of Sparta, with a despotic oligarchical government, and the Ionian state of Athens which became notably democratic. Variety and diversity in thought and institutional life marked the city-states generally. No two were exactly alike. Therein the Greek world shows a significant contrast with the uniformity in thought and institutions of Oriental peoples.

Real unity the Greeks never attained. Great natural barriers separated the city-states, and, unlike Rome, Greece never built paved roads. The "wet ways of the sea" were the highroads of Greece, and the gods of the sea build civilizations different from those built by the gods of inland rivers.

Cretan-Mycenaean Society and Education

At the height of its development (2000-1200 B.C.) the empire of Crete bristled with agricultural, industrial, commercial and military activities, and large cities had emerged, Knossos, with a population of perhaps 100,000, becoming the capital. Well-built roads linked the cities with the ports through which passed their industrial products to the mainland, the Mediterranean islands, Egypt and other lands. This first great empire of the sea came to be ruled by kings who exercised not only political but religious, legislative and judicial authority. An earlier clan system gave way in later times to a strong family one, in which women, all of them priestesses of the Great-Mother goddess and apparently closely restricted to domestic pursuits, held a place of respect and importance. Freedom to engage in some non-domestic pursuits was not denied them.

Systems of pictographic writing were invented early by the Cretans and were carried to other lands by their traders, who used them in keeping their accounts, as did the government in keeping its records. An arithmetical system was also developed, and formal schools of these 2 R's probably existed. We know much more about the physical life and education of these people from the excavated remains of the palace at Knossos than we do about their mental education. Their soldiers and sailors were trained for their several duties and in the use of the weapons and implements used in war—swords, shields, daggers, bows and arrows, spears, slings, etc. Chariots were introduced from Syria, as was a superior breed of horse, and were extensively used in war and hunting in the last centuries of Cretan civilization. Hunting was a national sport. Bull-fighting and professional bull-fighters, delights of the Great-Mother goddess, were the crowning glory of the athletic life. Women engaged, as did Spartan women later, in acrobatic contests. Boxing, wrestling, running and swimming were common sports. The Olympic games were here in embryonic form. Music and dancing, of which the Great Mother was a patroness, had a prominent place in the life of the people, and women were the chief performers in the religious dances. Not only was dancing dear to the goddess, but nearly all military and sporting activities as well. Concern for personal cleanliness is evidenced by the discovery of public and private baths. Games of chance and skill, some of them associated with religion, had a place in the education of the people.[3]

Cretan power fell, probably about 1200 B.C., before the southward sweep of the Achaeans. Then ensued the "golden" Heroic Age of Greece under the leadership of Mycenae. Homer in the *Iliad* and *Odyssey* depicts the gods, heroes and institutions of this age, but whether or not his account is accurate is a debated question. The Mycenae of Homer's story was ruled by strong kings in the interest of a nobility served by professional aids, commoners and slaves, the last having no legal rights. Women, both wives and concubines, were regarded as salable property and were held in subjugation. Agriculture was deemed a dignified occupation even for the nobility, although slaves did most of the work. The arts and crafts were assigned almost entirely to free artisans and slaves. The religions of the period will be described later.

There is but little in Homer that casts light upon the formal education of the time, and what there is refers only to the nobles, who apparently were illiterate. Cheiron, probably a health specialist, taught Achilles hunting, running, and the rules of diet and health, while Phoenix taught him to be a "speaker of words and a doer of deeds." Oratory, physical training and music, provided by private tutors, thus constituted the formal training of some nobles. Fathers, no doubt, assumed most of the responsibility for the education of their sons, who are represented by Homer as attending the social functions of their elders. Music, singing and dancing, associated

[3] T. Woody, *Life and Education in Early Societies* (New York: The Macmillan Co., 1949), pp. 197–215.

with religion and war, had a leading place in the experience of youth. Homer's nobles were not brought up to prize the inglorious arts of peace. Running, jumping, hunting, swimming, boxing, wrestling, archery, throwing the spear and discus, riding and driving the chariot were among their exercises. Girls were taught by their mothers domestic pursuits. Younger children, both boys and girls, played many games; and older folks, a variety of competitive gymnastic exercises and sports, which seem to be the forerunners of the games and contests of later times, and which survive in the Olympic games of our own day.[4] The life and education of Spartans and Athenians, as indeed of all later Greeks, were thus foreshadowed by the practices of earlier times, which were dictated by the needs and interests of the ruling class whose chief occupations were government and war. While they enjoyed much leisure, they were not given to a life of inactivity.

Spartan Society and Education

Little is known with certainty about Dorian history prior to the eighth century B.C. Then the curtain rises to reveal Sparta in a two-centuries struggle with the city-states around her, which resulted in her military domination of the Peloponnesus. There were revolts against her iron rule, and at last her power was broken by Thebes in the battle of Leuctra (371 B.C.).

Sparta had a total population of about 400,000, of whom about 225,000 were *Helots,* or slaves, and 130,000 *perioikoi,* who were not citizens but enjoyed personal freedom and other privileges. The *Spartiatae,* or citizens, to whom the name Spartans belonged, numbered about 45,000. In these estimates women and children are included. The Helots were the descendants of the conquered people whom their Dorian masters reduced to slavery. They were made hewers of wood and drawers of water. Occasional revolts but accentuated their distress and the barbarity of their treatment by their masters. They performed personal services for Spartan soldiers and sometimes served as soldiers in battle. An occasional one was admitted to the military training program of the citizen class. For bravery and loyal service some of them were granted freedom, but as a group they remained hostile to the state.

The *perioikoi* were probably descendants of the pre-Dorian people who accepted without much opposition the rule of their conquerors. Occasionally, however, they revolted against their rulers. The problem of the citizens was that of defending the state, as estab-

[4] *Ibid.,* pp. 215–32.

lished, from enemies within and enemies without. Slaves and underprivileged persons have no reason to be loyal to those who oppress them. That work of defense devolved upon the *Spartiatae.* The state became after the seventh century B.C. a military communism in which the citizens lived on a basis of equality in political and economic rights and their corresponding duties. The partially democratic constitution, attributed by tradition to Lycurgus (*c.* ninth century B.C.), largely failed in practice to preserve for the citizen the freedom and privileges which it would accord him. By the sixth century B.C. the tyranny had hardened, and individualism was almost completely destroyed in order that the state might be strong. Among the many aspects of the Spartan system were the exclusion from citizenship of those who did not submit to the approved discipline, which included eating unsavory common food in common mess halls, wearing scanty common dress, avoidance of manual occupations, the acceptance of the state system of iron money designed to root out avarice, obedience to a rule forbidding travel outside of the state, and compulsory marriage. It was a harsh discipline, but the citizen bore it. Men, when properly conditioned and indoctrinated, have accepted tyranny with apparent equanimity.

State authorities decreed at the birth of a male child whether it should be permitted to live or not. Over their children parents exercised little or no authority. Indeed, the home, as we know it, did not exist in Sparta. Mothers had charge of their sons until they reached the age of seven, but thereafter all education was in the hands of the state. That education had become by 600 B.C., when patronage of music, poetry and art had ceased, entirely physical and military, and was consciously designed to make men physical and moral brutes. The reason for this cultural decline was probably a fear of some internal disorder.

Education was drastically affected by the social and cultural change. The physical and military discipline was, at times, so severe that weaker youths died under the strain, but Sparta rejoiced because she had discovered weaklings whose deeds of bravery and brutality would not redound to her glory. From seven to eighteen, when they became *ephebi* (cadets), boys were subjected to increasingly severe physical and character discipline. Boys sought to prove their courage by submitting to excruciating whipping before the altar of Artemis. They wore only a single light cloak, had to go barefoot, slept on beds of reeds and rushes, and subsisted on light, coarse diet. They were frequently whipped by a hierarchy of officers from whose eyes they could never escape. Here laughter seems to have been unknown. Running, wrestling, boxing, hunting, swimming, riding, archery, ball-playing, throwing the javelin and weights, and dancing were their chief exercises. There were public contests in all of these and in the brutal, free-for-all, individual encounter between individual boys called the *pancration*.[5] From eighteen to twenty they did garrison duty. Marauding bands of *ephebi* were sent out occasionally to murder groups of unsuspecting Helots so that they, in their youth, might learn to despise the enemies of Sparta, become accustomed to the shedding of blood, and be brutalized for the task of defending the state. From twenty to thirty their military training continued as they guarded the frontiers of the state. At thirty they were admitted to citizenship and compelled to marry, but they remained soldiers in training and war until death or incapacitation.

Gymnastic and military exercises, moral and religious training, patriotic songs and music—all designed to form the patriot soldier in body and spirit—formed the content of their education. If Spartan boys learned to read and write, they did so privately, for the state was not a patron of such intellectual pursuits. Yet mental training was not neglected, for Spartans were trained to think and speak with brevity, clarity and precision. The officer, according to Plutarch, bit the finger of the boy whose answer to a question was not brief and to the point. Girls were given a physical training and discipline similar to that of boys, but less strenuous, in order that they might produce sturdy sons. Running, jumping, dancing, throwing the javelin and discus, wrestling, ball-playing, and riding were practised by them. What effect the freedom and privileges of Spartan women had upon the fall of the state is a matter of dispute among Greek writers. Plato and Aristotle thought it was detrimental.

The Spartan educational system achieved its end, the preservation of the selfish interests of the *Spartiatae* and their political system, but it contributed nothing to the building of a nobler world or to the betterment of humanity. The student of the history of education ought to read the significant, if not entirely reliable, story of Sparta's political and educational practices in Plutarch's *Life of Lycurgus*. That Spartan system stands in marked contrast with the political and educational practices of democratic Athens where men first learned to live the life of freemen.[6]

[5] *Ibid.*, pp. 378 f.

[6] H. Blümner, *The Home Life of the Ancient Greeks* (London: Cassell & Co., Ltd., 1895), pp. 99–102; C. A. Forbes, *Greek Physical Education* (New York: Appleton-Century-Crofts, Inc., 1929), pp. 12–43; James, *op. cit.*, I, 205, 220–34; K. J. Freeman, *Schools of Hellas* (London: Macmillan & Co., Ltd., 1912), pp. 11–41.

Athens and Athenian Society

PERIODS OF DEVELOPMENT. What is called Athens comprised the whole territory of Attica which, between 1000 and 600 B.C., was unified under the leadership of Athens, its principal city. Athenian society and education passed through four loosely democratic and overlapping periods of development: (a) the prehistoric, with which we shall not deal, when the people named Pelasgians, who spoke a pre-Hellenic tongue, inhabited the territory; (b) the Old Athenian Period of 1,000 years, which ended about 500 B.C. when outside influence—Cretan, Mycenaean and Dorian—made itself felt, and the Dorians imposed Hellenic speech upon the inhabitants; (c) the Transition Period, beginning about 500 B.C., and ending with the Macedonian Conquest in 338 B.C.; and (d) the Hellenistic Period, beginning in 338 B.C. and ending in A.D. 529, when the Christian emperor, Justinian, closed the pagan University of Athens.

THE ENVIRONMENT. (1) ECONOMIC ASPECTS. In the Old Period, one of peaceful infiltration, social blending and cultural interchange, economic developments were slow. The population subsisted mainly by agriculture, and the soil was, on the whole, unproductive. During this period, industry and trade were undeveloped, and craftsmen were neither organized nor influential. Poverty of the soil and population pressure forced Athens, eventually, into industry and commerce, and she became, in the Transition Period, the wealthiest of Greek states. Poverty in culture, in the Old Period, went hand in hand with poverty in material possessions. Geographic and climatic conditions were, however, favorable to the development of commerce and an advanced culture. Until 600 B.C., Athens had produced no literature and her art was rudimentary.[7] Life in Old Athens had been simple, and society remained unchanged over a long period prior to 600 B.C. From that date forward economic changes came, and came suddenly, and society and education were profoundly influenced by them.

At the beginning of the Transition Period, the lawgiver, Solon, introduced many economic and social reforms and did much to develop foreign trade.[8] From that time on, industry and trade flourished, and the wealth of the citizens, as well as of the state, increased rapidly. Among the sources of that wealth were industry, commerce, gold and silver mining, duties on imported merchandise and a tax on foreigners. Old impoverished Athens thus became quickly

[7] *C.A.H.*, III, 572–85, 595–97; A Boeckh, *The Public Economy of Athens* (London: Parker, 1842), pp. 31–39.

[8] *C.A.H.*, IV, 32 ff.

a land flowing with gold.[9] Because of this increase in wealth, Athenian citizens came to enjoy much leisure and had greater opportunities for public service.

(2) SOCIAL ASPECTS. In Hellenic Athens, throughout her history, there were three social groups: (1) citizens, (2) *Metics*, or foreigners, and (3) slaves. In spite of the growth of democratic government, Athens was, and always remained, a society founded upon the institution of slavery. The state and communities owned some of these slaves and employed them as policemen, clerks, watchmen, attendants, etc., and paid them in food, clothing, and money. Most slaves, however, were individually owned and were bought and sold in an open market. Wealthy citizens owned as many as fifty, middle-class citizens as many as twelve, but there were poor citizens who could not afford to buy even one. Some slaves, for faithful service, were manumitted and acquired a status similar to that of *Metics*. Slaves were generally well treated, and some earned enough money to buy their freedom. Most Greek philosophers considered slavery a natural and useful institution and never questioned its justice.[10]

During the Transition Period, the *Metics*, who numbered about 40,000, dominated the industrial and commercial life of the city. Not a single important business was owned by citizens, and most shopkeepers, artisans and laborers were either foreigners, freedmen, or slaves. Citizens filled the ranks of public officials and the more important army positions, or engaged in agriculture. Until the end of the fifth century, Athens denied naturalization to *Metics*. It was considered vulgar and servile to work for another individual for pay, and all so employed, whether citizens or not, were despised. Such a stigma has attached to various trades and pursuits even to our own day. Ordinary laborers and even artisans were poorly paid for their services. It was not considered servile to accept pay from the government for public services, but to engage in private trade or labor for profit was considered disgraceful and unbecoming a citizen and a freeman. The *Metics* always enjoyed much personal liberty, but were heavily taxed and subjected to other burdens including military service.

The citizens comprised, at any time, but a small portion of the entire population. Estimates of the total population of Athens differ, sometimes widely. The total population probably never exceeded 350,000, of whom probably never more than 100,000 were citizens. Among the citizens there were always economic inequali-

9 Boeckh, *op. cit.*, pp. 309–19, 329–33, 336–77.
10 *Ibid.*, pp. 184–87, 207–8, 260–63; *C.A.H.*, V, 5–6.

ties and resultant social inequalities. Some citizens were very rich and some were poor. It is probably not true, as some writers have stated, that profound social distinctions existed among the citizens, and that the rich lived by exploiting the poor. Among male citizens there were no rigid political or social distinctions. Indeed, here, probably, citizens were more nearly equal than in any other society in history.[11] This equality was a product of liberal forces at work chiefly during the Transition Period, and did not exist in the earlier centuries of Athenian history.

Status and education of women. Women held a very inferior position in Athens throughout its history. Their status was one of economic, social, and political enslavement. In ordering their own lives they had no voice, but were subject, before marriage, to their fathers and, after marriage, to their husbands. Divorce for them was difficult; for men, easy. They were, indeed, forced to live in a world of their own, removed from that of men. In their homes, women and girls were cloistered in separate women's apartments. Poorer women were permitted to go to the wells for water, and appear alone, at other times, in public, but richer women never appeared in public without a chaperon, in the person of a husband, servant, or slave. Athenian men or servants did the household marketing.[12]

Athenians, generally, put a very low estimate on a woman's ability and strength of character. Greek writers, with a few notable exceptions, made them an object of jeers, sneers, scorn and contempt. "Who trusts a woman," said Hesiod in his *Work and Days*, "that man, I ween, trusts knaves." The sudden social changes of the Transition Period were accompanied by a general disregard of the old morals, and a class of women, called *hetaerae,* commonly represented as immoral, made their appearance in the city. Some of these were educated and attractive, and became the mistresses of prominent Athenian men, such as Pericles, Plato, and Aristotle. These enjoyed a freedom and opportunities for culture which wives and legitimate daughters were denied. One writer asserts that the education of European women began with the cultural privileges enjoyed by these *hetaerae,* and that they began the struggle of European women for emancipation from male tyranny. There was a school for *hetaerae* in Miletus, and Aspasia, mistress and, later, wife of Pericles, who was educated there, established a similar school

[11] La R. Van Hook, *Greek Life and Thought* (New York: Columbia University Press, 1923), pp. 80–81; James, *op. cit.*, pp. 96–99.

[12] Blümner, *op. cit.*, p. 191.

in Athens.[13] The disabilities which custom and marriage laws imposed upon wives and daughters were numerous and oppressive. The home was almost their only sphere of activity. They were permitted in time to practise midwifery, and we hear of one who practised medicine.[14] There were girl entertainers who performed as dancers, acrobats, and musicians, but they were not sprung from respectable stock.

For Athenian girls there were no formal schools and, with the exception of a few who were given some literary training by exceptionally kindly husbands, girls received no education except the training given them by their mothers in the rearing and education of children, superintending nurses and slaves, cooking, weaving, making the family clothing, and other household tasks. One field of activity which, generally, in Oriental lands, and throughout the world, both past and present, has been a male prerogative was open to Athenian girls and women. That was the priestly office. Girls and women occasionally acted as temple priestesses, but the number so employed was very small. This liberalism was due to the facts that there was no priestly class in Greece, as in the Orient, and that the Greeks had no religious dogmas which called for an education preparatory to temple service. The Greek men wanted their women to be religious. Like Napoleon I, they wanted women who believed, not women who reasoned.[15]

(3) POLITICAL ASPECTS. In a unique way, Athens is the cradle of Western democracy, liberty, and individualism. True it is that Christianity stressed the value and sacredness of the individual soul, and that the ancient Teutons enjoyed a form of political equality in their "hundreds." But when all the facts have been examined, the conclusion is unavoidable that our democratic ideal goes back to the Demos of Athens. Roman genius for practical politics made it possible for this idea of liberty to survive in the West. During the Middle Ages there was a return to certain forms of spiritual and intellectual repression, but then the spirit of Greece, fostered by favorable conditions, awoke and, in the Renaissance, returned men again to the ways of freedom.

From a monarchical government, in the Old Period, Athens progressed, in the seventh century B.C., to an aristocratic republic, ruled

[13] A. Heilborn, *The Opposite Sexes* (London: Methuen & Co., Ltd., 1927), pp. 111–19.

[14] J. A. St. John, *The History of the Manners and Customs of Ancient Greece* (London: Bentley, 1842), I, 115.

[15] S. Reinach, *Orpheus* (trans. F. Simmonds; New York: Liveright Publishing Corp., 1930), p. 97.

by the nobility, and finally, in the Transition Period, to a most liberal democracy, ruled by all male citizens. The democratic movement really began with the reforms of Solon in 594 B.C., and was significantly advanced by the reforms of Cleisthenes between 510 B.C. and 508 B.C. By this latter reform, all male Athenians of pure birth were enfranchised, and sovereignty was vested in the *Ecclesia*, or Assembly, of all the citizens. It was, indeed, a "popular" assembly. It passed all laws. A Council of 500, chosen by lot by the Assembly, put the laws into execution. The Council was but a committee of the Assembly, and no individual could be a member of it more than twice during his life. Citizens were paid for attending all meetings of these bodies, as well as for every public service they rendered. This attracted the poorer citizens to public office. Should any citizen arouse the indignation of the public, the Assembly could exile him for ten years from the city, if it were able to muster 6,000 votes against him. Still further privileges were extended to poorer citizens by Pericles in the period 460-430 B.C. Thus were men's rights protected from would-be tyrants, and thus did Athens create and preserve that liberty which it bequeathed to the West. While it does not tell the whole story, Aristotle's treatise on *The Athenian Constitution,* readily accessible to students, is an interesting account of the development and practice of democracy in Athens.

(4) MILITARY ASPECTS. Coincidentally with the increase of wealth and freedom went a great increase in the power of Athens. In the long struggle of Greece with Persia, Athens distinguished herself above all other Greek states and, from leader of nearly 300 cities, called the Confederacy of Delos, in that struggle, she became ruler of them. While Sparta defeated her in the Peloponnesian War (431-404 B.C.), Athens retained her position of military greatness until all the Greek states were finally subjugated by Macedon in 338 B.C. Like all other Greeks, Athenians regarded war, plunder, and even treachery, as legitimate in national defense, and as inevitable and indispensable.

(5) RELIGIOUS ASPECTS. Greek religion was a blend of many elements, Minoan, Hellenic, and Oriental. The ancient Cretans worshiped a virgin goddess and her son, and a cult similar to this extended in time throughout the pre-Christian Mediterranean world. One of the sacred objects of the Cretans was a marble cross, in form like that used by orthodox Greek Christians.[16] On this earlier culture were superimposed that of the Achaean gods, of whom Homer sang in his *Iliad* and *Odyssey,* and of the Doric gods, of whom

[16] Montgomery, *op. cit.,* pp. 257–67.

Hesiod sang in his *Theogony* and *Work and Days*. Some of these gods were national, such as the Olympic deities, and others were local deities, worshiped only in individual city-states. Many of the gods reflect the cosmology of the people. Zeus, for instance, was the sky god, and Poseidon, the god of the sea. The following important characteristics, presenting significant contrasts with other systems, are marks not only of the Athenian religion but of that of all Greeks.

Unlike Oriental peoples, the Greeks had no religious dogmas, nor sacred writings. Here no deity, like Osiris, pretended to judge the lives of men. Greek gods, while immortal, were neither holy nor omnipotent, but anthropomorphic beings somewhat better than ordinary mortals. No inspired teacher arose here. Their religion had no divine founder, nor a uniform priesthood. Priests and priestesses existed, but were appointed by the government and were subject to its authority. In religious matters the voice of the government was final. Greek priests were but masters of ceremonies in the temples and were neither teachers nor preachers. Such a system was more conducive to progress than the ecclesiastical despotisms of the East.

Among the Greeks, who burned their dead, a clearly defined ghost world did not arise, as it did among the Egyptians and others who buried their dead. Life, not death, was the center of interest. Here, religion was concerned with man as a living, working, moral and political being, and on it, in a very special way, the social structure rested. The practical and social character of Greek religious thought can be seen in Hesiod's brief treatise *Work and Days*.

In the Transition Period, in Athens, this foundation of the social structure was seriously weakened. Rich, powerful, and free, Athens had fallen heir to a great heritage of science and philosophy which freemen had been creating for two hundred years. That heritage was devastating to the old myths and superstitions. In the new age of reason and enlightenment, the old beliefs were challenged on philosophical and moral grounds. But the old culture and folkways did not die without a struggle. Anaxagoras and Protagoras were tried, and Socrates put to death, for their public questioning (private questioning was never prohibited) of traditional beliefs. But, while Athens was perpetrating these acts of intolerance, Aristophanes and Euripides were presenting their burlesques of the gods in the theater for the amusement of the public. At last, the old religion failed to meet the needs of an enlightened people, and philosophical speculation began to take its place as an answer to man's intellectual and religious problems. Freemen were now seeking "unknown" gods, and a flourishing period began for mystery cults, such as Orphism, which aimed at individual perfection and happiness on earth (to which the hope of a blessed immortality will contribute), and attempted to destroy any fear of death from which the members of the cult might suffer. These individualistic, personal cults had their counterparts in the individualistic philosophies of Skepticism, Stoicism, and Epicureanism.[17]

(6) INTELLECTUAL ASPECTS. It has been noted that, in 600 B.C., Athens was still quite primitive in culture. Yet, in common with most of the Greeks, Athenians always respected intellectual things. Over literature, art, and science there presided female spirits, whom the Greeks called Muses. There were nine of these, and each presided over her own branch of learning. The great era of Greek intellectual progress opened in the seventh century B.C., when the Ionian physicists began to investigate the nature of the physical world. While indebted to Babylonia and Egypt, these Greek physicists produced works which were original. With them European science began. They sought knowledge for its own sake rather than for the sake of a social or a religious system. This attitude the liberal Greek mind never entirely abandoned.

From a starting point in cosmology, Greek inquiry came to center, during the Transition Period, in man and society, and Athens became the home of this form of speculation. When Greece lost her independence, philosophy, thereafter, concerned itself chiefly with the nature of the divine and man's relation to it. Thus, Greek philosophy began with physical science, reached its zenith when it dealt with human and social problems, and ended as a system of theosophy or theology, in which form it passed over into Neo-Platonism and Christian theology.[18]

Anaximander (born 610 B.C.), Thales (flourished 585 B.C.), Anaximenes (lived *c.* 550-500 B.C.), Pythagoras (born *c.* 570 B.C.), Xenophanes (born *c.* 571 B.C.), Heracleitus (lived *c.* 550-475 B.C.), Parmenides (born *c.* 515 B.C.), Empedocles (lived *c.* 500-450 B.C.), Anaxagoras (born *c.* 500 B.C.), Zeno (born *c.* 489 B.C.) and Democritus (born *c.* 460 B.C.) were early philosopher-scientists who sought an answer to the riddle of the universe and the something in the world of change which does not itself change—the underlying, constant reality.

[17] *Ibid.*, pp. 244–301; Reinach, *op. cit.*, pp. 87 ff.

[18] W. Windelband, *History of Ancient Philosophy* (New York: Charles Scribner's Sons, 1921), p. 22; F. Ueberweg, *History of Philosophy* (New York: Charles Scribner's Sons, 1893), I, 26–27.

Thales was an astronomer who, tradition has it, predicted eclipses of the sun and moon, and introduced mensuration from Egypt into Greece. Anaximander made a map of the world, and taught, among other things, that space and time are infinite, that the earth is round and is stationary in space because of its equidistance from other bodies, that life evolved from moisture evaporating in the sun, and that man evolved from a fish. Anaximenes taught that air is the basic, constant reality. Xenophanes proclaimed the existence of one supreme, motionless god who rules all things by his mind, who is not like men, as are the sinful gods of Homer and Hesiod, and he taught that earth and water are basic elements from which living things evolved. Empedocles held that water, earth, air and fire are the basic, constant realities out of which Aphrodite, the goddess of love, shaped all living creatures. Heracleitus taught that fire is the basic element, but that the universe is an eternal series of changes. "The order," he said, "which is the same in all things, no one of gods or men has made; but it was ever, is now, and ever shall be an ever-living Fire, fixed measures of it kindling and fixed measures going out. . . . God is day and night, winter and summer, war and peace, satiety and hunger; but he takes various shapes."[19]

What for us is most significant about this exploration of the physical world and, later, of the social world, is that it represents, apparently, the first time in history when men, exercising freedom, turned the light of reason upon all important phenomena. What the factors were which led them to embark on the great adventure in intellectual and political freedom no one can say with certainty. But it reveals their faith in reason and in scientific curiosity and inquiry. The motto "Know Thyself" inscribed in the shrine at Delphi stands in marked contrast with the motto of other peoples "Know God and Fear Him." The Greeks, particularly the Athenians, throughout most of their history, sought a natural cause and a rational explanation of phenomena, whether physical, social, or human. They were the first scientific discoverers of Nature and of Man. And Athens, the cultural capital of Greece, became in this intellectual adventure the "School of Hellas," as Pericles called his city-state.

Yet, in spite of great intellectual achievements, the Greeks long continued to accept some ancient superstitions that found their way into Homer; and even Herodotus, the father of history, attributed all occurrences to the will of the gods. They did not understand the influence of tradition upon the affairs of men. Even Aristotle did

[19] O. J. Thatcher (ed.), *The Library of Original Sources* (Milwaukee: University Research Extension Co., 1901), II, 149–50.

not see that his "self-evident truths," "first principles," the major premises of his syllogism, needed the support of scientifically verified facts.

Greek intellectual development reached its height in Athens in the Periclean Age (461-429 B.C.), but the period of greatness continued until the Macedonian Conquest (338 B.C.). The "glory that was Greece" was, indeed, the achievement of Athens alone. In architecture, sculpture, tragedy, comedy, history, and philosophy, Athens produced masterpieces that have never been excelled.[20]

The Social Crisis

Athenian society in the Old Period was a society built upon traditional culture and folkways which, for centuries, permitted very little change in its ideals and institutions. While freer here than in Sparta from state domination, the individual was, nevertheless, subordinated to the state, and his behavior was regulated by custom, law, public opinion and, if necessary, by force in everything that concerned the welfare of the state. In the Transition Period, the social changes which we have described occurred. They were sudden and deep-rooted changes, and their chief significance for us is that they resulted in the breakdown of the old folkways and the old culture and in the emancipation of the individual citizen from all the old agencies of control. The individual, for the first time in history, had become free in thought, speech and action, except in so far as he was restrained by laws which he himself made. It was a great and dangerous political adventure in which men turned to reason as their guide. Freemen had discovered the joys of liberty.

Although Aristophanes and Xenophon would have us think so, that liberty did not destroy the devotion of Athenians to their state. Liberty, rather, became a new and powerful force binding men to the state. Yet there were citizens, chiefly aristocrats, who hated the new democracy and were traitors to Athens in her war with Sparta. But the advent of freedom had created the problem of rebuilding society upon a basis new in the world, that of individual freedom. How were men to build a society in which the individual would be free and society itself be stable and enduring? And so Athenian statesmen and philosophers faced that problem, which is the chief problem of every democracy, theorized about it, and left to the world a rich heritage of political and social ideals which have been an inspiration and a guide ever since. Thus, out of the Athenian crisis,

[20] M. Maeterlinck, *et al.*, *What Is Civilization?* (New York: Duffield, 1926), pp. 81–95; H. J. Muller, *Uses of the Past* (New York: Oxford University Press, 1952), pp. 99–121.

men began, for the first time, to build consciously and deliberately the ideal society and the ideal world.

In the building of the new and better world, Athenian philosophers recognized the indispensable contribution that education must make to the process and the product. But before considering the new educational practices which mark the Transition Period and the social and educational theories of the philosophers, we must now pause to consider briefly the educational practices of Athens in the Old Period.

Education in the Old Period

GENERAL ASPECTS. (1) Formal Education. In Old Athens, unlike Sparta, the home was a very important institution, and parents enjoyed great freedom and responsibility in regard to the education of their children. The father had almost unlimited authority in the home. He decided the question as to whether or not his newborn child should be permitted to live, a question which, in Sparta, the state decided. He decided, also, most questions regarding the education of sons before they entered the state military corps at about the age of eighteen. Influenced, no doubt, by public opinion and by love for Athens, as well as by laws, fathers educated their sons for their duties as citizens. Female infants were frequently abandoned at birth and permitted to die. For girls who were reared, no formal education was provided.

Until the age of seven, a boy was in charge of his parents, and was instructed and disciplined in the way customary in Athenian homes. Mothers, sometimes assisted by nurses, were the chief teachers of their daughters until marriage, and of their sons until they entered the *palaestra.* Spartan nurses, because they were thought to be good disciplinarians, were in demand. Stories of hobgoblins and ancient heroes were told children to inspire or frighten them into good behavior, but the appeal through the anatomical posterior was often resorted to. A wide variety of playthings, most of them still popular, were in common use. Many girls, no doubt, participated in the childhood games of their brothers. At the beginning of his eighth year, the boy was separated from his sisters and younger brothers and placed in charge of a slave, called the *paidagogos,* who continued to be his attendant and guardian at home, in school, and in his sports, until he reached the age of eighteen. The *paidagogos* advised him in matters pertaining to modesty, politeness, and self-control.

During the Old Period, but perhaps originating near its close, Athens provided two schools for boys: (1) the *palaestra,* or physical training school, and (2) the *didascaleum,* or school of music and letters. Rich and poor citizens were educated in different schools and for different lengths of time, the rich remaining in school until the age of sixteen or seventeen, the poor leaving much earlier.[21] There is still much uncertainty about the exact plan of school organization in this Old Period.[22] Occasionally, the sons of the rich were instructed privately at home.[23] The *palaestra* and *didascaleum* were the only schools of whose existence in 600 B.C. we are reasonably certain. It is unlikely that the *gymnasium,* an institution for more advanced bodily training, existed in the Old Period.[24] On leaving these schools, the sons of the poor went to their various trades or domestic labors, but the sons of the rich, it is reasonably certain, continued their gymnastics in some way, for in bodily exercise and physical contests Athenian boys and men of leisure never lost interest.

In the time of Pericles there were three public *gymnasia* in Athens (the Academy, the Kynosarges, and the Lyceum), and others were added later. These were attended by boys who had finished their schooling but were not yet of military-training age. The chief teacher in these was the gymnast, who trained professional and amateur athletes. Poor boys had little time for these diversions after their school years had ended. At the age of eighteen or nineteen, every Athenian boy of pure blood took an oath of loyalty to the state and was enrolled as a citizen. The state in the Old Period probably provided some form of military training for boys between the ages of eighteen and twenty, a practice which, in the fourth century B.C., developed into the *Ephebic College.*[25] Young men of the ages of twenty to twenty-two were sent out to guard the frontier and continue their military training. That period of service completed, the formal education of Athenian boys came to an end.

(2) INFORMAL EDUCATION. To be born, live, and participate in the family, social, economic, political, and religious life of Athens was an education in itself. In that little state, youths learned the ways of life by participating in the activities of life. In the Old Period, only the few participated in political activities, but the democracy of the Transition Period changed all that. Social life was marked throughout Athenian history by a variety of functions such as feasts, festivals, games, sports, and temple worship, in which

[21] Freeman, *op. cit.*, p. 49; C. B. Gulick, *Life of the Ancient Greeks* (New York: Appleton-Century-Crofts, Inc., 1905), p. 87.

[22] Freeman, *op. cit.*, p. 54.

[23] Blümner, *op. cit.*, p. 103.

[24] *Ibid.*, pp. 115, 119.

[25] Forbes, *op. cit.*, pp. 111–78.

nearly all participated. Attendance and participation of Athenian men and boys in the great national games, such as the Olympic, Pythian, Isthmean, and Nemean games, as well as the great Athenian festival, the Panathenaea, had great educational significance.[26] The sports and games were related to war and the life of the soldier, to which most Athenians looked forward, and they were pleasing to the gods. Sons of farmers, artisans, etc., learned the skills of these callings by acting as apprentices to their fathers or probably to others thus employed. Athens never developed any formal vocational schools.

The education of girls, with very few exceptions, was always of this informal character, was provided by mothers and nurses, and was related to domestic activities, to which women were very closely restricted, as we have already noted. A few seem to have been able to read and write. The *hetaerae,* who often were public entertainers, had physical training and performed marvelous physical feats not countenanced for modest women.

EDUCATIONAL PRACTICES. (1) PURPOSE OF EDUCATION. Even in old Athens, the aim of education was the development of the freeman citizen, in body, mind and morals, for his own welfare as well as for that of the state. Here there existed traditionally a deep respect for the individual and his worth. It was not the Spartan ideal. Athens aimed to make citizens after its own ideal; to make men, who were really men and gentlemen, and not brutes. All Greek education had citizenship for its object, but the political ideal, as well as that of citizenship, varied from state to state. It was not an education designed to prepare men for the judgment of an Osiris in another world, or for an entrance into some *nirvana.* It was rather an education designed to prepare youths for life in the *polis,* the city-state. In as far as the ideal of developing body, mind, and morals for the sake of moulding men was embodied in the education of old Athens, that education was the forerunner of the ideal of a liberal education which marked the Athens of the succeeding periods. Professional and vocational skills were never aimed at in the schools. Solon's law, freeing sons from supporting fathers who had not taught them trades, had little or no effect upon education. While their civilization came to be based upon industry and commerce, Athenians scorned labor and the practical arts upon which their society was based, leaving these activities to slaves and foreigners. Yet, the Good Life depends upon these arts.

(2) CURRICULUM. **(a) Physical exercises.** The *palaestra* was an open-air school, generally enclosed, in which naked boys practised

[26] Blümner, *op. cit.,* pp. 351 ff., 372 ff.

wrestling, boxing, running, jumping, throwing the discus and spear, punching the bag, ball-playing and tug-of-war, and in which richer boys received, in addition, some military training. The work of the day ended with a swim in an adjoining stream.[27] The exercises, no doubt, were graded according to the age of the boys. The *pancration,* a combination of wrestling and boxing, and apparently brutal, was practised, and some boys were trained prematurely for the Olympic Games.

(b) Music. In the *didascaleum* boys were instructed in vocal and instrumental music, the Athenians being conscious of the moral, cultural, and patriotic influences of such training. Chiefly on moral grounds, the simple Dorian music was preferred to other forms as was the seven-stringed lyre to the soul-stirring flute. Dancing probably was never taught in old Athenian schools.[28]

(c) Letters and literature. Reading, writing, and poetry (especially Homer and Hesiod) were studied by all boys under a special teacher, probably in the *didascaleum.* Literature served a cultural, moral, and intellectual purpose. Throughout Athenian history, the poet was the most revered of men. Plato tells us in his *Protagoras* that poems were set to music by teachers, and were played and sung by the pupils to produce harmony and rhythm in their souls, while the thoughts and ideals of the poets would inspire them to noble deeds. Only actors, poets, musicians and professional athletes escaped the odium attaching to the acceptance of pay for labor or service, and of these the poet was most highly esteemed.[29] Actors and musicians were richly compensated for their work. If arithmetic was taught, it was a very unusual procedure since a liberal education, as then conceived, frowned upon anything practical. In later times, Socrates would teach it for useful purposes, and Plato stressed it as a means of mental discipline.

(3) Method and Discipline. Imitation, drill, and repetition were the methods used in the schools. From sunrise until sunset the school grind continued, but boys must have considered many exercises of the *palaestra* not work but play. Long poems were memorized; and while some of the stories told by the poets were interesting, the study of reading, writing, and music, as taught, was difficult and the methods very formal. Many years were required to master even fundamentals. Individual instruction was probably the rule, except in the case of singing. Discipline was severe at

[27] Gulick, *op. cit.*, pp. 80–82.
[28] *Ibid.*, p. 84.
[29] *Ibid.*, pp. 234–35.

home and in school, and flogging of boys was a common practice, for it was thought to be essential to learning.[30]

(4) Organization. Whether boys attended the *didascaleum* first and then, some years later, the *palaestra*, or did exactly the opposite of this, or actually attended both schools simultaneously, is a question which has not been definitely answered.[31] In these schools boys might remain for an indefinite time. No upper age limit was fixed but, by custom, rich boys withdrew about the age of sixteen or seventeen, and poor boys about the age of thirteen or fourteen.[32] Beyond this came some state scheme of military training for eighteen- and nineteen-year olds, as we have noted.

(5) Support and Control. The *palaestra* and *didascaleum* were largely private schools, conducted by individuals for private gain. The only school in Athens that the state ever owned and controlled was the military training school for youths between the ages of eighteen and twenty which developed, in the Transition Period, into what historians have called the *Ephebic College.* Ephebic training was the only schooling which was ever compulsory in Athens. Strictly speaking the *gymnasia* were not schools. From Solon's time, if not earlier, boys were required to be literate and be able to swim, but the laws did not prescribe any school for such purposes. There are records of Athenians who knew no music, but no record that any Athenian was illiterate. The state was interested in the morality of youth and placed its supervisors of morals in the private schools.[33] The laws forbade, under pain of death, persons older than the boys, with the exception of the teacher's son, brother or son-in-law, to enter the *palaestra* or *didascaleum* while pupils were there. The morals of boys exercising in the *gymnasia* were similarly safeguarded. In the Transition Period, and probably toward the end of the Old Period, subdivisions of Athens, known as the "tribes," were required to defray the cost of a part of the instruction in gymnastics and music, and they employed teachers for that purpose. The cost of any further instruction in these subjects and, apparently, the entire cost of literary education had to be borne by parents directly. In later times some distinguished teachers among the Sophists were paid by the state.[34] Poorer parents sometimes instructed their own children in letters, because the fees of teachers were too high.[35]

[30] *Ibid.*, p. 88.
[31] Blümner, *op. cit.*, p. 115.
[32] *Ibid.*, p. 113.
[33] *Ibid.*, p. 102.
[34] Boeckh, *op. cit.*, pp. 120–22.
[35] Freeman, *op. cit.*, p. 59.

The private character of education in old Athens is significant. It was primarily a parental duty, the state or the "tribe" merely assisting in work which parents recognized as their own.

(6) Teachers. Three special teachers had charge of a boy's education: the *paidotribes* taught him gymnastics; the *kitharistes,* music; and the *grammatistes,* reading, writing, spelling, and literature. In some schools the *kitharistes* taught reading and writing in addition to music. Flute players assisted the *paidotribes* in the *palaestra.* These teachers were often emancipated slaves or citizens of inferior economic and social standing. The profession of teaching was not an honored profession largely because men engaged in it for purely private gain, and sold their services to private employers. Most of them received but a mere pittance for their labors.

(7) Pupils. The sons of all Athenian citizens, both rich and poor, were educated in the way we have described. The studies were the same for all, but the rich pursued them for a longer time, and attended better equipped schools than the poor could afford to attend. This condition continued throughout Athenian history. Formal schooling was a male prerogative, and girls, with but few exceptions, received only the informal training essential for the discharge of household duties, a fact which has been noted earlier. It ought to be noted also that *Metics* were not excluded from the schools during any period of Athenian history.[36]

While the social changes of the Transition Period brought changes in educational practice, and prompted the writing of many treatises on ideal education, the traditional conception of the purposes of education was not abandoned, although the drift in the schools was in the direction of a greater emphasis upon intellectualism. Service to the state, a balanced development of the individual in mind, body and morals, and educational differentiation based upon social rank and vocational pursuits remained ideals, after they had been modified or abandoned in practice.

The New Education of the Transition Period

IN SEARCH OF THE IDEAL SOCIETY. The significant changes in Athenian society during the Transition Period, which have been noted, resulted in the breakdown of the old folkways; and the new freedom of the individual made men anxious regarding the well-being of the state. Athenian philosophers and statesmen were thus forced to seek a solution of the basic problem of all democratic societies—the problem of reconciling individual freedom with social

[36] Gulick, *op. cit.,* pp. 64–65, 87; Xenophon, *Economics,* chap. vii.

stability. Solutions of the problem were proposed by three groups in Athens: (a) the conservatives, who would reduce the individual again to subordination to the state; (b) the radicals, who, by a verbal defense of individualism or by catering to its demands, showed little concern for the state; and (c) the mediators, who would reconstruct society upon a new basis which would ensure social permanence and a supposedly adequate measure of individual freedom.

The Athenians were thus among the first to approach the fundamental problem of society rationally. The demons of Necessity and Change make men thoughtful. In Athens, educational change followed social change; educational theories followed social theories. Men who dreamt of ideal states dreamt of ideal educational schemes at the same time. These ideals, never realized in Athens, embodied the vision, new in the world, of building the perfect society on the basis not of what has been but on the basis of what ought to be—on the basis of the ideal.

CHANGING EDUCATIONAL IDEALS AND PRACTICES. (1) MODIFICATION OF OLD SCHOOLS. In the Transition Period, less time was given to the old courses in the *palaestra* and *didascaleum,* and for boys over fourteen or fifteen an advanced course in music and literature was provided in some of these old schools. It was because these old schools, though improved, did not satisfy the popular demand that the schools of the Sophists arose.

(2) NEW SCHOOLS. **(a) The gymnasium and Ephebic College.** Probably in the sixth century B.C., the first *gymnasium* was established in Athens. In some Greek states, the *gymnasia* were schools, but in Athens they were buildings and grounds, generally public, where young men who had passed from the *palaestra* and men of all ages, as well as professional athletes, engaged in physical exercises. The would-be professional athletes had coaches; the others received no instruction.[37] Only the rich attended the *gymnasia;* the poor had no time for such activities. Here were trained runners who would represent the tribes in city festivals.

Between 338 and 335 B.C., Athens provided a two-year course of compulsory military training for *ephebi,* or boys between the ages of eighteen and twenty. This institution is known as the Ephebic College. Traditionally, military training was a matter of private individual choice, the state providing it for soldiers' orphans alone. Wars have, nearly always, stimulated interest in physical and military education. In Athens, following the Persian War, that interest

[37] Forbes, *op. cit.,* p. 82; Woody, *op. cit.,* pp. 309 ff.

knew no bounds, but it suffered an alarming decline when youths became absorbed in the intellectual activities offered by the Sophists. To check that decline, Athens departed from a long tradition and made military training compulsory. The Ephebic College was a state program of strenuous gymnastic and military training provided in *gymnasia* reserved for the purpose and in frontier fortresses. Religion, as a patriotic duty, was stressed in the training of the cadet. At the age of nineteen, before he went on patrol duty, he took the famous Ephebic Oath of loyalty to his country, its property, its government and its gods. Earlier the oath was administered to young men at the age of eighteen.[38] From 322 B.C., fees were charged, and thus the College became aristocratic, and its compulsory feature was gradually abandoned. Under Roman rule, Athenians felt that they had all necessary protection, and the College became primarily academic in character.

(b) Ideals and schools of the radicals or Sophists. These peripatetic lecturers, some of them learned men and some impostors, were numerous in Athens in the fifth century B.C. They were the radicals whose individualistic philosophy delighted adventurous youths and liberals, but shocked the conservatives. As teachers for profit, they were despised by Plato who seems to have forgotten that fees were customary in the old schools; as radical thinkers, they were feared by many.

Protagoras, a distinguished Sophist, taught that the individual man is "the measure of all things, both the things that are seen and the things that are not seen," truth thus becoming what each individual perceives, or thinks it to be. Yet while he placed the individual, and not the state, highest in the scale of values, he would educate him for a life of practical service to society. In spite of such an individualistic philosophy as that of Protagoras and, no doubt, of many Sophists, youths and often adults flocked to their schools, for that liberal education, worthy of freemen, which liberates the intellect from ignorance, the soul from fear, the body from infirmities; which develops the whole man, and which, ever since the days of Athenian democracy, has been associated with the ideas of human liberty, leadership, and the rights of freemen. The Sophists provided the element of a liberal education which was most neglected in the old schools, the intellectual element.

[38] This famous oath, only slightly modified, has been in wide use in American schools and colleges, and civic and patriotic societies in some of our cities require their new members to take it. See F. H. Swift, *The Athenian Ephebic Oath of Allegiance in American Schools and Colleges* (Berkeley: University of California Press, 1947).

They neglected too much the physical element. From them youth sought those intellectual accomplishments necessary for leadership in public life. Since a liberal education means an education which meets the needs of freemen, its content in a modern liberal, industrialized society, where all men and women are politically free, and in an age of science and technology, must differ from that of ancient Athens and other societies of the past.

For two centuries, Greek scientists had been exploring the universe, but they had kept their wisdom from the people. In democracies knowledge is the people's right. One of the most significant aspects of the work of the Sophists is that they collected existing knowledge and offered it for sale in the open market to everyone who could afford to pay for it. And their prices were moderate.

(3) The New Curriculum. As a group, the Sophists taught everything that students demanded, and among their offerings were arithmetic, geometry, astronomy, natural history, grammar, etymology, rhetoric, logic, versification, history, mythology, political science, ethics, criticism of religion, mnemonics, drawing, painting, music, athletics, and military tactics.[39] Rhetoric they stressed most, the other subjects being taught with a view to forming an accomplished orator. The Rhetorical School of Greece and Rome thus originated. In democracies oratory is important; in despotisms men are puppets.

The Sophists, some of their critics asserted, taught logic not for the sake of truth, but for victory in debates. This has been called sophistry. The title of sophists, or wise men, was given them in derision. Many of them, no doubt, were not deserving of the contempt in which men like Aristophanes and Plato held them. Their schools no more caused the downfall of Athens than those of Tzarist Russia caused the downfall of the Tzars, or the schools of Colonial America, the downfall of British rule in the colonies. We have no proof that words and ideas have been the basic determiners of the course of history. If their teachings, and the intellectualism which they represented, had not been acceptable to most Athenians, the Sophists could not have flourished as they did. And the intellectualism they promoted was destined to become the glory of Athens and the brightest light in the Western world. A stable state or world cannot, however, be built upon such a philosophy as that of Protagoras. Man needs institutions, and every institution, in greater or less degree, restricts his freedom.

The Sophists represent the disintegration of the old folkways and the old mind, and the point of origin of an enlightenment and a

[39] Freeman, *op. cit.*, pp. 165–66.

new way of life which mark the beginning of modern progress. They played a necessary part in the shaping of the new way of life. Men had to be freed from enslavement to custom before the better society, intelligently, consciously, and freely built and directed, could be established. As servants of the new democracy, intellectualism and secularism, which created them, they helped to enrich the new order of things. But it remained for others to lay a philosophical basis for the good society which thoughtful men desired.

IDEALS OF THE CONSERVATIVES. Pericles, Aristophanes, and Xenophon were among those who, in varying degrees, were conservative in their views of the social problem. They looked back longingly to "the good old days" when the individual lived for the state. They praised the glories of the past; they bewailed, directly or indirectly, the ignominies of the present. In his famous Funeral Oration in honor of those who had died for Athens, Pericles lauded the greatness of Athenians, their traditional ideals, and the state. With probably the philosophy of the radicals in mind he said: "We alone regard a man who takes no interest in public affairs, not as a harmless, but as a useless character."[40] He commended briefly the traditional education. In addition to oratorical appeals for loyalty to the state which permitted men to live as they please, Pericles beautified the city so that Athenians might love it all the more. And Athens, even in defeat, remained the most admired of Greek cities.

Aristophanes, the comic dramatist and one of the immortals, used the theater to ridicule the new tendencies in Athenian life. The Sophists and their education he held up to public scorn. He condemned the new education as effeminate, and called upon youth to return to manly exercises, as in the following passage from the *Clouds:*

> If then you'll obey and do what I say,
> And follow with me the more excellent way,
> Your chest shall be white, your skin shall be bright,
> Your arms shall be tight, your tongue shall be slight,
> And everything else shall be proper and right.
> But if you pursue what men nowadays do,
> You will have, to begin, a cold pallid skin,
> Arms small and chest weak, tongue practised to speak,
> Special laws very long, and the symptoms all strong
> Which show that your life is licentious and wrong.[41]

[40] P. Monroe, *Source Book of the History of Education for the Greek and Roman Period* (New York: The Macmillan Co., 1919), p. 27. (By permission.)

[41] B. B. Rogers, *Aristophanes* (New York: G. P. Putnam's Sons, Inc., 1924), I, 357–58.

But the voice of the critic was heard in vain, for the old education no longer met the needs of Athens. The Sophists, whom he denounced, were not a cause of the changes, but only a symptom of what had taken place before they came as a result of economic, social, political, and intellectual forces which were at work in Athenian life. In the new Athens, rich, powerful, and free, a return to the old order was impossible.

Xenophon, in his *Ways and Means,* condemned the free economy of Athens and would nationalize industry and business, because he believed that free enterprise left some citizens without sufficient maintenance, thus weakening their loyalty to the state. He praised the Spartan system of government and education in his *Cyropaedia* and in the *Constitution of the Lacedaemonians.* In his books *Oeconomicus, On the Art of Horsemanship,* and *The Cavalry Commander,* he reveals his love of the old ways of life and education. The citizen-soldier, trained and hardened by a rigorous discipline in body and spirit for service to the state in war and peace, was the ideal he proposed. The intellectual education of the schools of the Sophists had little attraction for him. All of the Athenian theorists of the time, including Plato and Aristotle, considered war an inevitable, normal occurrence, and their views on education reflected that conviction.

Ideals of Constructive Theorists. Of paramount significance in the growth of Western social and educational theory are the contributions of (a) Socrates, (b) Plato and (c) Aristotle.

(1) Socrates (469-399 B.C.). **(a) Theories of society and knowledge.** Socrates sought a basis of social unity in knowledge. For the old folkways, now derided, he would substitute new folkways acceptable to a people enlightened and critically intelligent about social problems. He sought, by a process of free critical discussion in which he would have all participate, to bring men to an agreement on social questions. He would rebuild Athenian society on the basis, not of individual opinion, but of truth, knowledge or "ideas" universally acceptable and intelligently accepted by all men. Truth, he said, resides not in individual perception, as Protagoras' statement implies, but in the element common to all perceptions, the concept. The philosophy of Protagoras would destroy unity of thought; that of Socrates would create such a unity and make it the basis of a stable society, of which enlightened men could be proud. Thus "the father of philosophers" bequeathed to the world his faith that an enduring society could be founded on the basis of knowledge, and that men can build, consciously and intelligently, a society that will not mock the reason of inquiring men. That society

would respect the individual, for it originates in his own "ideas," and would be worthy of intelligent freemen. The individual he saw as the root and source of social virtue.

What Socrates taught, we know through the writings of Plato, Xenophon and Aristophanes. Here we see him as one of unbounded faith in the power of reason to guide man to the solution of all his problems, a faith in which Plato and Aristotle, whom he no doubt inspired, shared. While he emphasized intellectual and moral education, he knew the value for the individual and for the state of health and of physical training, and condemned what he considered to be the defects in the physical education and the training of the professional athletes of his day. He marveled at the performances of female athletes and, like Plato after him, questioned the belief that women are by nature inferior to men.

(b) Socratic method of teaching. This method is a process of arriving at a definition, or concept, inductively by conversation on moral and philosophical problems. Socrates taught boys by eliciting their opinions on such problems. His purpose was to bring, as he said, ideas of universal validity "to birth," by proving logically to boys that their original opinions were erroneous or but half-truths. Thus he would stimulate them to further inquiry. While Protagoras and, no doubt, other Sophists thought of man as essentially a perceiving being only, Socrates thought of him as predominantly rational. It is the intellect, especially, he taught, that leads man to knowledge and therefore to virtue which is based on knowledge. And virtue and wisdom, not individual success and happiness are, he held, the proper goals of education.

(2) PLATO (427-347 B.C.). **(a) Social theory.** Plato approached the educational problem by considering its fundamentals, the nature of man, the nature of society, and the nature of knowledge.

The perfect society was the goal he sought, and he saw education as an indispensable instrument of its attainment and preservation. Unlike Socrates, who was of humble birth and not a respecter of wealth or rank, Plato was an aristocrat, and his social and educational thought reveals a contempt for common men and a high regard for an intellectual, if not for a social, elite. While his thought was, no doubt, influenced by the Pythagoreans and the other mystery cultists, to whom he occasionally refers, one who reads the *Phaedo* will see in it unmistakable marks of the direct influence of Egypt, one of the countries in which he traveled, and to whose educational practices he refers in his book, the *Laws*. His doctrines of the immortality of the soul, judgment of the dead, and of rewards and punishments in the other world are strikingly Egyptian, and his theory of Ideas may well have been, as stated elsewhere, a development of the Egyptian concept of the *Ka.* His doctrine of temporary punishment in Tartarus for lesser crimes brings to mind that of Purgatory of Christian times.

Like Socrates, he was preoccupied with ethical questions. While an otherworldliness crept into his philosophy of Idealism—and in the *Phaedo* he said philosophy is "the practice of death"—the end of knowledge was viewed by him as virtue in the citizen and justice in society. In the *Theaetetus* he presents his theory of knowledge; in the *Parmenides* he develops further his doctrine of Ideas; and in the *Phaedo* he applies that doctrine to immortality. In his *Phaedrus* and *Timaeus* he states further his views on the soul. His treatises, however, of greatest social and educational significance are the *Republic* and the *Laws,* both of them revealing his opposition to democracy. In the latter, written in his old age, he abandons some of the positions and doctrines which he advanced in the *Republic,* the first great contribution in the West to the social sciences, and one of the world's great classics.

The "ideal state" described in his *Republic* is one in which there are three social classes, men of gold, men of silver, and men of iron. The gods, he says, made men thus. The universe, society, and man operate according to a divine plan. Just as man is an organism which works in harmony towards a divinely appointed end, so society is composed of similar parts for a similar end. The function of the men of gold, or philosophers, whose virtue is wisdom, is to rule the state; of the men of silver, whose virtue is courage, to be the military guardians of the state; and of the men of iron, whose virtues are obedience to superiors and self-control, to be the laborers of the state. Each man will perform that duty for which his god-given nature has equipped him. Thus would Plato build, upon this principle of "justice," a society which avarice and unrestricted individualism could not destroy. The ills of Athens, he felt, were due to an "unjust" division of labor, and these he would correct by abolishing private ownership of property in the case of philosophers and guardians, by restricting it in the case of laborers (slaves) and of farmers, artisans and tradesmen, and by assigning duties to men on the basis of the natural capacity of individuals and of groups. His ideal state is thus a communistic one. To get men to believe the myth of the divine institution of social classes, he would remove all over the age of ten from the state, and then indoctrinate the children. There have been many lies in education, but few have so frankly justified the practice as did Plato.

Theoretically, the social classes would not be hereditary, and a cobbler's son might be born a philosopher. But since the rulers would secretly see to it that only "the best" of either sex unite with "the best," and "the inferior," only with "the inferior," an hereditary class system would probably be the result. Thus would Plato build the ideal state with philosophers, who love wisdom, truth and justice for their own sake, and who have been properly educated for their tasks, as its rulers. And Plato remarked that, until kings are philosophers and philosophers are kings, the perfect state will not see the light of day. In practice, there would be very little individual freedom in such a state.

Plato's ideal state is a city-state, a closely-knit community, an association of virtuous individuals working, each one in his proper place, for a common end. The state is the like-minded citizens themselves, not a governing body distinct from them. Like the Nazis, Plato would not distinguish between society and the state. He knew that his state was a purely imaginary institution, the model of which could be found only in heaven, as he said. The social harmony ("justice") which he sought is beyond human attainment. To exclude the working classes from political life, as he suggested (and as did Aristotle later), would not insure lasting harmony. In reality his rulers would be an intellectual aristocracy rather than an ethical one, just as his supreme Idea, the Idea of the Good (God), is a metaphysical rather than an ethical idea. And the test of fitness for government is the ability to comprehend the Idea of the Good, the eternal, unchanging absolute. In Plato's state moral virtue is political virtue, and vice versa, but it finds its sanction in the will of the state as expressed by the philosopher-rulers. The idea of social duty is paramount in Plato's concept of morals, and the moral man is one who performs the duty assigned him in his appointed social place. Plato's moral code looks to the needs of only his city-state and does not extend beyond it.

Complete control of the individual by the state marks the thought of Plato. Nothing is left to his own choice. Women, children and property are communized. To preserve this economic, political and spiritual communism, a state system of education would be established. But this education would be indoctrination, not the free, natural growth and development of the capacities of the individual. The end he sought was the strong, harmonious state, and selfishness he saw as its chief destroyer. In the *Laws* we still find him in quest of the strong state, but he no longer suggests that, to that end, a communism in wives and children be established. He came to realize in his later years some of the evils of the extreme communism of the *Republic.* He still, however, clings to his doctrines of (1) caste based chiefly upon occupation, but partly upon ability, (2) the exclusion of artisans from citizenship, and (3) the equality of the sexes. He accepts slavery now as socially indispensable.

Position of women. Plato would accord women all the privileges enjoyed by men. The home and marriage he would abolish so that the state would be the only object of affection, women be free, and the breeding of a better human stock be provided for. Women are, he says, generally inferior to men, but some women are superior to some men. All fields of activity he would open to them, and he would have them educated in exactly the same way as men. Some, as philosopher-queens, would help to govern the state; others would engage in war in its defense; and others, fit only for drudgery, would be assigned to manual occupations. In his advocacy of the equality of the sexes he was two thousand years ahead of the world.

(b) The nature of man. Plato recognized individual differences, and would take cognizance of these differences in his scheme of education. While stressing the political and social aspects of man's nature he did not ignore its physical, religious, intellectual, and aesthetic aspects. Some of these he would develop more in one social class than in another. Laborers would be given little or no intellectual education because of their natural incapacity for it.

In analyzing the nature of man he created a cleavage between soul and body, the former conceived as spiritual, pre-existent and immortal, the latter as material and mortal. Sensation, passion, appetite and desire represent the lowest, or animal, aspect of the soul, and reside in the belly. Courage, shared in by nobler animals, is of a higher order and resides in the heart. These aspects of the soul are not pre-existent and immortal. They have their roots in the body and die with it. Of the highest soul, reason is the essence. This, the rational soul, created by a supernatural divine intelligence in its own image, is distinct from the body and is immortal. In its pre-existent state it saw the real objects in the world of Ideas, of absolute being, and it carried these innate ideas with it on its earthly sojourn, where its vision of true reality is, during life, dimmed by "the lusts of the body," the source of wars and every social evil. This rational soul resides in the brain. It is by education that the man gradually comes to know this Reason within him and to recognize her as a friend. In his youth, passion and appetite concealed her presence. The science of psychology in the West had its unscientific beginning with Plato, Aristotle and the Sophists. Plato and Aristotle were well aware of its social and political significance.

(c) Theory of reality and knowledge. Plato examined the nature of knowledge by considering its object, the reality with which it deals, and he formulated one of the great answers to the questions "What is reality?" and "What is truth?" By that answer, developed in many of his dialogues, particularly the *Theaetetus* and *Parmenides,* he became the founder of the philosophy of idealism in the West. A shorter exposition of it is found in the *Republic,* where he establishes its relation to social harmony in the state. In brief, his answer is that the only real things, with real existence, are abstract or universal Ideas and that these have an objective and independent existence in the metaphysical world, the world beyond and separate from the physical one. Goodness, beauty, truth, equality, justice, greatness, etc., exist in the world of Ideas as real entities, and the objects of the material, visible world partake of their reality. Great things are great, just things just, and beautiful things beautiful, only because they partake of the abstract realities of greatness, justice and beauty. He was, as we see in his *Parmenides,* afraid to assert with finality that there is an abstract idea of such things as hair and dirt or anything that is "foul and base," but he had no doubt about the existence of nobler abstractions such as similarity and goodness. The world of sense, of matter, does exist, and always did exist but it is not real. Only the changeless world of abstract ideas is real, and here only one finds truths that are real and changeless.

He thus created a cleavage between the ideal and the natural, and later Platonists and Christians accentuated the dualism he created between them. Mediaeval Christian ortherworldliness and contempt for the natural world owed much to later Greek thought. It was not such thought that made Greece or Athens great, and its spread reveals a doubt that, by natural means, man can achieve the good life. Such thought debases the world of nature, the only world that man can know with some degree of certainty, by declaring the human spirit to be superior and foreign to that world.

In the age of change which gave rise to such philosophy, the Greeks lost interest in civic life, and sought refuge for their souls in mystery religions and a life of spiritual contemplation. Stoic resignation to Necessity, and Epicurean quest for happiness through peaceful retirement from life's problems were logical outcomes of Plato's emphasis upon spirituality. The material, visible world, for him, is one of appearances or shadowy reflections of "Ideas," which are the causes of all concrete things, which were formed in time out of eternal matter by some divine, nonmaterial, eternal Intelligence, in whose mind the models existed. The highest Idea, or first cause, is the Idea of the Good, which is Plato's supreme god. These "Ideas," or perfect realities, are visible only to the "mind's eye" of contemplative philosophers. The material world is knowable by sense perception; the real world, only by a process of contemplation, pure reasoning, and intuition. Ordinary men can know the former; only men of gold can know the latter. Socrates' "truth" resides in the world of man's everyday experience; Plato's, in a world beyond the reach of such experience. The men of gold will bring to human society some of that justice, goodness, beauty, wisdom and truth which reside in the "Ideal" world.

While he rejected materialism as an explanation of life and the universe, Plato, like other Greek thinkers and unlike the Hebrew-Christians, held the view that matter always existed waiting to be moulded into myriads of concrete objects, patterned after the Ideas in the metaphysical world. In addition to many other rational arguments in support of his philosophy, he used his doctrine of innate ideas to justify his position, but proof of his theory, as the scientist understands proof, is lacking.

Knowledge in his view is one's mental image and understanding of realities, of the Ideas. Only God, who created them, has absolute and exact knowledge of them. Knowledge is not sense impressions, although some knowledge may be gained by reasoning about such impressions. Real knowledge, he tells us in the closing words of the *Theaetetus,* comes only when "the mind is alone and engaged with being," the world of true reality. Here we see that divorce of knowledge and education from life which long characterized educational practice. In the *Republic,* Plato says that the lover of wisdom has no time for the occupations and problems of men, which distract the mind from the contemplation of changeless realities, whose order and harmony he ought to imitate. Let lower men be preoccupied with their bodily needs, practical affairs and the quest for wealth, but in the life of the mind and spiritual contemplation let philosophers find the only true happiness. The doctrines of absolute ideas, of rule by philosopher-kings, and of the supremacy of dialectic, or the study of pure abstract being, are not stressed by Plato in the *Laws.* Presumably, by his closing years, he had modified his earlier thought.

While respecting the old folkways, Plato would found his ideal society, not upon custom and ancient belief but upon the basis of truth, as he conceived it. The idea of building society upon truth, but not necessarily Plato's truth, will appeal to reasonable men, for truth can make and keep men free.

(d) Plato's educational theory. In both the *Republic* and the *Laws* Plato says that the highest duty of the state is the moulding of virtuous citizens. Modern thought often falls short of that goal, but it has not gone beyond it. Plato's state is the secular state and his educational scheme is also secular. The otherworldliness of the *Phaedo* is not found in the *Republic* and the *Laws*. The ideal state of the *Republic* would have its temples and sacrifices, and its citizens would respect the gods, but fear of the other world robs soldiers of their courage in battle and must not be taught. Viewing education in a broad sense, and stressing character formation, he advocated censorship of art, literature and music so that the citizen might be loyal and virtuous, and the state a reflection of the "true," "the beautiful" and "the good," and an image of the order and harmony in heaven, the world of Ideas. His faith that education can bring human, social perfection brings to mind the faith of Pestalozzi and Dewey in modern times. The ideal state can be realized only through education.

Plato's views on the education of artisans, merchants and farmers—men of iron—are obscure. Presumably they would be trained by apprenticeship for their various occupations. The educational scheme of the *Republic* is reserved for soldiers and rulers. These two classes would be educated to the age of eighteen in music and gymnastics, girls receiving the same education as boys and exercising naked in the *palaestra* with them. The course for both sexes from eighteen to twenty would be military. At twenty, the soldier class would be eliminated from school. Up to this point the scheme is essentially the same as the traditional plan in Athens. But Plato would expurgate the poets in the interest of morality and the martial spirit, and would ban all music not conducive to moderation and courage, as well as all new music, since innovations in music are dangerous to the state. In the *Laws,* he approved Egyptian opposition to innovations in music and art. Thus, in his advocacy of censorship he was consistent to the end. He has much to say about the proper use of gymnastics in the training of youth. The ideal soldier must be a nice blend of mind, spirit, and body. Mere athletes are often sluggish and given to illnesses, and in battle tend to act like wild beasts rather than as intelligent strategists. Music alone makes men effeminate; gymnastics alone dulls the mind, destroys health, and makes men savages. Plato's soldier would be somewhat less a brute than his Spartan counterpart.

During these first stages of education some "natures" will be discovered who are fit to rule and to study philosophy. These "lovers of the vision of truth," whose marks and virtues he describes in the *Republic,* are designed by nature to be leaders, not followers, and for them he proposed the establishment of two new schools, or stages of education, the first for students to the age of thirty, when the less gifted would retire from school to engage in practical politics, the second for great-minded intellectuals for five years longer. Between the ages of twenty and thirty, all these philosophers would study arithmetic, geometry, and astronomy not for practical purposes but for the purposes of disciplining the powers of the mind, and of comprehending the great abstract truths, or "Ideas," underlying these sciences.[42] These studies lead to dialectic, or the contemplation of pure being, or absolute truth, for those retained in school after the age of thirty. At this stage, these philosophers would contemplate nothing perceivable by the senses, but only pure abstractions, for the purpose of catching a vision of the "Idea of the Good." From thirty-five to fifty, they would rule the state, and then retire from public service, to enjoy till death the vision of the "Absolute," the contemplation of which Plato considers the highest form of happiness. And when they have passed to the Islands of the Blest the state will honor them as demigods and divine.

In the *Laws* he urged compulsory education in music and gymnastics for boys and girls, under the control of a state minister of education, the goal being the moulding of virtuous citizens, not the acquisition of wealth or athletic honors. One should learn to do by doing the things which life will later demand, and the method of playful imitation should be used in forming citizens as in training future artisans and husbandmen. Plato goes into much detail in describing the essentials of music and gymnastics and justifying their use. The whole choral art, which includes rhythmical bodily movement, is the whole of education, and the infant should begin to develop harmony through play and listening to songs. For children between the ages of three and six education should consist of sports, self-will being curbed by corporal punishment. At six, the sexes should be separated, the girls, "if they do not object," engaging in the same physical exercises as the boys, although living apart from them. The formation of bad physical habits must be avoided. Respect for the gods and for antiquity must be inculcated at every stage of education. Because women are naturally different from men, the music marked by moderation and temperance, rather than

[42] He tells us, for instance, in Book VI of the *Republic,* that those who have studied geometry are infinitely superior in understanding to those who have not studied it.

the "grand" or manly music, is peculiarly appropriate for them. In gymnastics there should be no sex differentiation whatsoever, girls being trained for war in the same way as boys.

At the age of ten, the study of letters should begin and, at thirteen, a three-year study of the lyre, the length of study always to be determined by law. Boys should be taught by men; girls, by women. And all teachers should be state officials, paid by the state.

At the age of sixteen, presumably, the study of arithmetic, geometry and astronomy—studies "fit for freemen"—would begin. These are necessary for anyone who wishes to know the highest things and to be a man rather than a pig. But ignorance of these is far less fatal to the state than the cleverness and cocksureness of petty intellectuals, whose character has been badly formed. "A little learning is a dangerous thing" as Pope, perhaps prompted by Plato, remarked.

In the *Laws,* Plato sees education as a curbing of rebellious nature. A boy is a most unmanageable animal whom any freeman, as well as teacher, should be free to punish at will.

(e) Influence of Plato. The following are a few of many examples of Plato's influence: The government of the mediaeval church, while influenced by the Jews, was essentially Platonic, the priestly hierarchy playing the rôle of philosophers. The modern totalitarian state with its rejection of liberty and equality, and its practice of lying to the people, has marks in common with Plato's state, although he would oppose its brutality. "Platonic realism" and theological dogmatism are closely related. Mediaevalists tried to build an "absolute" society on the basis of otherworldly "truth," as did Plato. To them, as to Plato, the visible world is one of unrealities. This idealism was, for centuries, the chief obstacle to the growth of scientific inquiry.

Plato's formal disciplinary conception of education has exerted a great influence on curriculum and methods of instruction almost to our own day. His divorce of education from life and his disregard of vocational education were prophetic. His doctrine of innate ideas had a wide theological appeal in Christendom. And he was the first to formulate a definite philosophy of education, and to lay a philosophical basis of state education.

(3) Aristotle (386-322 B.C.). (a) Social and political theory. In his *Ethics* and *Politics,* Aristotle says that society and the state are natural institutions, and that man is by nature a "political animal." The state, he says, is the greatest achievement of nature and of man. His social and educational philosophies are founded upon his doctrine of "nature." Nature makes one man superior to another, and

designs some to be masters and others to be slaves. Slavery he considers a natural institution, and his "ideal state" would be founded upon it. Above slaves stands a social hierarchy headed by a governing elite. In that society, each man would be placed according to his peculiar natural gifts. Slaves, artisans, and merchants, Aristotle would exclude from citizenship, because their vocations are ignoble and impediments to "virtue." Only those should be citizens who have leisure for self-improvement and for the performance of public duties. All landed property should belong to the state, half of it being allotted to the citizens for their private use, and all farm labor should be performed by slaves.

Women's place in society. Women, he says, have, by nature, their own peculiar virtues and duties. They are, by nature, inferior to men, and their virtue lies in obedience to men, whose right it is to command. Silence, he says, is the natural ornament of a woman. Freedom for women, as in Sparta, is a menace to the state. The natural sphere of women's activities is the home and, here, it is the husbands' right to exercise complete authority in regulating the lives of women and children. Women, since they lack the power of foresight, were not designed by nature to be rulers. Yet since, unlike slaves, they are not niggardly and make things for one and not many uses, they must be distinguished from slaves.

Political theory. The state, we are told in the *Politics*, is the highest form of community, and includes every other social group within it. Its aim is the attainment of the highest good (*summum bonum*) for mankind. This *summum bonum* is happiness, not "justice," as with Plato. This, and this alone, men seek for its own sake, and is thus, by nature, the ultimate end of all individual and social action. Since the whole is prior to the part, the state, a creation of nature, is prior to the individual and the family, which, unlike the state, are not self-sufficient. Only a beast or a god has no need of the state. Like some modern totalitarian political theorists, Aristotle makes no distinction between society and the state, both of which, he says, are rooted in the social instinct of man.

The state is composed of individuals and families, and its happiness depends upon the existence of proper relationships between master and servant, husband and wife, parent and child, and upon the virtue and wisdom of its individual members. Its essential functions are, he says: the provision of food and the encouragement of the arts and crafts; defense against enemies; raising of revenue; care of religion; and, most important of all, the power to decide what is just and in the public interest. For the efficient performance of these functions, the people should be divided into occupational groups, war and government being the occupations of the citizen classes. Since the warrior can, if he wills, destroy the constitution, he should, upon his retirement from military service, be assigned a position in the government. The priesthood should be reserved for old men of the two citizen classes—warriors and councilors—since the gods would otherwise be dishonored. And religion should be supported by the state.

Aristotle's ideal state is a city-state located in a healthy locality and provided with an abundance of pure spring water. What he says about the architectural design of the city proper makes him a pioneer in city planning, now a preoccupation of many architects. Beyond the walls lies the rural section of the state, with its farms, forests, temples, etc., each being presided over by a magistrate or inspector.

Having examined various forms of government from pure democracy to tyranny, he advocated a republican, or constitutional, government as the best form in practice, although he believed that a benevolent monarchy is in theory the best. His final choice was in keeping with his doctrine of the "relative mean," that vice lies in extremes and virtue in the path between them. Only citizens, of course, would participate in the government. It is rather obvious that his supposedly liberal state would dominate the individual, who would be made, by education and law, its servant and tool.

(b) The nature of man: faculty psychology. Aristotle realized full well the importance of an understanding of human nature in the building of states and of educational systems, which are the servants of states. His psychology has a socio-political purpose. In the *Ethics* he discussed his doctrine of happiness and the way of its attainment by individual natures, and he returns to this fundamental matter at appropriate places in the *Politics*. Happiness is attained by every organism, vegetative, animal and human, when it performs its peculiar, natural function. Man has a life in common with plants and animals, and shares their peculiar vegetative or appetitive functions. But the life of reason and free moral action is peculiar to man. These are his unique functions and his highest happiness consists in their performance.

Happiness he defines as an activity of the soul in harmony with perfect virtue, and human virtue he defines as man's supreme natural excellence, whose attainment results in happiness. Man's peculiar virtue is not that of the body but of the soul. It is the prime duty of the physician to know the former; of the politician, the latter. What, in the word of translators, he called the "soul" has two parts, the "irrational" and the "rational." Of the irrational soul there are also two parts, one the "nutritive soul" which man shares with plants, and which is not related to reason, the other the "concupiscent" or "appetitive" soul, which, while opposed to reason, partakes of it and obeys its commands. The rational soul possesses pure reason itself and nothing else. He based his doctrine of the moral and intellectual virtues upon this analysis of the soul, the former being peculiar to the "appetitive soul"; the latter, to the rational soul. Wisdom and prudence, for instance, are intellectual virtues; liberality, courage and temperance, moral virtues. The former are acquired by "a process of inference," which requires long thought and experience; the latter, by habit.

It was in connection with moral education and the training of the irrational soul that he formulated his theory of "faculty psychology," a theory which he himself, probably in a lost treatise, applied to the training of the rational soul as well. This theory, accepted by St. Augustine in his treatise on free will, met no serious challenge until the nineteenth century.[43] Moral virtues, he says, are not natural to us, but we have a capability or "faculty" of acquiring them by acts, or activity. As in the arts we learn to do by doing (a principle stressed by Comenius and Dewey in recent times), so in morals we become moral by doing what is moral and by habituating ourselves to moral action.

Moral virtue results from the conditioning of moral faculties, and is a primary concern of every state. While necessary for all in society, moral virtue is not the same for all. A man's courage, for instance, consists in commanding; a woman's, in obeying. Slaves, women and children are largely irrational, and their virtues are moral, not intellectual. Thus, only male citizens are capable of intellectual activity in search of truth and in its application to statecraft, which is the sovereign art whose end is social happiness. When all individuals in a state are happy, each by performing his or her natural functions, the state will itself have attained happiness. Aristotle's ideal society is, then, one in harmony with human nature and reason, and in which the citizens are controlled by education rather than by external coercion.

Aristotle, as did Plato, created a dualism between mind and body which most modern psychologists reject. And the faculty theory of the soul, stressed by Aristotle, provided support for the formal disciplinary theory of education for centuries.

[43] W. B. Pillsbury, *The History of Psychology* (New York: W. W. Norton & Co., Inc., 1929), pp. 13–33; O. Klemm, *History of Psychology* (New York: Charles Scribner's Sons, 1914), pp. 47–55.

(c) The nature of reality and knowledge. Although a pupil of Plato, Aristotle rejected Platonic realism and made the physical world of time and change the center of reality. The things of the physical world are not mere shadows of "ideas." While these things change and perish, there is in them a reality that is constant. This reality, or "Form," is a something inherent in matter and is incapable of independent existence. It is the same in all objects of one class, and is the essence, or true nature, of the individual object. Aristotle's "Form," or "substance" and Plato's "Idea" differ mainly in that Plato gave independent existence to the "Idea," while Aristotle makes the "Idea" inhere in each concrete thing. Individual things, he held, are important chiefly as representative of the class of things to which they belong. For him Plato's universals, whose reality he denied, are but intellectual concepts useful in describing classes of similar things. Before assuming actual existence, individual objects existed as potential things (*in potentia*), and were transformed from the potential into the actual by the force of motion which determines the various types of individual concrete things in the visible world.

This doctrine of motion is one of Aristotle's central concepts in his explanation of phenomena. He uses it to explain everything in the world of Being, or existence, applying it to man's inner life in the *Ethics* and to his society in the *Politics*. Everything comes into existence, and moves, as a result of a progressive series of motions extending back, not to infinity, but to an eternal, necessary, living individuality, the "immovable First Mover," the creator of heaven and nature. This doctrine of motion called for the operation of many movers in explaining phenomena, and was quite acceptable to later Christian thinkers who endowed material objects with spirits, desires, and tendencies to motion. The modern mechanical concept of the universe, which needs no spirits to explain its behavior, is rooted in the "law of inertia" of matter, not in Aristotle's doctrine of motion and its later theological embellishments.

In explaining reality, he formulated a doctrine of causation, namely that every concrete thing is the result of four causes: the material, the formal, the efficient, and the final, the first two being the matter and form of the thing, the third being the maker, and the fourth, the final cause, being the purpose of its existence or creation. Apparently Aristotle believed that the universe has a purpose, as have the individual things that men make. This doctrine of purpose in life and the cosmos has been, and still is, a matter of debate. He saw reason in the universe, and God, the First Mover, a rational being engaged in pure thought and eternally contemplating his own essence. St. Thomas Aquinas and other scholastic philosophers found Aristotle's metaphysics, or his basic philosophy, easy to reconcile with their theology.

While he is best known as a philosopher, political theorist and logician, he was also the first great descriptive natural scientist in the West. He observed and described nature with remarkable accuracy within the limits set by his span of life. He wrote on biology, anatomy, embryology, zoology, physics and astronomy. While his observations were generally quite accurate, his explanatory theories were sometimes erroneous. He concerned himself more with the visible and the natural than with the invisible and the supernatural, and was thus a truly modern man. For him reality was in the visible world around him, the world of sense perception. But he classified "incomplex things" into basic "categories," such as "substance," "quality," "quantity," and invented a system of deductive logic by which, reasoning from the categories as first principles or major premises, men would predicate something, or draw conclusions, about particular things. This was a process of reasoning from the general to the particular, which became, as we shall see, an object of attack by scientific thinkers from the seventeenth century onward.

Aristotle's logical doctrines were presented in six treatises, known as the *Organon*, two of which, the *Categories* and *De Interpretatione* (on expression in words) were translated into Latin by Boethius and were in use in the schools of mediaeval Christendom.

While Plato would discover reality and truth by pure reasoning and intuition, Aristotle would begin the quest with sense perception, although he held that universal truths can be reached only by pure reasoning and intuition. His belief in the infallibility of syllogistic, or deductive, reasoning, retarded the growth of science, for here he assigned to sense perception a subsidiary place. Yet his own use of the inductive method in his scientific studies, if not his attitude, was favorable to science, for he insisted upon collecting all ascertainable facts.

(d) Educational theory. *Education and politics.* No one, perhaps, has formulated more forcefully than Aristotle the conception of education as a state function and of the dependence of its character upon that of political systems of which it is the servant and preserver. He presents these views in Chapters VII and VIII of the *Politics*. Education, said he, must serve the political system by conforming with its nature. It must also conform with the nature of the individuals to be educated. Its goal is the making of virtuous citizens. While opposing military states and offensive war, he recognized the need of a trained citizen army, to protect the state against attack and to ensure good government, and of a navy composed of non-citizens. The ideal state, however, should have as its ultimate aim the attainment of leisure and peace for its people. He thus rejected the Spartan ideal and way of life, although he approved state control of education there. For him education is more than formal schooling. It includes all influences and experiences that help to mould character: the influence of associates, stories, objects of art, games, the theater, etc., and all of these would be under the control of his "Directors of Education." Only the education of the citizen class is considered in his plan.

Education of the body and irrational soul. Aristotle's period of formal education ends at the age of twenty-one, and has five subdivisions, the first ending at the age of five, the second at the age of seven, the third at about the age of fourteen, the fourth at the age of eighteen, and the fifth at the age of twenty-one (an age later deemed politically and socially important by Western societies). To insure a healthy body for the future citizen, he advocated eugenic marriages, and discussed at length the proper age for marriage, the qualifications of would-be parents of citizens, the diet and exercises of pregnant women, etc. He recommended abortion when families are large and the destruction of deformed children, because such practices are essential to individual and social happiness.

During the first five years the care of the body by proper diet, exercise, and regulated exposure to cold (the "hardening process" of Locke and others) is all-important. During these early years no study or labor should be required, and the boy should be safeguarded against immoral influences, those guilty of indecent speech or shameful acts in the presence of children being subjected to disgrace and punishment.

From five until seven the boy, still at home but under the supervision of the state "Directors of Education," will observe the activities he will later learn to perform.

From seven until fourteen the boy's education will be exclusively physical and moral. He will now be instructed by state teachers of health and physical education. The exercises must be light so as not to impair the growth of the body. Here, as always, the principle of the mean should be a guide to practice. Too much or too little exercise, he says, destroys our health and strength, but moderate exercise produces and preserves them. Health, morals and happiness are acquired by habit and instruction, and good education is the formation of good habits. In all matters our acts determine the character of our habits and, therefore, everything we do must be in keeping with right reason. He developed this doctrine of the mean in the *Ethics*, and showed its application to physical and moral training. From fourteen to eighteen, the boy's education should consist of a study of reading, writing, music and drawing, gymnastics being given but little attention. Moral training will be continued. In this period, then, intellectual education begins, the purpose being the liberal one of intellectual enjoyment, the relaxation of the soul, and the enrichment of one's days of leisure. But he is still preoccupied with the training of the irrational soul and the preparation of it for control by reason.

From eighteen to twenty-one, a boy should be subjected to hard physical training for the sake of health and athletic performance rather than for war, although it is reasonable to infer from his political theory that military training would be given much attention in the plan—what is noble, not what is brutal, being the guide to practice.

Education of the rational soul. How Aristotle would educate the rational soul can only be conjectured. The *Politics* does not treat the subject and, if he wrote a special treatise on it, that work is lost. To Aristotle the "mind" is man's instrument of thinking and judgment, and its training, in keeping with his doctrine of habit formation, would probably consist of practice in thinking and in forming judgments. One might reasonably infer from his own interest in the natural and social sciences, particularly political science, and in logic and metaphysics, that he would use these subjects as a means of training the rational soul.

Liberal education and the curriculum. Aristotle distinguished between liberal and illiberal occupations, the former being worthy of, and the latter unworthy of freemen. He says that men disagree regarding the aim of education, utility, virtue and higher knowledge having, each, its advocates. While there are useful things which must be taught because they are necessary for freemen, it does not, he says, become free and noble souls to be always seeking the useful. Any occupation, art, or study which limits the freeman's exercise of virtue is vulgar and illiberal. All paid employments, since they degrade the mind, and any art which deforms the body are also vulgar and illiberal. Even arts liberal in themselves and worthy of freemen will, if carried to perfection, become vulgar and illiberal. One's motive in learning may affect the issue. Arts learned for one's own sake or for the sake of friends may be liberal, while the same arts pursued in the interest of others may be illiberal. Reading and writing should be taught to freemen because they are useful and necessary to further study. Drawing should be taught to enable them to judge the beauty of the human form.

But of all studies gymnastics and music are the most important, and he discussed them at length. Their purpose is the liberalizing one of purifying the soul of its passions and developing in it right habits of moral action. Gymnastics should not make athletes, or brutes, but men—men of health, beautiful form and noble character, who are virtuous and happy because their impulsive souls function temperately and enrich one's hours of leisure and peace. "Purification" (*Katharsis*) of the irrational soul of evil influences, and the habit of observing the principle of the "relative mean" in one's instinctive and moral behavior are the chief purposes of music, as they are of gymnastics. The music that slaves and laborers may hear may be as vulgar as their souls, but melodies of purification, played upon instruments that do not inflame the passions or distort the face, are appropriate to freemen. The liberally educated man is one whose body and irrational soul obey the commands of the rational soul—one who lives a life of reason as a follower or a leader in the state.

Education of women. Since Aristotle believed that women are incapable of rational activity except, perhaps, in the most rudimentary form, and of self-direction, they must, in a well-ordered state, be subjected to male authority and their activities be confined to the home, their natural sphere. There they should be trained in the virtues peculiar to their sex, particularly obedience to men, and in the performance of household tasks. They should marry at eighteen, and be taught to observe proper dietary habits and rules of light exercise during the child-bearing period. Care of young children, under state supervision, would be a duty of mothers. While the women of the citizen class would be free persons, their education would be planned in light of their inferior natures and of the domestic duties which nature had assigned them.

(e) **Influence of Aristotle.** It is hazardous to venture an appraisal of the influence of any man upon the world, but certain things may safely be said about Aristotle. He was perhaps the greatest intellectual genius of Western antiquity who, through his students in the Lyceum, which he founded, exerted a great influence upon the intellectual life of the ancient world until Justinian, in A.D. 529, closed the pagan schools of Athens. During the earlier Middle Ages in the West only two books of his logic (the *Organon*) were known, but from the twelfth century on his other works were gradually restored to the West, where he remained the supreme authority in philosophy and science until the seventeenth century, when modern science and new philosophies arose to refute his theories and challenge his thinking. His theories of knowledge and of the universe became the official philosophy of the church in the thirteenth century and were authoritative in the universities of Europe for four hundred years. The influence of his logic and formal syllogistic method of reasoning has continued into the present, although science has given us a new method of discovery since the seventeenth century, and a new dynamic logic has been formulated by Dewey and others in recent years in conformity with the world of relativity and change which science has revealed.

Among Catholics and the Neo-Thomists, Aristotle still holds the place of pre-eminence in the realm of philosophy which some theologians of the thirteenth century accorded him. In the hands of the latter, Aristotle's thought, made authoritative in the world of nature, retarded the growth of science, although he himself saw in science and the inductive method an essential, primary, source of a true knowledge of reality. And the sciences of ethics and politics owe much to this great Western pioneer thinker in these fields. His views, and those of Plato, on state education crept into Roman law, into the philosophy of Thomas Aquinas and Luther and, eventually, into modern educational practice. And the position he took on the nature of women probably contributed to their long-continued subjugation in the West. Most of his physical theories were unsound, e.g., his doctrine that earth, air, fire and water are the basic elements of earthly things, and ether of celestial bodies; that earthly motion is in a straight line, and heavenly motion is circular; and that weight determines the speed of falling bodies. And there were basic errors in his theories of biology and anatomy. Had the world, however, learned from him, as it might well have done, the value of critical thinking, instead of using his authority to stifle that spirit, the discoveries of recent times might not have been so long delayed.

Developments in the Hellenistic Period

THE NEW GREEK WORLD AND MIND. In the Hellenistic period, Greek culture spread through the Near East and the whole Mediterranean world, and we must get away in part from Athens to view a wider Greek scene. Cosmopolitanism implies devotion to no single state, and Greek learning and culture now assumed that characteristic. The stage for this was set in the conquest of Greece and the Near East by Alexander the Great, who claimed to be of Hellenic descent, and who, with his successors, founded some two hundred and seventy new cities, as centers of Greek culture, throughout his empire. To these, Greek settlers and traveling adventurers, attracted by trade and the lure of wealth, but occasionally by curiosity and wanderlust, carried the glories of their civilization, and added to them. In Greece itself, the period was one of economic, political and cultural decay, which drove exiles from their native lands, although Athens continued to be regarded everywhere as the light of the world. The ideas of humanity and of a universal world arose to replace that of the *polis,* the city-state, beyond which even Plato and Aristotle had not gone. It foreshadowed the dream of Rome, of Christianity, and of humanism and such modern developments as the United Nations and Unesco.

Freed from the burdens of war and petty political and social strife, and from the wranglings of philosophers, the transplanted Greeks turned to utilitarian activities. They planned and built beautiful cities, highways and harbors, keeping in view the health, comfort and prosperity of the people. This utilitarianism led to the rise of the specialist in the various fields of skill, research and learning. A great increase in trade and wealth conditioned the progress of the age. But it was a progress that did not lack beauty or respect for man and the human spirit. After Alexander's death, the empire was divided into kingdoms, which warred with one another with all the barbarities of the ancient city-states, until they all fell before the might of Rome. With all their glories, the Hellenistic kingdoms were marred and weakened by slavery and the poverty of a rural and city proletariat, and they were held together by military force.

Unlike Orientals who always had clung to it, the Greeks abandoned monarchical government early in their history. Alexander, however, returned to it and proclaimed his divinity, no doubt to make his rule acceptable in the East. Perhaps Aristotle, who was his tutor, had recommended such a policy. In Rome and Christendom the monarchical idea had a stronger appeal than any other idea of government. Whatever the reason, the Hellenistic Greeks did not extend democracy to the native peoples of their new kingdoms from whom they largely lived apart in their own isolated cities, although they mingled freely with the upper classes of the natives, thus ensuring much cultural exchange. Internal social conflicts, however, made the conquest of their kingdoms easy for the Romans who, in turn, failed in their attempt to govern the Hellenistic world successfully. The Near East and the Mediterranean world became an expansion of Greece, as America became an expansion of Europe, with striking analogies appearing between both developments which may have a lesson for us.

EDUCATIONAL DEVELOPMENTS. The chief developments of the period appeared in higher education, the lower schools remaining much as they were. In Athens, with the loss of independence, physical and military educational requirements were gradually relaxed, and schools became more academic in character. Around the year 300 B.C. compulsory ephebic training was abolished, and the course was reduced to one year. While the Ephebic College did not close until the end of the third century A.D., few Athenian boys enrolled in it and, in the second century B.C., foreigners were admitted to it. Physical and athletic training, also, suffered a general decline, although Athenians never entirely lost interest in physical education. With the decline of military training, the ephebi turned to intellectual studies and began to attend the lectures of philosophers, rhetoricians and grammarians on a part-time basis. The chief developments of the period in Athens itself appear in: (a) the intellectualizing of the Ephebic College, (b) the growth of philosophical schools which collectively have been called the University of Athens, (c) the endowment of chairs of rhetoric, the subsidizing of philosophy, and at times the appointment of teachers of the University by Roman emperors who wished to make Athens the cultural center of the empire, and (d) the closing of the University by the Christian emperor, Justinian, in A.D. 529.

While philosophy and rhetoric, particularly the former, were the great studies in the University, other studies, such as grammar and mathematics, were taught by private teachers to the regular students or to candidates for admission. Only four philosophical schools—those of Plato (the Academy), of Aristotle (the Lyceum), of the Stoics and of the Epicureans—acquired permanence, the first of these continuing until A.D. 529, and each clung closely to the dogmas of its founder. Student life and customs, as described by Gregory of Nazianzus in the fourth century A.D., were very similar to those of mediaeval university students.[44] Under Roman dominion, Athens became a great international center of learning which attracted many foreign students, including many Romans. Opposition of Christian leaders to the rational spirit which marked this learning led to the closing of the University by Justinian in A.D. 529. The growing popularity of rhetorical schools had already resulted (*c.* A.D. 300) in the closing of all of them except the Academy.

Outside of Athens, the Hellenistic Greeks established great new centers of learning, often referred to as universities, at Alexandria, Tarsus, Rhodes, Antioch and Pergamum. Of these, that of Alexandria, founded by the Ptolemies, became the most famous. It was not a university in the usual sense but a museum and library where poets, scientists, philosophers and students pursued research and

[44] Monroe, *op. cit.*, pp. 305–7.

study. The library contained about 700,000 volumes, and had a state endowment sufficient for the purchase of all important original works. In the reign of the Roman emperor Theodosius (A.D. 379-395), who decreed that the whole empire should be Christian, the library was broken up and plundered at the instigation of Theophilus, Bishop of Alexandria, who persecuted the pagans. At Pergamum in Asia Minor a similar, and a rival, library and research center was established, and had a collection of some 200,000 volumes. From all these centers, especially from Alexandria, philosophers, scientists, grammarians, schoolmasters, and physicians went out in large numbers carrying learning to the isles and coast of the Mediterranean and throughout the Near East. This age of specialists produced such famous men as Euclid in mathematics, Strabo in geography, Ptolemy in astronomy, Archimedes in physics and mechanics, Galen in medicine, Herophilos in anatomy and surgery, and Aristarchus in grammar. This last listed eight parts of speech and was the father of grammar as it has been taught in Western schools to our day. During these centuries of Greece there came a blending of Oriental and Graeco-Roman cultures which exerted a profound influence upon the religious and secular traditions of the West.[45]

But progress in learning suffered a serious check in the last centuries of the pagan world. The greatness of Athens declined rapidly following her defeat by Sparta and her allies in the Peloponnesian war (404 B.C.); and other Greek states, impoverished by the war, suffered a similar fate. The failure of the Greek city-states to create a united Greece was calamitous, as was the failure of their statesmen to solve the problem of social inequalities and tensions within their own borders. Economic and political decay gave rise to the philosophy of skepticism and the nonsocial and individualistic philosophies of the Stoics and Epicureans, while the Cynics ridiculed man's concern with civic affairs. The tendency away from the moral, social and political thought of Socrates, Plato and Aristotle, appearing in Stoicism and Epicureanism, ran itself out in the hedonism and nihilism of men who laughed at all philosophers and at all quests for truth or certainty. The new comedy, also, was individualistic. It stressed the joys of youth and of worldly pleasures. Life is ruled by chance, and the gods are not interested in men. Said Lucretius of Hellenized Rome:

> No God Almighty ever made for man
> A Universe of such imperfect plan.[46]

[45] S. Rappoport, *History of Egypt* (New York: Grolier Society, Inc., 1904), Vols. I, II.

[46] *C.A.H.*, VII, 246.

With the privileged class, philosophy gradually took the place of religion, or they turned, as many did, to the salvationist religions, the Eastern mystery cults. Ethics now was divorced from politics and became the science not of social but of individual happiness. Under Hebrew-Christian influence, it became the handmaiden of religion and theology, and the bond became so strong that modern states have found it difficult to separate both in public education.

In spite of scientific advance in the Hellenistic world, Westerners, influenced by the decay around them and by the salvationist cults, began to substitute faith for science and reason in the quest for truth, and then came the Middle Ages, an age of faith when scientific progress ceased. As a result Europeans, in A.D. 1800, had advanced no further in many sciences than had the Greeks in 200 B.C.

Our Debt to Greece

While Greek institutions, life and thought at their best show many defects, we have inherited many important ideals from this cradleland of our culture. Of these, the most significant are humanism, liberalism, naturalism, secularism, and faith in reason and man's own power to solve his problems. Perhaps all the others are but aspects of humanism, still considered by many, but not all, thinkers to be one of the really great isms. When Pope wrote that "the proper study of mankind is man," he stated a Greek ideal. From Homer's time their literature glorified the deeds of great men. Even their gods were human in their interests. To make free, fully developed men was the leading goal of their culture and their schools, although some states fell far short of attaining that goal. And their Olympian gods left them free to be courageous, self-reliant and happy in pursuit of their ideals. When Socrates, Plato and other writers caught a vision of a One God, they did not conceive of Him as a being restricting reason or the spirit of inquiry into human, social and moral problems. Whether or not such a secular humanism is sufficient for the needs of man and his world is a matter of controversy. On the educational side of the picture, the Greeks bequeathed to us a concept of a liberal education for freemen which, modified in some respects from time to time to meet the demands of our changing civilization, has endured in its essentials to the present day.

B. Roman Society and Education

Periods of Development

There were four periods in the development of Roman education: (a) the *Native Roman Period,* the first part of which ended about 600 B.C., when Rome had possession of an alphabet of obscure origin but probably borrowed from the Greeks of Cumae, and the second part of which ended when Livius Andronicus, a Greek resident of Rome, translated, about 250 B.C., Homer's *Odyssey* into Latin; (b) the *Transition Period,* when Greek culture and Greek educational ideals and practices were introduced widely into Rome, in spite of the opposition of Roman conservatives, the period ending with a victory for Greek ideals about 55 B.C., when Cicero wrote his *De Oratore,* in which the new education was fully approved; (c) the *Hellenized Roman Period,* ending about A.D. 200, during which there occurred a great expansion in the growth of educational institutions and practices, significantly Greek in form, but not entirely Greek in spirit, for the Romans added the utilitarian ideal to the purely liberal and cultural ideal of later Greeks; and (d) the *Period of Decline,* corresponding with and following the decline of the Roman state, a period which ended in A.D. 529, when the Emperor Justinian closed by law the pagan University of Athens, and thus officially approved the Christian and ecclesiastical domination of education in the West, a domination which had been growing gradually for two hundred years. During this last period, and as a result of the political changes which finally resulted in the absolute rule of imperial autocrats, the educational practices of the two earlier periods, which prepared men for a life of practical usefulness and leadership in Roman society, lost their former values and relation to life and, surviving by the force of tradition, degenerated into purely formal procedures, prized by an idle aristocracy of birth and wealth for their purely cultural and ornamental values.

The Changing Environment

RISE OF ROME AS MASTER OF ITALY. The earliest known inhabitants of Italy were the Ligurians whose culture has been traced back to about 10,000 B.C. Sometime around 3000 B.C., Indo-European settlers, of the same stock as the Hellenes, came into Italy from the north and acquired a foothold in northern Italy. By about 2000 B.C., these Aryans had spread out over all Italy. Migrations of other Aryans into Italy seem to have occurred from time to time. As a result of these happenings there came a blending of Ligurian and Aryan peoples and cultures, the product, in which the Aryan elements predominated, being known as Italian. From this stock sprang the people known as Romans. About 1000 B.C., new invaders, the Etruscans, of doubtful race, culture and origin appeared upon the scene and, by 550 B.C., they had become the masters of Italy but, thereafter, their power declined rapidly and was replaced by that of Rome. From them the Romans learned much about the building of houses and cities and about the arts of war.

While little is known with certainty about the Etruscan language or Etruscan influence upon the Roman alphabet, some Roman writers mention Etruscan literature, both secular and religious. There is some evidence that their priests provided formal religious education for the sons of the aristocracy. That the Etruscans left their mark upon the culture and ways of life of Italians is beyond doubt. Their conquest of Latium, of which Rome was one of the tribal communities, in the seventh century, helped to unify the Latins. Their sway at Rome, which they made their capital, was, however, short-lived and ended with the expulsion of their king, Tarquin the Proud, about 509 B.C.

Rome, which in time became the capital of a great empire, originated as a tribal village around 1000 B.C., when the Latins, a pastoral folk, settled in Latium, and established several tribal communities of which Rome eventually became the leader and ruler. By 338 B.C., Rome had become, by conquest of other Latin cities, the master of Latium. Seventy years later, her other enemies—the Etruscans, the Gauls and the Samnites—had bowed to her power, and Rome had become master of all Italy. And the building of the empire continued. The whole is a story of intrigue, lust for power, plunder and almost continuous warfare, until, in the first two centuries of the empire, the Roman world enjoyed a state of almost unbroken peace, the *Pax Romana*.

THE CHANGING ECONOMIC AND SOCIAL ENVIRONMENT. From a small, self-sustaining pastoral and agrarian tribal community, with a domestic economy, in the early Native Period, Rome grew, in the Transition and later periods, into a nation and an empire of great landed estates, great industrial and commercial activity, and great wealth. The significance of commercial activity in the blending of cultures in the Mediterranean world, while very great, cannot be presented here, except to say that it contributed notably to the mingling of Eastern and Western thought,[47] and the spread of Graeco-Roman culture. Great Roman engineers built a network of roads which extended from the Forum to the ends of the empire, and which served military, commercial, and cultural purposes.[48] Towns and beautiful cities, bristling with industrial, commercial, and political activity, arose. Gilds of artisans, with an apprenticeship system of technical education, appeared and, through them, the mechanical arts of the Orient and Greece were transmitted to Europe.[49] The *Pax Romana* kept the trade routes open and safe, and Rome reached the height of its prosperity at the end of the second century A.D. From the third century A.D., town life and commercial activity declined, and the townspeople were gradually reduced to a condition of serfdom on the great landed estates of the nobility.[50]

Throughout the entire history of Rome, agriculture continued to be a leading activity, but great wealth had to await the growth of industry and commerce. When private industrial capitalists, from about A.D. 300 on, frightened by internal political feuds and, later, by outside invaders, closed their doors, the state set up factories everywhere in the empire and compelled artisans to work in them. The output of these factories was varied and of high quality. Nero paid $170,000 for one Eastern brocade. Machinery, textiles, metal objects, furniture, shoes (some of them decorated with gold and jewels), pottery (some dishes sold for $50,000) and carriages were among the products of the factories. In A.D. 301, Diocletian fixed the maximum price of some 750 articles and of industrial and professional services in order to aid the masses and save the empire from ruin. Among those whose wages he fixed were baby-sitters and teachers. While the empire was expanding, it prospered because of plunder and new markets; when it ceased to expand, economic decay set in. The contempt of the senatorial ruling class for the mechanic arts, industry, mining and commerce, in which they were even forbidden to invest their wealth, although it was largely produced by these activities, must have hastened the decay. The state socialism of Diocletian and Constantine were desperate attempts to save the economy when the private-enterprise system had failed. Had Romans studied economics, and thought about their wealth instead of

[47] *Ibid.*, VIII, 652–58; X, 417.

[48] E. M. Hulme, *The Middle Ages* (New York: Henry Holt & Co., Inc., 1929), pp. 7–8; W. B. McDaniel, *Roman Private Life and Its Survivals* (Boston: Jones, 1924), pp. 171–76.

[49] Hulme, *op. cit.*, pp. 189 ff.

[50] *Ibid.*, p. 148.

merely seeking it for power and pleasure, the story of the empire might have ended differently.

The social system, as it developed, reflected the changing character of economic and political life. Roman society was always a society of marked social distinctions. In the Native Period, there were the patricians, an hereditary and land-owning aristocracy descended from the most ancient families, and the plebeians, who enjoyed a measure of personal freedom, but who depended for a livelihood upon the patricians, and engaged in manual, domestic and commercial occupations. Until 445 B.C., intermarriage between the patricians and plebeians was forbidden by law.[51]

Out of a successful struggle of the plebeians for economic and political rights came, in the fourth century B.C., a new landed nobility, composed of patricians and plebeians. Most plebeians, however, remained small landowners who, in competition with the great slave-operated estates, lost their property and were forced into the ranks of the city proletariat or of the army. While remaining legally free these lived in poverty and economic dependence. Between this dependent free class and the landed aristocracy there emerged, as a result of imperial and commercial expansion, a new middle, capitalist class who engaged in a variety of profitable occupations, military, administrative, and commercial. But at the very top of the social structure there always stood the nobles, so noble that they were expected never to engage in any mental or manual work, except agriculture, for profit.

Below all of these stood the slaves, who were few in the Native Period, but who numbered millions in Rome and Italy from the third century B.C. onward, every war bringing its new quota of slaves into Roman society. The prices paid for slaves on the Roman market ran from $100 for a laborer to $28,000 for a grammarian.[52] Eventually, all manual occupations and some professions, such as medicine and teaching, came to be, in varying degrees, in the hands of foreigners, slaves, and ex-slaves. Owners made great profit by the skilled labor and sale of slaves. As trained gladiators, slaves brought a high price when the public thirst for blood became intense. As many as 10,000 of these perished occasionally in a single day to whet the Roman desire for thrills. Contempt for slaves brought contempt for the occupations in which they engaged. Yet gifted slaves were respected and, when freed, sometimes rose to high positions.

With the decline of the empire, wealth passed into the hands of

[51] H. W. Johnston, *The Private Life of the Romans* (New York: Scott, Foresman & Co., 1903), p. 51.

[52] McDaniel, *op. cit.*, p. 93.

the senatorial nobility, who in the fourth century possessed nearly all the land of the empire, and the other classes were gradually reduced to forms of civil, industrial, and agricultural serfdom. In the fifth century, civil servants were placed by law in hereditary endogamous gilds. Similarly, the old industrial gilds became hereditary, and various forms of serfdom, under a wealthy nobility, were imposed upon European society.[53] Economic and social inequalities, and the discontent they produced, plagued the empire. Slavery kept wages low, and the masses lived in poverty in both cities and country. Unemployment became a chronic ill. The burden of taxation was, wherever possible, passed on by the rich to the ever increasing ranks of the poor, for whom at last, after class wars and rebellions had failed, only one hope of a happier life remained—an otherworldly heaven prepared for them by the dying-gods of Oriental salvationist cults, whose spread reflects the decline of Roman secular society.

STATUS OF WOMEN. In spite of male domination, founded upon the male prerogative of *patria potestas* which gave absolute power to the oldest living father in the family, Roman women enjoyed more economic advantages and much greater personal and social freedom than Athenian women. Yet, their status was one of inferiority. The family was one of Rome's most unique institutions, and loyalty to one's family, the crowning virtue of Roman life. The home, too, was the nursery of patriotism. The cult of the household gods—the *lares* and *penates*—continued long after the official religion of the state had disappeared. The home, recently weakened by economic and social change, was one of Rome's legacies to Western civilization. The strong family culture of Rome gave women an honored position in society but, as the scene changed, some of them sought more honor and privileges. Vesta, the goddess of the hearth, was the chief female deity of early times, and her temple with its Vestal Virgins symbolized the honor paid to Roman wives and mothers. Great social changes accompanied the expansion of the Roman state, and Cato proclaimed regretfully, in 195 B.C., that women were becoming the rulers of men.[54] His attempt to curb their extravagance by law failed.

The "emancipation" of Roman women progressed rapidly with the increase in the wealth and power of Rome and with the penetration of Roman society by Greek culture. Toward the close of the

[53] *Ibid.*, pp. 23–40; S. Dill, *Roman Society in the Last Century of the Western Empire* (London: Macmillan & Co., Ltd., 1898), pp. 145–66, 227–81; Hulme, *op. cit.*, pp. 10–13.

[54] Heilborn, *op. cit.*, pp. 121–22; McDaniel, *op. cit.*, p. 54; Livy (trans. B. O. Foster, *et al.;* Harvard University Press, 1919–), XXXIV, 1–8.

Transition Period, an exaggerated form of the hetaeradom had developed, and family ties, formerly supported by profound religious feelings, were seriously weakened. Never, probably, except for a time in Soviet Russia, was divorce more easily obtained than in the first centuries of the Roman empire.[55] In the Transition Period, Rome experienced a social crisis similar to that of Athens, and the old culture and folkways, the old morality, underwent a profound change. There were few Roman customs or traditions which were not affected by the new forces at work in society at that time, and the greater freedom which was accorded to women was but one aspect of the social change that had occurred. Before the law women and men were equal. Yet, Roman women never enjoyed the same educational opportunities as men.

THE CHANGING POLITICAL ENVIRONMENT. Rome grew from a small tribal community to an Italian nation, and then to a great empire of some 100,000,000 people, covering much of the Near East and all of Europe, except Germany. The *polis* had become *cosmopolis.* In government, Rome progressed from a monarchy (*c.* 754-509 B.C.) to a republic (509-27 B.C.), and then to an imperial autocracy (27 B.C.-*c.* A.D. 476). The crowning achievement of Roman statecraft was the preservation of republican forms, minus their substance, under the absolute régime of the emperors. Democracy developed slowly between 449 and 70 B.C. out of a protracted struggle of the plebeians for power, but at its best it was a restricted form of democracy. Under the empire, political life acquired a fixity of form, with the emperors wielding supreme power. Women, freedmen, and slaves continued to be disfranchised. Simple freemen, mostly tradesmen and artisans, and minor civil servants were permitted to vote but could not hold political offices. Above these came the full citizens, who might hold any office provided they met all legal requirements, but who were, in practice, barred by poverty from such positions. The highest political privileges and offices were enjoyed by the nobles, an aristocracy of birth and wealth.[56]

In the period 300-146 B.C., as a result of the Italian, Punic, and Macedonian wars, Rome became a great power, and Greek culture was forced upon her as a consequence of foreign contacts. From A.D. 200 onward, Roman power and prestige were declining as a result of economic, social, political, religious, and moral causes.[57]

[55] McDaniel, *op. cit.,* p. 57.

[56] Hulme, *op. cit.,* pp. 10–11; J. W. Duff, *A Literary History of Rome* (London: George Allen & Unwin, Ltd., 1927), pp. 92–95.

[57] G. B. Adams, *Civilization during the Middle Ages* (New York: Charles Scribner's Sons, 1914), pp. 77–84; Dill, *op. cit.,* pp. 227–81; F. Lot, *The End of the Ancient World* (New York: Alfred A. Knopf, Inc., 1931), pp. 185–86.

The separation of the Eastern and Western empires occurred gradually from A.D. 330, when Constantine made Constantinople the new capital. The Western empire, long decaying, fell to the Germans in the fifth century, but its shadow remained until Napoleon ended it in 1806. The Eastern empire continued until Constantinople fell to the Turks in 1453. At the beginning of the sixth century, the Eastern emperor, Justinian, restored Roman power in Italy for a brief period, during which he introduced into the West his Justinian Code with its provision against pagan schools. This Code became, later, the basis of legal study in the law schools of Europe.[58]

The Roman empire was a great "melting-pot" of races and cultures, but only the upper classes were really Romanized. The underprivileged lower classes were given little, or no, share in the culture of their masters. While schoolmasters, with designs upon the minds and souls of men, followed the conquering armies of Rome, and while emperors took control of education for the sake of cultural and political unity in the empire, the masses were touched but little by Roman culture. The empire died at the top, for the common people were never given a voice or a real stake in it; nor was any real effort made to educate them. The ancient idea of universalism was embodied in the empire, a political structure built, in theory, upon the principles of (a) the independence of citizens, (b) the sovereignty of the people, and (c) the supremacy of law, as supposedly an expression of the people's will. In the fields of government and law, Rome has been the teacher of the Western world.

The fall of the Western empire brought dismay and despair to Christians and pagans alike, for it was, indeed, perhaps the greatest political achievement of man. At the height of its greatness, Romans placed the word *Aeternitas* on their coins, and their poet Rutilius, in the fifth century, evidently unaware of the decay around him, called Rome the "Eternal City." Many Christians looked upon it as a divine institution and, at its fall, waited in fear and hope for the end of the world. St. Augustine, in his *City of God*, treated the empire as the last period in human history, and proclaimed that there is a more abiding city than worldly Rome, the otherworldly Heavenly City.[59] Rome fell, but the world did not end. Romania, the cultural Rome, survived, for dreams and ideas are difficult to destroy. It was its brilliance and glory, though not always undimmed, which make the age and civilization that followed it so dark and dismal. The Eastern empire, which lived on, was but a

[58] Adams, *op. cit.*, pp. 67–74.

[59] Lot, *op. cit.*, pp. 251–53; Dill, *op. cit.*, pp. 305–10.

mediaeval type of theocratic state which retained little of the fallen Rome of the West. But it preserved for the future West the culture of Greece.

No problem has interested historians more than that of the causes of the fall of the Western Roman empire. Opinions differ, and some stress one cause, and others another, as the chief factor in the fall. Rachel Carson suggests that the cruel northern sea and its inundations of northern Europe forced from their homelands the barbarian tribes who eventually overran the Western empire.[60] But what they overran had become weak by internal decay. The great plagues of the second and third centuries brought widespread anxiety and misery. The fall was, no doubt, the result of many factors—economic, political, social, moral and religious. Patriotism was weakened by the spread of the salvationist cults, but that spread was itself but a manifestation of the decay of a secular society that had no longer anything to offer to the oppressed. To what extent the fall of the empire was due to official neglect of formal mass education and to contempt for commerce, manufacturing and manual occupations is a matter of interesting speculation. Nor did the schools of grammar and rhetoric, attended by the ruling and privileged classes, provide Rome with the intelligence necessary in directing the affairs of her far-flung empire.

THE CHANGING RELIGIOUS ENVIRONMENT. The official gods of ancient patrician Rome were patrician gods, and religion was a state and patrician religion. Around the old city was erected a sacred wall, the *pomerium,* and, inside this cultural fortification, foreign deities might not be worshiped. Yet many early Roman gods, beliefs and religious rites were of Etruscan origin. The whole world of the ancient Roman was filled with spirits. Over every important event or activity in a Roman's life, whether birth, death, plowing, warfare, etc., a spirit presided, which Romans had to propitiate. Animism, polytheism and ceremonialism characterized religion. The plebeians, who had their own humbler gods and who were usually excluded from public ceremonies, were in time shown to be less loyal to the ancient faith than the aristocrats, who remained the last devotees of paganism in the dying empire. These earlier deities were abstract forces of nature, not anthropomorphic as were Greek gods, and they were practical forces which "bound" men firmly to their everyday duties without promising them any rewards in an after life. In time nearly all abstractions, among them the Roman state (*Respublica*) were deified. State priests, who were simply

[60] *The Sea around Us* (New York: Oxford University Press, 1951), pp. 181 f.

public officials, but never a caste, conducted the state worship under the direction of a "supreme pontiff." Here religion and patriotism were one, and here *pietas* (reverence for religious things) was man's bounden duty. Rome rose to greatness on this secular faith whose essence was patriotism. But it was always the official faith of the state rather than a matter of individual belief. Because of the common Indo-European heritage of Greeks and Romans, the native religions of both have many common features. Native Roman religion had no divine or inspired founder, no sacred books, no creeds and no dogmas. In it there was but little ethical content. It was essentially a system of rites devoid of creeds or formal beliefs. Yet Romans, largely unlike the Greeks, believed that their gods could influence men and determine their destiny. And unlike the joyful religion of the Greeks, that of Rome was a religion of fear and of a gloomy hereafter.

Between 500 and 200 B.C., as a result of national expansion, the worship of foreign gods, particularly Greek anthropomorphic deities, spread rapidly. From 399 B.C. onward, in spite of determined conservative opposition, Greek religions were introduced widely, and all the gods became, in time, so humanized that there occurred a great decline in religious fervor. Because of the growing democracy and individualism of Rome, men sought a personal rather than a social religion, and this personal element the traditional system lacked. The early emperors had themselves proclaimed and worshiped as deities for the purpose of cultural and political unity in the empire, but this was but another form of state, not personal, religion, and it did not satisfy the individualism and rationalism of the age. All official attempts to preserve the old faiths were in vain. Under the republic and the empire, Roman liberalism permitted very great freedom of worship, and the official state religion was but one of many in Rome. The masses were attracted in increasing numbers by Oriental mystery cults, such as Mithraism, and by their related cults of Judaism and Christianity; the intelligentsia, by intellectual systems, such as Stoicism and Epicureanism. The struggle for supremacy between an array of competing philosophies and religions passed into its last phase, in the fourth century A.D., with the imperial recognition of Christianity as the religion of the empire. Paganism, however, struggled on against the new cult for nearly two centuries and left its impress upon many church practices in Christendom.

In the triumph of Christianity, the rôle of Rome was of supreme importance. Without the political and cultural unity which Roman genius for government had created over what was to become the

Christian world, the religion of Jesus and Paul, who boasted of his Roman citizenship, might never have been preached to "all nations." Its official approval by Roman emperors was probably indispensable to its triumph. While the Roman empire became Christian, Christianity came to embody pagan elements as a result of its contact with the pagan world.[61]

FOREIGN INFLUENCE. While the Etruscan contribution was great, by far the most important foreign influence upon Roman life was that of Greece. From about 800 B.C., a stream of influence, first from the Greek colonies in southern Italy and Sicily, and then from Greece herself, flowed into Rome and Italy, the period of greatest borrowing from Greece dating from the first war with Carthage (264-241 B.C.) when Rome began a struggle for empire beyond Italian shores which culminated, in a little over a century, in her mastery of the whole Mediterranean and Hellenistic world. Sometime before 600 B.C., the Romans borrowed the alphabet probably from the Greeks of Cumae, and the art of writing spread throughout most of Italy between 800 and 200 B.C.[62] There was, however, little writing prior to the third century B.C. Thus Rome owes the beginning of her literary education to Greece. The earliest written Roman documents that have been found date from the sixth century B.C.[63]

In 449 B.C., as a result of growing democracy, the Laws of the Twelve Tables began, according to most scholars, to be put into written form, but the literary period proper began about 250 B.C., with the introduction of Greek literature, and Latin translations of the same, by Greeks who had settled in Rome. All that can be said here is that Rome soon inherited all the literary products of Greece, and that soon Greek and native Roman authors were producing a Latin literature modeled after the Greek. The "Golden Age" of Latin literature was reached in the period 70 B.C.-14 A.D., the age of Cicero and his younger contemporaries. When Cato, an enemy of Greek culture, wrote at the beginning of the second century B.C., he listed oratory, agriculture, war, law and medicine as subjects worthy of study. One hundred years later, Varro listed as studies, grammar, rhetoric, dialectic, geometry, arithmetic, astronomy, music,

[61] Montgomery, *op. cit.*, pp. 48–49, 316–43; Dill, *op. cit.*, pp. 74–111; Duff, *op. cit.*, pp. 53–59; Windelband, *op. cit.*, pp. 303 ff.; *C.A.H.*, X, 46 ff., 468–583; S. Angus, *The Mystery-Religions and Christianity* (New York: Charles Scribner's Sons, 1925); W. W. Hyde, *Paganism to Christianity in the Roman Empire* (Philadelphia: University of Pennsylvania Press, 1946).

[62] *C.A.H.*, II, 563–90; IV, 113–17, 122–23, 347–403, 413–68; James, *op. cit.*, I, 209–10.

[63] Duff, *op. cit.*, pp. 67–69.

medicine, and architecture. Cato's conception of education was essentially professional; Varro's, much more liberal.

In science, art, literature, philosophy, religion and education, Rome borrowed freely from Greece, and the culture of Hellas became the spirit that enlivened the republic and the empire. But the new culture met with determined opposition. There were Romans who thought that they could conquer the world without losing their souls, but in that they deceived themselves. In 161 B.C., the Roman senate, alarmed probably by Epicureanism, decreed the expulsion of philosophers and rhetoricians from the city. These outlaws were probably Greeks who lectured in Latin, but the law was not enforced, for Romans, thirsting for the new culture, continued to attend the lectures of Greek professors. In 92 B.C., Latin rhetoricians were expelled by a similar decree, because boys were "wasting their time" attending their lectures, all of which indicates that, at this time, only Greek teachers were thought to offer the genuine article to Roman youths. Greek physicians were likewise unwelcome for a long time, because Romans feared that they had murderous designs upon the lives of "barbarians." [64] The Transition Period was, then, one of struggle, which ended in a victory for Greek culture, although the Roman never fully accepted the Greek estimate of liberal values.

ROMAN MIND AND CHARACTER. While Roman history is a continuation of the Greek, the character of both peoples differed, for the Greeks were thinkers, the Romans, doers. Roman art was as utilitarian as their great roads, and Roman literature nearly always displays a practical purpose. Lucretius would destroy superstition; Virgil would glorify the empire and recall men to their sense of duty. Roman rhetoric, history, and philosophy bear the stamp of utilitarianism. In all literary fields, except satire, the Romans were imitators, not creators. While there were two languages, the Greek and the Latin, there was but one literature, the Greek. The Romans achieved practically nothing in natural science, for Greek scientific knowledge was enough for them. In mathematics their interest lay in arithmetic and surveying, while in architecture they stressed function. Their roads, bridges and aqueducts reveal their engineering genius. But in law and government they excelled most of all. The Greeks knew how to think about the world; the Romans, how to rule it. Roman law is one of the greatest of human achievements. It still lives in the legal customs of Spanish-speaking countries as well as in some aspects of English common law. Many of

[64] T. C. Allbutt, *Greek Medicine in Rome* (London: Macmillan & Co., Ltd., 1921), p. 62.

the earlier laws may be found in Livy, and the Justinian Code is readily accessible, or ought to be, to students.

The favored philosophies of the Romans were the ethical systems of Epicureanism and Stoicism. Lucretius (*c.* 98-*c.* 55 B.C.), author of the great philosophic poem, *De Rerum Natura,* represents the former school, while Seneca (*c.* 4 B.C.-A.D. 65), in his *Peace of Mind,* and Emperor Marcus Aurelius (A.D. 121-180), in his *Meditations,* represent the latter.

No one has ever stated the philosophy of materialism more eloquently than Lucretius. With Epicurus, he held that society and moral man, as well as nature, resulted from a purposeless mingling of atoms. From early pastoral and agricultural societies, founded upon friendship, there evolved the militarized, predatory states of later times. The fear of death, rooted in a belief in immortality, made man, as he struggled for survival, a wolf to his fellows. The goal of life, said he, is not the quest for immortality, by the nature of things impossible, but the enjoyment of nobler pleasures. Therefore, man should abandon religion and follow reason. The Epicureans organized societies of friends, opposed to war and the state, whose faith was an ethical creed promising only earthly happiness. Such views and practices aroused against them the enmity of the Roman government and later of Christian leaders. Karl Marx, who wrote his doctoral thesis on Epicurus, seems to have been influenced by his ideas and those of Lucretius. More acceptable than Epicureanism to influential Romans from Cato to Marcus Aurelius was Stoicism.

Stoicism called for calm submission to natural law as a means of destroying fear and desire, and the evils they produce. It was thus in harmony with the Roman ideal of self-discipline. It was a philosophy of fatalism and resignation to nature, but lacked the Epicurean promise of happiness. But for both schools, nature and reason are God.

> All life [said Seneca] is slavery: let each man therefore reconcile himself to his lot . . . and lay hold of whatever good lies within his reach. . . . He who fears death will never act as becomes a living man. . . . Disease, captivity, disaster . . . are none of them unexpected: I always knew with what disorderly company Nature had associated me.[65]

And Marcus Aurelius wrote in a similar strain:

> Life is a warfare and a stranger's sojourn, and after-fame is oblivion. What then is that which is able to conduct a man? One thing and only one, philosophy. But this consists in . . . doing nothing without a purpose, . . . accepting all that happens, . . . and, finally, waiting for death with a cheer-

[65] Thatcher, *op. cit.,* III, 343–45.

ful mind, as being nothing else than a dissolution of the elements of which every living thing is compounded. . . . For it is according to nature, and nothing is evil which is according to nature.[66]

The Stoics dreamt of a universal state, a brotherhood of wise men and a world citizenship to take place of the city-state, and they stressed the worth of the individual less than did the Epicureans. In the ideal world-state of Marcus Aurelius all men would enjoy equal rights and freedom of speech, guaranteed by a universal natural law revealed by reason, which would protect them from the tyranny of governments. Yet he himself inaugurated no social reform in his empire. His philosophy of resignation to nature was acceptable to the upper classes from whom "nature" demanded few sacrifices, but it was not adapted to the realities of the Roman imperial society. It had, however, more to recommend it to a liberal world than the political, authoritarian religion of Plato with its cosmic justification of social privilege and rule by the few.

As the glory and tragedy of the Roman empire unfold it is easy to lose sight of the contribution of Greece to its life and thought. The greatness of the ancient world passed with the fusion, in the early imperial period, of the best that Greece and Rome had contributed in the intellectual, artistic, legal, and administrative fields.[67] Rome, while making a contribution all her own, stands as a bridge over which passed into the modern world the culture and achievements of Greece.

Roman Education in the Native Period

INFORMAL EDUCATION. (1) Vocational and Practical. It is upon writers of the late republic and empire that we lean for information regarding the old education, and they probably give us a fairly reliable account, sometimes in the form of personal reminiscences, of the old practices.[68] In Rome, newborn children were "exposed," or reared, at the discretion of their fathers, an exercise of parental power (*patria potestas*) authorized by the Laws of the Twelve Tables and surviving in law to the end of the empire, as the Institutes of Justinian reveal. Before the alphabet was introduced, educational practices were like those of a pre-literate people living under similar conditions, and children were educated through actual participation in life activities. While a few Roman writers mention formal schools (*ludi*), the evidence for their existence is not conclu-

[66] *Ibid.*, p. 417.

[67] *C.A.H.*, X, 545, 586; Adams, *op. cit.*, pp. 20–23; Duff, *op. cit.*, pp. 1 ff.; Allbutt, *op. cit.*

[68] See Woody, *op. cit.*, pp. 503 ff.; Monroe, *op. cit.*, pp. 327 ff.

sive. Rome, however, was itself a school, where life was education and education was life. Children were given moral training by their mothers. At the age of seven, sons of patricians and plebeians became versed in their fathers' callings by acting as their apprentices, but plebeian youths were restricted to manual and menial employments until near the end of the period, when a few succeeded in achieving privileged positions. In the same way girls were instructed by their mothers in the domestic and social duties imposed upon women.

(2) Religious and Moral. In their homes and society children grew up in an atmosphere of religion and of moral discipline. Over all important events in the lives of individuals as well as over all important acts of government some spirit presided, and had to be duly propitiated if success were to be achieved. The practical Roman demanded his *quid pro quo* even from the gods, and worldly success, not a reward in another world, was his goal. Children learned religion and morals by participating in the religious life of their people in their homes and fields and by conforming with the moral behavior of their elders. When in time temples came to be established, the devout Roman attended services in them. Certain days were holy days when certain forms of labor were forbidden. The life of the ancient Roman was one of religious ceremonial from morning until night and his children followed his example. No doubt such learning was acquired by example rather than by precept.

The virtues which Romans prized as the marks of the ideal man were *pietas* (filial duty, respect for the gods, and patriotism), *virtus* (courage), *honestas* (trustworthiness), *gravitas* (seriousness), *constantia* (firmness of character) and *prudentia* (practical wisdom). Many of these virtues were, no doubt, seen as marks of the ideal woman also. Nostalgic writers of the later age of female license and extravagance applauded the thrift, industry, chastity, sobriety, dignity, obedience, truthfulness, courage, kindness, respect for in-laws and religious devotion of ancient women. In respect to some aspects of moral conduct, more seems to have been expected from women than from men. Livy mentions a few whose conduct fell short of the ideal.

(3) Physical and Military. Life on the farms and on the range provided physical education for ancient Romans. It was a hard life and demanded physical skills and stamina of a high order. Even the patrician who employed hired labor on his estate had supervisory work to perform which kept him constantly on the move.

But in addition to these activities, the Roman was called upon to be a soldier. For this, his rugged rural life helped to prepare him. Military service, earlier a patrician privilege, was made compulsory for all propertied citizens except those in the colonies. Many of the games and sports that Roman children, youths and adults engaged in had military value, but the play and games of younger boys and girls were similar to those of children nearly everywhere and had no special military significance, although many of them contributed to health and muscular co-ordination. The sports of older boys—running, jumping, wrestling, boxing, swimming, throwing weights, riding, and exercising with weapons—had soldiering as an objective. Perhaps the sport of hunting contributed also to the development of military skills. The Roman army kept increasing in size. All propertied citizens were enrolled and served in various capacities depending on their ability to buy armor and weapons. Only wealthier men could afford to serve in the cavalry. There was no pay for military service, but great public honors and indirect pecuniary rewards were bestowed upon heroes and distinguished military men. And youths were inspired to feats of heroism in war by listening to tales about the great soldiers of the past. The discipline in the army was severe, and the punishments for infraction of rules and for disobedience to commands of officers were brutal. In the *Campus Martius*, a public exercising ground somewhat like the Greek *gymnasium*, fathers taught their sons the arts of war. Here and in the army itself some formal training for war seems to have been provided. It is worthy of note that gymnastic training and the Athenian ideal of physical training for the sake of bodily grace did not appeal to Romans; nor did music and dancing, although Romans sometimes practised them, usually in connection with religious ceremonials.

(4) Apprenticeship Education of Boys. Boys at about the age of seven began to learn their life occupations by acting as their fathers' apprentices. Thus they learned farming, in its various forms, and the care of livestock. Boys were hardened to the tasks, some of them dangerous, by training and experience. Little is known about the training of artisans, although artisan gilds are said to have existed from Etruscan times. There can be little doubt that youths learned how to make tools, farming implements, boats, weapons, etc., by the apprenticeship method. The work of government and of administering the law demanded a special kind of training. Roman youths learned these by acting as apprentices to their fathers. With the exception of the period 100 B.C.–150 A.D., when the mer-

chant middle class challenged their ascendancy, the ancient patrician class had control of these services. Until the rise of formal schools in the Transition Period, youths learned the arts of legislation, government, and public pleading by the apprenticeship method. And, if we can trust the estimate of Cicero, Tacitus, and Pliny, that old method produced men better versed in the law than did the new one.

(5) Education of Girls. By law, a woman was subject to some male—a father, a husband, or a brother—and her behavior was closely guarded. Her duties consisted of cooking, weaving, spinning, supervising the work of daughters and servants, and of educating her children with the assistance of her husband. She looked after their health, taught them correct speech and the moral virtues dear to the Romans. Girls occasionally tended flocks where that work was not dangerous. Near the end of the Native Period, reading, writing and arithmetic were taught in some homes, perhaps by mothers, and some girls of better families were, no doubt, literate. A girl's home education ended with her marriage which was permissible for her at about the age of twelve.

THE FAMILY AS EDUCATIONAL AGENT OF THE STATE. Ancient Roman education was education for the state, although the state did not control it. The family served the ends of the state and served them well in moulding civic character and raising up a patriotic citizenry. It gave Rome men and women skilled in occupations, loyal to the state, the family, and their gods. As the state grew in size and complexity, many of the earlier educational functions of the family were transferred to formal schools.

FORMAL EDUCATION. Little is known about literary education in Rome prior to the publication of the Laws of the Twelve Tables. Thereafter, Romans gradually fell under the cultural spell of literature. The Tables were committed to memory by patrician and plebeian boys, but, until 304 B.C., only patricians knew the rules of conducting law suits. About 280 B.C., the first plebeian *pontifex maximus* (supreme pontiff or priest) opened a law school in Rome evidently for plebeian boys.[69] Instruction in reading and writing preliminary to the study of the Tables was, apparently until the Transition Period, given by fathers, and perhaps mothers, in their homes, for there is no conclusive evidence that special teachers were employed in the Native Period.[70] However, as we have seen, some later writers refer to *ludi*, or schools, in this period. The Tables

[69] Duff, *op. cit.*, p. 88.

[70] *Ibid.*, pp. 86–88; Johnston, *op. cit.*, pp. 74–75.

continued to be learned by heart until the time of Cicero, although the language of the Tables had passed out of use.

The utilitarian character of the old education deserves particular notice. Here was a liberal education, designed to keep freemen free, with little of the literary and intellectual element in it. The study of law, albeit through apprenticeship, with a view to its application to the science of government provided, however, an important form of intellectual discipline. In the Transition Period, when freemen were busy building an empire and robbing others of their freedom, the literary element gradually replaced, to a large degree, the old traditional practical education. The change to the new education was conditioned by the increase in wealth and leisure of a growing class of freemen who could enjoy the luxury of idleness.

Education in the Transition Period

INFORMAL EDUCATION. The old apprenticeship system of education continued in the fields of domestic and mechanical arts, commerce, navigation, diplomacy, civil service, war, and, to a remarkable degree, in law. In connection with commerce, our modern bookkeeping system began to develop, but boys learned it, not in schools, but through business practice. In the vocational fields, the apprenticeship system endured until the fall of the empire, and survived in the civilization of the Middle Ages, and well into modern times.[71]

FORMAL EDUCATION. In the cultural field, an expanding nation needed a more universal leaven than the native culture of the earlier city-state and, on the intellectual side, formal schools and formal education, fashioned after Greek models, emerged from about 300 B.C. onward. We have already noted the opposition of certain Romans to the new culture, and the failure of that opposition to stem the tide of change.

(1) The New Purpose. When Roman fathers, no longer able to prepare their sons adequately for an increasingly complex life, turned them over, perhaps regretfully, to schoolmasters, they demanded that these masters prepare them in a practical way for a life of usefulness and political leadership in the republic. In the Native Period, education prepared boys for the many duties, legal, military, political, economic, etc., which all citizens then performed, but, in the Transition Period, formal education came to embody a single practical purpose, the making of the perfect orator. The ideal was

[71] J. W. Thompson, *Economic and Social History of Europe in the Later Middle Ages* (New York: The Century Co., 1931), p. 449.

not, however, a narrow one, for by Romans an orator was conceived to be the completely educated man, possessed of all the knowledge and skill of a philosopher, lawyer, statesman, soldier, author, etc. Indeed, to the accomplished orator, all positions in public life, whether in peace or war, were open. For three hundred years, Romans continued to define the orator, as Cato did, as "a good man, skilled in speaking."[72] All education of boys, whether in the elementary, secondary, or higher schools, came to be guided by that purpose. Roman theorists, as Cicero and Quintilian, insisted that the ideal orator must work unselfishly in the service of society.[73] Yet Cicero was not averse to the pursuit of knowledge for the enjoyment of leisure, although knowledge for the sake of action and public service remained his ideal.

(2) THE NEW METHOD AND DISCIPLINE. In the Native Period, youths learned by imitation of their elders in the courts or on the farm, etc., and, when the Twelve Tables were introduced, they learned them by memorization. With the coming of schools and literature, imitation and memorization of literary models, as a method of instruction, were carried over from the apprenticeship system into the schools of letters, grammar, and rhetoric. Thus, a highly formalized method of memorization and imitation, strengthened by severe corporal punishment, came gradually into almost universal vogue and, in the Hellenized Period, was condemned by educational theorists and ridiculed by satirists.[74]

Flogging with a rod or leathern strap was apparently an almost universal practice. Quintilian condemned it but probably to no avail. The Greek theories of faculty psychology and formal discipline appear in such writings as those of Quintilian, whose views on method are, however, highly progressive. Adapting instruction to the age and capacity of pupils, the giving of prizes, the use of rivalry between students, and repetition and memorization were devices recommended by some Roman teachers of grammar and rhetoric. In the Transition Period, many older practices survived, and moral education continued to be acquired by example in the home; and many orators continued, as in the past, to learn the procedures of the law courts by attaching themselves to practising lawyers, while others learned by pleading fictitious cases in rhetorical schools under the instruction of a schoolmaster.[75] In the centuries following the

[72] H. E. Butler, *The Institutio Oratoria of Quintilian* (New York: G. P. Putnam's Sons, Inc., 1920), IV, 335.

[73] *Ibid.*, pp. 335 ff.; J. S. Watson, *Cicero on Oratory and Orators* (London: Bohn, 1862), pp. 346 ff.

[74] Butler, *op. cit.*, I, 57–61; Monroe, *op. cit.*, pp. 396 ff.

[75] Monroe, *op. cit.*, pp. 359 ff., 371 ff.

Transition Period, the formal method of the schools replaced, almost entirely, the apprenticeship method of the past.

(3) Organization and Curriculum. **(a) Ludus.** With the possible exception of the *ludus,* Rome borrowed her schools from Hellenistic Greece, and their form, with the exception of the university, had become fixed by about 100 B.C. They extended from the elementary school to the university. As we have seen, the date of the origin of the elementary school (*ludus*) is uncertain. The word *ludus* means "play," as the Greek word "school" means "leisure." The *ludus* became, at times, if not often, a school of terror, not play, if we can trust the testimony of such tormented eyewitnesses as Horace and Martial. The school began before cockcrow, and the torture continued for the children apparently until dark. The vacation period seems to have run from early July until late October. The curriculum consisted of reading, writing, and arithmetic. Until Cicero's boyhood, the Laws of the Twelve Tables were used as reading material. Arithmetic was stressed because of its many practical uses, and a special teacher (*calculator*) appeared. In teaching, he used the abacus and a finger-calculating system. The teacher of reading and writing (*litterator*) was usually one of low literary attainments. In teaching writing, he held and guided the pupil's hand, or had him trace letters grooved on a tablet until he no longer needed such aids.

Until the time of the empire, when they appeared everywhere, even in villages, these elementary schools were few, and the 3 R's were usually taught by private tutors in the home. Elementary education, whether in the home or *ludus,* began usually at the age of seven and ended at the age of twelve when boys, in the Transition and later periods, entered the grammar school. About the beginning of the empire there originated the practice, similar to that of Athens, of placing a boy at the age of seven under the supervision of a slave attendant (*paedagogus*), whose chief duty was to supervise his conduct. The *paedagogus* was usually a Greek, and he apparently gave the boy instruction in the rudiments of the Greek language.

(b) Grammar school. By the third century B.C. grammar had become a highly developed study in the Hellenistic world. It included not only grammar as we know it now but literature as well. The first teacher of grammar (*grammaticus*) in Rome was Livius Andronicus, a Greek born in Southern Italy, who was brought to the city as a slave in 276 B.C., and the second was Ennius, an Italian (born 239 B.C.). Both taught Greek and translated Greek literary works into Latin. While they apparently taught literature in Rome, there is no evidence that they established schools of grammar. Suetonius in his *Lives of Eminent Grammarians* considers Crates of Mallos, who came to Rome between 169 and 159 B.C., the first important organizer of literary instruction. Greek grammar schools date from his coming, or from an early date thereafter. About 100 B.C., when a Latin literature had appeared, Latin grammar schools were established. From Rome these schools spread quickly to the provinces. Many of the early teachers of grammar were Greeks and, in spite of marked official and private opposition to Greek culture, the progress of the new education suffered no serious check. Fallen Greece triumphed over the mind of her conquerors and did so without any plan of spiritual conquest.

While Romans considered the Greeks as their inferiors politically and morally, they had to admit their superiority in literature, philosophy, and art. Therefore, the Greek language and literature were long esteemed more highly by Roman intellectuals than the Latin language and literature. Quintilian, near the end of the first century A.D., said that the formal education of Roman boys ought to begin with a study of Greek, but that Latin should receive equal attention after this beginning stage. When Quintilian wrote, the study of Greek alone was the common practice. Indeed, there originated in Rome the practice of attaching greater importance to the study of foreign languages than to a study of vernaculars. The Greek language became a medium for learned men in the empire, a fact of great cultural significance.

Under some emperors, from Constantine's time, Latin was officially recognized as the language of the empire. After the fall of the Western empire, Greek prevailed in the East, and Latin continued to hold its place in the cultural life of the West.[76] But, the thought embodied in Latin literature was Greek more than Roman. Classical Latin was never the language of the common people of Rome, the *vulgus*. Their language was vulgar Latin, the Koinê, and the classes in Roman society were distinguished by their language as well as by many other marks of difference. This Koinê, the parent of Romance languages, spread widely through the empire, and the cultural unity of the masses, created by it, lasted until the eighth century.[77]

Roman boys entered the grammar school at about the age of twelve, remaining there for about four years. This secondary school represents the nearest approach of the Romans to the Greek view of

[76] Hulme, *op. cit.*, p. 4; Lot, *op. cit.*, pp. 272–75.

[77] H. F. Muller, *A Chronology of Vulgar Latin* (Halle: Max Niemeyer, 1929), pp. 5 ff.

a liberal education, for it provided a thorough literary training, but as a preparation, however, for the technical work of the higher rhetorical school. It should be noted that there was more than one Greek plan of a liberal education, or the education of freemen. The Spartan state, as we have seen, neglected the literary education of its citizens. Rome borrowed, but with modifications, the practices prevalent in the Hellenistic world, practices inspired more by the Athenian than by the Spartan tradition. The study of Greek and Latin grammar, technically understood, came, in time, to receive much attention. Early in the first century B.C., Varro wrote his grammatical *De Lingua Latina* and other works on grammar. This was followed, in the next century, by Palaemon's *Ars Grammatica* and, in the fourth century A.D., by the grammar of Donatus, which had great vogue in the Middle Ages. These texts laid down rules of grammar, and illustrated them by numerous quotations from classical authors. Generations of mediaeval students knew many of the popular classical authors only through quotations from their writings in the grammar of Donatus and, to a lesser extent, since it was less popular, in the fifth-century grammar of Priscan.

The curriculum of the grammar school included a wide selection of Greek and Roman literature, both poetry and prose, Homer's poems being favorites until Virgil's began to replace them in the second century A.D. Much less attention, however, was given to prose than to poetry. Until the Period of Decline, emphasis was placed upon the meaning of the thought in literature, and the grammar school thus provided instruction in a variety of subjects, such as history, geography and mythology, to which allusions were made by the authors. In addition to these studies, students wrote Greek and Latin compositions. The grammar school, at its best, seems to have provided a rich literary and mental education for Roman youths, an education focused upon the realities of the human and social world.

(c) Rhetorical school. There were enough Greek philosophers and rhetoricians in Rome at the beginning of the second century B.C. to alarm the conservatives, and the formal study of rhetoric dates from that time, although the rhetorical school, in its final form, did not emerge until, probably, about the close of the Transition Period. It was, however, Greek in origin. Indeed, for a long time after 55 B.C., the masters of the grammar schools gave instruction in oratory, although special schools of rhetoric existed for that purpose. Boys entered the rhetorical school at about the age of sixteen to study the techniques of oratory. The school was modeled after the rhetorical schools of Athens, and its procedures were based largely on the views regarding rhetoric of Isocrates and Aristotle, and later of Cicero and Quintilian. The chief studies of the school were oratorical theory and declamation, and these were studied and practised in a very thorough way. The grammar school aimed to provide a "general education," but the goal of the rhetorical school was to train public speakers. All the knowledge that a boy had previously acquired was now applied, in school debates and declamations, to problems related to actual public life.

Until near the close of the Transition Period, as Cicero's own education shows, oratorical training continued to be acquired by many youths, not in formal schools, but through their acting as apprentices to practising orators and statesmen of note. The formal school, however, soon replaced that system, and its procedures became highly formalized. There, students wrote compositions and speeches, each one conforming closely with an established form and, in delivering these speeches, practice came to be based upon established rules, even in such matters as facial expression and gesture. But, while showing formal tendencies, the work of the school, until after A.D. 200, was definitely related to social needs, for in a free society the orator plays an important rôle, and the school aimed to prepare him for that rôle.

Cicero and Quintilian felt that encyclopedic knowledge was essential for success in oratory. Cicero listed, for instance, as essential, a knowledge of military affairs, geography, political affairs, philosophy, physics, mathematics, law, and logic, and remarked that the "complete orator" is one "who can speak on all subjects with variety and copiousness." [78] Quintilian listed, among other studies, Greek and Latin grammar and literature, orthography, etymology, music, astronomy, geometry, mensuration, surveying, physics, philosophy, moral philosophy, history, and a little gymnastics for the sake of graceful gestures.[79] These theorists did not consider instruction in such subjects to be the duty of the teacher of rhetoric. They were thought of as the work of the grammar master, or private tutor. Both Cicero and Quintilian included philosophy; but philosophy, in spite of the interest of Roman intellectuals in it, never found a firm foothold in Roman schools.

(d) Universities. University education in Rome grew out of the study of philosophy which, in spite of opposition, became popular with the aristocracy. Many wealthy youths supplemented the work of the rhetoricians by traveling in Greek lands and studying at the

[78] Watson, *op. cit.*, p. 158.
[79] Butler, *op. cit.*, I, 61 ff.; IV, 355–409.

famous centers of Greek learning.[80] There was a famous school of rhetoric and philosophy at Massilia in the first century B.C., which rivaled for a time the University of Athens. But the most important step toward university education was taken when emperors, beginning with Caesar, founded libraries. The library established by Vespasian near the close of the first century A.D. became, under Hadrian's patronage, the Athenaeum, a center of university learning. Here students pursued the study of architecture, medicine, law, mechanics, literature, rhetoric and philosophy, but the last was the least popular of these studies.

Quintilian, as probably most Romans, thought of the philosopher as a visionary who talked convincingly about government but avoided practical political activity. The ideal orator of Quintilian ought to be a "wise man" who relates his wisdom to action. Since philosophy was not taught by rhetoricians, Quintilian advised students of rhetoric to attend the meetings and discussions of philosophers as often as possible.[81] By the close of the Transition Period, Romans had come to consider oratory as the queen of studies and the last step in formal education.[82]

(4) SUPPORT AND CONTROL. The schools of this period were private, and were supported by students' fees. An occasional, but very rare, one probably had some aid from the local community and from public-spirited philanthropists. Pliny proposed such a plan of support for a school in Como. The schools, however, had no state support, and education was not compulsory.

(5) TEACHERS. Wealthy Roman parents placed their boys in charge of a *paedagogus*, a slave or ex-slave, from the time they entered the *ludus* until they donned the *toga virilis*, at about the age of sixteen. The *paedagogus* was expected to supervise a boy's morals and his studies, help him with his homework, and discipline him when necessary. He was the boy's constant attendant at home and in school, but any teaching he did was incidental.

The teacher in the *ludus* was called the *litterator*, and was often a slave or freedman. He was not highly respected, and his salary was small. In the time of Emperor Diocletian, his salary was fixed by decree at $1.20 a month, which was one-fourth the salary of grammar teachers and one-fifth that of rhetoric teachers, as regulated at the same time. The *litterator* was generally a poor teacher whose chief virtue consisted in his capacity to inflict physical torture on his pupils.

[80] *Ibid.*, IV, 385 ff.

[81] *Ibid.*

[82] Johnston, *op. cit.*, pp. 79–80; Monroe, *op. cit.*, pp. 363–64.

The teacher of the grammar school was called the *grammaticus* or *litteratus,* and was usually a man well versed in literature. As a class, these grammarians were accorded a measure of respect which increased as the centuries passed, and the fees they received, while small, were much higher than those of the *litterator.*

The teacher of the rhetorical school was called the *rhetor.* Of all teachers, a distinguished *rhetor* stood highest in social esteem, and the fees paid him were higher than those received by grammarians. Distinguished teachers were sometimes paid salaries by their wealthy patrons ranging from about $5000 to $50,000 a year, but high salaries were very exceptional. Juvenal, however, tells us that Roman fathers were unwilling to pay, even to the greatest teachers, more than "two poor sestertia," and that the education of their sons cost them less than their daily baths. For a long time the fees were paid as gifts, but, by the first century A.D., teachers were charging fixed fees. The Romans disdained the idea of salaried professions.[83]

The character of teachers was sometimes immoral. Even Palaemon, author of grammatical works, led a life of debauchery. The language of grammarians and rhetors was not always edifying. Roman writers frequently stressed the importance of good morals in those whose duty it was to mould the morals and manners of youth. Since the schools were private, the selection of the teacher was a parental responsibility, and some parents appear to have been more interested in the literary attainments than in the morals of the teachers they selected. Many of the teachers were, in all probability, men of irreproachable character. But, whether good or bad, they were very generally harsh disciplinarians whose floggings contributed to the perpetuation of the practice of corporal punishment in the schools of the West.

(6) STUDENTS IN THE TRANSITION AND LATER PERIODS. **(a) Boys.** It would seem that a knowledge of the 3 R's was quite general in Rome in the Transition and later periods. Cato would have household slaves thus instructed, most likely because they would be more useful to their masters. The whole question of the extent of literacy in Rome at any time is one about which there is much uncertainty. Because of a number of duties intrusted to slaves and freedmen, it would seem that some of them must have had a knowledge of the 3 R's, but it is very unlikely that, in acquiring that knowledge, they sat side by side with the sons of freemen in the schools of the *litterator,* and it is quite certain that they were very seldom given an opportunity to study under the *grammaticus.* Since, moreover, only

[83] Monroe, *op. cit.,* p. 418.

citizens of the upper class could hold higher offices in the state, and since these offices went to those highly educated, an incentive to pursue such higher education was lacking in all classes below the aristocracy. Moreover, since the schools received no public support before imperial times, the poor, some of them Roman citizens in the artisan class, must have found it impossible to pay fees or gifts to teachers.

In imperial times, many scribes were needed in keeping administrative records throughout the empire, and these were drawn from the lower classes. Thus, the groups below the aristocracy must have had fairly free access to the *ludus* and grammar schools under the rule of the emperors. As the imperial centuries passed, however, the nobility came to consider education their exclusive prerogative. In connection with this question one must keep in mind the growing caste system of Rome which became hereditary, the differentiation of employments on the basis of caste, the exclusive hold upon all higher offices by the aristocracy, and the relation of rhetorical education to the duties of such offices.[84]

(b) Girls. Throughout Roman history, girls received an informal education acquired through participation in the activities of domestic, religious, and social life. A woman's sphere of activity was, however, that of the home, and her duties were those of spinning, weaving, supervising servants, and the rearing of children.[85]

There was an increasing number of exceptions to this domestic rule under the republic and the empire, when some women engaged in manufacturing, commerce, entertainment and medical practice. The mystery cults opened some new opportunities for them in the field of religious ceremonies. Those who engaged in entertainment and medical practice were mostly Greeks. For such activities some education was necessary, but it was probably chiefly self-education. The chief duties of women remained those of mother and housewife. Even before the Transition Period, mothers taught their sons and daughters reading, writing and correct speech. Fathers assumed responsibility for the education of their sons who had reached the age of seven, but mothers continued to supervise the literary and moral education of their daughters.[86] Each rich girl had either a *paedagogus* or an elderly slave woman to attend her and supervise her conduct. After the *ludus* had been established, girls probably sometimes attended it, but the practice was certainly not common, and

[84] T. Haarhoff, *Schools of Gaul* (London: Oxford University Press, 1920), pp. 124–32.

[85] McDaniel, *op. cit.*, p. 56.

[86] Johnston, *op. cit.*, p. 74.

many girls of the aristocracy had private tutors, this, undoubtedly, being the common practice. Moreover, the "salons" of Roman *hetaerae* and noblewomen were centers of intellectual life from 200 B.C. onward.[87]

From the fourth century A.D., it appears that rich girls frequently studied grammar and philosophy. The rule of early marriage, however, limited their opportunities for study. Since they were never given the legal right to practise law, the professional training of the rhetorical school could have little value for them. Many women of the aristocracy were, in the last centuries of the empire, noted for their literary attainments. Even St. Jerome approved their study of pagan literature, although he was more concerned about their moral education.[88] Yet, in spite of the greater freedom enjoyed by Roman than by Athenian women, only a few of them, and these of the upper class, received a literary training, for such training was not necessary in their domestic activities. Musonius, following Plato, recommended that women be given the same intellectual opportunities as men but, unlike Plato, he would limit their sphere of action to the home. But he expounds a theory; he does not describe a practice.[89]

In addition to literary education, wealthy girls occasionally received instruction in music and dancing, as did their brothers at times also. That Christian ascetics later prohibited these arts is evidence of their popularity.

Roman writers who discussed the subject generally showed respect for women's ability and for their right to an education. Quintilian, Seneca, Plutarch, Musonius, and the Stoics would accord them an intellectual training similar to that of men. While aristocratic women, particularly in the imperial period, enjoyed many literary opportunities, only a few attempted to write, and Roman women's contributions to literature were unimportant.

(7) Physical Education in the Transition and Later Periods. In the republic and empire, military training remained as one form of physical training. The army and navy came to be composed of paid, professional fighting men who served from twenty to twenty-six years. In spite of many ex-service privileges, later emperors were forced to conscript soldiers, many of them foreigners and natives of poor character. Roman patriotism was now dead or dying. When, after Constantine's time, children of soldiers were

[87] A. Heilborn, *The Opposite Sexes* (London: Methuen & Co., Ltd., 1927), pp. 121–23.

[88] Haarhoff, *op. cit.*, pp. 205–9; Dill, *op. cit.*, pp. 207–8.

[89] Monroe, *op. cit.*, pp. 401 ff.

required to be soldiers, military service became a form of servitude.

The training of the soldier was strenuous, and produced disciplined warriors who made the name of Rome, in the days of its greatness, feared, admired and, by some perhaps, hated. Every soldier learned a trade, or skill of military utility. Wrestling, jumping, swimming, marching, carrying heavy burdens, and use of the spear, bow, axe, sword and sling were included in his training. The peaceful centuries of the *Pax Romana* brought, however, a laxity in military discipline.

In the early empire, there was organized a widespread, aristocratic youth movement, *Juventus,* whose goals were patriotism and physical fitness. Little is known about the exercises in which these youths engaged. The movement, however, brings to mind the Greek *Ephebi,* Mussolini's *Balilla,* the *Hitlerjugend,* and the *Komsomols* of Soviet Russia.

While Greek influence on Roman military training was insignificant, Roman physical life and attitude toward physical culture were changed noticeably by Greek example. Sport for sport's sake or for personal pleasure did not appeal to early Romans, who subordinated natural impulses to practical ends. When competitive sports and professional athletes were introduced, under Greek influence, in the second century B.C., the proud Roman remained a spectator rather than a participant. A century later, city and private *gymnasia, palaestrae* and baths were common in Rome and the provinces. In the second century A.D., *gymnasia,* with public baths and swimming pools attached, had become an almost indispensable city service, and the daily bath, rather than the earlier weekly one, a common practice. The private pools and baths of the wealthy, with their furnaces, marble walls, silver spigots, and adjoining spaces for games and sun-bathing, etc., were extravagantly luxurious. Many emperors, to enhance their popularity, built and supported elaborate public baths and swimming pools throughout the entire empire, while private philanthropists built and supported others.

The growing practice of gymnastics and of Greek dancing was criticized by many writers, including Cicero, Horace, Martial, Tacitus and Plutarch, on the grounds that they were a poor preparation for military life and had a softening and demoralizing influence upon character. Yet the Romans in the days of their wealth, power and leisure found dancing a pleasant relaxation and continued to dance.

Whether or not the sports and games of earlier Romans should be considered play, since they served the utilitarian ends of health and state service, is a matter of opinion. In the later republic and empire the traditional exercises came to be pursued as play and a source of pleasure. Romans now found delight in many forms of exercise and amusement, such as hunting, rowing, wrestling, swimming, boxing, ball games, sun-bathing, walking, fishing, dice and chess, most of which they engaged in from the days of their childhood. Games of ball, of which there were a number, were the most popular form of play. To what extent these pastimes were engaged in by the masses is not clear, but there is little doubt that they were confined largely to the aristocracy of birth and wealth in the cities of the empire, the gentry of Rome itself setting the fashion. It was the Hellenistic Greek cities, not the independent city-states of Greece, that set the pattern of education and life in the empire, and their influence was felt until the end. We know from Bishop Sidonius of Gaul that the Romans there, in the fifth century, pursued the sports, games, bathing, etc., that they enjoyed at home, and that the aristocracy of Gaul adopted the ways of life of their masters. There is no evidence in the writings of Sidonius that Christian asceticism had yet begun to cast its shadow over Gallic life.

Custom continued to oppose formal gymnastic and play activities for women, although they were often spectators of public events in the imperial period. Girls occasionally played ball and danced. The public baths were open to them, and mixed bathing, while generally officially opposed, was at times permitted.

As wealth and luxuries increased, Romans became more concerned about their health, to which, they felt, exercise and diet contributed. Roman writers frequently offered advice on the rules of health. The earlier opposition to Greek physicians disappeared in time, and medicine became a lucrative and honored profession. Augustus exempted physicians in Rome from taxes, and later emperors extended this privilege to provincial physicians. Public, city physicians, paid by the cities, were common from the second century onward. Medical schools were established in many cities and were encouraged by local authorities. As a science, however, medicine made but little advance in the Graeco-Roman world, although Hippocrates, Galen, Celsus and a few others had laid the basis of such a science. Old superstitions stood in the way of progress, and Christians, with their reliance upon miracles, retarded further the emergence of a scientific study of disease.

Because they were unable to assimilate fully the ideal of a liberal education as they found it in the Hellenistic world, and because of their acquired enthusiasm for intellectual culture, which they long lacked, Romans neglected the education of the body in their schools.

While they established many *gymnasia* and *palaestrae*, these had no connection with the schools.[90] Public and private athletic contests, and gladiatorial combats, for which gladiators were trained in special schools supported by the nobility or public treasury, satisfied the public thirst for amusement, if not for the blood of dying gladiators.[91] Nero required noble youths to engage in contests in the arena and in Greek games, and he inaugurated national games similar to the Olympic games, but all of these practices ended with his death. Under Gordian the Third, in A.D. 240, the national games were reintroduced.[92] The grammar and rhetorical schools, however, remained indifferent to the education of the body. Thus Roman neglect and, after it, Christian mediaeval thought destroyed the Greek tradition of physical education for centuries.

The views of Roman educational philosophers were not entirely in accord with school practices. Cicero (140-43 B.C.) in his *De Finibus Bonorum et Malorum*[93] recognized man's natural craving for activity, but he viewed bodily activity as less gratifying and excellent than mental activity. Physical exercise, he held, should have as its goal health and strength—a utilitarian goal—not pleasure. In his *De Oratore*[94] and his *Tusculan Disputations*[95] he showed himself sympathetic with Spartan physical discipline. In his *Laws* he recognized the value of public, athletic games, but he condemned, in his *Republic*, the Greek system of public, athletic exhibitions. The perfect orator ought, however, to be of athletic appearance, and his gestures ought to be manly.[96]

Quintilian (*c.* 35-*c.* A.D. 95), the chief exclusively educational theorist of Rome, agreed, in the main, with Cicero. While he admitted the educational value of dancing, it was for him fit only for children.[97] He finds in Greek authors some justification for gymnastics in the training of the orator, but oratorical gestures should not be inspired by the dance. The extreme training of gymnasts should always be avoided.[98] But whether we turn to Cicero and Quintilian, or to Roman moralists, such as Seneca,[99] we find what was the

[90] Johnston, *op. cit.*, pp. 65–66.

[91] *Ibid.*, pp. 215–77.

[92] *C.A.H.*, X, 717–18.

[93] (Trans. H. Rackham; London: Heinemann, 1914), V, 11 *passim.*

[94] (Trans. E. W. Sutton and H. Rackham; Cambridge, Mass.: Harvard University Press, 1942), III, 59.

[95] (Trans. J. E. King; London: Heinemann, 1927), V, 27.

[96] *De Oratore*, III, 59.

[97] Butler, *op. cit.*, I, 191.

[98] *Ibid.*, 3, 10; II, 8, 14.

[99] See R. M. Gummere (trans.), *Epistulae Morales* (London: Heinemann, 1917–25).

predominant Roman view that the mind is more important than the body. The moral degeneracy that came to afflict Rome was seen by some as associated with athletics, Greek gymnastics, and the cult of the body,[100] and that view may have influenced the practice of the schools.

If a liberal education is to be defined (and some think it should be) as the education of the freeman-citizen for a useful social life, as well as for his own growth and happiness, and, if the health of the body is essential to that end, then the schools of Rome, in their neglect of physical education, did not provide a truly liberal education for Roman youth.

Education in the Periods of Hellenization and Decline

HELLENIZED PERIOD. The literary and rhetorical tradition, which had grown up slowly during the Transition Period, became fixed and formalized in the Hellenized Period. While many older practices, such as home training in morals, tutorial instruction, and some aspects of apprenticeship training continued here and there, and while some writers, such as Tacitus, looked back longingly to the old education, literary and rhetorical education had passed from the home to the school,[101] and the moulding of the orator had become the sole aim of school training. Quintilian argued in favor of the school as against home and tutorial plans of instruction.[102] Grammarians, rhetoricians, and their schools increased rapidly in number, and education gradually became bookish, artificial and formal, although it was still related to social and political needs, for society, under the early emperors, retained its republican characteristics, and in it the orator continued to perform his traditional functions.

During the period, the demand for literary education reached its height. Great crowds then rushed to hear a great orator, as they do today to hear a great singer or a great preacher.[103] Outside of the schools, a strong national spirit developed, interest in Latin literature grew, and a reaction against Greek influence appeared. The schools, also, tended to become more national in their literary emphasis. But the method of the schools and the themes upon which students wrote and declaimed became more and more formal and less and less related to life.[104] The subjects upon which boys wrote and declaimed in school were ceasing to be the subjects with

100 Woody, *op. cit.*, pp. 658–59.
101 Monroe, *op. cit.*, pp. 361 ff.
102 Butler, *op. cit.*, I, 39 ff.
103 Dill, *op. cit.*, p. 425.
104 Monroe, *op. cit.*, pp. 416–17.

which statesmen and lawyers were actually concerned. If we can accept the views of Tacitus and Juvenal, even moral education was now much neglected. When the period ended, life and the school were at the parting of the ways.

THE PERIOD OF DECLINE. (1) FORMALISM. In this period, rhetoric became an end in itself, for, with the growing autocracy of the emperors, it gradually lost its earlier usefulness. The decline in the value of rhetorical education followed the imperial decline and was hastened by the growing despotism of the emperors who made men of learning their puppets and favored servants who no longer found inspiration in reality. The sword took the place of oratory in pointing out to men their course of action. Imperial laws, the voice of despots, at times imposed upon men by force, replaced the eloquent and persuasive voice of the orator. The old institutionalized practices survived, however, by the force of tradition, and because of the fact that rhetorical education had become a distinguishing mark of the nobility. As the period progressed, the old studies were pursued for their purely cultural values and for the personal pleasure and prestige that literary accomplishments brought to gentlemen, and sometimes ladies, of rank, wealth, and leisure. Schoolboys now debated themes far removed from the actualities of life. Freedom of speech was dead for rhetor and student alike. The tendency of the earlier period to stress the form rather than the content of education now became a fixed characteristic of the schools. Linguistic niceties for their own sake, or at best for the sake of personal polish and agreeableness, became the goal of education. The old stern moral training which was considered so important in the earlier periods, and for which the home long held itself responsible, was now intrusted to schoolmasters, of whom some were utterly corrupt, and under whom boys learned morals by reading didactic fables and by writing and delivering flowery orations on moral subjects. This was a poor substitute for the old practice, for it lacked a living example of sound morality. Christian education was a protest against this defect in the pagan system.[105]

(2) CHANGING ORGANIZATION. Toward the end of this period, the *ludus,* which traditionally admitted children of the lower classes, seems to have largely disappeared, and the work formerly assigned to the *litterator* passed gradually into the hands of the *grammaticus* and his assistant, the *primus magister.* In the Theodosian Code (A.D. 438), elementary masters are not mentioned. The practice of employing private tutors, common among the nobility, and the

105 Haarhoff, *op. cit.,* pp. 201–5.

growing servitude of the lower classes account, no doubt in large measure, for this change. At a very early age, usually at five, but frequently in infancy, boys were placed in charge of tutors who prepared them for the grammar school. At fourteen, they left the grammar school and entered that of rhetoric, which they left not later than the age of twenty.[106] Though he might never publicly practise his art, the Roman gentleman still wanted to become an orator.

(3) Rise of State Support and Control. Plato and Aristotle advocated, what was a practice in Sparta and some other Greek states, the control of education by the state and for the state, and Roman emperors saw the wisdom in that practice and theory. The decline of the old private system had its beginning in the philanthropic efforts of public-spirited men to encourage education in their communities. Under the first Caesar, who granted citizenship as an attraction to all teachers of the liberal arts, there were twenty publicly-subsidized schools in Rome. Succeeding emperors—Vespasian, Hadrian, the Antonines, Alexander Severus, and Constantine—adopted the policy of paying the salaries of Greek and Latin rhetoricians in Rome and the provinces. Augustus, when he expelled foreigners from Rome, exempted teachers and physicians from the ban. Trajan founded libraries, and Hadrian was lavish in his support of teachers and schools in the empire. Nerva, Trajan and Antoninus Pius founded institutions for poor children. The last fixed the number of teachers for cities, and would aid cities in paying their salaries. Diocletian fixed the salaries of teachers to be paid, apparently, by the cities. Constantine bestowed many favors upon public teachers and their families, relieving them from taxes and other burdens.

Benevolence opened the door to control. Julian (363) forbade the teaching of grammar and rhetoric by Christian teachers; Theodosius and Valentinian (425) forbade the opening of schools without their permission; and Justinian, a pillar of Christian orthodoxy, forbade (529) the teaching of philosophy in Athens (thus ending the famous pagan "university") and of law except in three cities, including Rome. Justinian's decree was an important step in the rise of ecclesiastical control of education in Europe. Thus did Rome depart from her ancient private scheme of instruction, and set patterns of support and control of education which have been followed in modern Europe and America and, more recently, in the rest of the world. And political experience and expediency were evidently the most determining motives in the development.

106 *Ibid.*, pp. 104–6; Woody, *op. cit.*, pp. 613 f.

(4) PAGAN ANTECEDENTS OF CHRISTIAN EDUCATION. The most Roman section of the empire in the fifth and sixth centuries was Gaul. Here the sun of pagan culture declined and set in the sky of the ancient world, but it bequeathed some of its light to the night of the Middle Ages and, in the Renaissance, it rose again. The Greeks established a colony and schools at Marseilles as early, probably, as 600 B.C., and the Hellenic educational tradition was strong here at the time of the Roman conquest.[107] There were, also, many other schools of Gallic rhetoric in Gaul when the Romans came. It was not until the fourth century A.D. that the Latin language and literature replaced the Gallic. In Roman times, there were famous schools at Marseilles, Autun, Trèves, Lyons, Arles, Auvergne, Vienne, Toulouse, Poitiers, Narbonne, and Bordeaux, that of Bordeaux being the foremost rhetorical school in the empire and one deserving to be called a university.[108]

In the universities of the greater cities, such as Rome and Constantinople, there were departments of grammar, rhetoric, philosophy, and law. Philosophy, however, had declined everywhere in the empire, except in Athens; and, in the schools of Gaul, Plato's great science of dialectic had fallen to the level of formal logic or had become a hunting-ground for rhetorical imagery. Science, the sister of philosophy, was never cultivated in Rome, except in a most superficial way; nor did it fare better in the schools of Gaul. In many Gallic schools, law was taught, but probably not thoroughly, for provincial students often went to Rome for their legal training, and Justinian appointed lawyers to "stations" in the empire for the purpose of offering a five-year course in law.[109] At Bordeaux, and probably elsewhere in Gaul, there was offered instruction in medicine,[110] but that science was not yet divorced from astrology. Physicians, however, enjoyed all the privileges of teachers in the empire. The whole science of the period was a jumble of inaccuracies, as is evident from the treatise of Martianus Capella on the liberal arts which had an extraordinary vogue in the Middle Ages. At no time were the liberal arts anything but a privilege of the few.

Thus the curriculum of the last schools of heathendom was confined almost entirely to a study of grammar and rhetoric, a tradition which long prevailed in the secondary and higher schools of Europe. But Roman students were trained to be slavish imitators of literary models, and not creators of literature. These models be-

[107] Dill, *op. cit.,* pp. 406–7.
[108] *Ibid.,* pp. 167, 409–10; Haarhoff, *op. cit.,* pp. 68–89.
[109] Haarhoff, *op. cit.,* pp. 80–86.
[110] *Ibid.,* pp. 87–88.

came intellectual despots, to whose authority students submitted, as they did to that of their imperial despots. Eminent Greek and Latin grammarians and rhetoricians carried on, until the close of the pagan world, the literary tradition which Greece bequeathed to Rome, and, within the narrow and formal intellectual circle in which they moved, they did thorough work. With the decline of paganism, the schools of Gaul and of the whole empire were slowly transformed by Christian influence. It was a very slow process of transformation and, in the process, the Graeco-Roman, or pagan, educational ideals and practices blended, to a degree, with the Christian. Christendom thus inherited the literary tradition and ideals of heathendom, although that tradition was weakened by the asceticism of the Middle Ages, when religious hymns, the Scriptures, and the writings of the Church Fathers supplemented, in the curriculum, the few safe pagan authors, such as Virgil, who continued to enjoy some measure of popularity. The despotism of Roman emperors, and of Roman and Christian literary models, which were worshiped too well, conspired to destroy the free, critical spirit of Hellas, and thus dimmed for centuries "the glory that was Greece."

Selected Readings

Blümner, H. *The Home Life of the Ancient Greeks.* London: Cassell & Co., Ltd., 1895.

Burnet, J. *Aristotle on Education.* London: Cambridge University Press, 1903.

Capes, W. W. *University Life in Ancient Athens.* New York: Harper & Bros., 1877.

Clark, D. L. *Rhetoric in Graeco-Roman Education.* New York: Columbia University Press, 1957.

Cole, P. R. *Later Roman Education.* New York: Teachers College, Columbia University, 1909.

Dill, S. *Roman Society in the Last Century of the Western Empire.* London: Macmillan & Co., Ltd., 1898.

Dobson, J. F. *Ancient Education and Its Meaning to Us.* New York: Longmans, Green & Co., Inc., 1932.

Forbes, C. A. *Greek Physical Education.* New York: Appleton-Century-Crofts, Inc., 1929.

Freeman, K. J. *Schools of Hellas.* London: Macmillan & Co., Ltd., 1912.

Gulick, C. B. *Life of the Ancient Greeks.* New York: Appleton-Century-Crofts, Inc., 1905.

Gwynn, A. *Roman Education from Cicero to Quintilian.* London: Clarendon Press, 1926.

Haarhoff, T. *Schools of Gaul.* London: Oxford University Press, 1920.

Hyde, W. W. *Olympic Victor Monuments and Greek Athletic Art.* Washington, D.C.: Carnegie Institution, 1921.

Jaeger, W. W. *Paideia: The Ideals of Greek Culture.* 3 vols.; New York: Oxford University Press, 1939–44.

McDaniel, W. B. *Roman Private Life and Its Survivals.* Boston: Jones, 1924.

Monroe, P. *Source Book of the History of Education for the Greek and Roman Period.* New York: The Macmillan Co., 1919.

RIDINGTON, W. R. *The Minoan-Mycenaean Background of Greek Athletics.* Ph.D. thesis, University of Pennsylvania, 1935.

WALDEN, J. W. H. *The Universities of Ancient Greece.* London: Routledge & Kegan Paul, Ltd., 1912.

WOODY, T. *Liberal Education for Free Men.* Philadelphia: University of Pennsylvania Press, 1951.

———. *Life and Education in Early Societies.* New York: The Macmillan Co., 1949.

6 Christian Society and Education to the End of the Middle Ages

No exact date can be assigned to the beginning of the so-called Middle Ages and the emergence of mediaeval institutions, since Christian society came to its triumph gradually in the slow disintegration of the Roman empire, but it is safe to say that the Western part of the empire was but a fiction after the last Western emperor, Romulus Augustulus, was deposed in 476. A strong case can be made for the date A.D. 330 (the date of the founding of Constantinople as the capital of the Eastern empire) as the beginning of the Middle Ages, and for the date A.D. 1453, when the Eastern (Byzantine) empire fell to the Ottoman Turks, as the end of the mediaeval period.

To preserve the unity of the Christian story we shall deal not only with developments in the Middle Ages proper but also with those of the Early Christian Period, when the Western church rose to power over the ruins of the Western Roman empire. With that event Europe entered its Dark Ages, extending roughly from A.D. 500 to 1000. There followed the period usually referred to as the Later Middle Ages, when a social and intellectual restoration occurred. On the educational side, this restoration brought, among other things, the rise of universities.

A. The Social and Cultural Scene

The early expanding Roman empire succeeded fairly well in absorbing and Romanizing all conquered people, except the Jews, who retained their feelings of religious and national isolationism.

In examining the development of Christian society and education, the overlapping of cultures should be kept in mind. At least as early as A.D. 50 Christianity had entered Rome. It was the last important religion to enter the early empire. Of purely Oriental origin, it was an enemy of the materialism and secularism of the Graeco-Roman world. It was an offshoot of Judaism from which it drew many of its ideals and practices. Yet Greek influence upon it was also significant. When it arose there were four Jewish groups in Palestine—the Sadducees, strict adherents of the written law, the Pharisees, who held that oral tradition was also important, the Essenes, a very ascetical Pharisaical sect who emphasized the immortality of the soul, and believed in predestination, and the Qumran sect, apparently closely related to the Essenes, the beliefs of which are now coming to light. The recently (1947) discovered "Dead Sea Scrolls," presumably genuine, are the Scriptures of this last group and show some interesting parallels with the Christian Gospels.[1]

While Judaism is the chief root of Christianity, other Oriental cults and particularly the mystery-religions also influenced it profoundly, especially in the beliefs in immortality and otherworldliness. The important doctrines of the fatherhood of God and the brotherhood of man were, however, unknown to or ignored by the mystery-cults. We shall see later how historical Christianity was indebted to pagan philosophies as well as to earlier religions.[2]

The Teachings of Jesus and Christian Ideals

The New Testament and a few brief statements by pagan writers are our only sources of information about Jesus and early Christianity. While Jesus' message was brief, simple, direct and easy to understand, Paul, "the apostle of the Gentiles," and, afterwards, the theologians built it into the complicated system of thought and belief which has been known as Christianity.

There is much disagreement regarding the teachings of Jesus, especially as distinguished from those of Paul. For instance, some scholars hold that the doctrines of original sin and grace, a "gift"

[1] M. Burrows, *The Dead Sea Scrolls* (New York: The Viking Press, Inc., 1955), pp. 326 ff.

[2] J. B. Bury, *et al.*, *Cambridge Ancient History (C.A.H.)* (New York: The Macmillan Co., 1923–39), III, 488–98; J. A. Montgomery, *Religions of the Past and Present* (Philadelphia: J. B. Lippincott Co., 1918), pp. 254–55, 376–97; A. H. Sayce, *The Religion of Ancient Egypt* (2d ed.; Edinburgh: Clark, 1913), pp. 47–49, 229–50; W. W. Hyde, *Paganism to Christianity in the Roman Empire* (Philadelphia: University of Pennsylvania Press, 1946), pp. 46-108; S. Angus, *The Mystery-Religions and Christianity* (New York: Charles Scribner's Sons, 1925).

of God which no man could merit by his own works—doctrines that affected education for centuries—were added by Paul.[3] In regard to a number of doctrines, however, there is little or no dispute. Among these are the fatherhood of God and the brotherhood of man. Paul stressed the latter in his effort to make Christianity a universal faith, the religion of Jew and Gentile, Greek and barbarian, slave and free. Here was the beginning of a dream of a universal Christian democracy, which has remained a dream. These two basic doctrines of Jesus are to be found in the thought of Eastern reformers from the fourteenth century B.C. onward. Akhenaton, Buddha, Krishna, Zoroaster, Confucius, Lao-tse and Asoka taught similar doctrines.[4] Even among Homeric Greeks, Zeus was a "Father" god, but the concept of the brotherhood of man was foreign to Greek thought and practice. The idea of a universal state and culture, however, found its way into Greek thought, particularly Stoicism, in the Hellenistic age, and the Macedonian and Roman empires were approaches to the attainment of a universal ideal, dictated, no doubt, by political motives.

The "Golden Rule," found long before in the thought of the Far and Near East, was the basic ethical doctrine of Jesus, who rejected the Mosaic principle of "an eye for an eye and a tooth for a tooth," and called upon men to love one another as children of a loving Father God. From such a principle it would be reasonable to infer that he opposed war, but some doubt exists as to what his actual teaching about war was.[5]

His basic economic doctrine was that wealth is the root of spiritual evil and that the rich would find it difficult to enter into the kingdom of heaven. What he meant by the "kingdom of heaven" or "kingdom of God," and where it was to be, became a topic of much debate and uncertainty, but the church came to view it as an otherworldly kingdom in the hereafter, and thus the idea of otherworldliness gained a firm hold upon the Christian mind, as it had also upon the pagan mind from the third century B.C. onward.

Many of the social and ethical ideals of Jesus found expression in the "Sermon on the Mount." His appeal for their observance was not to the mind but to the hearts of men. These ideals were to him more important than written law, synagogue or state. In the state he showed little, if any, interest. To many of the Jews, several of whose customs, including some rules of Sabbath worship, he

[3] Hyde, *op. cit.*, pp. 159 ff.

[4] H. M. Woodward, *Humanity's Greatest Need* (New York: G. P. Putnam's Sons, 1932), chap. i.

[5] Hyde, *op. cit.*, p. 149.

ignored, he was a subversive. Yet he came, as he said, not to destroy the Law but to fulfill it, a statement which seems to imply that he did not intend to found a new religion. He remained to the end a devout, though rebellious, Jew who declared himself to be the Messiah. And Paul proclaimed him to be a Savior-God who, unlike other savior-gods, deliberately sacrificed himself for man's redemption.

Institutionalized, Historical Christianity

While disputes have raged between Catholics, Protestants and lay scholars regarding the rôle of Jesus in the founding of a church,[6] there emerged a Christian church and, with its growth, many doctrines and ceremonies which, apparently, were unknown to Jesus and Paul. The causes of the triumph of Christianity over competing religions in the Roman empire have produced many interesting speculations. It was but one of many salvationist religions there, and yet, after a long struggle, it was made, in 380, the official and sole faith of the state, the church thus becoming a state-church. While it was a personal religion promising men eternal salvation as a reward of faith, hope, charity and holiness, it was also, but to a lesser degree, a religion of social reform, as was the religion of the Hebrew prophets. It made a strong emotional appeal to the poor and oppressed who were attracted by the promise of a heaven, where men never hunger or thirst, although it promised them few comforts here and recognized Caesar's right to his taxes. The fact that early Christianity was a lower-class movement explains, to a great degree, its rapid early spread. Yet neither Jesus nor Paul considered slavery wrong, and church institutions came in time to possess slaves.[7]

Manumission, common among Roman pagans, came, however, to be considered a good work by Christians and, after Constantine's time, the church, with gifts from private and state sources, took over nearly all works of charity. Something had to be done for the poor who would "always be with us." To the promise of salvation there was thus added the promise of bread. But the millennium and an earthly "kingdom of heaven" remained in the distant future.

Paul, with all his zeal to promote the new faith and with his belief in the spiritual equality of all men and women, was socially and politically conservative, and his was essentially an otherworldly scheme of salvation. It is hard to understand why this man, who

[6] *Ibid.*, pp. 161–62.

[7] J. Burckhardt, *The Age of Constantine the Great* (trans. M. Hadas; London: Routledge and Kegan Paul, Ltd., 1949), p. 320.

declared that all men were one in Christ, should not have warred upon political systems which divided men and kept many in bondage. Tyrannical governments for centuries found their justification in his famous political dictum: "The powers that be are ordained of God, . . . and they that resist shall receive to themselves damnation." And the subjugation of women for centuries found justification in his ascetical views on sex and marriage.

In examining Christian social theory and practice, age-old questions arise. Must the church, for instance, concern itself only with men's souls and stand aloof from social problems, rendering to Caesar the things that are Caesar's? If it observes the teachings of the New Testament, can it be an agent of political reform, and can there be a truly Christian state? Whatever the correct answers may be, this is an historical fact: Institutionalized Christianity has identified itself with almost every conceivable social institution and practice—imperialism, feudalism, monarchism, democracy, slavery, war, persecution, humanism, humanitarianism, etc. Institutionalized Christianity defies definition. Early Christianity was, however, a protest against what were deemed the evil ways of the world. In politically corrupt Rome it seemed to many to offer the promise of a new state and a better society. When at last it came to power amid the ruins of the Roman empire, the result in part of Christian otherworldliness and the spread of other Oriental salvationist cults and beliefs,[8] it too fell into the ways of the world, and social evils continued in the Christian's so-called "vale of tears." Officially the church has held that man is responsible for all evil, while good always finds its source in God and the divine church.

The Church and the State

One of the conditions which made it possible for Christianity to triumph in Rome was the unity and political organization of the empire. Here we had a union of many peoples in which local cultural prejudices had been softened by membership in one state, with an efficient machinery of communication, and in which Latin and Greek were widely understood languages. The Roman empire, because it was polytheistic, was very tolerant of all religions. Yet, there was a state-religion, and all were expected to burn incense at the statue of the emperor, an act somewhat akin to saluting national flags today. The Christians, like the Jews, refused to do so, to participate in official political and military celebrations, to volunteer

[8] J. L. LaMonte, *The World of the Middle Ages* (New York: Appleton-Century-Crofts, Inc., 1949), p. 18.

for military service, or to participate in many other popular activities.[9] Moreover, their meetings were secret, and the government feared secret societies.

They were intolerant of all other cults, as they were of that of the state, and they aroused the hostility of merchants who traded with the temples by attacking the sale of religious objects and sacrificial animals. They were thus deemed officially and popularly to be "bad citizens," the result being a series of persecutions beginning with that under Nero, in the first century, and ending with that under Diocletian, in the fourth. No accurate information about the number of victims exists. When the last one occurred, the Christians, according to careful authorities, numbered about 1/15 of the population of the Western part of the empire and about 1/10 of that of the Eastern part.

The persecutions did not stop the expansion of Christianity, and "the blood of martyrs" may, in the words of Tertullian (late second century), have "become seed." A few years after the abdication of Diocletian (305), Galerius issued an "Edict of Toleration" (311), which was followed (313) by a similar proclamation, or act of official policy, by Constantine and Licinius, and known as the "Edict of Milan." Christianity thus became one of the "lawful" religions, and Christians could henceforth openly profess their faith.

The emperor Constantine the Great (306-337) was gradually converted to Christianity (312-337) and was the first of the Christian emperors. It is widely thought that his motive was political, although he seems to have become a devout Christian. However, he continued to support the state-cult, and retained, as did other later Christian emperors, the pagan priestly title of *pontifex maximus*. Because of his many reprehensible acts, Burckhardt could say that Christians would have nothing to lose, nor pagans anything to gain, by renouncing him.[10]

A temporary withdrawal of official approval of Christianity occurred in the reign of "Julian the Apostate" (361-363), but its final triumph came in 380 and 381, when Catholic Christianity and the dogmas of the Nicene Creed (325) were imposed by imperial edicts upon all the people of the empire, East and West. Paganism, however, continued to struggle against it, though feebly, for at least another century.

Without the church, the triumph could not have been achieved. The opposing faiths had no such well-knit organization. It evolved

[9] F. J. C. Hearnshaw, *Mediaeval Contributions to Modern Civilisation* (London: George G. Harrap & Co., Ltd., 1921), pp. 24–25.

[10] *Op. cit.*, pp. 283 ff.; Hyde, *op. cit.*, p. 194.

slowly, its officials, from the second century, gradually becoming a well-ordered hierarchy. By the end of the fifth century, bishops were elected by the clergy, not by the people. In the evolution of the church, councils emerged and acquired power to enact church laws and formulate creeds, bishops of larger "sees" having great influence in council decisions. Out of doctrinal disputes and political jealousies a split between the Eastern and Western churches which began in 344, when the Eastern bishops excommunicated Pope Julius I, culminated in the final rift, "The Great Schism," in 1054, when the Pope and the Patriarch of Constantinople exchanged excommunications. The Eastern, or Greek Orthodox church became the state-church of the Byzantine empire, as did the Roman church of the Western empire.

In the sixth century the Eastern emperor, Justinian, said that God created both church and state, but made the state the directing power, even in religion. The Orthodox church accepted and practised that policy, until the acts of Soviet Russia led to dissension between the state and the most important (the Russian) subdivision of the church. The Western church, however, took over state functions, became, indeed a state—an empire within an empire—and proclaimed its power even in secular, temporal affairs to be supreme. The Orthodox church has been ruled not from one but from four patriarchal centers, each directed by its own synod, and the services are conducted in the thirteen different languages of its subdivisions. In the West, on the contrary, all national branches of the church were brought under the rule of the pope, and Latin has been made, since the end of the third century, when the Western empire became Latinized, the official language of the church and its services, a fact of cultural and educational significance. In 1955, the pope permitted a mass to be conducted in English in Uniontown, Pennsylvania, another evidence of the inevitability of change, but it was Protestantism and nationalism that restored national languages to a state of dignity in the religious life of the West.

When wedded to the Roman empire, the church, "the Empire baptized,"[11] used the state to enforce orthodoxy. The state, thus, suffered politically by becoming involved in theological disputes, and the church morally by using its political power to convert pagans by coercion.[12] Did not Jesus ask his followers to love their

[11] A. C. Flick, *The Rise of the Mediaeval Church* (New York: G. P. Putnam's Sons, 1909), p. 148.

[12] M. Deanesly, *History of the Mediaeval Church* (London: Methuen & Co., Ltd., 1925), pp. 63–64; E. M. Hulme, *The Middle Ages* (New York: Henry Holt & Co., Inc., 1929), pp. 670–75; F. Lot, *The End of the Ancient World* (New York: Alfred A. Knopf, Inc., 1931), pp. 50–52.

enemies? Christians learned to hate them. The death penalty for heresy was officially sanctioned by the church, Pope Leo the Great in the fifth century being the first pope to endorse it.[13]

From the fall of Rome until the twelfth century, the Charlemagne régime excepted, the domination of the state by the church was almost complete. The "City of God" had triumphed over the city of Satan, and the bishops of Rome wielded the power of fallen or absent emperors. All this was justified by St. Augustine, the most influential of the Church Fathers, who, in his famous work, *Of the City of God*, viewed all history as a struggle between two hostile societies, the divine church, whose end is to be finally realized in heaven, and the earthly city of the world that has no end beyond itself and the achievement of temporal glory. He did not condemn the state, as such, but assigned to it the rôle of servant of the church in its work of suppressing crime and saving souls. The ancient theocratic doctrine of rule by divine right was taken over by the mediaeval church and, later, by European kings to justify their claims to autocratic power. In exercising their power of divine rule, many quite zealous churchmen acted in a very earthly fashion and invited attack even by devout Christians. But they also did much to end such practices as gladiatorial combats and the abandoning of infants; and they promoted charity toward the sick and poor. But to "heretics" they showed no charity. Government by God, through his human representatives, was in time, and for many reasons, to be replaced by popular, secular government.

While the status of the mediaeval church in relation to the state changed from time to time and from place to place, and while the papacy and local bishops were occasionally forced to submit to political interference, as monarchs were to papal interference, the great power of the church looms large in the total picture. It had its own civil and criminal courts, dungeons and gibbets. Its courts had wider powers than those of lay princes. It owned one-quarter of the land of Europe, and the state could not tax it. It determined the basis of economic life. It controlled all charity. Above all, it controlled ideas through its control of education, one of those ideas being that of the supremacy of church power.[14]

13 H. J. Muller, *Uses of the Past* (New York: Oxford University Press, 1952), p. 186.

14 F. J. C. Hearnshaw, *The Social and Political Ideas of Some Great Mediaeval Thinkers* (New York: Henry Holt & Co., Inc., 1923), pp. 14–16; C. H. McIlwain, *The Growth of Political Thought in the West* (New York: The Macmillan Co., 1932), p. 206; G. G. Coulton, *The Mediaeval Village* (London: Cambridge University Press, 1931), pp. 189–91, 248–49.

The acts of men should perhaps be judged by the standards of their time. Many acts of mediaeval churchmen are reprehensible as judged by modern standards of conduct. Catholic writers take the position that the church cannot be held responsible for such acts of churchmen. This question of an institution's responsibility for the conduct of its members is an interesting academic and highly controversial one. Can a church, a nation, a school or any other institution do wrong? Can it logically claim credit for the good its members do while, at the same time, it refuses to accept responsibility for their evil acts? These are questions to be answered by moral philosophers and theologians rather than by historians whose primary concern, as scientists, is to assemble and narrate facts, although, as men, they, too, may evaluate and moralize.

From the twelfth century onward, modern national states slowly emerged, and the power of the church declined. Since the beginning of the nineteenth century, the secular state has, largely by education, controlled the lives of individuals for the glory and power of the state, as the church once did for its glory and power. But the tendency to secularize education in the interest of the modern state has created a serious concern in some people for the religious and moral education of children. That problem some states have solved in one way and some in another but, in no case, to everyone's satisfaction.

Pagan Philosophies and Christianity

As it spread, Christianity came into contact with the philosophies of the Graeco-Roman world. Unlike its competing religions, it had to its advantage a Book, the Old (older than the Roman empire) and the New Testaments, answering the problems of creation, the universe, life and the whole divine and human drama. It was hard for some philosophers to accept the story, which, with similar stories, they often called "superstitions." But Christian "Apologists," such as Clement and Origen of Alexandria, reconciled the Christian story with Greek philosophy, particularly that of Plato, as did Philo for the Jewish story.

Two centuries later, Augustine said that the Incarnation was the only Christian doctrine not mentioned by Plato.[15] The striking similarities between some Christian and some Stoic and Neo-Platonic doctrines suggest that reconciliation was easy to effect. Plotinus (205-270), the leading Neo-Platonist, was a mystic who

[15] Muller, *op. cit.*, p. 77.

saw all things as an emanation from God with the human soul being the highest thing in the order of created beings. Its entrance into earthly life was said to be a fall, and its passage from earth a resurrection. The Neo-Platonists were pagan ascetics, but they probably contributed much to Christian asceticism and monasticism. St. Augustine was strongly influenced by them.

The religion of Jesus and Paul was one of faith rather than reason, of the heart rather than the mind. To Jesus, the man who believed without seeing was more blessed than the man who had first to see. And to Paul, though debtor "both to the wise, and to the unwise," and who defined faith as "the evidence of things not seen," the wisdom of the world is foolishness and, without faith, man cannot be saved.

In the centuries to follow, reason and philosophy were suspect. One might compile a long list, running down the centuries, of Christian advocates of the principle that faith rather than reason is the key to knowledge, wisdom and salvation. In the second century, Tertullian summed up his faith in the famous words "I believe *because* it is absurd" (*impossible*), and St. Augustine said that man should accept nothing except on the authority of the Scriptures, the final authority on *all* questions.[16] For a long time indecision on the issue of faith *versus* reason marked the official thought of the Catholic church, but ultimately, as we shall see, the position of the Apologists came to be officially approved. The "foolishness" of the philosophers was found, even in the first Christian centuries, to be indispensable in the conversion of pagan intellectuals and in settling the numerous doctrinal issues which arose in the Christian community.

Thus, in contact with the world, Christianity, as a religion of faith, was changed, and the wise who were not to be called were called. Evidences of this intellectualizing movement, to mention only two of many, may be seen in St. John's Gospel where Jesus is identified with the Greek concept of the *Logos* or "Word," and in the profoundly philosophical language of the Nicene Creed (325) which, unlike the Sermon on the Mount, simple folks could not understand. Christian theology, with its many dogmas, resulted from this union of religion and philosophy, and Christian culture, with its universal ideal, became a divisive one, for not all could ac-

[16] E. E. Kellett and F. H. Marseille (trans.), *Monasticism—Its Ideals and History, and the Confessions of Augustine* (London: Williams and Norgate, Ltd., 1901), p. 123; S. H. Mellone, *Western Christian Thought in the Middle Ages* (Edinburgh: William Blackwood & Sons, Ltd., 1935), pp. 49–56.

cept the dogmas. The dogma of the Trinity, for instance, turned the Jews away, nor would Islam later accept such a doctrine. Even sincere, devout Christian theologians were, in consequence, often expelled from the kingdom of God. Variety of thought and disagreement on matters of belief became heretical and unthinkable. Man's reason was seen as a dangerous faculty, and the principle of "don't think" in religious matters became a law of heaven, as it threatens to become again in our own, even liberal, societies in matters of economics and politics. The early "Creeds," of which there were four,[17] represent a triumph of philosophy and reason in the struggle with faith, but reason suffered from its victory, since the dogmas of the creeds were made matters of faith which orthodox believers might no longer question. In the struggle to establish the dogmas of "the true faith," the authority of the church was finally accepted as the criterion of truth.

St. Augustine, while recognizing the infallibility of the Bible, proclaimed the church, not councils which sometimes erred, to be its authoritative interpreter. Luther, centuries later, could agree with Augustine on the infallibility of the Bible and on "salvation by faith," but rejected the doctrine of infallibility of councils or church, for which he substituted the doctrine of private interpretation of the Scriptures. For Catholics the issue was finally settled on July 18, 1870, when the Vatican Council proclaimed the dogma of the "Infallibility of the Pope" when he speaks *ex cathedra* on religious and moral questions. In the Catholic plan, councils are no longer necessary to decide doctrinal issues.

In the intellectual life of Christendom, the conflict between reason and faith has a central place. The Greek spirit of inquiry produced many "heresies" in early Christendom, and all questioning of "orthodox" thought since then has reflected that spirit. While the early Christian Fathers would use philosophy to "rob the Egyptians," they saw that in it lurked a threat to the faith, and Christian opposition to pagan literature and learning became marked in the third and fourth centuries. The *Apostolic Constitutions* (*c.* 254), addressed to clergy and laity, while not officially sanctioned, can, in the light of other evidence, be taken as an expression of the attitude of the church on the question. The following is a brief quotation from this document:

> Refrain from all the writings of the heathen; for what has thou to do with strange discourses, laws, or false prophets. . . . For if thou wilt explore history, thou hast the Book of Kings; or seekest thou for words of wisdom and

[17] Hyde, *op. cit.*, pp. 212–14.

eloquence, thou hast the Prophets, Job, and the Book of Proverbs, wherein thou shalt find a more perfect knowledge of all eloquence and wisdom for they are the voice of . . . the only wise God. Or dost thou long for tuneful strains, thou hast the Psalms, or to explore the origin of things, thou hast the Book of Genesis. . . . Wherefore, abstain scrupulously from all strange and devilish books.[18]

Tertullian and Augustine thought that divine studies were incompatible with the secular. St. John Chrysostom and St. Jerome warned Christians against the pursuit of pagan studies. The Fourth Council of Carthage (398) forbade the reading of secular books,[19] and Pope Gregory the Great (590-604) said that God's word does not need the aid of grammar. It has, however, been observed that the Latin Church Fathers denounced classical pagan literature in a classic style derived from their own study of it. Book burning originated in the reign of the Christian Emperor Theodosius the Great, and the famous library of Alexandria was, probably, destroyed by Christian zealots in 391.[20] Hypatia, the famous woman professor of philosophy at Alexandria, was brutally slain by a gang of monks in 415. But such hostility could not change the fact that God's word needed the aid of grammar in the work of "robbing the Egyptians," and "divine eloquence" needed the enrichment provided by "the filthy writings of pagan poets." [21]

Not only did pagan literature and philosophy suffer from Christian opposition, but science, already weakened by Roman indifference, also suffered a serious decline. The belief in the resurrection of the body made, for instance, the study of anatomy irreligious. The belief that God made the earth and that it would soon be destroyed checked man's interest in geology and geography. No science could thrive in an atmosphere where capricious supernatural powers were substituted for immutable laws as the causes of things. The period to the end of the Dark Ages was preeminently the Age of Faith. While this was due, in part, to Roman neglect of Greek science and to barbarian invasions and the disintegration of European society, it was due, in a marked degree, to the hostility of Christians to Graeco-Roman learning generally. The Christian mind was a believing mind. Its peaceful certainty was based upon faith, not upon reason or scientific discovery.

[18] J. B. Mullinger, *Schools of Charles the Great* (London: Longmans, Green & Co., Inc., 1877), p. 8.

[19] Hyde, *op. cit.*, p. 199.

[20] LaMonte, *op. cit.*, p. 200.

[21] H. Waddell, *The Wandering Scholars* (London: Constable & Co., Ltd., 1938), pp. xvii–xviii.

Against such a mind the philosopher and scientist were later forced to struggle.[22]

There is, however, a brighter side to this picture of intellectual decay. There were early Christians who were "transmitters" of ancient classical learning. Boethius, who in *The Consolation of Philosophy* attempted to reconcile Plato and Aristotle, also translated Greek books on some of the seven liberal arts. Aristotle's logic (*Organon*) was made known to Christendom chiefly through the work of Boethius, and he may well have been the instigator of the realist-nominalist controversy which we shall examine later.[23] Donatus (fourth century) and Priscian (fifth century) wrote Latin grammars in which they used many illustrations from the leading classical Roman authors and thus transmitted at least the names of those writers to the mediaeval world. And the monk Cassiodorus, himself a notable author and transmitter, influenced the Benedictine monks to undertake (*c.* 526) the copying of classical manuscripts, a work without which many classical books might have been lost. To this incomplete list of transmitters should be added the name of Isidore, Bishop of Seville (died 636), who, while not as learned as his predecessors, was the last important Christian transmitter of ancient secular learning to the West. His treatise on the seven liberal arts was a compendium of existing secular knowledge, and was long used as a textbook and authoritative reference work. That his hodge-podge of fact, fable, and superstition should have been then considered erudite is evidence of the decline in learning that had occurred in the West. Christianity, while against antiquity, was thus, in part, its preserver and transmitter.

There were some Christians who were creators rather than transmitters. Boethius should be placed among them, since he was more than a critic and translator. In poetry the Christian creator performed best, and the tone is sometimes secular, sometimes religious. The historical writing of the time was generally ecclesiastical, apologetic, and designed to edify—interest centering on the lives of saints and the triumph of Christianity over paganism. Eusebius, an Eastern writer of the fourth century, and Orosius, a Spaniard of the fifth century, were the chief historians of the early period. While Eusebius wrote secular history, his *Ecclesiastical History* was his

[22] A. D. White, *History of the Warfare of Science with Theology in Christendom* (New York: Appleton-Century-Crofts, Inc., 1896); J. W. Draper, *History of the Conflict between Religion and Science* (New York: Appleton-Century-Crofts, Inc., 1927).

[23] H. R. Patch, *The Tradition of Boethius* (New York: Oxford University Press, 1935), p. 31.

most influential work. Orosius wrote *Seven Books of History against the Pagans* to prove that God willed their destruction. Interest in the national history of the Goths and Franks appears in the works of Cassiodorus, Isidore and Gregory of Tours. With all these activities, however, the first three centuries of Christian cultural dominance were unproductive of significant original thought, except in the field of theology, a new field, and one which aroused as much interest then as, let us say, economics and communism do today.

From the time of the Charlemagne revival of learning, at the end of the eighth century, respect for learning gradually returned, and the tempo of progress increased rapidly as the Dark Ages came to a close (*c.* 1100). While individual, observational sciences were given a humble place in the scheme of knowledge as it was organized in the later Middle Ages, they were nevertheless recognized as the base of the structure. Above them stood philosophy, which included physics, mathematics and metaphysics as its theoretical parts, and logic, ethics and political science as its practical parts. Theology was placed at the apex of the structure. But with this recognition of the material world, there remained a fear of knowledge. Plato and Aristotle believed that a rational understanding of the causes and meaning of things was man's highest capacity and delight. When their civilization was dying, Greek thinkers viewed knowledge merely as a guide to a good life, as many moderns view science. There then appeared thinkers (*e.g.* Seneca of Rome) who thought it intemperate to know more than we need to know for the ends of life. This question interested later mediaeval thinkers. St. Thomas Aquinas (1225-1274) said that it is lawful to seek any kind of knowledge which helps man to save his soul and to glorify God. A century earlier, St. Bernard of Clairvaux had said that it was impious to seek knowledge merely for the sake of knowing.

The position generally accepted by the theologians was that there are things which Christians should not try to know and which God forbids them to know, things with which the devil could mislead them to their damnation. A legend had Gerbert, the distinguished teacher at the cathedral school of Rheims and later Pope Sylvester II, invent a mechanical figure which could speak and always speak the truth, but he misinterpreted one of its pronouncements, and died as a result.[24] The earlier Christian view that the visible world was but a revelation of its creator, and that all knowledge had to do with God, was modified by later theologians who viewed the created world as an independent object of investigation and knowable by sense perception and reason. This discovery of

[24] Mellone, *op. cit.*, pp. 35 f.; LaMonte, *op. cit.*, pp. 244 f.

Nature came in the twelfth and thirteenth centuries, but man might, apparently, still know too much about it. The devastating plague known as the Black Death (1348-1350) did something to dispel that belief. Some wondered how it was communicated from one to another, while most saw in it the work of devils and Jews, or a divine punishment of sin. It would seem that the motive of curing disease was historically the most potent factor leading man to an accurate observation of nature and of man. There were Christians who did not want to go to heaven prematurely, and were ready to find a way to extend their earthly sojourn. The progress made was in many ways a rediscovery of the intellectual life and interests of pagan antiquity in an age when social developments demanded a looking back to the wisdom of the past.

Christianity against the World: Monasticism

ORIGIN, EARLY DEVELOPMENT, AND IDEALS. The otherworldly tendencies of Christianity found concrete embodiment in monasticism, a movement in which, over an extended period, millions of Christian men and women fled from the world into monasteries where, by leading a life of asceticism, they hoped, in the words of Byron, "to merit heaven by making earth a hell." Asceticism was common in Eastern and Greek cults for centuries before Christian ascetics began to flee into the deserts of Egypt and Syria in the third century A.D.[25] Three different forms of asceticism can be identified: (1) the religious, largely Oriental, (2) the ethical, largely Greek but influenced by the Orient, and (3) the philosophical, which was essentially Graeco-Roman and which reached its fullest expression in Stoicism and Neo-Platonism. Christian asceticism, while influenced by all of these, was predominantly religious. In about a century the movement had spread throughout Eastern and Western Christendom. Gradually colonies of monks and nuns, or monasteries, emerged throughout the Roman empire, East and West. In the rural areas of the West, the monastery became the chief depaganizing agency at work among the heathen peasantry and, until the ninth century, the chief center of education. In missionary and educational work in the British Isles and on the Continent, the influence of Irish monks was all-important.

The first Egyptian monks were hermits who lived in caves.

[25] W. M. F. Petrie, *Personal Religion in Egypt before Christianity* (London: Harper & Bros., Ltd., 1909), p. 62; J. W. Swain, *The Hellenic Origins of Christian Asceticism* (Ph.D. thesis, Columbia University, 1916); A. Harnack, *Monasticism: Its Ideals and Its History* (trans. by C. R. Gillett; New York: The Christian Literature Company, 1895).

Anthony (252-357) lived in a tomb. Devils, sometimes in the form of naked women, tempted them. They practised excessive fasting, tortured their bodies and spurned all bodily comforts, including a bath. St. Simeon Stylites (died 459) stood for some thirty years on top of a pillar, went without food sometimes for months, never bathed, and permitted his excoriated flesh to be tortured by vermin and maggots. It is said that, at his death, he ascended into heaven in a great odor of sanctity.[26] The need to organize the increasing multitude of hermits was soon felt, and three Eastern saints, Basil, Anthony and Pachomius, drew up, in the fourth century, rules of community life for them, which substituted manual labor and prayer for extreme asceticism. Monasticism was introduced into the West at the end of the fourth century. Here, too, many monks, including St. Benedict (*c.* 480-543), practised rigid austerities. Benedict established, in 529, the monastery of Monte Cassino, near Naples, which became a model for thousands of others, and drew up his celebrated "Rule" for his monks there.

Among the causes of Christian monasticism were: (1) economic insecurity and the general decay of Roman society, (2) the secularization of the church, evident in the lives of many bishops steeped in worldly pomp, in the majestic grandeur of church buildings and ritual, and in the moral corruption of many of the Christian laity, especially the aristocrats, (3) the beliefs that life is evil, sin is real, the flesh is an enemy of the soul, and that salvation comes only as a reward of holiness and of avoidance of the things which the world calls good, and (4) the belief, not universal however, that the world would soon end.

The Christian ascetic, fearing hell, warred against the world, the flesh, and the devil, and tried to stifle every urge of his aesthetic nature. The ascetical ideal found embodiment in the vows of poverty, chastity and obedience, by which all monks renounced the chief bases of attachment to the world—property, family and personal freedom. Contempt for the state and secular society finds its clearest expression in these vows. In addition to these vows, the Benedictine Rule enjoined upon monks constant manual labor, to keep them from sin, and some reading, preferably sacred reading, each day.[27] It was this reading requirement that led to the copying of manuscripts and some intellectual activity. The attitude of monks, other than the Celtic, toward pagan literature was not, how-

[26] C. Kingsley, *The Hermits: Their Lives and Works* (London: Macmillan & Co., Ltd., 1890), pp. 170, 205.

[27] Deanesly, *op. cit.*, pp. 36–40; Hulme, *op. cit.*, p. 172; E. P. Cubberley, *Readings in the History of Education* (Boston: Houghton Mifflin Co., 1920), pp. 56–59.

ever, one of respect prior to Charlemagne's revival of learning, when it began to become less scornful.

By the twelfth century, asceticism was declining rapidly as a result, among other things, of changed social conditions, the supposed safety of the church, and the belief in the efficacy of the sacramental system as a means of salvation. By then, the church in the world and the church against the world had, generally, become alike in their worldliness. They could not avoid it. Thus in a feudal world, the church became feudal, and many feudal bishops and abbots lived as luxuriously as lay feudal noblemen. The kingdom of God has often found enchantment in the *gloria mundi.*

Despite "Rules," monastic life came to need reform. The reform movement, which placed all new monastic "orders" directly under the authority of the pope, began with the founding of the monastery of Cluny (910) and its exemption from local episcopal and lay control. There followed a system of Cluniac monasteries which followed the rules of the mother abbey. The Benedictine monasteries had no central abbot-general directing them, and each one led an independent life. A revised Benedictine Rule was adopted for the whole Cluniac system, with less emphasis upon manual labor and prayer and more upon singing, copying manuscripts and reading. Pagan literature was respectfully read by Cluniac monks. For two centuries, their schools were the best of monastic schools, although harsh corporal punishment of the boys was the practice in them. The Cluniacs were noted for their works of charity among the needy, but they became rich and, in competition with new orders, their work and prestige declined. Those of extreme ascetical tendencies now turned away from the cultured urbanity of Cluny, and founded the Carthusian "order" (1084), which came to have many branches, and the Cistercians (1098) which, by 1300, had some seven hundred branches. Both of these groups practised extreme asceticism, and the latter repudiated scholarship, even to the point of despising education, as did St. Bernard of Clairvaux (1090-1153), their most famous member.

In addition to these monastic orders, there were organized groups of secular clergy called cathedral canons who lived a community life under the rule of St. Augustine. They originated in Germany in the eighth century, but were few until the twelfth, when they spread throughout Europe. Among their duties was that of teaching in cathedral schools. Like monks proper, they took vows of poverty, chastity and obedience.

All of these groups secluded themselves from the world, to a greater or lesser degree, in order to save their souls. There was felt, however, a need for an order of monks given to a life of activity outside of the cloister, and the mendicant orders, the Dominicans and Franciscans, known as the Friars, and some seven or eight other groups were founded to meet that need. There are few who have not read of St. Francis of Assisi (1182-1226), founder of the Franciscans, the divinely mad mystic, lover of all living things, advocate of total poverty, and enemy of learning.[28]

St. Dominic (1170-1221), founder of the Dominicans, was a more practical man who demanded an educated clergy who, by preaching, could advance the Gospel and save Christians from the wiles of heretics, then becoming numerous. The Franciscans did not follow their founder in the matter of ownership of property. Both of these orders produced the leading theologians of the later Middle Ages (*e.g.* the Dominicans, Albert the Great and Thomas Aquinas; and the Franciscans, St. Bonaventura and Duns Scotus), and both were active in the work of universities.

EFFECTS OF MONASTICISM. Monasticism probably saved the church from complete secularization by stressing spiritual values. By aiding the distressed, it upheld Christian ideals. For a time, it set an excellent example of industry for the peasants and dignified manual toil but, after the tenth century, many monks preferred the choice of Mary to that of Martha.[29] While the monks helped to preserve ancient intellectual treasures, they were not friendly to the liberal education of the Graeco-Roman world. But they were the products as well as, in a degree, the moulders of a transition age in the history of the West.

Economic and Social Life

FEUDALISM. Mediaeval economic and social life was linked to feudalism. On its economic side, it originated in declining Rome; on its political side, it arose in the late eighth century because of the decay of central government and the insecurity of life and property. Under it, political power was, in theory, delegated by the king to subordinates, and sub-delegated from one to another of these through a hierarchy of nobles. In practice the state, under feudalism, lost its ancient prerogatives, and government was completely decentralized. In return for personal and military service, each overlord in the hierarchy bestowed great tracts of land upon his subordinate nobles. Roman political unity was thus at an end.

[28] H. O. Taylor, *The Mediaeval Mind* (London: Macmillan & Co., Ltd., 1938), Vol. I, chap. xviii.

[29] Coulton, *op. cit.*, pp. 208–22.

The story of the rise of nationalism is, largely, the story of the decline of feudalism.

THE ECONOMIC SYSTEM. The economy was agrarian; industry was domestic; and commerce, though never dead, was, until the twelfth century, poorly developed. Agriculture and war were the chief activities in which men engaged. The history of feudal society is a chronicle of war, barbarities, and anarchy from which the church tried, with some success, to rescue it through the "Truce of God," in the late tenth century.

SOCIAL CLASSES. There were three clearly defined groups in mediaeval society: the clergy, the nobility and the peasants. If we classify the higher clergy with the nobility, as some prefer to do, then there were only two classes, the nobility and the peasants. War was the profession of the lay nobility, ecclesiastics seldom bearing arms, though engaging others to do so. In time an hereditary caste system developed within the feudal hierarchy itself. The peasants, unorganized, impoverished and illiterate, were at the mercy of the aristocracy.

The peasantry comprised: (a) serfs bound to the soil, (b) semi-free *villeins*, or renters, and (c) slaves. St. Ambrose (340-397), St. Jerome (340-420), and other early Christians approved of slavery,[30] as did canon law.[31] Ambrose felt that slavery provided slaves with an excellent opportunity to practise the Christian virtues of humility and love of enemies.[32] In the sixth century, the Franks were forbidden by church decrees to kill their slaves, to sell them to distant purchasers, or to separate married couples. The souls of slaves were declared to be as precious as those of their masters in the eyes of God, and manumission was included among the works of piety.[33]

We should add here that Christians as a religious group never protested effectively against the institution of slavery. The Pennsylvania Quakers (1696) were the first sect to succeed in stopping slave-trade in any state. The institution of Sunday as a day of rest helped to lighten the burden of laborers. As a day of worship, Sunday gradually replaced the Jewish Sabbath from Paul's time onward. Tertullian advised Christians to abstain from labor on Sunday, the Lord's Day. In 321, Constantine the Great proclaimed Sunday as a day of rest for slaves. The "Day of the Sun" was long held sacred

30 S. Dill, *Roman Society in the Last Century of the Western Empire* (London: Macmillan & Co., Ltd., 1898), p. 161.

31 Coulton, *op. cit.*, pp. 166-72.

32 Muller, *op, cit.*, p. 188.

33 D. C. Munro and G. C. Sellery, *Mediaeval Civilization* (New York: Appleton-Century-Crofts, Inc., 1917), pp. 73–74.

by pagan solar cults, but Constantine's decree was the first law making it a day of rest. That law was enforced later by civil and church law, and the observance of Sunday as a day of worship and abstention from labor was made very stringent by Charlemagne in 788.[34]

Mediaeval thinkers found warrant for the social system of the period in Holy Writ, and in the writings of pagan philosophers. St. Thomas Aquinas, the Christian Aristotle of the thirteenth century, said that the state needs a stupid, brawny peasantry divided by distrust of one another.[35] For a long time, Christians felt that the caste system reflected the "will of God." The church and the monasteries acquiesced in the social injustices of the time. Under feudal bishops and abbots, as under lay lords, the serfs were degraded. Relatively few of humble birth were canonized. It was chiefly through the monastery that a poor boy had a chance to better his position, for the aristocracy had almost exclusive preference for high positions in the church in the world.

EMERGENCE OF THE BOURGEOISIE. Mediaeval life was essentially rural prior to the thirteenth century. There were towns, whose chief institutions were the gallows, the church, and the cemetery, "God's Acre." In these towns, there was always some industrial and commercial activity but, from the tenth century onward, there was an increase in that activity. Beginning with the twelfth century, the growth of cities in number and the increase of commercial activity in them were very rapid. Contact of Europeans with the East and the Muslim world was the chief cause of this revival.[36] Eyes of discontented and often rebellious peasants began to turn from the castle to the town, and to the towns the population began to drift, in spite of efforts to stop it. Great landowners became more humane, and an agrarian middle class appeared.

The cities, however, were the nurseries of the new bourgeois class, bankers, manufacturers, merchants—capitalists—men interested in wealth and power. A new Europe was emerging as a result of commerce. The old Europe was feudal, ecclesiastical, and agricultural; the new, bourgeois, lay, and commercial. The new burgher class, the Third Estate, worldly and lay in its interests, has played a leading rôle in destroying feudalism, converting Christian universalism into nationalism, and secularizing the world—for profit. Its political victory came in the democratic revolutions of the eighteenth century, and, against the growing power of the proletariat,

[34] Hyde, *op. cit.*, pp. 257 ff.

[35] Coulton, *op. cit.*, p. 253.

[36] R. A. Newhall, *The Crusades* (New York: Henry Holt & Co., Inc., 1927), chap. iii; Hulme, *op. cit.*, p. 490.

it recently turned to Fascism.[37] Out of political and economic urban developments came the worldly legal profession which substituted, for feudal law, Roman law, the first serious rival of the Scriptures in Christendom. This new profession was lay and bourgeois. Wealth and knowledge, weapons once almost entirely in the hands of the church, passed gradually into possession of the city bourgeoisie, and power eventually passed with them.

THE GILD SYSTEM AND INDUSTRIAL SERFDOM. With the revival of commerce came the organization of merchant and craft gilds to protect their members from unfair competition. Weavers, shoemakers, fishmongers, etc., were so organized, and each gild had its patron saint. These gilds became autocratic, and lower class workmen were barred from many privileges. To become a master craftsman, a boy, at about the age of thirteen, was apprenticed to a master for about seven years. Then, for more experience, he went from town to town as a "journeyman" artisan. Lastly, he presented his "masterpiece" to gild examiners, and, if it was considered of sufficient merit, he was enrolled as a gild member, and became himself a master over apprentices. The gilds, in time, tried to prevent men from becoming masters. Strikes of journeymen against the masters sometimes occurred, and the gild system was not as ideal as some writers would have us believe. Out of it came an urban social hierarchy, running through many levels from commercial magnates at the top to unskilled laborers at the bottom. Poverty and ignorance continued, and an industrial serfdom appeared.[38] Lower class workers were exploited by the gilds; riots occurred from 1250 onward, but ended, about 1400, in a victory for the industrial barons. But the struggle between the proletariat and the bourgeoisie had begun.[39]

WOMEN IN MEDIAEVAL SOCIETY. Christendom inherited various traditions in regard to women's nature and status. We have seen how they were treated in Greece and Rome. In later Hebrew society they lost an earlier independence which they once enjoyed.[40] Ancient German women held an inferior position, as the word *weib*,

[37] G. B. Adams, *Civilization during the Middle Ages* (New York: Charles Scribner's Sons, 1914), pp. 275–301; J. W. Thompson, *Economic and Social History of Europe in the Later Middle Ages* (New York: Appleton-Century-Crofts, Inc., 1931), pp. 126–79, 224–55.

[38] H. Pirenne, *Mediaeval Cities* (Princeton, N.J.: Princeton University Press, 1925), p. 160.

[39] C. H. Haskins, *Studies in Mediaeval Culture* (London: Clarendon Press, 1929), pp. 198 ff.; Thompson, *op. cit.*, pp. 396–414.

[40] T. Woody, *Life and Education in Early Societies* (New York: The Macmillan Co., 1949), pp. 96, 107 f.

of neuter gender, still reminds us. Until the late eighteenth century a European woman was often considered her husband's "property" and could be sold by him.[41] The freedom acquired by Roman matrons in the empire might have survived had not St. Paul ordered them to obey their husbands and keep their heads covered in churches. Christian ascetics, following Paul, often saw women as a snare set by Satan for the ruination of souls, but monasticism, while segregating them, gave them many opportunities enjoyed by monks.[42] The spiritual equality of women and the sacredness of marriage were church ideals, though often disregarded in practice.[43] Worship of Mary helped to raise women to a high moral plane but, stressing modesty, it retarded their entrance into public life. Chivalry, with its ideal of gallantry, both refined and debased the "gentler sex."

In theory and practice, woman's world was different from man's. Socially, morally and intellectually she stood on a different and inferior plane. Under later feudalism, great ladies often enjoyed great privileges, even intellectual, but they also suffered great disabilities. Some of them were not paragons of virtue. When noblewomen became nuns, as superannuated ones, especially, often did, they sometimes carried their vices with them into the nunneries. The duties of the women of the castle and the nunnery, as those of the hovel, were the traditional domestic ones. Feudalism, however, tended to emancipate them from the home. St. Thomas Aquinas taught that women, by their natural weakness, are subject to men, and that children should love their fathers more than their mothers. Such an estimate, mediaeval women accepted.[44]

The field of medicine was not entirely closed to mediaeval women. Some branches of medicine, connected with nursing, had always been open to them. Athenian women, for instance, were permitted to practise midwifery, and we hear of one female Athenian physician.[45] Women were on the staff of a medical school at Salerno, Italy, in the ninth and later centuries.[46] Where health was

[41] A. Heilborn, *The Opposite Sexes* (London: Methuen & Co., Ltd., 1927), pp. 123–32.

[42] E. Westermarck, *A Short History of Marriage* (New York: The Macmillan Co., 1926), pp. 44–46.

[43] F. W. Cornish, *Chivalry* (London: George Allen, 1911), p. 286.

[44] Monroe and Sellery, *op. cit.*, pp. 282 ff., 288 ff., 299.; W. S. Davis, *Life on a Mediaeval Barony* (New York: Harper & Bros., 1923), pp. 9 f., 74 ff., 99, 100 ff.

[45] J. A. St. John, *The History of the Manners and Customs of Ancient Greece* (London: Bentley, 1842), I, 115.

[46] T. C. Allbutt, *Greek Medicine in Rome* (London: Macmillan & Co., Ltd., 1921), pp. 431 ff.

concerned, some ministrations of women were, thus, not held in contempt.

Views regarding women's mentality differed. Tertullian, Ambrose, Augustine, and Jerome, for instance, had respect for the female mind. Yet, the opposite view prevailed generally throughout the period, and women were not permitted to develop their talents and their tastes in their own way. The Middle Ages produced no women of intellectual greatness.

Chivalry

Chivalry was the social and moral code of the feudal nobility, but it was an ideal rather than a practice. Its ideal, summed up in the phrase "death rather than dishonor," was given final expression in the *Chanson de Roland,* about A.D. 1110. Its rules applied chiefly to one's conduct in war, religion, and love, and required the knight to serve his lord, God, and his lady according to fixed forms of conduct. To base-born men it did not apply, but only to those of noble blood. Under chivalry, the nobility despised the poor, and the consecration of knighthood by the church prolonged the bondage of the masses. A regular system of apprenticeship education in the services due to one's feudal lord, for the purpose of moulding the finished "gentleman," grew up and became formalized. Gentleness, honor, loyalty, homage, courage, courtesy, liberality, respect for women, faith, and piety were the knightly ideals of virtue. Like the monk, the knight had his vows. He swore to fear and worship God, serve his lord, uphold the rights of widows, the weak, and defenseless, and protect the church. In practice, the knight was a paragon of virtues and vices, at the latter of which ecclesiastics connived, although there was some criticism of the tournament and the debaucheries connected with feminine chivalry as practised in the courts of love.

The chivalric code was a union of religious and worldly ideals, to the growth of which the knights, the clergy and the so-called ladies contributed. From the altar, where the ceremony of knighthood was performed, the knight marched out into the world as the Christian soldier, but a soldier more than a Christian. While knighthood was originally a military and economic institution, it eventually became largely social and a mark of membership in an exclusive social group. Chivalry ended in the fifteenth century with the fall of the cavalry system of warfare long pursued by feudal soldiery. When the horse fell from power, at the hands of base-born infantry, many ideals fell with him. While chivalry lasted, one of its leading characteristics was its international code of manners, based upon caste. The literature it produced, though non-national, laid the basis of national vernacular literatures and cultures.[47]

Intellectual Aspects of Mediaeval Society

THE MEDIAEVAL MIND. We have examined above the impact of the pagan world upon early Christian thought, and the reaction of the Christian mind to its worldly, decaying environment. Out of these happenings, Christians set up a system of values and ideals which, while not exclusively Christian, marked their outlook and aspirations for centuries. Among these ideals, we find (a) otherworldliness, (b) the supreme value of spiritual things, (c) the nobility of labor and (d) the unity of mankind and the spiritual equality of all men. Underlying these was the belief that man was created to serve God, his fellows and his own soul.

The Christian set for himself high moral ideals, but practice fell far below them, for the mediaeval mind accepted existing things, many of them vicious, as a manifestation of the will of God. The mediaeval mind was an ascetical, believing, submissive mind, filled with fears and superstitions. It was a Christian mind—though largely, but unconsciously, pagan—ready to make every sacrifice for Christianity. It was a clerical mind, exalting the ecclesiastical above the lay, or lewd, life. It was a herd mind, intolerant of heterodoxy. Above all, it was a mystical, otherworldly mind which, like cathedral spires, looked from earth to heaven, from the limited to the unlimited, from the temporal to the eternal.

FACTORS PRODUCING MENTAL CHANGE. All the worldly developments we have considered—commerce and the revival of political interests, the revival of interest in Roman law, the emergence of the bourgeoisie, chivalry and the Crusades—hastened the process of secularizing the mediaeval mind and making it critical about its surroundings. Closely related to these developments, and of great intellectual significance, were (a) the realist-nominalist controversy, (b) the introduction of Arab learning into Europe and (c) the re-emergence of local cultures.

(1) The Realist-Nominalist Controversy: From Mysticism to Scholasticism. Leading Greek thinkers accepted the principle of the supremacy of reason, and moderns accept that of the su-

[47] Cornish, *op. cit.*, pp. 68–83, 157–231, 267–80, 310, 365; Alfred Lord Tennyson, *The Idylls of the King;* E. Prestage, *Chivalry* (New York: Alfred A. Knopf, Inc., 1928).

premacy of observation and experiment, in discovering truth and in interpreting man and the universe. The idea that God has revealed truth in history was the controlling mediaeval idea. God who has repeatedly spoken to man "hath in these last days spoken unto us by his Son." In history the mediaeval man saw a divine purpose, and revelation and faith became, for him, the foundations of all truth and all knowledge. Faith was opposed to reason which, in the pagan world, led man into skepticism, and Holy Writ and the voice of the church became final authorities on all questions, earthly or divine.[48] This idea was most perfectly embodied in mysticism, a process by which holy men became united with God, as an actual experience. The basis of that union was not the intellect, but the heart; not knowledge, but love. To mystics, the material world is an illusion, the senses deceptive, multiplicity and change unreal, and God, though invisible, the one and only reality, through whose omnipresence all things become one unity.

Mysticism is a very old phenomenon, and it came into Christian thought through Platonism and Neo-Platonism. St. Paul who gazed upon God from the "third heaven," an Aristotelian astronomical sphere that never existed, was a mystic. His transportation was immediate and instantaneous. Dialectic soon changed this earlier view of the "flight of the alone to the Alone," as the pagan Neo-Platonist, Plotinus, spoke of the soul's flight to God. The pseudo-Dionysius, a Christian Neo-Platonist, whose authority became al-

[48] The intellectual aspects of mediaeval life have given rise to much debate. Here, as elsewhere in history, generalizations are hazardous. Yet, from out the mass of facts and interpretations of life in the Middle Ages, one fact constantly intrudes itself upon the view: Faith, not reason or science, was then man's guiding light, and reason was but the servant of faith, to be cast aside if it became a threat to faith. That we find a few men who clung to reason as their guiding light does not destroy the validity of the generalization. The general picture of the mind of the time reveals reason and faith in opposition. That opposition must be kept in mind as we try to interpret the intellectual life of mediaeval Europe. H. Wildon Carr, in F. J. C. Hearnshaw's *Mediaeval Contributions to Modern Civilisation* (p. 91), puts his finger upon the very heart of the question. Says he: "Throughout the whole period of mediaeval philosophy we find two factors in continual opposition, a principle of reason and a principle of faith. The whole philosophic effort is an attempt to reconcile them, to justify authority by an appeal to reason in the interest of faith. It ended in failure. It was bound to do so, for the only principle the philosopher could invoke to reconcile the contradiction was the principle of reason of the Greek philosophy, and this principle was itself one of the opposing factors. It is this inherent contradiction in the mediaeval mind which gives to its philosophy throughout the whole period that negative character which it assumes even in its most enlightened exponents. *Credo quia impossibile, Credo ut intelligam*—these are its watchwords. The Pauline doctrine of justification by faith is the embodiment of the contradiction. The faith to which Paul appealed was not intuition or any form of the mind reconcilable with reason. It was an irrational and an anti-rational principle, and this was the tragedy so far as philosophy is concerned."

most apostolic, said that there are three steps in the soul's flight: (a) purgation, (b) illumination, and (c) perfection. His book, *Celestial Hierarchy,* was translated into Latin by John Scotus Eriugena (*c.* 810-875), and had a deep influence upon Christian mysticism. Later logical analysis of the steps to a mystical union with God increased their number, and the flight, once instantaneous, now often required a lifetime. Mysticism rendered philosophy futile by transferring its goal from earth to the ethereal realm beyond.

The breakdown of mysticism was accelerated by the work and writings of Rhabanus Maurus (*c.* 776-856) and Eriugena. The former, a German abbot, stressed the indispensability of logic in the struggle against the intellectual trickery of heretics, and his interest in it foreshadowed scholasticism.[49] Eriugena, an Irish scholar who was head of the Palace School of Charles the Bald, offered a logical defence of church dogmas against certain current heresies. In doing so he went beyond the doctrines of the Church Fathers, and used Neo-Platonic philosophical arguments as a support for the orthodox theology. In his treatise, *De Divisione Naturae,* he urged the view that all things are one, that created things have no independent reality but exist in God, that true philosophy and true religion are one, that theology must agree with philosophy and that authority is derived from reason, not vice versa. Reason and Holy Writ, he said, spring alike from God's wisdom, and reason is the only safe guide to the interpretation of God's word. All church dogmas must, since they are true, be in harmony with reason, the supreme arbiter in matters of faith and theology. In his work, he constructed, in Platonic fashion, a hierarchy of being running from natural objects to the divine absolute. His mysticism and semi-pantheistic thinking led him to deny the existence of evil and hell. When pantheistic thinkers in the twelfth and thirteenth centuries invoked his support for their views, the church condemned many of his teachings. What, however, he tried to do was to make a corrected Platonism and Neo-Platonism the servants of theology, as Augustine had previously done. Soon Aristotelianism was to be used by others to modify Platonism, but it did not destroy it. Eriugena was the one great philosopher-theologian of the Dark Ages and his problems were the basic ones involved in the realist-nominalist controversy and in its offshoot, scholastic philosophy.

Two centuries after Eriugena wrote, the realist-nominalist controversy was disturbing Western Christendom. The debate between St. Anselm (1033-1109), the realist, and Roscellinus (*c.* 1050-1121),

[49] Taylor, *op. cit.*, I, 223 ff.; M. L. W. Laistner, *Thoughts and Letters in Western Europe, 500–900* (New York: Dial Press, Inc., 1931), p. 252.

the nominalist, centered on the question of the nature of universals, or class names. Anselm held that only universals, genera and species, are objectively real and that individual things are but appearances or shadows of reality, patterned on universals existing in the mind of God. These universals, he held, exist independently of time, place and circumstances or of our knowledge of them. They are eternal verities, not mere abstractions from objects of sense experience. Roscellinus held, on the other hand, that universals are but names (*nomina*) and that individual things perceived by the senses have objective independent reality. The realists, then, held that the universal is prior to the thing—*universale ante rem;* the nominalists, that it is posterior to the thing—*universale post rem.* Both claimed erroneously that Aristotle supported their views. His position was that the universal is in the thing—*universale in re.*

This whole issue had been pointedly dealt with by Porphyry (*c.* 233-304), an Eastern Neo-Platonist, in his *Introduction* to the *Categories* of Aristotle, a work which Boethius translated from Greek into Latin. It was, indeed, Boethius who first introduced Aristotle into Western Christendom. While Boethius took a neutral position on the question, he seems to lean to the view of Abelard or of the Moderate Realists of the twelfth century. Eriugena is hard to classify since he leans now toward Platonism and again toward Aristotelianism. The nominalist position, clearly presented by Boethius, goes back to Greece, where Democritus, the Epicureans and leading Sophists advanced it.[50]

In the twelfth century, Abelard (1074-1142), while denouncing Roscellinus, took a position close to nominalism, which he rejected only in its extreme form in which universals were said to be mere "words." For him, individual things are real, but universals are concepts derived from our vision of elements common to all members of a class of things. The universal "man" has no existence as a thing, but individual men are one in that they are men, and the mind sees their common qualities by forming concepts. From particulars, he said, we arrive at concepts; the process is not the other way. If there were no individual things there could be no universals. His position, known as "conceptualism," was essentially Aristotle's, and it came to be widely accepted.

The controversy had serious implications for religious beliefs. If, for instance, the universal element of humanity does not make all individual persons one, then that of divinity does not create a unity in the Trinity of God. Indeed, the church as an existing institu-

[50] M. H. Carré, *Realists and Nominalists* (London: Oxford University Press, 1946), pp. 33–64.

tion was itself a universal, but nominalism would reduce it to individual congregations. The doctrine that the substance of bread and wine is changed into the body and blood of Christ (Transubstantiation) rests on the realist view that there is a universal substance underlying the accidental properties of individual things. Thus the controversy was fraught with danger for orthodoxy and faith. It should be noted, too, that realism was linked to social ideas and practices. Corporations, with their universal sweep, found justification for their universality in realism. Church schools, universities, monastic orders, gilds, towns, etc., could look to realism for justification of their corporate structure. And authoritarian states in our own day have turned to the related philosophy of idealism in support of their practices. Those who insist upon the corporate, or totalitarian, character and supreme authority of the church or state belong to the school of extreme realists; while those who stand for individual rights and political democracy are modern nominalists. The seemingly faraway conflict is still with us.

This mediaeval debate was entirely between theologians, and it involved not only the question of the nature of reality and truth but also that of the method of discovering and knowing them. Extreme realists, like Anselm, held that faith is the path to reality and truth, and that it precedes reason. "I believe," said Anselm, "in order that I may know." The nominalists held that reason precedes faith; that the senses and reason are the foundations of all knowledge; and that dogmas and revealed truths must be demonstrable by reason. Roscellinus was condemned by the church in 1092 [51] and, thereafter, few such "heretics" expressed their views openly until William of Ockham (*c.* 1280-1349) became again a champion of their position. He, however, held that religious doctrines are incapable of rational proof, and relegated them exclusively to the sphere of faith. Abelard defended men's right to question all dogmas and all *dicta* of Church Fathers. In his treatise *Yes and No,* he compiled a list of contradictory statements found in the Bible and the Fathers as a justification of such questioning. Said he: "A doctrine is not to be believed because God has said it but because we are convinced by reason that it is so." [52] The church condemned his "errors" in 1141, and even Roscellinus thought that action just.

The system of thought which emerged from this controversy is known as scholasticism, and St. Thomas Aquinas (1225-1274), whose

[51] F. Ueberweg, *History of Philosophy* (New York: Charles Scribner's Sons, 1893), I, 372.

[52] R. L. Poole, *Illustrations of the History of Mediaeval Thought* (London: Williams & Norgate, Ltd., 1884), p. 153.

views became authoritative among Catholics, perfected the system. He regarded the teachings of Aristotle on logic and the "natural order," which he Christianized, as the last outpost on the path to truth attainable by reason. Thomism teaches that philosophy and theology are separate subjects, the former surveying the natural, and the latter, the supernatural order. Since, said Aquinas, revelation is a "fact"—and philosophy must not question that "fact"—true philosophy and theology can never be in opposition when they deal with the same questions; and revealed truths, incomprehensible to the intellect, must be accepted on faith. The finite reason can never comprehend the infinite, but it can prove the validity of the preambles of faith and show that faith is not unreasonable. Whether or not he made philosophy the "handmaiden of theology" is a matter of debate. It is, however, clear that he considered theology the supreme study of supreme things, to the attainment of whose goals he found philosophy useful, if not indispensable. His position is presented in his famous work *Summa Theologica.* St. Augustine created a sharp cleavage between *scientia* (the knowledge of nature), with which reason deals, and *sapientia* (the knowledge of supernatural things), with which faith deals, and he subordinated the former to the latter. Aquinas attempted to restore the equilibrium between them by making them allies, although he gave reason a very humble place in the partnership.

With Aquinas, scholasticism reached its climax. But, no sooner had he reconciled faith and reason than Duns Scotus (*c.* 1274-1308) began to show the futility of reason as the servant of theology, and to carry the use of the syllogism to such a ridiculous extreme in proving his case that stupid boys have come to be given his name, Dunce. In the hands of William of Ockham, the Thomistic reconciliation broke down completely, and faith and reason, and the spheres with which they deal, were completely separated. From his position that religious beliefs must be accepted entirely upon faith it was but a short step to Luther's rejection of scholasticism and to his doctrine of "justification by faith." Luther represents a return to Augustine and a turning from dialectical theology to the simple teaching of the Scriptures.

Every philosophy is a reflection of the institutions and struggles of its time. Scholasticism, in its striving for intellectual unity, reflects the strivings for political, social, and ecclesiastical unity in the scholastic age. Order in knowledge was viewed as necessary to order in the church, in the Holy Roman empire, and in the new national states of Europe which the unifying papacy was struggling to direct and control. Vincent of Beauvais' (1190-*c.*1264) great encyclopedia, the *Speculum Majus,* embodies the desire for unity and order, as does the Gothic art of the time. And Dante's *Divine Comedy* and *On Monarchy* are pleas for universal unity and peace on earth under the rule of pope and emperor, as it is in heaven under the rule of God. In the world that has emerged since then, liberal thinkers have come to view disorder as often preferable to order, and disagreement, to agreement, although all agree that some measure of unity is essential to the strength and preservation of every nation. We have found, however, that unity in philosophy and religion is not essential to the welfare of nations. The mediaeval efforts to create and preserve unity did not save the City of God from disintegration. The rising revolt against scholasticism by humble Christians as well as by scholars such as Ockham, who was excommunicated, coincides with the rise of opposition to the papacy and of political unrest.

The rediscovery, in the twelfth century, of all the surviving works of Aristotle had much to do with the finished product of scholastic thought. In addition to his complete work on logic, the *Organon,* his works on metaphysics, physics, psychology and ethics, with their subdivisions, were introduced into Europe. Although Jewish scholars did much to carry ancient philosophy from place to place, it was the Arabs who contributed most to the rediscovery of Aristotle. As interpreted by the Arab scholars, Avicenna and Averroës, many views of Aristotle vital to Christian orthodoxy varied from those of the church. The Averroistic interpretation was condemned by the Bishop of Paris in 1270.[53] When the original Aristotle was discovered, after the capture of Constantinople by the Crusaders (1204), it became easier to reconcile his views with those of the church. His works, with the exception of his *Organon,* continued, however, to be proscribed under pain of excommunication. When purged by a papal commission and officially interpreted, they were all, following their approval by the University of Paris in 1254, sanctioned for the use of students and teachers. Thenceforth, for three hundred years, they were the core of the liberal arts course in universities. It was the Dominicans, Albert the Great and Thomas Aquinas, who did most to capture Aristotle for the church in a period of dangerous speculation.

Stamped with ecclesiastical approval, Aristotelianism became an enslaver of the human mind. The written word of Aristotle, as interpreted by orthodox theologians, became in the sphere of reason and the "natural order" as authoritative as the written word of God in the sphere of faith. However, the Franciscan theologians, Sco-

[53] Carré, *op. cit.,* p. 67.

tus, Ockham and Bonaventura, continued to stand for Christianized Platonism, and opposed the preference of their Dominican rivals for Aristotelianism as the best setting for the dogmas of the church. The latter liked Aristotle's doctrine of the unmoved mover, a force outside of nature, which set everything in never-ending motion, because it fitted the Christian theistic conception of God.

Aristotle was a physician and a naturalist who viewed the senses as a valid source of knowledge. His acceptance by the church helped Christians to rediscover nature. Yet, he was often in error. He rejected, for instance, any mechanical explanation of natural events and the mobility of the earth, and made the heart, not the brain, the center of the nervous system. He taught, too, that the earth is the center of the universe. And he took a Greek mathematical theory regarding the movement of the planets and "spheres," the latter an empty nothing, and made it a scientific fact. Those are but a few of his errors. The blind acceptance of Aristotle as an infallible authority in the realm of nature is one of the greatest intellectual tragedies in history. His psychological postulate of an "active," immortal Reason, as the highest grade in mental life which functions independently of the body, helped to perpetuate the dualistic conception of man's nature and to promote in education the practice of pure intellectualism.

In the scholastic age, however, it was impossible to find one more enlightened to turn to. Then, the materials of knowledge were very limited, a fact which must be considered in evaluating the work of the scholastics. Their perfected system of knowledge retarded the Renaissance and the scientific movement, and their method of inquiry, that of appeal to authority, impeded progress. Abelard rejected in part the argument from authority, and Aquinas said that it was the weakest of all arguments in matters falling into the sphere of reason. And yet, in practice, the teachers and students of the time went to books even to solve such problems as the number of teeth in a horse's mouth. Interest, too, came to center in matters of no practical importance, such as the problems of the number of angels that could stand at the same time on the point of a needle and of whether or not horsiness could exist apart from a horse. We should, however, note that students and teachers in American colonial colleges were still discussing similar questions. Attachment to intellectual subtleties made scholasticism ridiculous and helped to bring reason and faith to the parting of the ways. In the thirteenth century some thinkers were advocating the experimental method of inquiry, and Roger Bacon (1214-1294) actually formulated a method of observation and experiment as a universal method of scientific inquiry, thus becoming the first European to do so.[54] The modern mind was slowly emerging.

(2) Introduction of Arab Learning into Europe. The votaries of spreading Islam assimilated, in the early eighth century, Greek learning, which had survived among the Hellenized Christians of the East, and brought it back to the West, where they ruled over all northern Africa and Spain. While in the later Middle Ages the West was in direct contact with the East through the Crusades and otherwise, the indirect contact through the Arabs was more influential. The greatest contribution of the Arabs to the West was the restoration of Aristotle's philosophy. Their work in mathematics, astronomy, physics, chemistry, botany, biology, geology, geography, surgery, medicine, pharmacy, and history, was notable and contributed to the awakening of scientific interest and to the rediscovery of the observational and experimental method in Western Christendom. They were practising surgery when Christians were still using the bones of saints to cure disease.

Long in contact with India, and students of Hindu learning, the Arabs brought to the West Arabic notation, a Hindu product, which has been of great value in arithmetic and algebra. In commerce, wealth, the beautiful and very modern cities they built, agriculture, engineering, and the arts, as well as in learning, they led the world and, in contact with them, Christian Crusaders saw the discrepancy between the real world and the church's picture of it. Every large Muslim city, in the East and West, had its college or university, staffed by the best scholars, Arab, Jewish, or Christian, and often enrolling as many as 10,000 students. Thus Arabs helped notably to pass on the torch of Greek learning to the West.[55]

(3) The Vanishing of Unity and the Rise of Local Cultures. As we have noted, the unity of mankind was one of the ideals of the mediaeval world, and thinkers dreamt of a universal Christian empire ruled by pope and emperor as representatives of God. The history even of the Christian world shows the vanity of that desire. The pagan Roman empire came much closer to its achievement than did the church, the "empire baptized." Roman cultural unity, as evidenced by the spread of the Koinê, or vulgar Latin, through Western Romania, was due as much to the great Roman roads as to

[54] L. Thorndike, *History of Magic and Experimental Science* (New York: The Macmillan Co. and Columbia University Press, 1923–40).

[55] Hulme, *op. cit.*, pp. 214–37, 439–54; F. M. Stawell and F. S. Marvin, *The Making of the Western Mind* (Garden City, N.Y.: Doubleday & Co., Inc., n.d.), pp. 48–51; F. J. C. Hearnshaw, *Mediaeval Contributions to Modern Civilisation*, pp. 107–48; Ueberweg, *op. cit.*, I, 402–17; Allbutt, *op. cit.*, pp. 289–99, 394–95, 422.

Roman military power and administrative efficiency. It was the language of the commonality, not the elite, of Rome and her provinces, although many of the latter respected it and, probably, used it at times in conversation. It remained a bond of cultural unity in Italy, France, Spain, and Portugal—Romania—until about 750, when modern Romance languages were emerging. It was essential in the work of the church, and its use by Christian missionaries was important in the preservation of the unity of Romania,[56] although it was a religious rather than an intellectual and political unity which they promoted. Many of the missionaries were themselves almost illiterate.[57]

The economic and social bases of cultural unity were disintegrating rapidly in the eighth century. Roads collapsed; commerce declined; travel became less frequent; missionaries, having depaganized Romania, were back in their monasteries; and the Koinê was passing into village dialects. The West was now cut off from the East by Arab power in the Mediterranean, and the Germanic states of the West had now been welded into the Frankish empire of which Charlemagne (768-814) was the last great ruler. He received his imperial crown from Pope Leo III on Christmas day, 800, in St. Peter's cathedral in Rome, and by this act of papal power the seat of the Roman empire was transferred from the Bosphorus to the Tiber; and thus was born the phantom known as the Holy Roman empire of the Germans, of which it has accurately been said that it was neither holy, nor Roman, nor an empire. But the phantom remained until Napoleon I put it to political rest.

Charlemagne, the greatest of mediaeval statesmen, made a valiant and, for a brief period, a highly successful attempt to re-establish political and cultural unity in the West. While a few other kings, notably Alfred the Great of England, concerned themselves with the education of their subjects, he was the leading protagonist of the educational prerogatives of the state in the Middle Ages. We shall examine his educational activities later, but here we should say that they represent a significant effort to preserve the unity of his empire by creating a homogeneity of culture based upon Latin literary learning. The attempt failed because the economic and social bases of unity were gone. Following a tradition of German tribal kings, he divided his empire among his sons, and political disintegration followed rapidly, culminating in the decentralization of power which marked the feudal régime.

56 H. F. Muller, *A Chronology of Vulgar Latin* (Halle: Max Niemeyer, 1929), pp. 123–25.

57 *Ibid.*, pp. 12 f., 21 ff., 28, 39 f.; Haskins, *op. cit.*, p. 93.

The breakdown of economic, social and political unity was accompanied by the rise of vernacular literatures. In the Europe of the Middle Ages, Latin was the language of international affairs, of the international church, of prayer, theology, philosophy, and, with a few minor exceptions, of all schools and textbooks. The Latin of the period was mediaeval Latin. Being a living language, it added many new words and grammatical forms that would shock Cicero. But it was still Latin. It was basically the vulgar Latin now become the literary language of Western Christendom. The complete corruption of classical Latin appears in the Romance vernaculars, not in mediaeval Latin. Here it should be noted that the Koinê never became the language of the people of the British Isles or of Germany, although it did become the language of their schools. Charlemagne considered Latin indispensable in all important matters. It was the clergy who perpetuated it, for few laymen, except some later feudal aristocrats, could read or write. The laity, however, created vernaculars and narrated in them, first orally and then in writing, the legends of Europe. A vernacular literature began to appear in England in the seventh century; in France, Germany, and Scandinavia in the ninth; and in Ireland, Wales, Spain, and Italy in the twelfth and thirteenth centuries.[58] Its earliest form was poetic, and it shows an interest changing from heroic deeds to love, and then to adventure. Chivalry inspired much of it, and its tone was worldly. A later literature, born in the cities, was satirical, rationalistic, and, sometimes, communistic. These new writers mocked theology, the clergy, and the nobility, and showed utter contempt for women and marriage.[59]

Much worldliness, obscenity, frivolity, and mockery crept into the Latin songs of wandering students, pilgrims not to Rome or the Holy Sepulchre but to shrines of knowledge, the new universities rising up in awakening Europe from the late twelfth century onward. The church disapproved of wandering, but it could not stop it forever. Crusades, pilgrimages, wandering friars and merchants created an interest in the world beyond mountains and seas that authority could not suppress. Organized gilds of students, stationary and wandering, arose, and many of their members showed as much interest in wine, women, song, and heresy as in serious learn-

[58] Stawell and Marvin, *op. cit.,* pp. 57 ff.; H. E. Barnes, *An Intellectual and Cultural History of the Western World* (New York: The Dryden Press, Inc., 1937), pp. 444 ff.

[59] Hulme, *op. cit.,* pp. 493, 808–36; Hearnshaw, *Mediaeval Contributions to Modern Civilisation,* pp. 176–87; Prestage, *op. cit.,* pp. 45 *passim,* 167–80; F. A. Ogg, *A Source Book of Mediaeval History* (New York: American Book Co., 1908), pp. 445–47.

ing. Their vices were legion, and their songs show a drift from the mediaeval to the modern world.

The rise of vernacular literatures, lay, worldly, satirical, and radical, indicates the collapse of the cultural unity of Romania and a changing attitude toward religious, social, and intellectual traditions. In every way, they show heretical tendencies. In the tenth and eleventh centuries, though appearing earlier, vernacular Gospels spread and, finally, the Reformation gave Holy Writ to the common people in their own languages. Schools for the common people, the elementary schools of modern nations, arose on this new cultural foundation, as did modern nations themselves. The sixteenth century saw not only the unity of Romania gone, but the universalism of Christendom replaced by localism.[60]

B. Early Christian And Mediaeval Education

Transition from Pagan to Christian Education

In the process of disintegration of the Roman empire, the church gradually assumed the rôle of educator of Europe and made the school its servant. The Christians of the first century were generally poor and illiterate and had little interest in education. But, as the rich and wise were called to the faith, they brought with them the desire of their class for education, and sent their children to the pagan grammar and rhetorical schools, since, for a long time, the church did not provide similar schools in the West. The practice of sending Christian youths to pagan schools and of Christians teaching in them created a problem for the church and the state. Until the death of Julian the Apostate (363), such Christian teachers were politically suspect, and some Christian leaders considered it improper for them to accept positions which demanded participation in pagan ceremonies and the teaching of a literature permeated by respect for pagan gods and culture. While Tertullian (*c.* 160-230), in his treatise *Idolatry*, stood opposed to any use of pagan schools by Christians, he saw no alternative for them then. The Apologists, as reconcilers of pagan and Christian thought, offered the first practical solution of the dilemma in the catechetical schools of the East. Pagan learning was found to be useful in refuting the

[60] J. A. Symonds, *Wine, Women and Song* (London: Chatto & Windus, 1907); Waddell, *op. cit.*, pp. 161-94.

arguments of pagans, and the Church Fathers, themselves educated in pagan schools, used it effectively to that end, but their contact with it disturbed them.

St. Jerome (*c.* 340-420) tells us that he dreamt that he had died and was condemned before the bar of Heaven because he was a Ciceronian rather than a Christian.[61] While he tried to create a Christian literature, his love of the pagan classics continued until his death, but he remained disturbed by that love. Others suffered from the same anxiety. St. Augustine (354-430) was more fearful of a compromise with pagan culture. In his *Of Christian Doctrine* he proclaimed Holy Writ and the writings of the Fathers to be of far greater value than pagan learning in the quest for truth. History, geography, science, natural history, grammar, and the rules of eloquence could, he said, be learned as well from the Scriptures as from the classics. And he recommended outlines of the liberal arts to conserve students' energy for the study of religion.

In spite of all such examples of apologetic indecision—and they are many—it is the growing attitude of hostility, especially in the West, to pagan learning and ways of life that emerges clearly from the records. That attitude is revealed well in the *Apostolic Constitutions,* already cited, and in a letter of Pope Gregory the Great (*c.* 540-604) to Bishop Desiderius of Vienne, in which he said that "the same mouth cannot sing the praises of Jupiter and the praises of Christ" and that it is "an abominable thing . . . for a bishop to recite verses which are unfit to be recited by a religious layman." [62] Such a faith, operating in a climate of social decay, could have only one result—night and darkness.

Between the fourth and the sixth century Roman public grammar and rhetorical schools disappeared, and the Western church had done little to replace them. These schools, already infiltrated by disloyal Christian teachers, received their final blow from the new faith and its devout adherents. Then ensued the Dark Ages. Evidences of the decline of literary education are numerous. We may cite the very ungrammatical Latin of Bishop Gregory of Tours (538-594) in his *History of the Franks* as a significant example of that decline. By the sixth century education was in the hands of bishops, priests and monks, many, if not most, of them nearly illiterate. In the East, as we have seen, the emperor Justinian outlawed pagan education when, in 529, he closed the University of Athens because

[61] P. Schaff and H. Wace (eds.), "Letters of St. Jerome," XXII, 29–31, in *A Select Library of Nicene and Post-Nicene Fathers of the Christian Church* (New York: The Christian Literature Company, 1890–95), ser. 2, VI, 34 ff.

[62] F. H. Dudden, *Gregory the Great* (New York: Longmans, Green & Co., Inc., 1905), I, 287.

it was a center of Neo-Platonism, the last great philosophical enemy of Christianity.

EDUCATIONAL AIMS AND IDEALS. In the transition from the secular to the Christian state, the ideal of education for death and eternity replaced the Graeco-Roman ideal of education for life and the world. The Christian did not feel at home in this "vale of tears." Heaven was his home. The plagues that swept Rome and the destruction of life and property by invaders but confirmed the belief of Christians that "all is vanity" except serving God and one's immortal soul. That otherworldly ideal did not end with the Dark Ages; indeed, it still continues to challenge the secular ideal in modern education. A liberal education in the Graeco-Roman world was the education of "freemen" for citizenship and public service. As regards individualism, it differed in emphasis from state to state. In mediaeval Christian society, it became the education of the "servants" of God and the church for otherworldly and ecclesiastical ends. To know God was far more important than to know the world. During the Dark Ages particularly, all knowledge was seen as having God and his purposes as its true object.

The change to the Christian state brought the rejection of the Greek ideal of education of "the whole man" in all aspects of his nature for a life of personal satisfaction and social service. The education of the Christian "servant of God" was, certainly until the twelfth century, anti-intellectual, anti-aesthetic and anti-physical, and concessions to pagan ideals came slowly and reluctantly even then. Christian education placed a supreme emphasis upon moral and religious training and, for a time under monastic Rules, upon manual labor as a moral discipline and a safeguard against sin. Irish monastic schools [63] and a few surviving lay schools in Italy were exceptions to the general anti-intellectualism of the Dark Ages. Mental education was not, however, the only important victim of the Christian victory.

Physical culture, dear to the Greeks, suffered a sharp rejection, inspired by Christian asceticism. Pagan Neo-Platonists and other pagan ascetics were equally opposed to the education of the body. The Neo-Platonist Plotinus, like the monk St. Simeon Stylites, did not bathe, and showed the utmost disregard for his health.[64] The body was viewed by all these ascetics as a dangerous thing which

[63] H. Graham, *The Early Irish Monastic Schools* (Dublin: The Talbot Press, 1923); B. Fitzpatrick, *Ireland and the Foundations of Europe* (New York: Funk and Wagnalls Co., 1927), pp. 178, 208; Hearnshaw, *Mediaeval Contributions to Modern Civilisation*, p. 198.

[64] C. Kingsley, *Alexandria and Her Schools* (London: Macmillan & Co., Ltd., 1854), p. 109.

must be tortured. In his *City of God,* Augustine declared "the corruptible body" to be an enemy of the soul. Bishop Isidore of Seville, in the seventh century, advised the healthy to become sick for their souls' sake.[65] Voluminous records attest the prevalence of this view in the Dark Ages and far beyond.[66] Bathing, sports, athletic contests, etc., were condemned by Christian ascetics as obstacles to salvation. And art and its appreciation also suffered.

Christians considered it sinful to gaze upon some beautiful works of pagan art. Yet Christian borrowing from this art is evident in the architecture, sculpture, and wall-painting of mediaeval Christendom. The earliest Christian art appears in wall-paintings around the graves in the catacombs. In the fourth century, great churches, elaborate in architectural design and in ornamentation, began to appear. The glory of God and the church and the drama of death and eternity inspired Christian art. But the Christian artist was a creator, often of beauty, even in the atmosphere of the grave. In the eleventh and twelfth centuries, Romanesque and Gothic art emerged, the latter, especially, being strikingly original and beautiful. Both expressed religious ideals and Christian conceptions of the beautiful, although a secular, naturalistic craving appears in Gothic art. That art attained its greatest beauty when (*c.* 1200) it passed out of monastic control into the hands of artisan gilds in the cities. The new cathedrals were the finest examples of the art of the time but, in the thirteenth century, there appeared also the fortified city and the city hall, both architecturally impressive. It may be true, as some assert, that the Renaissance but formalized the free, creative art of the later Middle Ages.

The arts of dancing, seen as a sinful bodily display, and of secular music, its unholy attendant, met pronounced Christian opposition. Gregorian chant, with its otherworldly laments, was created to replace secular music and to save Christians from the evil influence of the world's songs.[67] The Gothic period produced a Gothic music which expressed both a sacred and a secular ideal, and France led in the creation of a purely secular music. There, the *troubadours* and *jongleurs* began, in the late twelfth century, to entertain the feudal nobility with their worldly songs, music, and dancing. And the practice soon spread throughout Europe. The triumph of Christianity was the death of the theater, as the Greeks knew it,

[65] E. Brehaut, *An Encyclopedist of the Dark Ages, Isidore of Seville* (New York: Columbia University Press, 1912), p. 70.

[66] T. Woody, *Liberal Education for Free Men* (Philadelphia: University of Pennsylvania Press, 1951), pp. 93 ff.

[67] E. Dickinson, *Music in the History of the Western Church* (New York: Charles Scribner's Sons, 1925), pp. 65 ff.

because Christian leaders considered the influence of comedy and tragedy immoral.

All of these changes represent a sharp break with the Graeco-Roman past. However, shadows of that past remained, and the Christian, whatever his final destiny, had to live in the world and meet the demands of life. In addition to needs for food, clothing and shelter, which even ascetics had to satisfy, there were positions in civil and church administration and service which had to be filled, and so mediaeval education had a vocational purpose. All church positions and, until the fourteenth century, many civil positions were in the hands of the clergy (clerks). The general training of the schools was, however, about the only form of preparation provided for these vocations. That, too, was the practice of the Graeco-Roman world, and it has endured through the centuries as the European mode of training civil servants. There was very little special training for professional or vocational fields in the Middle Ages, although a beginning of such training in law and theology and in the work of city vernacular schools appeared near the close of the Dark Ages; and the universities, when they arose later, were professional schools. In the total picture of aims and ideals one thing stands out clearly: a moral and religious purpose predominated in the thought and practice of the Dark Ages, and yielded ground reluctantly to secular influences in the closing centuries of the Middle Ages.

THE CURRICULUM. In education, the most significant form in which the pagan past survived is seen in the curriculum of Christian schools. The content of the Roman curriculum had become fairly definitely fixed by the year A.D. 300, and consisted of what came to be called the *seven liberal arts.* In the late empire, outlines of various subjects were often preferred to the reading of entire works of ancient authors.[68] Martianus Capella, an African pagan of the fifth century, compiled a compendium of knowledge similar to these, and gave it the title *The Marriage of Mercury and Philology.* It became a very popular mediaeval textbook, and did much to fix the content of the mediaeval liberal arts. At the allegorical wedding on the Milky Way, the seven attendants of the bride, Philology, recited their attributes, and these recitations are Capella's textbook on the seven arts: Grammar, Rhetoric, Dialectic (the literary arts), Arithmetic, Geometry, Music, and Astronomy (the mathematical arts). In Christian schools the first three, regarded as lower studies, were known as the *Trivium;* the last four, or higher studies, as the *Quad-*

[68] LaMonte, *op. cit.,* p. 81.

rivium. Capella borrowed from Varro, but excluded architecture and medicine which Varro had included. His sugar-coating of subject matter probably accounts in part for the popularity of his treatise in Christian schools. The other encyclopedias of the liberal arts which attained much vogue were those of Cassiodorus (*Institutes of Divine and Secular Letters*) and of Isidore of Seville (*Etymologies*), the latter becoming especially popular in later centuries. There were other less systematic compendiums of the liberal arts which were used, no doubt, in some mediaeval schools. These included those of Boethius, the Venerable Bede (673-735), Alcuin (735-804) and Rhabanus Maurus (786-856).

The seven liberal arts contained nearly everything of a general nature which mediaeval clergy needed to know and, for them, they were vocational studies as well as a prerequisite to a study of theology and the Scriptures. While Isidore, who wrote about everything he had ever thought of, included law and medicine in his treatise, he apparently did not deem these studies liberal, for he gave "seven" a sacred significance by declaring the arts to be the Biblical "seven pillars of wisdom." In the scholastic period, when men sought unity in the universe, the sevenness of the arts was further confirmed by the Aristotelian doctrines of the seven spheres and planets, and by the Christian doctrine of seven corresponding orders of angels presiding over them. The encyclopedias lack originality. Isidore, for instance, borrowed his geography from the Roman author, Solinus, who, in turn, had borrowed from Pliny's *Natural History*. And the most fantastic tales had the greatest attraction for the Bishop of Seville. He wrote with finality about geography, astronomy, animals, men, angels, medicine, etc. The bizarre nature of his wisdom shows to what depths learning had fallen in Western Christendom.[69] It is unlikely that, until late in the Middle Ages, the *Trivium* and *Quadrivium*, as taught, were richer in content than they were presented in the encyclopedias.

(a) THE TRIVIUM. *Grammar*, *rhetoric*, and *dialectic* were the chief, if not the only, studies pursued in many of the schools. Latin, the language spoken by teachers and students, was the medium of instruction in all subjects. Until the ninth century, Greek, the official language of the church until A.D. 200, remained a study in the schools of Great Britain and Ireland. On the Continent, it disappeared with the Latinization of the Western empire in the third century. The books used as special Latin grammar texts were those of Donatus and Priscian, and the latter was filled with fragments

[69] Sandys, *A History of Classical Scholarship* (London: Cambridge University Press, 1903–8), I, 228 *passim;* Laistner, *op. cit.*, pp. 22 f., 169 f.

from Latin literature. Students began with Readers, and advanced gradually to some Latin classics, interest in which was very low until the twelfth century. Aesop's Fables and the Distichs of Cato were occasionally used as readers. There was a fair supply of classical literature available,[70] but it was evidently little used until the twelfth century. The monks, it should be recalled, made copies of many of the Latin classics. During the Dark Ages, the rules of grammar were not respected. Gregory of Tours, for instance, wrote his *History of the Franks* without any regard for the agreement of nouns and adjectives, or for the proper use of the moods and tenses of verbs. It is hard to understand how the word of God survived in such a climate of neglect. Interest in classical grammar was finally revived in the eleventh and twelfth centuries, under the leadership of the cathedral school of Chartres and its famous teachers, Bernard and John of Salisbury (1110-1180). Thereafter official church records were written in grammatical Latin.

The twelfth century brought a wave of interest in classical literature, usually called the Twelfth-Century Renaissance. It centered in the cathedral schools of Chartres and Orleans.[71] In John of Salisbury's account of his student years (1136-1148), given in his *Metalogicon,* we get an excellent picture of the schools at Chartres and Paris. While dialectic was the center of interest in Paris, grammar, the writing of prose and verse compositions, and the reading of classical Latin authors were stressed in Chartres. John shows some contempt for the dialecticians, but only the highest respect for the classics. This first literary renaissance was checked in its growth by the rise of scholasticism, but it prepared the way for later humanism.

In comparison with grammar, which included literature, the other six liberal arts received scant attention in the Dark Ages and, thereafter, interest in them fluctuated from time to time and from place to place. *Rhetoric,* as the Romans taught it, disappeared until Renaissance scholars revived it. *Dictamen,* or the writing of documents and letter writing (epistolography), replaced it in mediaeval schools. The monk Aleric of Monte Cassino wrote a manual on letter-writing in the eleventh century, and the letters of the chancellor of Emperor Frederick II were studied as examples of perfect letter writing. Very generally, the clergy were the penmen of the time, and the word *clerk* became synonymous with *clergyman.*

[70] H. Buttenwieser, "Popular Authors of the Middle Ages," *Speculum,* XVII (1942), 50–55; J. S. Beddie, "Ancient Classics in Mediaeval Libraries," *Speculum,* V (1930), 3–20; P. Abelson, *The Seven Liberal Arts* (New York: Teachers College, Columbia University, 1906), pp. 11–51.

[71] L. Thorndike, *University Records and Life in the Middle Ages* (New York: Columbia University Press, 1944), pp. 7–9.

In the Dark Ages, *Dialectic*, as a school subject, was but a study of the rules of formal logic. Cassiodorus gave much more space to logic in his encyclopedia than did Capella or Isidore.[72] Interest in it increased from the eighth century when church dogmas began to need syllogistic defense. Yet, the West knew only the elements of logic until Aristotle's complete *Organon* was rediscovered late in the period.[73] From the eleventh century onward, we find teachers and students applying the rules of logic in disputations usually on topics arising out of the realist-nominalist debate. The scholastic age produced many dialecticians, masters in the art of verbal hairsplitting. Disputations were a universal practice in universities, but they were not entirely unknown in cathedral grammar schools.

(b) THE QUADRIVIUM. *Arithmetic* was studied as a mental discipline as well as for its use in keeping accounts, but its content was very elementary until the thirteenth century.[74] *Geometry*, also, was studied as a mental discipline, but seems to have found some practical application in surveying and settling boundary disputes.[75] *Astronomy*, while pursued for a similar mental purpose, was of practical value in fixing the dates of movable holy days. It was Ptolemaic in its theory. While all the arts looked toward God, astronomy especially turned eyes and minds heavenward. *Music*, as a liberal art, was studied only theoretically. The texts of Boethius and Isidore were made the bases of the study. The former, from whom Isidore borrowed, divided music into three categories: the "mundane" (the music of the spheres), the "human" and the "instrumental." It was such philosophical conceptions that the teacher dealt with. The encyclopedists say little about singing, but they treat the types of musical instruments and their uses.[76] A few monastic schools became famous for their theoretical and practical work in music, and the latter was given special attention in the song schools of the period.

(c) OTHER STUDIES. An occasional school gave some attention to history as found in Isidore's treatise and in Orosius' *Seven Books of History against the Pagans*. Everything in history, however, was seen as an unfolding of a divine, supernatural plan at work in man's world. Above the seven liberal arts, as preparatory studies, stood the Scriptures, theology, and canon and civil law, all of which were given attention in some schools of the British Isles in the Dark Ages.

[72] Sandys, *op. cit.*, I, 253.
[73] Poole, *op. cit.*, p. 220.
[74] Hulme, *op. cit.*, p. 802; Abelson, *op. cit.*, pp. 90 ff.
[75] Abelson, *op. cit.*, pp. 113 ff.
[76] L. Ellinwood, "*Ars Musica*," *Speculum*, XX (July 1945), 290–99.

It is doubtful that Continental schools did anything similar at that time since, there, learning was in a state of decay. Civil law first came into prominence as a study in the city states of Northern Italy, where it was taught as a branch of rhetoric. Roman law was studied in the city school of Ravenna from the ninth century, and in the city school of Pavia from the eleventh century. One such school, that of Bologna, became a university and the center of legal study in Europe.

From the time of Eriugena onward, interest in theology increased, and it blossomed in the work of the scholastics, becoming after 1100 the queen of studies and even more important than that of the Scriptures themselves. As for science, the Middle Ages were the second childhood of scientific thought. At the end of the Middle Ages, Christians were just beginning to discover Nature, and science, in the Greek and modern sense, had no place in the curriculum of mediaeval schools. A Gerbert and even a Roger Bacon were but strange voices in a great wilderness, unknown until the Arabs and Aristotle began to direct attention to its mysteries.

METHOD AND DISCIPLINE. Mediaeval education was a disciplining of man's nature regarded by Augustine and his followers as corrupted by the Fall. Only the Fall-doctrine could substantiate the need for a Redeemer in the human tragedy. Man, without the grace of God, was considered helpless in the quest for salvation. He was viewed as a dual being composed of a passive, mortal body and an active, immaterial, immortal soul, the only precious part of man. The sinful body was but a vicious tabernacle of the soul, and capable of destroying its immortal treasure unless its physical, emotional, and aesthetic urges were curbed by discipline. John Cassian would chastise his body that he might not lose his soul.[77] And other ascetics, as we have seen, were of the same mind. St. John Chrysostom, in his *Golden Book concerning the Education of Children,* would have youths acquire habits of prayer, chastity, and heroic self-restraint. Fear of the rod, in childhood, and of hell, in adolescence, would provide the motivation. Parents should discipline all the senses of their children, and keep their minds preoccupied with death.[78] Jerome expressed a similar view.[79]

These attitudes, more than the psychological doctrines of Augustine or Aquinas, determined the method of instruction. Underlying them, however, was the doctrine, held by all mediaeval theologians, that human nature is dualistic and that the body and soul are com-

[77] *The Twelve Books of John Cassian,* V, 16–17, in *A Select Library of Nicene and Post-Nicene Fathers,* ser. 2, XI, 524 f.

[78] J. Evelyn, *Miscellaneous Writings* (London: Colburn, 1825), I, 115 ff., 124 ff.

[79] Cubberley, *op. cit.,* pp. 60–63.

pletely separate elements. Thought, understanding, and will are, in Augustine's view, the soul's chief faculties or activities, the will guiding the other faculties aright only if enlightened by the grace of God, without which man, depraved by the Fall, is a helpless victim of the forces of evil. For him, thought (which he calls, in Latin, *mens*) is identified with mind, and includes reason (*ratio*) and understanding (*intellectus*), the latter capable of the highest function of grasping infallible, spiritual truth. His psychological views are found in his *Confessions, City of God, Concerning the Teacher,* and elsewhere in his writings. While they are essentially Platonic, his analysis of the mind into vegetative, animal, and rational activities, or faculties, resembles the position of Aristotle.[80] He follows Plato in holding that truth is not found in sense-experience, which he separates from thought. Our mental images are not produced by the body but by the mind itself, and, indeed, it is the latter that produces sensation from its own substance. Words, symbols, and other sense objects are but stimuli of the faculties, or capacities, already existing in the mind, and an invitation to the student to discover the truths that dwell there. He abandoned Plato's Doctrine of Reminiscence, or the view that the image is innate and was impressed upon the mind in its wandering through the world of Ideas. Thomas Aquinas, unlike Plato and Augustine, assigned to sense-experience a basic rôle in forming mental images and in acquiring knowledge of reality. He, with other scholastics, accepted the principle that "there is nothing in the mind which was not first in the senses." But Aquinas did not question the traditional dualistic conception of human nature nor the view that education is a process of mind building through intellectual experiences.

The records available do not show with any clarity what practical effect, if any, these psychological theories, as such, had upon the methods of teaching used in mediaeval classrooms. They themselves are but a reflection of asceticism, religious beliefs, and, with the scholastics, of respect for reason as it explores the preambles of faith. As for the actual methods of the schools, definite evidence exists. With some exceptions in universities and a few grammar schools, near the end of the period, where discussion and debate had come into use, individual expression was curbed, authority was stressed, and corporal punishment was universally used for infractions of school rules, and probably frequently for neglect of study. Reliance upon books as the only sure source of truth was universal, and the authors of the books were often unenlightened. Monastic

[80] J. Morgan, *The Psychological Teaching of St. Augustine* (London: R. Scott, 1932).

rules imposed upon monks the duties of toil to the point of exhaustion. One good monk is reported to have burned, at the end of each year, everything that he had made so that he might always have work to do.[81]

The concept of discipline thus pervaded education. In the classroom, texts were memorized, students were drilled in the use of words and forms, and the catechetical method was much used, particularly with younger students. We find Alcuin using that method in instructing Charlemagne's son, Pepin, in science. And Pepin memorized a long list of the "correct" answers. "What is frost?" said Alcuin, and Pepin learned the response: "A persecutor of plants, a destroyer of leaves, a fetter of the earth." [82] John of Salisbury tells us how Bernard of Charters (died *c.* 1130) drilled his boys in grammar, literature, and composition, and punished them for their failures, in order to develop their mental faculties. The record states in part: "Because memory is strengthened and talent is sharpened by exercise, he urged some by admonitions to imitate what they had heard and others by blows and penalties. Each was obliged to review on the following day something of what he had heard on the preceding day. . . . They daily wrote prose and poems and drilled themselves in mutual collations." [83] Pierre Dubois, writing in 1309, also emphasized drill and memorization in the study of grammar and composition.[84] A speaking knowledge of Latin was acquired in all church schools by the conversational method.

In 1350, we find an anonymous author, supposed to have been a German clergyman, calling the attention of teachers to the importance of recognizing individual differences, mental, physical, and emotional. He says that there are many degrees of mental ability, running from extreme dullness to extreme brightness. He attributed these differences to climate and "the elements which no scientist or even physician can precisely measure" because "various aspects of the stars" contribute "to these differences and their quasi-innumerable influences upon conception, formation, and birth of children, which somehow spread occult affections in human bodies." And he said that the mind "follows the body in its dispositions." The teacher should correct "the timid by words" and master "the frivolous with rods." And he recommended physical diversion and play to refresh the mind after "the tedium of classes." [85] Today we are trying to measure precisely what he, apparently, desired to see meas-

[81] Haarhoff, *op. cit.*, p. 196.
[82] Cubberley, *op. cit.*, p. 88.
[83] Thorndike, *University Records and Life in the Middle Ages,* pp. 7–9.
[84] *Ibid.*, pp. 141 f.
[85] *Ibid.*, pp. 223 ff.

ured, but we ignore the influence of the stars upon the capacities we measure. While we find some thought being given to individual differences in late mediaeval times, it was the humanist educators who first gave its importance the prominence it deserves.

SCHOOLS. (1) CATECHUMENAL AND CATECHETICAL SCHOOLS. These, the first Christian formal schools, arose for the purpose of instructing pagans in Christian beliefs as a preparation for baptism. The students were known as *catechumens,* or listeners, who learned by *catechesis,* or oral instruction. The course became gradually one of two or three years, and was instituted to test the sincerity of applicants, to safeguard Christian ideals as well as to prepare pagans for baptism, then the last, not the first, step to membership in Christian society. Bishops were the first teachers of catechumens. When all pagans had been converted, this early episcopal function was transferred to the family and to formal church schools. Catechumenal schools appeared first in the East in the second century, and one of them, that at Alexandria, became (*c.* 200) a school of higher learning. That it arose in the shadow of a pagan university and that among its first teachers were the converted philosophers, Clement and Origen, is significant in the history of Western thought and education. Origen was pronounced a heretic because he reconciled pagan and Christian thought too well.[86] This Alexandrian school taught the Scriptures, theology, philosophy, Greek literature and the sciences. Jerusalem, Antioch, Edessa, Caesarea, Rome, and other cities soon had similar schools.[87] These higher schools, an evolution from catechumenal instruction, are known as catechetical schools, and were established chiefly to train leaders who would defend Christianity against paganism. They survived in the cathedral and theological schools of later Christendom.

(2) CATHEDRAL SCHOOLS. At episcopal seats, schools were established from the third century onward to train secular priests for parish work. The first of these probably gave instruction only in pastoral duties, since Christians were then receiving literary education in Roman schools. In Continental Europe, Spain led in organizing cathedral schools. The Council of Toledo (531) requested bishops to establish such schools apparently because of alarm over the spread of the Arian heresy to which secular priests were much exposed. Bishop Isidore in his *Etymologies* remarked that grammar is better than heresy. It was, however, in England that cathedral schools flourished most prior to the eighth century. There, they

[86] Montgomery, *op. cit.,* p. 389; J. T. Shotwell and L. Loomis, *The See of Peter* (New York: Columbia University Press, 1927), pp. 78, 87–89, 93.

[87] Haarhoff, *op. cit.,* p. 176.

began with the establishment of a grammar school at Canterbury (*c.* 598) modeled after those of heathen Rome. It survives today as King's School. Bede (673-735) tells us in his *Ecclesiastical History of the English People* that King Sigebert of East Anglia established a similar school there. Both schools were adjuncts of the church. This type of school had a healthy growth in England even in the Dark Ages, and it is the one true Christian representative of the grammar schools of pagan Rome. It served both clerical and lay students during the early centuries of its existence, a very unusual practice, if it existed at all, in Continental cathedral schools. In Europe, generally, it was a school for those preparing for church positions, and in England it became more and more clerical in purpose as time went on. Poor boys were rarely admitted to cathedral schools.

The Third Lateran Council (1179) of the church ordered that funds be provided in every cathedral for the free education of the cathedral clergy and of poor students "lest the opportunity of reading and education be denied poor children"; and other churches and monasteries, if in the past they ever provided free education for the poor, were ordered to re-establish that practice. Such a decree indicates that many cathedral and other ecclesiastical schools were not providing free education for the poor at the time. Whether or not the order of the Council was obeyed cannot be determined.[88] The Fourth Lateran Council (1215) decreed that every cathedral must provide a grammar school and every archiepiscopal cathedral a professor of theology.[89] It is worth noting here that the son of an unemancipated slave could not be ordained, and that few of servile birth ever rose above the status of servants in mediaeval church positions.[90]

While the bishops themselves were, apparently, the first teachers in cathedral schools, they later delegated this duty to their subordinates, the *cantor* (in charge of the song school) and the *magister scholarum* (in charge of the grammar school). This latter became in time the diocesan chancellor and superintendent of schools in the European episcopal school system. As *magister scholarum* (teacher of students) he, earlier, taught everything from the 3 R's to theology, but, later, used assistants to teach the rudiments. Generally throughout Europe, the cathedral school, prior to the Charlemagne revival of learning, did not teach the liberal arts. The number of these schools in the Dark Ages, and even later, is very uncertain.

88 Thorndike, *University Records and Life in the Middle Ages*, p. 21.
89 LaMonte, *op. cit.*, p. 403.
90 Deanesly, *op. cit.*, pp. 32–33.

There were many bishops then, but it is doubtful that many of them provided grammar schools for their future clergy. Some priests were illiterate, or nearly so, even as late as the fourteenth century.[91] Boys entered cathedral schools at the age of six or seven and pursued a course of study which varied in length from time to time and from place to place. In the later Middle Ages lay students were admitted to these schools, but they did not meet lay needs well.

The earliest church law pertaining to these schools seems to have been enacted in the East. It granted to every priest the privilege of sending a relative, presumably as a free student, to such schools. A second Eastern law authorized priests to establish, in villages and towns, free grammar schools for Christian students in order, apparently, to counteract the influence of Roman schools. The dates of these laws are uncertain, but they probably are earlier than that of the Council of Toledo already referred to. In 797, Bishop Theodulph of Orleans re-enacted these early laws for his French diocese. In 826, the General Church Council of Rome admonished bishops to select "teachers of grammar and the liberal arts" with care, presumably because the existing schools needed to be improved. This official concern appears in the acts of later councils as, for instance, the Lateran Council already referred to. One must not infer, certainly from the earlier pronouncements, that everything was well in church education. The Capitularies of Charlemagne, soon to be examined, reveal a tragic state of educational decay on the Continent at the turn of the ninth century. But, thereafter, the cathedral school grew in importance.

From the eleventh century onward, some cathedral schools became noted centers of learning, many in Northern France attracting students from many lands. Such schools as Chartres, Laon, Paris, and Orleans became very famous. In the twelfth and thirteenth centuries, France became the cultural leader of the Western World. Chivalry, monastic and religious reforms, and Romanesque and Gothic art are among the cultural products of France in those centuries, and from France they spread to neighboring countries. And improvements of cathedral schools there are but a phase of that general cultural advance. It was in the twelfth century that the liberal arts were definitely separated from theology in cathedral schools, the so-called grammar department becoming preparatory to the higher department of theology. The earlier *magister scholarum* was now the bishop's chancellor, head of the theological school and diocesan superintendent of schools. His earlier position passed into the hands of the grammar schoolmaster, a position usually given, after the rise

[91] Coulton, *op. cit.*, pp. 200 ff.

of universities, to those holding the degree of master of arts. With the rise of reformed monastic orders many bishops transferred the direction of cathedral schools to monks, but the secular clergy continued to be the teachers there. These schools, however, remained under episcopal control.

(3) MONASTIC SCHOOLS. Although monastic Rules required monks to read, Continental monasteries prior to the year 800 were mental wildernesses. Yet, when we view Western Christendom as a whole, they were more important centers of learning than cathedrals prior to the year 1000. They were established as spiritual refuges, not as schools, but moral and religious needs made them educational agencies. In spite of Rules, the light of learning had almost gone out in them prior to the Charlemagne Renaissance. They had *scriptoria* and scribes, and prepared manuscripts for reading purposes, but formal schooling they neglected. Their libraries, too, long remained small, many of them having only a few hundred volumes and these mostly of a religious nature. As a result of Charlemagne's commands to abbots and of the influence of Irish monasteries, Continental monastic schools were greatly improved. The seed of the revival, if it should not be called a birth, was brought from Ireland where the light of learning had not yet grown dim.

In the eighth century Ireland was the brightest star in the educational firmament. This was because she had been saved from invasions, had a rich pagan tradition, and developed a church different in organization and ritual from that of Rome. Here, the tribe was the social unit, and the episcopacy, a city institution dominated by the papacy, did not acquire the power it held on the Continent. The Irish monastery, often embracing a whole tribe, and having its own Rule, became the center of ecclesiastical life and administration, and even an abbess, like St. Bridget, sometimes exercised semi-episcopal jurisdiction.[92] Pre-Christian Ireland probably had Celtic Druid schools of higher learning similar to those of Gaul, of which Caesar wrote. When the monks replaced the Druid priests as teachers, they permitted their secular practices to remain in the form of schools of Irish literature and law operating by the side of the monastic school. In the seventh and eighth centuries, these Irish schools drew many students from England and the Continent. From Bede's account, it is reasonable to infer that the monastic schools of Ireland were open to the laity and that maintenance and instruction in them were free to some, if not all, students. While Latin seems to have been the language of instruction, the monks also taught the vernacu-

[92] J. Ryan, *Irish Monasticism* (Dublin: The Talbot Press, 1931), pp. 179–84.

lar language and sometimes became teachers of Irish law and literature in the secular schools. This ancient glory ended with the Viking invasions (795 onward), but round towers and old monastic ruins still stand as reminders of that past.[93] Perhaps more important than their work at home was the missionary and educational work of Irish monks in Britain and on the Continent. In the sixth and seventh centuries they founded such famous monasteries as Luxeuil and Bobbio, forerunners of many later ones. The work of these monks is the one bright spot in the dismal picture of monastic education in the Dark Ages.

From the tenth century onward, such new orders of monks as the Cluniacs, the Franciscans and the Dominicans showed greater respect for learning than the older Benedictine monks, although they preoccupied themselves with theology and preaching. The other new orders were generally extreme ascetics and unfriendly to literary culture. In the twelfth and thirteenth centuries these new orders established thousands of houses all over Europe, and all presumably had schools at least for their own *oblati*. There are records, however, which show that literary education was badly neglected in some English monasteries on the eve of the Reformation, and that some monks there were almost illiterate.[94] And there are other records which show some English monasteries of the time providing grammar school education for the sons of aristocrats.[95]

There were two types of monastic schools: one for *oblati*, or those entering monastic life; the other for *externi*, or outsiders. Only Irish monasteries had the latter. We read of abbots who provided instruction in handicrafts for the orphans of serfs, and of other abbots who fined their peasants for sending their sons to school.[96] What any individual monastery or monastic house did depended, obviously, upon the views of the abbot or upon the purposes of the rulers of monastic orders. It can, however, be said with certainty that, in the total mediaeval picture, the monastery contributed less to the spread of literary culture than did the cathedral. Its chief contribution appears in its upholding of a moral ideal and in dignifying manual toil, particularly in a barbaric age when some bishops were setting a very bad moral example for the people. The rule requiring seven hours of manual labor each day introduced a

[93] Graham, *op. cit.*

[94] Cubberley, *op. cit.*, p. 263.

[95] A. F. Leach, *Schools of Mediaeval England* (London: Methuen & Co., Ltd., 1915), p. 115.

[96] Coulton, *op. cit.*, pp. 78–79, 184.

useful form of physical education into monasteries.[97] Later monks, such as those of Cluny, gave more time to study and prayer and less to labor, although other later orders (*e.g.* the Cistercians) clung to the labor ideal, perhaps in part because it had proved its worth in building great monastic estates.

(4) SONG SCHOOLS. Singing was deemed important by the church. Pope Gregory the Great, a pioneer in the founding of song schools, forbade bishops to confer "orders" upon boys who could not sing, and nearly every cathedral came to have a song school which, in the later period, was sometimes connected with the cathedral grammar school, particularly in England. A similar school, known as an "almonry school," was conducted by English monasteries for the children of beggars.[98] The song school was generally for poor boys who were boarded and instructed free in return for choir and other church services. In addition to singing, they were taught elementary Latin and, occasionally, arithmetic. A few of these boys later became priests and received instruction in grammar and theology. In the later Middle Ages, non-choir boys were admitted to song schools which, with parish schools, came to be the chief elementary schools of the church. The cantor, who was head of the song school, became, in some places, a supervisor of elementary schools with authority to grant teaching licenses.[99]

(5) PARISH SCHOOLS. Outside of episcopal towns, it appears that few parishes, if any, had schools prior to Charlemagne's time. Individual bishops occasionally requested parish priests to instruct youth in singing and morals, as did the Council of Vaison, in 529. Other church councils in the ninth century made similar demands, but continuing admonitions of councils and bishops indicate that many parish priests neglected to do so. In the later Middle Ages, parish schools increased in number, but they apparently taught little more than singing and prayers. The Bishop of Winchester, England, in 1295, asked priests to "take care that boys in their parishes know the Lord's Prayer, the Creed, and the Salutation of the Blessed Virgin, and how to cross themselves rightly."[100] The song and parish schools were the chief schools provided by the church for poor lay students. In England, late in the mediaeval

97 E. F. Henderson, *Select Historical Documents of the Middle Ages* (London: George Bell & Sons, Ltd., 1892), pp. 274 ff.

98 Leach, *op. cit.*, pp. 229 f.

99 Thorndike, *University Records and Life in the Middle Ages,* pp. 239–41; Cubberley, *op. cit.*, pp. 124 f.

100 Cubberley, *op. cit.*, p. 124.

period, there appeared, in connection with almshouses, so-called Hospital Schools for young inmates, but their relation to the church is not clear.

(6) Collegiate Church Schools. From the twelfth century, some churches were administered by communities of secular priests who lived under a Rule and conducted grammar schools which were among the best schools of the late Middle Ages. While these schools attracted some lay-minded students, their work had church service as its primary goal. Great noblemen occasionally endowed these communities of priests especially, it seems, for the purpose of providing grammar schools for their sons as well as for boys intending to become priests.

(7) Other Later Mediaeval Schools. The merchant and craft gilds usually employed priests to conduct their religious services and pray for their dead members. Many of these priests conducted schools for members' children and sometimes for other children of the community. These schools, known as *gild schools,* occasionally developed into grammar schools.

Rich men sometimes endowed a chapel and priests to chant prayers for the donors' souls and often required them to provide free grammar schools for all boys seeking admission. These *chantry schools* were confined mostly to England where there were about one hundred of them in 1500. There were schools known by such names as *Stipendiary Schools* and *Morrow Mass Schools,* but they were endowed and conducted in almost the same way as the chantry schools.

The chief significance of gild, chantry and other similar schools is that, while their teachers were priests, they were not under the direct control of the church. Lay interest and participation in education increased in the fourteenth and fifteenth centuries. Winchester College, England, founded in 1382, and Eton College, founded in 1440, were established for an educational, not a clerical, purpose. In fifteenth-century England, principalships of grammar schools began to be opened to laymen. Lay activity in education never entirely ceased in the Middle Ages, and it increased as the period came to a close. It appears clearly in (1) Lay Schools of Italy and Ireland, (2) Royal Schools, (3) the Schools of Chivalry and (4) private and municipal vernacular schools.

(8) Lay Schools Controlled by the Laity. **(a) Schools of grammar, rhetoric, and law.** Schools of the Roman type never entirely disappeared from Italy, and they seem to have been encouraged, if not supported, in part by towns. We have noted earlier that

law was studied in "city schools" of Ravenna, Pavia, and Bologna. Their teachers were referred to by ecclesiastics as "lay philosophers," and were looked upon with suspicion. These schools served a lay educational purpose, not that of professional training of the clergy. In 1051, Wippo of Burgundia exhorted Emperor Henry III to introduce the Italian lay system into Germany where only clerical students attended school.[101] In Ireland, as we have seen, there were lay schools of history, poetry, and law which continued, apparently, until the Viking invasion in 795, if not to a later date.[102]

(b) Royal schools. Some of the royal successors of the barbarian kings who conquered Rome took an active interest in education. Among these were Theodoric of the Ostrogoths, who ruled in Italy, and King Chilperic of Gaul. The former attempted to preserve the old Roman grammar schools, and the latter ordered the towns in his kingdom to provide schools of Greek and Latin letters. Both these kings lived in the sixth century. King Sigebert of East Anglia, in England, established a school about the year 700, as did Alfred the Great later.[103] In Aquitaine there appeared a group of royal schools.[104] The most significant royal effort was, however, that of the Frankish king Pepin, who founded a Palace School, and of his emperor son, Charlemagne (768-814) who made the school famous as a literary model for his empire. We shall say more about this school and its teachers when we describe the Charlemagne Renaissance.

(c) Schools of chivalry. The feudal nobility, pursuing their own worldly life, needed an education different from that of servants of the church whose needs were met by the liberal arts, particularly grammar, and by theology. The nobility had little need for literary education, since the clerk (clergyman) was available to keep records. The church established its schools primarily for its own servants, not for the laity, even the lay nobility. In earlier centuries, some nobles were illiterate, but some others, such as Chaucer's squire, could read and write. Even in later centuries, noblemen, while mostly literate, displayed a marked lack of literary culture. In their training they received only a modicum of literary education. Chivalry became after the eleventh century the way of life of the nobility, and boys learned that way through an established mode of training and by participation in chivalric life.

[101] Poole, *op. cit.*, pp. 81 ff.; Deanesly, *op. cit.*, pp. 209 f.

[102] Fitzpatrick, *op. cit.*, p. 341.

[103] E. P. Cheyney, *Readings in English History* (Boston: Ginn & Co., 1908), pp. 52 f., 63 ff.; Ogg, *op. cit.*, pp. 235 ff.

[104] Poole, *op. cit.*, p. 29.

The boy of the lesser nobility to the age of seven was instructed by his mother in reading, if she herself could read, and in morals and religion. Thereafter, he became a page and, from the age of fourteen to twenty, a squire in the castle of his father's overlord, where he was instructed with his overlord's own sons. To the age of fourteen he was under the supervision of the ladies of the castle who taught him the rules of love, the proprieties of personal service, singing, dancing, family duties, morals, and chivalric virtues, while the men taught him running, riding, wrestling, the use of toy weapons, and how to dress his overlord. As a squire, he was instructed by men only, and now he was taught the rules of dress, general etiquette, wrestling, jumping, swimming, hunting, hawking, duelling, riding in heavy armor, and other sports and arts related to war and the tournament. He also waited upon his lord both inside and outside the castle, performing all kinds of personal service, including waiting at table. Now, too, he learned parlor games and, often, music so that he might be agreeable to the ladies. He spoke the language of his own country or neighborhood and, in later centuries, received some instruction in Latin and in reading and writing his own vernacular language.

While the nobles were far from eminent in letters, they were patrons of vernacular literatures when the church neglected them. No boy, however noble by birth, could earn the honor of knighthood unless he had pursued this formal course of training, which ended with the formal ceremony of dubbing. On the night before the ceremony, the young man fasted and prayed; and in the morning he bathed, put on clean garments and confessed his sins to a priest. The rest of the ceremony, usually performed in a church, was quite formal, and in it an officiating knight and friends and relatives had a part. It ended with the girding on of the sword. Often many young men were knighted in a general ceremony. A banquet and a tournament followed. Food was distributed to the guests, and the left-overs went to the poor. Minstrels were there to sing and recite tales of heroic knights of old, and the ceremony sometimes lasted for weeks.

This whole scheme of training was lay and secular, and it did not end with the age of chivalry. Wherever we find in later schools an emphasis upon gentlemanly character, honor, politeness, generosity, devotion to duty, and sportsmanship, there too we find the ideal that permeated the mediaeval schools of chivalry at their best. The church helped to mould these ideals in its efforts to Christianize the barbarian warrior. But the knight, as indeed many churchmen, did not live according to the ideals. Indeed, from the failure of ideals to influence conduct in mediaeval and other times, some observers have concluded that a negative correlation has existed between ideals and practices in civilized societies, but fortunately that conclusion is still but an opinion.[105]

(d) Private and city vernacular schools. The revival of town and city life had most important results for education in the later Middle Ages. The walled cities bristled with commercial and political activity. Town life demanded a new education to meet the new needs for penmen, bookkeepers, and those engaged in civil administration. These needs were first met by private, lay scriveners who conducted schools of writing, reckoning, and bookkeeping. This type of school probably never disappeared thereafter, and it was these private teachers who were most daring in keeping the unlicensed schools that are often mentioned in the records of the time.[106] By the thirteenth century, there were few large towns which did not have their own schools. The first of these were taught by priests and controlled by the church, although they were supported, in varying degrees, by the towns. The last step in this development appears in the rise of the *Burgh Schools* of Scotland and Germany, which were maintained by the towns, and whose teachers, usually laymen, were often appointed by the town authorities. Church chancellors claimed the right to inspect these schools, and to license their teachers, but the cities were not always friendly to church control.[107]

These city developments brought an emphasis upon the vernacular tongues and practical arithmetic in education. The private teachers of writing and bookkeeping seem to have used the vernacular exclusively. The *Burgh Schools,* as they acquired freedom from church control, stressed practical training in the vernacular and in arithmetic for business and civic ends. Church schools neglected the vernacular in favor of Latin, the professional language of the clergy, and they taught arithmetic as a liberal art rather than as a useful instrument. Practical arithmetic was thus something to be learned on the job, but such apprenticeship training could not serve the urgent needs of growing industry and commerce. A new type of leadership was demanded by city life, and the Burgh School arose to supply it. Only about one-tenth of the people of the cities were burghers, or full citizens, and the Burgh School originated as a school for middle-class citizens. Its purpose was secular and utilitarian.

105 Cornish, *op. cit.,* pp. 47–83; Davis, *op. cit.,* pp. 123 f., 176 ff., 200 ff.; Hulme, *op. cit.,* pp. 239–65; LaMonte, *op. cit.,* pp. 383 ff.

106 Thorndike, *University Records and Life in the Middle Ages,* pp. 239–41.

107 J. W. Thompson, *The Literacy of the Laity in the Middle Ages* (Berkeley: University of California Press, 1939), p. 501.

The public vernacular school of today is, thus, a child of mediaeval cities, although the Reformation was an influential factor in the spread of such schools. Vocational, rather than religious and national, demands brought it into existence, and gave the 3 R's the vocational significance which, in part, marks them still.

The Charlemagne Renaissance

While the increased educational activity of the later mediaeval centuries was due to a complex of factors which we have already considered, the beginning of the end of the Dark Ages dates, in a special way, from the efforts of Charlemagne (716-814) to revive learning. The example had been set for him by earlier kings, as we have seen, among whom was his father Pepin. But Charlemagne seems to have grasped the political importance of education better than his predecessors. He was not only a conqueror who built an empire embracing almost all Europe but an able legislator and imperial administrator as well. In return for favors, Pope Leo III, in the name of the Maker of empires, placed the crown of the Roman empire upon his head on Christmas Day (800), and Charlemagne, servant and master of the church, accepted the honor with seeming humility.

Charlemagne's intellectual revival centered in the Palace School for nobles at Aix-la-Chapelle to which he brought as teachers the leading scholars of England, Spain and Italy. The most notable of these teachers were Alcuin of England, and Peter of Pisa and Paul the Deacon, both of Italy. The school was to be a model for his empire, whose people he wished to elevate by "a study of letters, well-nigh extinguished" he said "through the neglect of our ancestors."[108] In addition, however, to creating this model school, he addressed "capitularies" to all bishops and abbots in which he commanded them to establish schools. These edicts were probably written by Alcuin who seems to have played the rôle of his minister of education from 782 to 796. The first one, issued in 787, expressed alarm over the incorrect language of monks, which he viewed as an obstacle to an understanding of the Scriptures, and requested the clergy to devote themselves to study.[109] The second capitulary (789) commanded that bishops and abbots require the clergy to associate with the children of both freemen and serfs, and establish schools of reading for them, presumably in parishes and in monasteries. And the last capitulary (802) recommended that all boys

[108] Mullinger, *op. cit.*, p. 101.

[109] A. J. West, *Alcuin and the Rise of the Christian Schools* (New York: Charles Scribner's Sons, 1892), p. 49.

study grammar and remain in school until they had become well instructed.[110] To insure the co-operation of church officials, he had his traveling representatives (*missi dominici*) act as school inspectors.

While, as we have seen, other kings were active in promoting education, Charlemagne was the most forceful and effective upholder of the educational prerogative of the state in the Middle Ages. Although the church Council of Aachen (817) forbade monasteries to admit *externi* to their schools, the bishops generally supported the royal encouragement of learning. In 829, the bishops of Gaul requested Charlemagne's son, Louis I, to follow his father's example in establishing schools.[111] It was Louis' son, Charles the Bald, who brought Eriugena to the Palace School. His presence there links the Charlemagne Renaissance, thinly no doubt, with the later scholastic controversies. And in the Italian section of the empire, divided at Charlemagne's death, the emperor Lothaire issued, in 825, an edict calling for the establishment of nine city schools, because he found learning extinct there. That edict apparently prompted the ensuing church Council of Rome to order bishops to establish schools. These developments provide some tangible evidence of the immediate effect of Charlemagne's efforts to revive learning. While a second decline followed the disintegration of his empire, learning never again reached the depths that it had gone to in the early centuries of the Dark Ages.

Alcuin (735-804), who came to the Palace School from the cathedral school of York, England, was perhaps the leading light in the revival, although his chief writings were but dialogues on grammar, rhetoric, and dialectic. Paul the Deacon and Einhart are better known for their writings. The former wrote a *History of the Longobards*,[112] and the latter wrote *The Life of Charlemagne*,[113] a work in fairly good classical Latin. Charlemagne's own interest in history brought an order to each monastery to keep a yearly record of all local and national events, and some of the annals resulting from this order are now of much historical value. Of the individual thinkers and teachers stimulated by the revival Eriugena was the most original and most influential. And the revival was not confined to the Continent.

110 *Ibid.*, p. 56.

111 Poole, *op. cit.*, p. 24.

112 Trans. by W. D. Foulke in *Translations and Reprints from the Original Sources of Mediaeval History*, ser. 2 (Philadelphia: The University of Pennsylvania, 1907).

113 Reprinted in J. F. Scott, A. Hyma, and A. H. Noyes, *Readings in Mediaeval History* (New York: Appleton-Century-Crofts, Inc., 1933), pp. 149–66.

In England, Charlemagne's work stimulated a similar revival under the leadership of kings, of whom Alfred the Great (871-899) was the most notable performer. A decline of learning had previously occurred in England as a result of Danish invasions,[114] and Alfred attempted to check it. He, therefore, established a Palace School, and asked the church to increase its educational efforts so that "all free-born youths," of necessary wealth and "not fit for any other occupation," should remain in school until they could "read English well," while the better ones should remain longer to study Latin.[115] While Charlemagne had to come to England for aid in his work, Alfred now had to go to the Continent for scholars. Unlike Charlemagne, he was himself a scholar, and he translated into Anglo-Saxon Boethius' *Consolation of Philosophy* and the histories of Orosius and Bede. In addition, he founded the *Anglo-Saxon Chronicle* which, until it ceased (1154), was the leading vernacular historical journal in the West.

These activities of monarchs show that state interest in education never ceased in Western Christendom. And it is significant that the state apparently feared the darkness of the mind more than did the church, the asceticism of which was perhaps the most influential factor in the making of the Dark Ages.

Women's Education

We have examined earlier the status of women in mediaeval society and the views of influential Christians regarding their rôle in the world. The theory and practice of women's education reflected their status in society and the Christian conception of the ideal woman. Some of the Church Fathers were not opposed to a literary education for girls, but they were more concerned about their moral training. Thus, St. Jerome, who approved a literary education for them, would have "boys with wanton thoughts" and attendants of "loose" and "worldly" character kept away from them. A mother, he said, in rearing her daughter should "not pierce her ears or paint her face," nor "load her with jewels," nor "redden her hair," suggestive of the fires of hell. A girl should always be accompanied in public by her mother, and no "young dandy with curled hair" should be allowed to "greet her with smiles." A girl should spend her day in prayer and pious reading, and she should learn "to spin wool, to hold the distaff, to put the basket in her lap, to turn

114 A. F. Leach, *Educational Charters and Documents* (London: Cambridge University Press, 1911), p. 23.

115 *Ibid.*, p. 25.

the spinning wheel and to shape the yarn with her thumb." She should be educated in a monastery and remain ignorant of the world.[116]

Jerome's liberal view of literary education for girls disappeared with the growth of asceticism, but his other views survived. Many Christian women entered the cloister from the days of declining Rome. There, the Rules usually required nuns to read, but the records are silent regarding their pursuit of the liberal arts in mediaeval nunneries, where the emphasis was placed upon their moral and religious training. Nunneries, however, had small libraries, and a few nuns in the late Middle Ages were engaged in copying books. Sewing, weaving, and other domestic arts were probably taught to all entrants to nunneries, but nuns of aristocratic birth usually had their own private maids and did not engage in manual work.[117] Irish nunneries were apparently more liberal in educating their *oblati* and, perhaps, their *externi*, than were nunneries generally. The twelfth-century Austin canonesses were forbidden by their Rule to teach so that they might give all their time to manual work and prayer.[118]

Outside of the nunneries—which until late in the period seldom had schools for outsiders—and the castles of the nobility, the mediaeval woman's education, with the exception of the practice in the medical center at Salerno, and domestic apprenticeship training in fifteenth century England,[119] was the informal domestic, moral, religious and physical training demanded by life and the environment. The family and the church were the chief agencies providing that training. Charlemagne seems not to have included girls in his scheme of education. While the word "children" appears at times in his edicts, the words "boys" and "sons" are the most frequent ones used by him. He apparently did not consider the literary education of girls a necessity. No one, as far as we know, has yet attempted to discover the relationship between literacy and sainthood, but the records reveal that the mediaeval world produced relatively few female saints. We hear little at all about women of the period, except those rich ladies who became notorious for their scheming and their moral irregularities. The mass of women, no doubt, led normal lives for the time, and passed on into the heaven of the ascetics without leaving behind any evidence of their influence upon human

116 Cubberley, *op. cit.*, pp. 59 ff.

117 A. C. Flick, *The Decline of the Mediaeval Church* (London: Routledge & Kegan Paul, Ltd., 1930), II, 442.

118 Deanesly, *op. cit.*, pp. 218 f.

119 T. L. Jarman, *Landmarks in the History of Education* (London: The Cresset Press, 1951), p. 124.

destiny. The world of the Middle Ages was an anti-feminist world, but the daughters of the nobility enjoyed in it a freedom and an opportunity for culture denied to women generally and even to nuns.

Girls of the nobility were often taught by private tutors in their castles. While polite manners and religious and moral conduct were stressed, reading and writing in Latin and French and, occasionally, the elements of arithmetic and astronomy were also included in their instruction. In a less formal way the ladies were instructed in the healing properties of herbs and in practical nursing, since among their duties was the care of wounded warriors. Noblewomen, too, instructed their daughters in housekeeping and in wifely duties. Nor was physical training of these girls neglected, for they participated freely in such sports as riding, hunting, hawking, etc.

The instruction of women in medicine, surgery, midwifery, and nursing at Salerno, Italy, was apparently confined to this one center. While nearly all mediaeval women performed nursing duties, there existed neither a nursing profession nor formal schools of nursing. The Salerno school was exceptional. With the exception of those in nunneries and castles, mediaeval women were almost universally illiterate. Formal educational opportunities for boys, until late in the period, were very limited; those for girls, far more limited still. By the fourteenth century opportunities for girls outside of the cloister and castle were increasing. Previously, a few were probably admitted to song schools, and some nunneries had begun to instruct well-to-do girls as a source of income. We hear of girls attending reading schools in Florence in 1338,[120] and of Parisian schools for girls, taught by women, in 1357. In Paris and its suburbs, at that time, there were twenty-one women teachers, some of whom apparently taught Latin grammar, but to girls only, for women were not permitted to instruct boys.[121]

While mediaeval thought frowned upon learned women, one voice at least, that of Pierre Dubois, spoke out in opposition. He was a political theorist who, in 1309, urged the public education of selected youths, both boys and girls, from the age of four to maturity, for service in the Holy Land and the Orient. While he would have boys instructed in Latin, Greek, Arabic, the other liberal arts, medicine, military tactics, etc., the girls would be instructed chiefly in medicine, surgery and related subjects, and in Latin, another foreign language, logic, and the rudiments of natural science. Said he: "These girls . . . namely the noble and other more prudent

120 *Ibid.*, p. 120.

121 Thorndike, *University Records and Life in the Middle Ages,* pp. 239–41.

ones, suited in body and form, will be adopted as daughters and granddaughters of the greater chiefs of those regions . . . so that they may be given as wives to the greater princes, clergy and other wealthy Orientals."[122] This proposal remained on paper, but it is important as an example of the most original thought of the time on the problem of women's education.

Physical Education

Asceticism, as we have seen, brought an end to physical education in Christian schools of the Dark Ages but, from the twelfth century, we find English cathedral schoolboys playing ball games on festival days,[123] although these games were not yet a part of the school program. The schools of chivalry were the only ones that then provided systematic physical education, which, for the nobility, was a preparation for war and such sports as the joust, the duel, and the tournament.

Largely from the sports of the nobility, popular sports arose, but the church frowned upon such delights of the common people. Dancing, the church denounced as satanical, but the people danced.[124] Wrestling, juggling, and feats of strength performed by common men at fairs were also denounced. Ecclesiastics outlawed the ball games of peasants but not the sports of the nobility. Royalty, too, forbade many games of boys because these killed interest in archery and shooting. Priests sometimes set a bad example by playing dice and quoits.[125] Village football was a fairly common sport in the fourteenth century, and schoolboys in England were playing it even earlier but not on the school grounds. Interest in physical diversions never entirely disappeared, even in the most ascetical centuries. As, however, in every society and period, physical education was generally of the informal variety, springing from the demands of man's physical nature and from the need for survival. The life of the peasant was a physical life, as was that of many monks and nuns who observed the letter of their Rules. Some monks were skilled artisans who pursued their several trades and offered their products for sale in the markets of Europe. The Irish monasteries enforced the duty of manual labor. When the Benedictines grew lax in enforcing this duty, other orders of monks arose and enforced it upon their members. The military life, too, provided physical education for the soldier and sailor.

122 *Ibid.*, pp. 138–49.
123 Jarman, *op. cit.*, pp. 82–83.
124 Coulton, *op. cit.*, pp. 559 ff.
125 *Ibid.*, pp. 93 ff., 480 ff., 561 f.

Charlemagne had no regular army or navy, but he required all freemen to bear arms, some as cavalry and some as infantry. His soldiers, however, were given no special training but were recruited hastily from farmers and nobles for each campaign. The Norsemen, however, had, apparently, regular armies and navies, and Alfred the Great was led by their example to reorganize his army and to found a navy.[126] The military training records of the Dark Ages are not plentiful, but there is an abundance of records which reveal the mode of military training of the later feudal warrior.

Hunting and sports seem never to have entirely disappeared in the Dark Ages. The sons of Charlemagne and Alfred the Great engaged in both. And all children, no doubt, laughed and played in the midst of the gloom created by ascetics. By the twelfth century, when the epidemic of asceticism had subsided, we find youths and adults enjoying many forms of diversion. There were, for instance, at local and international fairs, all sorts of amusements, including cockfights, racing, dancing, acrobatic displays, etc. Nature had again begun to compete with supernature on more equal terms.

Educational Control and Support

The dominating agency of educational control was the church, each bishop and abbot exercising that function under authority delegated to them by the pope and the church councils. The pope exercised some direct control over city vernacular schools by reserving to himself the licensing authority over them. And laymen in universities had to pay fees to him for attending lectures in law and physics.[127] Ecclesiastical control was never, however, complete, as is evidenced by the existence of lay schools in Ireland and Italy, and by the existence of royal and other schools, in the operation of which the church was but a partner of the lay agencies which founded them.

Support of monastic, cathedral, song, and parish schools came, in part, from church revenues and, in part, from fees paid by students, and from gifts of their relatives and friends to teachers and schools. *Oblati* in monasteries and a limited number of poor students in nearly all church schools were taught gratuitously, and some later schools, as we have seen, were privately endowed for the benefit of the poor. The records seem to indicate that it was the policy of the church to provide free instruction for desiring students who could not afford to pay for it. Many, however, in later centuries, who

[126] LaMonte, *op. cit.*, pp. 159, 197.

[127] Flick, *The Decline of the Mediaeval Church*, II, 120 ff.

could afford to pay fees went to lay schools, sometimes kept by unlicensed private teachers, whose competition with church schools met with sharp clerical opposition.

In these later centuries, teaching became a profitable activity in which the church tried, though vainly, to establish a monopoly. Burgh School buildings were provided by the towns, but the teachers in them were supported by tuition fees. The lay town schools of Italy, previously referred to, seem to have had some support from town revenues, and the Palace Schools of Charlemagne and Alfred were, no doubt, supported, in part at least, by their founders. Charlemagne and other noblemen gave gifts to bishops and abbots to aid them in providing education, and these gifts were probably the first examples of Christian philanthrophy as a mode of school support. Since the church came to possess great landed wealth, its revenues were sufficient to provide fairly adequately for schools, especially when the priests and monks taught, as they did, without salary. Had the church schools been responsive to the needs of the laity in a changing world, competing schools would have disappeared and others would not have arisen. Church control declined when the church was unable or unwilling to provide the education which the public needed.

The Extent of Popular Education

In spite of the seeming variety and number of schools in mediaeval Europe, the masses were illiterate. Mediaeval Europe had no school system or compulsory education. The ecclesiastical and feudal nobility viewed the servile condition of laborers as a reflection of God's will, a fact which creates a strong presumption against the literacy of the peasantry. Favorable decrees of church councils and bishops prove little with regard to actual practices, for good intentions and practices were far apart in the Middle Ages. Peasants sinned shockingly in spite of the most solemn prohibitions of God and the church.[128] Of the Bible, the mass, and other religious matters the masses, excepting an occasional heretic, knew practically nothing. Indeed, many of the clergy did not know the meaning of the ritual and prayers they themselves recited. The enlightenment of a nearly primitive peasantry was not easy, and churchmen knew that knowledge brought unbelief. But some priests spent time in driving away evil spirits which might have been more profitably used in dispelling ignorance.[129] The church did much, but it might have done much more.

[128] Coulton, *The Mediaeval Village,* pp. 561–62.
[129] *Ibid.,* pp. 265–66, 268.

Secular rulers and nobles were often greater enemies of popular enlightenment than churchmen. Rulers such as Charlemagne and Alfred the Great were exceptionally progressive, but their efforts bore little fruit as far as the masses were concerned. In the later Middle Ages, England seems to have been far ahead of her neighbors in providing education for the poor, but even here the provision was inconsiderable. Poor boys were the chief beneficiaries of Song Schools, Hospital and Almonry Schools, but these reached only a few.[130] How many poor were thus provided for elsewhere in Europe is impossible to determine. The school constantly mentioned in the records is the Latin grammar school of the church, a school designed to educate a celibate clergy. The transmission of a respect for knowledge from father to son was prevented by the practice of celibacy. The gradual spread of liberal learning among the lay aristocracy restored education, in time, to the secular status and respect it held in ancient times and accelerated its transmission.

The peasant-laborer group comprised probably 90 per cent of the European population. God must, indeed, have loved them because he made so many of them. Under feudalism they lived in little villages; never wandered far from home; knew few outsiders; had no reading matter; and felt no need for even a knowledge of the alphabet. They were taught in the school of life and of the realities of their humble existence. Their lives were spent in almost unceasing labor. When the lord's tax-collectors were humane, they burned holy candles. An occasional bright peasant boy, guided by a local priest, found his way into the priesthood, and peasants spoke in wonderment of any such boy who ever rose to the episcopal rank. Generally, peasants lived and died in filth, poverty, and ignorance. With the rise of cities, the facilities for the education of laborers improved, the improvement being greatest in Italian cities, where the rate of literacy in the fourteenth century was fairly high. In Northern European cities, a high rate of illiteracy seems to have continued.[131]

Vocational Education and Apprenticeship Training

We have noted that the formal education of the clergy was for them vocational as well as general. Many priests, too, learned their jobs by the practical, apprenticeship method.[132] It was by ap-

[130] A. F. Leach, *English Schools of the Reformation* (Westminster: Constable & Co., Ltd., 1896), pp. 229 f.

[131] Thompson, *Economic and Social History of Europe in the Later Middle Ages*, pp. 457–58; J. W. Thompson, *The Literacy of the Laity in the Middle Ages.*

[132] G. G. Coulton, *Europe's Apprenticeship* (New York: Thomas Nelson & Sons, 1940), chap. iii.

prenticeship that all crafts and practical skills were learned and transmitted in the Middle Ages. That practice was institutionalized by the craft gilds in the twelfth and thirteenth centuries, and shows some similarities with the procedures used in the training of the knight. Like the future knight, the applicant for gild membership became an apprentice to a master craftsman at about the age of seven, and remained in his service generally for about seven or eight years. Thereafter, he became a journeyman or hired laborer, in the shops of other master craftsmen. As such he fell into the ranks of the city proletariat. When he had acquired sufficient experience, he was examined by gild examiners and, if he passed his examination, he was enrolled as a master member of the gild. The master under whom he was an apprentice was required by the terms of a written agreement to feed and clothe him, teach him reading and writing and supervise his morals, but the records do not show how well he discharged this obligation. As a master craftsman, the new gild member could employ apprentices and journeymen in his own shop, where the tools and raw materials were exclusively his property and where he sold his products directly to the consumer. In the late Middle Ages, Italian masters sold their services to merchants, the first middlemen in European commerce. While these gilds in time disappeared, the apprenticeship system of training did not, and it has only been in recent times that schools have assumed the function of training craftsmen.

Teachers

Although lay teachers were tolerated, the preacher was officially the teacher prior to the Reformation. The most learned among the clergy taught the liberal arts. The rudiments were taught apparently by the junior clergy, or by priests not distinguished for their attainments.

There was no teaching, as separate from the clerical, profession until near the close of the Middle Ages. The duty of teaching and supervising schools came in time to be assigned, as a special activity, to designated regular and secular priests such as the *magister scholarum* and the chancellor, who gave all of their time to education. It was, however, with the advent of universities that a distinct teaching profession arose which, with the professions of law and medicine, gradually became a serious rival of the clerical profession. The university professor, very often a layman even from the beginning of universities, was held in high social esteem until, in our own day, the popularization of higher education and the lowering of academic requirements for his position have adversely affected his social status. Generally, however, throughout the total sweep of the Middle Ages, the teacher was poorly qualified, and the masses were poorly instructed.

Wandering students, in university times, were sometimes employed as assistant teachers. Burgher schoolmasters had to pay the wages of their assistants out of meager incomes, and they sometimes employed men of low character and little learning. With an awakening desire for learning among the poor, despicable men often opened schools in hovels and workshops for laborers' children, and the feeling grew among the masses that anyone with a knowledge of the 3 R's was qualified to keep school. Under the Roman and mediaeval systems the common people accepted degradation and ignorance as their lot. The priests who, as teachers of the 3 R's, preceded the lay vagabond teachers of the fourteenth and fifteenth centuries were often nearly illiterate. The Middle Ages contributed nothing significant to the development and acceptance of the idea that the poor have a right to the services of a good teacher.

Teaching was generally a male activity. In nunneries and castles, as we have seen, some nuns and all noblewomen had certain teaching functions to perform. As we enter the fourteenth century, we find lay women conducting schools for girls in Paris and its suburbs, and the practice probably prevailed also in other French cities. The Middle Ages, however, did little to create the "female peril" in education, frequently referred to in the nineteenth century.

Mediaeval Universities

ORIGIN. No modern institution is more mediaeval in origin than the university. While the Graeco-Roman world had somewhat similar schools, it was the mediaeval world that established the pattern of the universities of today. Although the medical school at Salerno, originating in the late ninth century, is generally called a university, the University of Bologna, dating from the early twelfth century, when it became a famous center of legal studies, deserves the distinction of being the first of our universities. The earliest universities were not planned or legally "founded," but just grew up by an addition of the new studies of Roman and canon law, Aristotelian philosophy and Arabic science to the old liberal arts. The change made these schools more attractive to lay-minded students. The fame of great teachers, such as Abelard at Paris, attracted many foreign students interested in the debate between realists and nominalists. Students from England, Scotland, Ireland, Flanders,

Germany, Normandy and other faraway places came to hear Abelard defend his views against the realist position of William of Champeaux.[133]

It was out of the enrichment of the program of some cathedral schools and the revival of interest in learning that universities arose. The term *universitas* was then applied to all chartered gilds, and the gild of professors or students was given this general designation. Its own distinguishing title was *studium generale,* or school privileged to grant a universal teaching license, as opposed to the *studium particulare* whose graduates could teach only within a diocese of the church. For a time, universities chartered by kings could grant licenses valid only within the kingdom. Such a school was known as a *studium generale respectu regni,* but all of these, in time, came to be recognized as *studia generalia.* Those which, like Paris and Padua, could not show a papal or imperial charter were known as *studia generalia ex consuetudine* (by tradition). In some universities the students held the charter; in others the masters held it. By the fifteenth century the terms *universitas* and *studium generale* had become synonymous.

CAUSES. Associated with the rise of universities were (1) an intellectual awakening produced largely by the realist-nominalist controversy and the contact of Christians with Arab, Jewish, and Greek scholars; (2) the rise of cities and a burgher class interested in the profits they could get from a student population as well as from some forms of worldly learning which the universities promoted; and (3) the inadequacy of the old schools to meet the needs of a changing world. The "Wise Men" and citizens of Ferrara, in 1442, voted to re-establish a university there, because it would bring honor to the city and keep youths at home "where they can learn without expense, and our money will not fly away."[134] Moreover they thought that outside students are of the "greatest utility" to the city "through their purchase of victuals, lodgings, and other necessaries."[135] But the greatest return to cities and states came through the training of doctors, lawyers, and teachers, now demanded by the new life of Europe. All factors which helped to change the otherworldly mind of Christendom contributed to the rise of universities. In addition to such general causes, a special interest in law, medicine, philosophy, or theology stimulated the rise of individual institutions, such as Bologna, Salerno, and Paris.

By the fifteenth century universities existed everywhere in Eu-

[133] Carré, *op. cit.,* pp. 42 f.

[134] Thorndike, *University Records and Life in the Middle Ages,* pp. 333 f.

[135] *Ibid.,* p. 310.

rope. There was one in every important Italian city, those of Bologna (twelfth century), Padua (1222), and Naples (1224) being the leading ones. In France there arose the University of Paris (twelfth century) called "the mother of universities," and now known as the Sorbonne; Montpellier, which was a famed medical center as early as the eleventh century;[136] the universities of Orleans and Toulouse, founded in the thirteenth century, and others later. In England there were Oxford (*c.* 1180) and Cambridge (1209), the latter arising by a *cessatio* in Oxford. In the fifteenth century, the Scottish universities of St. Andrews, Glasgow, and Aberdeen appeared. In Spain, there was the University of Salamanca, chartered in 1220. In Germany, the first universities were Vienna (1365), Heidelberg (1385), Cologne (1388), and Erfurt (1392). The University of Prague, in Czechoslovakia, was founded in 1348. Poland, Hungary, Sweden, and Denmark had universities by 1450. The rapidity with which the movement spread indicates the existence of a need for the new institution.

GENERAL CHARACTERISTICS. The universities of the twelfth and thirteenth centuries were marked by (1) poverty, resulting from lack of private, church, and public support; (2) laicization, the purposes being largely lay and secular, the teachers frequently being laymen, although often holding the minor clerical mark of tonsure, and many, if not most, of the students being attracted to lay professions; and[137] (3) a large measure of freedom from church and state control although both of these powers, particularly the church, kept an eye upon them, and sought to control them by their right to charter and bestow privileges upon them. In time the papal charter became the most desired.

PRIVILEGES. Among the privileges conferred upon universities by their charters were (1) freedom of teachers and students to travel unmolested by governments, and the protection of their persons from violence; (2) the right of student debtors or criminals and of professors to trial by special university courts, a privilege which made the university largely independent of church and state; (3) *cessatio* (suspension of lectures), or the right of a university, or part of it, for stipulated cause, to secede from the parent institution or location; (4) the *jus ubique docendi,* or the right of graduates to teach anywhere, a degree thus being a teacher's license; and (5) exemption of teachers and students from taxes upon personal property and from military service. This last privilege was enjoyed

[136] *Ibid.*, pp. 10 f.
[137] Hearnshaw. *Mediaeval Contributions to Modern Civilisation,* p. 202.

by many Roman teachers and by the clergy since the days of early Christian Roman emperors; and the securing of one's person against violence was traditionally a privilege conferred upon the clergy by canon law. We find the pope, occasionally, making special rules governing the conduct of universities and their officials, most of which were designed to protect students and teachers from mistreatment. Thus, in 1231, for instance, the pope forbade the chancellor of the University of Paris to keep a prison for student criminals, who henceforth must be sent to the bishop's prison, and declared the practice of arresting students for debt to be against canon law.[138] And, as supreme authority for the licensing of teachers, the pope, in 1255, conferred the *jus ubique docendi* upon graduates of the university of Salamanca, a king-chartered institution, but withheld their right to teach in Paris or Bologna without undergoing a special examination for positions there. Some universities, disregarding papal authority, refused to recognize this right of graduates. Thus, for instance, the professors of Paris once complained that their graduates were not permitted to teach in England and Montpellier.[139]

ORGANIZATION. The universities were international, and students, and often teachers, were grouped into "*nations*" according to the land of their birth. The number of "nations" appears from the records to have run from about four to seven. These "foreigners" often created serious problems for the officials, because they brought with them their peculiar national customs—feasts, music, games, spectacles, etc.—sometimes described in the statutes as "superstitious" and "wanton." [140] Oxford University had originally four nations but, by 1250, this number was reduced to two, and then, in 1274, the nations were abolished there because of the disturbance and fights which they created. The "proctor" was the elected representative of each "nation." Teachers were divided into "*faculties*," those of theology, canon law, civil law, and medicine being "superior," and that of the liberal arts being "inferior." Not all universities had all the "superior" faculties. The head of each faculty was the "dean." In the organization, the church was represented by the *chancellor*, an official who controlled examinations and the conferring of degrees and thus, indirectly, determined who the teachers in universities would be. At the head of the whole university stood the "rector," an elected officer who was sometimes a student and sometimes a teacher, the former practice appearing only

138 Thorndike, *University Records and Life in the Middle Ages*, pp. 37 f.
139 *Ibid.*, p. 123.
140 *Ibid.*, p. 255.

where the students held the charter. The rector was often a foreigner, and usually held office for about a year. All of these officials emerged gradually, but they existed everywhere by 1375.

A special aspect of organization appears in the rise of university colleges, as separate but constituent parts of the whole institution. They appeared in Paris in the twelfth, and in Oxford in the late thirteenth century, and the movement spread to other universities. They originated generally as hospices or halls for poor students, whose miseries attracted the sympathy of rich benefactors. The Sorbonne, founded about 1260 and which became the center of theological studies in the University of Paris, was the first of these colleges. Fifty-six others were founded in Paris before 1500. Merton College, Oxford, and Balliol College, founded a few years after the Sorbonne, were the first of these in England, where they have survived in both Oxford and Cambridge as one of the unique features of these oldest of British universities. All the ancient colleges of Paris have disappeared, but the name Sorbonne lives still, but only as a name. In Paris, unlike England where the colleges enjoyed great independence, the University exercised much control over the colleges. In Scotland, North Germany, and the Low Countries, the college system did not develop to the same extent as it did in France and England, and the universities remained largely single institutions in which college and university were almost identical. The Scottish universities were the first to have a permanent staff of professors. Generally the masters wandered from one university to another at will, thus exercising their privilege of *jus ubique docendi.*

PURPOSE AND CURRICULUM. The universities grew up to prepare men for the professions of law, medicine, theology, and teaching. The "arts" course prepared the "arts" teachers of universities, but many graduates of the course became teachers in cathedral grammar schools. While no uniform practice marked all universities, some study in the arts faculty, if not graduation in arts, was a prerequisite for admission to the superior faculties.

Keeping in mind variations based upon time and institutional peculiarities, the studies were as follows: The arts course included grammar, in the narrow sense, philosophy, logic, rhetoric (largely *dictamen*), metaphysics, moral and natural philosophy, and mathematics. Natural philosophy covered such fields as physics, astronomy, zoology, botany, and psychology. The curriculum was a required one for everyone seeking the degree. The authority of Aristotle was viewed as final on all subjects upon which he had written. The classics are absent. The course in arts varied in length from four to seven years, and fell into two, or sometimes three, parts, each one leading to a degree or formal academic honor. Successful completion of the whole course entitled the student to a master's degree. While a grammar school education became, by the year 1300, a prerequisite for admission to the arts course, the universities came to have their own special teachers of grammar. Entrance examinations were apparently a common practice in the fourteenth century, and many applicants for admission were rejected. Upon graduation the young man might become a university teacher, if he could find students, though faculties in time subjected him to further tests of his qualifications; a priest, if he could find a bishop to adopt him; a civil servant, if he could find such employment; or he could proceed to a study of civil law, canon law, medicine, or theology, the course in theology, often in charge of the Dominican and Franciscan Friars, being the longest and requiring about eight years for the highest theological degree, the doctorate of divinity. Few students were enrolled in the theological course. Most priests, however, were not university graduates, but cathedral school graduates.

The courses in law and medicine, leading to their appropriate degrees, were usually five- to eight-year courses. A fairly extensive knowledge of civil law was a prerequisite to the study of canon law, which prepared men for administrative positions in the church, and which was a popular course with ambitious young men. It was mainly through their work in civil law that the universities, though international, became defenders of the rights of national states against the claims of the papacy to be the supreme arbiter of the affairs of men. The decline of church jurisdiction over civil affairs coincided with this rebirth of interest in civil law. Rhetorical composition and, apparently, *dictamen* were stressed in the civil law course, which was based on Roman law.

In medicine, Galen was almost as authoritative as Aristotle was in philosophy. The course was a book course. Then, the best physicians, at bedsides of patients, recited learnedly in Greek and Latin the views of Galen, or Hippocrates, or some of their Arabic commentators, and considered their obligations discharged. The influence of surgeons, long despised by medical faculties, brought, in the fifteenth century, a more practical approach to the study of diseases.[141]

The surgeons in Bologna, in 1405, still taught chiefly by lecturing and directing disputations on material found in the works of Galen, Avicenna, Bruno, and Almansor. [142] But, at the same time,

141 Allbutt, *op. cit.*, pp. 486 f.

142 Thorndike, *University Records and Life in the Middle Ages*, pp. 284 f.

rules governing the dissection of dead bodies appear in the university statutes, and the doctors rather than the surgeons seem to have performed the dissections. A few years later, we find the gild of surgeons prosecuting in the *Parlement* of Paris a woman who engaged in surgery without a license. Apparently many unlicensed men and women practised medicine in Paris in the fourteenth and fifteenth centuries, a practice forbidden by the medical faculty of the university in 1352.[143] There was a need for physicians which the universities were not meeting, and unlicensed practitioners arose to meet it. Perhaps the knowledge of the "old wives, monks, rustics . . . and herbalists" engaged in illicit medical practice was often as scientific as that found in the books used in the medical course in the universities. The gilds, however, had a right to protect themselves against usurpers. While medicine was recognized as a profession by about 1200, barber-surgeons, herbalists and exorcists long provided the medical assistance sought by the sick, and some such practitioners are still with us.

METHOD AND DISCIPLINE. All teachers used the method of lecture, dictation and disputation, syllogistic argumentation settling issues even in medicine and law. Books were few, and students relied much upon class notes, which they often memorized. The masters in Paris showed a keen interest in method when, in 1355, they prohibited "after diligent examination" the slow method of lecturing which encouraged note-taking, and ordered all "masters of philosophy" to use the rapid method of lecturing under the penalty of being suspended from teaching and faculty privileges for one year.[144] In 1366, masters were forbidden to read their questions and lectures from a manuscript, although they might have on their desks some notes to aid them in recalling and presenting the chief points in their arguments.

While universities pursued no uniform practice governing the use of their libraries by students, some of them restricted their use to masters and degree-holding students, as did Oxford in 1412,[145] so that serious students might not be impeded in their studies "by the excessive tumult of popular concourse." [146] Basic dependence upon the few existing texts and upon formal lectures thus marked method everywhere. The master sat at his desk on an elevated platform, and the students sat usually on chairs or benches. In 1366, the students of the arts in Paris were required by a new rule to sit

143 *Ibid.*, pp. 235 f., 284 f.
144 *Ibid.*, pp. 237 f.
145 *Ibid.*, pp. 318 f.
146 *Ibid.*

on the ground "so that the occasion of pride may be removed" from them.[147] To aid students in their work, quiz classes conducted by "reviewers," or assistant teachers, sprang up. In 1405, the University of Bologna adopted rules governing the work of its "reviewers" and the fees they might charge. All students were given an opportunity to dispute on some questions, as they would generally be required to do in their final examinations for degrees. In these examinations they were tested on their knowledge of the books used in the courses and on their ability to defend a thesis or theses suggested by the books. A lucky student might know only one book and still get his degree, if the chancellor or professor happened to examine him on that solitary book. A reliance upon books marked all university teaching with the exception of anatomy and surgery, in which dissection of corpses and experiments on animals were being used from the late fourteenth century.

Mediaeval university students were not angels, as the "rules" show, but they were forced to live, after the fashion of monks, under close supervision and rigorous discipline. Imprisonment, rustication, and expulsion were the penalties for such crimes as stealing, entering a college through windows after the gates had been closed, witchcraft, forgery, wearing daggers, and taking women inside the gates. They were forbidden to keep dogs, monkeys, bears, etc., to play dice, or to visit taverns and theaters. After 1400, they were frequently flogged for crimes and pranks,[148] but excommunication, imprisonment, and fines were more frequently used as punishment for misconduct. Excommunication was the penalty for more serious crimes such as rape, burglary, and for organizing groups intent upon such crimes. Adolescent delinquency is not a new phenomenon. Chancellors and bishops sometimes received fees for removing excommunications, as papal rules forbidding the practice imply.[149]

SUPPORT AND CONTROL. The first universities had no buildings of their own, or costly equipment, and their teachers lectured wherever they could find a room or, lacking a room, in a vacant lot or a churchyard. Paris, very early, gave the faculty of arts a small street exclusively for school purposes. The first professors were supported by student fees which long continued to be paid directly to them, the amount of the fees coming to be fixed by university statutes. Occasionally we read in the statutes that masters overcharged stu-

147 *Ibid.*, p. 246.

148 Haskins, *op. cit.*, pp. 56–57, 75–76.

149 Thorndike, *University Records and Life in the Middle Ages*, pp. 37 f.; Haskins, *op. cit.*, pp. 56 f., 75 f.

dents for rooms they rented to them but not for instructing them.[150] The paying of salaries to professors originated in Italy in the thirteenth century. This practice was inaugurated by cities, Bologna in the lead, in order to save professors from humiliating restrictions placed upon them by the student gilds. The fee system, however, continued long after that time in universities generally. Almost from the start, each university collected graduation fees from students. The "nations," too, collected fees from new graduates to defray the cost of their services. Unlike the rich students, who had their servants and lived in comfortable rented houses, the poor ones had to live in stables or any available shelter. Then came the endowment of hospices for these indigent students, as we have previously noted. In these, our first university buildings, older students began to tutor younger ones, and soon masters rented rooms in them and began teaching there. Philanthropy was thus one of the oldest sources of university support. Emperors, kings, nobles, and churchmen were among the first to endow university colleges. Others made gifts of manuscripts to them, and libraries slowly arose. The main source of early support was, however, the tuition paid by students. The fees were small and varied with the subjects taught. It is probable that some teachers exempted an occasional student from fees, but that occurrence was, no doubt, rare.

While the control of the early universities differed in certain details from country to country and institution to institution, and struggles occurred from time to time between the claimants to authority in the government of universities, the control was vested in the gild which held the charter. In Italy and Southern Europe the students usually held it, while elsewhere in Europe it was usually held by the masters. In the student universities the masters sometimes found themselves subjected to fines for cutting or coming late to class, or for disobeying other rules laid down for them by the students. It was, however, the claims and acts of bishops and chancellors that provide the most interesting aspects of the problem of control. The civil authorities showed but little desire to deprive the corporation of their claim to self-government. The control of cathedral schools was completely in the hands of the local bishop and his chancellor, who was the head of the school. Although some universities, as those of Scotland, were founded by bishops, most of them could claim their independence from the control of local churchmen on the ground that they derived their existence and privileges from the pope, the emperor or the king, not from the local bishop. The chancellor, however, as the bishop's

[150] Thorndike, *University Records and Life in the Middle Ages,* pp. 274 f.

representative, claimed great power in those universities where his appointment came from the bishop. In Oxford, however, he was soon elected by the professors, and thus ceased to be under episcopal control, although he still remained a churchman. His functions everywhere were assigned him by the university statutes, which were laws binding all officials and students. Those holding the charter made the statutes.

In all universities, the trend was to restrict the chancellor's power and, by 1500, the chief function left him was that of making arrangements for examinations and of granting licenses to successful candidates. By that year, the professors, generally, had become the supreme masters of the universities, and were ready to challenge all attempts at interference with them by civil or local church authorities. Struggles with these authorities helped to unite and strengthen the university corporations. The threat to the independence of the earlier universities came from local sources rather than from popes and emperors. The students in Bologna provoked the threat there by acts that resulted in the payment of teachers by the city. Yet the city in this case left the University very free. The records of the University of Paris show that the pope stood with the masters in their disputes with the chancellor and the bishop. The hard-won freedom from local interference, won by most universities, ended in the Reformation era, when national kings and national churches wrested the control of universities from the teachers, and forced them into the rôle of servants of church and state in both Catholic and Protestant countries. The fact that the support of most of them came from student fees and private sources did not save them from interference in a period of grave conflict.

EXAMINATIONS AND DEGREES. When a student, as any gild craftsman, had produced his masterpiece, he was inducted into the gild of master scholars. The degree of the master craftsman in learning came to be called the Master's or Doctor's degree, the latter coming to be used for graduates of the "superior" faculties. At first, there was no Bachelor's degree. It arose out of the practice of permitting students, after four or five years of study, to lecture on the *Organon* of Aristotle for a few years prior to their graduation. Such a lecturer was called a bachelor, a title long borne by younger knights in the service of older ones. In time, a formal examination was set up to test candidates for these lectureships, and the successful ones were given the title of Bachelor. The examination consisted of a disputation with his own master, an examination on books by an examining board, and a lengthy defense of a thesis against opponents. This defense of a thesis came to be termed a "determination" (*determinatio*), and in Paris the examiners were officially called "*temptors.*" The numerous rules pertaining to cheating indicate that not all the students and masters could be trusted.

The typical student was, when he became a bachelor, about nineteen years old. For about two or three additional years, he was both a student and an apprentice-professor, and an accepted candidate for the mastership. Then he presented himself to the chancellor for a license, and his master presented him to the other masters as a candidate for membership in their gild. He was first examined by the chancellor who was aided by a few masters. If they were satisfied with his knowledge of the books he had read, the chancellor granted him a license, and he became a "licentiate." Without this license, he could not be admitted to mastership. Having received it and the approbation of his "nation," he then disputed before the masters and, if they approved his performance, he was ceremoniously capped with the Master's biretta, a symbol of membership in the gild. Thereafter he had a right to wear the formal robes of a master as previously he wore the clerical dress of a student. Elaborate and lengthy ceremonies grew up in connection with the granting of degrees, some of which, in modified form, have survived to the present. This same general procedure prevailed in the "superior" faculties also. Practices, however, differed in some details in the different universities and faculties, and Oxford abolished the final examination and required only that the student be recommended to the chancellor by ten masters and that he take an oath that he had studied the required books. As a master he could now take apprentices and open his own school. When students who did not want to teach earned a Master's degree, a distinction in name came to be made in Paris and Bologna between the two groups although the studies remained the same for both. The age when students might receive their degrees was fixed by statute, but no uniformity prevailed regarding it.

STUDENTS AND STUDENT LIFE. University students were a motley group of old and young, rich and poor, studious and indolent, orderly and disorderly. St. Nicholas was the patron saint of them all. Boys, generally, entered the arts faculty at the age of fourteen or fifteen. Charitable persons gave work and gifts to poor ones, not a few of whom lived by begging from door to door. Aimless ones drifted from school to school and from teacher to teacher. Organized gangs of wandering students roamed between universities, begging and stealing as they went, until, finally, their vagabondage brought reprobation and outlawry upon their heads. Europe was restless in the twelfth and thirteenth centuries, and many types of *vagi* were abroad, of which student *vagantes* were but one.[151] Many masters encouraged their students to take work in other universities, and they themselves frequently went to other institutions for an enrichment of their experience. Not all of the wandering was aimless, and it provided a form of physical education when stadiums, intercollegiate athletics and departments of physical education were not yet dreamt of.

Of those enrolled in universities, we hear more of the disorderly than of the more numerous orderly ones. Extravagant ones incurred debts and bedeviled their fathers with heartrending stories of their financial miseries. Some of them exhausted the whole gamut of mediaeval vices. Many carried weapons; wounded one another frequently; and often made violent attacks upon townspeople and their property. Their vices provided preachers with material for many a blood-and-thunder outpouring. But preachers denounced, also, the thirst of students and masters for worldly learning and emoluments. Congregations were told of conceited masters whom God struck dumb, and of dead students who returned to warn teachers that their pursuit of worldly wisdom might lead to damnation.[152] We hear of a very bright student in Paris, in 1445, who was deemed by some professors to be "a magician and full of the demon" and even "antichrist because of his incredible knowledge of the scriptures."[153]

Yet, in spite of what preachers said, youths, in great numbers, were attracted to academic life. There was a glamour about it which made them reluctant to quit it. In addition to a summer vacation, of varying lengths, there were numerous holidays, all of them connected with church festivals. These provided an opportunity for physical diversion and healthy relaxation.

University education was a male privilege, and women were frequently forbidden to enter the buildings, or even the grounds, because they were looked upon by the authorities as "an occasion for sin."

The practice of hazing a freshman, then called a *beanus*, or greenhorn, was well established in the fifteenth century. This "beast" had to be properly tamed before he could be accepted into university society, and the older students tamed him well in many a ridiculous but, no doubt, impressive ceremonial, in which the rector often played a part. For a glimpse into the life of students, one

[151] Waddell, *op. cit.;* G. G. Coulton, *Life in the Middle Ages* (2d ed.; London: Cambridge University Press, 1928–30), II, 119–20.

[152] Haskins, *op. cit.*, pp. 49–50.

[153] Thorndike, *University Records and Life in the Middle Ages,* p. 343.

will find Seybolt's translation of the *Manuale Scholarum* (1481) both interesting and instructive.

THE UNIVERSITY TEACHER. The teacher was one holding the degree required for membership in the faculty in which he taught. In the faculties of theology and canon law he was also a priest. In Paris, no one under thirty-five years of age could teach theology, and then only if he had studied his subject for eight years. And students and masters in theology were forbidden to speak in the vernacular. There were some priests on the arts faculties, but most of the arts masters were, as we have noted, laymen. Theoretically the number of teachers on any faculty was unlimited, since any one with the necessary degree had a right to teach.

The appearance of Dominican and Franciscan Friars as teachers of theology, first at Paris (1217-1231) and then at other universities, was an important development. While their special field was theology, their pretensions in the field of philosophy affected the work in the arts faculties. It was chiefly they who made the University of Paris the philosophical and theological center of Europe.

While they were rivals of each other, they both found themselves engaged in a common rivalry with the secular clergy and laymen on the staff. By a statute of Paris (1228), they were permitted to study only theological works, and were, after their first coming, specifically forbidden to study "the books of the Gentiles and philosophers" or "the secular sciences" and the liberal arts.[154] In 1261, a new statute forbade them to hold jointly more than four full professorships in the university. While they were a small minority of the faculty, prominent names, from many lands, appeared on their list. There were Thomas Aquinas and Bonaventura from Italy; Albert the Great, from Germany; and Alexander of Hales, Roger Bacon, Duns Scotus, and William of Ockham from England and Scotland. Bologna provided the greatest names in civil and canon law. There, Irnerius lectured on Roman law, as Gratian did on canon law. Irnerius was the forerunner and inspiration of a distinguished list of jurists. Gratian's work in canon law helped to create, for centuries, a better relationship between civil and ecclesiastical courts and the legal systems they administered. The earlier universities gave us no great names in medicine. The need to isolate patients suffering from contagious diseases was discovered in the thirteenth century, but it is doubtful that the medical faculties deserve the credit for its discovery.

Within the faculties, the teachers were not specialists. The Master of Arts, for instance, taught his students all the subjects in

[154] *Ibid.*, p. 30.

the curriculum. Special teachers of grammar, however, appeared in the universities and, in the University of Toulouse, were granted exclusive rights to teach the subject in 1426.[155] Logic, too, became a subject of specialization. These were the only two subjects which teachers in the University of Paris were permitted to teach privately, and they were apparently taught at times by teachers who were not masters or even aiming to become masters.

ACADEMIC FREEDOM. The teachers and students enjoyed a measure of freedom of teaching and learning, but it was never complete. Averroism and Judaism were denied a fair hearing. The *Talmud* was burned by the theological professors of Paris, in obedience to a papal mandate, and "the impious perfidy of the Jews . . . and the blindness which is characteristic of Israel" were cited by Pope Innocent IV, in 1244, as a justification of the act. The censorship of books was a function of the theologians of Paris, and they banned many great books.[156] Within the bounds of Christian orthodoxy and its tolerated fringes, the teacher and student enjoyed freedom. Roger Bacon and William of Ockham were on the theological faculty at Paris. When circumstances demanded audacity, an occasional professor dared to speak for justice and truth. A Doctor of the University, said a professor at Paris, is bound to declare the truth. Said he: "'Few there are to be found who can be blamed for excess of frankness; but many indeed for their silence,'"[157] a remark which suggests that intimidation is an old experience of university professors, and that their freedom of thought and expression was never complete.

CONTRIBUTION OF THE UNIVERSITIES TO WESTERN CULTURE. The early universities display a more liberal attitude to new knowledge than the church schools of mediaeval Christendom. Yet, they could not free themselves from the shackles of traditional learning and scholasticism. However, in the greater freedom of discussion of any subject which masters and students enjoyed, particularly in Germany, the universities mark an era in man's intellectual progress. When the new Aristotelian intellectualism became institutionalized in them, they themselves became conservative and antagonistic, in turn, to the humanities and the sciences, particularly to the latter. Their curriculum was, on the whole, narrow, and their methods of presenting truth, or what passed for it, became highly formalized. To the discovery of scientific methods of accumulating knowledge,

155 *Ibid.*, p. 305.
156 *Ibid.*, p. 257.
157 M. M. C. J. De Wulf, *Philosophy and Civilization in the Middle Ages* (Princeton, N.J.: Princeton University Press, 1920), p. 5.

they contributed practically nothing. Yet, the professors, by their courageous defense of truth, as they saw it, did much to stimulate a desire for truth among educated people in an age of widespread popular ignorance. The influence of the universities in the spread of knowledge and of new ideas was, undoubtedly, great, for they were the first centers of the book trade, and their teachers and students traveled widely. Not only were they centers of intellectual leadership, but they contributed much, either directly or indirectly, to such developments as the growth of nationalism and the reform of the church. The universities of Oxford, Prague, and Wittenberg, for instance, launched damaging attacks upon the papacy, ecclesiastical corruption, and even upon dogmas. Movements for political, religious, and moral reform were strongly supported by the universities.

Selected Readings

Abelson, P. *The Seven Liberal Arts.* New York: Teachers College, Columbia University, 1906.

Baldwin, C. S. *Mediaeval Rhetoric and Poetic.* New York: The Macmillan Co., 1928.

Carr, A. *The Church and the Roman Empire.* New York: Longmans, Green & Co., Inc., 1898.

Cornish, F. W. *Chivalry.* London: George Allen, 1911.

Coulton, G. G. *The Mediaeval Village.* London: Cambridge University Press, 1931.

De Labriolle, P. *History and Literature of Latin Christianity.* New York: Alfred A. Knopf, Inc., 1925.

Duchesne, L. *Early History of the Christian Church.* New York: Longmans, Green & Co., Inc., 1913.

Duckett, E. S. *Latin Writers of the Fifth Century.* New York: Henry Holt & Co., Inc., 1930.

Flick, A. C. *The Decline of the Mediaeval Church.* 2 vols.; London: Routledge & Kegan Paul, Ltd., 1930.

Graham, H. *The Early Irish Monastic Schools.* Dublin: The Talbot Press, 1923.

Haskins, C. H. *The Rise of Universities.* New York: Henry Holt & Co., Inc., 1923.

———. *Studies in Mediaeval Culture.* Oxford: Clarendon Press, 1929.

Hitti, P. K. *History of the Arabs.* New York: The Macmillan Co., 1952.

Leach, A. F. *Schools of Mediaeval England.* London: Methuen & Co., Ltd., 1915.

Mullinger, J. B. *Schools of Charles the Great.* New York: Stechert-Hafner, Inc., 1911.

Norton, A. O. *Readings in the History of Education: Mediaeval Universities.* Cambridge, Mass.: Harvard University Press, 1909.

Pirenne, H. *Economic and Social History of Mediaeval Europe.* New York: Harcourt, Brace & Co., Inc., 1936.

Rashdall, H. *The Universities of Europe in the Middle Ages.* 3 vols.; Oxford: Clarendon Press, 1936.

Stephenson, C. *Mediaeval Feudalism.* Ithaca, N.Y.: Cornell University Press, 1942.

Taylor, H. O. *The Mediaeval Mind.* 2 vols.; London: Macmillan & Co., Ltd., 1938.

Thompson, J. W. *Economic and Social History of the Middle Ages (300–1300).* New York: Appleton-Century-Crofts, Inc., 1928.

———. *The Literacy of the Laity in the Middle Ages.* Berkeley: University of California Press, 1939.

Thorndike, L. *History of Magic and Experimental Science.* 6 vols.; New York: The Macmillan Co. and Columbia University Press, 1923–40.

Waddell, H. *The Desert Fathers.* New York: Henry Holt & Co., Inc., 1936.

West, A. J. *Alcuin and the Rise of the Christian Schools.* New York: Charles Scribner's Sons, 1892.

Part III

SOCIAL AND EDUCATIONAL CHANGE FROM THE RENAISSANCE TO THE FRENCH REVOLUTION

7 Social Change from the Commercial to the French Revolution

Significant changes were occurring in Christendom from the tenth century onward, and evidences of the decline of mediaevalism accumulated rapidly in the twelfth and following centuries. The "Commercial Revolution" and the rise of the bourgeoisie, the emergence of modern nations, the humanistic literary revival, the Reformation, and the scientific movement show the paths of progress along which society was traveling. These closely interrelated movements were but so many phases of change in a society emancipating itself from the traditions of mediaeval Christendom. On the economic side, the Industrial Revolution, and, on the political side, the American and French revolutions represent a culmination of these earlier tendencies—the end and the beginning of an era.

Economic Change

The five centuries prior to the French Revolution were marked by great commercial and industrial activity. When they opened, the Commercial Revolution was well advanced, and cities were thriving along the trade routes of Europe. Italian cities, because of the geographical location of Italy, and because of the Crusades and Eastern trade, were the first to rise to wealth and power. North of the Alps, the tide of commerce soon flowed rapidly. Great wealth, of a new form, resulted from industry and foreign and domestic trade. Agriculture ceased to be an exclusive basis of wealth, and its decline in importance increased progressively. Yet farmers shared in the growing prosperity, for the cities were good markets for their produce. Political and geographical developments added impetus to the expansion of commerce.

Aided by the bourgeoisie, there emerged powerful states with central governments able and willing to regulate commerce in the interest of industrial and commercial magnates. Kings protected commerce, and merchants supplied the kings with money needed to wage their wars and increase their power. Commercial and then cultural leadership passed to such nations as France, Spain, and England, where national unity was first attained. When trade supremacy passed from the Mediterranean to the Atlantic, cultural leadership passed with it. England, Holland, and America succeeded Italy and Spain, first in commercial and then in cultural greatness. Commerce had now ceased to be urban; it had become national, and culture was eventually to follow a similar course.

Geographical discoveries, such as those of Columbus and Vasco da Gama, made possible by the invention of the compass, scientific cartography, and improvements in shipbuilding, widened the market; and trading companies, encouraged by governments, undertook the exploitation of new lands. While some European settlers came to the American colonies "for conscience sake," the political rivalries of the Old World and a thirst for profit inspired the capital investment which made colonization possible. Colonial America, nurtured by cupidity, was but an expansion of Europe. The thirst for gold heightened nationalistic feeling and international distrust.

The change from an urban to a national and then to an international economy was accompanied by the growth of the economic system of capitalism. Money was scarce and little used under feudalism, although the church and some individuals held vast amounts of movable treasures, an idle wealth which commerce set in motion. Mediaeval economy was a natural economy, and barter was the usual means of commodity exchange. Commerce demanded a money economy; and international commerce, requiring foreign commercial exchanges, produced the international capitalism and banking operations of the fourteenth and fifteenth centuries. Money became itself a commodity and was traded in for private gain. Industry, once controlled by corporate gilds, passed under the control of private capitalists; and commerce followed a similar course. Fabulous wealth was thus often accumulated by men who neither produced nor marketed anything. Commerce was separated from industry, and financial magnates acquired a grip upon both of them. The church, seeing moral issues, as well as its own interests, at stake, attempted to control these mercenary enterprises, as its war on usury shows. However, merchants and governments soon grew tired of ecclesiastical restrictions upon private business. The commercialism of the age did not leave even the church untouched. To secure gold to promote their ends, the popes and their subordinates resorted to oppressive taxation, trafficking in benefices and in indulgences, nepotism, and to other methods of raising revenue which created sharp resentment.

In principle, Catholicism continued to oppose the materialistic tendencies of the changing world, while Protestantism, in many of its forms, promoted the new spirit of commercial enterprise. Franciscan poverty is not a Protestant ideal. Calvinists, Puritans, and the sects to their left stressed the prudential virtues and attached high ethical values to sobriety, industry, thrift, profit-seeking, prosperity, and judicious honesty. The so-called Anabaptists, the most austere of the early Protestant moralists, were the first to advocate total abstinence from alcohol.[1]

This ascetical, bourgeois, worldly morality stressed the virtues that make for success in the economic struggle, but salvation remained as their by-product. Work was now raised to the dignity of prayer, and the hermit ideal of a contemplative spiritual life and world-renunciation, surviving even in later monasticism, was rejected. Such a practical moral idealism, while not causal, hastened the secularization of Western society. The fact that, as a general rule, agrarianism declined much more rapidly in Protestant than in Catholic countries suggests that an ideal may have a significant influence upon even the economic life of a people. And educational thought and practice reflect prevailing ideals and conceptions of value. In keeping with their economic idealism, left-wing Protestant groups were utilitarian in their educational philosophy. Educational dissent followed religious dissent. Catholics, and those Protestants who remained close to the old orthodox position, tended to remain educationally conservative. Educational conformity followed religious conformity.

The economic changes of the time were hastened by inventions. Textile machines, pumps, water-driven saws, magnifying glasses, gun powder, linen paper, the compass, guns and cannon, printing, glass bottles, watches, pendulum clocks, microscopes, telescopes, barometers, air pumps, the steamboat, and the lightning conductor were among the inventions of the period. Of these, printing, which originated in China,[2] was the most significant, for it gave wings to thought, made communication of ideas easy, and, eventually gave power to the powerless by popularizing knowledge which is power.

[1] R. H. Bainton, *The Reformation of the Sixteenth Century* (Boston: Beacon Press, Inc., 1952), p. 97.

[2] T. F. Carter, *The Invention of Printing in China and Its Spread Westward* (rev. ed. L. C. Goodrich; New York: The Ronald Press Co., 1955).

After printing, in importance, comes the clock. In an industrial world time has a great commercial value, and wasting it is a deadly sin. The educational as well as the industrial machine now runs "by the clock."

Thus the Commercial Revolution shook the foundations of the old society, and completed the demolition of the mediaeval economic and social structure, with its gild system of production and social organization, its commercially autonomous towns, its meager commerce, and its curb upon individual enterprise. Developing, it released the energy of "personal initiative" which, unrestrained, became a threat to social well-being. Democratic states now restrain it by law; autocratic states, by substituting the initiative of dictatorial government for that of individuals.

Out of this economic change came the social, political, religious, and intellectual changes of the time. The old order did not pass, nor did the new triumph, without a struggle, a continuous cultural or spiritual struggle, at times marked by violence.[3]

Social Change

THE CLASSES AND THE MASSES. We have previously noted the rise of the bourgeoisie as a product of the Commercial Revolution and of the cities. As this new class developed, there appeared within it an upper, a middle, and a lower stratum, the lower edge comprising the working masses and shading off into a new social element, the proletariat. The Middle Ages had vagabonds and beggars, scattered over wide rural areas. The new "rabble" was a product of gild and capitalistic economies, and it was born in cities. Below the proletariat stood the slaves, whose number actually increased in the enlightened fourteenth and fifteenth centuries. Christians justified the traffic on the ground that the slaves were Muslims or heathens, but many of them were Christians. A greedy merchant class promoted the traffic, and Americans were soon importing their cargoes of slaves. The fifteenth century saw all our modern social elements in existence.

Until the French Revolution, the old landed nobility capped the social structure. At the head of this nobility was the despotical monarch. This "divine" luminary had his satellites, the great nobles

[3] G. B. Adams, *Civilization during the Middle Ages* (New York: Charles Scribner's Sons, 1914), pp. 275–301; J. W. Thompson, *Economic and Social History of Europe in the Later Middle Ages* (New York: Appleton-Century-Crofts, Inc., 1931), pp. 3–19, 81–125, 224–55, 284–97, 396–429, 462, 487 ff., 502 ff.; G. G. Coulton, *The Mediaeval Village* (London: Cambridge University Press, 1931), pp. 328 ff.; P. Smith, *A History of Modern Culture* (New York: Henry Holt & Co., Inc., 1930–34), I, 8 ff., 376 ff.

and church prelates, who radiated his glory. As in mediaeval society, the higher clergy of the right-wing churches ranked with the lay nobility. Below this nobility stood the bourgeoisie, whose upper stratum gradually secured political recognition as the Third Estate, in France, or the Commons, in England. Between the nobility and the peasantry lay a great gulf. Royalty bestowed such privileges upon the nobility as exemption from penalties for crime, freedom from taxation, large pensions, etc. The peasants had few rights which the nobles were bound to respect. Comprising about one-hundredth of the population, the nobles owned nearly two-thirds of the land of Europe. As a class, they were unproductive and worthless.

The new commercial aristocracy aped the grandeur of the landed nobility. Great merchants built houses as palatial as the castles of noblemen. They wore costly silks and furs; were secular and anti-clerical in their outlook; and built great warehouses rather than churches. Below this upper bourgeois group, there was a gradual shading off through various social subdivisions down to the proletariat.

The lower classes both in town and country had no political rights, and proletarian and peasant revolts occurred occasionally, and sometimes at the same time, as in France, in 1382, and in Germany, in 1525. In the latter about 100,000 peasants were butchered.[4] Governments served the interests of the rich. In times of labor scarcity, wages were fixed by law in order to protect employers and to make the transition from a lower to a higher social class as difficult as possible. Other laws, designed to protect privilege, prescribed the style and quality of dress of different classes, how one's hair was to be worn, when one should go to bed, what games he might play, etc. Colonial Massachusetts enacted similar laws, some of them for religious or moral reasons but many of them designed to preserve the social and economic privileges of the propertied class.

Distrust marked the relationship between the classes and the masses. In the late eighteenth century, England had about two hundred and fifty crimes punishable by death, most of them being crimes against property.[5] Executions were public and their method was brutal, many prescribed for women being particularly cruel. Prisons were veritable hells. Much of this barbarism was inspired

[4] R. H. Bainton, *Here I Stand* (London: Hodder & Stoughton, Ltd., 1951), p. 280.

[5] C. Beard, *Rise of American Civilization* (New York: The Macmillan Co., 1930), I, 295.

by the desire to safeguard the possessions of an aristocracy of birth and wealth, and some of it reflected the religious fanaticism of the time.

The eighteenth century witnessed a gradual humanizing of the laws throughout Europe. American colonial laws were generally more humane than those of England, the Massachusetts code of 1641 being the most humane of that century. Religious developments give evidence of the social struggle. The sects, such as the Anabaptists and Quakers, were largely proletarian in origin and sympathy. The Puritans, and those allied to them, were essentially bourgeois. The Catholic and Anglican churches remained right-wing churches, clinging to the old social orthodoxies as they did to the old theological orthodoxies. The sects were persecuted because they were religious and social radicals who used a dangerous weapon, that of religious faith, to effect their ends. To a less degree than the sectarian revolt, the great revival movements of the eighteenth century, led by Swedenborg, Francke, Count von Zinzendorf, Wesley, Whitefield, and Jonathan Edwards, were revolts of the common man against social injustice. A democratic idealism, of various shades, permeated the left-wing religious groups, an idealism which, with the sects, centered around the lower classes and, with the Calvinist-Puritan group, around the middle class. Methodism appealed to the lower classes. It gave them some instruction and a little freedom of speech, but it robbed them of the spirit of aggressiveness in political and social matters. The English middle class supported it, for it thwarted radicalism and acted as a substitute for an armed revolt such as the French Revolution.

The social struggle was reflected in literature throughout the whole period, the writers voicing various forms and degrees of social prejudice. The verbal war reached its height in the bitter, but humane, outpourings of the rationalists, the *philosophes,* of the eighteenth century. While Locke made a powerful plea for the rationalistic and humanitarian approach to social problems, it was the French rationalists, particularly Voltaire, who made the most telling attack upon the social injustices of the time. La Mettrie, author of *Man the Machine,* contended that hunger deprives man of power to choose between right and wrong, and that crime is a disease of which social injustice is the chief cause. The Age of Reason was an age that promised a better world.

COLONIAL AMERICAN SOCIETY. The one important difference between American colonial society and that of Europe was that, in the English colonies, there was no lay or ecclesiastical nobility. At the top of the structure here stood a fairly rich middle class, some of them landowners and some of them merchants. Below these stood smaller landowners and shopkeepers, and the hierarchy descended through skilled artisans, indentured servants, and redemptioners, to slaves. The social system of Europe, beheaded, was thus transplanted to North America, and our aristocrats tried to perpetuate it. Thus a Puritan aristocracy in New England reserved, by law, titles of honor for itself, and seated persons in church and in college according to a nicely established scheme of social ranking. Everywhere in the colonies, ownership of property or the payment of a tax was a legal requirement for suffrage.[6] In America, land and liberty have stood in close relationship. Here, land was cheap and plentiful, and few long remained in the propertyless class. American democracy, as it took form in the nineteenth century, was largely a creation of those who, dissatisfied with conditions in the older settlements, sought freedom and opportunity on the frontier and, through labor, found them there.

SOCIAL POSITION OF WOMEN. On all social levels a woman's position was inferior to that of her male "lord and master." Luther, whose views were fairly typical, said that man was created first and, therefore, should rule his wife. Her sphere is the home. God, he said, gave her large hips so that she might stay at home and sit on them.[7] Her natural duty is to bear children. " 'If a woman,' wrote Luther, 'becomes weary or at last dead from bearing, that matters not; let her only die from bearing, she is there to do it.' "[8] It was difficult to change the mediaeval agrarian idea that the purpose of marriage is to preserve the family and its possessions, an idea firmly supported by the sacramental view of the institution. Prior to the Industrial Revolution woman's sphere of activity was the home. There were very few exceptions to that rule. An occasional woman operated a small store or hotel, kept a millinery shop, made, sold and administered medicines and aids to feminine beauty, acted as a nurse or wet-nurse, or dressed the dead for burial. Women sometimes conducted "petty" schools for the children of the poor. In England and her American colonies, these were called "Dame" schools. With such rare exceptions, a woman's duties were those of her own home.

Increasing wealth reacted favorably upon the women of the aristocracy, who became objects of lavish expenditure. The wives

[6] A. E. McKinley, *The Suffrage Franchise in the Thirteen English Colonies of America* (Philadelphia: University of Pennsylvania, 1905).

[7] Bainton, *Here I Stand*, p. 299.

[8] O. Shreiner, *Woman and Labor* (New York: Frederick A. Stokes Co., 1911), p. 56.

of commercial aristocrats aped the grandiose life of noblewomen. Among these women of privilege, interest in literature, art, and science grew. Poets and novelists wrote to satisfy the taste of a female as well as a male cultural elite. Thus, from the Renaissance onward, there were women who collected a "dowry" of education and who acquired a reputation for learning, and sometimes for feminine wiles and political intrigue. The freedom, however, which a female aristocracy enjoyed, particularly in the Latin countries, was not enjoyed by their socially inferior sisters, nor even by their equals, in Germany and England. In the North American colonies, women were accorded a respect and a freedom denied to European women. Everywhere, middle- and lower-class women were restricted to the sphere of domestic activities. Their duties, according to middle-class moralists, were obedience to husbands, chastity, frugality, bearing children, and housekeeping.

Men feared women, and endowed them with the mysterious powers of witchcraft and sorcery. Since, it was felt, women are weaker than men, they fall victims more readily to Satan's wiles. Husbands were given the legal or moral right to inflict corporal punishment upon their wives, the English law restricting them to the use of a stick not thicker than one's thumb. The Massachusetts code of 1641 forbade such indignities. Protestantism contributed to a growing sanity by stressing the civil character of marriage, thus preparing the way for the legalization of divorce. The Catholic church considered celibacy superior to marriage, although the latter, paradoxically, was held to be a sacrament, while the vow of celibacy was not. The Protestants, by rejecting celibacy, exalted marriage and substituted the home for the monastery and the priesthood as the best source of a virtuous Christian life. Chivalry, under the influence of women and the courts of love, viewed true love as something possible only outside of marriage. By the fifteenth century, the view came to be advanced that such romantic love should end in marriage. Then, finally, the view came to prevail that when love ceased marriage should be dissolved. Neither Protestantism nor Catholicism, however, looked with favor upon romantic love, upon passion as opposed to duty.

While the period was not wanting in women of intellect and accomplishments, most writers of the time show little respect for a woman's mentality, which they sometimes fearfully proclaimed to be inferior. Lord Chesterfield, in the eighteenth century, voiced a general conviction when he said: "Women are only children of a larger growth; they have an entertaining tattle and sometimes wit;

but for solid reasoning and good sense, I never knew one that had it."[9]

Not only intellectually, but morally, as well as physically, women were deemed weaker than men, a dogma which was not seriously challenged until the nineteenth century. Even women of fashion took the view that a woman's social rôle is an ornamental one. To dance gracefully, play an appropriate musical instrument, make a home attractive for a husband, and elevate social tastes, were the rôles that the female elite accepted as peculiarly women's.[10]

GENTLEFOLK AS A SOCIAL AND EDUCATIONAL IDEAL. In mediaeval days, the saintly ascetic and the knight, with his ascetic vows, were considered to be embodiments of ideal character. After the year 1500, the ideal of the "gentleman," an ideal entirely worldly, supplanted the mediaeval one, although the character of the "gentleman," in practice, fell far short of the ideal. In his class, the observance of formal etiquette was deemed the supreme mark of good breeding and caste. Burgher tastes and manners were uncouth in comparison with those of the old feudal nobility, but the new aristocrats were willing to improve their ways. Formal rules of etiquette appeared in many languages, after the thirteenth century. One set of rules reads in part: "Eat with three fingers; . . . don't pick your teeth with your knife; . . . don't butter your bread with your finger; . . . don't spit on or over the table."[11] After the invention of printing, numerous books on courtesy and etiquette appeared. Among books stressing the importance of courtesy and formal manners were Castiglione's *The Perfect Courtier*, Caxton's *Book of Courtesy*, and Peacham's *Compleat Gentleman*. Similar works were addressed to "ladies." The last important counselor of men was Lord Chesterfield, whose letters on conduct addressed to his son and godson appeared between 1738 and 1770.

The literature for men dealt, generally, with the conduct proper to a gentleman in public or private life. The cultivation of friendships, personal cleanliness, proprieties in dress, suavity, and elegance were deemed of first importance. Profane and obscene conversation were condemned as social errors, as were moral vices that led to a social downfall. Regarding religion, "gentlemen" and "la-

[9] Cited in Smith, *op. cit.*, II, 604.

[10] T. Woody, *A History of Women's Education in the United States* (Lancaster, Pa.: Science Press, 1929); Smith, *op. cit.*, I, 528 ff., 537 ff.; II, 142 f., 299 ff., 600 ff.; J. E. Mason, *Gentlefolk in the Making* (Philadelphia: University of Pennsylvania Press, 1935), pp. 54 ff., 208–18.

[11] C. H. Haskins, *Studies in Mediaeval Culture* (Oxford: Clarendon Press, 1929), p. 80.

dies" were advised to worship God, read the Bible, and attend church services. The books often dealt with the origin of natural inequalities among men. To serve the king, by filling some courtly office, ought to be the first ambition of a "gentleman." Next to this, as suitable pursuits for him, were listed the professions of law, medicine, and the office of justice of the peace.[12]

By the eighteenth century, deceit and hypocrisy had found their way into the ideal of the "gentleman." Gentlemanly conduct, moreover, usually fell far short of even the degraded ideal. There were some aristocrats of real refinement, but the vast majority were given to intemperate eating and drinking, and to profanity and obscenity in their vilest forms. It was such a gentry, rich, lazy, and cruel to the masses, that controlled European society prior to the French Revolution.

Political Change

GROWTH OF NATIONALISM. The centuries prior to the French Revolution witnessed the rise of powerful national states. That development, as we have seen, was hastened by the alliances between kings and the new-rich. For education, nationalism was destined to become the most momentous development of modern times.

In the Middle Ages, the church and state existed as two forms of government ruling over one society, the Christian theocracy. While generalizations for such a long period and such a large area are hazardous, it can be said with a high degree of accuracy that the church dominated the state, and that all European Christians lived under its authority, claimed to be divinely instituted. In mediaeval society, baptism and religious orthodoxy were required for citizenship and other privileges. Economic, social, political, and intellectual aspects of life were controlled by the church. By requiring the confession of sins, it controlled the individual; by marriage laws, the family; by interdicts and excommunications, nations and kings; by price fixing and its war on usury, commercial and industrial practices; by its schools and universities, and by its persecution of heretics, the cultural and intellectual life of men. So all-encompassing was its power that the state might be said to have been non-existent.

ROYAL ABSOLUTISM. In the thirteenth century, strong political, national states were again emerging, and political theory, earlier subordinated to revealed ethics, or theology, began to receive separate consideration. National patriotism, as an ideal, began to per-

[12] Mason, *op. cit.*

vade literature. The rights of secular political authority as against that of the church were asserted, in the fourteenth century, by Dante in his *On Monarchy,* by Pierre Dubois in his *The Recovery of the Holy Land,* and by Marsiglio of Padua in his *Defender of the Peace,* and traces, at least, of national patriotism appear in their writings. The fifteenth century saw the birth of the spirit of nationalism in a struggle between England and France. The life of Jeanne d'Arc reflects the rise of that spirit. In England, Henry IV honored his country's spirit by speaking English rather than French, and Chaucer, even earlier, wrote his *Canterbury Tales* in the vernacular. In Italy, however, patriotism continued to be local rather than national.

In the sixteenth century, Machiavelli, Luther, Cervantes, and Shakespeare appealed not to the universal consciousness of a united Christendom, but to national feelings. By that time, strong national states, as a vehicle of culture, had replaced the universal state of Christendom. England, France, Spain, Portugal, Sweden, Holland, and Denmark had become such states by the year 1600. In political theory, Machiavelli (1469-1527) is the most telling advocate of power politics and the rights of national states in the period we are reviewing. His *The Prince* and *The Discourses* express his views with great intensity. So forcefully did he defend nationalism and the rights of the national state, that Pope Paul IV saw fit to put his books on the Index, the Catholic list of forbidden books. *The Discourses* is more important than *The Prince.* In it, he advocated (1) republican government based upon mass consent, (2) the unification of the state under the rule of a leader, (3) the creation of mass military power to defend the state, (4) the founding of a national religion to unite the people and strengthen their morale, not to keep their minds on eternity, and (5) the adoption of ruthless measures to promote the ends of the state. One can find here the doctrines of Nietzsche and of the totalitarian statesmen of recent times.[13] In Machiavelli we behold the full birth of the theory of modern national statecraft.

The new national states did not conform with many of Machiavelli's proposals. However, at the head of each stood an autocrat, who exercised sovereign power, symbolized national unity, and bent all institutions to his will. The nobility and the merchant plutocracy bowed to that will. Both Protestantism and Catholicism became vehicles for the expression of national patriotism. Christian universalism was gone. By the principle "*cujus regio ejus religio*" (whose region, his religion), accepted at the Treaty of Augsburg (1555),

[13] N. Machiavelli, *The Prince and the Discourses* (trans. L. Ricci and C. E. Detmold; New York: Modern Library, Inc., 1940).

Christianity itself was officially nationalized. Kings, as formerly did the popes, now claimed to rule by divine right. Monarchy, said James I of England, "is the supremest thing upon earth . . . as to dispute what God may do is blasphemy, . . . so is it sedition in subjects to dispute what a king may do in the height of his power."[14] "I am the state," said Louis XIV of France, whose despotism culminated in the Revolution. Leading the forces opposed to royal despotism stood the new-rich bourgeoisie. They deposed two English monarchs (1649 and 1689), and forced their kings to accept the principle of the omnipotence of Parliament. In France, the combined strength of the monarchy, nobility, and clergy checked the bourgeoisie until 1789. Then came the triumph of new wealth over the "old régime."

Royal tyranny rested on the theory of the divine right of kings. Opposing theories were often advanced. Among these was the view that government originated not in heaven but in a social contract, a binding agreement between rulers and their subjects, and that it has no other grounds to stand on. Aeneas Sylvius, about 1450, and other later writers such as Hobbes, Spinoza, and Locke advanced that theory. Hobbes used it to justify royal absolutism; Locke and his disciple, Rousseau, to overthrow royal absolutism by force.

THE DISFRANCHISED MASSES. Under the royal despots, the masses were politically voiceless. Outside of England, even the bourgeoisie, of all grades, were completely dominated by the monarchy. In England and her American colonies, where a degree of democracy existed, ownership of a considerable amount of property was essential for voting and for holding political offices. Universal suffrage was unknown before the nineteenth century. In the American colonies, as we have seen, more than half the adult male population was disfranchised. Everywhere, the mere idea of woman suffrage was well-nigh inconceivable. Elsewhere, we shall see how a changing world brought these conditions to an end in the nineteenth and twentieth centuries.

Religious Change

Religious unrest, culminating in the Protestant revolt, accompanied the social changes we have described. The Reformation was an adaptation of religion and morals to the demands of the new European social order. Economic, political, social, and intellectual factors operated to bring it about. The influence of religious and

[14] F. A. Ogg, *The Governments of Europe* (New York: The Macmillan Co., 1916), p. 24. (By permission.)

moral motives, as a separate and independent factor, in producing the reform in theology, ritual, and church government is one of dispute, as is also the basic question of the rôle religion has played in determining the mode of man's worldly affairs. The dispute is one between the economic and sociological determinists, on the one hand, and the ideological determinists, on the other. The arguments of both groups—and they are always supported by selected facts—are impressive, but the issue still remains unresolved. The central fact here is that the Reformation occurred in an age of significant social change. However, we must not, therefore, conclude that all, or even most, of the new religious slogans were inspired by worldly motives. The Reformation must be seen as the result of a complex of forces so intricately intertwined that it is difficult to isolate any of them. And one other factor remains to be added to those listed above: the dynamic personality and zeal of Martin Luther, the main personal instrument of the Reformation. But even a leader of such ability could not have succeeded if the age and its forces had not been co-operative.[15]

CAUSES. (1) Economic Cause. The Reformation was one aspect of a general reaction against the feudal social order with which the church had become closely identified. Church institutions derived most of their revenue from their land holdings and the labor of their serfs. The creation of a new social order was impossible until the church in its feudalized form was reformed. In the centuries preceding Luther's revolt, the serfs and free peasants struggled to escape from economic exploitation. The need of cities for laborers offered the serfs one avenue of escape. Feudal lords themselves, both lay and clerical, discovered that hired labor was more profitable than serf labor and, consequently, often freed their serfs. However, the Black Death plague (1348-1350) changed the whole picture by depleting the ranks of labor and forcing up the wage scale. The result of this epidemic and of commercial competition for labor was a sharp decline in the value of feudal lands and the weakening of the economic basis of ecclesiastical power. Kings and merchants, moreover, had been looking with envy upon the great wealth of the church and of the higher clergy, many of whose estates had for centuries enjoyed the privilege of *immunity* which, among other privileges, gave them freedom from taxation by kings. Besides, the clergy traditionally were free from taxes upon their

[15] J. Mackinnon, *Luther and the Reformation* (New York: Longmans, Green & Co., Inc., 1925–30); Bainton, *Here I Stand;* Bainton, *The Reformation of the Sixteenth Century;* Smith, *Erasmus* (New York: Harper & Bros., 1923); J. Davis, *Readings in Sociology* (New York: D. C. Heath & Co., 1927), pp. 184–90.

personal property. The first royal attack upon immunity came when Louis VII of France imposed a levy upon ecclesiastical property in order to raise funds for the Second Crusade (1147-1149). Pope Boniface VIII protested and claimed for the pope absolute control over the taxation of the clergy everywhere, but he was eventually forced to agree to such a levy in France for the purpose of national defense. Following this dispute, many governments forbade the church to acquire new landed possessions, but the old possessions still disturbed them.

The confiscation of church estates, in process for two centuries, ended in wholesale confiscation in Protestant lands after the Reformation. Ecclesiastics, generally, resisted these intrusions upon their "rights," thus inviting a revolt against church power. Insight into the forces at work is revealed by the fact that Protestant Europe was largely commercial and industrial while Catholic Europe remained chiefly agricultural and feudal.[16] A feudal economy had proved its worth to the church which, declining, struggled hard to preserve it.[17] There are many important details in the struggle which a picture of basic things does not reveal.

Financially, the papacy had become, by 1500, the wealthiest institution in Christendom, deriving its revenue from numerous sources.[18] The luxury and extravagance of the papacy had become a scandal. Kings who themselves needed the money saw foreign ecclesiastics carry it away to Rome to enrich the papal treasury.[19] Pope Leo X, in 1517, brought 500,000 ducats into it by creating thirty-nine new cardinals, and he borrowed an equal amount from bankers and other cardinals. With regard to interest rates, the papacy had solid reason to support Thomas Aquinas' principle of a mutual-risk contract rather than one of a fixed return. By 1550, the popes were spending about 55 per cent of their income to pay interest on their loans. While not friendly to capitalism they found themselves involved in capitalistic activities, and encouraging capitalism.[20] When the old sources of church revenue were drying up as a result, mainly, of diminishing land values and royal competition in the tax field, the church devised new forms of taxation in an area

16 Thompson, *op. cit.*, pp. 81–125, 284–97, 415–29.

17 D. C. Munro and G. C. Sellery, *Mediaeval Civilization* (New York: Appleton-Century-Crofts, Inc., 1917), pp. 159–201.

18 J. L. LaMonte, *The World of the Middle Ages* (New York: Appleton-Century-Crofts, Inc., 1949), p. 393.

19 J. W. Draper, *History of the Conflict between Religion and Science* (New York: Appleton-Century-Crofts, Inc., 1927), p. 267.

20 Bainton, *The Reformation of the Sixteenth Century,* pp. 236 ff., 248.

free from competition, the religious sphere itself. The sale of indulgences was one of the most lucrative of these devices, and it was such a sale which was the immediate occasion of the Reformation. While the poor paid no fee for indulgences, they were expected to pay for such services as masses for the dead. The means of salvation had become unfair, since the poor could not pay for such favors. Luther opposed this as he did all commercialism and even capitalism. He loved the agrarian life, but neither he nor the papacy could control the new force which historical events had brought into operation. Luther, however, unwittingly stimulated the spirit of capitalism when he advocated the abolition of monasticism and the confiscation of church property, and when he exalted labor and declared poverty, long a monastic virtue, to be either a sin or a disgrace.

(2) Social Cause. In the struggle which brought the Reformation it is easier to identify the working of economic prejudices than those associated with the class alignments of the time. The two, however, are closely related. The Reformation was, in the main, a bourgeois revolt, a revolt of men seeking freedom from arbitrary control whether of their economic or religious life, and demanding a stern morality as a path to worldly success as well as to Paradise. Where its success was greatest, it had the support of the masses, but their influence upon its rise and character seems to have been of minor significance.

Luther stirred them to revolt by advocating the freedom of Christ's men, but when they asked Luther to support their demands for social justice, they found that their trust had been misplaced. In his tract "Against the Robbing and Murdering Hordes of Peasants," he denounced them as "rebellious thieves, robbers, murderers and blasphemers," and said that they ought to be shot like "mad dogs." Said he, "I think there is not a devil left in hell; they have all gone into the peasants."[21] In the hope that a change might bring them some relief, the peasants and laborers, where conditions permitted, stood with the Reformers. While ignorance and superstition had long been their lot, the intellectual developments of centuries and the invention of printing had not left the poor untouched. Some pre-Reformation heresies spread among the poor,[22] and, after the Reformation, it was the sectaries, predominantly proletarian, who

[21] *The Works of Martin Luther* (Philadelphia: A. J. Holman Co., 1931), IV, 249 *passim*.

[22] Haskins, *op. cit.*, p. 245.

moved farthest away from the old religious orthodoxy.[23] It is unlikely that women had no part in creating the disturbance, but the records throw no light upon the question of the part they played in it.

(3) POLITICAL CAUSE. The ideals of a universal empire and a universal culture, and of the unity of mankind and of church and state dominated mediaeval Christian thought. In practice, the unity of Western Christendom after A.D. 750 was ideal rather than real, for many factors, as we have seen, brought disintegration. The protest against a church-imposed universalism expressed itself, among other forms, in national political opposition to papal interference in temporal matters. In the thirteenth and fourteenth centuries, the French and English nations successfully challenged papal temporal power as claimed by Pope Boniface VIII in the bull *Unam Sanctam.*[24] Nations, too, were aggrieved by the partiality shown by popes in disputes between rival nations. The decline of papal political power began in a struggle between France and Italy for the control of the papacy. The Avignon Papacy (1305-1378) was dominated by France. All of the Avignon popes were Frenchmen, and their acts reveal their national prejudice, with the result that they aroused bitter feelings in England, Germany, and Italy. The Avignon Papacy was followed by The Great Schism (1378-1409) in which at first two and, finally, three rival popes sat on the papal throne at the same time, each one claiming to be the legitimate occupant. National rivalries caused that schism, and it marks the end of the universal papacy. It was followed by the Conciliar Movement, in which general councils, not popes, directed the affairs of the church. Thus the Council of Constance (1414-1418) finally settled the Great-Schism dispute by a vote of the bishops and abbots of Italy, France, Spain, Germany, and England. Later general councils gave rise to the issue of whether a council or the pope should be the supreme authority in church affairs. That issue was finally decided in favor of the pope, and a strong papacy, Italian in sympathy, emerged. But the popes of the fifteenth and sixteenth centuries, though strong, were generally corrupt, the stench of Rome becoming too much for Luther's nostrils. A strong German nationalist, as Luther was, could not bear to have his nation despised by

[23] Smith, *History of Modern Culture,* I, 357–75, 380 f., 392 ff.; F. M. Stawell and F. S. Marvin, *The Making of the Western Mind* (Garden City, N.Y.: Doubleday & Co., Inc., n.d.), pp. 151 ff.; Thompson, *op. cit.,* pp. 378–86, 403–4; Coulton, *op. cit.,* pp. 540 f., 547 ff.

[24] For the text of the bull see LaMonte, *op. cit.,* pp. 441 f.

Italians and its religion controlled by popes who were more interested in political scheming than in spiritual affairs.[25]

Thus nationalism and national pride and prejudice were at work in the Reformation struggle. The period was the age of youth of national states, filled with that fervor which youth knows best. Before the Reformation, nationalism had made the church its servant even in lands that were to remain Catholic. Thus the Galican movement in France had forced Rome to permit Paris to direct many important church affairs, and the drift generally was in the direction of national churches independent of Rome in all but purely spiritual matters. It should be noted, however, that pre-Reformation kings stood for one religion as an essential bond of unity within each state. The problem of religious dissent became a grave issue for national governments in the post-Reformation era. The "whose-region-his-religion" clause of the Peace of Augsburg approved national churches but, at the same time, denied the citizen the right to dissent.

Germany, the center of the actual revolt, unlike Spain, France, and England, was not a united nation, but a people divided into small, independent states. The Holy Roman empire, with its head in Germany, was not a German state. There was no king here to protect the people from papal exploitation and Italian sneers. Luther was but one of many who were irked by Roman exploitation and insults.[26] The spirit of nationalism pervades his thought. "I thank God," he wrote in the preface to a book, *Ein Deutsch Theologia,* "that I thus hear and find God in the German tongue."[27] The idea of a German theology fascinated him, and his translation of the Bible into German was inspired largely by his national patriotism. He still remains Germany's national hero, patriot, and Protestant saint. He would "make Moses speak so that you would never know he was a Jew."[28]

When the Reformation came, papal claims to all power, both temporal and spiritual, were rejected by Protestant states, and religion, in them, became a state function. Christianity was thus nationalized. Even Catholicism, while it has tried to cling to its international ideal, has been significantly nationalized, and the saints seem to have become instruments of national sentiment.[29]

[25] *Ibid.*, pp. 720 ff.; Mackinnon, *op. cit.*, I, 259 f.

[26] Bainton, *Here I Stand*, pp. 130 ff.

[27] J. Mackinnon, *op. cit.*, I, 212.

[28] Bainton, *The Reformation of the Sixteenth Century*, p. 62.

[29] C. J. H. Hayes, *France—a Nation of Patriots* (New York: Columbia University Press, 1930); A. C. Flick, *The Decline of the Mediaeval Church* (London: Routledge & Kegan Paul, Ltd., 1930), I, 30–46, 54 ff., 243 ff., 347 ff.

(4) Intellectual Cause. Ever since the beginning of the realist-nominalist controversy, Western Christendom was in a state of intellectual ferment, the intensity of which deepened rapidly in the thirteenth and following centuries. An age of doubt and inquiry succeeded the age of faith. In the making of the Reformation, no one of the many important developments in the realm of the mind is of greater significance than the rediscovery of the ancient classics and the growth of classical scholarship. However, it was the spirit of free inquiry and man's right to reason, which the humanists espoused, which link the humanist movement and its scholarship to the work of the Reformers. Erasmus, Luther, Melanchthon, Calvin, Zwingli, and other leaders in the reform movement of the sixteenth century were all men trained in the use of linguistic tools. These were all Northerners, but the reforming spirit appears also in many Italian humanists. The writings of Luther and Melanchthon appeared in Italian translations.[30] Luther believed that the meaning of the Scriptures would become completely clear if those seeking it were equipped with the languages and the tools of critical inquiry. That belief was supported by such discoveries as that of Lorenzo Valla (1407-1457), an Italian humanist, who proved by internal evidence that the Donation of Constantine, by which the popes claimed temporal power over Italy, was a forgery.

Fate could not have chosen a better time for the birth of Luther. Humanism, from which he profited so much, espoused man's right to apply reason at every step in his pursuit of truth. This was not the spirit dominant in the church and the university, and it actually produced such pagan humanists as Poggio (1380-1459) and Valla, to mention only two of them. Germany got its humanism from Italy, but here it stayed within Christian bounds and became allied with the forces of social reform. Erasmus, at once both a scholar and a reformer, was the master spirit of German humanists. In his knowledge of Greek and Latin he outshone all his contemporaries. He applied Valla's method of historical criticism to the Scriptures and the writings of the Church Fathers, and edited a critical version of the New Testament in Greek which he published in 1516. He was the true Christian humanist who would, like Luther, revive Christianity by providing Europe with the Scriptures in their correct form. His critical humanist spirit appears in his many writings and in his courageous attacks upon the corruption and hypocrisy of churchmen, as well as upon the ceremonialism and superstitions of Catholic religious practices. He spared none in his denunciation of human folly. Teachers, lawyers, philosophers, theologians, monks,

[30] Mackinnon, *op. cit.*, IV, 344.

kings, and popes all felt his lash, and the ridicule was, no doubt, deserved. The theologians, he describes as a "supercilious crew . . . armed with six hundred syllogisms" and hiding their confusion behind "a wall of imposing definitions, conclusions . . . and explicit and implicit propositions." [31]

Humanism of the Valla-Erasmian type was an almost indispensable prelude to the Reformation, and the leading Reformers were all indebted to Erasmus and his humanist spirit.

While Luther was never a professed humanist, he studied the classics and recognized their value in reforming religion.[32] He found, for instance, that the sacrament of penance rested upon a mistranslation of the Latin Vulgate,[33] and that discovery heightened his respect for scholarship. He was, however, a theologian, rather than a humanist, but he made wide use of the results of the new learning in carrying out his reforms.[34] His theological training was of the nominalist variety of William of Ockham.[35] The humanists and he were closest together in their common rejection of scholastic theology and in their common struggle for an enlightened Christianity. Luther's friend, Melanchthon, as a humanist and a Reformer, symbolizes the blending of humanism and the Reformation. He went over to Luther's side unreservedly, but many humanists, when the storm was breaking, were not sure of themselves as they contemplated the ways of God, and, therefore, clung to the authority of the church rather than risk their salvation by following the fervid irrationalism of the new Augustine, Luther, as embodied in his doctrine of "justification by faith." And Luther, the nationalist, while he spoke in loudest praise of Erasmus as a critic of the church, could not accept his Christian humanism, because that humanism was opposed to nationalism. Nor could Erasmus, who chose to remain neutral in the controversy between Luther and Rome, entirely endorse a Reformer who was ready to break completely with the church.[36] The story of the relationship between humanism and the Reformation is long and involved, but this can be said with certainty: had it not been for the humanist ideals of individualism and respect for freedom of inquiry and reason, and for enlightenment provided by the new learning, the Reformation might have been long delayed; and it might well have become a reform from within,

[31] L. F. Dean (trans.), *The Praise of Folly* (New York: Hendricks House–Farrar, Straus & Co., Inc., 1946), pp. 95 f.

[32] Bainton, *Here I Stand*, p. 64.

[33] *Ibid.*, p. 88.

[34] *Ibid.*, pp. 93 ff.

[35] Mackinnon, *op. cit.*, I, viii.

[36] *Ibid.*, pp. 123 ff.

as attempted by the counter-Reformation, rather than a reform from without and a division of Christendom.

While humanism was, thus, important in directing the thought of the Reformation, its basic doctrine of human dignity and worth was soon to be rejected by Calvinists who made human degradation the central fact of history. Humanist optimism and faith in man and his world were rejected in the pessimistic supernaturalism of Calvinists and the sects related to them. A more radical naturalism and rationalism than that of Christian humanism was needed to ensure the triumph of humanist faith. But the Reformation in its general effects, if not in Calvinism, prepared the way for a wider acceptance of that faith in the eighteenth and nineteenth centuries.

(5) THEOLOGICAL CAUSE. Whether the theological controversy was a cause or merely an occasion of the revolt is a matter of dispute. While the moral, religious, theological, and ecclesiastical issues were a sufficient reason for it, they would have been ineffectual were not the time, in its basic social aspects, ripe for a change. The secularized church needed reform from its very beginning, and many attempts were made to reform it. Among them were monasticism, the Conciliar Movement, and numerous heretical movements. Thinking men were always inclined to wander away from "the faith," as numerous church regulations to preserve orthodoxy indicate. Separatist churches, such as the Nestorian and Coptic, date from the early Christian centuries. The twelfth and thirteenth centuries saw a resurgence of heresy, the most dangerous one being the Albigensian, Zoroastrian and Manichean in its tenets, which proclaimed the church to be the servant of the devil. The extremely pagan fanaticism of its devotees was a lesser threat to religious orthodoxy than was the contemporary Waldensian heresy.

The Waldensians, originating with Peter Waldo (*c.* 1172), preached a gospel of poverty. They advocated universal reading of the Bible and the preaching of its doctrines by all men and women. As do Quakers, they opposed war and oaths and, like Jehovah's Witnesses, taught that God only should be obeyed. And they demanded, also, that the vernacular be used in all church services. Other like-minded heretics soon appeared.

In England, John Wycliffe (*c.* 1324-1384), a professor of theology at Oxford, became a champion of British nationalism against papal support of France, and declared that the pope had no more possession of the Keys of Heaven than any ordinary priest. The pope condemned nineteen of his statements as heretical, but the faculty of theology at Oxford proclaimed that they were true. Like Luther later, he would make no distinction between the clergy and the laity in the government of the church, and denied that priests could forgive sins. For him the Scriptures are the one and only source of faith, and he found in them no support for the doctrine of transubstantiation.

The story of Wycliffe parallels fairly closely that of John Huss (1369-1415), of Bohemia, who translated his writings into Czech. Huss was declared a heretic, was condemned by the Council of Constance and was executed in 1415. His teachings were almost identical with those of Luther.[37] Besides these, there were heresies of an academic, philosophical nature which appealed only to the learned, but which were a serious threat to orthodoxy. Christianity was threatened also by a new wave of mysticism, which, stressing the nearness of God, tended to make unnecessary the rôle of Christ in the world. Associated with it, as a general rule, was a rationalism which led to the rejection of dogmas, such as the Trinity, which had to rest for their acceptance on church authority. Some of these mystics, as, for instance, Johann Tauler, of Germany, Gerard Groote, of Holland, and Thomas à Kempis, of England, were accepted as orthodox Christians; but Michael Servetus, a Spaniard, and Faustus Socinus, founder of Socinianism, were pronounced heretical. Groote was a member of the Brethren of the Common Life in whose schools Erasmus was educated. The Renaissance, too, produced a group of Neo-Platonic mystics who saw the same truth in all the great religious systems.[38] Against all heretics and mystics who moved too far to the left the papacy reacted violently.

In 1209, Pope Innocent III launched a bloody military crusade against enemies at home. Besides, the papal Inquisition got to work to snuff out and stamp out heretics, scores of whom were burned to death "in holocausts 'very great and pleasing to God.'"[39] The weakness of the papacy in the sixteenth century saved Luther from that fate. In 1520, the pope excommunicated "that son of iniquity," as he called him, and ordered that his books be burned.[40]

There were certain central positions which nearly all later heretical groups held in common. The most important of these were that the Bible is the basis of religious truth and ought to be accessible to the laity in the vernaculars; that religion is an internal experience; and that external acts, such as almsgiving, the sacraments, and acts demanded for indulgences, are foreign to true religion. Confession of sins and transubstantiation were held to have no Scriptural foun-

[37] LaMonte, *op. cit.*, pp. 647 ff.
[38] Bainton, *The Reformation of the Sixteenth Century*, pp. 124–39.
[39] Haskins, *op. cit.*, p. 223.
[40] Bainton, *Here I Stand*, pp. 147 f.

dation. Papal claims to temporal power, the supremacy of the pope in church affairs, the holding of secular offices by the clergy, the greed of ecclesiastics, clerical immorality and celibacy were commonly denounced both by friends and foes of the old system.

THE REFORMATION IN GERMANY: LUTHERANISM. The immediate occasion of Luther's revolt was the preaching of an indulgence by Tetzel, a Dominican friar, for the purpose of raising money for the new archbishop of Maintz to enable him to pay a debt to the bank of the Fuggers and the pope, a debt which he contracted in accepting his office. The vending of this indulgence was scandalous.[41] Bainton in *Here I Stand* gives a full account of this sale which provoked Luther to publish his famous ninety-five theses and to attack openly the doctrine and practice.[42] He had long been shocked by the use made of relics in the dispensing of such favors, and was, no doubt, disturbed also by the failure of the Conciliar Movement to reform the church from within.[43] The theses were a denunciation of the practice. In one month, all Christendom had heard of them and, in one year, the Reformation had become an accomplished fact, for Christendom was ready for a change. Orders for Luther's publications poured in from many countries,[44] and the new evangelism spread rapidly into Sweden, Denmark, Norway, and Holland.[45]

Among many other doctrines and practices, Luther rejected the Catholic sacraments, except baptism, and he reduced the mass to the Lord's Supper. A separate priesthood was, thus, no longer, necessary, and the faith of the individual became the only channel of grace and salvation. The kernel of his views appears in his doctrine, Pauline and Augustinian in origin, of "justification by faith" and in his doctrine of "private interpretation of the Scriptures." For him, each individual is responsible for his own salvation, but this was not the humanist ideal of individualism. In the actual work of organizing a new church, many practical difficulties were encountered—difficulties of belief, ritual, and of the disposal of Catholic church properties and endowments. All that can be said here is that Luther, faced with the actual problems and often against his own wishes, was forced to accept, as a solution, religious conformity

41 *Ibid.*, pp. 74 ff.

42 For some of the theses see E. P. Cubberley, *Readings in the History of Education* (Boston: Houghton Mifflin Co., 1920), pp. 231 f. For all of them see O. J. Thatcher (ed.), *The Library of Original Sources* (Milwaukee: University Research Extension Co., 1907), V, 112 ff.

43 For an interesting detailed account of the collection of relics in Wittenberg see Bainton, *Here I Stand*, pp. 69 ff.

44 *Ibid.*, pp. 121 ff.

45 Mackinnon, *op. cit.*, IV, 337–49.

and control of the church by the state. His city of Wittenberg was the first (1521-1522) to adopt the reforms and, from here, the movement of practical reform spread throughout Northern Germany and beyond. Those who had broken with Rome—among them, bishops, monks, nuns, princes, and common people—were not themselves united, and Luther was shocked by the diversity of the new evangelicanism.[46]

Luther faced opposition not only from a militant Catholicism but from rulers who saw in his work a threat to political unity. Many Protestant extremists, hankering for a return to the purely spiritual Christianity of primitive Christian times, demanded a church of the spirit either dominating the state or separate from it.[47] But political Lutheranism, in reality, came as a reaction to political Catholicism. The Second Diet of Speyers (1529) divided Germany into two camps, the Catholic and the Lutheran, and reaffirmed for Catholic territories the edict of the Diet of Worms (1521) which required Lutheran territories to grant religious liberty to Catholic minorities, however small, whereas weak non-Catholic minorities were denied such liberty in Catholic territories. The Evangelical groups protested against this invidious plan and were consequently called Protestants. A "Protestant" is, thus, historically one who demands equal religious liberty for Catholics and non-Catholics.[48] The principle of religious liberty in the Christian world originated in the conflicts of the Reformation.

While Southern Germany remained Catholic, Lutheranism was accepted by the majority of Germans and became an expression of the national spirit. Bloody struggles between Catholics and Protestants followed the break with Rome, and the warring factions temporarily settled their strife when, at the Peace of Augsburg (1555), they agreed to the principle of "whose region, his religion," which accorded kings the right to determine the religion of their subjects, and made religion legally a state function. But the wars between Protestant princes and the Holy Roman emperors, as allies of the papacy, ended only after the Thirty Years' War (1618-1648) and the Peace of Westphalia (1648). That treaty recognized the claims of national states to independence from the Holy Roman empire, and gave kings the right to determine the religion of their people. That was a victory for institutionalized Protestantism but not yet for religious liberty as a practice. It was a triumph of nationalism rather than of Protestantism. There are many documents available which

[46] *Ibid.*, pp. 311 ff.
[47] *Ibid.*, pp. 251 ff.
[48] *Ibid.*, pp. 311 ff.

reveal the ideas of the Reformation but none is so completely revealing as The Augsburg Confession (1530) which was drawn up by Luther's friend, Melanchthon, and written in German.[49]

THE REFORMATION OUTSIDE OF GERMANY: CALVINISM AND ANABAPTISM. While Germany is considered the land of the Reformation, the revolt, as we have seen, did not begin there. Nor did it end in the acceptance of Lutheranism by all discontented people. In Switzerland, John Calvin (1509-1564), a French humanist, led a revolt which eventually left a deeper mark upon Christendom than did Lutheranism. From its headquarters in Calvin's theocratic city of Geneva, Calvinism spread rapidly into France, the Netherlands and Scotland, and eventually became firmly rooted in British North America. Its basic tenets may be seen in Calvin's *Institutes of the Christian Religion,* a profoundly intellectual analysis of religion devoid of Luther's stress upon its emotional basis. For Calvin, more important than one's faith is the sovereignty of God as he works out his inexorable plan for man in the unfolding historical process. Everything that happens or exists reflects the inexorable will of God. Man, evil in mind and morally depraved by Adam's fall, should not waste his energies struggling for a destiny, whether of salvation or damnation, to which at his birth he was already predestined. He should submit heroically to the unknown will of God, and go about his worldly concerns with stoical indifference to the hereafter. Calvin, however, gave a place in his scheme to grace and redemption through Christ. It was a harsh doctrine, and later Calvinists, like Milton who accorded to man the power to repair the ruins created by Adam, encouraged men to believe that living well was a proof of one's election to glory. A moral code, based upon personal responsibility, became possible under later Calvinism, which made personal liberty indispensable to virtue. The Christian's right to dissent was thus at last recognized by Calvinists.

Calvin's conception of the state was that of an authoritarian theocracy, or divine government, in which the political power would be the servant of the ecclesiastical, and in which ministers would control every activity of man and government, including education. The doctrines of liberty and of the right to dissent of later Calvinism may be seen in the life and works of Roger Williams, who would save both the individual and the community of "the elect" from any externally imposed conformity. This was a far cry from Calvin's theocratic Geneva where church and state were made one tyranny for the glory of God, and the individual was subjected to harsh con-

[49] For a translation see Thatcher, *op. cit.,* V, 151–78.

trol[50] on the grounds that no man should be left free to go to hell in his own way, a view held also by Catholics.

Calvinism should be viewed, perhaps, as a reformation of Lutheranism. The so-called Reformed church is Calvinist. But there were those who would reform both Lutheranism and Calvinism by returning Christians to the simple faith and moral life of the Sermon on the Mount. These dissenters originated in the teachings of Zwingli, Calvin's predecessor in the Reformation in Switzerland, and are known as Anabaptists. Their goal was the restoration of primitive Christianity, as revealed in the Scriptures and in the lives of martyrs. Neither tolerated nor state religions, they held, are truly Christian, since they know not persecution. It is impossible to Christianize the state, which is always the ally of the devil, and the Christian, like Jesus, must always expect persecution and death. While Luther stressed beliefs, the Anabaptists stressed morals and a Christian life, as exemplified in the life of Jesus. In their own strict morality, they astounded their contemporaries of different faiths. Those who were moral nonconformists were banned from their church, but they would never use the power of the state to that end. The church, which is a community of saints, should always be separate from the state, the symbol of sin. The true Anabaptist, they held, should pay no allegiance whatsoever to the state, since it cannot be Christianized. Even though it restrains sinners it should be left completely in the hands of sinners, and the saints should have nothing to do with it.

The Anabaptists opposed war, capital punishment, and oaths, and challenged the world with their peculiar conception of religious liberty. They acquired such a wide following in various localities that Lutherans and Catholics united at the Diet of Speyers (1529) to exterminate them by death. They accepted martyrdom in thousands, and Germany destroyed all of them who arose there. Those who survived the persecutions repudiated the earlier extreme positions, but clung to their practices of abstention from worldly affairs and a strict moral asceticism. Menno Simons, the founder of the Mennonites, helped to shape their final doctrines and ways of life. The last remnants of these religious rebels found some peace in Holland, Switzerland, and then in America, where Mennonites and Amish still lend color to our national panorama. The Anabaptists, more than any other groups, laid the basis for the ultimate triumph of the principle of dissent, and of man's right to be different. And those who know the Amish country know how different modern

[50] H. Baker, *The Wars of Truth* (Cambridge, Mass.: Harvard University Press, 1952), pp. 292 ff.; Bainton, *The Reformation of the Sixteenth Century*, pp. 111 ff.

Anabaptists can be. Their nonconformity in education has caused no little concern to the educational authorities of Pennsylvania in recent times.

In spite of these leading departures from Catholic orthodoxy, the Reformation did not bring immediately any important theological revision. A trinitarian God, the incarnation, redemption, resurrection, miracles, prophecies, angels, demons, witches, etc., were among the beliefs retained by both Protestant and Catholic churches on a dogmatic basis, a fact which seems to indicate that, on the religious side, the Reformation was a revolt against moral and ecclesiastical abuses rather than against traditional theology.[51]

THE COUNTER-REFORMATION. (1) CHRISTIANS AGAINST CHRISTIANS. Protestant action brought Catholic reaction. This led to reform within the Catholic system and to attempts to win back Protestants to Catholicism. Both violent and peaceful methods marked the reaction. Kings, no doubt, found the religious dispute a convenient motive to promote their own ambitions. For over a hundred years, Europe was wrecked by "religious" wars in which the masses were butchered ostensibly for the glory of God and the kingdom of Christ. Christians, forgetting the ideals of the Master, still showed their capacity to hate.

Persecution of "heretics," an old phenomenon, marked the general period. The Roman and Spanish Inquisitions judged heresy, witchcraft, blasphemy, and other offenses, and turned convicted ones over to the executioner. In Spain, great church festival days were chosen for the spectacular public butcheries. Moors and Jews, also, were barbarously treated. In France and Italy the Protestants were savagely persecuted and murdered. Where Protestants were in power, as in some German states, England, and the American colonies, the Catholics were subjected to persecution and legal disabilities. War, bloodshed, and persecution thus accompanied the Counter-Reformation, both groups being about equally fanatical. The Catholic church, however, adopted other forms of counterattack.

The Council of Trent (1543-1563) was convened by the pope, who dominated it, for the purpose of defining Catholic doctrine and regulating morals. Reactionary in its spirit, it made no concessions to discontented ones either on matters of theology or church govern-

[51] W. S. Lilly, *Renaissance Types* (London: George Allen & Unwin, 1901), pp. 103–74, 231–302; Smith, *Erasmus*, pp. 33–48, 119–27, 159, 192 ff., 209–29, 242 ff., 372 ff., 386 ff., 421–41; Smith, *History of Modern Culture*, I, 357–75, 378–97; II, 265–72, 546–66; F. A. Ogg, *A Source Book of Mediaeval History* (New York: American Book Co., 1908), pp. 445 ff.

ment. It stressed the need for catechising children in the old beliefs. Supplementing these other measures, on the Catholic side, was the establishment of new religious societies such as the Jesuits, Oratorians, and the Christian Brethren. Such groups engaged in missionary, charitable, and educational activities. They were not contemplative in their purpose as were earlier monastic societies.

(2) THE JESUITS. The Jesuit Society was incorporated by the pope, in 1540, to promote Catholicism, evangelize heathens, extirpate heresy, and educate children and ignorant persons in Christianity. The document canonizing Ignatius Loyola, founder of the Society, declared that he had been sent by God to combat Luther, "foulest of monsters."[52] While the Dominicans continued to operate the Inquisition, the Jesuits became the spearhead of the Catholic attack upon Protestantism, new heresies and new philosophies. They attained great power by dominating, through their schools, the minds of influential Catholics, and by their political shrewdness. They were feared by their rivals and hated by their enemies. In 1773, Pope Clement XIV suppressed the Society, chiefly for the good of the church. It was re-established early in the next century. As educators the Jesuits did not aim to develop in their students free minds, critical of authority. It was rather their aim to make them intellectual adherents and defenders of official Catholic orthodoxy, and harmlessly virtuous, though history shows a few notable cases in which they failed to make their students orthodox. Obedience to authority was, for them, the crowning virtue. The Society was itself founded on that principle.

Supplementing their educational work were their foreign missionary activities. Both Protestants and Catholics struggled to dominate heathen minds. Cultural conquests abroad were good for business, although merchants rather than the missionaries realized that. Numerous and reliable authorities, however, have observed in Jesuitism a combination of astute worldliness and religious piety. The *gloria mundi* allured them little less than did the *gloria dei*. With the laboring masses, always unimportant if ignorant and obedient, they were but little concerned. Through their influence with the powerful, they themselves became powerful, to the advantage, for a time, of the Catholic church.

(3) THE CHRISTIAN BRETHREN. Inspired by a spirit of charity and deep concern for the well-being of the degraded Catholic poor, whom he wished to keep within the Catholic church, Jean Baptiste de la Salle founded, in 1682, the Christian Brethren. Originating in

[52] Smith, *History of Modern Culture,* I, 364.

France, the Brethren carried their work, in time, into many other countries. They were not a society of priests but of lay "brothers," whose primary purpose was the religious indoctrination of poor Catholic children. The members were trained elementary school teachers. As such, they strengthened the position of Roman Catholicism among the socially underprivileged, as did the Jesuits among the Catholic aristocracy. Unlike the Jesuits, whose schools were of secondary and higher rank, the Brethren long devoted themselves to the field of elementary education.

(4) Other New Catholic Societies. From the late sixteenth century onward, many other Catholic societies were established mainly for charitable, missionary, and educational purposes. There were about thirty of these established between 1525 and 1700, about half of them being congregations of women. Among these were the Fathers of Christian Doctrine (1593), the Brothers of Charity (1538), the Ursuline Nuns (1535), the Oratorians (1558), the Sisters of Charity (1634), the Passionists (1725), and the Redemptionists (1732).[53] The establishment of these groups was prompted by the need for aggressive methods in combating Protestantism. Charitable needs existing under our economic system have been used by both Protestant and Catholic churches to extend their influence. The assumption of charitable functions by lay agencies and governments has weakened the influence of the churches.

CHURCH AND STATE IN THE POST-REFORMATION WORLD. In the confusion resulting from the break with Rome, a grave problem, as we have seen, arose for princes and church leaders. Religious tensions and rivalry put a severe strain upon political machinery. In Poland, in 1573, Calvinists, Hussites, and Lutherans accepted the principle of religious liberty, and agreed to live together and yet differ. The alternatives were bloody strife or territorial churches, the latter being adopted at the Peace of Augsburg. The political ruler would thus determine the religion of his subjects, legalizing, if he desired, more than one denomination.

The struggle became, however, largely one for the recognition of a single national faith, and established churches eventually emerged, the Lutheran church of Sweden (1527) being the first Protestant national church. In England, the Anglican church was established in 1533, and other state churches were soon established in other lands, including colonial America where the Puritan and Anglican churches were the privileged ones. St. Paul's dictum that

[53] P. J. Marique, *History of Christian Education* (New York: Fordham University Press, 1924–32), II, 128.

"the powers that be are ordained of God"[54] shaped all Christian political theory. Because of human nature and the intrinsic evil of the world, society, in Luther's opinion, could never be Christianized, and men must be forced to do good. The sword is thus made again an instrument of God. What a ruler demands, God demands, but politics falls, nevertheless, into the orbit of nature. The natural man can be good and just if he acts within the law, but he must not be permitted to pursue his own selfish ends in contravention of law. To kill the body of an evildoer is not, according to Luther (and here he follows Augustine), incompatible with Christian love. In a truly Christian society, in Luther's view, there would be no need for law or the sword, but such a society, even in the form of a church, is impossible. Both church and state are of the earth, earthly, and always reflect the conflict between good and evil, the divine and the satanic. The dualism between God and nature he saw permeating all human institutions. And a dualism exists even in the nature of God, who is both a vengeful and merciful ruler. On earth, the state administers his vengeance; the church, his mercy; and the church should guide the state in administering justice. Luther would not separate them, but he declined to say which one should be dominant. Calvin, however, showed no hesitancy in choosing theocracy, or rule by God and his dominant church. Luther, in his indecision, contributed to the acceptance of the view of a single church-state power, or caesaropapism, as it is called. Perhaps, in practice, this could mean only political absolutism and the supremacy of the state. But, while Luther opposed rebellion, as in the case of the Peasant Revolt, he believed that men are sometimes, in religious duty, bound to disobey the state. For him, religion is man's first duty. The political doctrine of Calvin is clearer and easier to interpret than that of Luther.

For Calvinists, the ideal society is a theocracy designed exclusively for the glory of God, and in which clergy and magistrates work together in a community of God's elect. The perfect society is a Holy Commonwealth in which church and state, the single community of the saved, are equal partners in God's business. Both Lutheranism and Calvinism, then, contributed in different degrees to the doctrine and practice of the union of church and state, but neither would give the state the power to suppress the true religion, which, for each group, was its own. In Anglican England, the Stuart doctrine of the divine right of kings made the monarch the supreme head of the church, and dissent from its teachings an at-

[54] *Romans,* 13.

tack upon his sacred person. All these working arrangements and theories, however, did not work well.

The separation of church and state came with the spread of dissent from established forms of religion and with the growth of rationalism, nationalism, and political liberalism. The Anabaptists died for that ideal. Nations found by harsh experience that religious conflict was an enemy of national solidarity, and that coercion of dissenters weakened the national community. Even in nations such as Sweden and England, where the separation of church and state has not yet been achieved, the principle of toleration has won out over that of suppression. The doctrine of "one land, one king, one law" did not work in the sphere of religion, where pluralism has come to stay. To achieve national unification in the midst of religious pluralism was one of the chief purposes for which national school systems were established.

The problem of federal aid to education in the United States touches upon all the timeworn issues involved in the conflict between church and state. While the problem still exists, the state has become the dominant institution for the advancement of civilization in modern times. Mediaeval cities were built around great churches, which gave them their distinctive character. State and business buildings now tower above the churches, and this visible change symbolizes the change in the conception of values that has taken place in the Western world. The Reformation was but a passing phase in the transition to the secular world of today.

THE REFORMATION IN ENGLAND AND SCOTLAND. Because of peculiar local history and traditions, the reform of the church displays the marks of local coloring as we go from one land to another, although the basic grievances against the old order were everywhere the same. The church in England had acquired a large measure of independence before the break with Rome occurred. Here heresies had been stamped out, and theological issues were not a major problem. Papal interference in national affairs, however, caused resentment. The occasion of the break was the question of the annulment of the marriage of Henry VIII so that he might have a son to succeed him. In the conflict with the papacy, an English national church was proclaimed, and the monasteries were suppressed, although many of the abbots supported the king in his demand for a divorce.[55] During the controversy, Henry ordered that an English Bible be used in the churches, and Coverdale's translation, the fore-

[55] Bainton, *The Reformation of the Sixteenth Century*, p. 194.

runner of the King James Bible, was officially approved. But the break was one without heresy, although blood was shed in the rupture. Thomas More, humanist, author of *Utopia,* and opponent of Henry's divorce, was one of the prominent victims. England, however, produced no really new theology, and Puritan attempts to bring the nation into line with Lutheranism and Calvinism had but little effect upon religious thought and practice. The Thirty-Nine Articles of the Anglican faith are, however, Protestant.

In the British plan, the national church was empowered to regulate beliefs, and the state was given the power to regulate the public aspects of religion. England was more concerned about national unity than about theological truth, and here appears the chief difference between Anglican and Lutheran-Calvinist Reformers. In purely religious matters, the British solution was a compromise between the old and the new, and a mixture of both.[56] The new national church of England became not only the instrument of the national spirit at home, but also the promoter of British national interests in British colonies, including those of colonial America.

Across the border, in Scotland, Calvinism became firmly entrenched and left an indelible mark upon Scottish national character. The English were less concerned about creeds than about prayer, as is evidenced by the Anglican *Book of Common Prayer.* The Scot stressed a creed, the well-known Westminster Confession. It was John Knox, the pupil of Calvin, who shaped the revolutionary spirit of Scotland. There, Calvinism became a phase of the political struggle with England, as Catholicism did in the struggle between England and Ireland. Irish Catholicism, somewhat paradoxically, became an ally of Irish nationalism. The struggle between Scottish Calvinism and Anglicanism was carried to British colonies and, in America, the Calvinist fear of an imposed Anglican orthodoxy contributed something to the growth of the desire for independence. While English officers, who called the Revolution a "Scotch-Irish rebellion," [57] may have been guilty of an overstatement, there is little doubt that the force of religious dissent was at work in the conflict. What happened in England and Scotland in the Reformation era had a special bearing upon political and educational developments in America, although the happenings there were but a part of the whole European struggle.

[56] *Ibid.*, pp. 183–209.

[57] H. M. Jenkins, *Pennsylvania: Colonial and Federal, A History, 1608–1903* (Philadelphia: Pennsylvania Historical Publishing Association, 1903), II, 28.

Intellectual Change

HUMANISM. Intellectual change accompanied the other changes we have described. The period opened with the protest of Renaissance thinkers against scholasticism and Aristotelianism, and it ended with the Enlightenment which, rejecting traditionalism in thought and postulating the infallibility of reason, represents a complete negation of mediaevalism. The chief steps in the intellectual development were the Renaissance, the Reformation, the scientific movement, and the rise of the philosophies of rationalism, empiricism, and skepticism.

As a progressive force, the Renaissance was the least important of these steps. It was a gradual spiritual awakening which can be dated back, with certainty, to the twelfth century. The commonly accepted view that the "rebirth" of the human spirit occurred in the fourteenth and fifteenth centuries is indefensible in the light of our present knowledge of the intellectual activities of the preceding centuries. The "rebirth" was inspired chiefly by the study of the ancient classics, and eventually touched all aspects of human life and thought. The term humanism, which has been applied to the literary and educational aspects of the rebirth, suggests the new outlook and theory of values that marked the movement. Man, as a human being, and his worldly problems became a primary concern of the humanists. Literature, art, theology, education, politics, science, and the natural world became things of interest and inquiry in this age of intellectual awakening. The fourteenth century saw a blossoming of the humanist spirit in the cities of Italy. There it stood for individualism and man's unrestricted right to direct his thought and life by reason.

Most of the humanists, both earlier and later, have been called Christian Humanists because, although they would restore the thought of pagan classical antiquity, they were not anti-Christian. While extravagantly honoring Plato and the moral ideals of the Stoics and of Cicero,[58] as some of these did, they would not substitute these teachings for those of Christ, but, rather, reconcile both, as did early Christian Apologists. Many Italian votaries of classical antiquity abandoned their Christian faith, and are known as Pagan Humanists. Some of them would even revive the old pagan cults. Those who have become known in our own time as Secular Humanists differ from both of these groups in that the only cult they stress is that of humanity without any limiting labels attached to it. The

[58] Baker, *op. cit.*, pp. 110 f.

humanism that came to prevail was, however, Christian humanism. Humanism, as the cult of man and humanity, originated in Greece. There, even the gods were humanized in a culture which recognized the humanity of the gods and the divinity of man. The interest of the Pagan Humanists was literary and artistic, rather than moral, but, when forced to choose, they favored pagan moral ideals and practices. They would free the individual from the restraints of Christian morality, and allow him to follow nature rather than any traditional moral law. The naturalistic conception of man, which blossomed in Rousseau, originated in the cult of individuality of Italian humanists. In attacking clerical immorality, they were not, however, consistent with their own doctrine, which made individualism a principle even of moral conduct.

The movement, as it developed in the fourteenth century, was one marked by optimism, faith in reason and in man's ability to conquer evil and build the perfect world. Those ideals, confirmed later by man's actual achievements in social and religious reform and in his advancement of scientific knowledge, found their most optimistic expression in the Enlightenment of the eighteenth century, with its doctrines of the perfectibility of man and the inevitability of progress.

An examination of humanism, whether in its Christian or pagan form, shows it to have been unproductive of new ideas. While the humanists were critical thinkers, they were, with a few notable exceptions, worshipers of the past and preservers of inherited values. They would purify man's inheritance; they would not create something boldly new. For them, the golden age was in the past, not in the future. And their criticism of existing institutions sheltered itself behind the walls of conservative thought. The educational theorists among them were preoccupied with the education of princes and the social elite; and their political theorists were generally reluctant to defend the national state, although it had become a reality. For wisdom in reforming the world, they would turn to a Plato, a Marcus Aurelius, or a Cicero. In medicine, they looked to the wisdom of such ancients as Hippocrates and Galen; in history, to that of Pliny, etc. They were restorers, not creators, but that seems to have been a necessary step to the "great renewal" of the scientific movement, which was a revolt against all authority and the worship of the past. Yet, in spite of this conservatism, humanism represents a great intellectual revival. In the ferment, scholasticism and clericalism were attacked, and the intellectual achievements of antiquity were again made known to Europeans. And, in the effort to rebuild the intellectual structure of Christendom, a spirit of skepticism developed which was of inestimable value in later centuries.[59]

The skepticism generated by humanism was soon, however, to be turned against its own faith in man and reason. Even Petrarch (1304-1374), a leading champion and popularizer of the ancient classics, once wrote that he could not trust his reason,[60] but such doubt did not become widespread for some two centuries later. As it developed, it brought a questioning of humanist optimism, of the doctrines of the dignity of man, the adequacy of reason, and of the new education with its emphasis upon verbalism and intellectualism. Some of the questioning of humanist ideals was inspired by religious beliefs and mysticism. Among the numerous religious critics was Cornelius Agrippa (1487-1535), a wandering German teacher and a dabbler in magic and occult philosophy. In his book, *Of Uncertainty,* he attacked secular learning and the cult of words, reason, and worldly success; but he stood on common ground with the humanists and the Reformers in their scorn for scholastic philosophy as an attempt to achieve a rational theology. And the Reformation, with all its indebtedness to humanism, as a revival of a literary and scholarly tradition, was a revolt against humanist ideals.

Protestant theologians rejected the humanist doctrines of the dignity of man and of his right to free development and a life of joy. For them, as for mediaeval ascetics, man is born but to die and face the judgment of God. The Renaissance never succeeded in changing that attitude entirely. Giannozza Mavetti, in his *On the Excellency and Dignity of Man,* tried hard to refute traditional Christian pessimism and asceticism, but few humanists ever saw man as a glory in himself and in the realm of nature. For them, with few exceptions, he remained but a noble thing in a theocratic universe, plodding his glorious way toward the grave. Luther and Calvin rejected the optimism and aestheticism, limited though they were, of humanist thought. For the former, as for Augustine whom he followed, man is by nature weak and dependent for salvation upon the regenerating power of God's grace. For Calvin, human prestige is the gravest of fallacies, and man's degeneration through the Fall is an established fact. In his natural state, man is no better than a worm. Religion thus challenged the optimistic view of the humanists regarding man's nature and his rôle in the universe.

However, neither the humanists' glorification of man, nor Calvinist degradation of him proved to be a satisfactory answer to the question of man's significance, and a synthesis between the views of

59 *Ibid.,* pp. 1 ff.
60 *Ibid.,* p. 147.

humanists and supernaturalists remained to be established. It was found in the view that man is a link between the worlds of matter and of spirit, in both of which his nature shares. In his spiritual and moral nature he is, in this view, an associate of God and, as such, little less than the angels in dignity. This view preserved the optimism of the Renaissance, but those holding it saw in the visible world a moral purpose and asserted the moral responsibility of man to study the achievements of the race and the book of nature as revelations of God and the moral universe. Whether knowledge be derived through faith, reason, or scientific observation, it was thus assigned a moral end, to be realized in a better and happier world and in salvation in the hereafter.

Milton (1608-1674), in his *Paradise Lost* and *Samson Agonistes,* and in spite of his acceptance of the Fall-doctrine and its implications, upheld the view of man's dignity by attributing human sinfulness to Satan who perverted man's nature and will. And he presents us with a man possessed of freedom to sin or not to sin, not the hopeless victim of the Creator's will. A century earlier, Peter Ramus (1515-1572), a French Calvinist and humanist, effected a similar compromise between humanism and pessimism. And the thought of Ramus and Milton came to prevail generally in Puritan lands. Renaissance optimism was thus saved from the threat directed at it by a gloomy supernaturalism.[61] But a skepticism of a rationalist sort also posed a serious threat to humanist faith in man and his reason.

Montaigne, in his essay *Apology for Raymond Sebond,* sneered at man's vanity and pride in his own achievements. Instead of being but little less than the angels, he is rather little better than the brutes. He, like the other animals, is but a part of nature, and no dearer to Heaven than the rest of living things. Man's conflicting philosophies, filled with ridiculous dogmas, reveal his inability to know anything. All his works testify to his pride, arrogance, and insignificance. The anti-intellectualism and distrust of reason expressed in this essay is the high-water mark of philosophical skepticism of the humanist age. Richard Burton, in *The Anatomy of Melancholy,* made a similar attack upon reason and man's pride in his achievements. For him, also, man is but a beast who, in his folly and arrogance, uses his gift of words to conceal his own inadequacies. Skeptics like these could not, however, destroy humanist optimism. And, while the skeptics were trying to annihilate reason, the early scientists were at work discovering new objects of knowledge and inventing a new method of discovering it.

[61] *Ibid.,* pp. 25–50.

Related to all the intellectual unrest of the humanist age was the discovery of the literature of the Graeco-Roman world. Beginning in the twelfth century,[62] the rediscovery of the classics was completed by approximately 1400. Petrarch is the first great Renaissance humanist. He was a poet and a popularizer of the classics, whose *Familiar Letters,* addressed to ancient Roman writers, stimulated great interest in their thought. He did not know Greek, and wrote both in Latin and Italian as did his contemporary humanist, Boccaccio (1313-1375). The latter had learned some Greek, but the spread of knowledge of the Greek language and literature dates from the arrival in Italy (1393) of Manuel Chrysoloras of Constantinople (1350-1415). Other distinguished Greek teachers followed him and continued his work. When Constantinople fell to the Turks (1453), Italy was deluged with Greek scholars, but nearly all the ancient Greek authors had been rediscovered by that date. One of the great achievements of early Italian humanists was the gathering of Latin and Greek manuscripts and the founding of classical libraries. In the mid-fifteenth century, the Vatican Library was established by Pope Nicholas V, but, before this time, classical libraries had been established by many city despots. Until the development of printing, all of these libraries were small, the largest being that of the Vatican with less than 4000 volumes.

Some popes of the time fell under the spell of the classics, and promoted the new intellectualism. Both laymen and churchmen thus played a part in the revival of interest in the pagan past and the literature it produced. That was then, as it still remains, one of the greatest of literatures. After centuries of literary decadence, the humanist found in this ancient literature a storehouse of wisdom. In spite of the later rise of vernacular literatures, Graeco-Roman literature is still deservedly known as "the classics." That it aroused so much enthusiasm in the fourteenth and fifteenth centuries should not be a matter of surprise. It was then the only great literature which the Western world had produced. And, before we leave the subject, it should be noted that humanism and the classics, in this age of early nationalism, knew no national boundaries, or sectarian or party lines, and promised men a unity in an age of growing disunity. Humanism as an international culture, however, was fated to be wrecked by the forces of sectarianism and nationalism. The ideal of "humanity," closely related as it is to that of the brotherhood of man, still, however, offers hope to would-be reformers of the

[62] C. H. Haskins, *The Renaissance of the Twelfth Century* (Cambridge, Mass.: Harvard University Press, 1927).

world. But to label it Christian, or Buddhist, or anything else, limits its usefulness as a unifying force in a sharply divided world.

PROTESTANTISM. The Reformation, while reactionary in its worship of the "golden age" of early Christianity, made a significant contribution to individualism, intellectual freedom, and progress. All authority and all beliefs were weakened when the Reformers disrupted the unity of Christendom. Protestantism, though without intent, made it increasingly difficult to stifle freedom of thought and speech. In the evolution of dissent from mediaeval orthodoxy there arose so many sects that unity of belief could no longer be enforced upon Christians. Thus, indirectly, Protestantism promoted intellectual progress.

Protestant rejection of scholastic philosophy and the rational theology of Aquinas and his followers had a direct influence upon the future course of intellectual life. In contempt for scholastic subtleties, Protestant theologians were one with a long line of humanists. The scholastics assumed that nature could be understood by a process of logical reasoning created by man himself and embodying his own preconceptions of the reason and order which the intelligent Designer must have given to nature. But to Luther and, particularly, Calvin, both of whom were followers of Ockham, the ways of God in every realm are inscrutable, and man must rely upon revelation and faith for an understanding of them. From that point the step was a short one to the view that things knowable by reason fall exclusively into the realm of nature, a realm which must be sharply separated from that of revelation and theology. In the sphere of nature, things happen in ways that are not dependent upon, nor revealed by, any scheme of thought or logical analysis.

Indeed, logicians, like Aristotle and Aquinas, had attributed to nature properties and happenings which were not in accord with observable facts. The Reformers insisted that revelation, not a moral philosophy or a rational theology, was the sole foundation of faith and belief in the ways of God. Reason should not invade the realm of the supernatural. Its sphere is nature, and natural knowledge is a thing apart from religious belief. Calvin, the theologian, and Francis Bacon, the scientist, demanded, with equal force but for different reasons, the separation of the natural from the supernatural. Calvin would save supernaturalism from attacks by naturalists and skeptics, while Bacon would save nature and man's freedom to explore it from scholastic supernaturalism and its ally, Aristotelianism. Calvin would, by the separation of nature from God, save Christian dogmas; Bacon would save science and natural knowledge from all dogmas.

While Protestantism contributed to the advance of science and natural knowledge by giving its blessing to worldly enterprise, its most significant link with the scientific movement is seen in its advocacy of a separation of nature from the supernatural. Man might now explore the world without fear of hell provided, of course, that, in working out his salvation, he did not substitute nature for God. But all this apparently happy rapport between Protestant nominalism and science does not mean that Protestant leaders showed a friendly spirit to the new scientific theories of the sixteenth and seventeenth centuries. Indeed, the opposite was often the truth. Out of the intellectual ferment of the Renaissance and Reformation era and the new social scene reflected in it came the most significant of all modern Western developments—the scientific movement.

THE SCIENTIFIC RENAISSANCE. From the twelfth century onward, interest in the natural world and its physical truths, while it had never entirely ceased, slowly returned. That awakening culminated in the scientific renaissance of the sixteenth and seventeenth centuries, when intellectual interest, once centered in the supernatural and then in the human world, came to center in the physical world and its laws. The greatest discovery of the period was science itself; the greatest invention, that of a new method of discovery, namely, observation and experiment. All the great changes in thought and social institutions which distinguish the modern from the mediaeval world are traceable to science. Above all, it gave to the world a new mind, born in an agonizing clash between new and old ideas.

Some minor spiritual shocks resulting from the geographical discovery of a new earth prepared men for the greater shock of the astronomical discovery of new heavens. The importance of man, in the scheme of nature, faded with the importance of the earth, now pushed out of the dignified central position in the cosmos which pre-Christian scientists and their Christian debtors had given it. Among the final results of the scientific exploration of the heavens were the substitution of a new infinite complex cosmos for the old one of Genesis, Aristotle, and Ptolemy; a weakening of Scriptural and theological authority; and the partial liberation of the Western mind from the tyranny of ancient wisdom and of herd beliefs.

Though the old cosmology was pagan, fundamentalist theologians, Protestant and Catholic, persecuted its opponents. Bruno was martyred, in 1600, for his interpretations of astronomy, and Galileo was forced by the Roman Inquisition, in 1616, to recant his cosmological views as "contrary to holy Scripture." Luther and his leading associate, Melanchthon, denounced the Copernican theory on

Biblical grounds; and Comenius, then the leading advocate of a realistic education, was anti-Copernican.[63] Even the skeptical Montaigne and Francis Bacon condemned the Copernican system for reasons then considered philosophically profound but which now appear childish. The universities, enslaved by Aristotelianism, long opposed the new knowledge. Professors in church-controlled universities were required to take an oath not to teach the Copernican system.[64] The telescopic method of investigation was denounced by those theologians who, following Aquinas, held that the only true method was that of reasoning theologically from the Scriptures, and by those who believed that Aristotle had said the last word about the world of nature. Telescopic observation, it was held, could reveal nothing in the heavens which Aristotle did not know. Some believed that there was a devil in the telescope that deceived the eye. Books teaching the Copernican theory remained on the Catholic *Index Expurgatorius* of forbidden books until 1835.[65]

Despite opposition, scientists organized societies to conduct experiments in such fields as physics, chemistry, geometry, astronomy, geography, anatomy, medicine, navigation, statics, magnetics, mechanics, etc.[66] The first important one was the Academy of Experiments established in Florence in 1657; and the second was the British Royal Society, chartered in 1662. Other similar societies were soon established in France, Germany, Russia, and Ireland. In America the American Philosophical Society arose out of a proposal of Franklin in 1743.[67]

By the seventeenth century, visionaries, aware of the great progress that had been made in the fields of discovery and invention, were predicting the coming of a worldly Utopia.[68] A new faith was in the making, a faith in science and scientific research as a remedy for all the ills of life and society. Objective, verified knowledge would, according to this faith, give man the power to control and shape his worldly destiny. "Knowledge," said Francis Bacon, "is power." For these enthusiasts the tree of knowledge is not the tree of death, and their faith, which has become a unique element in Western culture, still inspires the rapturous expression of its

[63] H. Butterfield, *The Origins of Modern Science, 1300–1800* (London: G. Bell & Sons, Ltd., 1949), p. 43.

[64] A. D. White, *History of the Warfare of Science with Theology in Christendom* (New York: Appleton-Century-Crofts, Inc., 1896), I, 128.

[65] *Ibid.*, I, 156–57.

[66] Smith, *History of Modern Culture*, I, 164–72.

[67] J. Bigelow, *Works of Benjamin Franklin* (New York: G. P. Putnam's Sons, Inc., 1904), II, 67 f.

[68] L. Mumford, *The Story of Utopias* (New York: Liveright Publishing Corp., 1922).

devotees.[69] The scientific movement was a rejection of ecclesiastical and Aristotelian authority in the realm of science—a veritable intellectual revolution. The Renaissance and the Reformation merely reordered the mediaeval Christian tradition, and they remained within it. Science, on the other hand, created something new and revolutionary. It created a new way of thought about man and his world and, in it, the modern mind and the modern world had their real origin.

In the Dark Ages, scientific knowledge had suffered a sharp decline from the heights it had reached in ancient Athens and Alexandria. In the later Middle Ages, some few men were observers of nature, but they tended to explain what they observed in terms of traditional religious conceptions. The rediscovery, chiefly through Arab channels, of Greek works on science opened up new vistas of thought, and therein also lay the significance of the Renaissance for the development of experimental science, a significance much greater than that of later nominalist and Protestant separation of the natural and supernatural realms. Protestantism, however, had an elasticity which eventually brought it into alliance with science and the philosophies related to it. Of all aspects of the revolution which we call science that of the scientific method of inquiry is by far the most important. By the seventeenth century, visionaries, aware of the great progress that had been made in the fields of discovery and invention, were predicting the coming of scientific Utopias. Campanella, Andreae, Bacon, Hartlib, and Comenius envisaged a world made perfect in every way by science. These enthusiasts believed that, by scientific research, men would soon possess all knowledge, the *pansophia* of Comenius, and thus acquire the power to remedy all the ills of life and society.

THE SCIENTIFIC METHOD AND EARLY PHILOSOPHERS OF SCIENCE. The method by which the scientists had come to a knowledge of a great variety of startling new truths was that of observation and experiment. In the fifteenth century, medical men at the University of Padua were performing experiments in anatomy, but for the purpose of illustrating the "truths" found in the writings of the Greek physician Galen (*c.* 130-200). Even Vesalius (1514-1564), a professor at Padua, who made anatomy a science was at first shocked when his experimental data differed from the findings of Galen. The spirit of secularism permeating the city life of Italy left its mark upon the work of the medical faculty in Padua. Here, Fallopio (1523-1562), discoverer of the Fallopian tubes, and William

69 For example, see S. O'Casey, *Rose and Crown* (New York: The Macmillan Co., 1952), pp. 181 f.

Harvey (1578-1657), discoverer of the circulation of the blood, demonstrated the futility and the evil of reliance upon authority, even of a Galen or an Aristotle. As explorations and experiments went on, old theories and old errors were discarded one by one. Floods of new and tested data were released as the old authoritarian walls were broken down.[70] Experiments were not something new, but the old ones were few in number.

The most famous of the early experiments of our period was the testing of Aristotle's supposed teaching that the speed with which falling bodies approach the earth is in proportion to their weight. Galileo, apparently erroneously, has been given credit for the discovery that the Aristotelians were wrong. He suspected that they were wrong and probably tried, as did a few others, to test the theory experimentally. Who actually proved it wrong still remains in doubt.[71] The problem itself was a significant one since it touched upon the primary qualities of matter and the mechanism of the universe. In the realm of matter, the early scientists saw that things were capable of exact measurement. When the Renaissance scholars unearthed the mathematics of antiquity they gave scientists one necessary instrument of such measurement. The new mathematicians united the algebra of the Hindus with the geometry of the Greeks to provide scientists with an essential tool of measurement of the physical world. Descartes saw mathematics as a general science related to every quantitative phenomenon in the realm of matter, and without which there could be no exactness in the physical sciences. For him, as for Galileo, Spinoza and others, reality must be thought of in terms of mathematical relationships. It should be noted, too, that the discovery of the work of Archimedes (*c.* 287-212 B.C.) in mechanics and hydrostatics influenced experimentation in physics, as mathematics did in the general field of science. The seventeenth century witnessed the invention of important scientific instruments, such as the telescope, microscope, pendulum-clock, barometer, and thermometer. Without such devices, exact measurement would be impossible.

As far as the method men should use in exploring nature was concerned, two schools of thought appeared. The first, that of the rationalists, represented by Descartes and Spinoza, viewed the universe and natural processes as rational, and the deductive method of comprehending it all as the correct method. That was essentially the view of Plato and, to a lesser degree, of Aristotle. The rationalists, as they are known, of this school ignored sensation as an impor-

[70] Butterfield, *op. cit.*, pp. 28 ff.
[71] *Ibid.*, pp. 59 ff.

tant step to knowledge and truth, and looked upon deductive reasoning and intuition as the essential keys to an understanding of nature. The second school, that of the empiricists, represented by Bacon, Locke, and Hobbes, gave sensation a primary place in the process of discovering the truths of nature. The empiricists are pre-eminently the philosophers of science. For them systematic observation, sense experience, and experiment are the necessary steps to a knowledge and control of nature, and the method they recommended was the inductive method.

Though there was basic disagreement between the rationalists and empiricists in regard to deduction versus induction, both agreed that a new method of inquiry was needed, and that man could never understand the world unless he freed his mind from the accumulated errors and superstitions handed down from the past. The inductive method which came to prevail in science was not a creation of the seventeenth century rationalists and empiricists. Leonardo da Vinci (1452-1519) was an empiricist through and through.[72] He was not interested in any realm of thought which was closed to critical scrutiny. Galileo, while approving the mathematical-deductive method, experimented and observed nature so closely that he saw the universe as a perfect machine. Francis Bacon, the leading formulator of the inductive method during the early scientific movement, was thus heir to a rich heritage of scientific thought and achievement. While he was not able to tear himself completely away from the errors of past,[73] his books *The Advancement of Learning*, the *Novum Organon* and *The New Atlantis* did more to advance the causes of science than the works of any other single individual.

These works of Bacon are landmarks in the history of science. He not only issued a call to the world to build anew the edifice of knowledge from its very foundations, but he outlined, as well, the method by which that should be done. He showed utter scorn for Aristotelian logic and scholastic philosophy, and he rejected humanistic skepticism as more pernicious than Platonism or Aristotelianism, since it led men to despair of finding truth. The effort of the Reformation was to reconstruct the basis of religious knowledge; the effort of scientists and of Bacon was to free man's knowledge of nature from traditional theology, Aristotelianism, and scholastic philosophy. Bacon had unbounded faith that the human mind could be delivered from error, or what to uncritical thinkers had been deemed truth. The first step of the new methodology, described in

[72] H. E. Barnes, *An Intellectual and Cultural History of the Western World* (New York: The Dryden Press, Inc., 1937), p. 573.

[73] Butterfield, *op. cit.*, pp. 76 f.

his *Novum Organon* ("The New Logic"), is the shattering of the idols, or prejudices, which have kept man's mind in error and in chains. Man must rid his mind of mere opinions. He must in the future seek a knowledge of things, not what men of the past thought were things or properties of things. The starting point of inquiry is sensation, but the human senses need help. And the help is presented in his rules of induction.

The first help is a compiling of a sound natural and experimental history in which facts are presented in a systematic and orderly fashion. This would be a catalogue of facts, and of unsolved problems as a guide to further inquiry. From these data man should proceed by an inductive process of successive steps to lesser, middle and then larger generalizations. The lowest of these are little more than mere particular experiences, while the highest ones are hazy mental abstractions. Those in the middle, he said, are solid and of great practical value to man. Bacon would thus have men end with generalizations, not begin with them, as the deductive reasoners did, but each new generalization would suggest the need for further experiments. Deductive thinkers either jumped to final generalizations from a few observed particulars or, ignoring particulars entirely, set up their generalizations on a purely speculative or *a priori* basis. And often the generalizations, or "first principles," with which their thinking process began, were but untested assumptions which had become a part of men's cultural heritage. Bacon would reverse that procedure, and the generalizations in his scheme would always be subject to modification in the light of new discoveries. This is the inductive method, as Bacon conceived it. He failed to see that men might misinterpret data and observe in them things that were not there. It was his revolt against the old method rather than his suggested technique which was of greatest significance. He failed to see the importance of mathematics in describing natural occurrences; and the need for the hypothesis, as a technique of research, did not even occur to him. He had, however, a clear vision of a new kind of knowledge.

By reaffirming the ideal of human dignity and by asserting the ancient Greek doctrine that knowledge is man's highest function, Bacon did much to preserve a most significant element in European thought. And the knowledge he would promote was natural knowledge which he would have man use for utilitarian ends. Where Socrates equated knowledge with virtue, he would equate it with power, the power to control nature and make it man's servant in the enrichment of life. The scholastic philosophers, he said, neither served God nor man by uniting natural and divine knowledge.

Their baseless generalizations about nature kept the mind in darkness and in ignorance of natural phenomena and their causes. The scientist, he held, should not seek final causes, as the scholastics did. That should be left to philosophers and theologians. But the scientist should not stop with a mere collection of data. Like the bees, he should extract honey from these flowers; that is, he should interpret what observation and experiment have revealed, and extract generalizations from his data. He criticized many "natural philosophers" of his own day for going beyond facts and building untrue pictures of the world out of the empty fabric of their own thought. He thus saw nature as a field of exact and useful knowledge within the reach of man, but attainable only if he will seek it inductively. Bacon brought the importance of method into the foreground and, in a few decades, Descartes' famous *Discourse on Method* was published.

As a starting point in the search for knowledge, Descartes would doubt everything except his own existence. The position "I think, therefore I exist" was the foundation of his system. He would abandon all inherited systems of knowledge and ideas and, like Bacon, build a new system. In this rebuilding he would rely, not upon sensation, but upon reason and man's capacity to see things distinctly. The eye of the mind, he held, sees more clearly than the eye of the body. God, according to Descartes—and here he accepts as valid Anselm's ontological proof of God's existence—is one of man's clear ideas. Without God, man could not be sure of anything, and life and thought would be but a dreadful confusion. The Cartesian universe, starting with matter and reaching up to God, was an orderly one, designed by an immutable Creator, and mathematically precise and uniform in its nature and operations. Descartes saw experiments as subordinate to mathematical insights in uncovering the truths of nature, but he would combine both of them. His is a clockwork universe which operates with mechanical and mathematical precision, indeed so perfectly designed that Newton feared it could keep running without God.[74] Thus, in spite of his recognition of God, Descartes helped to glorify the mechanization theory. He himself tried to save God, the human soul, thought and religion from mechanization, but such mathematicians as Kepler (1571-1630) and Leibnitz (1646-1716), and such experimental scientists as Boyle (1627-1691) saw no escape from mechanism as an explanation of life and the physical order. In the sciences, however, mathematics came to be subordinated to observation and experiment as methods of inquiry. While Bacon contributed most to

[74] *Ibid.*, p. 95.

the ultimate triumph of empiricism and the experimental method, John Locke (1632-1704) gave influential support to his position.

Locke, in his *An Essay concerning Human Understanding*, made a devastating attack upon scholastic rationalism and the doctrines of innate ideas and *a priori* truth. For him, sensation and experience are the only sound sources of true knowledge. It is experience that provides the furnishings of the blank paper (*tabula rasa*) which is the mind. Nominalist as he was, he saw universals as merely verbal "learned gibberish" and particular "things" as the only reality. Ideas of these things enter the empty mind through the senses, are retained in the memory, and are given names, groups of them being given general names, the only real universals. It is with these objects of sensation that reason works. While error is likely to arise in this sensory knowledge, a limited truth, sufficient for man's practical needs, can be extracted from it, if the mental processes are properly disciplined.

While Locke did not formulate a definite statement of the inductive method, his general theory of knowledge is empirical, and the method of acquiring knowledge a completely inductive one. For him, all deductive intellectual systems are not worthy to be considered as providing anything higher than hypotheses, or untested paths to a knowledge of nature. Newton, he remarked, was only able to show the limited value of mathematics in exploring the universe. He himself viewed the universe as incomprehensible, since man can never have direct experience of the basic qualities and properties of matter. Man has the power, however, to draw useful inferences from the data of sensation and, using his experience, to achieve a practical morality. Eternal ethical absolutes, if they exist, are beyond his reach. Of greatest importance, in Locke's view, was man's use of his natural faculties to acquire sufficient knowledge to live well and agreeably with others. The whole tone of his thought, as of Bacon's, was secular, utilitarian, and naturalistic. What in modern educational thought is called functionalism can be found in all its basic elements in the thinking of early empiricists, particularly Locke.

SCIENCE AND MORAL AND POLITICAL THOUGHT. The freeing of nature from its old theological moorings had significant moral implications. We have just seen Locke's emphasis upon a practical morality derived from experience. The use of scientific tools of research could not reveal a moral purpose in nature, and scientists did not examine it as a symbol of moral value. The separation of natural and religious truth, approved by both religious and secular philosophers, led some to separate morals from revealed religion, as Spinoza

(1632-1677) did in his *Ethics.*[75] Morals, he said, should be studied as natural phenomena and in the same way as "lines, planes, and solids." [76] Descartes' universe was mathematical rather than moral. The approach of Spinoza and Hobbes (1586-1679) to an understanding of morals was through physiology and psychology. Pleasure and pain were for them the sources of good and evil in human conduct. Hobbes' position was completely materialistic. In his *Leviathan* he depicts the life of man as a restless, continuous desire for power that ceases only with his death. The only goal and glory of life is to come out on top in every struggle. To repent or despair is misery and death. This was a complete rejection of Christian and humanistic moral values. Hobbes took morality out of the sphere of reason and placed it in that of man's wildest emotions and beyond any possible control through education and discipline. He showed scornful contempt for supernatural religion and the use of the fear of otherworldly punishment to make men good. For him nothing exists but matter and motion; and everything, even the soul, is corporeal. For man there is no freedom of choice; nature has determined everything for him. Yet, with all this ironclad naturalistic pessimism, Hobbes saw man's natural state as social. The brute must live with other brutes in a society governed by natural or mechanical, not moral, law.

There is no place in Hobbes' thinking for the Golden Rule, as a rational principle of conduct, or for natural law as a law of God. He recognized, however, a law of nature devoid of moral meaning, and a Golden Rule dictated by instinct alone. Man's instinct for self-preservation tells him to respect the power of others. The natural law forbids him to jeopardize his own life. He can best preserve his life by living in peace with his fellows according to the law of nature, now completely secularized by Hobbes. His natural "right" to do as he pleases to others must give way to natural "law" which preserves him from the violence of others. To preserve themselves men entered into a social contract in which they agreed to submit their private wills to the will of an absolute, ruthless monarch, a "Mortall God" who will protect their lives against all enemies,[77] and who may, for the common good, destroy even his own subjects at his will.[78] A sinner, in Hobbes' view, is one who disobeys the king and his written laws. There is no place here for

[75] R. H. M. Elwes (trans.), *Philosophy of Benedict de Spinoza* (New York: Tudor Publishing Co., 1933).

[76] *Ibid.*, p. 128.

[77] T. Hobbes, *Leviathan* (New York: E. P. Dutton & Co., Inc., Everyman's Library, 1950), chap. xvii.

[78] *Ibid.*, chap. xxi.

the Ten Commandments or any other religious, universal moral code. There is no sin except that of disobedience of the civil law. Hobbes demanded a state church whose function should be to destroy liberty of conscience and to aid the king in enforcing conformity. But, for salvation only two things are necessary: faith in Christ and obedience to civil law.[79]

While the Christian view that morals must be assigned to the realm of the supernatural and find their sanction in religion was retained by the Catholic and Protestant churches, we now find that view challenged by the naturalists of the early scientific era. The view, too, that government is a natural thing, and that the relation between subject and sovereign is contractual gained more and more adherents. The tyranny of kings and their established churches forced Presbyterian, Puritan, and Catholic thinkers to accept the secular, contractual conception of government. The doctrine, for instance, of the "divine right" of kings was a threat to papal claims and to the rights of dissenters from Protestant orthodoxies. Much better, many churchmen felt, to see government as a secular and natural institution with no theological trappings.[80] The naturalistic political theorists of the time would thus separate political morality from religion in the name of reason and natural law. Hobbes' view that public morality must be conceived in terms of national interests was eloquently refuted by the Dutch Jurist, Hugo Grotius, who, in the name of reason and natural law, urged an acceptance of international law and international morality. For Grotius, natural law exists, but it knows no national frontiers. Machiavelli preached the law of the jungle—each for himself—but nature, revealed in the universally demonstrated desire of men for social order, shows law to be a rational and moral necessity rooted in nature. Grotius thus saw the law of nature as supernational and immutable. Even God could not change it without contradicting his own essence.[81]

What we have presented here is but the thinnest outline of the effect of the religious, political, and intellectual struggles of the seventeenth century upon the moral thought of the time. The same issues which confronted the thinkers of that century confront us still, and the problems of private and public morality and of moral education still stand as perhaps the greatest challenge to the wisdom and ingenuity of modern man.[82] The view that morals, like all

[79] *Ibid.*, chaps. xxix, xl.

[80] H. Baker, *op. cit.*, pp. 267 ff.

[81] *Ibid.*, p. 271.

[82] The leading issues in moral education and various modes of their solution have been significantly presented in the *Yearbook of Education,* 1951, published by the London University Institute of Education.

other phenomena, fall within the realm of scientific inquiry is now generally accepted. To attach politics and morality to divinity, as was long the Christian practice, placed them outside of the field of natural science, where the modern scientific world has come at last to place them.

SCIENCE AND RELIGION. The spiritual and intellectual struggle appeared in the spread of Deism and in the religious revival movements, particularly Methodism, in the seventeenth and eighteenth centuries. Great evangelists, such as Whitefield, Wesley, and Edwards, checked the spread of religious indifference among the masses. It was easier for these champions of Christianity to save the masses from science than to refute the philosophy of an intelligentsia whose God was no longer the God of theology but the God of nature. The new religion of the devotees of science was Deism. When kings were claiming to be above the law, Deists taught that even God was bound by law, the immutable laws of nature, with which He must act in harmony. Revelations and miracles are, said the Deists, incredible because they negate established laws, and thus destroy truth, which is the essence of God. Thus, they went to the Bible of nature and discovered the truths of natural religion, many of them, but not all, similar to traditional beliefs, such as the existence of God, immortality, and divine rewards and punishments. To have taken the irrational element out of Christianity, as the Deists attempted, would have destroyed its hold upon the masses and weakened it as a social force. However, only a small intellectual class knew or accepted the tenets of Deism. In America, it had a number of influential advocates, among them Washington, Franklin, and Jefferson.

Criticism of the old religious themes was not confined to Deists, scientists, and the philosophers of science. The rationalism of the age invaded even the precincts of theology itself. To a divine like John Donne the Hebrew-Christian story, which Dante called a comedy, and as embellished by theologians, made no sense. "Adam sinned," said Donne, "and I suffer; . . . I had a punishment before I had a being, and God was displeased with me before I was I; I was built up scarce 50. years agoe, in my mother's womb, and I was cast down, almost 6000. years ago, in Adams loynes; I was borne in this last Age of the world and I dyed in the first." [83] This questioning spirit of the seventeenth came to blossom in the Enlightenment of the eighteenth century.

[83] J. Donne, *Complete Poetry and Selected Prose* (ed. J. Hayward, 1929), p. 556, cited by Baker, *op. cit.*, p. 60.

THE ENLIGHTENMENT. A nonagenarian living in the year 1700 had lived in two eras, the mediaeval, as restored and modified by Christian humanism and the Reformation, and the modern, with its stress upon rationalism, naturalism, utilitarianism, and worldly progress. He had witnessed one of the greatest changes in the history of man's intellectual life. The intellectual revolt of this transition era culminated in the rationalism of Voltaire and the Encyclopedists who aimed to bring all social institutions into harmony with reason and the rules of logical thinking. Whatever, in the judgment of great intellectuals, conflicts with reason must, they held, be cast away. Freedom of thought and inquiry are indispensable in guiding men in their quest for the good world. Even the atheist should be left free from external restraint. Voltaire (1694-1778) was the most eloquent defender of the principle of freedom of thought, speech, and action. For him, any form of persecution of men for their beliefs is "absurd and barbarous." Such persecution is "the law of tigers; nay, it is even still more savage, for tigers destroy only for the sake of food, whereas we have butchered one another on account of a sentence or a paragraph." [84] Tradition has it that, in a letter to Helvetius, a contemporary who rejected his intellectual snobbery, he said: "I wholly disapprove of what you say but I will fight to the death for your right to say it." An important result of the Enlightenment, of which Voltaire was but one voice, was the publication of the *Encyclopédie* (1751-1772), of which Diderot (1713-1784) was the editor. It was the first compendium of knowledge in which man and his institutions were dealt with from a completely rational standpoint. Voltaire and Diderot attacked traditional religion, the former making Catholic supernaturalism the main object of his attack, while the latter, who wavered between deism and atheism, condemned as evil all theistic religions and asserted that natural religion is sufficient for man.

The social thought of the Enlightenment, as indeed of Locke who contributed much to it, was aristocratic. The contempt which the intellectuals of the movement showed for the mentality of the masses aroused telling opposition from Helvetius (1715-1771) and Rousseau (1712-1778). Helvetius challenged the prevailing view that observed differences between the mentality of the masses and the classes were due to nature, not to lack of educational opportunity. He proposed, therefore, that they be given the opportunity to develop their natural talents. And Rousseau, a son of the laboring masses, denounced the political and social inequalities of his time, and demanded a new education as a servant of a society freed

[84] From "Treatise on Tolerance," in Thatcher, *op. cit.*, VI, 387.

from such evils. The rationalist dogma of the infallibility of reason brought forth a telling reaction, led by Rousseau, who saw not in reason, with its intellectual uncertainties, but in human feelings and emotions the most enduring basis of social well-being. In the building of democratic states, philosophers appealed not to reason but to nature as revealed in the hearts and sympathies of common men. Yet science and the Enlightenment gave to the world a faith in the inevitability of progress and the perfectibility of man and human institutions. While these were new ideas born out of the secularization of knowledge in the scientific movement, they existed in embryonic form in the optimism of the classical Renaissance and in all questioning of the ancient theory of decline. By the Prophets of Reason the world was not viewed as cursed, nor evil as a permanent thing. That they ignored man's emotional nature was their most serious error. The heart knows truths which reason cannot comprehend, and human feelings must be considered in any attempt to reform society.

BEGINNINGS OF MODERN PSYCHOLOGY. In the general drift in the direction of naturalism and secularism the question of man's nature and of the learning process attracted the attention of thinkers. The view that man is a natural, not supernatural, being whose mental states and activities are subject to natural law came to be widely accepted. The list of those who discussed the nature of man and his physical and mental processes is a long one. The treatise *On the Soul and Life* of Jan Luis (Ludovicus) Vives (*c.* 1492-*c.* 1540) was the first in which psychology was approached physiologically and empirically. Vives considered man's physical and emotional mechanism important in analyzing his mental behavior. Descartes, on the other hand, made a sharp distinction between mind and body, as he did between matter and spirit in the universe, and thus gave support to the traditional dualistic conception of man. While he would study the body and the material universe mathematically, he would study the mind by the method of introspection. For him, the brain has no part in the process of pure thought, which originates in the soul. Man's basic ideas, such as that of God, mathematical axioms, and of space and time, are innate. Of all living things only man possesses the power of thought.[85]

Spinoza and Newton, also, viewed mind and body as separate, although there is interaction between them. For Descartes and Spinoza, God remained a determining force in human thought, and the originator of basic ideas. The most extreme exponent of the doc-

[85] *Ibid.*, pp. 42 ff.

trine of innate ideas was, however, Leibnitz (1646-1716) who, in his *Monadology*,[86] saw mental life as an inner unfolding of "monads" or "spiritual atoms" which exist, though in different forms and manifestations, in inanimate and animate things. Ideas are attributes of the "monads" of self-conscious life, peculiar to man, and are innate and independent of stimulation from without. While Leibnitz was one of the greatest minds of his time, he failed to see the scientific approach to the study of man.

Materialism and the view of a mechanical universe, however, gave rise to the mechanistic psychology of Hobbes and Locke. Hobbes, like the Epicureans, placed man in the category of atoms in motion in the universe of nature. With him, there is no dualism between mind and body, and all human behavior, mental as well as physical, can be reduced to atoms in motion. This was a complete rejection of the doctrines of the separation of mind and body and of innate ideas. Everything in mental life originates in sensation, the brain and the nervous system, as a result of stimulation by the external world. Man interprets these sense experiences through symbols and communicates them through the symbols of words and thought systems built with words. Locke's position differed from that of Hobbes in only minor details. For him, too, there are no innate ideas. At birth, the mind is a blank paper (*tabula rasa*) to be furnished with ideas by sense experience. Ideas are simple and complex, the latter resulting from a combination of the former by a process of association. Previous discoveries in anatomy supported the mechanistic views of Hobbes and Locke, and, after their death, medical research continued to support their views. Friedrich Hoffman (1660-1742), a professor of medicine at the University of Halle, assailed the dualistic conception of man and taught that life is a mechanistic process which can be explained without reference to a soul. A little later, Julien de la Mettrie, a French physiologist, said that human life is similar to that of plants and animals, and that thinking is but a reflex action explicable without any appeal to a soul. The discovery of reflex action by Robert Whytt confirmed the views of the mechanists.[87]

Regarding the learning process, the associationist psychology of Hobbes and Locke had a considerable following, especially in the eighteenth century. It viewed mental life as an association of ideas, considered as mechanical units originating in sensation and having their own power of association. The associationists linked social well-being with the direction of the mental process, and their influ-

[86] *Ibid.*, pp. 79 ff.

[87] Smith, *History of Modern Culture,* I, 110.

ence was felt in movements to educate the masses, particularly in the English charity school movement. Their theory of association they reconciled with traditional faculty psychology, a theory that lent itself easily to mechanistic interpretation. In harmony with the notion of inborn faculties, with a traditional view of human nature, and with political and ecclesiastical domination of the individual was the conception of education as a discipline of man's nature in all its aspects, and that was the conception that prevailed until the late nineteenth century. The psychology of the period was introspective, not experimental, in its method, although a few men caught a glimpse of the scientific approach to the study of human nature.

Selected Readings

BACON, F. *Advancement of Learning and the Novum Organon.* New York: John Wiley & Sons, Inc., 1944.

BAINTON, R. H. *Here I Stand.* London: Hodder & Stoughton, Ltd., 1951.

———. *The Reformation of the Sixteenth Century.* Boston: Beacon Press, Inc., 1952.

BATES, M. S. *Religious Liberty.* New York: Harper & Bros., 1945.

CATLIN, G. *The Story of Political Philosophers.* New York: McGraw-Hill Book Co., Inc., 1939.

DESCARTES, R. *Discourse on Method.* London: J. M. Dent & Sons, Ltd., 1949.

ERASMUS, D. *The Praise of Folly.* (Trans. L. F. Dean.) New York: Hendricks House–Farrar, Straus & Co., Inc., 1946.

FÜLÖP-MILLER, R. *The Power and Secret of the Jesuits.* New York: The Viking Press, Inc., 1930.

HARKNESS, G. E. *John Calvin: the Man and His Ethics.* New York: Henry Holt & Co., Inc., 1931.

HOBBES, T. *Leviathan.* New York: E. P. Dutton & Co., Inc., 1950.

LEA, H. C. *A History of the Inquisition in Spain.* 4 vols.; New York: The Macmillan Co., 1906–7.

MACHIAVELLI, N. *The Prince and the Discourses.* (Trans. L. Ricci and C. E. Detmold.) New York: Random House, Inc., The Modern Library, 1940.

MASON, J. E. *Gentlefolk in the Making.* Philadelphia: University of Pennsylvania Press, 1935.

PAINE, T. *The Age of Reason.* New York: Liberal Arts Press, 1948.

SARTON, G. *Introduction to the History of Science.* 2 vols.; Baltimore: The Williams and Wilkins Co., 1927.

SMITH, P. *A History of Modern Culture.* 2 vols.; New York: Henry Holt & Co., Inc., 1930–34.

THOMPSON, J. W. *Economic and Social History of Europe in the Later Middle Ages.* New York: Appleton-Century-Crofts, Inc., 1931.

THORNDIKE, L. *History of Magic and Experimental Science.* 6 vols.; New York: The Macmillan Co. and Columbia University Press, 1923–40.

WEBER, M. *The Protestant Ethic and the Spirit of Capitalism.* New York: Charles Scribner's Sons, 1930.

WHITE, A. D. *History of the Warfare of Science with Theology in Christendom.* 2 vols.; New York: Appleton-Century-Crofts, Inc., 1896.

8 Educational Theory and Practice, 1400-1800

Under the surface of a universalism, imposed upon Europeans by the Roman empire and its successor, the church, the seeds of native cultures survived in a congenial soil, awaiting a new life and growth. Rome, with all her military and cultural conquests, failed to Romanize the masses completely, and the church did less than emperors to transmit to them the foreign literary culture of which she became custodian. Latin, the repository of that culture, was given only to a few. The masses, however, eventually created vernaculars which were soon to become the souls of nations, of reformed Christianity and of the schools of the people, citizens not of a universal Christian cosmopolis but of national states founded basically upon pre-Christian cultures. The change came gradually. The period of transition from universalism tò localism witnessed a revival of classical literature among the social and intellectual elite and those aspiring to elitehood.

These literary developments were but a reflection of social struggle and change. The ghost of the Roman empire, surviving in the papacy, became more ghostly as nations arose and released the pent up flood of local cultures. In the change, even God was made to speak to men in their own tongues, and the Scriptures were made instruments of national patriotism. Indeed, even the classics, the very heart of humanist learning, glorified a spirit of patriotism better suited to a nationalized than an internationalized world. And humanists, like Petrarch and Ariosto in Italy, and Northern humanists, later, desired to create vernacular literatures as rivals of the classics. Vernaculars were destined to meet the needs of nations, Protestant faiths, science, and commerce better than Latin could. Many early scientists wrote and lectured in the vernacular to popularize the new knowledge; and Luther could not have reached the masses if he had not appealed to them in their own tongue. Even Aeneas Sylvius, later Pope Pius II, said: "It is unworthy of a prince to be unable without an interpreter to hold intercourse with his people." [1]

The story of the recognition of the importance of vernaculars is but one aspect of the worldly realisms that came to dominate educational thought in the modern world. The real things that post-mediaeval men have sought have not been the eternal verities of the philosophical-theological world of pure thought or of religious faith but the verities of life and of visible realities. Modern man has not abandoned the quest for metaphysical truths, but those that have interested him have been the ones that promised to give him mastery over the physical world and his social environment. Man and his worldly problems and needs, social realities, and the truths of the physical world and their application to human problems became matters of supreme concern to the new worldly man of the West, and they left their mark upon his educational thought and institutions. For a time, the theory of education as a discipline of man's natural powers, and primarily for discipline's sake, turned men's educational thought away from immediately utilitarian goals, and checked the growth of socially realistic education. As the story of education in the post-mediaeval world begins, we find the humanists occupying the center of the stage both as theorists and practical reformers.

Development of Educational Theory

Humanist Educational Theory

ITALIAN AND NORTHERN THEORISTS. The century 1350-1450 saw the blossoming of Italian theory in the writings of Vergerius, Bruni, Sylvius, and Guarino.[2] The last Italian theorists of note were Sadoleto [3] and Castiglione,[4] the former emphasizing the earlier ideas, and the latter setting the fashion for those preoccupied with the education of the governing class. After 1500, the banner of leadership in thought passed to Northern humanists, on the list of whom, to mention but a few, we find such notable names as Erasmus

[1] W. H. Woodward, *Vittorino da Feltre and Other Humanist Educators* (London: Cambridge University Press, 1912), p. 142.

[2] *Ibid.* Here is a translation of their treatises.

[3] W. H. Woodward, *Studies in Education during the Age of the Renaissance* (London: Cambridge University Press, 1906), pp. 166 ff.

[4] *Ibid.*, pp. 244 ff.

of Holland, Melanchthon of Germany, Budé of France, Vives of Spain, and Elyot, Ascham, and Milton of England. While all of them were "Christian humanists," their main outlook was secular, and the secular emphasis increased as the years passed. Erasmus and Vives are the most eloquent spokesmen of the Christian international ideal in humanism. The former believed that a world elite, drawing its wisdom from Christianity and the classics, and communicating with one another in Latin, would create international understanding and reform social and religious evils of which ignorance was the fruitful mother.[5] Yet Erasmus accepted the state as a fact, and education of rulers and citizens as a necessity. He himself preferred to be a citizen of the world, not of one city. Vives would make Latin a universal language and an instrument of international understanding and of a universal religion.[6] Both of these men remained Catholics in the Reformation struggle. In the humanist age, however, the city-states of Italy and the nations of the North were facts—facts which made a deep impression upon humanist thought.

THE SCHOLAR-CITIZEN IDEAL. Much of humanist theory is but the thought of the Graeco-Roman world modified here and there by the Hebrew-Christian tradition. Of the ancient theorists, Quintilian made the deepest impression upon the humanists. They revived the ancient ideal of the "humanities" as the proper content of education.[7] Pope spoke their views when he said that "the proper study of mankind is man." Intellectual power, literary taste and eloquence, polished manners, worldly success, leadership and public service were deemed by the humanists to be the noblest attainments of the noblest of beings, man, "in action how like an angel!" said Shakespeare, "in apprehension how like a god!"

EDUCATIONAL AIMS. The purpose of the new education was said to be the moulding of the whole man (*homo universalis*) for his own happiness as well as for citizenship and service to his state. The *homo universalis* is a man fully developed intellectually, physically, morally, and aesthetically. Above all, he must be a man of scholarship and virtue. Such a one is seen as capable of playing every leading rôle in the world, whether it be that of courtier, teacher, explorer, artist, businessman, churchman, general, etc. In

[5] W. H. Woodward, *Desiderius Erasmus concerning the Aim and Method of Education* (London: Cambridge University Press, 1904); S. Zweig, *Erasmus of Rotterdam* (New York: The Viking Press, Inc., 1934).

[6] Woodward, *Studies in Education during the Age of the Renaissance*, pp. 180–210.

[7] Guarino's "On the Method of Teaching and Learning," in Woodward, *Vittorino da Feltre and Other Humanist Educators*, p. 177.

a broad sense this liberal education was thus a practical one. Vergerius said that eloquence "is no slight advantage in negotiation, whether in public or private concerns."[8] Narrow vocationalism the humanists scorned. Personal enjoyment and the worthy use of leisure were included among their aims, but citizenship was the chief goal they sought. Many modern followers of the humanist tradition look upon citizenship as a by-product of individual development, and not worthy to be made the primary goal of a liberal education.

In the sixteenth century, Castiglione in the *Courtier* (1528) and Thomas Elyot in *The Boke Named the Governour* (1531) saw a liberal education as the special prerogative of courtiers and princes, and thus restricted its end to a special field of public service. Their universal man would not perform universal service functions. The ideal governor, whose needs were their chief concern, was a combination of the knight—the Christian military gentleman—and the scholar. All humanists aimed at moulding men of gentlemanly conduct, but Castiglione, Elyot, and their followers, placed a special emphasis upon that purpose. For them the purpose of a liberal education is the moulding of the gentleman-scholar-governor, skilled in the arts of government, war and peace, for the service of king and country.[9] That idea continued to be stressed by others such as Humphrey Gilbert in *Queen Elizabeth's Academy* (1572), Roger Ascham in the *Scholemaster* (1570) and John Milton in *Tractate of Education* (1644). The welfare of the state looms large in the thought of humanists. Melanchthon, reorganizer of education in Lutheran Germany, stressed it in his treatise *On the Education of a Prince,* which he wrote in Latin. Erasmus and Budé (1468-1540), a French theorist, wrote treatises with the same title. The latter, who wrote his book in French, reveals strong national sentiments. The development of the "universal man" for citizenship and leadership in private and public life was thus the basic aim of the humanists. That was not the mediaeval purpose.

THE LIBERAL CURRICULUM. (1) INTELLECTUAL STUDIES. Vergerius (1349-1420) said: "We call those studies liberal which are worthy of a free man; those studies by which we attain and practise virtue and wisdom; that education which calls forth, trains and develops those highest gifts of body and of mind which ennoble men. . . . For to a vulgar temper gain and pleasure are the one aim

[8] *Ibid.,* p. 104.

[9] Woodward, *Studies in Education during the Age of the Renaissance,* pp. 244–94.

of existence, to a lofty nature, moral worth and fame."[10] While they recommended many other studies, the humanists considered the Graeco-Roman classics (and the list of authors is a long one) the most excellent source of practical wisdom. Grammar, composition, logic, rhetoric, music, arithmetic, geometry, astronomy, history, geography, politics, ethics, and natural history were usually listed as liberal studies. The theorists, generally, attached great importance to oratory and broad knowledge as essential to it. Music, however, received but little emphasis. Elyot considered instrumental music a recreative art, not a study, as he did also painting, sculpture and drawing, the last being of practical use in war. The writings of churchmen whose style was pure were often recommended as sources of moral wisdom on a par with those of pagan moralists. Philosophy, as a guide to a good rational and moral life, was rated among the best of subjects.

From all these studies it was believed that the student would acquire a good literary style and the wisdom and virtue that come from universal knowledge. God, said Vives, demands that man examine "all facts and all truths" and "survey the whole universe as it were our own domain."[11] For him the best book on natural science is not Aristotle but the Book of Nature, and he thus foreshadowed the later emphasis of the scientists. In his view on the importance of nature study he was ahead of his contemporary educators. The view that vernacular literatures are not liberal studies is expressed or implied in many of the treatises on education. Erasmus despised vernaculars. Some recognized the vernacular as a necessary medium of instruction and of communication between rulers and their subjects. Vives asserted that no educated man should be ignorant of his native tongue; and Elyot, author of the first *Latin-English Dictionary* of its kind and translator of Plutarch and Isocrates into English, would use ancient literature to enrich the English tongue, so that Englishmen might express their feelings "more abundantly."[12]

(2) MORAL AND RELIGIOUS STUDIES. Here the emphasis was moral rather than narrowly religious, and the theorists believed that moral lessons were equally available in Graeco-Roman and Hebrew-Christian writers. Plato, Aristotle, Cicero, Seneca, Plutarch, and the Graeco-Roman "Historians" were considered most valuable sources

[10] Woodward, *Vittorino da Feltre and Other Humanist Educators,* p. 102. (By permission of The Macmillan Co.)

[11] Woodward, *Studies in Education during the Age of the Renaissance,* p. 188.

[12] *Ibid.,* p. 270.

of moral wisdom. The perfect citizen must, however, show a regard for the Christian faith and its ideals. Hebrew-Christian literature that expresses these ideals in good literary style ought to be read. The active virtues of a man of the world rather than the contemplative ones were stressed by all the theorists. In moral matters they would not give free rein to individuality. The austere virtues of ancient Romans appealed strongly to them. Courage, patriotism, devotion to duty, temperance, and sincerity represent the type of moral virtues which they stressed. The scholar should possess them if he would be a successful leader of men. The mediaeval saint was not the ideal which guided their thought. They sought a more practical type of morality than his.

(3) PHYSICAL EDUCATION. The importance which the theorists attached to physical training as a part of liberal education is a significant revival of the Greek idea.[13] To give health and strength to the body as well as to train the ruling class in the arts of war, they recommended a variety of sports and exercises for students as a part of their liberal training. The education of a freeman's body is as important as that of his mind, for bodily infirmities destroy his happiness and restrict his public usefulness. The ideal of "a sound mind in a sound body" (*mens sana in corpore sano*) runs through all of their theory. "Both mind and body," said Aeneas Sylvius, "should be developed side by side." [14] Erasmus, opposing war as folly, stood opposed to military training, and he showed less concern for physical education than did most other humanists.[15] Vives took a similar position. But these views were exceptional. Vergerius said that "arms" and "letters" are the two chief liberal arts, and he enumerated the games, sports, and military exercises which he deemed suitable educational activities.[16] Unlike Elyot, whose list of exercises is similar, he considered dancing an unworthy mode of relaxation.[17] Diet and the rules of health received much attention from the theorists. Rabelais, a French monk turned physician, carried the health and physical training emphasis to an extreme in the education of his giant monstrosity, Gargantua.[18] All of the theorists saw physical exercises as a cure for mental fatigue and a stimulus to learning.

[13] See Woodward, *Vittorino da Feltre and Other Humanist Educators*, pp. 92 ff., 137 ff., for the typical views of Vergerius and Aeneas Sylvius.

[14] *Ibid.*, p. 134.

[15] D. Erasmus, *The Education of a Christian Prince* (trans. L. K. Born; New York: Columbia University Press, 1926), p. 226.

[16] Woodward, *Vittorino da Feltre and Other Humanist Educators*, pp. 114 ff.

[17] Woodward, *Studies in Education during the Age of the Renaissance*, pp. 291 ff.

[18] F. Rabelais, *Gargantua and Pantagruel* (ed. D. Douglas; New York: Random House, Inc., The Modern Library, 1928), pp. 12–56.

A few of them set the fashion for Locke and his followers by advancing the disciplinary theory of the "hardening process" as a guide in developing the body. Elyot, for instance, wanted strenuous exercise to make his gentlemen hardy, but it was Montaigne (1533-1592) who, in his essay *On the Education of Children,* formulated the doctrine clearly. He would build bodies so strong by rigorous exercise that they would be indifferent to pain and hardships. And he would build strong minds in the same way. This disciplinary theory we shall examine more fully elsewhere.

METHOD AND DISCIPLINE. In their scheme of liberal training the humanist thinkers gave almost as much attention to method as to content. A wrong method could defeat the ends which they sought. Teachers must be guided in their work by the mental and physical differences found among students. Find the natural bent, interests, and capacities of students and follow them, said the theorist. All studies should be made interesting and never be carried to the point of mental fatigue. Erasmus knew, however, that some students will never show any more desire for some studies than a donkey for playing a violin.[19] Meanings should always be stressed rather than mere words and forms. This theme runs through the pedagogical thought of Europe since then. Praise and emulation are the best stimuli to learning; and corporal punishment is an indignity to freemen and detrimental to learning and the building of good character. Erasmus despised "the whole tribe of grammarians" who beat the "wretches" under them with "ferrules, rods or straps" and "rage dogmatically in all directions at once."[20] Yet the theorists did not advocate the mollycoddling of students. Some would use moderate corporal punishment, but only as a last resort, as did Vives, perhaps the most original thinker on method of them all. Repetition, drill, writing of prose and verse compositions, speaking conversational Latin at home and in school, were usually recommended. Erasmus and Elyot recommended the use of pictorial illustrations, an idea soon to be developed further by Comenius. Many of the Northern humanists deemed tutorial instruction a better plan than the group plan of the school. This preference was due, in part, to the fact that the Northern gentry were largely a rural gentry. Guarino thought that the school plan promoted rivalry and created a fear of failure, but he would not have the classes large.[21] The play method was recom-

[19] Woodward, *Desiderius Erasmus concerning the Aim and Method of Education,* pp. 195 f.

[20] Erasmus, *The Praise of Folly* (trans. L. F. Dean; New York: Hendricks-Farrar, Straus & Co., Inc., 1946), p. 90.

[21] Woodward, *Vittorino da Feltre and Other Humanist Educators,* p. 163.

mended particularly for younger students. Guarino and Vives speak approvingly of examinations as teaching devices. The history of examinations has still to be written. With the exception of the practice in ancient China, we know little about them prior to their use in mediaeval universities. The humanists would use them to stimulate the student to greater effort.

While the theorists asked teachers to be guided by the nature of the learner, Vives did most to show them how. Among his writings is the treatise *On the Soul and Life,* the pioneer European work on educational psychology. He is a faculty psychologist who saw memory, reason, and imagination as the faculties of the soul but possessed by individuals in different degrees. Some studies—and he names them—are best for developing one faculty; some, for another, and each individual inherits a special genius for some one study, or for either the practical or theoretical aspects of it.[22] His views were derived from his own observations as a teacher, not from traditional doctrines. Learning, he says, originates in sensation and reflection, and continues by a process of mental association of perceptions. In the learning process, emotions play an important rôle. For retention, drill, repetition, and frequent testing are of great worth. Vives was thus the modern forerunner of educational psychologists. And he would psychologize instruction to enlighten men and reform the world, as Pestalozzi and others would also do.

ORGANIZATION. In the home, children should be instructed in morality, refined tastes, Latin and, according to some, vernacular grammar and conversational Latin. Those who preferred the school to a tutor would send the boy to school at about the age of five, but not later than the age of ten. Most of them preferred a boarding school to a day school, since parents tended to spoil their children. An elementary as distinct from a secondary school was not thought of, but reading, writing, arithmetic, drawing, conversational Latin, the rudiments of grammar, prayers and hymns seem to have been considered elementary studies.[23]

The classical school was to provide a complete liberal education and not be preparatory to the university, for which humanists showed not a little contempt. Vives, however, said that the professional training of universities should have a liberal education as its foundation. The length of the course was not discussed but, obviously, many years would be needed to complete it. Elyot made the most specific suggestions regarding organization. He recommended three levels of instruction: the first, ending at the age of fourteen

[22] Woodward, *Studies in Education during the Age of the Renaissance,* p. 196.
[23] Woodward, *Vittorino da Feltre and Other Humanist Educators,* p. 200.

and including mainly literary studies; the second, ending at seventeen, and including oratory in Latin, logic, history, geography, and political and military training; and the third, occupied chiefly with philosophy and moral training and ending at the age of twenty-one.[24]

CONTROL AND SUPPORT. Humanist writers say little about the control and support of education. It is, however, clear that they would accord the laity everywhere a prominent rôle in directing it. Vergerius said that the state is the "proper sphere" of education,[25] and Erasmus held that parents, church, and state should co-operate in education, and that the provision of good teachers and education is "a public obligation in no way inferior . . . to the ordering of an army."[26] However, if the argument from silence be a good one the humanists must have preferred the private school to the public one. Free education, moreover, was not a humanist idea. The view that a liberal education was the almost exclusive right of a social elite that could pay its own way was almost universal. The question of support, therefore, did not occupy their thought.

STUDENTS. The humanists thought almost entirely of the needs of the socially privileged classes, aristocrats of birth and wealth. Those whom a social system condemned to a life of toil did not fall within their purview. Even Erasmus, so-called "Christianizer of the Renaissance," held the "vulgar" masses in low esteem and would deny them political power.[27] Yet he would not deny them instruction in "the teachings of Christ," and he would have state and church remove the handicaps imposed by poverty upon the talented poor. How that was to be done he does not say. An upper-class prejudice, while it appears everywhere, is most flagrantly apparent in the writings of men like Castiglione and Elyot who thought exclusively of the training of princes and noblemen. Yet even these recognized the existence of a few gifted minds outside of the ranks of born aristocrats which princes might well make use of.

TEACHERS. The selection of teachers of the highest moral and mental qualities was deemed of supreme importance. Those, like Elyot, who were preoccupied with the training of gentlemen-rulers, would have the teacher well-born and courteous, according to the manners of the class whose sons he was to instruct. The ideal

[24] Woodward, *Studies in Education during the Age of the Renaissance*, pp. 279 ff.

[25] Woodward, *Vittorino da Feltre and Other Humanist Educators*, p. 99.

[26] Woodward, *Desiderius Erasmus concerning the Aim and Method of Education*, pp. 209 f.

[27] P. Smith, *Erasmus* (New York: Harper & Bros., 1923), p. 201.

teacher should be a profound scholar, of excellent character, who rules with kindness and who adapts his teaching to his students' interests and abilities. And, quite significantly, he would be a layman. Harsh criticism of teachers of the time runs through the writings of the theorists. Erasmus and Elyot were particularly caustic in their denunciation of the teachers. This demand for the good teacher came when the poor still felt that teachers who were nearly illiterate were good enough for their children, and it came from men who did not bewail the lot of the poor.

VIEW ON GIRLS' EDUCATION. The Renaissance brought no significant change in the European tradition regarding woman's ability and social destiny. Heaven and society made the home her sphere. Therefore, a liberal education defined in terms of a life of public service was not her prerogative. Most of the theorists are silent on the question of women's education. Yet, the rôle of mothers in educating preschool boys received much attention, and some writers apparently deemed it desirable that they should be able to converse with their sons in Latin. Leonardo Bruni's *Concerning Studies and Letters,*[28] Vives' *On the Education of a Christian Woman,*[29] Cornelius Agrippa's *On the Nobility and Super-excellence of the Female Sex,*[30] and Elyot's *Defense of Good Women*[31] are the most important treatises on the subject. Agrippa, a German, showed greater respect for women's ability than did the others. Vives, Erasmus, and Sadoleto considered women weak and frivolous and in need of education to counteract their shortcomings. Erasmus and Sadoleto considered a mother's influence upon her sons bad. Boys should, therefore, be turned over to tutors at an early age to save them from that influence.

The humanist writers, while they disagreed regarding woman's character, would have her educated intellectually and morally for her own welfare and the uplift of the home and society. Vives and Elyot recognized the importance of her moral influence upon social life. Both of them—and their views are fairly typical—would educate her in preparation for marriage, household duties, and a worthy life. Elyot, who followed the Italian humanists and Erasmus closely, would have girls instructed in classical literature, moral philosophy, and the social graces proper for noblewomen, with whom he was preoccupied. Vives, who would have them taught by women, said

[28] Woodward, *Vittorino da Feltre and Other Humanist Educators,* pp. 119–32.

[29] Woodward, *Studies in Education during the Age of the Renaissance,* pp. 204 ff.

[30] *Ibid.,* pp. 264 ff.

[31] Woodward, *Desiderius Erasmus concerning the Aim and Method of Education,* p. 153.

that their studies should be vernacular speech, Latin and Christian literature, moral philosophy based upon pagan and Christian authors, nature study as related to nursing, household management, the rearing of children and cooking. Such studies as mathematics, rhetoric, and political science he viewed as unsuited for women. He does not mention such ornamental studies as music, painting and dancing which, later, became the vogue in girls' education. Silence, he held, is the greatest ornament of a woman. While household cares should be the main guide in educating women, the theorists would not deprive them of the joys of leisure and social intercourse. All of them were, however, preoccupied with the needs of the female aristocracy.

THE GENTLEMAN-SCHOLAR IDEAL. Of the humanists, some, as we have seen, became preoccupied with the needs of a governing elite to be drawn almost entirely from the ranks of the nobility. While princes and courtiers should be scholars, they should above all be gentlemen, trained in the manners of their class. "Manners maketh man" runs an adage of aristocrats. The ideal of the gentleman-scholar is a combination of the ideal of the mediaeval knight and that of the citizen-scholar of the humanists. Castiglione, Elyot and their group would preserve the knightly ideal but freed from its earlier asceticism. Their views on the purpose, content and method of a liberal education have been already presented, but we may add here that their thought was marked by an emphasis upon social realities linked to the interests of the governing class. The arts of war as much as the arts of peace loom large in their thought. In his dress, gait, posture, speech, and modes of reaction to all personal and social situations, whether humorous or serious, the gentleman must respond in ways that become a man of good breeding, learning and refinement. Here we should note that, by the sixteenth century, the courts of Europe had become the centers of cultural life and were setting the standards of social life. It is not, then, surprising that the education of "governors" received special attention from men close to the summit of social life.

THE RISE OF NEW THEORIES. Looking back at the humanist conception of a liberal education, one sees in it a secular, socially utilitarian emphasis which stands out in marked contrast with the otherworldly, theological ideal of mediaeval Europe. A demand, however, for a different type of utilitarian education arose in the soil of middle-class Europe. The cultural leadership of the court and high society was gradually passing to the merchant aristocracy and, as it did, the demand for a less verbal, more modern and scientific form of education arose and found eloquent advocates from the sixteenth century onward. The new theory was both negative and positive. On the negative side it appeared as criticism of humanistic verbalism and the formal practices of the classical schools.

CRITICS OF HUMANISTIC EDUCATION. The list of critic-theorists is a long one. The earlier ones denounced the prevailing emphasis of the schools upon linguistic forms, their neglect of the ideas and wisdom to be found in ancient literature, and the brutal discipline used by teachers. Erasmus in his *Ciceronianus* denounced those teachers who made Cicero an infallible authority in wisdom and the use of words. He makes his Ciceronian say: "For seven whole years I have touched nothing except Ciceronian books. . . . There is not a word in all the books of that divine man which I have not set in order in an alphabetical lexicon."[32] In his *Praise of Folly* he says: "It is amusing to see a clique of scholars trade compliments and scratch each other's itch. . . . When one makes a verbal slip, and another has the luck to notice it, what an uproar!"[33]

Others went deeper than Erasmus in their criticism of word worship and the narrow curriculum of the schools. Rabelais (*c.* 1490-1553) satirized the schools, and proposed a broadened curriculum which would include many languages, mathematics, astronomy, history, geography, the sciences, philosophy, law, medicine and a complete course in health and physical education. His scholar would be "ignorant of nothing that exists." Montaigne was, however, the most penetrating thinker of them all. We have examined his views on the education of the body. He would not have youths study for the sake of mere knowledge and amusement but to develop, by a process of mental discipline, the faculties of memory, reason, judgment, and understanding. As for the content of education, he would seek it not in the great books (valuable, however, when read properly) but in "the great world" with its many sects, opinions, laws, customs, etc. which teach us how to evaluate our own thought and ways of life. And he would limit studies to those of "real utility." If, he said, teachers will but furnish their pupils with "things," words will come easily to them. Of ancient literature, he considered Plutarch's *Lives* the best source of practical wisdom for the "gentlemen" he wished to mould. And philosophy, as a guide to a good life, he viewed of great educational value. He considered the vernacular the most useful tongue and, though a classical scholar himself, he would use no language unknown in the markets of Paris.

[32] Erasmus, *Ciceronianus* (trans. I. Scott; New York: Teachers College, Columbia University, 1908), pp. 23 ff.

[33] P. 90 (Edition listed in preceding chapter).

At the start, the humanists were "progressives" but their theories and practices soon became out of date in a rapidly changing world. The new "progressives" who came after them wanted "things" rather than words, but by "things" they meant ideas and wisdom found not only in the classics, but in modern languages and in the thought and ways of life of contemporary peoples. The humanist conception of the universal man and of the suggested mode of his education, while attractive as an ideal, did not fit well into the social and political pattern of the time. The class prejudices of the humanists, and even of their early critics, often blinded them to the real needs of nations.

Humanistic education in practice created a cleavage between the learned classes and the masses, and that was its major defect. And the sons of the aristocracy, often living in idleness and debauchery, symbolized the failure of education to serve either class or common interests. The first critics saw the remedy in an expanded humanism. Humphrey Gilbert recommended for gentlemen's sons a curriculum which would include modern languages, science and law. Mulcaster considered the vernacular more important than Latin. Said he: "I love *Rome,* but *London* better, . . . I honor the Latin but I worship the English."[34] Roger Ascham, in the *Scholemaster,* and others urged the importance of the vernacular in educating the aristocracy. Milton in his *Tractate of Education,*[35] while ignoring the vernacular which he used in his own writings, would not have students spend seven or eight years studying "miserable Latin and Greek." He would add to the classics many modern languages, mathematics, politics, economics, various sciences, law, medicine, etc. For him language is but a path to "things." Locke held a similar view. Daniel Defoe (1660-1731) saw the classical scholar as "a Learned Fool" who knows nothing about men or things.[36] Such criticisms as these foreshadowed the greater emphasis of those who would give men an education based upon science and the realities of the physical and social world as found in the books of Nature and Experience.

Sense-Realist Educational Theory

SCIENCE AND EDUCATIONAL THOUGHT. To know and control the natural world for the benefit of mankind became with the devotees of science the most worthy end of human effort. Knowledge

[34] R. Mulcaster, *Elementarie* (ed. T. L. Campagnac; Oxford: Clarendon Press 1925), p. 269.

[35] New York: The Macmillan Co., 1895.

[36] H. Barnard, *American Journal of Education,* XXVI, 426.

which, in Bacon's words, is "power" is the knowledge of nature and its laws. The most real and most important things are not, in the new thought, the ideas in literature or the ideas one gets through traveling in one's own and in foreign lands but the realities of the world of nature. Real things, in the words of Leibnitz, are *vera physica* (physical truths); and the devotees of science, and their educational debtors, asked men to conquer nature in the interest of man. This new ideal became a basis of a new type of utilitarianism in the educational thought of the time. Significant traces of the new emphasis appear in the writings of Rabelais, Vives, Montaigne, Milton, Ramus, and others.

Peter Ramus (1515-1572) is linked to the new realism by his work in reforming the University of Paris where, in his Master's examination, he defended the thesis that "Everything that Aristotle said is false." He is better known for his attack on Aristotelianism in his *Institutes of Dialectic* and *Animadversions on Aristotle* than for his teaching that the principle of utility should guide all educational practice. Like Dewey in our own day, he held that the value of knowledge, whether ancient or modern, is determined by its applicability to existing social problems. By attacking clerical control of education he prepared the way for the admission of science and applied mathematics into the work of universities. No one in his century attacked the practice of uncritical appeal to authority more devastatingly than he. Nature, he held, not books should guide men in their quest for knowledge.

The discovery of science and its method coupled with the growing consciousness of national and commercial needs brought a demand for more realistic studies, for a reform of methods of teaching and for the extension of educational opportunities to the people generally. Religious strife had weakened the confidence of men in theological systems of knowledge and in the value even of classical wisdom as man's guiding light. The classics had become in practice instruments of theological orthodoxy and of social conservatism. Indeed, the classical schools, as servants of conservative social forces, maintained their pre-eminence until the middle classes won political power in the French and American revolutions. Theory, however, ran ahead of practice. The new theory was rooted not only in science and its philosophy but even more basically in the economic, social, political, and religious changes of the time. Protestantism, for instance, opened the door to critical inquiry, to the new philosophies and to science, not, however, because it espoused rationalism and naturalism but because it created conditions favorable to intellectual adventure. One form of dissent from orthodoxy led to others, and education soon felt the impact of the revolt, as it did of other social forces as well.

The seventeenth century saw the tide of revolt running high. The central emphases in it were (1) that the vernacular and its use as a path to knowledge are of primary importance, (2) that the method of teaching foreign languages and method generally should be reformed by an approach to learning through sense experience of things rather than through words, (3) that the things and laws of the material world and studies that enable man to master physical forces should be given a place of central importance in education, and (4) that the gates of learning should be opened to all classes. As far as studies were concerned the new theory increased the emphasis upon science and technology found in Milton's *Tractate of Education* and decreased the emphasis upon languages and literature. Because of the stress placed upon learning by sense experience and observation of things, the philosophy of these theorists is often called "sense realism." Bacon set the stage for the demand that the school become a promoter of science and that knowledge be sought through the method of induction, a method both certain in its results and usable by anyone whose perceptive senses are normal. In spite of the progressive theory of the humanists, the schools of the time taught little but Latin and Greek, with an emphasis upon grammar and form. Indeed, Latin occupied most of the students' time. The vernacular was almost completely ignored, and mathematics received, at best, but elementary treatment. Demands of humanists for a reform of method show a preoccupation with the study of the classics. Even Bacon himself wrote his chief works in Latin and had little faith in the value of modern languages. Two of his contemporaries, Wolfgang Ratke, of Germany, and John Brinsley, of England, made strong pleas for the teaching of the mother tongue but not for the teaching of science.[37] The first great herald to the educational world of the Baconian philosophy and its practical utilitarianism was John Amos Comenius (1592-1671), a bishop of the Moravian church.

COMENIUS AND HIS WORKS. A Christian, desiring social justice and the well-being of the masses, Comenius saw in science an instrument of social regeneration. In his *Pansophiae Prodromus* (Forerunner of Pansophy) and his *Didactica Magna* (The Great Didactic) he gave expression to his ideal of *pansophia* which embodied his belief that the world could be reformed by teaching everyone the causes and purposes of all important things in the

[37] J. W. Adamson, *Pioneers of Modern Education 1600–1700* (London: Cambridge University Press, 1921), pp. 18 ff.

world. He strove to bring education and teaching into harmony with the nature of man. In the *Didactica Magna,* he presented educational principles and, in the many textbooks he wrote, he attempted to apply them. His most significant texts are the *Janua Linguarum Reserata* (The Gate of Languages Unlocked) and the *Orbis Sensualium Pictus* (The World of Sensible Objects Pictured). The texts embody an effort to teach things rather than words. "Why," said he, "should we learn the works of Nature of any other master rather than of these our senses? Why do we not, I say, turn over the living book of the world instead of dead papers? . . . If we have anywhere need of an interpreter, the Maker of Nature is the best interpreter Himself." [38] The idea of using pictures in teaching is found in the writings of earlier theorists, but it was Comenius, however, who first applied this visual method well.

COMENIUS AND THE CURRICULUM. To perfect the natural powers of learning, virtue, and piety within man, so that he may master himself and all things and conform with God's design is, says Comenius, the end of education. Therefore, he would teach the causes and meanings of all the main facts in the world and would stress the vernacular and the things of nature rather than the classics and words. Languages he would retain, but for the practical end of understanding the things of the visible world. Harmoniously with his idea of an encyclopedic or pansophic curriculum, he would have every mother teach her infant children the first elements of metaphysics, physics, optics, astronomy, geography, chronology, history, arithmetic, geometry, statics, mechanics, dialectic, grammar, rhetoric, poetry, music, economics, politics, morals, etiquette, and religion. On this curriculum of the so-called School of the Mother's Lap he would build the encyclopedic curricula of the vernacular school, the Latin school, and the university. And all instruction would have in view the application of knowledge to the various needs of life.

COMENIUS AND METHOD. Methods of teaching, Comenius viewed as of equal importance with the curriculum. "Follow nature" is his fundamental rule of method. Traditional teaching failed, says he, because it ignored that rule. Among his principles of method, some of which the humanists stressed, are the following: (a) approach learning through the senses; (b) teach things before words; (c) proceed from the easy to the difficult, from the known to the unknown; (d) organize subject matter according to its difficulty;

[38] R. H. Quick, *Essays on Educational Reformers* (New York: Appleton-Century-Crofts, Inc., 1897), p. 149.

(e) harmonize instruction with the age, interests, and capacity of the pupil; (f) let children learn to do by doing, by their own activity and experience; (g) make schools cheerful and equip them with illustrative materials; (h) let teachers be sympathetic; and (i) let merit be rewarded. The inductive method of Bacon he would bring into the school: "As far as is possible," said he, "[men must] be taught to become wise by studying the heavens, the earth, oaks, and beeches, but not by studying books; that is to say, they must learn to know and investigate the things themselves, and not the observations that other people have made about the things." [39]

COMENIUS AND SCHOOL ORGANIZATION. More significant even than these other reforms was his proposal to reform the traditional school organization of Europe. He would create a Christian democratic state by providing equality of educational opportunity for all boys and girls regardless of their social status. Three hundred years had to elapse before America led the nations toward a realization of that dream. The Europe that Comenius knew had a dual school system, a very defective vernacular system for the masses, and a system of socially exclusive and expensive secondary classical schools for the classes. Such a dual system, Comenius would abolish. In its place, he would establish a single-track system of schools, from the lowest grade to the university, for all youths, male and female, of every nation, in which all, to the age of twelve, regardless of wealth or rank, would pursue the same studies, students thereafter being selected for the secondary school and university on the sole basis of ability and merit. Yet, unable to escape all the prejudices of his world, while admitting the intellectual equality of women and men, he would instruct a woman in "all that enables her to look after her household and to promote the welfare of her husband and her family." [40]

From the Mother's School of every home, youths would go to the vernacular school at the age of six, attendance at which, for six years, would be universal and compulsory. Above this school stands the six-year secondary school and, then, the six-year college, admission to both of which would depend on a student's natural capacity for further education. This ladder-plan of organization, then but a Utopian dream, was first realized in the United States.

Out of the pansophic ideal of Comenius came his plan to have established, somewhere in the world, a "School of Schools or Didactic College," wherein learned men would co-operate to advance science, and spread wisdom throughout the world, by supplying to the

[39] *Didactica Magna* (trans. M. W. Keatinge; London: Black, 1896), XVIII, 28.
[40] *Ibid.*, IX, 7.

world's schools the knowledge which would guarantee their vitality and the well-being not of any race or nation but of all humanity. That all humanity has a right to the benefits of knowledge and science is an ideal often ignored under the stress of exaggerated nationalism. Science, too, has often been perverted to ignoble ends, and the tree of scientific knowledge threatens to become a tree of ruin and death. Comenius did not even dream of such a perversion.

FRANKLIN AND OTHER SCIENTIFIC UTILITARIANS. The new utilitarianism of Bacon and Comenius found early eloquent spokesmen in Samuel Hartlib, William Petty and John Drury, in sixteenth-century England. In colonial America, Franklin, perhaps the leading spirit of his age, a voice not only of science but of its philosophical expression, the Enlightenment, was the first influential advocate of schools devoted to the vernacular and science as the essential paths to American well-being and human comfort. Franklin, unlike most of the European theorists, said practically nothing about method, but he listed, in great detail, the studies which he deemed important.

Reform thought in England was closely linked to Puritanism, and was inspired by the disturbances of the Cromwellian régime and the needs of the middle class. Hartlib, Petty, and Drury saw the need for a scheme of public education, open to all classes, through which knowledge would be disseminated widely among the people for the benefit of the nation and the material well-being of all. All of them would promote science and technology as means of human welfare.

Drury had quite definite views regarding the organization of a system of public schools.[41] He, however, in common with Hartlib, thought of the poor as a class with its own social destiny much more than did Petty who would open his "literary work-houses," as he called his schools, to "all children" and exclude none by reason of poverty.[42] The curriculum proposed by Petty was extremely utilitarian. Foreign languages, but not literature, should be taught but only to those who need them. Observation of sensible objects should precede instruction in reading and writing. Drawing, arithmetic and geometry, health and physical education should be required studies because of their utility. And no student, however well born, should be exempted from learning a trade or handicraft. Mathematics, physics, mechanics, and the "History of Art and Nature" are indispensable sources of "reall Learning." Following

[41] Adamson, *op. cit.*, pp. 155 f.
[42] *Ibid.*, p. 132.

Bacon's idea of Solomon's House, presented in the *New Atlantis,* he proposed the establishment of two research institutions, one of which would promote "mechanical arts and manufactures" and the other, furnished with samples of all the "things" in the world, serve as a center of research in pure science. If a child, he remarked, had seen these "things" before learning to read and write, he would be able "to understand all good books afterwards, and smell out the fopperies of bad ones."[43] Petty, unlike Milton, would make the study of languages optional, and would make education universal. In curriculum and method he was a thorough sense realist. His method of learning by doing and by personal observation and sense experience follows the empirical philosophy and the principles of Comenius and anticipates much of the later thought of Pestalozzi and Froebel.

In America, Franklin would educate young men for a useful life. Since they cannot learn everything, they should "learn those Things that are likely to be *most* useful and most ornamental. Regard being had to the several Professions for which they are intended."[44] There is a marked vocational emphasis in his educational philosophy. Among the many studies he proposed were English language and literature, drawing, arithmetic, geometry, astronomy, bookkeeping, history, geography, natural history, medicine, study of foods, gardening, grafting, inoculating, history of commerce, natural philosophy, Latin, Greek, French, German, and Spanish. Foreign languages should be compulsory only in connection with the professional training to which they made some special contribution. Thus, French, German, and Spanish were said to be suitable for students designed for commercial life. His view of the importance of the vernacular appears in his plan for the English School of the Philadelphia Academy which was designed to prepare youths for business and "the several offices of civil life."[45] Thus science and the intellectual outlook of the age were having effect upon the educational thought of America near the eve of the Revolution, and the realism reflected in them was soon to find a congenial soil in a land where nature, not, as in the Old World, the foibles and prejudices of men, presented the chief challenge to man's ingenuity.

[43] *Ibid.,* pp. 130 f.

[44] B. Franklin, *Proposals Relating to the Education of Youth in Pensilvania* (Philadelphia, 1749), p. 11.

[45] B. Franklin, *Idea of the English School,* reprinted in T. Woody, *Educational Views of Benjamin Franklin* (New York: McGraw-Hill Book Co., Inc., 1931), pp. 120 ff.

The Theory of Education As a Discipline

Throughout history, educators have appealed either to the principle of utility or that of discipline as a justification of the studies and activities which have comprised the content of liberal education. Studies of no direct value in meeting immediate, practical ends could be justified, however, by an appeal to their value as means of mental, moral, and physical discipline of one's nature and its capacities. It is difficult, however, to justify any educational practice except on grounds of utility, either immediate or remote. Even Plato, the father of the formal disciplinary theory in the West, viewed his plan of mental training for philosophers as a practical preparation for their rôle as rulers in his ideal state. And mediaeval Christian thinkers saw the Seven Liberal Arts as useful paths to church service and salvation.

Means have, however, sometimes become ends, and formal mental, moral, and physical training became with some almost the be-all and the end-all of education. Make men by strengthening their natural powers and, then, it was believed, they will perform well every activity demanded by the needs of life and the world. Thus, no study or activity is useless if, and only if, it provides suitable discipline and exercise of man's natural capacities. With the disciplinarians, then, the goal of liberal education should not be training directed to any immediate utilitarian goal but the building of mind, body, and character without reference to the use to which one might later put his abilities. Romans justified the study of Greek, and the humanists the studies of Latin and Greek on utilitarian grounds. For them, these studies provided some skill or wisdom of practical value in achieving their goals. When their practical value became less apparent with the rise of vernaculars, their retention as studies could best be justified on grounds of their value as mental training to which some added a general cultural and ornamental value. But the principle of formal training of the mind came to be used as a justification not only of the retention of the classics in the curriculum but of the measure of the educational value of all studies. Thus such studies as arithmetic, geometry, and even manual training and home economics had, when the demand arose for them, to be justified on disciplinary grounds before they acquired educational respectability. Their difficulty as mental exercises and the amount of effort they demanded for mastery were considered the chief measure of their worth as studies. Indeed, as Mr. Dooley said, it doesn't matter what you teach a boy so long as he doesn't like it. Spartan discipline, on the physical side, Plato's doctrine, on the mental side, and Hebrew-Christian asceticism, on the moral side, contributed, each its part, to the development of the general theory of education as a discipline.

While Montaigne, among others, was largely a disciplinarian, it was Locke who first stated the doctrine most clearly in modern times. Though an empiricist in philosophy and an advocate of utilitarian training for gentlemen, he gave forceful expression to the disciplinary theory of physical, moral, and mental training. He would harden the body from infancy by subjecting it to exposure, discomforts, and rigorous exercise.[46] Right moral conduct, too, can come only by persistent crossing of one's desires and by practice of virtue. A child should be given only what is good for him, and nothing that merely pleases him. The education of the mind, as of the body, he said, is achieved by the exercise and use of its inborn faculties or powers. Man, for instance, becomes rational through the exercise of his faculty of reason, and mathematics provides the best exercise for its development. He would, he says, teach mathematics not to make one a mathematician but to make him a reasonable being, and the training thus acquired would carry over into other subjects whenever the occasion arose.[47]

The doctrine of formal mental discipline and its corollary, that of the transfer of training, are thus clearly stated by Locke. While he himself advocated a broad and varied curriculum, his disciplinary followers would restrict studies to those of permanent and general value as mental exercises, with a view to forming the cultured man, not the utilitarian man, even as conceived by men as far apart as Vergerius and Comenius. The utilitarian goal of pansophia and universal knowledge was rejected by the disciplinarians in the name of mental culture and in their adherence to the doctrine of faculty psychology. Even Franklin, eloquent spokesman of vocationalism, agreed with Plato regarding the value of mathematics in forming minds and training them to reason exactly even in nonmathematical subjects.[48]

Thus the idea that it is not what is learned but the power acquired in the process of learning that is important came into vogue as a justification of subjects of study, and of methods of teaching aimed at making learning as difficult and uninteresting as possible. All was going well in the educational world so long as Johnny was having a rough time in learning to read and to become a man of

[46] J. Locke, *Some Thoughts concerning Education* (Cambridge University Press, 1913), pp. 2 ff.

[47] J. Locke, *Conduct of the Understanding* (Oxford: Clarendon Press, 1901), VII.

[48] Woody, *op. cit.*, pp. 129, 159, 183, 232.

parts. In secondary schools and universities, Latin and Greek held a most honored place because of their difficulty and the supposed power they gave students to master other subjects. Schools, it was believed, should not stress the acquisition of knowledge for the sake of skill in its use. Knowledge, however useful, has in itself no educational value. The only such value it has lies in its use as a means of developing mental powers and putting the mark of general culture upon men. Such useful studies as the vernacular, the sciences, the vocational subjects, etc. were considered unworthy to be pursued by freemen of ability, men who should scorn the lowly motives of utility and profit. The whole theory was destined to be rejected by the builders of industrialized nations as unsuited to the realities of the modern world.

Since 1890, the doctrine of transfer of training has been subjected to experimental testing, and the results show but little transfer. With a few exceptions, we have now returned to an emphasis upon useful content directed to general and specific ends, and have abandoned the doctrine that it is mind training and not knowledge that is important.[49] Many studies that used to be pursued as mental disciplines are now defended on the grounds that they are essential in the "general education" which makes men expert citizens as distinct from the studies which prepare them to become experts in some vocation or art.[50] Professional men, too, recognize the value of general education for successful practice of their professions. Doctors, for instance, were recently told by a leader of their profession that it is as important for them to know men and women, and how to think about patients, as it is to know their own technology. "A general cultural education," says Ernest E. Irons, M.D., "not only is one of his [the doctor's] most important useful tools but also is a source of professional effectiveness in the art of medicine."[51] And so, after a night of fitful disciplinarian fever, we sleep well again in a comfortable utilitarian bed.

The Ideal of Public Universal Education

The ideal of public, universal, compulsory education, as we know it in our state systems of today, had its origin in the Reformation. Sparta provided free, public education for boys of the citizen

49 T. Woody, *Liberal Education for Free Men* (Philadelphia: University of Pennsylvania Press, 1951), pp. 216 ff.

50 *General Education in a Free Society,* Report of the Harvard Committee (Cambridge, Mass.: Harvard University Press, 1945).

51 "Medical Education Looks at General Education and the Universities," *The Journal of the American Medical Association,* CLIX (Oct. 8, 1955), 538.

class and made it compulsory, but non-citizens and girls were excluded from it. The scholarship system dates back to imperial Rome; and mediaeval Christendom provided free education for some poor students. Such piecemeal provisions did not satisfy Luther. He urged the establishment of public, universal, compulsory elementary schools for the children of the masses, and presumably he had vaguely in mind some mode of public support. The humanists would limit education for citizenship almost entirely to the upper classes; Luther would make it universal. His concern for the masses was rooted in his doctrine that God had imposed upon each one the duty to read and interpret the Scriptures as the only way to salvation. His advocacy of universal education was thus an expression of his religious beliefs.

But he was a German as much as a Christian salvationist, and thought of the needs of Germany while he contemplated the plans of God. In 1524, he wrote that not only had God imposed upon rulers the duty of instructing youth, but that it was also to their own best interests to do so. He advocated compulsory attendance of boys at school for two hours daily, and of girls for one hour, and the instruction of boys in trades and of girls in household duties, although he did not suggest the establishment of vocational schools. "There is . . . an urgent necessity, not only for the sake of the young, but also for the maintenance of Christianity and of civil government, that this matter be immediately and earnestly taken hold of, lest afterwards, . . . we shall . . . feel in vain the pangs of remorse forever." [52] And he remarked further: "Though there were no soul, nor heaven, nor hell, but only the civil government, would not this require good schools and learned men more than do our spiritual interests? . . . For the establishment of the best schools everywhere, both for boys and girls, this consideration is of itself sufficient, namely, that society, for the maintenance of civil order and the proper regulation of the household, needs accomplished and well-trained men and women." [53]

Thus the idea that education must have regard for the nature of man as a citizen found many advocates. Vergerius, an early humanist, called upon states to educate their citizens, and declared that the man of mere literary and intellectual accomplishments is a useless citizen. Stressing individualism and a liberal education, the humanists, as a group, identified the "complete citizen" with the fully educated man. Social and intellectual change, however, tended to

[52] F. V. N. Painter, *Luther on Education* (St. Louis, Mo.: Concordia Publishing House, 1928), p. 201.

[53] *Ibid.*, pp. 194–96.

divorce the ideal of scholarship from that of citizenship. Luther's masses would be socialized through the most rudimentary instruction, and even Comenius would limit the education of the great majority to six years of elementary instruction. Yet, both Luther and Comenius recognized the capacity of all for citizenship, whereas the humanists, with a few notable exceptions, were preoccupied with the task of educating the few for social leadership. The humanists' Republic of Letters was an international society, and social leadership was, for many of them, a world, not a national, leadership. While Erasmus, the humanist, considered education "a public obligation as much as the training of an army," his internationalism stands opposed to the nationalism of Luther, the Reformer. The one was influenced by the common cultural element in European tradition; the other, by the cultural peculiarities of the various national groups.

Melanchthon, the first organizer of education for Lutheran Germany and the chief reconciler of humanism and the Reformation, also advocated universal education. The obligation, he said, to make children virtuous "extends to the entire youth of the state whose training demands corporate supervision. For the ultimate end which confronts us is not private virtue alone but the interest of the public weal." [54] The idea of public schools for the masses was also stated by, or implied in the writings of, Hartlib, Petty, Drury, and Comenius in the sixteenth and seventeenth centuries. The inductive method of the sense realists gave strength to the idea, since in it was implied a faith in the value of the sense experience of all men and in their capacity to acquire knowledge. The disciplinary theory, on the other hand, stressing mental ability, with which all men are not equally endowed, retarded the acceptance of the idea of universal education.

That universal education should be of the liberal variety is not a view promoted by the Reformers. Luther would have in every state higher schools for the training of preachers, teachers, and civil officials, while he would train the masses for a life of toil; and Melanchthon's chief interest centered in the reform of classical schools. The view that all classes have a right to a liberal education was inspired by political liberalism, the needs of industrial nations and the world struggles of the past two centuries. The conception of a liberal education has, moreover, been transformed under the impact of a changing world.

[54] Woodward, *Studies in Education during the Age of the Renaissance,* p. 224.

B. Development of Educational Institutions

Education of the Masses

VERNACULAR ELEMENTARY SCHOOLS. (1) City Vernacular Schools. From the thirteenth century onward, city Latin grammar schools and vernacular schools, embodying the lay spirit, arose. The Latin schools were attended by children of merchant aristocrats, were preparatory to universities or to church and civil positions, and had no connection with the vernacular schools, attended by socially inferior groups.

In these vernacular schools were taught reading, writing, and arithmetic as a preparation for minor positions in industry and commerce. Arithmetic long continued to be considered an advanced and difficult study of post-elementary character. Special writing and reckoning schools arose offering training for business, and the teachers of these subjects organized a gild to safeguard their interests. These vernacular schools were, then, vocational, not cultural in their ends. Some of them, particularly in Germany, were municipal in control, but most of them were conducted by private teachers as a source of livelihood. In the fifteenth century frequent disputes arose between the church and town councils in Germany over the question of city schools. The basis of the dispute was usually the loss of revenue suffered by the church through city competition in education, particularly in Latin education.

(2) Extension of City Vernacular Schools. In the fifteenth and sixteenth centuries, the vernacular schools, chiefly in the cities, increased in number. These were usually private schools attended not by the destitute but by the near-destitute who could afford to pay a few pennies for instruction. The teachers were usually poorly qualified in learning and character, and taught but little for their little fees. The invention of printing, the multiplication of books and newspapers in the vernacular, and increasing interest in the Bible contributed, slowly but surely, to the growth of vernacular schools for the common people, national and religious motives for their establishment supplementing the earlier vocational motive. The religious motive, intensified by the Reformation, was seized upon by governments to advance the education of the masses for civic and national ends.

Before the Reformation, the city proletariat and the peasantry were almost completely neglected. When their worth to states, churches, and industry was realized, organized movements to educate them began. What came to be called the folk-school (*Volksschule*) in Germany, the common school in America, the public elementary school in England, and the primary school in France represent the extension of the city vernacular school, with a predominantly vocational purpose, to the proletarian slums, the peasant hamlet, and the countryside. In that development the various churches in their anxiety to hold and win adherents played an important rôle in the post-Reformation era. Sectarian rivalries, thus, brought a significant expansion of educational provisions for the common people. The Protestant denominational school stands as the foremost representative of the transition from the mediaeval church school to the state school of today. The Reformers, perhaps without intending it, placed religion upon the side of state education. The state-church educational system of Protestant lands was a steppingstone to the state systems of today, some of which have become almost completely secularized. Until the national states became the dominant controllers of education, the story is concerned chiefly with the educational activities of the various churches. Among Lutherans and Calvinists the education of the masses was viewed as a public service which the state and its church owed to themselves. Among Anglicans, Catholics, and others it was viewed as a charity to be provided by churches and philanthropists prompted entirely by religious and charitable motives.

LUTHERANISM AND VERNACULAR ELEMENTARY EDUCATION. Since Luther made one's salvation depend on his ability to read the Bible, it became incumbent upon the new ecclesiastical authority to equip the people with that ability. The interests of society being also involved, Luther asked the state to help the new church in educating the masses. While public action was taken earlier in sections of North Germany, under the leadership of John Bugenhagen (1485-1588), Württemberg (1559) was the first state to provide for free "German schools" for the masses in rural villages, in which reading, writing, religion, and music were to be taught. Secondary and higher pay schools for the socially superior, as Luther suggested, were planned at the same time. In 1642, the state of Gotha established a system of state schools, in which were taught the Bible, the Lutheran catechism, prayers, the liturgy of the Lutheran church, and "the natural and useful sciences," according to the suggestions of Comenius, and music, composition, and spelling. Among the many useful sciences suggested by the School Code of Gotha were the points of the compass, sun dial, observation of the weather, herbs, trees, animals, cities, towns, streams, laws, taxes, rules of domestic life, surveying, carpenter's rule, and weights and measures. The children were required to attend church and write outlines of the sermons. Cleanliness, good manners, and moral conduct were to be diligently required by the teachers. Parents whose children failed to attend school were to be fined. Pupils were required to enter school at the age of five. The work of each class, of which there were three, was tested in an annual examination given by the teachers, ministers, and inspectors of the schools. The teachers were carefully chosen and supervised. Prince Ernest, who planned this system of Gotha, was ahead of his time, but his work became a model for later German educators, among them August Francke whose educational institutions at Halle, established later in the seventeenth century, advanced the movement of social reform through education.[55]

Thus did Lutheran Germany begin to lay the basis of its state system, but progress was slow. Lutheran influence upon educational reform soon extended also into Sweden and Denmark. All Lutheran church regulations proclaimed education to be a church function, but the church itself was a state institution deriving its educational authority from the states, whose educational power was supreme. Before 1700, nearly all German states had made legal provision for popular education, but the laws were poorly enforced, and the folk-schools remained very inefficient until the nineteenth century, largely because of the opposition of property owners and of parental indifference. Lutheranism, however, promoted the governmental acceptance of the principle of free, universal, elementary education, and the laying of the legal basis for such education.

CALVINISM AND ELEMENTARY EDUCATION. While Calvin's own interest centered in secondary and higher education, he would have everyone instructed in the Bible, the vernacular, and arithmetic. God, he said, had given to everyone the spark of reason in order to discover and understand truth. When he organized his schools in Geneva he provided elementary schools as the first level in the system. Here pupils received instruction in religion, the French vernacular, and arithmetic. Calvin looked upon the Scriptures as the foundation of all learning. From Geneva, Calvinism exerted a mighty influence upon education wherever the religion spread. In England, its influence appeared in the Puritan penetration of Oxford and Cambridge but, for England, it largely ended there. Many graduates of Cambridge, however, carried its doctrines to colonial

55 Barnard, *op. cit.*, XX, 576–84.

Massachusetts. In France, the Huguenots established many elementary and secondary schools and eight universities. It was, however, in Holland, Scotland, and colonial America that Calvinism had its greatest effect upon education. Following the Geneva practice, the state in Holland, New Netherland, Scotland, and New England was a church-state partnership in which the church dominated.

(1) IN HOLLAND AND NEW NETHERLAND. In 1618, the Dutch national synod of Dort demanded that parents, teachers, and ministers instruct all children in Christian doctrine. Earlier national synods, beginning with that of Wezel in 1568, laid down similar regulations. The church was made primarily responsible for providing schools in all cities, towns, and rural areas, in which the poor were to be instructed free. The civil authorities were called upon to provide suitable teachers and pay their salaries. Careful provision was made for the frequent visitation and inspection of schools by church and state supervisors. The synods viewed with greatest concern the religious orthodoxy of the teachers and the religious education of youth. Teachers were required to sign a pledge of loyalty to the Reformed church, and were required to bring all their pupils to church services and have them report upon the sermons they had heard.[56] The curriculum in the elementary schools consisted of the vernacular, the Heidelberg Catechism, the Epistles and Gospels, the Commandments, prayers, and the story of Dutch wars. Patriotism was taught as a religious duty. These practices of the mother country were carried to America and continued in Dutch settlements even after the British conquest of them in 1664.

(2) IN SCOTLAND. John Knox (1505-1572), the Scottish Reformation leader and a personal friend of Calvin, introduced the Genevan ideal of education into Scotland. In his *First Book of Discipline* (1560), in which he formulated his plan for a national church, he called for the establishment of schools, free to the poor, running from elementary schools of the rudiments and religion to "great schools called universities." He would have the church compel all parents to rear their children in "learning and virtue," and he would make the church directly responsible for providing and supporting schools for all classes and both sexes. Under his plan all bright students would be required to continue in school until their talents had been fully developed for service to the "Commonwealth."[57] The Scottish Parliament rejected his proposals in 1567, as did the

[56] W. H. Kilpatrick, *The Dutch Schools of New Netherland and Colonial New York* (Washington, D.C.: Government Printing Office, 1912), pp. 20 f.

[57] D. Laing, *The Works of John Knox* (6 vols.; Edinburgh: Bannatyne Club Publications, 1846–65), II, 209 ff.

church as well. Knox had hoped that his Presbyterian schools could be supported from revenues derived from confiscated Catholic properties, but these properties were seized by the nobles, and his plan consequently failed. Parliament, however, in 1567, made the church the supervisor of schools and, in 1592, the authority for licensing teachers. In 1640, the presbyteries were given legal power to levy a tax for parish schools and, in 1646, every parish was legally required to maintain a teacher. These laws lacking enforcement, elementary education was provided mainly by private teachers until the eighteenth century, when a general system of parish schools was established.

(3) In British American Colonies. While the Scotch and Scotch-Irish Presbyterians were active in Pennsylvania, New Jersey, and parts of the South, it was the Puritan founders of Massachusetts, Connecticut, and New Hampshire who made the chief Calvinist contribution to education in the New World. Massachusetts was founded as a Biblical commonwealth, exclusively for Puritans, non-Puritans enjoying only the freedom to stay out of it. Puritan exclusiveness, however, soon broke down, because the worldly business of the Puritans made it impossible for them to escape the influence of the world. In the state, as founded, only Puritans could vote or hold public office. The state was Puritan, and its towns were Puritan towns. Its laws were Puritan laws, passed by Puritans in their civil capacity. Its town schools were Puritan schools, supervised by Puritan ministers, taught by tested Puritan teachers, and the religion of the schools was Puritan. Though the state and its schools were denominational, this Puritan state was a state; this Biblical commonwealth, a commonwealth, whose laws were civil laws, albeit they bear the stamp of Puritanism.

To make children Puritans, the General Court of Massachusetts (1642) required, by law, the selectmen of towns to see that all children were properly employed and were able "to read & understand the principles of religion, & the capitall lawes of this country," and to apprentice children neglected by their parents. In 1647, the Court ordered every town of fifty families to employ a teacher of reading and writing whose fees should be paid either by the parents or the town community. Connecticut legislated similarly, in 1650, as did New Hampshire, in 1680, when it ceased to be a part of Massachusetts, although the latter law was ignored until 1719, when more careful provision for schools was made.

Through Calvinism came the New England town elementary school, public in character, although that public was, in the beginning, a Puritan public. That school survived (although pioneer conditions and social change militated against it) as the influential forerunner of the public, elementary, secular, common school of our modern American states. The Calvinist doctrine of total depravity, and its corollaries, the total helplessness of man to avoid sin, to follow the Gospel or even to repent, unless God made the first move, were accepted completely by the Puritan church. God's grace was viewed as irresistible, but given only to the elect. Conversion was proof of election, and some were bewildered by the choice of God when, in revival meetings, more girls than boys were converted.[58]

The Puritans made no distinction between the child and the adult, and gave both the same religious food. Parents and preachers were alarmed when children showed little concern about religion, because their moral and spiritual welfare was their first consideration. Children of six and seven years were dressed as adults and expected to act as adults. The child psychologist was not there to question the prevailing views of child nature. On the gloomy New England sabbath, the child sat motionless in the church listening to the story of his eternal doom and waiting for a gloomy eternal sabbath which to many children offered no joy. From the first Sunday after his birth the child was brought to church to listen, through the dreary years of childhood and adolescence, to long prayers and sermons, which caused many a youthful scofflaw to "larf" and whisper during public worship. And what a crime it was when a little boy threw "Sister pentecost perkins on the ice it being Saboth day . . . between the meting hous and his plaes of Abode"![59] To be converted, children, like adults, had to be "'willing to be damned'" and some of them, no doubt, felt that their God was a cruel God. Hell was filled with children and adults alike. The Bible was the chief book for children, and they were required to read and study it from beginning to end. Some read it in its entirety four times a year, and with fear, trembling, and tears. The books for children were all of a religious nature, but the *New England Primer* is deservedly the most famous of them.[60] It reveals clearly the spirit of Calvinist education in colonial America.

The New England Primer. Widely used in the schools of New England and in those of Dissenters everywhere was this children's reader. First published about 1690, it was republished and reprinted for nearly 200 years,[61] and, for 150 years, had an average

[58] S. Fleming, *Children and Puritanism* (New Haven: Yale University Press, 1933), pp. 55 f.

[59] *Ibid.*, p. 63.

[60] *Ibid.*, pp. 78 ff.

[61] *Vide* reprint of the 1777 Draper edition published by Joel Munsell Sons, Albany, N. Y., 1885.

sale of 20,000 copies yearly. The alphabet, illustrated and in rhyme, syllables, words of one to six syllables, moral and religious lessons from the Bible, the Westminster *Shorter Catechism,* and usually John Cotton's "Spiritual Milk for American Babes Drawn out of the Breasts of Both Testaments," the martyrdom of John Rogers and his last poetic advice to his children, and a lengthy "Dialogue between Christ, a Youth and the Devil" were included in it. Even with the alphabet, the child drank from the religious spring:

A. In *Adam's* Fall
We sinned all.
B. Heaven to find
The *Bible* Mind.

. . . .

N. *Noah* did view
The old world & new.

. . . .

R. Young pious *Ruth*
Left all for Truth.

. . . .

T. Young *Timothy*
Learnt sin to fly.

. . . .

Z. *Zaccheus* he
Did climb the Tree,
Our Lord to see.[62]

All blessings and powers come from God:

The Praises of my Tongue
I offer to the Lord,
That I was taught and learnt so young
To read his holy Word.

God has decreed our final end:

I in the burying place may see,
Graves shorter there than I,
From death's arrest no age is free,
Young children too must die.
My God may such an awful sight,
Awakening be to me!
Oh! that by early grace I might
For death prepared be.

This primer rapidly disappeared from the schools of America after 1800, due to the growth of the secular, national spirit. That secularism has now almost completely triumphed over denominationalism in education, although a militant reaction against it has recently appeared. The modern state spends money to make citizens and craftsmen, but not a cent for the salvation of souls. Nor is it clear that the present growing demand in America for religious

62 From the Edward Draper edition, Boston, 1777.

education, as a part of our public school program, is actuated by an otherworldly motive.

ANGLICANISM AND "CHARITY" ELEMENTARY EDUCATION. In Anglican England, where the established church had great power, attempts, though ineffective, were made to impose the official orthodoxy upon everyone. The school was particularly watched. Unorthodox teachers were forbidden to teach, under heavy penalties, and their employers were fined, under a law of 1580. The Act of Conformity (1662) required all teachers to sign a declaration of loyalty to church and state, and forbade them to teach without a bishop's license, the latter being a legal requirement after 1603. "The Five Mile Act" (1665) added further restrictions. Teachers of certain endowed schools were exempted from these legal burdens, and about 1,100 endowed elementary schools were founded before 1730. The Anglican church, being a national church, was the state's educational agent, the state itself performing no direct educational function until the late nineteenth century. The idea that free education is a charity, not a right of youth or a public service, came to prevail in England and her colonies. The idea, however, was not confined to the English-speaking world, and usually the interests of a church rather than the altruistic love of the poor prompted the promoters of charity schools, although, as we shall see later, the movement did not lack a social motive.

The Anglican Reformation, because of the perversion of church property for secular ends, nearly destroyed the elementary schools of England. Philanthropists, however, began anew to endow charity schools for the poor, while private masters provided cheap schooling for the lower bourgeosie. But destitution, ignorance, and crime increased among the lower social elements. In 1698, the Anglican church organized the Society for Promoting Christian Knowledge (the S.P.C.K.) and, in 1701, the Society for the Propagation of the Gospel in Foreign Parts (the S.P.G.). From the start, these two societies established schools for the limited end of teaching reading, writing, and the Anglican catechism. The enrollment in the schools of the S.P.C.K. reached a height of about 50,000, in 1750.

In the North American colonies, particularly Pennsylvania, New York, New Jersey, parts of New England, the Carolinas, and Georgia, the S.P.G. conducted schools similar to those of the S.P.C.K. in England. Anglican indoctrination of the poor was the primary motive of these educational activities. Philanthropic and social-reform ideals were, however, at work in the movement.

NON-CONFORMIST CHARITY SCHOOLS. The Dissenters in England also established charity schools for the poor, but these were few in comparison with those of the S.P.C.K. The motives which inspired this activity were the same as those of the S.P.C.K.

QUAKERISM AND ELEMENTARY EDUCATION. Of the smaller dissenting sects, the Society of Friends was probably the most active in education, that being one of the chief cares of their various Meetings. In the British Isles and America, they provided for the "guarded education" of their own children and for the free education of the poor of Quaker and other faiths. In New England, New York, New Jersey, Pennsylvania, Delaware, and parts of the South, they conducted schools. Many of their schools are still among the most excellent in America. The curriculum in their early elementary schools comprised religion, reading, writing, arithmetic, and probably bookkeeping. Becoming conduct, everywhere and always, was constantly enjoined upon their pupils, as was the use of the "plain language" for Quaker children.[63]

CATHOLICISM AND ELEMENTARY EDUCATION. Catholic interest in the education of the poor appeared most noticeably in France. In the sixteenth century charity schools for the poor in cities were encouraged and established by the nobility and the clergy, and city authorities were challenging the claims of the church to dominate the education of the masses. The laity at times demanded even a system of compulsory elementary education.[64] These reform activities which aimed to provide education in the mother tongue for French children foreshadowed the work of the Christian Brethren.

The most notable early Catholic achievement in educating the poor was that inaugurated by Jean Baptiste de la Salle, founder of the Brethren of the Christian Schools, in 1682. In 1684, he opened his teacher training seminary at Rheims. In 1792, the Brethren had 127 houses and were instructing some 36,000 boys. Their schools, designed for the poor, were free, but, in time, paying students from the lower middle class were admitted to them to pursue advanced commercial studies. The Catholic religion had a prominent place in the curriculum of all the Brethren's schools. In addition, in most of their schools, only reading, writing, spelling, and arithmetic were taught, but always with a practical emphasis. Occasionally, boys were taught a trade. The Brethren's discipline was, for a long time,

[63] For an example of their work, see T. Woody, *Early Quaker Education in Pennsylvania* (New York: Teachers College, Columbia University, 1920).

[64] Adamson, *op. cit.*, p. 199.

severe, and the school atmosphere repressive. When whipped, a boy was compelled to kneel and thank the teacher for his kindness.[65]

Among the pedagogical contributions of La Salle were the substitution of class instruction for the usual individual recitation; the careful organization of subject matter to facilitate group instruction; and the individual and orderly promotion of students from one unit of subject matter to another. In these respects the Brethren were ahead of their time. And their work for the poor of France was carried on against the opposition of many aristocrats.[66]

ELEMENTARY EDUCATION FOR GIRLS. In spite of Protestant solicitation for girls' souls, and the actual legal provision made for them in such states as Württemberg and Gotha, girls were but meagerly cared for in most Protestant countries, Anglican England almost wholly neglecting them. The Quakers and Moravians deviated notably from this rule. Catholic governments showed no interest at all in the problem but, from the sixteenth century onward, congregations of nuns and of lay women made some provision for a few Catholic girls. The most notable Catholic work centered in France where the Sisters of Notre Dame (founded 1597) established free elementary schools for poor girls. These pupils were to be taught "reading, writing, sewing and divers manual arts, honorable and peculiarly suited to girls." [67] The Catholic schools were of the convent type where, with the rudiments, girls were taught to stifle their natural desires and to neglect their bodies, "destined to serve as food for worms." [68] The practices of the period show little concern for girls of the laboring classes.

SCHOOL LIFE AND DISCIPLINE. Thus were the masses cared for prior to the rise of national school systems. Their portion, where accessible, was instruction in the 4 R's: religion, reading, 'ritin, and rudimentary 'rithmetic. Private masters and dames, poorly qualified in learning and character, were numerous, but taught little for their little fees. The churches, and their societies, did something for the poor, conditions being best where the church and state co-operated to educate the masses. Denominational indoctrination characterized education. The school atmosphere was Biblical and sepulchral. Children everywhere shared the ponderous religiosity of their eld-

[65] P. Smith, *A History of Modern Culture* (New York: Henry Holt & Co., Inc., 1930–34), II, 431.

[66] For an interesting, scholarly account of La Salle, see E. A. Fitzpatrick, *La Salle, Patron of All Teachers* (Milwaukee: The Bruce Publishing Co., 1951).

[67] P. J. McCormick, *History of Education* (Washington, D.C.: The Catholic Education Press, 1915), pp. 307 f.

[68] E. P. Cubberley, *Readings in the History of Education* (Boston: Houghton Mifflin Co., 1920), p. 282.

ers. James Janeway in his *Token for Children,* in which he tells stories of their conversion, holy lives and "joyful deaths," tells how Elizabeth Butcher, born in Boston in 1709, asked herself, when two and a half years old, "What is my corrupt nature?" to which she made answer, "It is empty of Grace, bent unto Sin." At the age of seven, her happiest day was "catechizing day."

The post-Reformation world was a world of catechisms, and catechizing children was a leading activity of home, church, and school. The catechetical method of memorizing answers to questions of religion was used even where formal catechisms were not available for reading and study. A Massachusetts law of 1641 and other later New England laws urged the duty of catechizing children upon all church elders, parents, and schoolmasters.[69] The catechetical method of memorizing formal subject matter was not limited to religious material. Understanding of the subject matter was not stressed, and no attempt was made to depart from a logical presentation in order to make the difficult things easy for the child mind. There was no joy within the walls of the school any more than within the walls of the church. In John Wesley's rules for schools, we read: "As we have no play days, so neither do we allow any time for play on any day; for he that plays as a child will play as a man." [70]

In school and out, the rod was the means of discipline. A well-known case of school torture is that of the Swabian teacher who, in fifty-one years of teaching, gave 911,527 blows with a rod, 124,010 blows with a cane, 20,989 taps with a ruler, 136,715 blows with the hand, 10,235 blows on the mouth, 7,905 boxes on the ear, and 1,118,800 blows on the head. He made boys kneel on peas 777 times, and on a three-cornered piece of wood 613 times, while he made 3,001 students wear the dunce's cap.

The life of the teacher was not pleasant either. Said Goldsmith: "If you are for a genteel, easy profession, bind yourself seven years apprentice to turn a cutler's wheel, but avoid a school by any means." [71]

THE UNREALIZED IDEAL OF UNIVERSAL ELEMENTARY EDUCATION. Before the nineteenth century the universal, vernacular schools, which men like Luther and Comenius had proposed, remained in the realm of pious wishes. The churches, sometimes in partnership with the state, attempted to reach the masses. While their activities enlarged the opportunities of the poor, they lacked effective organ-

69 Fleming, *op. cit.,* pp. 110 ff.

70 Smith, *A History of Modern Culture,* II, 422.

71 *Ibid.,* II, 425.

ization and the power to enforce official requirements. They were handicapped, too, by the scarcity and cost of books in the vernacular and by lack of funds to carry on their work. Yet the work of the churches and philanthropic agencies was extensive and significant. Universal, popular education had, however, to wait for the building of a smooth-running state machinery of public education, and for the acceptance by the public of its national necessity.

VERNACULAR EDUCATION AS CLASS EDUCATION. Just as vocational education was long considered that of the lower classes, so also was vernacular education until national governments, in their own interests, removed that stigma from it. While many theorists, as we have seen, stressed the dignity and necessity of vernacular education, the privileged classes clung to the classics, and found the social exclusiveness they desired for their children in their own segregated secondary schools and universities. But the triumph of the common man and his culture was not to be long delayed in a nationalized and industrialized world. When elementary education was removed from the category of charities and made a national service, the mark of caste was gradually removed from it.

VOCATIONAL EDUCATION. As we have seen, vernacular schools arose as vocational schools designed to prepare penmen and bookkeepers to serve the needs of commerce. Our first vocational schools were these commercial, vernacular schools of the cities. In Germany and the Netherlands they had their most rapid early development. All of these were schools chiefly of the lower middle class. The opening of trades to the poor was hindered by the gild system whose privileges came to be restricted largely to children of members. Luther would have all children taught a trade, although he had no clear plan of how that should be done. Sir William Petty would have all children, rich and poor, taught a trade or useful art,[72] and called for a system of trade schools to meet that need. Bookkeeping and manual trades were taught by the Christian Brethren in some of their schools in France.[73] John Locke proposed the establishment of "working schools" for the poor in every English parish.[74]

The idea that vocational education was peculiarly suited to the needs of the poor or near-poor prevailed everywhere. By the English Poor Laws of 1562 and 1601 overseers of the poor were directed to apprentice pauper children and to provide workhouses for those not apprenticed. These laws took beggars off the streets and forced them into the army of laborers where competition kept wages low.

[72] Adamson, *op. cit.*, pp. 133 f.
[73] *Ibid.*, p. 222.
[74] *Ibid.*, p. 203.

This enforced apprenticeship system was carried to the American colonies. The Massachusetts education law of 1642 required parents and masters to teach their children a trade and, in 1692, the overseers of the poor were authorized, but not compelled, to apprentice poor children. William Penn would have all children over twelve taught some useful trade so that "the poor may live to work, and the rich, if they become poor, may not want."[75] Compulsory apprenticeship training of the poor became almost universal in the Southern colonies. In colonial America, the apprenticeship laws generally required that the apprentice be taught to read and write. Here as in Europe vocational training bore the mark of caste.

Developments in Secondary Education

THE LATIN GRAMMAR SCHOOL. (1) In Italy. The rediscovery of Graeco-Roman literature and the revival of interest in classical and, with the Reformation, in Biblical antiquity led to the establishment in Europe and America of schools in which Latin and Greek, especially Latin, came to comprise almost the entire curriculum. These first arose in Italy, the most famous one (established *c.* 1420) being that of Vittorino da Feltre, who aimed to mould learned Christian gentlemen through an education embodying the classical, Christian, and chivalric ideals. A classical education, based upon pagan and early Christian authors, he provided to that end, the immediate aim being to give a youth eloquence, an ornate literary style, and sound moral, physical, and intellectual experiences. Vittorino stressed the content of the Greek and Roman classics as well as their form and, in the curriculum, added to them music, mathematics, natural philosophy, natural history, astronomy, ancient philosophies, and physical exercises.

In its literary emphasis, the Latin school was a re-creation of the grammar and rhetorical schools of pagan Rome. That old tradition being again re-established, it has been difficult for men to accept the view that any non-literary education can be liberal. Vittorino's ultimate goal was the moulding of the complete citizen through the harmonious development of his mind, body, and character. He would, like all humanists, train the youth to be a man, not a technical expert. All humanist education was man-centered, not job-centered, and Vittorino's school represents the ideal at its best. There were earlier city Latin schools in northern Italy, but they stressed language, not classical literature, and their aim was narrowly practical and job-centered. The Marquis of Mantua became the patron of

[75] *Colonial Records of Pennsylvania,* I, 41.

Vittorino's school. To it flocked the sons of the northern Italian aristocracy. A few daughters of the nobility also studied there. Vittorino admitted, and supported at his own expense, some poor boys of great promise. Students entered the school at ages as far apart as six and twenty-one. To all of them it was a home, and Vittorino, a kindly father. Corporal punishment was practically unknown. Of special significance was the broad compulsory program of health and physical education, including a variety of games and athletic exercises popular at the time, many of which had come down from ancient Greece. The reputation of this Mantuan school spread into northern Europe and left its mark upon many schools there.[76]

Schools similar to that of Vittorino were established or patronized by the princes of other Italian cities, but none of them attained the excellence of his. The relation of the courts of Italian city tyrants to the new education was one of its unique features. While an occasional poor boy of promise found admission to these "court schools," the city aristocracy made them almost exclusively their own. The middle and lower classes had to be satisfied with the vernacular writing and reckoning schools, or with private or city Latin schools designed for practical rather than liberal ends. Some few students, however, went from these inferior Latin schools to the higher classical "court schools" to complete their literary education. It should be noted that these "court schools" were not preparatory to universities, but provided a complete liberal education for those who often despised the professionalism of the universities. And it should also be noted that all of these new city developments represent the passing of clerical control over the education of Italian youth.

(2) In the Netherlands. As in Italy, city life north of the Alps stimulated a revival of learning which looked beyond the needs of the church to that of society and of laymen. The burghers of the free cities of Holland and Flanders first followed the lead of Italian cities in reviving learning. Town schools had existed in the Netherlands from about the year 1200. In the closing years of the fourteenth century the Brethren of the Common Life, a charitable religious society, began to supervise and reform these schools. By 1550, they had over 150 grammar schools in the Netherlands and Western Germany under their control. Their schools were carefully organized and, unlike the classical schools of Italy, formed a single system. From 1450, the humanistic studies were introduced into the curriculum, and the schools became models for later classical schools

[76] Woodward, *Vittorino da Feltre and Other Humanist Educators,* pp. 27–92.

in northern Europe. Under the principalship (1465-1498) of Alexander Hegius, the Brethren's school at Deventer had some 2,000 students and an eight-year course. In the first six classes the studies were almost exclusively classical. Philosophy was added in the seventh grade and theology in the eighth. The schools of the Brethren were the nurseries of most of the leading educators of northern Europe in the sixteenth century. Among their students were Erasmus and John Sturm, the latter the reorganizer, in 1537, of the Strassburg city Latin school to which he gave the name *gymnasium*.

(3) In Germany. Philipp Melanchthon (1497-1560), Luther's friend and associate in religious reform, was the first leading organizer of Protestant humanist schools in Germany. He saw the need to reorganize German education on the secondary and university levels. Previously the city Latin schools were sending their graduates to the universities at the age, often, of thirteen. Melanchthon, as did others earlier, saw the need for an intermediate school between these Latin schools and the universities, and somewhat similar to the schools of the Brethren of the Common Life. Such a school, stressing both Latin and Greek literature, Melanchthon deemed necessary to make young Germans wise in matters important to the nation and its new national faith. In spite of Melanchthon's guidance, classical schools established at Eisleben (1525) and at Nuremberg (1526) fell short of his ideal. Strictly classical schools, moreover, did not appeal strongly to the merchant class in northern Europe, and only larger ones in larger cities attracted sufficient patronage for survival. Princes and the landed gentry, however, found classical schools to their liking. Many German merchants sent their sons abroad to learn more useful languages than Latin and Greek. One of the early classical schools of Germany which prospered and became a model for later schools of its type was the Strassburg *Gymnasium*. John Sturm took the old mediaeval Latin school of the city, gave it a humanistic purpose, and made it a nine-class school. It taught Latin grammar, not as preparatory to logic, but as an instrument of correct expression; and it taught classical literature for the sake of liberal training and the moulding of church and civil leaders.

Following Luther's views, the education of church and state leaders continued to be a purpose of secondary education stated in school and church ordinances in Germany throughout the sixteenth century. The *gymnasium* embodied that purpose. In it, students studied, almost exclusively, Latin and Greek, emphasis being placed upon grammar and the style of Cicero, whose works comprised a large part of the curriculum. In Sturm's school, logic, rhetoric, and the elements of mathematics received a little attention in the upper grades, but the mathematical studies were given the barest recognition. Greek had a minor place as compared with Latin. Physical education was neglected entirely. The writing and speaking of Latin were the chief work of the school.

Many schools of the Strassburg type emerged in Germany, but they were schools which catered to the upper aristocracy, and were preparatory to the universities, which, until recent times, catered also to the few. In the control of the *gymnasium* church and state participated. While publicly aided, it was an expensive school from which the masses were excluded not only by cost but, perhaps still more, by class prejudice. Originating in the atmosphere of the Reformation, the stamp of denominationalism was also on it. In its excellence as a classical school it has never been surpassed. We shall refer later to its changed place in the German national school system.

(4) IN FRANCE. In the closing years of the fifteenth century, humanism invaded France, where the University of Paris stood as a stronghold of scholasticism and an enemy of the lay spirit in education, as universities generally were. When Guillaume Budé, through his treatise *On the Education of a Prince* (1516), secured the sympathy of King Francis I for the new education, the humanist cause was notably advanced in spite of the opposition of the university and the church. In 1530, Budé organized the College of France, in Paris, for the study of Latin, Greek, Hebrew, and mathematics. The first humanist secondary school in France was the Collège of Guyenne at Bordeaux, established by the city in 1534. Montaigne was one of the famous pupils of this school. The sympathy of some of its faculty for Protestantism as well as its lay outlook aroused the opposition of the church, and even the King was led to believe that the school was an enemy of the state. In spite of these charges, largely unfounded, and of the establishment, in 1572, of a rival Jesuit school in the city, the Collège survived and influenced the development of later humanist schools in France. In the Reformation struggle it stood against a break with Rome. It was a twelve-grade school. Boys entered at the age of six, and were introduced to Latin, with the aid of the vernacular, in the first grade, where emphasis was placed upon prayers, the alphabet, reading, writing and spelling. During the first ten years of the course, Latin grammar and literature comprised nearly nine-tenths of the course, with Greek and mathematics constituting the rest of it. The last two years of the course were spent in the study of philosophy based

chiefly on the works of Aristotle, and were known as the Faculty of Arts. All but the younger students, who might use French, were required to converse in Latin at all times. The lay humanistic spirit, embodied in this school, was checked by the rise of Jesuit schools in France and other Catholic lands.

(5) IN ENGLAND. About the year 1510, Dean Colet, assisted by Erasmus, refounded St. Paul's School, London, on the humanistic plan. Its stated purpose was the attainment by its students of wisdom, good manners, and eloquence. The curriculum consisted of the catechism in English, the Greek and Roman classics, and the works of Christian authors who wrote in "clene and chast latin." English secondary education has, with some modifications in recent times, borne that general character ever since.

The British state did not establish or control these secondary schools of the humanistic period, although Henry VIII and other monarchs ordered that only *Lilys Grammar* be used in Latin schools. They were founded by individual philanthropists and private organizations for the intellectual, religious, and moral development of the individual youth rather than for the moulding of church and civil leaders. The earlier schools were generally free and open to all classes though intended primarily for the poor. The poor, however, were soon robbed of their gift. In Holinshed's *Chronicle*, for 1573, we are told that Oxford and Cambridge "were erected by their founders at the first only for poor men's sons, . . . but now they have the least benefit of them by reason the rich do so encroach upon them. . . . In some grammar schools likewise which send scholars to these universities it is lamentable to see what bribery is used; for ere the scholar can be preferred, such bribage is made, that poor men's children are commonly shut out, and the richer sort received."[77]

While the control of these English classical schools was vested in a private board of trustees, the Anglican church licensed the teachers, tested their orthodoxy, and supervised the religious instruction they offered. Allied to Anglican orthodoxy, the classics became firmly entrenched in the secondary schools of England as well as in the Anglican universities of Oxford and Cambridge, for which many of them, particularly the Great Public Schools, became almost exclusively preparatory.

(6) IN AMERICA. (a) In New England. In America, our first secondary schools were imported European Latin schools, all alike

[77] Cited by R. B. Morgan, *Readings in English Social History* (London: Cambridge University Press, 1923), pp. 297–98. (By permission of The Macmillan Co.)

in purpose and curriculum. In methods of control and support, they differed because of national or religious tradition. In Puritan Massachusetts, following the practice of Calvinist countries, the church and state co-operated to establish the schools. In 1635, the citizens of Boston voted to appoint a town schoolmaster and, in 1636, Daniel Maud was appointed the "free schoolmaster" of the town. Thus arose the Boston Latin School, the first secondary school in the colonies. The citizens of Boston established it by vote, but only those could vote who held much property and were members of the Puritan church. The support came from voluntary subscriptions until, in 1650, a compulsory town rate was adopted. The state granted land to aid in supporting the school.

Other Massachusetts towns followed rapidly the example of Boston and, in 1647, the General Court legalized the practice by passing the "Old Deluder Satan Act," whose preamble reads: "It being one of the chief projects of that old deluder Satan to keep men from the knowledge of the Scriptures, as in former times by keeping them in an unknown tongue, so in these latter times by persuading from the use of tongues, that so at least the true sense and meaning of the original might be clouded by false glosses of saint-seeming deceivers, that learning may not be buried in the grave of our fathers in the church and commonwealth, the Lord assisting our endeavors." To these ends, the Court ordered every town of a hundred families to appoint a grammar master capable of preparing boys for the university, a fine of £5 (raised gradually to £30 by 1718) being imposed upon towns violating the law. Thus did the Puritan state create Latin schools "to advance learning," says *New England's First Fruits,* "and perpetuate it to posterity; dreading to leave an illiterate ministry to the churches, when our present ministers shall lie in the dust." That is not the purpose of our modern high schools, for our society has changed and our schools have changed with it.

Generally, the Massachusetts Latin schools were controlled by the selectmen of the towns, and were inspected by Puritan ministers who passed upon the orthodoxy of the teachers. Boston, in 1709, appointed laymen to accompany the ministers on their rounds of inspection, and the ministers protested, but in vain.

Connecticut and New Hampshire adopted the plan of Massachusetts. The New England town Latin school, however, was not popular, for it was not suited to the economic life of a population pioneering under difficult conditions. Latin had little to contribute to one's success in farming, industry, or commerce. The Latin school was the school of the rich, although an occasional talented poor boy was admitted to it. The marked class distinctions of society pervaded the schools of the Puritan state. Harvard continued to list students, not alphabetically, but by their social rank until the eve of the Revolution. Significant social change brought eventually the free high school for all the children of all the people, regardless of wealth, rank, or belief. Yet the Puritan Latin school, in its public aspect, contained an essential element of the purpose embodied in the high school of today.

(b) Outside of New England. The Dutch, in New Amsterdam; the Quakers and other religious groups, in New Jersey and Pennsylvania; and the Anglican English settlers, in Maryland, Virginia, and the Carolinas established Latin schools, similar in purpose and curriculum to those of New England, but different from them in matters of control and support. In keeping with Quaker utilitarianism, a higher English school existed from the start side by side with the Latin school in the Quaker system of Pennsylvania. William Penn's plan of public schools was not realized, and colonial secondary schools in Pennsylvania were provided by denominational groups and private schoolmasters. In 1696, Maryland provided by law for the establishment of classical schools, to be supported by gifts and duties on merchandise. Only King William's School, now St. John's College at Annapolis, resulted from that law. In Virginia, bequests were made for schools by Benjamin Symms (1635), Thomas Eaton (1646), and by others later, and a few "free schools," or classical schools, resulted from such philanthropies. In 1724, the ministers of twenty-nine parishes reported to the Bishop of London the existence of three schools of apparently classical character, one of which was the grammar school of William and Mary College. Private effort in Virginia accomplished much less than public effort in New England. In South Carolina, in 1710 and 1712, and in North Carolina, in 1745 and 1764, the governments aided and encouraged the establishment of secondary schools. In the South Carolina school, under Anglican control, practical mathematics, bookkeeping, navigation, and surveying were taught in addition to the classics, a practice followed also in a school authorized by the New York legislature, in 1732. Such studies as these and such a school as the Quaker English school foreshadowed the coming of the academies and high schools. Ministers of various denominations, the Presbyterians being most active, established Latin schools in connection with their churches, the practice being quite prevalent in the Carolinas and Pennsylvania.

(c) General characteristics of colonial American Latin schools. In aims and curriculum, our early Latin school was the European humanistic school carried to the New World. The immediate aim was college preparation; the remote, the training of leaders for church and state. Our colonial colleges, with the exception of the College of Philadelphia, and to a degree of King's College, were largely theological seminaries. Latin and the rudiments of Greek comprised nine-tenths of all colonial grammar school instruction. In the cities, the private master appeared in answer to a popular demand for practical studies. Until 1745, when arithmetic was first required, Latin and the rudiments of Greek were the only requirements for admission to colleges. Princeton was the first college in America (1819) to make a knowledge of English grammar a requirement for admission.

In the Latin schools, the morals of boys were rigorously supervised and their spirits suppressed. Corporal punishment and expulsion were usually inflicted for graver offenses. The school day began at six or seven in the morning, and ended at four or five in the afternoon. The enrollment was low, the average school having about thirty students. Generally, the teachers were laymen or men preparing for the ministry. Denominational orthodoxy was a prime requisite for teaching. Teachers' salaries, with a few exceptions, were very low in present-day values. Girls were not admitted to the Latin schools, for they were barred from colleges, pulpits, and public offices. From 1700 onward, the Latin school slowly declined and, first in Europe and then in America, the *Realschule* and academy began to replace it.

THE JESUIT AND OTHER CATHOLIC SCHOOLS. In the struggle between Protestants and Catholics for the minds of men, the Jesuits were the most influential educators on the Catholic side. While many Catholic orders of priests, nuns, and lay brothers established elementary schools for poor Catholics, the Jesuits confined their efforts to the fields of secondary and higher education. They established hundreds of schools, called colleges, in many lands, during the Reformation period. Their first college was opened in Portugal in 1542. In large centers, like Rome and Paris, the enrollment rose to from 2,000 to 3,000 students. Usually some rich benefactor founded the schools and provided free board and lodging for boarding students.

The studies of the Jesuit secondary schools were almost exclusively classical. After nearly sixty years of teaching experience, the Jesuits published, in 1599, their *Plan of Studies*, which fixed authoritatively the curriculum and methods of their secondary schools and colleges until its revision, in 1832. In the sixteenth and seventeenth centuries, their schools were excellent. Their teachers were well trained, and their work was carefully organized and efficiently performed. Students entered the secondary school between the ages of ten and fourteen, having received their elementary instruction elsewhere. There were generally five classes in each school, but students spent two or, sometimes, three years in the last, or rhetoric, class. There, Jesuit secondary education ended, but above it was organized, in a college or university, the two- or three-year philosophical course, a theological course of five or six years capping the whole organization. No one was permitted to teach in the classical school until he had completed the philosophical course. That was a guarantee of his orthodoxy. Besides, for some time, the work of the beginning teacher was supervised by older men. The *Plan of Studies* was every teacher's guide, and the whole system rested upon the principle of authority. New opinions on questions already settled by others were officially condemned, and new questions pertaining to religion might not be asked by anyone without the permission of designated officials. Obedience to rules and approved practices was required. The authoritatively approved methods of memorization and repetition were everywhere used. Effort was stimulated by competitions, emulation, and prizes. Corporal punishment was practically unknown in Jesuit schools.

In moulding Catholic minds, the Jesuits used the combined influence of humanism and religion. The philosophical-theological discipline imposed upon their teachers guaranteed the result. They gained a monopoly of secondary and higher education in Catholic lands, beginning with France. In 1773, when they were temporarily suppressed by the pope, they had over 700 schools and about 200,000 students. Though catering to a social elite, they constantly sought youths of exceptional ability, whether rich or poor, for membership in the Society. Their schools were free, and, therefore, of great propagandist value. In 1814, another pope restored the Society but, having lost their endowments, their schools since then have not been free. Their suppression was never complete, and we find them establishing Georgetown University in America in 1791.

In France, two other teaching orders, the Fathers of the Oratory (founded 1611) and the contemporary Port Royalists established schools less hamstrung by the classical tradition than those of the Jesuits. Both groups were influenced by the rationalism of Descartes; and a form of Catholic puritanism, called Jansenism, pervaded the Port Royal community, thus arousing the hostility of the Jesuits to their schools, which lasted only from 1646 to 1660. Both groups gave prominence in the curriculum to history, mathematics, natural science, and French, in addition to the classics. When the

Jesuits were expelled from France (1764), Oratorian teachers were called to take their place. After the Port-Royalist schools were closed, some of their teachers turned to writing on education and, thus, their progressive thought remained as a stimulus to the growth of French education.

HUMANISTIC SCHOOLS AND THEIR LIMITATIONS. Thus arose the classical secondary school of Europe and America. In Lutheran and Calvinist countries, the church and state co-operated in providing it. In England, private agencies, supervised by the Anglican church, provided it. In Catholic lands, religious societies, authorized by the pope, were its chief supporters. Seldom was the school free from sectarian domination. Generally its basic aim, though not always stated, was the training of an intellectual elite for the service of church and state. Latin grammar was its fundamental study, and to it was added the acquisition of a useful Latin vocabulary, Latin conversation, Latin prose and verse composition, the reading of Latin authors, especially Cicero and Virgil, Latin declamations, performance of Latin plays, elementary Greek, religion, and, occasionally, rudimentary mathematics, such other studies as history, geography, etc., being taught incidentally in connection with the classics. Students after they had been taught the Latin rudiments through the medium of the vernacular were, generally, forbidden to speak their native tongue in school. Latin conversational texts called *Colloquia* were widely used. The *Colloquies* of the French Huguenot schoolmaster, Corderius, was the most popular of these books.[78] While dead, or rapidly expiring, Latin was used in the schools as a living tongue, because it had been useful in ecclesiastical and civil affairs when vernacular literatures were in a formative state, and because a classical education was a badge of social distinction.

When humanized schools first arose and, again, when religious controversies revitalized them, the spirit and ideas in literature were exalted above its forms. But instruction in all of them eventually degenerated into the barren formalism which Erasmus called Ciceronianism. The graduate knew words; their significance for life and the world, he did not know. His intellect had been enslaved by a worship of the words of the new tyrant of the intellect, Cicero. Said Voltaire of his Jesuit training: "The fathers taught me nothing but Latin and nonsense." And the same might be said of all classical schools of the time. The true spirit of humanism—life, and thought and knowledge—had departed from the schools.

[78] Woodward, *Studies in Education during the Age of the Renaissance*, pp. 155 ff.

The Latin schools, though occasionally free, were the schools not of the people but of the social elite. Even today, the poor cannot always afford to accept free education. Still less could they accept it from the fifteenth till the eighteenth century. And the education which the classical schools provided ignored the most pressing needs of national states and the demands of national cultures.

Though their schools degenerated, the ideals of the humanists have lasting values. To understand life and human problems for the sake of building a nobler world; to unite mankind by a common culture; and to free man's soul from fears, his intellect from ignorance, and his body from infirmities were ideals of lasting worth. And, with all their faults, the humanistic schools promoted an exact scholarship in the literary field that inspired directly the creation of scholarly works in the humanities and history, and, indirectly, in other fields.

Citizenship has become the right of all men and women in the advanced nations, and industrialization has demanded a new type of leadership and of service. While these changes have called for modification in the traditional conception and practices of a liberal education, there are some educators who still cling to the old classical tradition as if the rôle of the freeman citizen is still what it was in ages past. While industrial efficiency and technocracy have called for a new emphasis in education, we are not, as modern satirists would have the uncritical believe, moulding mere "monkeys minding machines." Science, technocracy, and democracy have not annihilated humanism. Many there are who feel that they have enlarged and enriched it. Technocracy, however, continues to pose a threat to it.

RISE OF REAL SCHOOLS AND ACADEMIES. (1) ORIGIN. An education stressing mere words and forms ignored the realities and needs of life. Men needed practical training for political office and for industrial and commercial life. By ignoring vernaculars and the sciences the Latin school did not keep pace with social progress. Criticisms of it, as we have seen, were numerous. There thus arose new schools stressing modern studies, such as the vernacular, modern languages, history, geography, and a long array of practical sciences. These first arose in France and Germany to prepare young gentlemen for courtly life.

(2) THE COURTLY ACADEMIES. The gentry of Europe, whose needs were stressed by men like Castiglione, Elyot, and Milton, sought what for them was a more realistic education than that pro-

vided by the classical schools. In the seventeenth century, many European noblemen employed private tutors for their children, and sent them to so-called "academies" to complete their education. These "academies" provided an education in the "accomplishments" proper to a gentleman of rank and had their origin in France, one of the most famous of the earliest ones being the Cardinal Richelieu Academy (1640). In 1638, the Oratorians, at the request of Louis XIII, opened a similar school, the Academie Royale, at Juilly. Horsemanship, training in arms, fortification, dancing, singing, music, drawing, mathematics, geography, physics, French, French history, and modern languages were the chief studies pursued in these schools.

Somewhat earlier, academies for nobles, *Ritterakademien*, were established in Germany under French influence. Many others were established there between 1650 and 1750. They came in answer to the demand of the German nobility for a courtly and military education. Because of the ascendancy of French culture at the time, French language, literature, and manners were given more attention than German culture in the *Ritterakademien*. In shaping their curriculum, Francke, the father of the *Realschule,* and the philosopher, Leibnitz, a strong advocate of scientific realism, were very influential.[79] Many modern languages and sciences were substituted in them for Latin and Greek. While some English parents were attracted by the courtly academies of France, schools of this type did not appear in England. This was due in part to the conservatism and power of the Anglican church in education and to the decline in influence of the aristocracy. English theorists, such as Elyot, Milton, and Locke, were, however, in accord with the general aristocratic and realistic goals of these schools for the gentry, and with their emphasis upon science and "modern" studies.

(3) THE DISSENTING ACADEMIES OF ENGLAND. If England had no "courtly academies" she had academies. These were established by Nonconformist educators when the laws forbade dissenters to teach in the established schools. Thus arose some sixty schools known as Dissenting Academies in which the sciences and modern studies were stressed. Their aim was to promote the realistic education recommended by Milton, Petty, Drury and other educational reformers. Some of them went beyond the level of instruction in the classical schools and might well be deemed of college rank. The earliest of these schools (1663-1690) were purely private, but later ones were often established and controlled by corporations.

[79] Adamson, *op. cit.,* pp. 178 ff.

While Latin and Greek were taught in them, modern studies, such as science, history, geography, and the modern languages, were given equal, if not greater, attention. One of them, Warrington Academy, where the scientist, Joseph Priestley, taught, had courses in law, medicine, and commerce. The goal of these schools was the preparation of the English middle class for life, business, and the professions. They were a protest against religious and educational orthodoxy and the unrealistic studies of the classical schools. In England, as elsewhere, religious dissent and the rise in influence of the middle class brought progress in education.

(4) THE GERMAN REALSCHULE. In Germany, the striving for a school preparing youths for real life culminated in the establishment of Hecker's *Realschule,* in Berlin, in 1747. That school embodied the spirit of science as man's servant in his economic struggle. Like the English academies, it was also the child of religious dissent, for its creators were Pietist dissenters from Lutheranism. Its forerunners were the *Pädagogium* established by the Pietist minister, Francke, at Halle, in 1696, and the Mathematical and Mechanical Real School, established by Semler, another Pietist, in 1706. Hecker, in his *Realschule,* aimed to prepare middle-class boys for practical pursuits. It was not a trade school. It provided instruction in writing, arithmetic, Latin, French, German, history, geography, drawing, geometry, mechanics, manufactures, economics, and architecture. It was the educational counterpart of the economic, social, religious, and intellectual changes of the sixteenth and seventeenth centuries, and it embodied much of the educational philosophy of which Bacon and Comenius were the leading representatives. It looked toward the encyclopedic goal of Comenius.

In their attempt to do too much, schools of the new type often did little well. They were the result of the economic, social, political, religious, and intellectual forces of the time, all of which, in a greater or less degree, helped to bring into education the new utilitarian purpose, the new inductive method, and the new curriculum which mark them off from the humanistic schools.

(5) THE RISE OF THE AMERICAN ACADEMY. While the academy became the American secondary school only after the Revolution, it had its beginning earlier. The view that Franklin's Philadelphia Academy, proposed in 1743 and 1749, and opened in 1750, was the first academy here is only partly correct. Certainly, many modern and practical subjects were taught, particularly by private schoolmasters, from about 1700 onward. Besides, regarding support and control, many post-Revolutionary academies show a long advance

toward the public high school beyond that of Franklin. While we shall look only at the Philadelphia Academy here, the social changes out of which it grew lie back of the whole academy movement.

The Philadelphia Academy, as were all our academies, was a product of our rapidly changing society. Back of it lie the Commercial Revolution and the rapid economic expansion of the New World; the rapid increase in our population and the emergence of a strong middle class; the growing heterogeneity of our population from the standpoints of national origins and religion; the spread of religious dissent and the breakdown of established churches and denominational exclusiveness; the growth of democracy which, in its earlier stages, was an aristocratic democracy; and the Enlightenment and scientific movement abroad, of the influence of which there is an abundance of strong circumstantial evidence.

(6) THE PHILADELPHIA ACADEMY. Franklin's school was not a town or a church Latin school, or a private school, or, when established, a college preparatory school. While designed especially for the racially and religiously heterogeneous population of Pennsylvania, all Americans were welcome to use it, if they could pay the tuition fees. It was, in a degree, a national institution designed to create unity among a people soon to become citizens of a new nation. In support, it was semi-public. In its control, its faculty and its students, it was nonsectarian from the start in practice and, after a struggle, in spirit. Its purposes, as stated by Franklin, were utilitarian from a social, professional, and vocational standpoint. He urged in his newspaper, the *Pennsylvania Gazette,* its establishment because "a proportion of men of learning is useful in every country" and because "those, who of late years come to settle among us, are chiefly foreigners, unacquainted with our language, laws and customs." The Germans were then the dreaded foreigners. Addressing the City Council of Philadelphia, Franklin stated the following as purposes of the Academy: (a) the education of civil officials in a country swarming with foreigners, and (b) the training of rural teachers. The latter remained a purpose of our academies throughout the nineteenth century. The original trustees defined the purpose in terms of social well-being and political unity, and one of them, Richard Peters, said the Academy would preserve civil and religious liberty. Franklin defined its purpose in terms, also, of the preparation of youths for useful living. He would have them taught the things that are "*most useful* and *most ornamental,*" attention being paid to their future vocations. Franklin said that the purpose of the English School was preparation for business and civil life.

As organized, the Academy had a Latin and English School, a teacher of mathematics being employed to teach apparently in both. A mathematical school emerged later. With the granting of a college charter (1755), the Latin School was combined with the college, the English and mathematical schools remaining as the Academy. In 1762, Provost Smith said that the boys in the Academy proper were preparing for "Merchandize, Trade, Navigation, and the Mechanic Professions." The English School, with its utilitarian goal, similar to that of our later high schools, was permitted by the trustees, during Franklin's long absence, to become but a shadow of its creator's ideal. As an old man, Franklin complained bitterly of that neglect of duty.

Developments in Higher Education

CHANGING AIM AND CURRICULUM. The universities, long strongholds of scholasticism, were eventually forced to give recognition to the classics. The humanists viewed the university education of their day as unsuited to a scholar or a gentleman. In the fourteenth century, Italian universities gave a place to the new liberal learning which princes, bankers, and even popes had come to approve. North of the Alps, the University of Paris, long the chief center of Catholic theology and mediaevalism, saw in the classics the seeds of heresy. That opposition was partly broken when, in 1530, King Francis I, under the influence of the French humanist, Budé, established chairs of Greek, Hebrew, and Latin in a new college of the University called the College of France.[80] French municipal governments in larger provincial cities also established higher classical schools approaching university rank. The value of the classics in religious and social reform being apparent to Protestant leaders and German princes, chairs of the classics were established, in the early sixteenth century, in the older German universities, and, later, in the new ones. Such reform of university instruction was among the lasting contributions of Melanchthon to education. Here, as in Italy and France, the princes played an important rôle in transforming the universities.[81] While a beginning appeared earlier in England, it was Henry VIII who was chiefly responsible for the reform of education in Oxford and Cambridge, but the opposition to the new learning was strong in both. A great impetus was given to classical scholarship at Cambridge by the lecturing there of Erasmus

[80] Woodward, *Studies in Education during the Age of the Renaissance,* pp. 127 ff.

[81] *Ibid.,* pp. 227 ff.

from 1510 to 1514. Oxford adopted the new studies enthusiastically in 1535. In that year, the king ordered all teachers in Cambridge to promote classical learning, Protestantism, and gentlemanly conduct. Such royal decrees did much to sweep away the mediaeval curriculum and provide something more suitable for the liberal education of the English "gentleman." The new curriculum, like the old one, became a required one for degrees. Indeed new courses, leading to degrees, and the practice of free election by students of courses and studies were practically unknown before the nineteenth century.

Thus, by the sixteenth century, the classics had a place in the arts program of the universities, although the old studies of theology, philosophy, law, and medicine continued to stand first in dignity. The theological struggle of the Reformation age brought, indeed, an increased emphasis upon the Bible, theology, philosophy, and moral philosophy. Philosophy and science remained in bondage to Aristotle and a few other ancients, such as Galen and Hippocrates in medicine, until the end of the seventeenth century.

The secularism that was now beginning to enter the universities made them less serviceable to the churches and to poorer boys, who were those chiefly attracted to the preaching profession. The great merchants and nobles who sent their sons to Oxford and Cambridge did not wish them to become preachers. A new aim, that of moulding the young "gentleman," thus came to mark universities, particularly Oxford and Cambridge. In Protestant lands, however, universities remained nurseries of the clergy and, consequently, some poor students were always found in them. American colleges and universities have always been a meeting place of rich and poor. The ideal of the "gentleman" found its way, however, into our colonial colleges, but our democratic ideal since the beginning of our national period has not been friendly to it.

THE UNIVERSITIES IN BONDAGE. Political and ecclesiastical tyranny robbed the universities, in post-Reformation days, of their earlier freedom from external control. Pre-Reformation universities, however, tried to control all thought by controlling the minds of the clergy who were then the chief moulders of thought. Post-Reformation Catholic governments required professors to take oaths of loyalty to the church and its dogmas. Censorship of books and lectures was so effective that heresies in Catholic universities were almost unknown. The Spanish Inquisition forbade the study of anatomy. The once powerful and free University of Paris fell a victim to religious fanaticism and Jesuit opposition. The French government imposed religious and intellectual orthodoxy upon its professors.

In 1624, the *Parlement* of Paris forbade, under penalty of death, any questioning of Aristotle. So conservative was the University forced to become that it refused to license the greatest scientific works of the time.

In Protestant states, a similar bondage was imposed upon universities. The state-supported University of Leyden was compelled to uphold the Reformed faith, and to accept Aristotle as the sole authority in philosophy. The law forbade even the mention of the name of Descartes, the rationalist, in the institution. In Lutheran Germany, the universities fell under the domination of the several states, which appointed and paid the professors, the church making its will felt through state action. The practice of having one university in each state, which state residents were required to attend, became so general that eighteen universities were established between 1500 and 1700. In all of them, Aristotelian intellectual tyranny and Lutheran orthodoxy were imposed upon faculties and students.

In England, Henry VIII and Edward VI recast the curriculum of Oxford and Cambridge in order to purge it of Roman Catholicism. Anglican orthodoxy was imposed upon professors and students by state law, as was, after 1640, the dogma of the divine right of kings.

Thus, everywhere in Europe political and ecclesiastical despotisms destroyed the freedom of universities. In chains, they could provide no light to guide men and societies to greater achievements. In medicine only could they experiment. Indeed, the universities offered little that would stimulate any youth to intellectual effort.[82] Toward the sciences they were as unfriendly as formerly they had been toward the classics. Except in medicine, research was practically unknown in them. For science study, they lacked laboratory equipment. A few astronomical instruments, and terrestrial and celestial globes comprised the scientific interests of most of them before 1700. Academic tradition and the disciplinary theory of education were largely responsible for their opposition to science as, in later times, to other innovations in the curriculum.

In the eighteenth century, the universities drifted toward rationalism and further secularism, and governments began to challenge the right of churches to dominate human minds. First in Germany, the universities ceased to be theological seminaries. There, royal patronage lent new dignity to the professoriate which, freed from church domination, began to stress research and new intellectual adventure. The University of Halle was the first center of an intellectual revolt, led by Thomasius, the rationalist, and Francke, the

[82] Smith, *A History of Modern Culture,* I, 344.

Pietist. Here, original research, even in theology, and free from the bondage of authority, was substituted for bookish intellectualism. The search for new truth was substituted for the worship of old errors, and a principle of academic freedom was defended in theory and respected in practice. But Halle was Pietist and, therefore, in a degree, propagandist. Freedom of research and teaching became even more complete at the University of Göttingen, chartered in 1734 by the state of Hanover. Here, German was exclusively the language of instruction and, as at Halle, science was stressed as much as literature. In the later eighteenth century, higher technical schools, such as the Collegium Carolinum of Brunswick, were established in Germany to prepare youths for the new professions like that of engineering. All these developments were largely due to the demands of the merchant middle class, and reflected the utilitarian educational needs of that class and the new rationalism and scientific intellectualism of the time.

Outside of Germany, university progress continued to be checked by church and state and by the heavy hand of tradition. Scotland was a notable exception, however. There, the universities from 1740 onward offered instruction in many utilitarian studies. In Italy, Spain, France, and England, universities were custodians of official orthodoxies. Oxford and Cambridge excluded all non-Anglicans. Puritanism, however, attained a foothold, especially in Cambridge. In both, the aristocracy enjoyed most of the privileges. All Souls College, Oxford, required only that its Fellows be *optime nati, bene vestiti, mediocriter docti* (excellently born, well dressed, and moderately educated).

THE RISE OF AMERICAN COLLEGES. In the New World, imperial Spain founded the first universities: in 1551, in Peru; in 1551, in Mexico; in 1619, in Chile; in 1622, in Argentina; in 1624, in Bolivia. Latin America had twelve universities and many classical secondary schools, most of them in charge of Catholic religious societies, before the English colonies in North America had established a single higher institution of learning. In the English colonies, Harvard College, founded by the Puritans, in 1636, was the first higher institution. To advance and perpetuate learning, to supply the Puritan pulpits with learned ministers and the colony with teachers and magistrates were the chief motives for its establishment. Church and state participated in its control,[83] and its support came from public and private sources. To promote learning and maintain poor students, every family was asked by the General Court, in 1644, to

[83] *Records of the Governor and Company of the Massachusetts Bay in New England,* II, 30.

contribute a peck of corn or a shilling to the college.[84] In 1642, the admission requirements were a mature knowledge of Latin and an elementary knowledge of Greek; and the requirements for degrees were: for the B.A., good character and the ability to read "the Originalls of the Old and New Testament in the Latin tongue, and to resolve them Logically"; and for the M.A., the writing of "a System . . . of Logick, Natural and Morall Phylosophy, Arithmetick, Geometry and Astronomy," and a defense of "the Theses or positions," plus a "godly life and conversation." Established to meet the civil and religious needs of New England, Harvard, in its earlier years, was the cradle of Puritan theological orthodoxy. It was a college, after the fashion of European university colleges, and not a university.

Elsewhere in the colonies, other denominational colleges arose: in Virginia, the Anglican College of William and Mary (1693); in Connecticut, the Congregationalist Yale College (1701); in New Jersey, the Presbyterian Princeton College (1746); in New York, the Anglican King's College (1754); in Rhode Island, the Baptist Brown College (1764); in New Hampshire, the Congregationalist Dartmouth (1769); and in New Jersey, the Dutch Reformed Rutgers College (1770).

With the sole exception of the College of Philadelphia, chartered in 1755, though a college since 1752, all our pre-Revolution colleges were denominational in control and, almost entirely, in spirit, though that spirit was weakening here and there. Yale was established as a protest against the impiety and, what Cotton Mather called, the "foolosophy" that had begun to taint Harvard. Franklin's College of Philadelphia was the only college in the colonies whose control was nonsectarian.

Theology and the classics were the core of our colonial college curriculum. Around these were grouped logic, rhetoric, ethics, politics, arithmetic, geometry, astronomy, and, occasionally, Hebrew. Here we have the mediaeval liberal arts, modified by Aristotelianism, humanism, and the Reformation. Truth in colonial America meant divine truth, and knowledge without God was not deemed to be knowledge. In King's College, and still more in the College of Philadelphia, the spirit of rationalism and secularism invaded our higher institutions. The course proposed for the Philadelphia College, in 1756, comprised Latin, Greek, mathematics (including trigonometry, conic sections, and fluxions), logic, rhetoric, metaphysics, botany, zoology, physics, astronomy, and French. That represents a recognition of the new scientific elements in culture and

[84] *Ibid.*, p. 86.

of some of the needs of our changing civilization. It is at least worthy of note that the trustees of the College of Philadelphia communicated with the authorities at Halle and received from them their plan of education.

Everywhere in Europe and America universities and their colleges possessed the faith that they were the guardians of truth, and that the highest truths are attainable only by theological and philosophical speculation. Likewise, a common interest in man and his institutions, a bequest of humanism, characterized all universities. As our period closed, science and rationalism were beginning to transform the older notion of truth, and the universities were beginning to admit the new scientific intellectualism which was destined, for a time, to preserve their common character. The changing world of the nineteenth and twentieth centuries has, at last, destroyed the unity of purpose and of knowledge which long marked the universities of the world.

Post-elementary Education for Girls

The expansion of the middle class and its increasing wealth brought a demand, particularly from 1700 onward, for an education in the "accomplishments" for girls. The daughters of aristocrats had long been in receipt of their "dowry of education," characterized by much of the "polite" and a modicum of the "solid" studies. It was provided as a rule by tutors. Practice, no doubt, fell short of the theory of the humanists. The daughters of the new rich and near-rich soon began to seek their dowry of education. In the eighteenth century a host of writers, both men and women, pleaded the cause of women's educational rights. Among them was Benjamin Rush, of Philadelphia, whose views represent an advanced position near the close of the century. Franklin, earlier, had written on the question, and stood for an instruction for girls in French, music, religion, morals, and the domestic duties of women. Rush would adapt their education to "the state of society, manners, and government of the country in which it is conducted," [85] and he recommended for them a fairly full program, for the time, of liberal and useful studies.

Among European theorists, Fénelon (1651-1715) took an advanced position. A Catholic archbishop, born of the nobility, he strove to win back French Huguenots to Catholicism by attracting their girls to Catholic schools under his supervision. His treatise *On the Education of Girls* reveals his rather conservative views on the question. Women, because they are excluded from public and

[85] *Essays, Literary, Moral and Philosophical* (Philadelphia, 1798), p. 75.

ecclesiastical offices have, he held, no need for learning in politics, law, philosophy and theology. Their sphere is the home and their education should be directed to the duties of the household. He saw women as frivolous and empty-headed, but he saw education as a way to correct those supposed defects of nature. He would limit their instruction to reading, writing, arithmetic, painting, music, home management and religion. He advocated, also, reform in the methods of instruction for both boys and girls, and was one of the most forceful early advocates of the use of play in teaching young children. Fénelon was, however, in advance of his European contemporaries in his views on women's ability and influence. When he wrote, the dominant view was that women were mentally inferior beings capable of playing a most insignificant rôle in human affairs.

The forces of rationalism and, then, of democracy led to a questioning of traditional conceptions regarding woman's ability, social sphere and her education. It is not easy to appraise accurately the influence of pioneer America upon the status of women here and abroad. In the economic struggle in colonial times, women demonstrated their worth, and acquired the respect of men and a degree of freedom greater than their European sisters enjoyed. The forces at work in the revolutionary period brought some animated protests from women against the disabilities imposed upon them. Priscilla Mason, a student at the Philadelphia Female Academy, addressing the commencement audience in 1793, said: "Our high and mighty Lords . . . have denied us the means of knowledge, and then reproached us for the want of it. . . . The Church, the Bar, and the Senate are shut against us. Who shut them? *Man.* . . . But Paul forbids it! Contemptible little body! The girls laughed at the deformed creature. To be revenged, he declared war against the whole sex: advises men not to marry them; and has the insolence to order them to keep silence in the Church—: afraid, I suppose, that they would say something against celibacy, or ridicule the old bachelor." [86]

In practice, but few girls received an education beyond the rudiments prior to the nineteenth century, and practice was confined usually to instruction in religion, morals, domestic arts, and the "accomplishments." Singing, instrumental music, dancing and such arts as embroidering stool cushions with puppy dogs, and decorating mirrors with humming birds, had a prominent place in their education. Proprietary schools, found usually in cities, gave

[86] J. Mulhern, *A History of Secondary Education in Pennsylvania* (Lancaster, Pa.: Science Press, Inc., 1933), p. 389.

them a chance to study "solid" subjects. Other schools, mostly under church influence, clung to the "orthodox" training of girls. Catholic nunnery schools, sepulchral in atmosphere, stressed religious and moral training. The Quakers and Moravians were the most liberal of the sects in providing a broader and useful curriculum for girls. Universities and colleges had not yet begun even to dream of the female specter within their halls. Until the nineteenth century, girls' education bore the mark of Kingsley's familiar view of the ideal woman:

> Be good, sweet maid, and let who will be clever;
> Do noble things, not dream them, all day long;
> And so make life, death, and that vast forever
> One grand, sweet song.

By 1800, a secondary school, usually called in America the "female seminary," had appeared. It was for girls what the academy was for boys, and furnished the steppingstone to the women's college of the nineteenth century.

Teachers

From ancient Greek until quite recent times the requirements for teaching were stated in terms of moral and religious character and mastery of subject matter. The faith and morals of the teacher and his loyalty to state or church were viewed as his most important qualifications. He found himself at various times the servant of masters who required him to develop in youth the type of character they desired. These masters were never entirely indifferent to the practical demands of life, and, therefore, looked to teachers to instruct youth in a variety of studies. Pedagogical training in the professional sense was, however, a late historical arrival, although theorists from the days of Socrates were not unaware of the importance of pedagogical experience and skill in teaching. Many ancient writers, such as Socrates, Cicero and Quintilian, particularly the last, enriched the profession with a wealth of pedagogical thought. Erasmus, Montaigne, Locke, Comenius, Vives, Elyot, to mention but a few, built upon the foundation laid by these earlier Western theorists.

Many of the criticisms of the schools from the fourteenth century onward were directed at the teacher. Vives complains that many of the teachers of his day were drunkards, criminals, or worthless men, while some became teachers as a steppingstone to a more honored profession.[87] If this was true of the schools of the upper classes, with which Vives was concerned, how much worse must conditions have been in the schools of the poor? What Vives says could scarcely hold true for such teachers as those of the Brethren of the Common Life. Elyot and Erasmus complained of the ignorance and brutality of the teachers of their day and, with Vives, complained of the meager stipends paid them.[88] The need for properly qualified teachers was increasingly felt in Europe from the Renaissance onward. The Jesuits started a teacher-training plan in 1599, but they had no special training school. La Salle's Normal School at Rheims (1684) was probably the first such school in the world.

In colonial America, the most important qualification of the teacher was religious orthodoxy. The elementary teacher was, however, required to be able to read and write and maintain discipline. Secondary teachers were usually well educated. Until 1712, when the selectmen of the towns took over the function, Massachusetts ministers approved the teachers. Connecticut, in 1742, required that teachers be licensed by the General Assembly. Earlier even than this, the Provincial Council of Philadelphia, which had appointed Enoch Flower as teacher in 1683, rebuked (1693) Thomas Meaking, a teacher in the Friends' Public School for teaching without a license.[89] Generally, colonial teachers were required to hold licenses from colonial governments or from church authorities. The Bishop of London was the licensing authority in Anglican colonies. The practice of licensing teachers originated with Roman emperors, was continued by the mediaeval church, and gradually became in modern times a function of the state.

With the probable exception of the Quakers, who trained some teachers by the apprenticeship method in "the Art, Trade and Mystery of a School Master,"[90] there was no systematic plan of training teachers in colonial days. Franklin was the first one to propose that teacher training be made a purpose of an American school. He would have the Philadelphia Academy educate "a number of the poorer sort" to be schoolmasters in rural areas where the teachers were, he said, frequently "vicious imported Servants, or concealed Papists."[91] The Academy, however, did not achieve that purpose, but later academies did. With the rise of universal education, as

[87] Woodward, *Studies in Education during the Age of the Renaissance,* pp. 190 f.

[88] *Ibid.,* pp. 290 f.

[89] Mulhern, *op. cit.,* p. 28.

[90] *Ibid.,* p. 50.

[91] *Ibid.,* p. 187.

an adjunct of national states, teacher training, often in special schools, became, as we shall see later, an important feature of national school systems.

Selected Readings

Adamson, J. W. *Pioneers of Modern Education.* London: Cambridge University Press, 1905.

Brinsley, J. *Ludus Literarius or the Grammar Schoole.* London: Constable & Co., Ltd., 1917.

Eby, F. *Early Protestant Educators.* New York: McGraw-Hill Book Co., Inc., 1931.

Elsbree, W. S. *The American Teacher.* New York: American Book Co., 1939.

Fénelon, F. *On the Education of Girls.* (Trans. K. Lupton.) Boston: Ginn & Co., 1891.

Fitzpatrick, E. A. *La Salle, Patron of All Teachers.* Milwaukee: The Bruce Publishing Co., 1951.

———. *Saint Ignatius and the Ratio Studiorum.* New York: McGraw-Hill Book Co., Inc., 1933.

Hyma, A. *The Brethren of the Common Life.* Grand Rapids, Mich.: William B. Eerdmans Publishing Co., 1950.

Keatinge, M. W. *Comenius.* New York: McGraw-Hill Book Co., Inc., 1931.

———. *The Great Didactic of John Amos Comenius.* London: Adam & Charles Black, 1896.

Laurie, S. S. *Studies in the History of Educational Opinion from the Renaissance.* London: Cambridge University Press, 1903.

Leach, A. F. *English Schools of the Reformation.* Westminster: Constable & Co., Ltd., 1896.

Locke, J. *Conduct of the Understanding.* Oxford: Clarendon Press, 1901.

———. *Some Thoughts concerning Education.* London: Cambridge University Press, 1913.

Milton, J. *Tractate of Education.* New York: The Macmillan Co., 1895.

Montaigne, M. E. de. *The Education of Children.* (Trans. L. E. Rector.) New York: Appleton-Century-Crofts, Inc., 1899.

Painter, F. V. N. *Luther on Education.* St. Louis, Mo.: Concordia Publishing House, 1928.

Robbins, C. L. *Teachers in Germany in the Sixteenth Century.* New York: Teachers College, Columbia University, 1912.

Stowe, A. M. *English Grammar Schools in the Reign of Queen Elizabeth.* New York: Teachers College, Columbia University, 1908.

Swickerath, R. *Jesuit Education: Its History and Principles in the Light of Modern Educational Problems.* St. Louis: Herder, 1904.

Watson, F. *The English Grammar Schools to 1660.* London: Cambridge University Press, 1908.

Wood, N. *The Reformation and English Education.* London: Routledge & Kegan Paul, Ltd., 1931.

Woodward, W. H. *Vittorino da Feltre and Other Humanist Educators.* London: Cambridge University Press, 1912.

Woody, T. *Fürstenschulen in Germany after the Reformation.* Menasha, Wis.: George Banta Publishing Co., 1920.

———. *A History of Women's Education in the United States.* 2 vols.; Lancaster, Pa.: Science Press, Inc., 1929.

———. *Liberal Education for Free Men.* Philadelphia: University of Pennsylvania Press, 1951.

Part IV

SOCIAL AND EDUCATIONAL CHANGE FROM THE FRENCH REVOLUTION UNTIL RECENT TIMES

9 Social Change Between the French Revolution and the Early Twentieth Century

Prior to the American and French revolutions, great changes had occurred in Western society. Geographical discovery and commerce had created a middle class hostile to the old feudal nobility. Exclusive trade privileges enjoyed by great merchants restricted the freedom of others. Trade had been nationalized, and mercantilism prevailed. The religious unity of Christendom had been destroyed. Great nations and colonial empires, ruled by "absolute monarchs," had arisen. An intellectual revolt, rooted chiefly in science, had occurred, and interest was drifting rapidly from theology and philosophy to the natural and social sciences, the conviction that society itself is governed by natural law growing constantly stronger. Glaring social injustice had brought a demand for sweeping social reform. In reason and science the faith of the intelligentsia had come to center. From the "golden ages" of the past, minds were turning to the "golden age" of the future when the ideal society, a gift of science, would appear. The foundations of the modern world were thus being laid. Science and democracy, and their allies, naturalism, nationalism, and the Industrial Revolution, have been the most potent forces in the building of the modern world.

The Rise of Political Liberalism

THE WORLD IN REVOLT. The late eighteenth century witnessed the dawn of a new era. In America and France, the middle class revolted successfully against the old tyranny. A bloodless revolution had accomplished a somewhat similar purpose in England, although the English masses were denied political rights until the late nineteenth century. The principles embodied in the English Bill of Rights, accepted by William of Orange in 1689, were: (a) the sovereignty of the nation, (b) the omnipotence of Parliament, and (c) the supremacy of law. Parliament was not, however, a truly popular body until 1867, and its own disregard for the liberties of the American colonists brought the Revolution and the rise of the American nation.

THE REVOLUTIONARY ENVIRONMENT. (1) ECONOMIC ASPECTS. The governments of Europe long pursued the economic policy known as mercantilism in order to increase the gold and silver holdings of their nations. To that end, they restricted trade by putting high taxes upon manufactured imports and low taxes upon imported foods and raw materials. They encouraged home manufactures and hindered those of their colonies. Thus, the American colonies were forbidden to manufacture any article which England could manufacture, and they were required to buy all their imports in England and to export many of their products to England alone. In these restrictions lay the basic cause of the Revolution. While the principle of civil and religious liberty was found useful in stirring up revolutionary ardor, the struggle in America was basically one against the practice of taxation without representation, against restrictions upon freedom of trade, and against the whole mercantile system of economics. It was a bourgeois revolt against privilege.

In France, the pre-Revolution economy was essentially feudal. The king, nobles, and church owned each one-fifth of the land while the cities and peasants owned, or had the use of, the other two-fifths. The peasants and bourgeoisie supported the unproductive royalty, nobility, and clergy. The feudal aristocracy, including the higher clergy, lived luxuriously at the expense of the toilers whom they taxed almost to starvation. In the French cities of 1789 lived, by commerce, 2,000,000 people, or about one-tenth of the national population. In Paris, particularly, many merchants had become very rich through their control of industrial gilds, or through foreign trade, or speculation in grain under government protection. Legal or *de facto* monopolies existed in many commercial fields, and restricted freedom of trade for the great mass of the merchant class. Wars and royal extravagance had brought France to the verge of financial ruin. She had struggled with England for colonial empire and world mastery, and she had lost, to the alarm of her bourgeoisie. But the whole internal economic system was unjust. The nobility and clergy were exempt from many heavy taxes which the poor had to pay. The privileged few enjoyed many exclusive rights in land, game, property revenues, and commerce, while the masses had few rights but many heavy duties. Many pre-Revolution lists of grievances (*cahiers*) were protests against such injustices. The social reformer, Turgot (1727-1781), Louis XVI's Minister of Finance, established free trade in grain and abolished many private monopolies, but the privileged groups thwarted his designs, thus hastening the Revolution, for the Third Estate eventually saw no other course open.

(2) Social Aspects. As we have seen, the Commercial Revolution created a middle class whose wealth and power steadily increased. Except for less than a dozen noblemen, the North American colonists were drawn from the European middle and lower classes, a fact highly significant in the growth of American democracy. Our colonial aristocracy was one of wealth, not of birth, and colonial fortunes were modest as compared with those of the European aristocracy. The superabundance of unoccupied land and the growing industry and trade of the colonies produced a rapidly increasing middle class, owning property in varying amounts from small holdings to fairly large estates and fortunes. Colonial society extended downward from greater landowners and traders through smaller farmers and shopkeepers, free artisans, indentured servants, and redemptioners to chattel slaves, and the social boundaries separating these groups were fairly clearly marked. The upper two classes, bourgeois, capitalist, and practical in ideals, directed American destinies in the revolutionary and early national period. Economic, social, political, and religious differences marked the several colonies, but the threat to their common economic interests soon welded them into a unity strong enough to overthrow the old tyranny.

French society, following the economic order, was composed of a hierarchy of classes. At its base stood the unemployed rabble, many of them criminals by necessity. Above these stood the laboring class—peasants, servants, apprentices, journeymen, and unskilled laborers. To these two classes belonged three-fourths of the total population. Above them stood: (a) the lower middle class—small merchants, lower ecclesiastics, poor nobles, and prosperous peasants; (b) the upper middle class—professionals, civil officials, great merchants and manufacturers; and (c) the upper class—the royal family, the nobility and great ecclesiastics, numbering less than 500,000 out of a population of 20,000,000. Privilege and underprivilege, power and helplessness, wealth and poverty marked, in glaring contrasts, the society of France. Discontent was widespread, as many historical records indicate. The *philosophes* attacked privilege in church and state, the oppression of the masses, the occupational and professional restrictions imposed upon men and classes, and the enforcement of religious orthodoxy. In the Revolution, the Third Estate, the bourgeoisie, directed events, proclaimed the Declaration of Rights, and drafted the first French constitution. Sieyès, a conservative revolutionary, asserted, in 1789, that the bourgeoisie, among which he included all laborers, performed all the necessary work of the nation. He wrote: "If the privileged order should be abolished, the nation would be nothing less, but something more. Therefore, what is the Third Estate? Everything; but an everything shackled and oppressed. What would it be without the privileged order? Everything, but an everything free and flourishing. Nothing can succeed without it, everything would be infinitely better without the others. . . . The Third Estate embraces then all that which belongs to the nation; and all that which is not the Third Estate cannot be regarded as being of the nation. What is the Third Estate? It is the whole."[1]

(3) Political Aspects. In an earlier chapter, we have noted the despotism of kings prior to the republican era. In spite of growing liberalism in England, reactionary forces were at work. The Tories clung to the dogma of the divine right of kings, while the Whigs upheld the idea of popular sovereignty. Under the Tory Government of George III, there was no actual nullification of the Bill of Rights in England, but the king ruled the colonies according to the principle of absolute autocracy, thus provoking the Revolution which resulted in the establishment of the American republic. Thomas Paine and other revolutionary leaders, including James Otis, Patrick Henry, John Dickinson, and Thomas Jefferson, opposed the Tory rule of the colonies on the political ground, among others, that it denied the colonists the constitutional liberties of Englishmen. The stubborn denial of British liberties to the colonists brought the demand for independence. Politically, the Revolution was a struggle for the "rights of man," that of freedom from political oppression being one of his fundamental rights. Liberty and equality became the catchwords of the Revolution, but liberty was the strongest idea-force in the movement.

In France, also, the political issue loomed large. French monarchical despotism had been more wickedly intolerable than elsewhere in Europe. Fénelon, Montesquieu, Voltaire, Rousseau, and many other individuals attacked the evils of the old régime. The "protests" of eighteenth-century *parlements*, or provincial law

[1] O. J. Thatcher (ed.), *The Library of Original Sources* (Milwaukee: University Research Extension Co., 1907), VII, 397–98.

courts, attacked monarchical autocracy and urged the equality of their own power with that of the king as well as the idea that supremacy resides in the nation. Similarly the *cahiers* of the clergy, nobility, and commoners attacked royal despotism. Thus the demand for political reform in France was widespread.

(4) Religious Aspects. The revolutionary spirit of the eighteenth century was anti-clerical. The world had grown tired of ecclesiastical privilege, dogmas, superstitions, and religious intolerance and strife. The nations, generally, had their established churches, dissenters from which were, at most, but grudgingly tolerated. Thus the Anglican was the legal church of England; the Roman Catholic, of France. The American colonies, with a few exceptions, had their established churches. Everywhere these privileged churches tried to use the power of the state to enforce upon all their "orthodox" beliefs. Dissenters were compelled to support these churches in the same way as were conformists. Worse still, they were frequently persecuted, expelled from the state, or forced to conform. The American colonies witnessed sectarian strife. Anglican divines denounced dissenters, and dissenters hated Anglicanism and feared its representatives, who sought to introduce into America the episcopal system of England. Fear of Anglicanism helped to create enthusiasm for the cause of independence. Prosperity and opportunity hastened the secularization of the colonial mind, while witch-hunting, in Massachusetts, and the cupidity of Anglican clergy, in Virginia, among other causes, resulted in a questioning of clerical leadership and a weakening of clerical influence. Though never so marked as in France, American anti-clericalism thwarted the designs of established churches and prevented the Anglican church from dominating religious life in the colonies. With the revolutionary demand in Europe and America for civil liberty went the demand also for religious liberty for the individual citizen. Thomas Paine considered "the free exercise of religion, according to conscience" the most important of all liberties.

In France, Protestantism never secured a firm foothold and, after the revocation of the Edict of Nantes (1685), the Catholic religion alone was recognized by the government. The church, allied to the state, was rich and powerful. The king appointed the bishops, nearly all of them being of noble rank. The lower clergy, drawn mostly from lower bourgeois stock, had but little voice in shaping church policy. The bishops upheld the king in his most vicious acts, and lived as luxuriously as the lay nobility.

The church was attacked not only for financial reasons but still more because it restricted religious liberty, persecuted heretics, stifled freedom of thought and speech, tampered with purely secular affairs, demanded privileges denied to the laity, and claimed a power superior to that of the state. The grievances against the church may be gleaned from Voltaire's *Law* (1764) and from the *cahiers* of the Third Estate. "The Civil Constitution of the Clergy" adopted by the revolutionary National Assembly, in 1790, reflects the mind of the bourgeoisie, on church reform. It required the election of bishops and priests by the vote of all citizens, Catholic and non-Catholic, and that their salaries be fixed and paid by the state. It further required that papal authority be restricted to matters of religious belief. Most of the legislators felt that priests should teach not dogmas but practical morals as a basis of citizenship, and that, therefore, non-Catholics ought to have a voice in their appointment. Only one-third of the priests and only seven of the 138 bishops took the required oath of allegience to this "Constitution." This and other laws of the Assembly indicate the nature of popular discontent with the church. The bourgeoisie, in power, would prevent the church from injuring the nation in its own interest. They would abolish religious distinctions between citizens; they would grant freedom of conscience to all and would prohibit the exercise of arbitrary authority over the human mind; they would make the church the servant, not the master, of the state; and they would not permit the state to perpetrate atrocities, such as the burning of heretics, at the behest of the church. The new secular bourgeois liberalism was thus challenging the liberty of the church to dominate the lives of citizens.

(5) Intellectual Aspects. Political change is a reflection of economic, social, and intellectual change. Prior to the French Revolution, a significant intellectual revolt had occurred. Though partly of ancient origin, it was rooted mainly in science. Old beliefs were challenged, and an optimistic secularism was substituted by the new Sophists for a gloomy supernaturalism. Reason was made the final authority in all matters, and written authority was rejected. The new philosophers sought absolute truth (the existence of which they did not question) not in the Bible or the classics but in nature's laws as revealed by science, then the new revelation. But that was not all. Philosophy they subordinated to science, and theology to history. History, it was found, furnished significant facts about man and society. The new intellectualism spread quickly among the upper bourgeoisie, but the unenlightened masses did not share in it, perhaps fortunately, for mass emotionalism, when aroused, can destroy the spirit of intellectual adventure. The period was rich in social theory.

ECONOMIC THEORY. It is unpleasant for rich men to reason about their wealth, but sometimes they are compelled to do so. Seventeenth-century theorists, generally, defended mercantilism, although Locke and a few others dissented from that view. Locke's theory that labor is the basis of property and property rights was further developed by the French physiocrats, in the eighteenth century, who held that soil is the source of wealth; and labor, of property. They advocated a laissez-faire policy of government in trade affairs, thus representing the demands of the bourgeoisie, although a few of them, anticipating socialist and communist demands, wrote in the interest of the proletariat.[2] Goldsmith bewailed governmental neglect of the masses, whom he saw

> Forced from their homes, a melancholy train
> To traverse climes beyond the Western main.

In *The Deserted Village* he wrote:

> Ill fares the land, to hast'ning ills a prey
> Where wealth accumulates and men decay.

The theory of free trade was rapidly accepted in England after the publication of Hume's *Political Essays* in 1752. There, Adam Smith gave final expression to this economic theory in his *Wealth of Nations* (1776). Holding that labor and natural resources are the basis of wealth, he opposed government interference with man's freedom to labor. While in matters of education and national defense the government, said he, may interfere, in economic matters it ought to abolish all obstacles to free competition between individuals. Had he written twenty years earlier, the American Revolution might have been averted.

POLITICAL THEORY. (1) INTELLECTUAL SETTING. The new worldly intellectualism embodied the belief that man and society, like inanimate nature, are governed by scientific laws, which can be discovered by the method employed by physical scientists. History, politics, psychology, education, ethics, religion, and all other social studies were soon to be viewed as sciences embodying natural law. The first aim of the revolutionary intellectuals was to harmonize society with reason as grounded upon accurate knowledge of facts. Back of this practical social-reform aim lay an almost religious belief in the natural goodness (not the Biblical depravity) of man, the perfectability of human nature and the inevitability of progress, beliefs that must be kept in mind by anyone who would understand the spirit of the new intellectualism.

[2] P. Smith, *A History of Modern Culture* (New York: Henry Holt & Co., Inc., 1930–34), II, 218–19.

Believing the individual to be the instrument of progress and of social reform, the revolutionary philosophers demanded freedom of thought and speech, so that truth might not be stifled; the rationalizing of religion and the substitution of natural religion for Christianity; the secularization of morals; and the humanizing of law. In politics, many of them preferred an enlightened despotism to democracy, but, while conservative, they prepared the way for the arch-reformer of the time, one who trusted the heart as man's guide and distrusted the intellect, who trusted nature and distrusted science, and whose faith in the worth of the individual and goodness of common men was such that he would bring government into harmony with their will. That man was Rousseau (1712-1778). In him the political spirit of the time reached its maturity and, through his voice, it spoke in prophecy of a new era approaching its dawn.

(2) ROUSSEAU'S POLITICAL FORERUNNERS. Rousseau would establish a society in harmony with nature, that is, a society, as he finally viewed it, in which government exists by the consent of the governed. The idea was not new. Athenian citizens had such a government. Capitalism, the source of modern republicanism, and its ally, Calvinism, had already created republican states. Thus the Mayflower Compact and the Fundamental Orders of Connecticut were freemen's contracts that embodied republican ideas. A Puritan republic was established in England under Cromwell; and Puritans, like Milton, espoused the cause of liberty, though others felt that Puritan liberty was a tyranny. The idea that political despotism is natural and rooted in a social compact was advanced by Thomas Hobbes (1586-1679) in his *Leviathan,* and he justified despotism on that ground, as Rousseau later justified the democratic state on the same ground. Search for a universal law of nature, underlying human conduct everywhere and superior to the laws of separate states, is as old as the Stoics. That idea was embodied in the Roman *jus gentium,* and later in the Christian "Law of God." The idea, modified by circumstances of time and place, survived. Seventeenth- and eighteenth-century political philosophers, influenced mainly by science, turned to nature as a justification of existing governments, or as a basis of ideal government.

The view that government arose by a social contract, designed to protect life and property, had thus influential advocates, among them Hobbes and Locke. Locke asserted that the motive for the social contract and the surrender of some of our liberties to government was, and is, the protection of property. Liberty, property, and labor are, he held, natural rights which no one can surrender, and labor gives a man a moral right to property. In America, John Wise (1652-1725) taught that, by nature, all men are free and equal and that the people are the source of civil power. Franklin, however, was the most influential defender of the social-contract theory in colonial America. In France, the principle of popular liberty was eloquently sponsored by Montesquieu. All of these, and others, were forerunners of Rousseau.

(3) Rousseau and Society-According-to-Nature. In his *Social Contract* (1762), Rousseau wrote that, by a contract, men renounced certain liberties they enjoyed as savages but gained, in return, civil liberty and the right to private property. Born free and equal, men surrender their natural liberties only for their own good. Prior to the contract, each was the sole defender of his natural liberty; after the contract, the whole community defended his civil liberty and his ownership of property. A clash of individual interests made the contract necessary, but individuals accepted it voluntarily. That contract, embodying the collective general will, is the basis of sovereignty, and popular consent is the basis of true, natural government. Every act of government must be in accord with that general will, for government holds its power by contract with the people. The only law, however, which must have unanimous consent is the social contract itself, the consent of the majority being sufficient in other cases. The government must treat all individuals exactly alike for no individual or class has a right to special privileges.

Having discussed civil liberty, Rousseau went on to define equality. It meant, he said, that no one should have enough power to become violent nor enough wealth to buy another; nor should anyone be so poor as to be forced to sell himself. Within these limits there would be degrees of wealth and power. Politically, however, all men are equal by the social contract. The perfect democracy is the ideal to be sought, although difficult to attain. "Were there a nation of gods, they would doubtless have a democratic government. Such a perfect system is, however, beyond the reach of men." [3]

(4) Naturalism. Allied to the whole democratic movement was the conviction that nature is good, and that social ills arise from man's ignorance of nature or his refusal to conform with it. Interest in the natural way of life was intensified, in the eighteenth century, by the accounts of travelers who depicted savage life as

[3] J. J. Rousseau, *Social Contract* (trans. the author; Paris: Garnier Frères, n.d.), Bk. III, chap iv.

natural, noble, innocent, and carefree. In contrast with the "noble savage" civilized man was depicted as vicious and irrational. Others found the ideal life in the Orient and made, for a time, the Chinese sage a rival of the "noble savage" as a philosopher of life. The revolt against civilization in favor of natural living reached its height in the earlier writings of Rousseau. In an essay written in 1750, he advanced the view that the arts and sciences had demoralized mankind. Science, he said, was a curse, and civilized man's legion of vices has resulted from his abandonment of his original "happy state of ignorance." That earlier view, Rousseau modified considerably in his *Social Contract.*

(a) Naturalism and the doctrine of equality. In his essay on "The Origin of Inequality," Rousseau deduced, from supposed principles of nature, a notion of equality, which he later modified. In it, he opposed the natural man to the civilized man. Self-preservation and compassion for his fellows are man's primary natural urges. A study of man's nature would, he said, reveal the permanent natural foundations upon which society should rest. Although nature created some inequalities, as in health and strength, social inequalities are man-made and unjust. While, in this essay (1754), he condemned private property as the basis of all social inequalities, in the *Social Contract* (1762) he approved it as essential to equality. Monarchical despotism he denounced, as he did later in the *Social Contract,* on the ground that no man can alienate his natural rights to life and liberty. Property and other acquired rights he may transfer, but he cannot surrender his natural rights. Governmental usurpation of men's natural rights has been a fruitful cause of social inequalities and corruption. In contrast with the primitive state, "the real youth of the world," in which "men were meant to remain," we have, said Rousseau, the civilized state in which men are slaves. The naturalism of the early democratic era, of which Rousseau was but one of many voices, expressed itself politically in a quest for the natural and inalienable rights of man, as the revolutionary documents of France and America reveal.

(b) Naturalism in literature. The spirit of an age finds its way into literature, and naturalism found expression in the literature of the republican era. Rousseau said that cities are the graves of humankind, and Byron caught that spirit in the lines:

> I live not in myself, but I become
> Portion of that around me; and to me
> High mountains are a feeling, but the hum
> Of human cities torture.

In Wordsworth, among English poets, the naturalistic spirit reached its height. Of the French Revolution he wrote:

> Bliss was it in that dawn to be alive,
> But to be young was very heaven.

For him, the Revolution was the beginning of a better social order and, like Rousseau, he regretted the calamity of civilization in which man alone, of all living things, knows no hope or joy. Unlike Milton, who sang of gods and angels and of "knights and barons bold," Wordsworth sang of simple, natural people like Lucy Gray, Simon Lee, and the Solitary Reaper. Like Rousseau, his sympathy extended to all feeling things, and he besought us "never to blend our pleasure or our pride with sorrow of the meanest thing that feels."

Beyond the lake country of England the *zeitgeist* found a receptive soul in Bobby Burns of Scotland to whose national poetry it gave, at times, the universal touch of naturalism. Nowhere in literature is the feeling that man has sinned against nature so appealingly expressed as in his lament at seeing a terrified mouse flee at a plowman's approach:

> I'm truly sorry man's dominion
> Has broken nature's social union,
> And justifies that ill opinion
> Which makes thee startle
> At me, thy poor earth-born companion,
> And fellow-mortal.

A thought revolution separates the romantic poets from the author of *Paradise Lost,* a revolution which exalted the natural above the supernatural and gave man and his works a place, not among angelic throngs, but among the things of nature. The ideas that everything natural is good, that existing society is unnatural and vicious, and that the bond between man and nature must be re-established, found frequent expression in the literature of the period.

(5) Common-Man Idealism. Linked to these other social yearnings of the time was a growing respect for the common people, the folk, who, it was said, had most nearly escaped the "blight of civilization." A common-man idealism, which glorified the lowly toilers and the poor, and endowed them with dignity and nobility, pervades much of the literature of the early democratic era. Rousseau, Wordsworth, Burns, Carlyle, Ruskin, Dickens, Thackeray, Emerson, Whittier, and later writers, such as Whitman, Tolstoy, Shaw, and Anatole France, have thus idealized the common people. This glorification of common folk is closely related to the development of nineteenth-century nationalism.

(6) The Triumph of Social Interests. While interest in the physical world, predominant in the sixteenth and seventeenth centuries, continued, an interest in man and his social problems has, since then, become prominent in the thought of the world. Embodying the belief that man and society, like the physical world, operate according to immutable laws of nature, and using the scientific method of discovery, the social sciences have come to occupy a leading place in the intellectual field. Their advance was stimulated by the theory, older than Darwinism but greatly strengthened by it, that social institutions have grown up by a process of evolution. That men can, consciously and intelligently, direct that process, if their knowledge of social facts be accurate, is a fundamental postulate of the faith of the social scientist.

The Intensification of Nationalism

DEMOCRACY AND NATIONALISM. If the discovery of the common man has been the most significant social phenomenon of the modern world, the intensification of nationalism, a phase of that discovery, has been next in importance. Patriotism, as a mass phenomenon, became a great emotional force in the nineteenth century, when political power was transferred from the classes to the masses and national school systems were perfected for nationalistic ends. Voiceless, powerless, and hungry, the masses of the predemocratic régime felt no urge to national loyalty. Accorded an increasing modicum of privilege, provided with free vernacular schools, and systematically indoctrinated with national ideals through the press, the theater, national games, and a host of other devices, of which the radio and television have been the most recent, they have become the sinews and souls of the nations. Improved means of communication, which focused attention upon social evils; an increase in wealth, which made the rich more generous; and the softening of social barriers, which was hastened by growing wealth, better education, and greater freedom of the masses themselves, contributed to the social elevation of the common people. In empires, monarchies, and democracies alike, the common people, in the nineteenth century, took on a new importance in varying degrees. That is a significant aspect of the new nationalism.

Nationalism was a movement which strove, among other things, to build political states out of groups having a common language, a common history, and a common culture. In the process there emerged the nationalist mind based upon a fusion of patriotism and cultural differentiation and prejudices. A common language and literature and common institutions are the distinguishing marks of a nation. We have noted earlier that, out of a once united Christendom, there had been emerging from the twelfth century onward strong, autocratic, national states. Each of these came to have its own language and literature, its own traditions, its own economic interests protected by its army and navy, and its own national church and religious ideals. Nationalism is one phase of that secularization of the world which has replaced the supernaturalism of the Middle Ages.

The principle of national democracy, based upon that of popular sovereignty, and advanced by such men as Locke, Rousseau and Jefferson, had its first triumph in revolutionary America and France, where nationalism as a mass phenomenon originated. Here arose the belief that any people with the same history, culture, and institutions have a right to self-government. The American nation was the first one founded on these ideas. Fostered by the bourgeoisie for materialistic ends, nationalism was made the greatest ideological force in modern times. Patriotism, though related to commercial rivalries, was made the motive of all the revolutions of the nineteenth century in Europe and Latin America. Where monarchy survived the democratic storm, kings became gentle fathers, as in England, or benevolent despots, as in Germany. Everywhere, the common man was exalted in varying degrees. Humanitarianism, the belief in man's perfectability and in the inevitability of progress, and a faith in the doctrines of liberty, equality, and every man's right to happiness were among the unselfish ideals of early democratic social reformers. Slavery, intemperance, poverty, unemployment, old age, crime and prison systems, war, and the emancipation of women occupied the attention of these social leaders.[4]

While the spirit of benevolence loomed large, there were those who would make the idealism of the age serve the ends of the national state. In the nineteenth century, democracy was defined mainly in terms of political liberty, although women were not enfranchised until after the First World War, and then only in a few democracies, and Russia. In the twentieth century, philosophers of democracy have stressed the ideal of equality of opportunity for all citizens so that the nation may have the service of its best brains without regard to the social or racial origin of individuals, or to sex differences. While the democracies led in fostering nationalism, aristocratic and authoritarian states, such as Germany and Russia,

[4] Smith, *op. cit.*, II, 592 ff.

emerged in the nineteenth century as strong national units with their own national ideals.

MONARCHISM AND NATIONALISM. Democracy and nationalism, though natural allies, are not the same. Democracy is, among other things, a governmental policy; nationalism is a feeling which unites all classes and parties within the nation. That feeling was developed under despotic as well as under liberal governments. Germany furnishes an excellent example of that development.

Among the intellectuals of the eighteenth and the early nineteenth century, both within and without Germany, there were many whose hopes and desires were cosmopolitan. Among Germans, Kant and Fichte saw the universal state as the final goal of political organization. Others denounced nationalism. Said Lessing: "Love of country is at best but an heroic vice, which I am quite content to be without." [5] The Napoleonic threat to the independence of European nations stifled such yearnings for a cosmopolitan world. After the defeat of the Prussians by Napoleon at Jena (1806), Fichte, once ardent in his cosmopolitanism, became a most eloquent advocate of the nationalistic state, not, however, as a final goal but as a necessary step toward a world state. Giving the state a divine purpose, he made patriotism a religious duty. But he went further. He proclaimed the Germans to be the only pure European race, with a pure language and culture, who, being the most religious of peoples, have preserved in its purity the divine will and are thus alone capable of real patriotism and of furthering the divine plan among men. This deification of race, culture and the state culminated in the anti-Semitism and the worship of blood and soil of the Hitler régime.

Between Fichte and the philosophers of National Socialism stands Hegel, the philosopher of the "absolute state." He taught that only through the national state can the individual become a moral personality, the state being the transmitter of God's will to men. Only by destroying liberalism and individualism could the Prussian state achieve its divine destiny. The state "is the absolute reality," wrote Hegel, "and the individual himself has objective existence, truth and morality only in his capacity as a member of the State." [6] History, which is but the working of the spirit of God, knows not the individual Ego but only the national Ego. The state is the greatest of God's creations, and to it the individual must be

[5] C. J. Hayes, *Essays on Nationalism* (New York: The Macmillan Co., 1926), p. 43. (By permission.)

[6] J. Dewey, *German Philosophy and Politics* (New York: Henry Holt & Co., Inc., 1915), p. 110.

subordinate and obedient; indeed, the state is God made visible to men. The victory of one state over another is, for Hegel, a proof that the victor has become the bearer of the divine spirit which passes, at times, from one national Ego to another. The Prussian absolute state he viewed as the highest embodiment of the divine will, because its government was not constitutional and it welded the anarchic mass of individuals together into the state based upon Absolute Reason. Karl Marx was influenced by his idea that history is a process of struggle and change, the progressive force of one state of social evolution becoming reactionary in the succeeding one.

From Hegel's teachings it follows that any scheme of internationalism is a negation of God's designs, and that any world plan which would end the life principle of struggle would frustrate the designs of God. War thus becomes a necessity, and God its author. War is the very life of the national spirit. Without it the nation dies.

Following Hegel, many German patriots have believed in the divine mission and destiny of their nation. Mussolini, too, made Hegelianism the basis of his totalitarian régime, and National Socialism was a practical realization of the basic ideas of the philosopher of the absolute state, though the régime itself was marked by a contempt for intellectualism as opposed to action.[7]

After the triumph (1870-1871) of Bismarck, Germany became a united nation, under the leadership of Prussia, and as nationalistic in its spirit and policies as its neighboring democracies. National rivalries, and their underlying commercial rivalries, brought the First World War (1914-1918) and the more exaggerated nationalism and international ill-will of the post-war era.

THE INDUSTRIAL REVOLUTION AND NATIONALISM. While nations have become economically interdependent, the Industrial Revolution has tended to stimulate nationalism; and even the doctrine of economic nationalism has its votaries. Improved transportation and means of communication, both products of the machine age, have brought the masses into that close physical and spiritual contact which is indispensable for nationalism. From the West, nationalism has been carried to the East through religious, intellectual, and commercial channels. China, Japan, and Turkey, for instance, have thus been largely Westernized.

ROMANTICISM AND NATIONALISM. The literary movement called romanticism gave a great impetus to nationalism. It glorified the common people and fostered an interest in folklore and folk cul-

[7] *Ibid.*

ture. Each nation was viewed as having its own folk, whose culture and folkways were made the basis of nationality. There are similarities and differences in national cultures, but nationalistic writers have accentuated the differences, thus stimulating the growth of national sentiment.

NATIONALISM AS A RELIGION. Love of the national state became, in the nineteenth century, an emotion similar to that of the Christian martyrs or the devotees of Islam. Should his church oppose his state, the patriot will oppose his church. He has renounced the ideal of humanity and human brotherhood for that of national brotherhood. Thus, Rousseau would substitute civil religion for supernatural religion, and French statesmen introduced many forms of state worship, such as civic baptism. Indeed, French extremists would substitute the state for God. While such extreme practices were abandoned, loyalty to *la Patrie* was retained as a form of cult. Similar developments occurred outside of France. Each nation has its heroes, revered like the saints of Christendom. Rituals have been approved for the worship of flags and the singing of national anthems. Each nation has its national shrine, pilgrimages, holy days, and dogmas. Each one persecutes its heretics. National schools are the nurseries of national faiths, and the ideal citizen is one who does not question the faith of the Founding Fathers.

NATIONALISM AND MILITARISM. Breeding distrust of foreign nations, nationalism has produced militarism and war. The race for military supremacy culminated in World War I, and that war, which many had vainly hoped would end wars, resulted in another World War and an armament race which, if it continues, must bring economic ruin upon the entire world. This drain upon national economic resources has met but feeble opposition. Taxpayers often oppose outlays for productive enterprises, including education, but do not question outlays for armaments. Demonstrations of military strength are greeted with great popular acclaim. While, perhaps, most wars have been fought for commercial and imperialistic ends, the great masses have seen in them a struggle to preserve high-sounding ideals. Nationalism, militarism, and war have been closely interrelated phenomena.[8]

NATIONALISM AND PROPAGANDA. Nationalists are made, not born. During the nineteenth century the findings of philologists, anthropologists, and historians were perverted by the missionaries of nationalism to bolster up the dogma of the superiority of some race or nationality. Indeed, so-called scientists have sought "proofs"

[8] Hayes, *op. cit.*, pp. 127–49.

of such superiority, and found what they sought. Propaganda has often masqueraded as science. The bourgeoisie were the chief supporters of nationalistic propaganda. They founded and financed national museums, games, societies, and journals. Controlling governments, they had laws passed to protect national industries and commerce. Soon, the nobility, clergy and intellectuals followed the lead of the bourgeoisie and became missionaries of nationalism.

NATIONALISM AND EDUCATION. While democracy and the Industrial Revolution have played an important rôle in shaping modern education, the force of nationalism was by far the most potent influence affecting its development. In the changing scene, the churches, in different degrees in different lands, were made to surrender to the state what control of education they formerly exercised. The French republic made the church subservient to the state. It stimulated the worship of the soil—*la Patrie*—which has become the basis of French patriotism. National flags, anthems, and holidays originated in the revolutionary atmosphere of France. Here it was first suggested that all citizens be compelled to speak the national language. Elementary education, free, compulsory, universal, and secular, became the educational formula of the revolutionary radicals. It was neither Communists nor Nazis who first demanded the secularization of education, but the French and American republicans, for the sake of national unity.

The French revolutionary educational formula, except in regard to secularization, was accepted by the Western nations in the nineteenth century. America and France secularized their public schools. Other nations such as England and Germany retained religious instruction in their public schools, either to appease popular feeling or to mould citizens of the God-fearing type. Everywhere, the inculcation of national ideals became a fundamental goal of public education. Even the 3 R's assumed a national significance, for the faith of the illiterate citizen is hard to nurture. Literate, his economic value to the nation was increased. When the masses were made literate and patriotic, cheap newspapers and magazines catering to their tastes and prejudices appeared everywhere. Democracy hastened these developments.

Where the people rule, the state must educate its rulers. Popular government presupposes popular education, and the framers of democracy in Europe and America realized that.[9] While some other governments may flourish without popular education, democratic government is almost inconceivable without it.

[9] A. O. Hansen, *Liberalism and American Education in the Eighteenth Century* (New York: The Macmillan Co., 1926).

The French Constitution of 1791 provided that "There shall be created and organized a system of public instruction common to all the citizens and gratuitous in respect to those subjects of instruction that are indispensable to all men. . . . Commemorative days shall be designated for the purpose of preserving the memory of the French Revolution, of developing the spirit of fraternity among all citizens, and of attaching them to the constitution, the country, and its laws."[10] In 1794, Frederick William II of Prussia proclaimed that schools and universities are state institutions, and at all times subject to examination and inspection by the state.[11] Colonial New England having set a precedent, the American states, in their constitutions, gradually recognized the principle of state responsibility for the education of the future citizens of the nation. In the nineteenth century, the principle of free, universal, compulsory, elementary education for national ends had won almost the universal approval of the Western world, and, in the East, Japan set the pattern for the nationalism in politics and education which today is revolutionizing the Oriental world. China, India and Egypt are now doing what the leading nations of the West were doing a century and a half ago.

Wars and revolutions have been an important factor in the development of national education. In France and America, a revolution in educational thought accompanied the political revolutions. The defeats of the Prussians by Napoleon, in 1806, and of France by Prussia, in 1870, were followed by educational reforms in each country. The Civil War in America intensified the conviction that the public school is the saviour of our institutions.

National schools have been nurseries of national patriotism. National educators first strove to "liquidate" illiteracy, for loyalty to the nation is dependent largely on the ability of citizens to read the national literature. In state schools, literature, geography, history and civics have been taught for nationalistic ends. Pupils have been taught to worship the national symbols and heroes. Everywhere, the masses were thus made to believe that theirs is the best nation of them all and the happiest and fairest land on earth. Contempt for other nations and lands often resulted from such teaching, and the national school often stood as an additional menace to world peace.[12]

[10] E. Reisner, *Nationalism in Education since 1789* (New York: The Macmillan Co., 1927), p. 12. (By permission.)

[11] Hayes, *op. cit.*, p. 82.

[12] J. F. Scott, *Menace of Nationalism in Education* (New York: The Macmillan Co., 1926); Hayes, *op. cit.*, pp. 61–92.

The Industrial Revolution and Social Reform Movements

From 1750 onward there occurred an economic phenomenon which historians have called "The Industrial Revolution." Prior to this change commerce dominated industry, but, with the change, industry came to dominate commerce. By 1850 the Industrial Revolution was, generally, an accomplished fact. Under the earlier system, industry was carried on mainly in the homes of workers in town and country. While the peasant family was not busy with its farming it was busy with its needles or its looms. This way of rural life ended first in England, the earliest scene of the Industrial Revolution. Here wealthy retired merchants bought land, introduced farm machinery and applied capitalistic methods to farming. Unable to compete with these agricultural magnates, the peasant farmers lost their little holdings or were deprived of them by "enclosure" laws passed by Parliament at the behest of the rich.[13] Besides, the invention and improvement of textile machinery soon put an end to the old handicraft system of the home. The existence of the machine and a propertyless peasantry hastened the Industrial Revolution and the factory system of production. Science was an indispensable ally of these, for it taught man how to make coal and iron work for him.

During the industrial change, and hastening it, came machinery of great precision, made possible by improvements in the manufacture of iron and steel. By 1850, power-driven machinery predominated in English industries. Thus, the factory system of production replaced the domestic system, and industry passed into the hands of great capitalists. After 1850, the Industrial Revolution spread rapidly through continental Europe while, even earlier, America was experiencing her own industrial transformation. The Bessemer process of manufacturing steel, invented after 1850, made fine steel available at one-seventh of the former cost of an inferior product. Our ships, skyscrapers, bridges, and airplanes testify to the effects of steel upon modern life. Oil, electricity, and atomic energy have come to supplement steam power. Electric power, generated at a central point, can be used to operate far-away machines, and electric light has enabled factories to operate as efficiently by night as by day. In this machine age skills have become highly specialized.

SOCIAL ASPECTS OF THE INDUSTRIAL REVOLUTION. Rural depopulation resulted from the concentration of industry in the cities, for workers were forced to follow industry from the farm into the

[13] M. Knight, *Economic History of Europe* (Boston: Houghton Mifflin Co., 1928), pp. 346–47.

factory. The factory system had one important advantage for the laborers: it made their miseries a matter of public knowledge and of public concern. They lived in crude shacks in congested areas; and worked from dawn until dark, and had little home life. While women operators were inhumanly treated, the employment of very young children and their treatment by employers were the most inhuman aspects of the early factory system. In England, pauper children were farmed out as "apprentices" by overseers of the poor to manufacturers in distant cities, where they were at the mercy of their employers. They often died in hundreds from epidemics and starvation, for they were often forced to work from fourteen to eighteen hours daily for a few pennies. The life of the poor had long been thought valueless, and the factory system had inherited the brutality of centuries of human oppression.

Social evils connected with the factory system soon convinced the thoughtful that the well-being of the family, the nation, and of industry itself demanded reform. Humanitarians clamored for state regulation of factories, mines, and labor. In England, beginning with the Health and Morals Act (1802), a series of child labor laws appeared, the most important being that of 1833, which forbade textile manufacturers to employ children under nine years of age, or to compel those under thirteen to work longer than forty-eight hours weekly, or those under eighteen longer than sixty-nine hours weekly, while it prohibited night work for those under the age of eighteen. The principle that it is the state's duty to interfere was fully accepted in 1833. France, Germany, and Belgium, in the thirties and forties, regulated labor conditions in essentially the same way as did England.

NEW SOCIAL PROBLEMS. In the year 1800, the world's population was less than 850 millions; in 1900, it was more than 1,700 millions. During that century, the population of Great Britain rose from 16,000,000 to 41,000,000; that of Germany, from 21,000,000 to 56,000,000; that of European Russia from 39,000,000 to 111,000,000; that of all Europe, from 180,000,000 to 400,000,000; and that of the United States, from 5,000,000 to 77,000,000. That increase created a food problem in Europe, from which people emigrated in great numbers to foreign lands, particularly to the United States. The foreign countries soon had food problems of their own and had to restrict the exports of farm products to Europe, where the cost of living consequently rose and competition for foreign markets grew keener. The nations, therefore, sought colonies as sources of food and raw materials. An industrialized Europe had to have both of these, and it had to export its manufactured goods. National economic imperialism was the result of these needs, and European states became world states.

Within the nations, the population became concentrated in cities, and rural population declined. In Germany, for instance, there were, in 1871, only eight cities of over 100,000 population; in 1905, there were forty-one. In 1871, 63.9 per cent of Germans lived by agriculture; in 1910, that figure had fallen to 40 per cent.[14] Problems of poverty, crime, and disease arose mainly in the cities, and brought persistent demands for moral and social reform. Many looked to the school as a remedy against the blights of civilization. "Open a school," it was said, "and close a jail." Others would go deeper and attack social problems through their causes.

HUMANITARIANISM AND SOCIAL REFORM MOVEMENTS. The late eighteenth and the first half of the nineteenth century witnessed the growth of an idealism which, centering around the common man, embodied a hope for the coming of social Utopias and a desire to build them. Daniel Defoe (1660-1731), John Woolman (1720-1772), and many others, including Rousseau and the rationalists of the Age of Reason, prepared the way for the nineteenth-century reformers. The spirit of liberty, equality, fraternity, and of faith in the goodness and value of common people found its way into the literature of the romantic movement. Burns, Wordsworth, Shelley, Victor Hugo, Balzac, Dickens, Dostoyevsky, Tolstoy, Ruskin, Emerson, Thoreau, and Whitman breathe the spirit of an age marked by an interest in nature, in common people, and in social reform.

ABOLITION OF SLAVERY. The Commercial Revolution and European foreign conquests had reduced to slavery great hordes of native peoples, particularly in Africa and America. Quakers and Anabaptists denounced slavery among other forms of cruelty. In British colonies, slavery was abolished in 1833, and in French colonies, in 1848. The Civil War ended the practice in America. While the conviction that free labor is more profitable and efficient than slave labor hastened the movement for emancipation, humanitarian motives probably weighed most in turning the balance against an institution antedating the dawn of history.

TEMPERANCE REFORM. Temperance is a puritan-bourgeois-proletarian virtue. A commercial and industrial society thrives better on such stimulants as tea and coffee than on gin. The intemperance of the old European feudal nobility passes all belief, and England, Scotland, and colonial America attempted to curb drunkenness by

[14] *Ibid.*, p. 529.

law.[15] With the Industrial Revolution, the vice spread among city workers. Sickness and communicable diseases, often caused by impure water and lack of sanitation, coupled with long hours of laborious toil, made city unfortunates seek a release from their miseries in gin-mills. English philanthropists attacked the evil. Methodists and other evangelical groups in England preached and struggled against it, and their views permeated the middle class. In the United States, the first organized effort to abolish intemperance was made in Boston in 1826, when the first American total abstinence society was founded. The movement spread rapidly here. Dissatisfied with the results of voluntary methods of reform, the leaders demanded prohibitory laws. In 1846, Maine enacted our first prohibition law and, by 1856, thirteen other states had taken similar steps which, however, they modified later. Maine, New Hampshire, and Vermont retained their prohibition laws until 1919, when the federal constitution made prohibition mandatory for the nation.[16]

PRISON REFORM MOVEMENT. The barbarous treatment of criminals prior to the nineteenth century has been referred to earlier. Bourgeois humanitarian idealism demanded reform in the treatment of criminals and secured it. The whipping-post and pillory were gradually abolished in England, as was capital punishment for all but a few most vicious crimes.[17] In the eighteenth century, torture had been abolished in Russia, Prussia, Austria, Poland, Switzerland, Denmark, and other countries.[18] In Australia and Ireland, between 1840 and 1860, the prison reform movement made great progress.[19] In America, social idealists demanded more humane and rational treatment of criminals, and the idea that the purpose of prison detention is reformation, not punishment, was finally accepted. The nineteenth century saw imprisonment for debt, which was an English tradition, abolished in America. Such suffering fell mostly upon the laboring class and the unemployed. The spread of humanitarianism in our eastern states and of frontier democracy brought an end to that practice.

Such movements as these aimed to correct the growing abuses of an industrialized world. But humanitarianism did not end with these. The nineteenth-century world came to accept the philosophy that everyone born into society has rights which society may

15 Smith, *op. cit.*, I, 534–35.

16 A. M. Schlesinger, *Political and Social History of the United States* (New York: The Macmillan Co., 1925), p. 76.

17 C. J. Hayes, *A Political and Social History of Modern Europe* (New York: The Macmillan Co., 1921), II, 115.

18 Smith, *op. cit.*, II, 580.

19 J. Davis, *Readings in Sociology* (New York: Heath, 1927), pp. 912–13.

not ignore. Institutions for the treatment and care of physical, mental, and moral defectives were established everywhere in the Western World, and older ones were improved. The Industrial Revolution, while it created evils, produced an increase of wealth which made it possible to alleviate suffering and distress. National school systems and a host of educational improvements arose, or were significantly expanded, during this era of idealism and social reform.

THE ORGANIZED LABOR MOVEMENT. Until 1824, combinations of working men were forbidden by English law. After that date, the policy of the British government toward labor unions gradually changed. In France, workingmen's bargaining unions were outlawed until 1884.[20] Restrictions placed upon union activity in England, after 1834, brought a militant clamor among laborers for political reform and, eventually, universal male suffrage. The triumph of industrial capitalism, by 1850, stimulated the growth of unionism and socialism. Marx and Engels, in the Communist Manifesto (1848), called for unity among the proletariat of the world. Continental unionism, unlike that of England, was marked by a notable degree of proletarian unity and socialistic idealism.

In America, changed labor conditions, resulting from the rise of the factory system, forced labor to organize in defense of its rights. Here, as abroad, factory conditions were degrading, wages were low, and working hours were from "dark to dark." Educational advantages enjoyed by the children of the rich were denied to those of the poor. On April 16, 1831, the *Mechanics Free Press*, a Philadelphia labor organ, demanded the following reforms: universal education, abolition of chartered monopolies, equal taxation, revision or abolition of the militia system, a less expensive law system, all officers to be elected directly by the people, a lien law for laborers, and no legislation on religion. Beginning in 1828, "Working Men's" parties were organized in the northeastern seaboard states, but in five years they had been replaced by trade unions which, in 1834, were linked together in a central National Trades' Union similar to the American Federation of Labor. The demands of organized labor for humanitarian and educational reforms were highly influential in the growth of common-man democracy in America.[21]

STATE SOCIALISM AND THE WELFARE STATE. The social problems created by the Industrial Revolution eventually forced govern-

[20] Knight, *op. cit.*, p. 403.

[21] R. V. Curoe, *Educational Attitudes and Policies of Organized Labor in the United States* (New York: Teachers College, Columbia University, 1926).

ments to regulate economic activities in their own interests as well as those of society and of laborers. State socialism arose in Germany out of Bismarck's efforts to destroy the political power of labor groups organized into political parties after 1863, when the German Social Democratic Party was formed. To thwart real socialism, Bismarck, between 1883 and 1889, had enacted social legislation which embodied many demands of the Social Democrats.

In England, the abandonment of laissez-faire economic practice coincided with the growth in power of organized labor following the Reform Act of 1867, which enfranchised urban laborers. Here was organized the Marxian Democratic Federation, in 1880; the Independent Labor Party, in 1893; and the present Labor Party, in 1900. Social legislation in England has followed a course similar to that of imperial Germany, and the government has often interfered in economic affairs without, however, undermining the system of private property.

In France, since 1898, the state has interfered in economic matters through laws enacted to protect the interests of workers and of the nation. The Fascist states of Italy and Germany went much farther than the European democracies in regulating the economic activities of their citizens, although they retained the institution of private property. Only in Russia has private capitalism been destroyed.

In the Scandinavian countries, Sweden being the most successful experimenter, a reformed capitalism has been adopted, which is a combination of state capitalism and private co-operative activities. Here, the state actively participates in industry, while the consumers are organized to protect their own interests. Through social education, within the schools and without, the people have been brought to see the superiority of this system over the older one, as far as their own small nation is concerned.[22]

To placate the laborer, governments, generally, have turned to state socialism or social security schemes. Such plans have sometimes resulted from the attacks of the proletariat and landed gentry upon the bourgeoisie. Thus the English middle class forced the curtailment of the political power of the nobility, in 1832, and the nobility retaliated by uniting with the proletariat in a demand for humanitarian reforms of the industrial system. The industrial aris-

[22] W. H. Dawson, *Bismarck and State Socialism* (London: Sonnenschien, 1890); C. Gide and C. Rist, *A History of Economic Doctrines from the Time of the Physiocrats to the Present Day* (trans. R. Richards; London: George G. Harrap & Co., Ltd., 1948); J. L. and B. Hammond, *The Rise of Modern Industry* (New York: Harcourt Brace & Co., Inc., 1926); J. A. Hobson, *The Evolution of Modern Capitalism* (New York: Charles Scribner's Sons, 1926).

tocracy itself has promoted movements of social reform to protect the capitalistic system. Much of the wealth of some of them, such as Andrew Carnegie and Henry Ford, has been given back to society to promote the public welfare. Business leaders have contributed generously to social relief funds, and the ablest among them have striven for industrial conciliation to preserve the existing order.

Nineteenth-Century Science and Intellectual Outlook

DARWINISM. While the evolutionary theory in its biological aspects found expression in early Babylonian writings and in the writings of Aristotle and other Greeks, it was not until the eighteenth and nineteenth centuries that the factual basis of the theory was firmly established. Linnaeus (1707-1778) suggested a common parentage for different botanical species. Erasmus Darwin (1731-1802) advanced the theory of adaptation to environment, and Malthus (1766-1834), that of the struggle for existence. Charles Lyell (1797-1875) was an evolutionist in geology, and Lamarck (1744-1829) taught a definite theory of organic evolution, which embodied the doctrine of the mutability of species, based on the assumption that acquired characteristics are inherited. Building upon all of these earlier concepts, Charles Darwin (1809-1882) formulated the theory of biological evolution.

The general theory of evolution demanded a significant intellectual revision. It implied that the cosmos is trillions of years old and that time, while useful as a working hypothesis, is largely a mental fiction. It further implied that change is inevitable and that everything is moving toward a different state, either better or worse. Moreover, it implied that man is a biological being and an animal, although prince of the animal kingdom. It reduced man to a very insignificant place in geologic time (for he emerged but yesterday), and in astronomic space, where he is but an infinitesimal speck. Within the unexplored reaches of the cosmos there may be beings far superior to him, but on the earth's surface he has become master over living things. While comparative anatomists have shown convincingly man's affinity to the ape, comparative psychologists have not yet conclusively proved that mental similarities are implied in physical likeness. Many riddles regarding the mental life of primates and of man remain to be solved.

The notion of social evolution was clearly stated, or implied, in many writings of eighteenth-century philosophers. The idea of the inevitability of progress, widely accepted by the social reformers of the early democratic era, embodied a belief in social evolution. It remained, however, for Herbert Spencer (1820-1903), a philosopher and sociologist, to see the laws of evolution at work in all fields. With him, the theory of evolution, as a general doctrine, made its first definite appearance. His view of a linear social evolution has been found not to be in harmony with facts.[23]

As a result of his views, a great impetus was given to the social studies. The position of Spencer was forcefully restated, and placed upon a sounder factual basis, by W. G. Sumner in his *Folkways* (1907). Therein, Sumner contends that all of our culture and institutions are the results of an evolutionary process and that many vicious elements, originating in the remote or less remote past, have been transmitted to us as a part of our cultural heritage.

THE IDEA OF PROGRESS. "Is there a thing whereof men say, See this is new? it hath been already in the ages which were before us."[24] It is hazardous to call any idea new, but that should be said of the idea of progress which found definite expression in the Enlightenment of the eighteenth century. The idea was evolving since Roger Bacon, in the thirteenth century, predicted future technological advance, but it took form slowly. It represents a revolt against the Augustinian doctrine of degeneration and against the scholastic doctrine of a fixed, static universe. To it, the humanist optimistic view of man's possibilities and, then, the discovery of nature and of science made large contributions. The age in which it germinated was, however, still one in which the theologians saw the world moving on toward its final destruction and the Last Judgment. The triumph of the idea, if we may yet call it that, had to await the secularization of knowledge which came in the seventeenth and eighteenth centuries. The idea was formulated in this age of boundless faith in reason and in man's capacity to reform the world, an age which gave the democratic world its basic ideals, among them the promise of indefinite worldly progress and universal human harmony. The devotees of this new faith told men that they could build the City of God here by turning the light of reason and of critical, independent thought upon the institutions which the past had bequeathed to them. These creations of self-seeking ecclesiastics and kings were declared to be unnatural and opposed to reason. Some, however, such as Rousseau, rejected reason as a guide to the better world. While most thinkers of the Enlightenment saw Nature as fixed and static, they viewed progress as a natural tendency and individual freedom as essential to it.

[23] See chap. i.
[24] Ecclesiastes, 1:10.

Men had to abandon the Augustinian concept of Nature before the idea of worldly progress could take shape. Saint Thomas Aquinas contributed to that change by declaring that the truths of nature are discoverable by reason. The nominalists and Calvin, no doubt without intent, isolated Nature from Super-Nature, science from theology. When Francis Bacon asked men to direct their intellectual energy to an investigation of Nature, and they did so, such significant advances were made in secular knowledge that thinkers could scarcely have escaped the idea of the inevitability of progress and the coming of the millennium. While many, such as Francis Bacon, Descartes and Pascal promoted the idea, it was Bernard de Fontenelle (1657-1757) who first formulated a definite theory of progress. These men and others saw their world as decidedly in advance of the ancient one, and a worship of the past as a serious obstacle to progress. Vico (1668-1744), the Italian philosopher of history, Turgot (1727-1781) and Condorcet (1743-1794) of France, Herder (1744-1803) and Hegel (1770-1831) of Germany, and William Godwin (1756-1836) and Herbert Spencer (1820-1903) of England, among many other distinguished social philosophers, promoted the idea. They asked man to set his eyes upon the Golden Age of the future and work to build the earthly City of God. Perhaps the history of the past century shows them to have been too optimistic, but their hope still encourages men to work for a better world, in the building of which education is seen as an indispensable instrument.[25]

DEVELOPMENTS IN PSYCHOLOGY. Discoveries in biology, anatomy, and chemistry suggested the need for a scientific study of the human mind. Franz J. Gall (1758-1828), an Austrian physician, made a scientific study of the brain and laid the foundations of neurology and scientific psychology. His work, misconstrued by others, led to the rise of phrenology in Europe and in the United States. In Germany, E. Weber (1795-1878) and G. T. Fechner (1801-1887) used the science of physics to explain the operations of the mind, Fechner using the term "psychophysics" to describe his work. With E. B. Titchener, of Cornell University, psychophysics reached its maturity. The theory of evolution suggested another approach.

G. Stanley Hall (1846-1924), following the lead of Huxley, es-

[25] J. B. Bury, *The Idea of Progress* (London: Macmillan & Co., Ltd., 1921); W. A. Dunning, *History of Political Theories from Rousseau to Spencer* (New York: The Macmillan Co., 1926).

tablished genetic psychology on a biological basis, thereby using the theory of evolution to explain mental phenomena. Alexander Bain (1818-1903) and Herbert Spencer attempted to study mental processes by introspection, using established knowledge in the fields of biology, physiology, and psychology to guide them in their investigations. It remained, however, for Wilhelm Wundt (1832-1920), of Leipzig, to make the first significant experimental laboratory approach to the problems of psychology. Hall, Titchener, and William James, in the United States, fell under the influence of Wundt. James' *Principles of Psychology* (1891) represents the last outpost reached by psychologists at the close of the nineteenth century. But they had taken a long step forward toward an understanding of the human mind and, influenced by the theory of evolution, they had begun to investigate the mind and behavior of animals as a basis of understanding the mind of man.

The psychology of the present century rests upon the sciences of neurology, endocrinology, biology, and physiology. Psychological research is pursued mainly in laboratories equipped with precise instruments for experimentation. Different schools of psychologists, distinguished from one another by an emphasis upon some peculiarity of man's mental life, have appeared. Among these are the biological psychologists, or functional school, to which William James, John Dewey, and E. L. Thorndike belong. These men have studied such mental activities as sense perception, emotion, and thought to see how they meet the needs of the human biological organism. The most extreme position taken by the biological or functional school has been that of the behaviorists, led by the Russian, Pavlov (1849-1936), and a group of Americans, of whom John B. Watson is the best known. Diverging somewhat from the functionalist position is the school of "purposivism," led by William McDougall, who has stressed the importance of instincts and of "purpose" in behavior. The Gestalt school also diverges from the functionalist view. Led by Köhler and other Germans, it insists that there is a unity in animal and human behavior that the functionalists have lost sight of in their preoccupation with the doctrine of specific responses to specific stimuli. To Freud goes the distinction of inventing a new approach, which still lacks a scientific foundation, to an understanding of mental abnormality as well as of normal mental life. The application of psychology to educational problems has elicited increasing attention on the part of psychologists and teachers in the past century. A notable succession of educators from Pestalozzi (1746-1827) to Dewey have worked to psychologize instruction.[26]

SOCIAL THEORY. Economic and social change produced by the Industrial Revolution and the expansion of democracy turned men's thoughts upon economic and social problems. Adam Smith and his followers formulated the philosophy of economic liberalism which, accepted, retarded social legislation favorable to the poor. Malthus (1766-1834), Ricardo (1772-1823), James Mill (1773-1836), John McCullough (1789-1864), and the English Manchester School of economists supported the laissez-faire theory. The doctrine that social evolution is natural and must not be interfered with lent support to that theory. John Stuart Mill (1806-1873) questioned the laissez-faire idea and prepared the way for government regulation in economic matters. Economists, political theorists, and sociologists thus produced a voluminous literature dealing with vital social problems. Intellectual interests, centered earlier on the physical world, were turned upon the social world which today remains the center of our interests.

The most radical social proposals were those of the Marxian Socialists, Anarchists, and Syndicalists. These aimed to transfer the control of the economic system from private capitalists to the proletariat. In 1848, Karl Marx (1818-1883) and Friedrich Engels (1820-1895) issued the Communist Manifesto. It proclaimed the doctrines of the inevitability of the class struggle and the final triumph of the proletariat through its seizure of political power. The Marxian theory that has attained widest popularity is that of economic determinism, or the materialistic interpretation of all institutions and events in the past and present. Following the leadership of Marx, the Socialists became a political force in Europe and forced governments to adopt many social reforms. Laissez-faire days are gone. In Russia, a socialism, which in practice has departed from Marxian ideals, has been established.

The philosophy of anarchism, which embodies a renunciation of all governments and of capitalism as inevitable instruments of oppression, was formulated by Michael Bakunin (1814-1876) and Peter Kropotkin (1842-1921). The latter advocated co-operative living and effort in a community free from agencies of force and private property. For the bourgeois principle and practice of competition, the anarchists proposed that of co-operation. Their aim is

[26] E. G. Boring, *History of Experimental Psychology* (New York: Appleton-Century-Crofts, Inc., 1929); W. B. Pillsbury, *The History of Psychology* (New York: W. W. Norton & Co., Inc., 1929); O. Klemm, *History of Psychology* (New York: Charles Scribner's Sons, 1914).

essentially the socialist aim but, unlike the socialists, they would attain it not by more state activity but by abolishing political authority altogether.

Syndicalism, too, aimed to destroy capitalism. Georges Sorel (1847-1922) has been its leading advocate. The syndicalists intended to destroy private capitalism and its defender, the national state, by strong labor unions, organized on industrial, not craft, lines and using the general strike and sabotage to demoralize and destroy the industrial capitalist. Their final goal is the establishment of a communistic society ruled by a government created by industrial unions.

Political problems, also, stimulated intellectual activity. Theory has its roots in experience. The capitalists, interested in protection of property, the enforcement of contracts and commercial freedom, fostered democracy, nationalism, imperialism, and constitutionalism. Constitutions, defining political power and the rights of citizens, and freeing business, by fixed law, from governmental and labor interference, were particularly desired by the bourgeoisie. Republicanism was deemed by them preferable to monarchism, because monarchies tended to be interfering things. Universal male suffrage was inaugurated in most of the Western nations in the nineteenth century, but female suffrage, in which New Zealand (1893) and then Australia led the way, made little headway until the United States and England adopted it after World War I. In practice the principle of majority rule has been largely nullified by the strategy of politicians whose party system, programs, and slogans have befuddled the masses and prevented them from thinking critically about vital issues.

DEVELOPMENTS IN THE PHYSICAL SCIENCES. Great advances have been made, since the end of the eighteenth century, in the physical sciences. In the year 1700, it was possible for one man to know all the important facts of physical science. Discoveries have come so rapidly since the year 1800 that it is now scarcely possible for one man to know all the established facts in a subdivision of one science. The value of science in industry has led to the support of scientific research by the great industries. The "Cold War" between Russia and the liberal world has brought a new emphasis upon mathematics, science and technology. In the eighteenth century, the greatest discoveries were made in chemistry; in the nineteenth, in biology and physics; and in the twentieth, in astronomy and electromechanics. Since 1800, great progress has been made in algebra and geometry, and higher mathematics has been applied to a variety of scientific problems from astronomy to statistics. With telescope, spectroscope, and, more recently, with the camera, astronomers have been exploring the heavens, and the accuracy of their predictions of celestial phenomena is one of the miracles of science. Heat, light, sound, and electricity have been reinterpreted, and the mathematical unification of the physical world has been demonstrated by the mathematician and the physicist. Experiments in physics conducted by James P. Joule (1818-1889) prepared the way for the confirmation of the principle of the conservation of energy. In 1847, Hermann von Helmholtz presented the facts upon which that law rests. The discovery of such laws was followed by their application to a variety of practical uses. Nineteenth-century discoveries in the field of electricity, particularly those of Ampère (1775-1836), Ohm (1789-1854), and Faraday (1791-1867), have led to the harnessing of this great force for practical uses. In the nineteenth century not only were new laws of quantitative chemistry discovered, but great progress was also made in organic chemistry. The relation between organic and inorganic matter was discovered, and it was shown that organic matter operates according to the same quantitative laws that govern inorganic matter. One practical result of chemical discoveries was the artificial production of many chemicals such as synthetic sugar, indigo, and rubber. The production by chemical processes of all the foods we eat or their nutritive equivalents is now within sight.

In biology, the most important discovery was the cellular nature of organic matter. That discovery has revolutionized the sciences of pathology and bacteriology. The science of embryology has thrown much light upon the question of heredity, and led to the formulation of the biological doctrine of recapitulation, which, while not entirely true, stimulated research in biology and genetic psychology. Research in the field of physiology gave rise to the widely accepted theory that life is but a chemical process. In the field of botany, the earlier classification of plants by Linnaeus was modified and harmonized with the theory of evolution.

Medical science was almost revolutionized by discoveries in related fields. Vaccination for smallpox was begun by Edward Jenner in 1796. The invention of the stethoscope by Laennec (1781-1826) helped physicians to detect many diseases of the internal organs. Chemistry supplied the surgeon with anesthetics, Crawford W. Long, of Georgia, being the first to use ether (1842). In addition, it provided many effective germicides. The publication of the germ theory of disease by Dr. Robert Koch, in 1876, put an end to many medical superstitions. In its discovery, Pasteur was very influential. Many a dreaded disease, such as anthrax, rabies, and tuberculosis, has been checked by these discoveries. Mental and nervous diseases, long associated with Satan's wiles, have been successfully investigated by neurologists and psychiatrists. With the exception of anatomy, nearly all great medical discoveries date from the year 1800. Yet "Nothing's known to what is yet to know."

To geologists and geographers the earth has surrendered many of its great secrets. Lyell's *Principles of Geology* (1830-1833) gave men accurate knowledge of the origin, age, and form of the earth. In addition, geology has aided in the development of the mineral industries. Great progress has also been made in geography. Karl Ritter (1779-1859), who assisted Pestalozzi in his educational reform, contributed much to our knowledge of physical geography, while explorers, such as Livingstone and Stanley, expanded the field of geographical knowledge. Most significant, however, was the development of a new point of view in the science itself which emphasized the effect of geographical factors upon human life and behavior. With Karl Ritter interest began to center in this anthropogeography.

THE CULTURE-LAG. Men often live in the midst of truths and wonders and see them not. The almost miraculous discoveries and inventions of the nineteenth and twentieth centuries have not yet aroused the masses out of their mediaeval slumber. Except for the highly educated few, men still interpret life and its problems in terms of traditional hopes and beliefs. Emotion, not science and reason, still rules the world. Because of the tenaciousness of ancient culture and folkways, it remains difficult to apply the truths of science to a variety of social ills that call for treatment. Teachers, preachers, statesmen, and, sometimes, even scientists themselves have vehemently opposed scientific truth and its social application, and modern dictators have renounced science when its truths have clashed with their political principles.

SCIENCE AND RELIGION. We have seen how science produced the Deism of the eighteenth century. The scientific principle of cause-and-effect was accepted by scientists as sufficient to explain all things in the world that we know by sense perception. The doctrine of evolution was applied to man and society as well as to the physical world. Modernist theologians adopted the new outlook and attempted to harmonize religion with science. The most important steps in this direction appear in the Biblical criticism of the "higher critics" and in the harmonizing of the Christian religion with the theory of evolution. The ninth edition of the *Encyclopaedia Britannica* (1875) did for the new rationalism what the

French Encyclopedists had done for rationalism in their time. This modernist movement occurred only within the circle of Protestantism, and there it was opposed by the Fundamentalists, who were the great majority during the nineteenth century, but who have lost ground in the twentieth. Among the Modernists, many, conceding the theory of evolution and denying that the Scriptures are inspired, retained their beliefs in the existence of God and the divinity of Jesus. Outside of organized religion, the Positivists, led by Comte, proposed a cult of humanity in place of all supernatural cults; and the Society for Ethical Culture attempted to bring together the highest moral teachings of all religions, while denying the supernatural character of them all, and insisting upon the human character of Jesus, for whose teachings they had great respect. These modernist movements were rooted in the theory of evolution, Biblical criticism, sociology, anthropology, and psychology.

The Catholic church effectively opposed Modernism within its own circle. Both in politics and religion it took a reactionary position. Pope Pius IX (1848-1876) condemned democracy and, in opposition to the naturalistic outlook of science, proclaimed the dogmas of the immaculate conception and of papal infallibility. The Catholic church made no attempt to harmonize its dogmas with science as it progressed. It opposed science, however, only when it conflicted with Catholic dogma.

In spite of progressive movements in religion, theological opposition stood as a threatening barrier to scientific progress, and some lay scientists boldly accepted the Fundamentalists' challenge to combat. Huxley, Haeckel, and Ingersoll denounced all theological orthodoxy as untrue. The Anarchist movement is atheistic, and Russian Communism took officially the same stand. The Rationalist Press Association and the International Freethinkers League were organized to combat theology in the interest of science. Critical accounts of the life of Jesus, embodying the skepticism of the higher critics, were written by David Strauss (1804-1874) and by Ernest Renan (1823-1892). These men rejected the doctrines of the divinity of Jesus and of the supernatural origin of Christianity. A group of German scholars at the University of Tübingen, led by Ferdinand Baur (1792-1860), advanced the view that Paul, not Jesus, was the founder of Christianity and that the gospels are pure myths, a view which attained wide vogue among intellectuals.

Kant, and Albrecht Ritschl (1822-1889) laid a firm intellectual basis for a new defense of religion. Kant asserted that in the phenomenal world, in which natural causes determine all happenings, the ideas of God and duty have no place but, in the moral world, they are essential as the rational bases of conduct. At a time when science was undermining the foundations of theology, Ritschl, in his work *The Christian Doctrine of Justification and Reconciliation* (1874), sought to free religion from dogmas by establishing it upon the basis of personal experience, and by making its goal the moral elevation of mankind. It is impossible, he held, to know God, but we can feel and experience him as a benevolent father guiding us toward a better life. God is thus an unknown power operating for the moral uplift of mankind, and pre-eminently through the moral leadership of Jesus.[27]

PHILOSOPHY. In the early part of the nineteenth century, Hegelian idealism held the center of the stage. It taught that there is an ultimate and idealistic reality which can be known by rational processes. Hegel's position was essentially Platonic. A reaction in favor of the Kantian position soon set in. Kant held that human knowledge cannot extend beyond the world of sense perception, and that the world of ultimate realities is unknowable. And since Hegel defended the idea of the "absolute" in government, and disregarded the struggle of the laboring masses, his philosophy was rejected by many for social reasons. While borrowing these fundamental views from Hegel, Karl Marx and others gave them a materialistic interpretation and thus laid the philosophical foundations of socialism. In America, Hegelian idealism, in its original form, found strong support from such men as W. T. Harris, best known as an educational reformer, and Josiah Royce, of Harvard, whose philosophical writings at the close of the century were the strongest American defense of a philosophy the principles of which were essentially opposed to our political and social traditions. While philosophers like Lotze (1817-1881), Schopenhauer (1788-1860), and Cousin (1792-1867) attempted to justify traditional idealism and reconcile it with scientific discoveries, there were others who formulated philosophies permeated entirely by the spirit of science.

Auguste Comte's philosophy, positivism, was an attempt to harmonize life and society with scientific laws, and to subordinate all other sciences to the new science of sociology, whose function it would be to apply the truths of the other sciences to the problems of society. Positivism was a religion in which humanity took the place of God, and in which all supernaturalism was cast aside. It

[27] F. S. Marvin, *The Century of Hope* (London: Clarendon Press, 1921); F. B. Mason, *Creation by Evolution* (New York: The Macmillan Co., 1928); A. C. McGiffert, *The Rise of Modern Religious Ideas* (New York: The Macmillan Co., 1915); G. H. Mead, *Movements of Thought in the Nineteenth Century* (Chicago: University of Chicago Press, 1936); A. D. White, *History of the Warfare of Science with Theology in Christendom* (New York: Appleton-Century-Crofts, Inc., 1896).

was an outgrowth of the need to solve scientifically the social problems created by the Industrial Revolution. In addition to positivism, a utilitarian philosophy of social reform was formulated by James Mill and John Stuart Mill and, justifying a measure of state interference in social matters, was a modification of the earlier individualistic utilitarianism of Bentham. In 1843, John Stuart Mill published his *System of Logic,* designed to end the Aristotelian deductive method of inquiry and to lay an observational experimental basis of philosophy, the principles of which would embrace all fields of scientific knowledge and embody a belief in the theory of evolution. For Spencer, the world of ultimate truths, of God and his purposes, is unknowable, and only the knowable world with which science deals is worthy of human inquiry.

In America, Charles S. Peirce (1839-1914), William James (1842-1910), and John Dewey (1859-1952) gave shape to the philosophical outlook of the New World. Peirce taught that experience and experiment are the only sound tests of truth. James taught that human thought cannot discover ultimate truths, nor final certainties, and that it is but an instrument designed to produce action or doing. Since he believed it to be impossible to know ultimate truths, he set up pragmatism as the test of the truth of all ideas and principles. Pragmatism teaches that what is useful—what works in a practical situation—is true; what does not work is false. Truth thus becomes not a fixed, eternal thing, but something that is subject to change. What is true today may be false tomorrow, for what works today may not work tomorrow. Thus tested, the ideas of Plato, Jesus, Augustine, Aquinas, Descartes, or even of James himself may be true at one time and false at another. Dewey accepted the fundamental tenets of James but, unlike James, who applied them to religion and ethics, has made his applications in the social field. Moreover, Dewey has expanded the philosophy of James into the theory of instrumentalism upon which his whole philosophy rests. For him, philosophy must not be a thing aloof from everyday life but must be constantly applied, as he himself has done, to political, social, economic, and educational problems.

Selected Readings

Ashley, W. J. *The Progress of the German Working Classes in the Last Quarter of a Century.* London: Longmans, Green & Co., Inc., 1904.

Babbitt, I. *Rousseau and Romanticism.* Boston: Houghton Mifflin Co., 1935.

Beer, M. *History of British Socialism.* London: G. G. Bell & Sons, Ltd., 1919–21.

Brett, G. S. *History of Psychology.* 3 vols.; London: Macmillan & Co., Ltd., 1912–21.

Bury, J. B. *The Idea of Progress.* London: Macmillan & Co., Ltd., 1921.

CONYBEARE, F. C. *History of New Testament Criticism.* New York: G. P. Putnam's Sons, Inc., 1910.

CREW, H. *The Rise of Modern Physics.* Baltimore: The Williams and Wilkins Co., 1935.

DAMPIER-WHETHAM, W. C. *A History of Science and Its Relation with Philosophy and Religion.* London: Cambridge University Press, 1940.

DAVIS, W., ed. *The Advance of Science.* Garden City, N.Y.: Doubleday & Co., Inc., 1934.

DUNNING, W. A. *History of Political Theories from Rousseau to Spencer.* New York: The Macmillan Co., 1926.

ERGANG, R. R. *Herder and the Foundations of German Nationalism.* New York: Columbia University Press, 1931.

GIDE, C., and RIST, C. *A History of Economic Doctrines from the Time of the Physiocrats to the Present Day.* (Trans. R. Richards.) London: George G. Harrap & Co., Ltd., 1948.

HOBHOUSE, L. T. *Liberalism.* New York: Henry Holt & Co., Inc., n.d.

KOCH, G. A. *Republican Religion: the American Revolution and the Cult of Reason.* New York: Henry Holt & Co., Inc., 1933.

KRIKORIAN, Y. H., ed. *Naturalism and the Human Spirit.* New York: Columbia University Press, 1944.

LASKI, H. J. *The Rise of Liberalism; the Philosophy of a Business Civilization.* New York: Harper & Bros., 1936.

MCGIFFERT, A. C. *The Rise of Modern Religious Ideas.* New York: The Macmillan Co., 1915.

MORAIS, H. M. *Deism in Eighteenth Century America.* New York: Columbia University Press, 1934.

MORLEY, J. *Rousseau and His Era.* London: Macmillan & Co., Ltd., 1923.

OSBORN, H. F. *From the Greeks to Darwin; an Outline of the Development of the Evolution Idea.* 2d ed.; New York: The Macmillan Co., 1913.

RILEY, I. W. *From Myth to Reason.* New York: Appleton-Century-Crofts, Inc., 1926.

SEDGWICK, W. T., and TYLER, H. W. *A Short History of Science.* New York: The Macmillan Co., 1917.

WALLIS, W. D. *Culture and Progress.* New York: Whittlesey House, McGraw-Hill Book Co., Inc., 1930.

WOLF, A. *A History of Science, Technology and Philosophy in the Eighteenth Century.* New York: The Macmillan Co., 1939.

10 The Socio-Psychological Movement in Education

Eighteenth-century France, as we have seen, was marked by intolerable political despotism, ecclesiastical evils and social injustice against which the Enlightenment directed a bitter attack in the name of reason, now substituted for authority. The social and intellectual unrest culminated in the Revolution and the overthrow of the monarchy. Political revolutions, when they embody fundamental changes in the economic and social spheres, invariably produce revolutions in educational thought and practice. The rise of political liberalism in the eighteenth century, rooted as it was in economic and social unrest, marked the beginning of new things, profoundly significant in education.

Theory of Education As Natural Development of the Individual

The principles of education in liberal states have changed with changing conceptions of liberalism, but certain fundamental positions taken by educational thinkers of the early revolutionary era have remained essentially unchanged. Foremost among these are the principles that (a) educational practice must be in harmony with the nature of the individual child and must develop his individuality to its fullest capacity, and (b) that the liberal state, the greatness of which depends on the greatness of the individuals who compose it, owes it to itself, for its own preservation, to educate its future masters and citizens, each one according to his natural capacities, for their own well-being as well as for that of society. The former principle gave impetus to a psychological emphasis in education; the latter, to a sociological emphasis, which was, however, not confined to liberal states alone but which, under the drive of nationalism, found expression in the establishment of national school systems for social ends as conceived mainly in terms of national interests. The most influential advocate of the individualistic-psychological emphasis was Rousseau, against whose supposedly extreme individualism more conservative reformers took an effective stand in the interest of society. Before examining the educational tenets of Rousseau, let us recall something of his forerunners and of the educational practices against which he protested.

ROUSSEAU'S EDUCATIONAL PROGENITORS. With the early Renaissance came a reawakening of the Greek respect for the individual in all of his natural aspects, aspects suppressed for centuries by the asceticism and otherwordliness of mediaeval ecclesiasticism. This discovery of man as a natural being, each one endowed with an individuality all his own, marked the beginning of an educational revolt which reached its height with Rousseau and extremists in the modern "progressive" school of educational thought. From the time of Vittorino da Feltre (1378-1446) until that of Rousseau, protest followed protest against the bookishness of education, harsh discipline, and the apparently general disregard of natural differences in individual capacities among students. With Mulcaster and Comenius, the idea, advanced by earlier writers, that education ought to be in harmony with human nature and a means of perfecting it was strongly emphasized. Comenius would make nature our guide in education; Rousseau would substitute it for education, and his views reflected the naturalism of his day.

Prior to the publication of Rousseau's *Émile,* French educational demand for the recognition and freedom of the individual found expression in Condillac's (1715-1780) *Treatise on the Sensations* (1754) and in Helvetius' (1715-1771) *De l'Esprit* (1757) and *On Man,* published after his death. The writings of the latter embody the most radically democratic educational and social philosophy of the eighteenth century. Both enlarged upon the sensationist psychology of Locke, and Helvetius carried it to its logical educational and social conclusion. As was Rousseau, both were indebted to Locke's view that sense experience is fundamental in the building of the mind and its faculties. In making sensation the basis of mental life, as Rousseau did, it followed that all individuals, because they all have senses, are intellectually equal. Condillac, however, did not stress that conclusion, while Helvetius did. The latter held, in opposition to the aristocratic prejudices of Locke, Voltaire and others, that the masses are not intellectually inferior to the classes, and that their seeming inferiority is due to their lack of opportunity to develop their capacities. Social differences, he held, are the result of educational differences, and equality of education will bring social inequalities to an end. The principle of equality of educational opportunity is quite clearly stated by Helvetius. He was a strong advocate of public education, of a free press as essential to progress and popular enlightenment, and of a rationalistic religion, rather than traditional Christianity, as a sound basis of a rational civic life. Rousseau was, no doubt, influenced by the psychological doctrines, if not by the social idealism, of his contemporary.

EDUCATIONAL DOCTRINES OF ROUSSEAU'S EMILE. As the economic and political theorists tried to bring economic and political institutions into harmony with supposed natural laws operating in society, so Rousseau tried to bring education into harmony with laws of nature governing the growth and life of the individual. He, no doubt, sensed the relation of "natural education" to the "natural state" which he described in the *Social Contract*. Yet, in *Émile*, his treatise on "natural education," he failed to indicate, in any clear way, the political and social implications of that education. That he recognized the political import of education is apparent not only in his *Social Contract*, but also in his *Discourse on Political Economy* and his *Considerations on the Government of Poland*. That he was at war with the society of his day is equally apparent. *Émile* is his protest against the degradation of men in that society, and against the educational practices which helped to degrade them. He would save children by a new education from that degradation. In the midst of the vices of civilization, Émile will retain unsullied the virtues of the savage, the natural man. The education which Rousseau recommends for Émile is designed to fortify him against the distortion of his nature by society. So sweeping is his negation of the old traditional education that he would preserve but the merest fragments of it. Do the opposite, said he, of what is customary and you will almost certainly be right. The essential tenets of his positive philosophy are the following:

(1) HARMONY OF EDUCATION AND HUMAN NATURE. Against the traditional view that human nature is evil and must be changed or disciplined in the interest of society or one's own soul, Rousseau taught that it is good and that no curb should be placed upon the freedom of its development. "All things are good as their Creator made them, but everything degenerates in the hands of man,"[1]

[1] *Emilius and Sophia* (4 vols.; London: T. Becket, 1763), I, 1. Our citations from the *Émile* are taken from this earliest English translation, and from that of W. H. Payne published by Appleton-Century-Crofts, Inc., in 1892, the latter being still the most valuable edition for students of education.

are the opening words of the *Émile*. The *Social Contract*, too, opened with the thought that, while men are born free, they are everywhere in chains. To free man he would reform the chief instrument of his oppression, education. He aimed to "form men," not by imposing upon children the ideas and modes of life of adults, but by allowing them freedom to grow according to those "tendencies" which are clearly a part of each one's original endowment. These natural interests and impulses are good because human nature is good and not vicious, as Christians were made to believe. Education must be in harmony with original and unspoiled human nature. Know child nature and bring instruction into harmony with it is the first indispensable law of education.

(2) Nature as Chief Teacher. We are educated by three teachers: nature, men, and things. "The constitutional exertion of our organs and faculties is the education of nature; the uses we are taught to make of that exertion constitute the education given us by men; and in the acquisitions made by our own experience on the objects that surround us consists our education from circumstances."[2] Over nature we have no control, and over things, only a partial control. Therefore, the education we control must conform with that which we cannot control. Nature he defined as our "natural tendencies" unchanged by reason, habit, or prejudices.

(3) Natural Interest and the Teaching Process. While Rousseau retained at many points the disciplinary conception of education, he urged the doctrine of natural interest as a guide to teaching with such persistent fervor that it overshadowed the other view to such a degree that the *Émile* stands as a revolt against the old education, with its emphasis upon the reform of nature by effort and exercises opposed to its tendencies. There are, said Rousseau, sharply defined stages in human development, paralleling in some respects the history of the race, each one marked by its own predominant and unmistakable interest which nature herself created. The transition from one stage to the next he views as a sudden one. The special interest, urge or demand of nature at each of the four stages of development is the guide which nature provides for the teacher, who must never anticipate the next stage but only perfect the child's development at the stage he has reached.

(4) Formation of Men as Goal of Education. Traditionally, education looked to some end outside of the individual, such as social well-being, the professions, or heaven. Rousseau would have it otherwise. He would make the attainment of the fullest natural

[2] *Emilius and Sophia,* I, 4–5.

growth of the individual the end to be sought. The teacher must train the man or the citizen; he cannot train both. But the natural man is greater than the citizen. He is the unit, and the citizen but the fraction. Were society itself natural, there would be no need to distort the nature of its future citizens. Said Rousseau:

> According to the order of nature, all men being equal, their common vocation is the profession of humanity. . . . It matters little to me whether my pupil be designed for the army, the bar, or the pulpit. Nature has destined us to the offices of human life. . . . To live is the profession I would teach him. When I have done with him, it is true, he will be neither a lawyer, a soldier, nor a divine. Let him first be a man. . . . All our wisdom consists in servile prejudice; all our customs are nothing but subjection, confinement and restraint. Civilized man is born, lives, and dies in slavery: at his birth he is bound up in swaddling clothes, and at his death nailed down in his coffin; as long as he wears the appearance of the human form he is confined by our institutions.[3]

Rousseau would thus free men from their bondage to society by educating them not for citizenship but for manhood. And yet no one was more preoccupied than he with the problem of reforming society. The natural state of which he dreamt needed as citizens natural men whose primitive natural virtues had not been stifled by the weeds of traditional social institutions. Not too hopeful of the emergence of the ideal society, Rousseau would immunize man's nature against the distortions which an unnatural society would inflict upon it. He realized that man must live in society, but he would not have him enslaved by it. Émile is a savage who must live in cities.

The preservation of individuality and the full development of manhood are the goals of education. Citizenship, professional and vocational preparation, or training for life in any social class are vicious objectives. Manhood is a vocation common to all men, and one who has attained it cannot discharge badly any vocation related to it. In a rapidly changing world, the individual should not be habituated to fixed institutions, but his powers should be so developed that he will be able to adapt himself to the changing environment and thus safeguard himself. To this end, the future needs of the child must be entirely ignored, and at each stage of his growth he will be taught to act according to his natural interest of the moment.

Under these broad principles all of the details of Rousseau's plan of education could be included. The greater part of the *Émile* consists of a description of the practices which he deemed

[3] *Ibid.*, pp. 13–16.

desirable. Following his view of the saltatory development of the pupil, he describes the education suitable to each of the sharply defined periods in his growth, those of infancy, early childhood, later childhood, and adolescence. For him age is the only safe guide in determining what a pupil is able to learn. The rule to be followed is not to gain time but to lose it.

NATURAL EDUCATION. (1) DURING INFANCY. The newborn child must be left free in body, not imprisoned in swaddling clothes. "Follow nature" is the guiding rule. Nature keeps the infant active, hardens him, accustoms him to grief and pain and thus strengthens him: "Inure them, therefore, by degrees, to those inconveniences they must one day suffer. Harden their bodies to the intemperance of the seasons, climates, and elements; to hunger, thirst and fatigue."[4] This is again the "hardening process" of Locke. In infancy also the basis of character is to be laid.

Throughout the entire educational period, ending at the age of twenty, nature has designed fathers to be the teachers of their sons, the most ignorant father being better than the cleverest schoolmaster. Were it possible to find an ideal teacher, a father might transfer his duty to him. Émile's teacher is the ideal one as conceived by Rousseau. He becomes his pupil's lifelong companion, counselor, and friend. The tutor's first duty is to give Émile a strong body, not by the deadly ministrations of physicians, but by hygienic living, temperance, and industry. Émile must be reared in the country, because of the vices and diseases of cities, but still more because men's "breath is destructive to their fellow-creatures,"[5] and Émile must be preserved from the death of his nature at the hands of society. Natural education begins, for everyone, with a strong body; where it ends depends upon the natural interests and capacities of each individual. Nature alone fixes its limits, for real education comes from living and experience. The tutor must be guided by Émile's interests and capacities which, in infancy, are those of the body and the senses. His wishes must be kept within the limits of his power, for otherwise they will destroy his liberty. Rousseau recognized, as do the modern activists, the importance of child activity which he would not curb since, in infancy, it cannot have destructive results because of the child's limited power. That the mental and moral gifts which nature bestowed upon him may not be perverted from their proper ends, Rousseau warned against the imposition upon the child of habits of thought

[4] *Ibid.*, p. 27.
[5] *Ibid.*, p. 57.

and behavior. "The only habit in which a child should be indulged is that of contracting no habit."[6]

Rousseau's war upon a wordy education, which he never abandoned, was begun in connection with infant training. "The school boy listens to the gabbling usher [teacher] of his class, with the same stupid attention as he did to the prattle of his nurse. Hence it appears to me to be a very useful mode of instruction to bring up children to hear nothing of it."[7] It is better to have clear ideas than a large vocabulary, and a child should not have more words than ideas.

(2) In Early Childhood. During this period, from the age of five until twelve, as in that of later childhood, from twelve to fifteen, Émile will remain in the country and be sedulously guarded against demoralizing influences. Where evil does not exist, the child will do no evil. In this period, sense interests predominate, and Émile's interest will center in the physical world which he will want to investigate by means of his senses. Now is the time to train the senses which nature has given him for a most vital end, that of life itself. This is also a period when moral training must not be neglected, and Rousseau lays down the following principles of moral instruction:

(a) Negative moral training. Émile must not be told anything now regarding moral action, unless he asks questions about such matters. Experience will teach him that he has no right to attack persons or things stronger than himself. Should he strike one stronger than himself, his blows should be returned with interest. Nature and environment will fix the limits of his liberty. Respect for private property, he must learn now, however, and Rousseau suggests that his natural urge for gardening be used to impress that duty upon him. Émile plants his garden in ground already planted by another gardener who, upon discovering what has happened, destroys Émile's plants. The saddened youth will now be told by his tutor that the other laborer was the first occupier and had a prior right to the garden, and that he has no basis of complaint. By such an experience he will learn the meaning of property, and the lesson will last because he was not told it but had discovered it himself.

(b) Learning by natural consequences. Should Émile break his window, let him sleep in the cold; should he lie, refuse to believe him even when he speaks the truth. Do not tell him he has done

[6] *Ibid.*, p. 66.
[7] *Ibid.*, p. 85.

wrong; let the consequences of his acts impress that truth upon him. The child is not by nature vicious, but a vicious environment makes him so. When a child lies, it is the fault of his elders. When they insist upon obedience, lying becomes a necessity for him. Should he, however, commit an offense, his act can be made to produce its own punishment.

(c) The importance of good example. In the realm of morals, the child learns by example, not by precept. Thus, acts of charity and kindness, performed in his presence, will make him charitable and kind. Nothing calling for an exercise of reason should be taught before the age of twelve, because the ability to reason does not exist earlier.

Since sense perception is the basis of thought and reason, nature has set aside these seven years for the training of the sense organs. Our first teachers are our feet, hands, and eyes; and books must not be substituted for them. By sense activities, the child learns the limits of his strength, the physical relation between himself and the external world, and the use of natural tools. Besides, such training lays the physical basis of later intellectual activity. Intellectual activity must yet, however, be sedulously avoided. Teach him now, said Rousseau, "the art of being ignorant." Instead of teaching him science, fashion the tools necessary in acquiring it. Develop now his senses and bodily organs by appropriate exercises. He saw clearly that sense interests and activities would create challenging problems for the child and an interest in solving them. Émile wants to pick cherries from a tree; he will learn quickly how to measure the ladder by which he hopes to reach them. Practical needs will urge him to draw, and thus he will learn the essentials of elementary geometry. But in drawing he must not copy copies. "I would have him have no other master than nature; no other model than the objects themselves." [8] Thus, during the period of sense training Émile will learn many useful things incidentally. His senses now developed, he is ready for adventures in reasoning. He has as yet few ideas, but they are precise because they have been derived from experience and from the book of nature.

He knows nothing at all of custom, fashion, or habit; . . . he pursues no formula, is influenced by no authority or example, but acts and speaks from his own judgment. . . . You will find in him a few moral notions relative to his actual state, but none on the relative situation in which he stands to society. . . . Speak to him of duty and obedience, and he will not know what you are talking about. . . . If you comply with his request, he will not thank

[8] *Ibid.*, p. 262.

you for so doing; but will be sensible that he has contracted an obligation. Whatever he may have a mind to do, he will undertake nothing above his abilities.[9]

(3) IN LATER CHILDHOOD. **(a) Curriculum.** During the period between the age of twelve and adolescence, the child's strength, says Rousseau, exceeds his wants. It is therefore the time for work, instruction, and inquiry, the time for developing the intellect. Only useful studies and such as contribute to human welfare should be selected for him. In selecting his studies, the guiding principle is to follow Émile's natural interests. Utility, however, must also be a determining factor, and Rousseau evidently assumes that natural interests are rooted in utility. Following these principles, Émile will be taught reading, the natural and physical sciences, and a trade. Though Rousseau hates books because "they only teach people to talk about what they don't understand,"[10] he considers reading ability indispensable, and Émile will learn to read from the book that best depicts life and education according to nature, *Robinson Crusoe.* The utility of his studies must always be apparent to Émile. His own experience, not that of his elders, is to be the measure of values. During this period of intellectual training, the question which the tutor must always be prepared to answer is "What is the use of that?"[11] In placing such exclusive emphasis, as he did, upon the study of sciences and a trade, during this period of supposedly predominant intellectual interest, Rousseau revolts against the disciplinary principle of selecting a curriculum, as well as against the classical and academic character of traditional schools. Rousseau had no aversion to the study of the ancient classics, but they should be read after the age of twenty. The period of intellectual interest is so short that it must be used very wisely. In early childhood, wasting time was a virtue; not so now. When, in a few years, his passions ripen, his intellectual interests will have been submerged. Therefore, he ought to be taught only the most useful sciences, but he ought to be given a taste of them all so that he may later pursue them alone when that taste matures.

(b) Trade training. Prior to adolescence, Émile has no sense of social relations, but a knowledge of skills essential to life will suggest to him the industrial interdependence of men. Their moral interdependence, he cannot yet grasp. Now is the time to teach him the arts that make men mutually useful. Émile must, therefore, be taken from one workshop to another, and must try his hand at

[9] *Ibid.*, pp. 302–5.
[10] *Ibid.*, II, 58.
[11] *Ibid.*, p. 43.

every trade. Now also is the time to instruct him regarding industrial exchange and such related matters as banking and transportation. In early childhood, he was taught how to preserve his life; now he must be taught how to live usefully to himself and others. Said Rousseau:

> Adapt the education of a man to his personal and not accidental abilities. Don't you see that, by bringing him up only to fill one station in life, you make him unfit for every other? You make a dependence on the actual order of society, without thinking that order subject to unavoidable revolutions. . . . The high may be reduced low, and the rich may become poor. . . . We certainly are approaching the crisis, . . . the age of political revolutions. Who can assure you what will be your lot? . . . There are no characters indelible but those imprinted by nature, and nature never made man royal, noble, or rich. . . . The man who earns not his subsistence, but eats the bread of idleness, is no better than a thief. . . . Rich or poor, strong or weak, every idle citizen is a knave.[12]

On the basis of that philosophy, Rousseau demanded a trade education for every boy. Manual labor is a natural pursuit and makes one not only useful but independent. With a trade "you have no need to fear or flatter the great, to creep or cringe to knaves."[13] In addition to these values, Rousseau saw still another one in trade education, that of mental discipline. Here again, this advocate of interest and utility, as principles of selection of studies, retains some elements of the old disciplinary philosophy.

> While I have accustomed my pupil to corporeal exercise and manual labor, I have given him insensibly a taste for reflection and meditation; in order to counterbalance that indolence which would be the natural result of his indifference to the opinions of mankind and the tranquillity of his passions. It is necessary that he work like a peasant and think like a philosopher lest he become as idle as a savage.[14]

(c) Methods of teaching intellectual subjects. To Rousseau, methods of teaching are of even greater importance than the things taught. Clinging to his fundamental principles, he states his views on the method of intellectual training:

> Let our senses then always be our guide, the world our only book, and facts our sole precepts. Children, when taught to read, learn that only; they never think; they gain no information; all their learning consists in words. Direct the attention of your pupil to the phenomena of nature, and you will soon awaken his curiosity; but to keep that curiosity alive, you must be in no haste to satisfy it. Put questions to him, . . . and leave him to resolve them.

[12] *Ibid.*, pp. 88–93.
[13] *Ibid.*, p. 98.
[14] *Ibid.*, pp. 114–15.

Let him take nothing on trust from his preceptor, but on his own comprehension. . . . If ever you substitute authority in the place of argument, he will reason no longer.[15]

Thus, Émile ought to study geography not from maps but from his own immediate surroundings, and he ought to make his own maps. It is better to know nothing than to be mistaken, or to have ideas that are not clear. The sciences he will learn by his own observation and by simple experiments. At all times, Rousseau stresses not the activity of the teacher but the activity of the child, an activity created by interest in problems that demand solution. Without formal instruction, Émile will acquire, by his own activity in workshops and by his own observation, an understanding of industrial relationships between men. Rousseau's revolt against book learning reached its height in such teachings as these.

(4) IN ADOLESCENCE. With the dawn of sex interest, nature demands that Émile's heart be brought into accord with the feelings of his fellows. Body, senses, mind, and heart compose the man. At the age of fifteen, only the heart remains to be developed. During the five succeeding years the goal of education is to make Émile loving and compassionate and "to perfect reason by sentiment,"[16] for he is "a savage destined . . . to inhabit . . . cities."[17] With sex interest comes an interest in all human relations. Love of all mankind and pity for all afflicted humans are the primary virtues to be acquired. These he will acquire by personal observation of the sufferings of the poor, the sick, and social outcasts. True pity springs from fear and is rooted in self-interest. The rich and powerful, having no such fear, know not pity. Émile must be made to fear that misery may one day be his own lot.

(a) Curriculum. In varying degrees of completeness, Rousseau discusses, as necessary studies, social inequalities, morality, religion, political science, history, courtship, marriage and parenthood, and interesting literature both ancient and modern. Generally, Émile will study men, as individuals and in their institutional relationships, in order that he may see that men have been depraved by society, and that he must respect the individual and despise the multitude. While history and biographies will help him to judge character, they are not sufficient. His tutor must have him tricked by conjurers, deceived by flatterers, misled by companions, and robbed by cheats. Only against the wiles of women must he be directly guarded. He must learn to be moral by experience, except

[15] *Ibid.*, p. 11.
[16] *Ibid.*, p. 116.
[17] *Ibid.*, p. 122.

when the risk is too great, and then he should have recourse to history, or fables, for the necessary experience.

(b) Religious education. Natural religion, as described at length in *Émile,* will be substituted for the supernatural religion of the traditional schools. Rousseau says that, at the age of eighteen, Émile may not know that he has a soul, for he has been taught only the things that he was able to understand. The dogmas of natural religion are said to conform with experience and reason. The existence of God, as demonstrated by reason and feeling, is the first dogma of natural religion, but little can be known of God beyond the fact of His existence. The second dogma is that of the existence of the soul and of rewards and punishments, a dogma founded upon feeling and desire, not upon reason or knowledge. Where reason fails in matters of religion, conscience is to be man's guide. Feeling and conscience are the measure of right and wrong. They never deceive us, and he who obeys them is following nature and, therefore, will not fall into an error of judgment or conduct. Philosophy leads men into error; feeling leads them to truth. Not to priests but to conscience and the book of nature, one ought to turn for light on questions of religion and morality. Émile must reject all authority and the beliefs of his countrymen regarding religion, and be guided entirely by his own reason and feelings in such matters. Since these natural authorities, implanted in him, can never discover the supernatural, his quest must end with natural religion. His tutor can guide him no farther.

(c) Sex education and training for parenthood. On the strength of the bond of confidence and affection established between the tutor and Émile the success of sex instruction will depend. Since marriage ought to be postponed until the age of twenty, Émile must be frankly informed of the dangers that beset him. At his present age restraint by knowledge is better than restraint by ignorance. Care must be taken that he receive all his sex information from his tutor. He must be protected from all harmful companions and influences, and be kept constantly engaged in physical exercises and hard work. Religious appeals to him are of no value. At appropriate times, the tutor will tell him of the laws of nature pertaining to sex, and the physical and moral evils which result from their violation. The dignity of marriage he must be constantly reminded of. At twenty he is ready to marry, and his tutor shall help him to find an ideal wife, but, before taking this final step, he must study the social and political institutions of neighboring nations so that he may determine under which system he wishes to spend his life.

(d) Instruction in economics and politics. To be a man among men Émile must know the world, and since books are of but little value for this purpose, he must travel with his tutor through neighboring countries and study their languages and institutions. One who is thus acquainted with a number of nations knows men. Now he will study governments and select the one under which he will live. He will study the origin of government, the various forms it has taken, and the advantages and disadvantages of each form. Questions of natural and civil liberty, of property rights, of sovereignty, of law, of the desirability of a federation of European states, etc., his tutor will discuss with him. Now, too, is the time to instruct him regarding the various occupations in which men engage, and the advantages and disadvantages of various pursuits. But this vocational guidance ought to lead Émile to farming as the safest and best way of living, and he should find a spot where taxes are low and homage has not to be paid to deputies, judges, priests, and to rogues of every kind.

(e) Other studies. During two years of travel, Émile will acquire a knowledge of national character, of two or three foreign languages, of natural history, political science, arts, and men. Then he is ready to marry and assume the responsibilities of a man, a husband, a father, and a teacher of his own sons. Rousseau viewed sex as important as age in guiding education.

(5) THE EDUCATION OF WOMEN. The perfect woman, Sophy, chosen since her childhood to be Émile's wife, is in many ways the opposite of Émile. The wisdom which her name suggests is that of the fox and not of the philosopher. "A perfect man and a perfect woman ought no more to resemble each other in mind than in features. . . . One must be active and strong, the other passive and weak."[18] Nature has designed her for man's delight, and her education should be directed toward that end. Motherhood and homemaking are her natural business. "Woman is worth more as a woman, but less as a man."[19] Whenever she usurps men's rights she becomes their inferior. While she has a right to think, she must always be humbly submissive to man's judgment. Unlike Émile, she must be subjected from childhood to many restraints. Says Rousseau: "The first and most important quality of a woman is gentleness. Made to obey a being as imperfect as man, . . . she ought early to learn to suffer even injustice, and to endure the wrongs of a husband without complaint; it is not for him, but for

[18] W. H. Payne, *Rousseau's Émile* (New York: Appleton-Century-Crofts, Inc., 1892), p. 260. (By permission.)

[19] *Ibid.*, p. 262.

herself that she ought to be gentle."[20] Her natural cunning makes her man's equal and his ruler, while she seems to obey him. Her teacher ought not to permit her to ask questions, but he ought to tease her into answering many. Religion is entirely beyond her grasp, but she must accept, on faith, first her mother's beliefs and then her husband's.

Rousseau considered women to be mentally inferior to men and incapable of abstract reasoning. Yet he would have Sophy taught reading, writing, and cyphering when she felt a need for them. All her studies should be practical. Among them should be a study of men and the accomplishments that make women agreeable to them. Her natural taste for finery and her native thirst for admiration should serve as guides in directing her education. Ornamental and plain needlework, and drawing, as a related study, should be taught her. Intellectual interests, however, destroy a woman's nature. Said Rousseau: "I would a hundred times prefer a simple girl, rudely brought up, to a girl of learning and wit who should come to establish in my house a literary tribunal of which she should make herself the president. A woman of wit is the scourge of her husband, her children, her friends, . . . of everybody."[21] The ideal natural woman is modest, gentle, patient, submissive, sensitive to rebukes, amiable, chaste, and charitable in her thoughts and words even toward other women. Viewed in the light of the freedom enjoyed by women of the eighteenth-century aristocracy, Rousseau's position was actually reactionary.

THE "EMILE" IN RETROSPECT AND PROSPECT. In the *Émile,* the protests of centuries against an education which ignored the nature of the individual, and made the book the center of all instruction, reached a culmination. That Rousseau had not in mind the needs of the masses, for whom his plan of individual instruction was completely impracticable, and that Émile is a child of the aristocracy, does not destroy the fundamental significance of his protest against an old education, psychologically unsound, practically unreal, and socially and philosophically unprogressive. In his fervent outpourings against the old, Rousseau gives us nothing scientific and much that is of doubtful wisdom. But he challenged the old practices with such bitter zeal and force that the world listened to his as to no other voice. The *Émile* marks, in a very special way, the beginning of an era of educational reform not only in psychology and methods of instruction but also in the movement to reform society by education. The anti-social implications of the *Émile,* negated

[20] *Ibid.,* p. 270.
[21] *Ibid.,* p. 303.

by Rousseau himself in other writings strongly nationalistic in their emphasis, brought other men to the defense of social institutions and helped, with other more potent forces, to stimulate a desire for social reform. Where men are still politically and spiritually free, many "progressive" thinkers, as Rousseau would have it, place the individual both at the beginning and end of the educational process. The individual does not exist for the state; the state exists for the individual. The individual does not exist for democracy; democracy exists for the individual, for the freedom of man and the growth of individuality. Where that ideal exists, there still lives the spirit of *Émile*.

Early Attempts to Reform Instruction

THE PHILANTHROPINISTS. We have already stressed the eighteenth-century preoccupation with nature as an infallible guide to which men should turn for light upon social problems. Rousseau and others, before and after his time, sought the guidance of nature in solving educational problems. Education must be in accord with nature, that is, as Rousseau taught, in accord with the native endowment of each individual. This native endowment might even be anti-social, but its free growth was justified either because of the conviction that traditional society was vicious or, more generally, because of the faith of intellectuals in the inevitability of social progress, supposed to result eventually in a free society of all humanity, an ideal thought to be attainable more rapidly through the freedom and natural growth of the individual. Rousseau rightly stressed the importance of developing the powers and organs which nature has given the child, but he erred in holding that this development is a spontaneous one, and its own end, without regard to the use to which the developed powers are to be put.

His concern with the natural development of children from their infancy had considerable influence upon the philanthropinists, Pestalozzi, Froebel, and, directly or indirectly, upon many others, including John Dewey and other modern progressive educators.

BASEDOW AND THE PHILANTHROPINISTS. The demand for natural education in the eighteenth century coincided with the demand for national education, first forcefully stated by La Chalotais (1701-1785) in his *Essay on National Education* (1763). In it he attacked the Jesuit schools for their failure to train their students for life and citizenship, and demanded a secular, national system of education, in which the children of the state would be educated by teachers in sympathy with the needs and ideals of the state. Although the basis of such a system had already been laid in some German states, the methods of instruction there needed reform. That work was undertaken by Johann Basedow (1724-1790), the first notable disciple of Rousseau, who would reform national education there by naturalizing the methods of instruction in conformity with the proposals of Comenius, Rousseau and La Chalotais. His *Elementarwerk* was modeled mainly upon the *Orbis Pictus* of Comenius, and his *Methodenbuch* embodied many of Rousseau's ideas of natural training. To reduce theory to practice he founded (1774) a short-lived school called the *Philanthropinum*, which was the precursor of many similar schools in Germany and Switzerland. The most influential propagandist for the philanthropinist movement was, however, Joachim Heinrich Campe (1746-1818) of Brunswick who, in collaboration with others, published a sixteen-volume work, *General Revision of the Whole System of Schools and of Education*, which contained practical suggestions for the reform of the curriculum and methods of instruction. The principle of utility was to be the guide to the curriculum, and the vernacular, physical education and handicrafts were elevated in importance. In Prussia, Baron von Sedlitz, minister of education of King Frederick the Great, saw the national significance of these reforms, and began to introduce them into the schools. In 1779, he established at Halle what was probably the first university professorship of pedagogy in the world, to train teachers in the new methods.

KANT AS DISCIPLE OF ROUSSEAU. Immanuel Kant (1724-1804), while professor of philosophy at the University of Königsberg, fell under the influence of the *Émile* and made Basedow's *Methodenbuch* the basis of his lectures on pedagogy, the essence of which appears in his brief treatise *On Pedagogy*. While he accepted in the main Rousseau's doctrine of natural education, he saw some measure of restraint in childhood essential to the attainment of true individual liberty. Like Rousseau, he denounced existing society, and saw in education, which he would make public but would preserve from control by selfish national rulers, the means to achieving the ideal world. It was in such an atmosphere of reform that Pestalozzi (1746-1827), a Swiss, appeared upon the scene.

The Pestalozzian Movement

Pestalozzi read the *Émile* soon after its publication, and was sufficiently converted to its philosophy to attempt the education of his own son according to its principles. In 1782, he published *Leonard and Gertrude*, in which he described the reform of a degraded Swiss village by Gertrude, his ideal teacher. He was author of many other works, including *How Gertrude Teaches Her Children* (1801), which provides the clearest exposition of his educational views. Pestalozzi fell heir to the view of earlier thinkers that man is a natural, not a supernatural, being, even in his mental life. That idea was strongly supported by Rousseau, who stressed the close relationship between mind and body. Yet neither Rousseau nor Pestalozzi abandoned the traditional dualistic conception of man's nature, which stressed the separateness of body and mind, though both of them leaned that way. Nowhere in Pestalozzi do we find suggested the experimental approach to a knowledge of the mind. Yet he labored to simplify instruction and to bring education into harmony with the nature and capacity of each individual child.

Pestalozzi's educational experiments, conducted in his native Switzerland, began in his orphan school at Neuhof (1774-1780), and continued in his schools at Stanz (1798), Burgdorf (1799-1804), and Yverdon (1805-1825). In these he attempted, in a homelike atmosphere, to improve the methods of teaching elementary subjects. At Neuhof, he combined industrial work for boys and girls with instruction in reading, writing, and arithmetic, the pupils supporting themselves by their own labor. This experiment demonstrated the beneficial effect of a good environment and of a systematic and active life upon the health, morals, and mental growth of children. The plan of combining the school with the workshop, which circumstances compelled Pestalozzi to abandon, was continued by Fellenberg in his Institute at Hofwyl (1806-1844), and gave rise to the "manual-labor movement," which reached America toward the close of the second decade of the century, and which assumed a sociological, much more than a psychological, significance. Having abandoned his first experiment, Pestalozzi, in his other three schools, with able and interested assistants at Burgdorf and Yverdon, devoted his time to reforming the methods of teaching the elementary subjects.

THE ABC OF OBSERVATION. Guided by his observation and experiments, Pestalozzi reached the conclusion that the fundamental principle of instruction is to reduce all subject matter to its simplest elements, which must be concrete in character, and make the observation of these elements by the pupil the basis of methods of teaching. That principle Pestalozzi called the "ABC of Observation." He thus made the observation of things, not of words and symbols, the basis of teaching, believing, as he did, that all knowledge is rooted in sense perceptions. This principle implied, among other items, the following basic procedures:

1. Reduction of subject matter to its simplest elements, objective and concrete in character
2. Grading these elements psychologically, or according to their difficulty for individual students, from the simple to the complex
3. Observation of these elements
4. Expression by the pupils of impressions regarding the elements thus observed.

These procedures Pestalozzi, with his assistants, attempted to apply in the teaching of elementary subjects, particularly in reading, writing, arithmetic, and geography. Believing that the senses are the gates to knowledge, he rejected the traditional book method of teaching in favor of object lessons and oral instruction. All of his teaching was a negation of the bookish and verbal method of the past, which filled children's minds with words, not with a clear understanding of things. The observation of objects familiar to the child would provide him with clear ideas of things, and give him the power to express in words those ideas.

Until Pestalozzi's day, the study of arithmetic, for instance, consisted in the memorization of rules, tables and symbols, meaningless to the child (because they lay outside of the pale of his experience), and the performance of mechanical written exercises with these symbols according to the letter of the rule, a rule usually lengthy and obscure. For such a procedure, Pestalozzi substituted mental arithmetic based upon observation not of words and symbols but of concrete objects, through the manipulation of which the child became familiar with arithmetical combinations, thus deriving from things clear ideas about number.

In teaching geography, he would make the subject a living one by having his pupils study physical conditions in the vicinity of the school and their influence upon the ways of life of the people. Beginning thus, the pupils would eventually make their own maps of the locality, or reproduce it in the form of a replica. Thus Pestalozzi would reverse the usual procedure by presenting the map last, and give that map a living significance for the pupil by having him construct it out of the materials of his own experience. From such a beginning the pupil would proceed gradually to a study of the geography of the world, with the purpose of seeing the relation of the physical environment to human life and activities. A similar practice was followed for other elementary subjects in Pestalozzi's school and, though much formalism marked the teaching even of Pestalozzi himself, the improvement over older methods was notable and attracted international attention.

OTHER PESTALOZZIAN IDEALS AND PRACTICES. Probably the most significant reform which he stressed was the cultivation of love and sympathy between the pupil and teacher, a reform which Rousseau forcefully demanded. The pre-Pestalozzian school, particularly that of the poor, embodied the belief that learning comes only through fear and terror. In addition, schools for the poor were cold, dreary, and filthy. Pestalozzi would transform them into houses of comfort and joy, in which the individuality of the child would be respected, and instruction be harmonized with his nature and abilities. The ideal school of Pestalozzi would resemble the ideal home and family. Education, as Pestalozzi defined it, is "the natural, progressive, and harmonious development of all the powers and capacities of the human being." That was a restatement of Rousseau's philosophy, but Pestalozzi, more than Rousseau, looked beyond the individual to a reform of society, a reform which, however, must begin with the individual.

The child's development, as he viewed it, is like the growth of a plant, a process of unfolding of inborn powers. That unfolding, however, he thought of as dependent upon observation and sense-perception. Indeed, it is difficult to reconcile the emphasis that Pestalozzi placed now on the growth from within, and then on the growth from without the individual. Yet, whatever be the process, the goal of education is the natural growth of the individual so that he may lift himself up through self-help and indirectly elevate society itself.

Unlike the plant, which is purely physical, the human organism has intellectual and moral aspects, and these too grow according to natural law. When these powers of body, heart, and head are fully developed and work in harmony, the goal of education has been reached. To knowing and feeling, Pestalozzi, like many predecessors, added "doing" as an important objective of education. The educated person must be skilful in applying knowledge to the problems of life. It is not so much knowledge as power and skill that count. Impressions ought to result in expression, in action. Pestalozzi's first experiment showed a concern for industrial, agricultural, and domestic training. His matured thought would have such training postponed until a general education had been provided. Yet, Pestalozzi saw that knowledge and judgment could be acquired by doing. So important did he consider practical activities and the training of children in practical skills that he would have developed a plan to that end had he had the opportunity to do so. Fellenberg and Froebel filled that gap in his work. Pestalozzi saw in such practical training not only a means for improving the life of the poor, but an educational device, psychologically sound.

In addition to intellectual and practical education, Pestalozzi also, respecting the emotional nature of man, stressed the need for religious and moral development—the development of the heart for the purposes of individual and social well-being. Out of the child's love for his mother, and such allied virtues as obedience and gratitude, develop the social and religious virtues of the grown man. Through good teaching the virtues of the infant are transformed into the virtues of the man. The method he used to develop these adult virtues was not the traditional one of catechizing, reading the Scriptures, or formal participation in church services, for Pestalozzi held that morals and religion could not be "taught." He led his pupils, as he would have other teachers do, toward morality and religion through personal experiences, and made their emotional response to that experience the basis of moral and religious instruction. Pestalozzi taught that the development of the basic emotions ought to precede intellectual training. It is the heart that gives meaning and value to the intellectual and practical activities of men. When the head and the hand operate in obedience to the urges of the heart, there is that harmonious development of the individual which Pestalozzi made the goal of education.

INFLUENCE AND SPREAD OF PESTALOZZIANISM. The contributions of Pestalozzi to educational progress are many and significant. Not the least of them was his ardent faith in education as a means of individual and social reform, which a world growing humanitarian, democratic, and nationalistic was ready to share in. Perhaps his belief that the good teacher can reform the world was a childish faith. While he contributed nothing scientific to psychological knowledge, he saw and, in an influential way, taught the world to see the dependence of sound teaching methods upon a scientific understanding of child nature and human development. All learning must begin with concrete human experience, and proceed from the simple to the complex by gradual steps in harmony with the gradual development of human powers. And the relationship between teacher and pupil must be one of kindness and sympathy, corporal punishment being permitted only as the last of all resorts. While modern experiments have disproved the validity or utility of the practices he himself used and approved, he laid the groundwork for fruitful reforms in the teaching of the elementary school subjects.

Into many of the cantonal schools of Switzerland, Pestalozzianism was introduced after the government had been liberalized in 1830. In France, largely, no doubt, because of the force of tradition there, little was done to promote such a reform. English statesmen and educators displayed a similar lack of interest for the same reason. In England, however, James P. Greaves and the Rev. Charles Mayo became active in promoting reform. Dr. Mayo, who studied Pestalozzi's methods at Yverdon, was responsible for the formalization of the object-lesson method, and it was in the Mayo form that Pestalozzianism had its widest reception in the United States. It was in Germany, especially in Prussia, that Pestalozzianism had its most notable development. Though introduced earlier, it was after the defeat of the Prussians by Napoleon at Jena, in 1806, that it was adopted nationally and for national ends. Frederick William III, Fichte, the philosopher of a new nationalism, and other prominent Prussians urged it as a means of regenerating the German masses and of building a strong state. The result was a general reform of the Prussian elementary school system as regards teacher training, school buildings and equipment, methods and school administration. That reformed system came to be known as "the Prussian-Pestalozzian school system."

The United States was touched by three waves of Pestalozzianism, the first being but a ripple. In 1806, William Maclure brought Joseph Neef, once an assistant of Pestalozzi, to Philadelphia, where he opened a school, in 1809. Neef's work in America, though it received some publicity, was not significant in its influence. Of far greater importance was the work of American educators who, beginning with John Griscom in 1818, visited Europe, studied the Pestalozzian reforms there, and reported their findings and impressions when they returned. William C. Woodbridge, editor of the *American Annals of Education,* Horace Mann, Henry Barnard and others did much in the eighteen-twenties and -thirties to promote reform here. Woodbridge, who visited Pestalozzi at Yverdon, published the *Rudiments of Geography* (1822) and *Universal Geography* (1824), both embodying Pestalozzian ideas. Lowell Mason, William Russell, and Herman Krüsi did much to introduce the new practice into schools in Massachusetts. Krüsi, a son of one of Pestalozzi's assistants, taught later at the normal school at Oswego, New York, which became the radiating center of the third wave of Pestalozzianism here.

In 1860, Edward A. Sheldon, Superintendent of Schools of Oswego, introduced, from Canada, into a normal school which he organized, the formalized Pestalozzianism of the Mayos of England. Through teachers trained in Oswego, the object-lesson method of teaching was spread throughout the United States. In 1865, a committee of the National Education Association gave the Oswego practices their approval. The object-lesson plan was thus the first major effort of American educators to psychologize instruction.

The Herbartian Psychological and Pedagogical Movement

More influential than Pestalozzi in laying the foundations of a psychological and scientific approach to education was the German philosopher and educator, Johann Friedrich Herbart (1776-1841). While indebted to Pestalozzi, whom he visited at Burgdorf, Herbart was, in many ways, an original and independent thinker, whose contribution was a necessary supplement to that of the Swiss reformer. Pestalozzi's ABC of Observation, while it explained for him the first step of mental development, left subsequent mental processes unexplained. Herbart went beyond sense-perception and observation to examine the phenomena of mental life, their bearing upon conduct, and the relation of instruction to mental growth and a virtuous life. At the University of Göttingen (1802-1808, 1835-1841), and at the University of Königsberg (1809-1835), he taught philosophy and pedagogy. At the latter institution he established a pedagogical seminar and a practice school for the theoretical and practical training of his advanced students. Of his many publications, *The Science of Education* (1806) and *Outlines of Educational Doctrine* (1835) are the most complete statements of his psychological and educational principles and recommended practices.

EDUCATIONAL AIM. Negating Rousseau's position, which represented a revolt against traditional morality and culture, Herbart made the ultimate goal of education the development of the religious and moral, or cultured, man. While not ignoring the importance of the physical environment and man's attitude toward it, he made man's relation to his social environment of greater import. To attain the ultimate goal, he set up, as an immediate one, the cultivation of "many-sidedness" of interest. While the doctrine of interest as a stimulant to learning was urged by Herbart and, still more, by his disciples, the doctrine of "many-sidedness" of interest pertained to the life-long scientific and ethical interests of the educated, cultured man, interests which are not means but ends of the educational process.

CONTENT OF EDUCATION. The sources out of which spring "many-sided interest" and, ultimately, virtue, are the physical and the human worlds. From these must be drawn the content of education, comprising the physical and natural sciences and the social and historical studies. While life-long interest in both these fields must be developed, the latter is the more important of the two, because it has a more intimate bearing upon moral conduct. Herbart's "cycle of thought" begins with knowledge, by which he meant not mere sense impressions, as did Pestalozzi, but clear ideas. The next step in the cycle is action, viewed as a product of clear ideas, and the final one is moral character. The final products are thus rooted in clear ideas about the physical and social worlds. The materials of instruction must be presented according to orderly procedures of mind-building if the ends desired are to be attained.

METHOD OF TEACHING. (1) HERBARTIAN PSYCHOLOGY. Herbart formulated a new psychology upon which he rested his whole scheme of method. Not only did Herbart negate the old idea of inborn faculties of the mind, but he denied the doctrine that the mind itself exists at birth. Body and soul exist at birth, but mind does not. Mind is merely the sum-total of ideas or impressions which enter into consciousness throughout one's lifetime, and is a result of contact between the soul and its environment. Ideas or "presentations," being particles of soul-stuff, are living and indestructible. That is true whether they reside in the realm of consciousness or of subconsciousness. Ideas keep passing between these two realms. Nor do they remain, each one as a separate and isolated entity. Rather, they group themselves into "apperceptive masses," according to similarities existing between them, by the process of "apperception," or the assimilation of new ideas by similar ones already in consciousness. This process of apperception is the learning process. The teacher's work is to direct that process. Instruction is the selection and orderly presentation of ideas by the teacher, who is both the architect and builder of minds. Such phenomena as feeling, willing and desiring are the product of ideas.

(2) INTEREST. The one indispensable condition of proper mind-growth, of learning, is interest. Interest is a force which, though distinct from ideas, has its origin in them and resides in them. It acts to retain ideas in consciousness and to recall them to consciousness. This power of interest is increased by the frequency with which the idea is presented to consciousness, and by the association of ideas in apperceptive masses. It is interest which determines what ideas or experiences shall occupy the realm of consciousness at any moment.

(3) Psychology Applied to Learning. Based upon his conception of the mind and his theory of apperception was Herbart's view regarding method. For him, there is a method, a general method, applicable to all subjects of instruction, because the mind assimilates all ideas, or experiences, in the same way. Since each new idea, experience, or "presentation" is interpreted and meaningful only in the light of past experience, the past experience of the pupil must be such as to guarantee the right kind of apperception or assimilation of the new idea. The first step of a teacher in presenting a new idea is to know what experiences already exist in the mind, call into consciousness, or supply, whatever may be needed for an assimilation of the new, and present the new when the mind can apperceive it properly. That is the first of five steps in the instructional process as modified by the Herbartians, and usually designated the *Five Formal Steps of the Recitation.* These steps are: (a) *Preparation,* or the preparing of the pupil's mind for the assimilation of the new idea; (b) *Presentation,* or the actual presenting of the new idea to be assimilated; (c) *Association,* or the actual assimilation of the new idea by the old; (d) *Generalization,* the forming of a general idea, concept, or definition upon the basis of the combined new and old experiences; and (e) *Application,* or the use of the acquired knowledge in solving problems to which it relates, and indicating the fields to which it applies. Herbart's followers applied them to each single recitation. These formal steps of instruction represent the practical application of Herbart's psychology and educational philosophy to the pedagogical process.

"CORRELATION," "CONCENTRATION," AND THE "CULTURE-EPOCH THEORY." Herbart taught that the subjects in the curriculum should be so interrelated that they form a unified conception of the world. The suggested practice of "concentration" differs from that of "correlation" in that, as a method of correlation, some one subject is to be made the core of the curriculum. Current in the thought of the time was the theory that each individual, as he develops, passes through stages corresponding to the stages of culture through which the race had passed in its development. That theory, accepted as valid by Herbart and his followers, is known as the "culture-epoch theory." It was applied to the psychological growth of the child and to the problem of method, but still more was it made to bear upon the selection of curricular material which, it was held, ought to parallel the cultural experiences of the race from the beginning of its development.

THE INFLUENCE OF HERBART. Among the chief contributions of Herbart were: (1) the effective negation of faculty psychology and a weakening of the doctrine of formal discipline, (2) the creation of a new psychology which he applied to education, and (3) the doctrine of interest both as a means and an end of instruction. The fact that Herbartian psychology and pedagogy have been since largely abandoned does not destroy their significance in our transition from the old to the new.

HERBARTIANISM IN GERMANY. After 1860, the universities of Leipzig and Jena became influential centers of Herbartianism. At Leipzig, Tuiskon Ziller (1817-1883) attempted to unify all instruction, beginning with the elementary grades, by a *concentration* of subject matter around history as a core study. He also developed the *culture-epoch theory* and applied it in constructing the curriculum. It was Ziller who reformulated Herbart's steps in instruction into the five formal steps which have been discussed above. And he inspired the founding of the Association for the Scientific Study of Education which spread quickly throughout Germany.

At Jena, Wilhelm Rein (1847-1929) followed the path of Herbartianism and made further practical application of its principles to the problem of the curriculum. In the form which it took at Jena, Herbartianism was carried to the United States by American students, who then frequented German universities for graduate work. It should be noted that, while Herbart himself was interested mainly in the improvement of secondary education, Ziller and Rein applied his theories mainly to the problems of the elementary school.

HERBARTIANISM IN THE UNITED STATES. After 1890, Herbartianism was spread quickly throughout the United States by teachers who had studied at Jena. Charles DeGarmo, of Cornell University, Charles A. McMurry, of the Illinois State Normal School, and Frank M. McMurry, of Teachers College, Columbia University, were the most influential of its early advocates. In *The Essentials of Method* (1889), DeGarmo began to popularize Herbartian theories. In 1892, Charles McMurry published his *General Method* and, in 1897, jointly with his brother Frank, *The Method of the Recitation*. Both of these works were based upon Herbartian principles. In 1892, The National Herbartian Society was founded to promote and adapt Herbart's system to American needs. Ten years later the name of the Society was changed to the National Society for the Study of Education. The rapidity of the spread of Herbartianism in the United States was almost phenomenal. By 1900, teacher training institutions had adopted it almost universally, and the tradition remained entrenched in them for two decades longer.

HERBARTIANISM AND THE CURRICULUM IN THE UNITED STATES. In addition to its influence upon the curriculum, Herbartianism stimulated an interest in the method of instruction. Between 1889, when DeGarmo's *The Essentials of Method* appeared, and 1920, pedagogical books, generally, sponsored the Herbartian "Five Formal Steps of Instruction," and students in teacher training institutions practised their application in the teaching of the several subjects of the curriculum.

THE DECLINE OF HERBARTIANISM IN THE UNITED STATES. After 1900, the worship of Herbart slowly declined in the United States. Darwinism, stressing the view of man as a biological organism, helped to destroy the foundations of Herbart's psychology and its educational implications. In Herbartianism there was too much emphasis on nurture and not enough on nature; too much on social heritage and too little on biological heritage. Besides, its own highly mechanical character and its perfection as a system brought a reaction in favor of less formal procedures. John Dewey, more than any other, weakened it by unanswerable objections to its shortcomings.

MERITS AND DEFECTS OF HERBARTIANISM. Among the merits of Herbartianism, John Dewey has listed the following: (1) the freeing of teaching from subservience to tradition by making it a planned, conscious, and precise process; (2) the abolition of the theory of innate mental faculties, which might be developed by any kind of exercise, if it were difficult enough, and the substitution for such exercises of definite subject matter consciously chosen in light of a definite educational aim; (3) the relating of method, now elevated in importance, to subject matter and to the immediate and ultimate goals of instruction.

Among its defects, Dewey lists the following: (1) it ignores the truth that man is a living, active, biological being who develops in response to his environment; (2) it magnifies the importance of the schoolmaster by making the human mind his handiwork, and by glorifying instruction and ignoring learning and student activity; (3) it worships the past and the intellectual aspects of the environment too much, ignoring the importance of sharing in the common experiences of living men; (4) it exaggerates the importance of formal methods; and (5) "it takes . . . everything educational into account save its essence—vital energy seeking opportunity for effective exercise."[22] The only objection that has been raised to

[22] J. Dewey, *Democracy and Education* (New York: The Macmillan Co., 1916), pp. 83–84. (By permission.)

Dewey's criticism, based, as it is, upon Darwinism and the psychology of functionalism, is that, in its preoccupation with biological evolution, it minimizes the import of social evolution, in which moral character is largely rooted.

The culture-epoch theory, stressing the notion of cultural recapitulation, as the later biological theory stressed biological recapitulation, helped to perpetuate the view that education ought to look to the literary and spiritual deposits of the past. That theory was in harmony with long-established traditions, but it lacked a scientific basis of fact. If life and learning were exclusively recapitulations of the past, there could have been no progress. Indeed, education ought to emancipate man from many restrictions which the past imposes upon him. To ignore the present environment to the extent that the Herbartians did is both unprogressive and unrealistic. While a knowledge of the past is vitally important for an understanding of the present and a control of the future, the individual must not be brought into complete spiritual accord with it, unless social stagnation is the goal we aim at. Dewey's view, which has found wide theoretical acceptance, that education is life and growth, not information about life in the past nor a preparation for life in the future, negates some of the most basic concepts of Herbart and his followers. And Dewey's position, based on a biological view of man's nature, claims the support of science rather than of metaphysical assumptions.

It ought to be noted also that Herbart's system of mind-building according to an exact plan and acceptable cultural patterns is better suited to conservative and authoritarian political and social institutions than to democratic societies, in which individualism is exalted, and change is recognized not only as inevitable but desirable. True it is that his psychological approach to education was an individualistic one and that he was concerned with private rather than public morality, but the Prussian state saw nothing subversive in his system. He himself may not have sensed its political and social implications but its conservatism was in keeping with Old-World traditions and official German interests.

The Froebelian Movement

In the line of reformers influenced directly by Pestalozzi and indirectly by Rousseau stands Friedrich Froebel (1782-1852). But there were other, and perhaps more profound, influences which affected him. The romanticism of his time, with its faith in man's kinship with nature; advanced scientific thought striving to find a principle or force permeating all forms of life and being; the Hegelian philosophy of history with its teaching that a divine principle of Reason has directed the evolution of society toward a final world unity, embodying the Absolute; the belief, fundamental to all of these other influences, that the universe has emerged by a process of evolution with which education ought to be in harmony; and his own observation of the activities of children are all reflected in the educational thought and practices of Froebel. He appeared at a time of intense German nationalism when, following the idealism of Hegel,[23] and the nationalistic demands of Fichte,[24] the ends of the state were made supreme, and individuality was viewed as opposed to their attainment.

THE DOCTRINE OF UNITY. In his book *The Education of Man* (1826), Froebel expounded the theory practised in his school at Keilhau, to which he, in the spirit of nationalism, gave the name the "Universal German Institute of Education."

All of his thought was linked to his mystical theory of the universe in which he viewed the whole cosmos as a unity sprung from the Absolute, or God. Within this all-inclusive unity, each individual thing, whether it be man, animal, plant, inanimate object, or human society, is itself an individuality and a unity, all these individual unities being bound into the one great cosmic unity, which is God, conceived of as a spiritual being. Froebel opens his *Education of Man* with the statement: "In all things there lives and reigns an eternal law. . . . This law has been and is enounced with equal clearness and distinctness in nature (the external), in the spirit (the internal), and in life which unites the two. This all-controlling law is necessarily based on an all-pervading, energetic, living, self-conscious, and hence eternal Unity. . . . This Unity is God. All things have come from the Divine Unity, from God, and have their origin in the Divine Unity, in God alone."[25]

From this mystical idealism followed the principle of the unity of man, nature, and God, from which all the educational principles of Froebel are deduced, either directly or indirectly. *Unity* and *continuity* in the development of the race and of the child, the *culture-epoch theory*, and *connectedness* in the studies which a pupil pursues were minor derivatives from his fundamental principle. Psychologically, man is viewed as a plant developing as a unity according to a law of nature unfolding within him. The intellectual, physical, and moral aspects of his nature are not sep-

[23] *Supra*, pp. 424 f.
[24] *Supra*, p. 424.
[25] Hailmann edition (New York: Appleton-Century-Crofts, Inc., 1887), pp. 1–2.

arate things but a unity. Mind, body, and soul are one. More important than these principles from the standpoint of educational practice were those of: (1) *Free Self-activity,* (2) *Creativeness,* (3) *Social-participation,* and (4) *Motor-expression.* Because Froebel rooted these principles in his mystical conception of the universe, their practical and psychological import were long lost sight of by his followers.

FREE SELF-ACTIVITY. Education, as Froebel viewed it, is a process of individual growth directed by inner forces in the child. This growth of the child differs from that of a plant in that, by conscious perception and reason, he can direct the process. He can be made conscious of the working of God within him. The divine spirit reveals itself in his activities, if these activities are permitted to be spontaneous. By divine law, this free self-activity directs his growth along the path of racial development, and merges his individuality with the spirit of humanity. In this humanizing of his spirit, the teacher will provide appropriate racial experiences, but, while directing the process, he must always follow nature, never thwart it, for he is but nature's assistant. Education, says Froebel, should not be *"prescriptive, categorical, interfering,"* [26] but should provide for "free self-activity and self-determination on the part of man, the being created for freedom in the image of God." [27]

Of the many forms of free self-activity, the play of childhood is of paramount significance. "The child is father of the man," and play is nature's way of directing his growth according to the social pattern, which is itself an expression of the unfolding divine spirit. In childhood, he observes the world and imitates it in play. In boyhood, he thinks about it, and now is the time to acquaint him with the Christian interpretation of it, with natural sciences, which reveal the working of God in nature, and with mathematics, which links the human mind with the physical world. To these studies, Froebel would add languages, because they point to the connection between the different things in nature, and arts, through which the soul expresses itself in a variety of ways, such as drawing, painting and modelling.

CREATIVENESS. Man is, by nature, an active, dynamic being, not a merely receptive, passive observer of events. United to the creative spirit of God, the Absolute, he, like God, is endowed with creative energy. He grows by the free play of his creative, self-active nature. *"God created man in his own image; therefore, man*

[26] *Ibid.,* p. 7.
[27] *Ibid.,* p. 11.

should create and bring forth like God."[28] His education ought to stimulate the exercise of his creative capacity.

SOCIAL PARTICIPATION. Man and all his activities are related by the nature of things, by necessity, to society, of which he is a part. He acts, and must act, in a social medium, and all his activities have social meanings and implications. His education must, therefore, take place in a social setting, and through his participation in the activities and life of society. Here we have a negation of Rousseau's anti-social philosophy. Social education looms large in the thought of Froebel. Each school he would make a miniature society, through the group organization and activities of which the child would be socialized.

MOTOR-EXPRESSION AND ACTIVISM. Related directly to his basic principle of "self-activity" is his principle of "motor-expression." Defending handwork as a school activity, he says: "To learn a thing in life and through doing is much more developing, cultivating, and strengthening, than to learn it merely through the verbal communication of ideas. Similarly, plastic material representation in life and through doing, united with thought and speech, is by far more developing and cultivating than the merely verbal representation of ideas."[29]

That principle embodies the recognition of the unitary character of human nature and of its growth through the activity of all of its parts. Head, soul, and hand are inseparable and interdependent parts of man which ought to be developed in unison. Mind and soul express themselves and grow through bodily activity and expression. Thinking must express itself in motor activity, in doing; otherwise the educational process remains unproductive.

The importance of motor activity had been urged by many educators from the sixteenth century onward. Thus we find the need for industrial training urged by Rabelais, Campanella, Andreae, Comenius, Locke, Budd, Francke, Rousseau, Basedow, Pestalozzi, Fellenberg, and many others. While recognizing the economic value of such training, many of these preferred to think of the training of the hand as an essential phase of a general education, and emphasized, as did Froebel, its educational rather than its vocational value.

SYMBOLISM. There is, according to Froebel and his forerunner Hegel, an Absolute goal toward which all things are growing. This Absolute is present, but only implicitly, in every existing thing. De-

[28] *Ibid.*, pp. 30–31.
[29] *Ibid.*, p. 279.

velopment, or growth, of anything consists in making this Absolute explicit by a gradual unfolding process. Hegel taught that this outward realization of the inner Absolute is realized through historical institutions, particularly the state, in each one of which some aspect of the Absolute resides. Froebel taught that the Absolute goal is realized through the presentation of symbols which represent the various aspects of the Absolute. Without such symbols that conception would remain dormant. Everything, for Froebel, possessed some inner symbolic meaning. Balls, spheres, cubes, forms of all kinds, motions, colors, words, play, games—everything—had, for him, a force which elicits in the child his innate notion of Unity, of the Absolute, or of some aspect of the Absolute. Since primitive times man has always used symbols to represent his ideas, but Froebel erred in reading into such a practice a mystical meaning.

THE KINDERGARTEN. In 1837, Froebel established the first kindergarten. It was to be, as the name implies, a garden in which children grow up as trees and flowers grow. In addition to this and a few other kindergartens, he established a school to train kindergarten teachers. Indeed, he believed that every mother should be so trained, and that every home should be a form of kindergarten. In his own school, Froebel practised his educational theories. Briefly, every child was presented with "gifts" in which Froebel saw appropriate symbolic meaning, and these "gifts" led to the "occupations" or activities of the child, through which his growth was supposed to proceed according to the laws of his inner nature. A ball, a sphere, a cube, and a cylinder were the first "gifts." To these, others were added as the child grew older. Froebel's view regarding the purpose and value of them all may be gleaned from his remarks on the value of the ball as an educational device. It ought to be given to the child at the age of three months. Its presentation will lead immediately to play. Symbolizing, as Froebel believed it does, the unity of the universe and the child's own nature, it elicits in him his own inner idea of that unity and his participation in it. The play it stimulates trains the senses and muscles and his power of attention, while giving him, at the same time, confidence in his own abilities. The moving ball, now in his grasp and now out of it, teaches him the meaning of such things as space, time, the past, present, and future. The mother or teacher sings in imitation and description of the motions of the ball, and the child thus learns the meaning of the words *up, down, out, around,* etc. As the child grows older, the motion of the ball becomes a symbol of life. The various ball-games can and ought to be graded according to the stage of growth reached by the child.

In addition to the "gifts," which reveal the nature mainly of inanimate things to the child, Froebel introduced into his kindergarten gardening and the care of pets, to develop a sympathetic understanding of living things, and nursery songs and rhymes, to reveal the inner life of animals and mankind. Games and songs were the chief features of Froebel's kindergarten.

MERITS AND DEFECTS OF FROEBELIANISM. Among the merits of Froebel's theory are to be listed: (1) a recognition of the importance of the native capacities of children, (2) the necessity of a sympathetic regard for these capacities on the part of parents and teachers, (3) the view that education is growth, the growth from within of native capacities, and must be in harmony with the natural evolution of the child's activities, (4) the recognition of the educational value of play, self-activity, motor activity, creative work, social participation, and learning by doing, and (5) the doctrine that knowledge is not the end of education but a means toward the end, which is the growth of inner capacities. These doctrines, divorced from the mysticism of Froebel, have been found to be psychologically, socially, and practically sound, and have been embodied in educational practices from infant schools to universities.

While many have condemned Froebel's views because of a too great significance he attached to play, and a too little significance to knowledge in the intellectual sense, the chief defect in his position, a defect about which there can be little doubt, is his view that there is some remote, mystical goal toward which the growth of the child must be directed, a goal which cannot be directly perceived. To look upon human actions and visible things as symbols of the Absolute and Eternal is to introduce into the realm of reality a concept that is unnecessary and vague. To insist upon the use of set symbols in the training of children must lead, as it did in Froebel's own kindergarten, to the imposition of external controls upon them, and to the stifling of the spontaneity and freedom of their activity, which Froebel stipulated as the most essential of all conditions of growth.

THE KINDERGARTEN MOVEMENT IN AMERICA. A reactionary Prussian government closed all kindergartens, in 1851, because they were suspected of socialistic and liberal leanings dangerous to the existing government. In the friendlier and more liberal atmosphere of America the kindergarten was destined to have its most significant development. The first of them were established here by German political exiles after the Prussian revolution of 1848.

Mrs. Carl Schurz led the movement when she opened a kindergarten at Watertown, Wisconsin, in 1855. Elizabeth P. Peabody opened the first English kindergarten in America, in Boston, in 1860. Thereafter, until 1900, kindergartens were provided by a rapidly increasing number of city school authorities, and by private philanthropic associations which, by the close of the century, numbered nearly five hundred. The rapidity with which the movement spread here was little short of phenomenal. Since 1900, the mysticism of Froebel, which marked our early kindergartens, has been abandoned by American kindergarteners, and the school has been brought into harmony with the spirit of the other schools in the system. Indeed, many earlier practices of our kindergartens have been abolished or modified.

THE MANUAL-TRAINING MOVEMENT. Indirectly, through Uno Cygnaeus (1810-1888), who introduced domestic hand work (*sloyd*) into Finnish schools in 1866, Froebel started the "manual-training" movement in education. The idea embodies the Froebelian principle of motor expression, and the movement embodies an attempt to carry it into practice throughout the various grades of schools. The development of the hand for educational, not occupational, ends was the purpose back of the manual-training practice. The movement aimed to produce manual dexterity through the use of tools, not to make craftsmen, but to develop the native capacities of the individual by providing an outlet for the inner urge to express one's ideas in an external form. It was, to a degree, a protest against the supposedly detrimental effect of factory occupations upon the life and character of workers, and against the drift toward narrow vocational training, which had no regard for the natural needs and urges of youth. As indicated earlier, emphasis had long been placed upon the educational value of hand training, and Americans were familiar with the idea. Indeed, Thomas Budd, of colonial New Jersey, had been one of the early advocates of it. Pestalozzian influence, as embodied in the manual-labor movement earlier in the century, directed attention to the educational value of such training, although its social and economic values were kept in the foreground. It was Froebel, however, who popularized the idea, arguing for it that doing preceded thinking in racial development, and that man, like God, should create things. For these reasons, he would have manual activity combined with study in all schools.

The Froebelian idea of manual training was brought influentially to the attention of American educators during the Centennial Exposition in Philadelphia in 1876, in which it was demonstrated as it was being practised in schools above the kindergarten in Finland

and Russia. President Runkle, of the Massachusetts Institute of Technology, made a report to the trustees which resulted in the establishment of a School of Mechanic Arts, the purpose of which was "not to fit the pupil for a particular trade, but to develop the bodily and mental powers in harmony with each other."[30] In 1879, the St. Louis Manual Training School was established and, in the eighteen-eighties, similar schools were established in Baltimore, Chicago, Cleveland, Philadelphia, and Toledo. In other places, about the same time, manual-training departments were added to schools of the old type. By 1900, the practice had spread widely throughout America.

Everywhere, the sponsors of the idea stressed the mental, disciplinary, and cultural value of the practice. While but few may have hoped to direct the enthusiasm for manual training into vocational channels, the movement did much to modify the age-old conception of education as a purely literary and intellectual process, and to prepare the way for a conception that would bestow upon industrial training for industrial ends a dignity equal to that traditionally bestowed upon literary or academic training. Indeed, in an industrialized society it may well be deemed an essential element of a liberal education.[31] In keeping with American democratic idealism, the traditional conception of a liberal education has been effectively challenged for more than half a century. Instead of defining it, as was wont, in terms of the rights and needs of a socially privileged class, and in terms of literary and nonpractical content, most American educators have come to define it in terms of the needs and capacities of individuals, and have insisted upon the principle of the equivalence of all studies, whether literary or practical, when they have been pursued for equal lengths of time.

BUSY WORK AS EDUCATION. It was not merely kindergartens and manual-training schools and departments that were haunted, a few generations ago, by the ghost of Froebel. Even the "little red schoolhouse" fell under his spell, though the teacher may not have known even his name. The belief that it is essential to keep children busy is probably as old as is teaching. Thus, Christian teachers insisted upon spiritual and mental drudgery to keep youths out of the clutches of the devil, and the formal disciplinarians made education formal, useless, disagreeable, and, sometimes, terrifying in order to

[30] Cited by T. Woody, "Historical Sketch of Activism," *The Thirty-third Yearbook of the National Society for the Study of Education*, Part II, 29.

[31] T. Woody, *Liberal Education for Free Men* (Philadelphia: University of Pennsylvania Press, 1951), chap. viii.

build strong mental faculties and to fix the habits of thought and behavior of men. Since primitive times, education has never, except possibly in a few isolated instances, been a joy of youth. Nor was keeping them busy motivated by a respect for the nature of children. Froebel's doctrine of free self-activity was a negation of the old formal discipline of the schools, and yet it produced another disciplinary formalism. In the eighteen-eighties, "busy work," designed to keep heads and hands busy, according to the principle of self-activity, made its entrance into the "little red schoolhouse," and pedagogues published books describing thousands of devices to keep the "young barbarians" harmlessly but profitably engaged. Making mud pies, designing worlds with beans, clipping and folding paper, and thousands of other activities were introduced for the purpose of "teaching the young idea how to shoot." Active natures called for a busy life, and teachers found in "busy work" youth's stepping-stones to heaven. The old education stressed knowledge as the path to a better society; the new, equally formal, and directed toward the same goal, stressed formal activities, many of them useless.

Dewey and the Progressive School Movement

HISTORICAL SETTING. For a century, America has been the world center of educational theory and experiment. While interest in child nature had been stimulated here by the followers of Rousseau, Darwinism opened up new avenues of thought which have had significant results for educational theory and practice. Ours was mainly a Calvinist inheritance which, while it stood for freedom of conscience and democracy, viewed human nature as corrupt and harsh discipline of children a religious necessity. The doctrines of faculty psychology and formal discipline fitted well into the pattern of theological authoritarianism of our Puritan past, as did also the conviction that education, rightly understood, is a mastery of formal subject matter. Before Dewey (1859-1952) entered the scene, Horace Mann and many others, largely under Pestalozzian influence, had demanded more humane treatment of children by more humane teachers. Closer to him in time were the humanitarian reforms of methods of teaching of Colonel F. W. Parker at Quincy, Massachusetts, and at the Cook County Normal School, Chicago.[32] But all these were practical reforms without a philosophical basis such as Froebel, in his *Education of Man,* and William T. Harris (1835-

[32] L. E. Patridge, *The Quincy Methods* (New York: Kellogg, 1885).

1909), a Hegelian idealist and United States Commissioner of Education, in his *Psychological Foundations of Education* [33] had provided.

On the philosophical side—and Dewey is primarily a philosopher—he owes much to his American contemporaries, Charles Peirce and William James, both of whom grounded their thought upon the realities of the world of experience and common sense, and placed their faith, in their search for truth, in experience and the scientific method. Looking back, as he did, over many centuries of sterile search for "abstract truth," and absolutes, and beholding the new world which science and democracy promised, he set out, as did Peirce and James, to bring absolutes down to earth and give them concrete expression in institutions and human life. Both scientific method and democracy are central in Dewey's thought. For him democracy is more than a system of economic, social, and political institutions. It is a way of life, of moral behavior, which should exist among men, and a faith in man's ability to build a society and a world in which it will be possible for him to achieve the possibilities of his nature. In philosophy, Dewey was indebted chiefly to James, but he was not a mere repeater of James or of anyone else. Much of his thinking is original. He always looked critically upon the views of his predecessors.

DEWEY'S PHILOSOPHY AND PSYCHOLOGY. Dewey is the leading exponent of biological pragmatism. Some, however, such as Professor John L. Childs, prefer to call his position experimental naturalism. The traditional philosophies sought a Reality behind the appearances and changing phenomena of nature and the visible world. For them, things are not as they appear, and men can come to know them not by sense experience but by reason and intuition. These thinkers formulated theories of general knowledge (epistomologies) in which they showed how knowledge of Reality is possible. They were not concerned with the mode of seeking the knowledge necessary in solving a practical problem, the type of knowledge acquired by experience and the scientific method. It is this latter type of knowledge which Dewey placed first in importance. In his naturalism there is nothing outside of nature which should occupy the thought of men. For Dewey, man is a purely natural being living in an ever-changing natural environment, knowable by experience and experiment, which should be the starting point of all philosophy and education. To this universe of uncertainties man must adjust himself by the indispensable, and only

[33] (New York: Appleton-Century-Crofts, Inc., 1901.)

serviceable, tools of experience, experiment and the exercise of his intelligence. Reality and meanings are not things separate from one's everyday experience. Principles and "truths" are rooted in such experience and are not, as were, for instance, Plato's Ideas, independent, *a priori* existences. In their precarious world, men have acquired control over their environment by the invention of tools and techniques, and by the use of the experimental method rather than by philosophical speculation about abstract truths, or by appeals to supernatural powers. The intellectual things of real value have never been divorced from the practical, and Dewey protested against schools for separating them. For him mind is not something fixed but a process of growth. The child acquires mind, or rationality, as he learns the meaning of things in his environment. It is but a phase of a unitary organism in the process of development, not a separate entity. Nor are sensory stimuli, ideas, and motor expressions separate things, as older psychology taught, but different functions of a "single concrete whole," the living organism.

The old dualistic conception of human life is thus negated. Mind, soul, and body are one. Ideas and acts are one. Mind is a product of activity, and it develops through activity. Dewey thus views man as a unitary psycho-physical organism acting and functioning in response to environmental stimuli. Thought is an instrument (instrumentalism) whereby the organism adjusts itself to its environment. The value, or the truth, of thought consists not in its grasp of some supposed ultimate or universal reality, as idealists would have it, but in its bearing upon the solution of practical problems. An idea, which is but a proposal for action, is valid if it solves the problem that gave rise to it, and the man in the street can have a valid idea as well as a scientist. Since man is an evolving organism adapting himself to a changing environment through mental processes, he ought to use his mental power now, as in his prehuman days, to solve the practical problem of his own preservation.

The biological foundation of such a philosophy and psychology is apparent. Religion, ethics, and knowledge are biological things, and life itself is a purely natural product resulting from the interplay of material forces. By human effort, however, nature can be controlled, and collective effort is more productive of desirable results than is individual effort. Therefore, Dewey and his school put a primary stress on society and social effort. Our world is one of change, of uncertainty, where action, not contemplation, brings success in man's struggle. Knowledge is but ability to direct change. Only such thoughts as change the world are true, for truth and usefulness are identical. The ideal society is one in which everyone is engaged in work which contributes to the common well-being.

DEWEY'S EDUCATIONAL PHILOSOPHY. On such a psychology and philosophy Dewey bases his educational theory. He abandons entirely the "faculty" view of the mind, and rejects the notion of a curriculum based upon fixed human knowledge, subdivided logically into subjects, and parts of subjects, woven into courses capable of being completed in fixed intervals of time. As opposed to the older position, he sees the child as a unity developing through its own activity, but in a social setting. Dewey's social emphasis is, perhaps, his greatest contribution to educational theory. Mind, being a social product, depends for its growth upon a social environment. It is a social experience which interprets for the child the meaning of physical stimuli such as light and sound. The mind is not developed through direct contact with the physical world, but through contact with that world as interpreted by the accumulated experience of men throughout ages of social development. The facts that have been labelled geography, arithmetic, etc., are not purely external, but facts rooted in social situations and needs. The teacher should not present them to the child as knowledge unrelated to his own needs and experience. All sciences and arts should be reduced to terms of pupil experience and need. Otherwise they will remain meaningless and lifeless symbols. Education is the reconstruction of the experience of the child until it expands into the organized experiences that are called "subjects." Seen by him as related to his own needs and experiences, the curriculum becomes vital for the pupil, and he learns with a purpose.

In all learning, action must precede thought, for mind is a product of activity, not the source of activity, as the older psychology would have it. Thought springs from needs created by practical difficulties, and it is never an end but only a means to an end, which is the satisfaction of a felt need, the solution of a problem recognized as significant. In education, action should hold the primary place. Education is purposeful activity in the solution of problems recognized by pupils as worth-while, and involving reflection as to means, ends, and consequences of one's actions. The activity must be inspired, not by the teacher, but by the pupil's own feeling of need for a solution of a problem. It must arise freely and spontaneously out of a life situation.

ACTIVISM IN EDUCATION. The idea of "learning to do by doing" can be traced back to antiquity. From the Renaissance onward, occasional writers, Comenius being a notable example, stressed it.

Rousseau, Pestalozzi, and Froebel did much to popularize it. The manual-labor and, still more, the manual-training movement brought a recognition of the importance of motor activity. Since 1896, when Dewey established his experimental school at the University of Chicago, the activity movement has made wide advances not only in the growth of schools embodying its philosophy but in stimulating educational reform in existing institutions of every grade. The new activists, following Dewey, stress social activism. In practice, however, the "activity school" and "activity method," in the free atmosphere of America, have almost as many meanings as there are men who interpret them. Upon one idea only is there universal agreement, namely that pupil activity, whether spontaneous or directed, is the best method of learning.

In his school in Chicago, Dewey taught by means of problems arising in life situations. Thus he aimed to develop thought and test it by action, on the theory that only the tested thought is really knowledge. Further, the social aspect of the educational process was stressed in his school. Yet, Dewey rejected the view that the child ought to be adjusted to the existing social order. Dewey's society is a changing one, not one that is fixed. His school was organized as a miniature society, the activities of which arose out of social problems, and led the students to an understanding of them and the way of their solution. Here, learning came by co-operative activity and living. Says Dewey of his experiment: "In intent, whatever the failures in accomplishment, the school was 'community-centered.' It was held that the *process* of mental development is essentially a social process, a process of participation; traditional psychology was criticized on the ground that it treated the growth of mind as one which occurs in individuals in contact with a merely physical environment of things. And . . . the *aim* was ability of individuals to live in co-operative integration with others." [34]

While Dewey rejects many views of his predecessors, he also approves many of them. Rousseau's ideas that education is the growth of native capacities, with which it must be in harmony; that it is imperative by natural necessity; and that personal experience is the best teacher meet with his complete approval. Froebel's principles of self-activity and social participation he accepts completely, and, in his experimental school, he attempted to apply them to older and younger children alike, but his symbolism he rejects. For the symbols, he would substitute real life experiences and occupations.

[34] Woody, "Historical Sketch of Activism," *loc. cit.*, p. 36; M. C. Baker, *Foundations of John Dewey's Educational Theory* (New York: King's Crown Press, 1955), pp. 136–57.

With Herbart, Dewey finds himself largely in disagreement, as we have seen.

To bring the school into touch with life as changed by the Industrial Revolution and democracy was the basic aim of Dewey's experiment. Existing schools failed to keep pace with the changes that had occurred. The modern child knows little about the processes by which his needs for food, clothing, and shelter are supplied. Unlike the child of the past, his ordinary life, practically, morally, and intellectually, lacks educational opportunity. As Dewey sees it, it has become the duty of the school in our industrialized society to abandon its tradition of bookishness, and provide those real life experiences of which the child has been robbed in the changed home and community environment of the present. For the listening school he would substitute the school of activity, in which morals as well as occupational skills are acquired by living and acting in real situations. Indeed, the school ought to be a reproduction of society, as it actually is, and in it the child should have actual experience with the needs and problems of social life. Thus, the economic, social, political, and all other activities and problems of society should constitute the curriculum of the school. The school, as Dewey stated it, should be life, not a preparation for life. Children should be made participators in the social and moral struggles of their communities. Since they are to live in a democratic society, they should help to organize one and live in it. The basic purpose of the school is to train pupils in "cooperative and mutually helpful living." Through the school's various activities, the pupil's native impulses will be directed toward the reform of society outside of the school. The school will thus serve to free society from its inherited evils by identifying itself with social and democratic life.

In Dewey the psychological and sociological movements in education thus converge. His books are landmarks in educational thought, and his influence has been marked not only in America but abroad as well.[35] *School and Society, How We Think, Interest and Effort in Education, Experience and Education* and the fullest single statement of his views, *Democracy and Education,* are his most important educational works. His influence may be seen in the rise of many "activity schools" at home and abroad, schools that have attempted to bring education and life together. Among these are: J. L. Meriam's school, Columbia, Missouri; Ethical Culture School, New York; Park School, Baltimore; Chevy Chase Country Day School, Washington, D.C.; the Lincoln School, New York; and many

[35] W. W. Brickman, "John Dewey's Foreign Reputation as an Educator," *School and Society,* LXX (October 22, 1949), 257–65.

others. There have been at work other influences than that of Dewey in the rise of activity schools here, as, for instance, that of the French psychologist, Seguin,[36] and of Madame Montessori, but these others have been of lesser significance. Other examples of the Dewey influence appear in such departures from traditional procedures as the "project method," and the Dalton and Winnetka plans of instruction. The fundamental psychological idea embodied in all of these is that of growth through self-activity.

Of all of these reforms in method, that of the "project" has been most widely adopted. It rests upon Dewey's principle that a complete act of thought results only from a felt need and the actual solution of a problem arising from that need. Professor William H. Kilpatrick has been the chief elaborator and popularizer of the "problem-project" method. It represents an attempt to have children learn with a purpose, and to foster thinking rather than memorizing by beginning each act of learning with a problem that creates interest and thought. The psychology back of it is the physiological conception of the mind which Dewey and Thorndike, though not always in agreement on details, accept as a substitute for the Herbartian.

The project method has political as well as psychological import. The purposeful thinking and acting which the method is intended to stimulate are viewed by Kilpatrick and his followers as essential in the life of free men, and in the preservation and improvement of democratic society. If the schools of our democracy are to serve society as they should, it is their duty to train youths to act with a purpose, for the worthy life is the purposeful life. The worthy life, Kilpatrick views as one directed toward social goals; and the good citizen, as one who lives and acts with worthy social aims in mind.[37]

This reform movement has been, in a notable way, an expression of the educational implications of the American concept of democracy as it emerged during the nineteenth century. That concept recognizes the right of every individual to equality of educational and economic opportunity, and to the fullness of growth of his native spiritual endowment. It repudiates the doctrine that special privileges are the birthright of any man or group. Liberty, individualism, and equality are its central elements. Where the unrestrained lib-

[36] H. Holman, *Seguin and His Physiological Method of Education* (London: Sir Isaac Pitman & Sons, Ltd., 1914).

[37] W. H. Kilpatrick, *The Project Method* (New York: Teachers College, Columbia University, 1918), p. 6; B. H. Bode, *Modern Educational Theories* (New York: The Macmillan Co., 1927), pp. 141–67, 171–92; *The Thirty-third Yearbook of the National Society for the Study of Education,* Part II (1934); W. H. Kilpatrick, *The Foundations of Method* (New York: The Macmillan Co., 1925).

erty of a selfish few threatens the equality of the many we demand that that liberty be restricted. We place the common good before that of the few. Our democracy implies a continuous readjustment of the social order toward a fuller recognition by all of the interests of all. And it is our faith that education will bring that more enlightened understanding of our common problems which is essential to a just solution of them.

EVALUATIONS OF DEWEY. To say that Dewey has become a storm center is an understatement. By some he is seen as the modern philosopher of nihilism who would destroy all philosophy and drag America and the world into chaos and perdition.[38] Others see him as the herald of a new and better day for America and the world. Between those who view him as a devil and those who view him as a saint stand the open-minded critics who, while they see some flaws in his thought, are in sympathy with his basic proposals and ideals.[39] That so much has been written about him, during his lifetime and since his death, both by friends and foes, is, in some measure, an indication of his greatness. His own writings would fill a small library. The world of the future will have to wrestle with the thought of this son of a small-town grocer of Vermont, and it may find him a prophet. No student of education can afford to ignore his educational philosophy.

While, no doubt, his demand that the problems of modern society be taught realistically alarmed social conservatives, his caustic criticism of traditional education in all its basic aspects became a matter of widespread questioning. Here was a social reformer who carried his respect for individuality to a point viewed by many as dangerous. To have stressed "change" and have rejected the "eternal verities," as Dewey did, appeared to some of his critics to be an unsound approach to education. Leading the attack upon what they deemed Dewey's anti-intellectualism and his brand of naturalism were Robert M. Hutchins (1899-) and Mortimer J. Adler (1902-) who, followers of Aristotle's naturalism and his doctrine of the uniformity of nature, hold that there are natural truths that do not change and that such truths should be made the fixed intellectual content of education. Since human nature and truth, they hold, are everywhere the same, education and its basic aims should be always and everywhere the same. Dewey agrees that human nature is everywhere the same but argues that the mode of satisfying its needs

[38] P. K. Crosser, *The Nihilism of John Dewey* (New York: Philosophical Library, Inc., 1955).

[39] S. Hook (ed.), *John Dewey, Philosopher of Science and Freedom* (New York: Dial Press, Inc., 1950).

differs in different environments, and that environmental conditions, rather than human nature, should be the guiding factor in education. And he rejected all "absolutes" and all doctrines of unchanging "truth." [40]

While other naturalists such as Frederick R. Breed [41] and the "essentialists," such as William C. Bagley, reject Dewey's educational theory but for different reasons, the supernaturalists, led by the Catholics, have rejected his exclusive naturalism on religious grounds, and have singled it out for special attack. While there are common elements in Dewey's naturalism and Marxist materialism, Stalinist writers have branded him as the leading voice of the American bourgeoisie and of Western imperialism.[42] The last word still remains to be spoken about Dewey, if indeed it will ever be spoken. This much we can say with a large degree of certainty: no one in our time has had such a profound influence upon modern educational thought and practice.

PROGRESSIVE EDUCATION. The efforts of many reformers of education in the past two centuries, of whom Dewey was the most influential modern representative, culminated in America in what we have called "progressive education." Its central concepts were: (a) that respect for the personality of the child is of primary importance; (b) that the child and his needs and interests are more important than subject matter; (c) that schools should concern themselves with developing the whole child, not with just some aspects of his nature, and (d) that good learning results not from external but from internal motivation.[43] The philosophy of "progressive education" thus stressed individual development, and was popular in the decades following World War I, when democracy seemed to have triumphed and the millennium seemed to be at hand. In 1918, the Progressive Education Association was organized to promote "child-centered" education and to reform the aims, methods and curriculum of schools in the interests of individuals. A storm broke over the whole movement in the 1930s when an economic crisis and totalitarianism posed a threat to democracy. Progressive education had moved away from the social-democratic emphasis in Dewey's

[40] R. M. Hutchins, "The Philosophy of Education" in R. N. Montgomery (ed.), *William Rainey Harper Memorial Conference* (Chicago: The University of Chicago Press, 1938), pp. 35–50; M. J. Adler, "In Defense of the Philosophy of Education," *Philosophies of Education, The Forty-first Yearbook of the National Society for the Study of Education,* Part II, chap. v (Bloomington, Ill.: Public School Publishing Co., 1942).

[41] *Education and the New Realism* (New York: The Macmillan Co., 1939).

[42] J. Cork, "John Dewey and Karl Marx," in Hook, *op. cit.*, pp. 331–50.

[43] H. L. Caswell, "Progressive Education," *NEA Journal* (November 1955), 474–76.

position, but the world crisis brought the demand that the emphasis be again placed upon the moral life, the social aspects of democracy, and the social responsibilities of the individual. That demand came both from within the teaching profession and from socially conservative elements in the population.[44] On the educational side, the "Great Tradition," with its intellectualism, stood in stubborn opposition to the forces of "progressivism." Various forms of opposition brought an end to the Progressive Education Association which, in 1944, changed its name to the American Education Fellowship. The central concepts in its philosophy are, however, still forcefully defended.[45]

Thorndike and Functional Psychology

Darwinism, as we have seen, was very influential in the field of educational psychology. William James, in his *Talks to Teachers,* called for an acceptance of the biological approach to teaching. G. Stanley Hall (1846-1924), author of *Adolescence* (1904), a landmark in the scientific study of the child, based his pedagogy upon the doctrines of organic and racial evolution. The psychology of Dewey, as we have just seen, falls into the Darwinian category. All of these accepted a functionalist view of psychology and, to all of them, Edward Lee Thorndike (1874-1949), the leading functionalist psychologist, was indebted.

To understand human learning, Thorndike experimented with animal learning and, upon the basis of his findings, formulated his "laws of learning," the chief ones being those of exercise and effect. Learning becomes, in the Thorndike view, a matter of stimulus and response, and his psychology has been, consequently, named the S-R Psychology. In his research, he subjected the doctrine of transfer of training, the corollary of faculty psychology, as James had begun to do, to the experimental test, and concluded that, where transfer occurs, it is due to common elements in the learning areas rather than in the building of mental powers by exercise. Numerous experiments since 1890 have been conducted to test the hypothesis of the transfer of training, and some have shown that the degree of transfer is high, while others have shown it to be low.[46] The tradi-

[44] G. S. Counts, *Dare the School Build a New Social Order?* (New York: John Day Company, Inc., 1932), p. 7.

[45] H. L. Caswell, *loc. cit.;* L. A. Cremin, "The Progressive Movement in American Education: A Perspective," *Harvard Educational Review,* XXVII, No. 4 (Fall 1957).

[46] P. T. Orata, "Transfer of Training and Educational Pseudo-Science," *Mathematics Teacher,* XXVIII (May 1935), 266 f.; E. L. Thorndike and R. S. Woodworth, "The Influence of Improvement of One Mental Function upon the Efficiency of Other Functions," *Psychological Review,* VIII (1901), 247–61, 384–95, 553–64.

tional claim of a sweeping transfer has, therefore, had to be abandoned in the light of experimental evidence, as had its foundation, the ancient theory of faculty psychology. Learning must, it seemed to follow, be viewed as specific, and the resultant powers and habits as specific rather than general. The doctrine of the specificity of learning is central in the theory of Thorndike's educational psychology. Learning, in his view, consists in the establishment of bonds between the stimulus and response, resulting in the conditioning of thought and behavior. Mental life thus becomes largely a matter of conditioned reflexes, although it was the behaviorists, led by John B. Watson (1878-1958), who carried this doctrine to its extreme.

The stimulus-response psychology, which explains human behavior in terms of instinct, habit, and adaptation to environment tends to weaken our democratic ideal in as far as it minimizes the importance of intelligence in reshaping the environment and securing an enlightened adaptation to it. It arose, in part, as a protest against the undemocratic character of the older schools. Faculty psychology did not demand the liberation of human intelligence for the sake of social progress. It demanded the development of mental faculties by intellectual exercises, and taught that mental "powers" thus developed would transfer automatically to every possible field of human activity. Those whose "faculties" had not been trained by suitable exercises, or who were deemed lacking in "faculties," as the masses were sometimes thought to be, had to be content with lowly social positions. That was a psychology which made for social stagnation and injustice. The Herbartian doctrine of "ideas" and mind-building replaced that of "faculties." It elevated the importance of the teacher and made the pupil a listener, whose mind was to be moulded according to a preconceived plan of studies and by formal steps of method that showed little regard for his active nature and individual capacities and needs.

Thorndike's psychology is a protest against these older doctrines on both scientific and social grounds. Without attempting here a detailed exposition, worthy though it be of a lengthy treatment, it must be noted that the Thorndike system, which has been widely accepted by American teachers and trainers of teachers, is, in its idea of learning as habit-formation, in accordance with the laws of readiness, exercise, and effect, at least moderately behavioristic. To reduce thinking to habits, formed with mechanical preciseness according to fixed laws, destroys thinking. That position seems to be implied in Thorndike's teachings. John Dewey in his *Human Nature and Conduct* views habit not as a substitute for thinking but as an indispensable aspect of thinking. Any psychology which reduces learning to mechanical habit formation eliminates the need for the concept of intelligence and wrecks the foundation upon which our democratic faith rests.[47]

Professor Bode, one of the leading critics of recent trends in the educational and psychological fields, regrets, as do many with him, that the preoccupation of many with scientific technique has obscured their vision of the importance of many things which do not lend themselves to scientific inquiry. Education, he says, which ought to be concerned "with the free operation of intelligence," has "a right to protest when intelligence is dropped out of the picture, just because it simplifies matters to do so." "It seems," he goes on, "reasonably clear that a democratic system of education has nothing to look for from a psychology that explains intelligence by explaining it away. . . . An adequate theory of education requires both an adequate social program and an adequate conception of the 'mind' or 'intelligence' with which the teacher has to deal."[48]

Such is the psychological movement in education. It implies the recognition of the principle that sound educational practice must be based upon an understanding of the nature of the being whom we educate. That, however, is but one basis upon which education must rest. Since man must live with his fellows, education must also rest upon an understanding of the nature of human society, a truth recognized by thoughtful ones since Plato wrote, and given great emphasis during the past two centuries.

Selected Readings

Adams, J. *The Herbartian Psychology Applied to Education.* Boston: D. C. Heath & Co., 1897.

Anderson, L. F. *Pestalozzi.* New York: McGraw-Hill Book Co., 1931.

Baker, M. C. *Foundations of John Dewey's Educational Theory.* New York: King's Crown Press, 1955.

Boyd, W. *The Educational Theory of Jean Jacques Rousseau.* London: Longmans, Green & Co., Ltd., 1911.

Childs, J. L. *Education and Morals.* New York: Appleton-Century-Crofts, Inc., 1950.

Cole, P. R. *Herbart and Froebel: an Attempt at Synthesis.* New York: Teachers College, Columbia University, 1907.

De Garmo, C. *Herbart and the Herbartians.* New York: Charles Scribner's Sons, 1895.

Dewey, J. *Democracy and Education.* New York: The Macmillan Co., 1916.

———. *Experience and Education.* New York: The Macmillan Co., 1938.

[47] E. L. Thorndike, *Educational Psychology; Briefer Course* (New York: Teachers College, Columbia University, 1927), chap. xii; Bode, *op. cit.*, chap. viii.

[48] *Op. cit.*, pp. 190–91. (By permission.)

———. *How We Think.* Rev. Ed.; Boston: D. C. Heath & Co., 1933.

Fletcher, S. S. F., and Walton, J. *Froebel's Chief Writings on Education.* New York: Longmans, Green & Co., Inc., 1912.

Froebel, F. *The Education of Man.* (Trans. W. N. Hailmann.) New York: Appleton-Century-Crofts, Inc., 1887.

———. *Pedagogics of the Kindergarten.* (Trans. J. Jarvis.) New York: Appleton-Century-Crofts, Inc., 1900.

Green, J. A. *Life and Work of Pestalozzi.* London: University Tutorial Press, 1913.

Guimps, R. De. *Petalozzi, His Aim and Work.* (Trans. M. C. Crombie.) Syracuse, N.Y.: Bardeen, 1896.

Hook, S., ed. *John Dewey, Philosopher of Science and Freedom.* New York: Dial Press, Inc., 1950.

Hutchins, R. M. *The Higher Learning in America.* New Haven: Yale University Press, 1936.

Krikorian, Y. H., ed. *Naturalism and the Human Spirit.* New York: Columbia University Press, 1944.

Krüsi, H. *Pestalozzi: His Life, Work and Influence.* Cincinnati: Van Antwerp & Co., 1875.

Lange, A. F. *Herbart's Outlines of Educational Doctrine.* New York: The Macmillan Co., 1901.

Lange, K. *Apperception.* Boston: D. C. Heath & Co., 1893.

Monroe, W. S. *History of the Pestalozzian Movement in the United States.* Syracuse, N.Y.: Bardeen, 1907.

Murphy, G. *Historical Introduction to Modern Psychology.* New York: Harcourt, Brace & Co., Inc., 1929.

Pestalozzi, J. H. *How Gertrude Teaches Her Children.* (Trans. L. E. Holland and F. C. Turner.) 2d ed.; Syracuse, N.Y.: Bardeen, 1898.

———. *Leonard and Gertrude.* (Trans. E. Channing.) Boston: D. C. Heath & Co., 1896.

Rousseau, J. J. *Émile.* New York: E. P. Dutton & Co., Inc., 1950.

11 The Emergence of Education as a State Function

The forces at work in the changing social scene of the eighteenth and nineteenth centuries brought into education an increased social emphasis. This tendency, in its earlier phase, was an embodiment of sectarianism, humanitarianism, and ideals of social reform for all humanity. Under the influence of growing nationalism, the broader ideals of the earlier movement gave way to that of reform within each nation for nationalistic ends. The tendency thus culminated in the establishment of compulsory systems of education, controlled not by the church but by the secular state, and supported by governments for their own ends.

Social unrest and change, as we have seen, resulted from the breakdown of the mediaeval social system and ecclesiastical authoritarianism. The political upheavals of the eighteenth century added greatly to the tempo of that unrest. Yet, the greatest single force which helped to transform Western societies was the Industrial Revolution. The social problems created by these changes, especially from about 1800, demanded a much more thoroughly organized and systematic control than older agencies, such as the church, could provide. Among the social functions which organized lay society operating through secular government wrested from the hands of the church was education. The movement for state control of education which, as we have seen, was rooted, in a very special way, in the Reformation, culminated in the establishment, at different times during the nineteenth century, of public, national systems of education in Europe and America.

PHILANTHROPY IN EDUCATION. Education for social as well as ecclesiastical ends marked the eighteenth-century tendency, confined largely to England and America, which is usually described as the philanthropic movement in education. Until then hundreds of activities, such as water supply, road building and poor relief, which today are performed by governments, were performed by private agencies. When it became apparent that the state could perform these necessary activities more efficiently than private agencies, society placed them, one by one, under government control. In the socializing of education, philanthropic agencies played an important early rôle. While their activities were not confined to a few countries, their largest contributions were made in England and America in the eighteenth century and the early nineteenth. The provision of education by philanthropic agencies was not something new. In the Middle Ages, as we have seen, individuals, motivated chiefly by a concern for the salvation of their souls, established schools for the poor. Others made gifts to universities for the purpose of housing poor students. The need for such effort increased in the rapidly changing world of the sixteenth and later centuries. Destitution and ignorance were widespread among the poorer classes. Sectarian and benevolent motives inspired the activities of the philanthropists who, from the late seventeenth century, undertook to educate the poor and ennoble their lives.

CHARITY SCHOOL MOVEMENT IN ENGLAND AND UNITED STATES. In 1699, there was founded in England the Society for the Promotion of Christian Knowledge (S.P.C.K.) to provide, among other things, Anglican religious instruction for poor children. In 1701, the Society for the Propagation of the Gospel in Foreign Parts (S.P.G.) was established by the Anglican church to do, in the British colonies, what the parent society was doing at home. These organizations undertook to establish and maintain schools for the poor, and to instruct them in reading, writing, spelling, arithmetic, and the Anglican catechism. They trained teachers, paid their salaries, provided texts, and supervised schools under their control. Their stated purposes were to make the poor "loyal church members, and to fit them for work in that station of life in which it had pleased their Heavenly Father to place them." [1] In addition to Anglican charity schools, others were founded by non-conformist churches. In the nineteenth century most of these schools were absorbed by the "National Society" among the Anglicans, and by the "British and Foreign Society" among the non-conformists.

In America, and particularly in the Anglican colonies here, the S.P.G. established and supported many schools. This Society was the principal bearer to America of the charity school idea. Following the Revolution, that idea found its way into some of our early state constitutions and laws pertaining to education. Thus the Pennsylvania Constitution of 1790 provided for the establishment

[1] E. P. Cubberley, *The History of Education* (Boston: Houghton Mifflin Co., 1920), pp. 449–50.

of schools "in such manner that the poor may be taught *gratis*." Many of our academies in many of our states were required, in return for state grants, to educate each year a stated number of poor children gratis. The view that the education of the poor is a charity rather than a public service was prevalent in parts of America until the eighteen-thirties, and persisted in England until the passage of the first public school law in 1870.

The practice of providing even charitable education for the poor met, in England, with the opposition of some of the gentry who were fearful of anything that might bring social change. Bernard Mandeville said, in the eighteenth century, that "the people of the meanest rank know too much to be serviceable to us."[2]

> To make the society happy [he wrote] and people easy under the meanest circumstances, it is requisite that great numbers of them should be ignorant, as well as poor. Knowledge both enlarges and multiplies our desires, and the fewer things a man wishes for, the more easily his necessities may be supplied. The welfare and felicity . . . of every state . . . require that the knowledge of the working poor should be confined within the verge of their occupations. . . . The more a shepherd . . . or any other peasant, knows of the world, and the things that are foreign to his labour or employment, the less fit he will be to go through the fatigues and hardships of it with cheerfulness and content.[3]

Mandeville would keep the laboring masses illiterate. Others would restrict their learning to the rudiments. The charity schools of seventeenth-century England and their continuation, the "voluntary" schools of the nineteenth century, seldom instructed children beyond the 4 R's, religion being the subject emphasized most. Ability to read the catechism and prayers of the churches and to understand simple sermons was a leading aim in these schools of the poor. And it was seldom, if ever, intended that they should raise the poor above the position in society in which their Heavenly Father had placed them.

In 1833, the British government showed its first marked interest in popular education when it appropriated £20,000 (later to be greatly increased) for that purpose, and divided it equally between the National and the British and Foreign societies. The Report of a Royal Commission, in 1861, showed that 1,675,158 pupils were enrolled in so-called public schools, of which nearly 90 per cent were controlled by the Church of England, and other millions in other types of schools. It was remarked that, without compulsory education, England had proportionately as many children in ele-

[2] B. Mandeville, *The Fable of the Bees* (London: Parker, 1723), p. 189.
[3] *Ibid.*, p. 179.

mentary schools as had Prussia, where education was compulsory. Few pupils, however, remained in school beyond the age of eleven, and the average attendance was about four years. The yearly cost per pupil in these schools was about $7.50, of which the government paid about one half, the other half being met by pupils' pennies, subscriptions, and endowments.

In addition to the National (1811) and the British and Foreign Society (1808), others had come into the field: the Home and Colonial School Society (1836); the Wesleyan Education Committee (1840); the London Ragged School Union (1844); the Catholic Poor School Committee (1847); and the Church Education Society (1853). All of these received state aid for their schools, and theirs came to be known as the "voluntary" system. Groups refusing state aid through fear of state interference remained outside of the "voluntary" system. The sectarian struggle was reflected in these schools and prevented the establishment of state schools until 1870, when the first national school law was passed in England. That law provided for the election of local school boards, and for the establishment of schools wherever existing accommodations were inadequate. Thus the publicly supported and controlled schools of modern England originated in the giving of public aid to religious and charitable education societies. Since 1870, the schools of nonconformist groups have been gradually absorbed by the national schools, but Catholic schools and many of the Anglican ones have retained their identity and, in the case of the Catholics, have increased in number.

MONITORIAL INSTRUCTION IN ENGLAND AND UNITED STATES. In 1798, Joseph Lancaster, a Quaker, established in a poor London district a school conducted on a plan designed to lower the cost of educating the poor and to enlarge their educational opportunity. To this end he employed older pupils as assistants, or monitors, and adopted new instructional devices, such as the use of sand to teach writing. It was possible for one teacher using Lancasterian methods to conduct a school of many hundreds of pupils. The plan attained instant popularity. In 1808, the British and Foreign Society was founded to direct and continue the work of the many schools organized, but mismanaged, by Lancaster. In opposition to the nonsectarianism of that society, the Anglicans organized the National Society, which took over most of the schools of the S.P.C.K. and introduced the monitorial plan into them. Under these two societies, schools for the poor multipled rapidly in the first half of the century. The monitorial system, though mechanical and basically imperfect in teaching procedures, helped to convince the public of the feasibility of public support of universal education.

In the United States, where the problem of paying for the education of the poor was also urgent, the monitorial plan became rapidly popular after 1806, when it was first introduced by the Free School Society of New York City. The rapidity of its spread here in two decades was phenomenal. In 1818, Lancaster came to America and taught in monitorial schools in New York and Philadelphia. Here the plan of instruction was adopted not only in elementary schools but also in academies and high schools. Despite its shortcomings, the monitorial system brought a rapid and significant enlargement of opportunities for the poor of early nineteenth-century America, and prepared the way for the adoption of free public schools, both elementary and secondary, for all the children of all the people. Many of our early public school laws provided for the establishment of monitorial schools. By 1850, the popularity of the monitorial practice had largely disappeared.

SUNDAY SCHOOL MOVEMENT IN ENGLAND AND UNITED STATES. In order to dispel ignorance and alleviate degradation among the poor, Robert Raikes, an English manufacturer, opened, in 1780, a Sunday school for children and adults in Gloucester. Though not the originator of the idea or practice, Raikes was its foremost popularizer. The movement spread rapidly and, in 1785, there was founded the Sunday School Society to direct it. The Royal Commission in its Report, in 1861, said that 2,411,554 pupils were enrolled in British Sunday schools. In addition to religion, the 3 R's were taught in the earlier Sunday schools, and the teachers were usually paid a little for the services. In 1786, Sunday schools of this type were introduced into America, where they also had a rapid growth. When the need for secular instruction had been met by other agencies here and in England, the Sunday schools abandoned all such instruction, but continued their work in the religious field.

INFANT SCHOOL MOVEMENT IN GREAT BRITAIN AND UNITED STATES. This movement was originated by Jean Oberlin in France in the late eighteenth century, but had its greatest development in Great Britain and the United States. In 1816, Robert Owen, a Scotch manufacturer and philanthropist, who had not heard of the French movement, opened an infant school at New Lanark, Scotland. Most manufacturers and mine owners then showed very little respect for the lives of children.

Owen would introduce them to life by providing them with healthy bodies, good morals, and the beginnings of an intellectual training. His school was designed for children between the ages of three and seven. It was then customary for institutions caring for foundlings and orphans to bind out their charges above the age of five as apprentices to masters whose treatment of them was often inhuman. In Owen's school there were no tasks assigned to rob children of the joys of childhood. Indeed, everything was done to create new joys for them, the primary objects of the school—the physical, mental, and moral growth of pupils—never being lost sight of. Under the influence of Samuel Wilderspin, who attempted to popularize the idea, later infant schools adopted the formal and mechanical practices of schools for older children. Thus the spirit of the New Lanark school passed from the movement. Yet, the movement continued and, in 1834, the Home and Colonial School Society was founded to train teachers for infant schools. That society checked the decay of schools by introducing Pestalozzianism, though only in a highly formalized plan of teaching by objects. Through the activities of the Infant School Society (1824) and the Home and Colonial School Society the infant school movement spread rapidly in Great Britain.

In the United States, the infant school idea found many advocates in the first half of the century, and schools designed for younger children were established in many cities. However, the public was slow to grasp the social need for such a practice. In 1818, Boston became the first city to appropriate money for such schools, there called "primary schools." In 1827, the New York "Infant School Society" was founded and, in the same year, infant schools were established in Philadelphia. Before 1830, infant schools had been established in Hartford, Baltimore, and other cities. Formal instruction, conducted on the Lancasterian plan, marked the earlier infant schools of America. Generally, until about 1850, they were supported by private philanthropic agencies actuated by respect for the rights and happiness of children, an ideal which, when dinned into public consciousness, resulted in the recognition by the public of the principle that education of younger children is a matter of public concern. In meeting the needs of the poor before governments became conscious of their obligations to them, philanthropic and religious agencies performed a significant service.

MANUAL-LABOR MOVEMENT IN EUROPE AND UNITED STATES. While the name of Pestalozzi is usually associated with the psychological movement in education, we must not lose sight of the fact that he was primarily a social reformer whose life and works were permeated by the faith that education, and education alone, is the remedy for the ills of society. He began his educational career as a teacher of children of poor peasants, whose lives he hoped to improve by education. "Ever since my youth," he wrote, "has my heart moved on like a mighty stream, alone and lonely, towards my one sole end—to stop the sources of the misery in which I saw the people around me sunk."[4] And again: "I suffered as the people suffered; and the people showed themselves to me as they were, and as they showed themselves to no one else."[5] Against the social institutions and vices which brought misery and degradation to the masses, Pestalozzi was inwardly at war, and his sympathy was always with the victims of oppression and injustice. He denounced the social injustice which robbed the poor of the educational opportunities enjoyed by the rich. On his tombstone are written the words "Saviour of the poor at Neuhof, at Stanz the father of orphans. . . . All for others, nothing for himself."[6]

Pestalozzi's experiment at Neuhof, in which he attempted to combine the school and the workshop, gave rise, through his friend Emanuel von Fellenberg (1771-1844), to the "manual-labor" movement in Europe and America. In 1806, Fellenberg, at the suggestion of Pestalozzi, opened on his large estate at Hofwyl, Switzerland, a school to train teachers in the Pestalozzian method. In a few years, the institution had developed into a school in which industrial and agricultural training were combined with Pestalozzian observational instruction, and the sons of the wealthy were instructed in the same practical studies pursued by the sons of the poor. However, to retain the sons of the rich, Fellenberg made provisions for their separate housing and special academic instruction in the "literary institute," while the poor attended the "agricultural institute" of the school. The rich were, nevertheless, required to engage in agricultural and other manual activities side by side with the poor. Literary education was provided for the poor but, for them, the stress was laid upon practical training.

The school at Hofwyl was a social as well as an educational experiment, and its success stimulated the growth of industrial and agricultural schools in Europe and America. However, Fellenberg's attempt to bring the children of all classes together into one school was not continued in later schools fashioned after the model which he established. The movement in practical education in which Pestalozzi and Fellenberg had a foremost place at the beginning of the nineteenth century came to be marked by a special emphasis

[4] J. H. Pestalozzi, *How Gertrude Teaches Her Children* (trans. L. E. Holland and F. C. Turner; 2d ed.; Syracuse, N.Y.: Bardeen, 1898), p. 30.

[5] *Ibid.*, p. 32.

[6] R. De Guimps, *Pestalozzi, His Life and Work* (trans. J. Russell; New York: Appleton-Century-Crofts, Inc., 1892), p. 367.

upon the needs of the poor who, it was felt, could be redeemed from the miseries created by industrial and social change by practical training in agriculture and the various trades. Switzerland was the first center of the movement in Europe. Here many farm schools and a few industrial schools were established before 1840, and industrial training came to be stressed in the normal schools. In Germany, France, and England, industrial training was introduced into orphanages and reform and continuation schools.

In the United States, Fellenberg's influence appeared in the rise of "manual-labor" schools. Here the movement developed between 1820 and 1840, and declined rapidly after the latter date. The idea that manual and intellectual training should be combined for educational ends, a view held by Fellenberg, was not stressed in America except by a few writers. The advantages of the manual-labor plan which were emphasized here were: (a) that it brought education, particularly on the secondary and college levels, within the reach of boys of humble means, by making it possible for them to defray the cost of education by their own labor, and (b) that the physical activities which it provided improved the health of students. Organized labor groups showed much interest in the plan, because they felt it threw the door of social opportunity open to their children who were debarred by high tuition fees from the traditional secondary schools and colleges.[7] While the manual-labor plan was popular in the older sections, it had its greatest vogue on the frontier where, it would appear, a majority of the academies and colleges established between 1830 and 1850 were of the manual-labor type. While they were not free, the tuition was much lower in them than in other schools. They were thus a reflection of the democratic tendencies of the time, and represent a transition from an undemocratic, class scheme of education to the publicly supported system, with its free high schools and its inexpensive state universities.

INDUSTRIAL EDUCATION. The Industrial Revolution and the factory system gradually brought an end to the apprenticeship plan of training youths for the various trades. Indeed, it resulted in the splitting of the old trades into separate processes, only one of which, as a rule, the factory worker needed to know. It ceased to be profitable for masters to train apprentices, or promising for apprentices to strive for mastery in the trades. Yet the need for skilled craftsmen continued. Therefore, schools had to be established to do what the masters once did for their apprentices. The movement,

[7] J. Mulhern, *A History of Secondary Education in Pennsylvania* (Lancaster, Pa.: Science Press, Inc., 1933), pp. 453–58.

however, had an earlier origin and grew by steps under many influences.

In sixteenth- and seventeenth-century England, many industrial schools for the poor were established and supported by philanthropic and, sometimes, public agencies. In 1641, legal provision was made by the Scottish Parliament for the establishment of textile schools in county towns. These steps were a departure from the traditional apprenticeship system. Industrial training schools for the poor, after the British model, were established in the American colonies. Thus the Virginia legislature, in 1646, made provision for the instruction of poor children in carding, knitting, and spinning in public flax houses. In the closing decade of the eighteenth century, industrial training was introduced into the *Volksschulen* of Germany, and special industrial schools for the poor were established in many German cities. The well-being of the poor and the commercial advantage to society, as well as the lowering of the cost of educating the poor, were the stated purposes of the German practice. A century earlier, as we have seen, the Pietist, Francke, was teaching trades in his school at Halle.

Before Pestalozzi and Fellenberg brought their influence to bear upon the practice, Rousseau and his immediate followers, Basedow and the Philanthropinists, promoted it both in theory and practice. In the schools of Basedow and Salzmann, trades were taught not only for practical ends, but also for health and the complete development of the whole man. The educational purpose of developing all the bodily powers, rather than a social purpose, underlay the work of the Philanthropinists. Froebel, who urged philosophical, educational, or psychological reasons for his practices, gave the trades a place in his school at Keilhau and exerted, as we have seen, a powerful influence upon manual training through his kindergarten.

The sloyd system, popular in England and America in the last quarter of the nineteenth century, was a Swedish application of Froebel's ideas to craft training, designed to preserve domestic industries, threatened by the Industrial Revolution, thus protecting peasants from their new enemy, the machine and the factory. The sloyd system embodied both an industrial and educational purpose. In America, after 1883, when it was favorably described in the *Annual Report* of the Massachusetts Board of Education, it became popular with those who felt that the manual training practice, which we borrowed directly from Russia, was too formal. Froebel's influence upon industrial education in America made itself felt in a native American modification of the kindergarten. In 1876, Emily Huntingdon, of New York, desiring to apply kindergarten ideas in the industrial field, substituted household utensils for Froebel's "gifts" in her school, which she called the Kitchen Garden. The idea spread quickly to other cities. In 1880, a New York Association was organized to promote the plan. That Association became, in 1884, the Industrial Education Association of New York. Between these years, in 1881, the Workingman's School of New York, stressing industrial training for older children, developed as an outgrowth of a kindergarten. Thus Froebel's influence tended to swing toward an emphasis upon the practical needs of youth and of our industrial society. While Herbart showed but little interest in industrial education, his disciple Ziller recommended special vocational schools or apprenticeship training for children of laborers. More fortunate classes, he said, have little need for such training. Of all the influences, however, contributing to the growing concern for industrial education in Europe and America, the Industrial Revolution was the most potent.

The first influence of the industrial change upon education appears in the efforts of philanthropists and of workingmen themselves to aid workers in meeting the problems which the factory system had created for them. Thus, Andrew Bell, in the Anglican monitorial schools of England, and Robert Owen, in the schools of New Harmony, Indiana, provided industrial training for the poor. In 1800, George Birbeck, of the University of Glasgow, offered lectures on applied sciences to industrial workers. That step led to the establishment, between 1823 and 1840, of Mechanics Institutes in many English industrial cities. In these, workingmen met for instruction in the application of science to industrial arts.

In America, comparatively few Mechanics Institutes were established. Here the lyceum movement took their place. The lyceum, established in numerous centers, large and small, from the eighteen-twenties onward, provided lectures on industrial and intellectual topics for everyone who wished for such an opportunity. The lyceum was one aspect of the broad, social reform movement which swept America prior to the Civil War, and which was inspired by the desire to build here an ideal society.[8]

The second large educational effect of the Industrial Revolution appears in the concern of governments for the training of skilled workers, so that each nation might hold its own, or more than its own, in international commerce. In the competitive commercial world, humanitarian idealism, which inspired earlier forms of indus-

[8] "American Lyceum," *American Annals of Education and Instruction*, I (June 1831), 378–79; "The American Lyceum," *Barnard's American Journal of Education*, XIV (September 1864), 535–37.

trial training, largely disappeared. After 1850, England, long supreme in world trade, found her supremacy challenged, first by France and then by Germany. In 1877, a British Royal Commission recommended the establishment and public support of technical schools. Laws were passed for Scotland (1887) and for England (1889) to make that recommendation effective. In America, also, the national motive had its effect. From the eighteen-twenties onward, technical education had been urged by individuals, among them Henry Barnard, as a national industrial need. In 1870, the Massachusetts legislature, aware of the international commercial struggle, required towns of over 10,000 population to give free instruction in mechanical drawing to older pupils. Maine (1870) and New York (1875) enacted similar laws.

Until the nineteenth century, the apprenticeship system of training artisans was practically the universal plan in America. A few theorists, such as Thomas Budd, recommended formal schools for the purpose. After 1824, a few Mechanics Institutes appeared. In 1824, the Rensselaer Polytechnic Institute was organized in Troy, by Amos Eaton, to teach science as related to agriculture and industry, and to disseminate such knowledge through the schools of America.[9] In 1862, the federal government, in response to urgent demands for aid in training industrial and agricultural workers, passed the Morrill Act, granting to each state for that purpose 30,000 acres of public land for each senator and representative it had in Congress. Thus began the federal endowment of vocational education which culminated in the passage (1917) of the Smith-Hughes Act and its later supplements.

From 1785, the federal government had granted land to the several states, with a few exceptions, for the purpose of general education. Since 1862, practical education has been the government's special concern. The Hatch Act (1887), the second Morrill Act (1890), and the Smith-Lever Act (1914) supplemented the first Morrill Act. Since 1917 federal benevolence has been directed chiefly toward vocational training. In 1937, a further grant of $14,000,000 was provided to meet the demands of the Smith-Hughes Act, and, in 1940, a special grant of $60,500,000, to meet the needs of the National Defense program. What has been done in England and America for industrial education has been done in other nations since 1850, the most elaborate provisions, until very recent days, being those of Germany. All of these developments reflect the

[9] E. M. McAllister, *Amos Eaton* (Philadelphia: University of Pennsylvania Press, 1941).

philosophy that education must be determined by social needs and ends.

EDUCATION AS A STATE FUNCTION. The view that education is a concern of the state and a preserver of political systems was expressed by Greek theorists, and found embodiment in Roman laws. Luther threw the influence of Protestantism upon the side of that principle. Having destroyed the unity of the Catholic church, the Reformation created the need for a new educational authority. We have seen that, under the new régime, responsibility for education was, in varying ways and degrees in Protestant lands, transferred to civil authorities. That was the beginning of the end of ecclesiastical control. Three hundred years after Luther's revolt, the Prussian state took over complete control of education, the legal basis for that step having been laid progressively during the eighteenth century. The last step was hastened by the defeat of the Prussians by Napoleon at Jena (1806). Immediately thereafter Prussian statesmen and philosophers demanded that the masses be instructed in their duties to the state. The result was the centralization of educational control in a national Department of Education, in which the church was not represented. Nationalism inspired that step.[10]

A revolution in educational thought accompanied the French Revolution. The radicals of the movement would establish a universal, free, compulsory, and secular system of elementary education for the moulding of citizens of the new social order. Eloquent protests were heard against the exclusion by the church of lay educators, as were also eloquent demands for the secularization of education and its control by the state. La Chalotais wrote, in 1763, "I dare claim for the nation an education which depends only on the State, because it belongs essentially to the State; because every State has an inalienable and indefeasible right to instruct its members; because, finally, the children of the State ought to be educated by the members of the State. . . . In every State the purpose should be to enkindle the spirit of citizenship." [11]

While the church continued to dominate French education until the establishment of the Third Republic (1870), the revolutionary ideal survived. In 1850, Edgar Quinet wrote:

> No particular church being the soul of France, the teaching which diffuses this soul should be independent of every particular church. . . . The teacher has a more universal doctrine than the priest, for he speaks to Catholic, Protestant, and Jew alike, and he brings them all into the same civil communion.

[10] *Infra*, pp. 527 f.

[11] G. Compayré, *The History of Pedagogy* (trans. W. H. Payne; Boston: D. C. Heath & Co., 1897), p. 345.

> The teacher is obliged to say: "You are all children of the same God and of the same country; take hold of each others' hands until death." The priest is obliged to say: "You are the children of different churches, but among these mothers there is but one who is legitimate. All those who do not belong to her are accursed. . . . Be, then, separated in time, since you must be separated in eternity." [12]

And Quinet demanded the secularization of education for civil ends, a step that was taken by law in 1882. While Napoleon, in 1808, brought secondary and higher education under a measure of state control, public elementary schools were not established until 1833, when the state assumed control of elementary education.

In England, ecclesiastical and class conflicts delayed the rise of a state system of education. The Anglican church, being the national church, claimed the right to be the national educator. Fearing such a development, the Dissenters opposed state interference in education on the grounds that it would destroy civil and religious liberty, while the Anglicans themselves opposed it since the government did not formally approve their claim, and since the outcome of the conflict was in doubt. Fearing that free, state education for the masses would make them restless and weaken social barriers, the aristocracy opposed it. When government was made nearly representative by the reform acts of 1832 and 1867, the Dissenters became supporters of a state system. On the passage of the act of 1867, Robert Lowe, member of Parliament and a leader of the reform group, shouted: "Now, let us educate our future masters."

In 1870, the Forster Elementary Education Act was passed, and in it was laid the foundation of the state system.[13] Support by the national government to the "voluntary" schools, inaugurated in 1833, continued, but they were refused a share in the taxes raised locally for the new "board" schools. Because of their long-established vested interest in education, and because they benefited by British respect (an outcome of a long struggle) for the rights of conscience, these sectarian schools won, in 1902, their fight for their share in local taxes. Public support, however, has brought a measure of public control over these schools. What other countries have done quickly, sometimes by revolutionary methods, England has done slowly and in an evolutionary way. There, respect for tradition has been strong, and progress has come by a tedious process of struggle and compromise between conflicting groups. What form the social

[12] F. Buisson and F. E. Farrington, *French Educational Ideals of Today* (Yonkers, N.Y.: World Book Co., 1919), pp. 1–2.

[13] *Infra*, pp. 553 f.

processes in the England of tomorrow may take can only be conjectured. Later, we shall examine the provisions of the Education Act of 1944 passed by the Churchill coalition government.

In the United States, the national and political motive in education found eloquent advocates in the early years of our nationhood. Our young republic was, however, an aristocratic one, and its educational philosophers were more concerned with the training of an intellectual elite for leadership than with the training of the masses for citizenship. To one principle, however, they gave prominence: that the success of the political experiment depended upon education, without which the democratic ideal could not be realized.

The common-man democracy, which succeeded the older form, was fashioned on our moving frontier. Since its first triumph in the election of Andrew Jackson to the presidency, and the rapid adoption of universal male suffrage in the conservative East, the American nation, operating through the governments of its several states, which the silence of the Constitution has made our supreme educational authority pending some future development, has made the training of the masses for participation in government and public affairs the primary goal of education. Theoretically, our schools exist for the leading purpose of providing our democracy with enlightened citizens who understand its problems, and who will participate intelligently in their solution.

In colonial and early national America, the sectarian and religious were, in practice, the controlling motives in education. Here, as in France, England, and elsewhere, the churches, long dominant in the moulding of minds, opposed the socializing and secularizing tendencies of the builders of the national democratic state. Here, the builders of the nation, conscious of the danger of involving the political authorities in theological controversies, and of the need for cultural unity among citizens, built a public school system completely lay and secular. Where, recently, local authorities have permitted children to attend their churches for religious instruction during the school day, their motive has been social rather than religious, in any sectarian sense. In the early days of the controversy with churchmen, Horace Mann in a reply to views of Rev. M. H. Smith, of Boston, stated the case against religious instruction in public schools thus:

> It is easy to see that the experiment would not stop with having half a dozen conflicting creeds taught by authority of law in the different schools of the same town. . . . One sect may have the ascendancy to-day; another to-morrow. This year there will be three Persons in the Godhead; next year

but one; and the third year the Trinity will be restored to hold its precarious sovereignty until it shall be again dethroned by the worms of the dust it has made. . . . This year the ordinance of baptism is inefficacious without immersion; next year one drop of water will be as good as forty fathoms. . . .

And he went on to say that it is the duty of the state to ensure that no sect shall, for its own ends, use the schools which the state has established for its own preservation.[14]

While, in America, Horace Mann was urging the establishment of state-supported and controlled schools on the grounds that "in a Republic ignorance is a crime," and that the wealth of a nation is in proportion to the intelligence of its citizens, property owners, while admitting the force of such arguments, fought against the public school movement because of their alarm over increased taxation. Why, it was asked, should a man who has educated his own children or the man who has no children of his own to educate be taxed to educate his neighbor's children? Mann reminded property owners that the state is a collective person, and that its property must bear the cost of saving youth from poverty and crime and of preparing them for the discharge of their social duties. The state must not allow selfish men to rob children of their rights, or the community of their best services. Henry Barnard and many others carried on the fight which Mann so ably led until, by the time of the Civil War, state schools were a general practice in America.

Thus, in Western nations, the socializing process progressed during the eighteenth and nineteenth centuries. The teacher, once a representative of a church, or a private adventurer who made teaching a business, is now a representative of society, and teaching has become a profession as socially necessary as the professions of law and medicine. To an even greater extent than in the fields of law and medicine, governments, throughout the world, have assumed the responsibility for the training of teachers, since their well-being depends upon those who mould the minds of youth and train their hands for industrial service. Not merely in matters of teacher training and administration has education been socialized, but its spiritual aspects, as involved in methods of teaching and curriculum, have been harmonized with social purposes and needs. The social studies—history, geography, civics, government, economics, problems of democracy—have come to loom large in the program of our schools. The aims of American education formulated, in 1918, by the Commission on the Reorganization of Secondary Education, in

[14] H. Mann, "Sequel to the So-called Correspondence between the Rev. M. H. Smith and Horace Mann," cited by E. P. Cubberley in *Readings in the History of Education* (Boston: Houghton Mifflin Co., 1920), pp. 575–76.

the so-called "Cardinal Principles" include, among others, health, worthy home membership, vocation, citizenship, and ethical character. In that statement of aims the social ideal is everywhere evident. In the growing tendency to emphasize the social motive, John Dewey and a host of influential followers have played a leading part in the past fifty years but, at the same time, they have been the severest critics of forces that attempt to control our schools for their own conservative ends. To the dogma of "social predestination" Dewey did not subscribe, much less to the belief that a democracy's schools should be instruments of such predestination.

Selected Readings

Bell, A. *An Experiment in Education Made at the Male Asylum of Madras.* London: Cadell, 1797.

Bell, S. *The Church, the State and Education in Virginia.* Lancaster, Pa.: Science Press, Inc., 1930.

Bourne, W. O. *History of the Public School Society of the City of New York.* New York: G. P. Putnam's Sons, Inc., 1873.

Brown, M. C. *Sunday-School Movements in America.* Westwood, N.J.: Fleming H. Revell Co., 1901.

Brubacher, J. S. *Henry Barnard on Education.* New York: McGraw-Hill Book Co., Inc., 1931.

Butler, J. E. *The Life of Jean Frederic Oberlin.* London: Religious Tract Society, n.d.

Cole, G. D. H. *Life of Robert Owen.* 2d ed.; London: Macmillan & Co., Ltd., 1920.

Curti, M. *The Social Ideas of American Educators.* New York: Charles Scribner's Sons, 1935.

Dunlop, O. J. and Denman, R. D. *English Apprenticeship and Child Labor.* London: Unwin, 1912.

Evans, D. *The Sunday Schools of Wales.* London: Sunday School Union, 1883.

Evans, O. D. *Educational Opportunities for Young Workers.* New York: The Macmillan Co., 1926.

Harris, J. H., ed. *Robert Raikes; the Man and His Work.* Bristol: Arrowsmith, n.d.

Hayes, C. B. *The American Lyceum.* U.S. Office of Education, Bulletin 12, 1932.

Humphreys, D. *An Historical Account of the Incorporated Society for the Propagation of the Gospel in Foreign Parts.* New York, 1853.

Kemp, W. W. *The Support of Schools in Colonial New York by the Society for the Propagation of the Gospel in Foreign Parts.* New York: Teachers College, Columbia University, 1913.

Lancaster, J. *British System of Education.* Washington: Cooper, 1812.

Noffsinger, J. S. *Correspondence Schools, Lyceums, Chautauquas.* New York: The Macmillan Co., 1926.

Pascoe, C. F. *Two Hundred Years of the S. P. G., 1701–1900.* 2 vols.; London: Society for the Propagation of the Gospel, 1901.

Salmon, D. *Joseph Lancaster.* London: Longmans, Green & Co., Ltd., 1904.

Southey, R., and C. C. *The Life of the Rev. Andrew Bell.* London: Murray, 1844.

Weber, S. E. *The Charity School Movement in Colonial Pennsylvania.* Philadelphia, Pa.: G. F. Lasher, 1905.

12 The Triumph of Science in Education

In the early centuries of the Christian era many streams of culture from the Orient flowed into the thought life of the West, and, blending with the native spiritual traditions of the peoples brought under Roman imperial sway, produced in time what we call Christian culture. In the cultural struggle of the first five Christian centuries some of the good ideals of pagan classical antiquity were submerged, as we have noted earlier. In the Renaissance, those ideals were again restored in another blending of paganism and Christianity. As a result, the classics came to be regarded as essential not only in the development of individuals and social leaders, but also, in post-Reformation days, as bulwarks of theological orthodoxies.

Science Enters Western Culture

With the scientific discoveries and inventions of the sixteenth and succeeding centuries, a development inspired in part by the Greek tradition, a new important element, science, entered into the cultural life of the West. Just as Christianity once struggled with the pagan tradition, so science was forced to struggle for its place in culture against the Christianized paganism of the classical heritage. In the pure classical tradition, it would be difficult to find any basis for intolerance of any form of human inquiry, but the classics became wedded to the supernaturalism of the Reformation era, and were thus made instruments of an ecclesiastical authoritarianism opposed to any form of inquiry likely to bring distrust of old conceptions. They had also become identified with the interest of a social elite. Moreover, three centuries of classical education had created a tradition so strong that the force of inertia itself presented a formidable barrier to the acceptance of science as an educational instrument. Indeed, the world had been transformed by science before its schools, always citadels of conservatism, became conscious of their academic fossilism. While here and there, in educational theory and in practice, science, as we have seen, was given a grudging recognition before the nineteenth century, that century was far advanced before the demands of an industrialized world, and of nations struggling for commercial supremacy, forced schools generally to give science a place in their work befitting its importance.

Science and Education

SPENCER AS PROPAGANDIST FOR SCIENCE. Ever since the sixteenth century, the study of science had many eloquent advocates, and it found its way into the curriculum of schools, but the opposition to it remained strong. In 1861, Herbert Spencer published his book *Education: Intellectual, Moral and Physical*, a collection of essays published separately some years earlier. In the first essay he treated the question "What knowledge is of most worth?" In answering that question, Spencer was thinking of individual needs, not those of society, because he was unalterably opposed to state interference in education. The purpose of education, he said, is "to prepare us for complete living." To attain that end, we must determine the leading forms of activity in which men engage as human beings living in organized society. These he set forth as follows:

1. Those activities which directly minister to self-preservation
2. Those activities which, by securing the necessaries of life, indirectly minister to self-preservation
3. Those activities which have for their end the rearing and discipline of offspring
4. Those activities which are involved in the maintenance of proper social and political relations
5. Those miscellaneous activities which fill up the leisure part of life, devoted to the gratification of the tastes and feelings.

It is the work of education, said Spencer, to prepare the individual to perform these activities (which, he says, are listed in the order of their importance) as efficiently as his economic and social position demands. Knowledge serves, he says, two ends, that of guidance and discipline. It guides him in the performance of his five basic activities, and it develops his powers through exercise in attaining it. Whether for guidance or for discipline, the knowledge of things is better than the knowledge of words. Spencer's answer to the question "What knowledge is of most worth?" is "Science." It is science that best prepares man to preserve his life, earn a livelihood, perform his parental duties, understand society and the ways of social behavior, produce and appreciate art, and develop his intellectual, moral, and religious nature. No religious devotee ever spoke more ardently of his faith than Spencer did of the blessings which science had bestowed upon men, and of its promises for the future.

Thomas Huxley, in his *Science and Education* (1868), gave influential support to Spencer's views. In America, they were defended by such men as Edward L. Youmans, Francis Wayland, and President F. A. P. Barnard of Columbia University. The voice of the opposition was, however, loud and, at times, bitter. In England and America, Spencer was denounced by some as a self-opinionated, ill-informed and, sometimes, blasphemous man. The controversy, from a standpoint of culture, was but one of many in the long struggle between science and theology. In its Spencerian stage, it was a struggle between Darwinism, with which Spencer was in accord, and the traditional fundamentalist view of the origin and meaning of life. It was a struggle between forces contending about the relative importance of material and spiritual values. Spencer and his school did not mock spiritual values, but they would re-interpret and re-evaluate them in the light of scientific discovery. They protested, however, vehemently against the neglect of the sciences, natural, physical, and social, and against the forces that would have man ignore his material well-being. Typical of the antagonism which Spencer's views encountered in America were those of Thomas Burrowes, long a leader in public education in Pennsylvania. In an editorial in the *Pennsylvania School Journal* (January, 1861), Burrowes denounced Spencer's utilitarianism and his scientific approach to ethics and morals as vicious and heretical.

SCIENCE AND THE DISCIPLINARY THEORY OF EDUCATION. One of the obstacles which science had to overcome in its struggle against traditionalism was the widely accepted disciplinary theory of education. The advocates of that theory struggled against the inclusion of the sciences in the curricula of schools on the ground that, since they are interesting studies, they are of no value in developing mental power which, like any other power, physical or moral, can be developed only by rigorous exercise. Because they were difficult and, as taught, uninteresting, the classics long enjoyed an almost universal distinction of being the best existing instruments of intellectual discipline, and they were taught generally for that purpose in the nineteenth century. The utilitarian argument for the classics had lost its force with the spread of vernacular literatures. Mathematics, also, had long enjoyed the same disciplinary prestige as the classics.

So widely had the disciplinary theory come to be accepted that every new study was called upon to prove its worth as a mental discipline. At this juncture, it was argued that discipline is of the essence of a liberal education.[1] That position was stated by Huxley in his description of a liberally educated man: "That man, I think, has had a liberal education who has been so trained in youth that his body is the ready servant of his will, and does with ease and pleasure all the work that, as a mechanism, it is capable of; whose intellect is a clear, cold, logic engine, with all its parts of equal strength, and in smooth working order; ready, like a steam engine, to be turned to any kind of work, and spin the gossamers as well as forge the anchors of the mind; whose mind is stored with a knowledge of the great and fundamental truths of Nature and of the laws of her operations; one who, no stunted ascetic, is full of life and fire, but whose passions are trained to come to heel by a vigorous will, the servant of a tender conscience. . . ."[2]

Here Huxley, a vigorous advocate of science as a worthy and useful educational instrument, identifies a liberal training with mental discipline. A knowledge of the facts and laws of nature is, he holds, an indispensable element of a liberal education. Without such knowledge there can be no complete training of one's natural powers, no adequate mental discipline. His book, *Science and Education,* was a forceful denunciation of the sterility of education, on all levels, in nineteenth-century England. After years of academic drudgery, meaningless to students, youths, said he, went forth from English schools ignorant of nearly everything they ought to know. They had been disciplined according to the accepted view of the time, but they knew nothing of modern geography, modern history, modern literature, nor of the physical, moral, and social sciences.

Huxley demanded that all that be changed, and that the schools recognize the importance of modern knowledge not only for practical ends but as a means of mental discipline as well. While he argued for an inclusion of the sciences in education on utilitarian grounds, he met the objection of the old disciplinarians, who considered them too easy and interesting to be of value as studies, by asserting that he could make the sciences as difficult, uninteresting,

[1] S. G. Noble, *History of American Education* (New York: Farrar & Rinehart, 1938), pp. 309 ff.

[2] T. Huxley, *Science and Education* (New York: Appleton-Century-Crofts, Inc., 1896), p. 86.

and disciplinary as they had made the classics. The force of Huxley's arguments did not end the debate regarding the value of the sciences in education. Some continued to deride the value of mere knowledge on the ground that the schools ought to aim at developing the intellectual power that makes men inventors rather than at giving students the rule-of-thumb knowledge of mere technicians. Mental power, it was said, not mere knowledge, must be aimed at, and to that end it is not knowledge but the process of acquiring it which is important educationally. The test of the value of any study was said to be its difficulty. What is taught is unimportant. It is the rigor of the mental exercise demanded which was considered to be the measure of the value of any study.[3]

Many were thus reluctant to acknowledge the disciplinary value of the sciences, and held to the view that the usefulness of a study was the surest proof of its educational uselessness. Yet, the view that the mind could be trained as well by useful as by useless studies attracted such an influential following in England and America that, in the last quarter of the nineteenth century, the sciences became respectable studies in our sanctuaries of learning. The classical strongholds of England (usually called "the Public Schools") and the older universities resisted the encroachment of the new studies more stubbornly than did American schools and universities but, even there, science had secured a firm foothold at the end of the century. In our American secondary and higher schools we do not now teach the sciences as mental exercises, although an occasional teacher will still justify one or another of them on such grounds. Seventy-five years ago, physiology, botany, geology, chemistry, physics, physical geography, and astronomy were taught, as one writer says algebra was then taught, not to make useful American citizens, but "for the purpose of developing patience and habits of persistence and of training a pupil in reasoning."[4]

We have seen that manual training was given a place in our schools for disciplinary reasons. Such studies as home economics, commercial studies, agriculture, art, music and physical education had to be proved of disciplinary worth before they were dignified with scholastic approval. To that end they were made to rest upon a suitable basis of related sciences and theory, and were thus taught in such a formal way that the recognition of their educational

[3] A. J. E. Fouillée, *Education from a National Standpoint* (New York: Appleton-Century-Crofts, Inc., 1892), pp. 36–37.

[4] D. E. Smith, *The Progress of Algebra in the Last Quarter of a Century* (Boston: Ginn and Co., 1925), p. 13.

worth could not be refused. Every new study had to be capable of formal logical organization before it could take its place in our schools with the older disciplines.

At last, the disciplinary theory itself was challenged by experimental psychologists, whose findings negated fundamental assumptions upon which it rested.[5] For over half a century its influence upon the curriculum of our schools has almost entirely vanished. Even before the psychological basis of the theory was seriously questioned, American educators had given approval to the principle of the "equivalence of studies" in order that our schools might serve better the needs of society and the individual. The Committee of Ten of the National Education Association, in its *Report* (1893), and the Committee on College Entrance Requirements of the same Association, in its *Report* (1899), endorsed that principle. It should be noted here that, from the time Franklin planned the Philadelphia Academy, with its separate schools or departments, the "elective system" found increasing favor in America. Our early academies and high schools, generally, offered students a choice of courses. Jefferson planned the University of Virginia (1818) on the elective principle and, when it opened (1825), students were left free to choose their studies on the basis of their interest rather than follow a prescribed course, as had been done in all other American colleges previously. Not until the closing quarter of the nineteenth century did American colleges, generally, adopt the elective system. The practice of free election of studies by students gave the sciences a chance to compete with the older studies for student patronage, and the result was favorable to science.

INSTITUTIONAL CHANGES. In an earlier chapter we have seen that economic and social change, and the early scientific movement, gave rise to a new type of secondary school called, in Germany, *Realschule* and, in England and America, Academy. This earlier interest in science was overshadowed by the greater interest produced by the Industrial Revolution, nationalism, and the cultural triumph of science itself.

In Prussia, physics and natural history were included by government order in the curriculum of the *Gymnasium* for the years 1812-1816. In 1859, a new type of school, the *Realgymnasium*, which gave more time to the sciences than did the *Gymnasium*, was established and officially approved. In 1882, came the establishment and recognition of another school, with a stronger scientific bias, the *Oberrealschule*. In addition to these, many special

[5] *Supra*, pp. 368 ff.

trade, or technical, schools were established in Germany in the nineteenth century. In the elementary schools, drawing, geography, and elementary science have been taught since the advent of Pestalozzianism.

France, because of its cultural indebtedness to ancient Rome and of marked Catholic, particularly Jesuit, influence, has shown a firmer attachment to the classics than Germany, America, or England. The Revolution resulted in the establishment of state schools, the *École Normale* (1794) and the *Lycée,* a secondary school (1802), in both of which science was taught. The sciences, however, were given slow and grudging recognition in secondary schools, and ranked below the classics in official and popular esteem. Drawing, geography, and natural sciences have had a prominent place in the curriculum of elementary schools since the establishment of the Third Republic.

In England, while the sciences had a place in the curriculum of the academies of the Non-conformists, the Anglican secondary schools remained classical. Industrial needs and the conservatism of the old institutions led to the establishment, in the nineteenth century, of municipal universities and national higher technical schools. In the last quarter of the century, against strong opposition by teachers, "modern" studies were introduced into the Public Schools where, to the present, they have held a place inferior to the classics. Since 1900, approximately, new schools, having a commercial and industrial bias, have been established and, since World War I, the "modern" studies have slowly secured increased emphasis in the older secondary schools. In the elementary schools, geography and elementary science have been required studies since the beginning of the century.

The British remain attached to the old disciplinary philosophy, and they send their children to secondary schools not so much to acquire knowledge and skill as to have their character formed and their social position preserved, or improved. To that end, the old disciplines, among which the classics are still ranked first in value, are considered best. Though the sciences have had a place in the traditional secondary schools for nearly a century, they have been taught in the main as formal intellectual exercises rather than with a view to their practical application. The laboratory method of teaching science, used by Amos Eaton in the Rensselaer Polytechnic Institute at Troy, New York, in 1825,[6] and, almost simultaneously, by Liebig at the University of Giessen, was not used in Oxford

[6] E. M. McAllister, *Amos Eaton* (Philadelphia: University of Pennsylvania Press, 1941), pp. 384 ff., 514 f.

and Cambridge universities until 1869. Industrial needs and national crises have, in the past generation, been dinning into the consciousness of Englishmen a realization that the welfare of the nation and the empire is linked to science, and that one of the first duties of the schools is to provide society with practical scientists capable of meeting all national needs.

In the United States, where European prejudices never became deeply rooted, and where pioneer conditions demanded practicality in life and a realistic emphasis in education, science has had a freer growth than in the Old World. In colonial times, numerous private masters taught science and its application to practical problems. While there was a little bookish instruction in science, according to the Aristotelian-mediaeval tradition, in our earliest colonial colleges, it was not until Franklin, in Philadelphia (1749), and Samuel Johnson, in New York (1754), laid new plans of higher education, which were embodied in the College of Philadelphia and King's College, that science was given a worthy recognition. To Franklin's plan we have referred earlier. Johnson would have taught, among other studies, the "Arts of *Numbering* and *Measuring*, of *Surveying* and *Navigation*, of *Geography* and *History*, of *Husbandry*, *Commerce* and *Government*: And . . . the Knowledge of *all Nature* in the *Heavens* above us and in the *Air*, *Water* and *Earth* around us, and the various kinds of Meteors, *Stones*, *Mines* and *Minerals*, *Plants* and Animals, and of everything *useful* for the comfort, the Convenience and elegance of Life in the chief Manufactures."[7] Until after 1825, however, the sciences received scant attention in American colleges. The most important early development came when, in 1847, the Lawrence Scientific School, at Harvard, and the Sheffield Scientific School, at Yale, were established. Similar steps were soon taken by other universities and colleges. Special private technical schools, such as the Rensselaer Polytechnic Institute (1824) and Worcester Polytechnic Institute (1868) also arose. Finally, public technical and agricultural schools, in the several states, were provided for by the national government under the Morrill Act of 1862 and its supplements of later years.

The academy, as previously noted, and then the high school, which have been the secondary schools of the national period, have shown no antagonism to science. The academy tried hard to meet the demands of our early democracy, and catered to popular needs and interests. The curriculum of the high schools preserved that tradition. Our probably first high school, established in Boston in

[7] E. G. Dexter, *A History of Education in the United States* (New York: The Macmillan Co., 1919), p. 255. (By permission.)

1821, offered instruction in geography, mathematics, surveying, navigation, astronomy, and natural philosophy. As the century advanced, physics, chemistry, botany, geology, zoology, natural history, drawing, and mechanical drawing appeared widely in the program of high schools. Since 1900, the laboratory method of teaching science, which had made its appearance in high schools earlier, has become almost universal, and the emphasis has been on applied rather than on pure science. In the elementary curriculum, geography was the first science to find a place. To it were later added physiology and nature study, in the form of "object lessons." These studies had a foothold by 1860.

THE "COLD WAR" AND SCIENCE

The "cold war" between the Communist and the liberal worlds has resulted in an emphasis upon science and technology as indispensable weapons in the struggle. William Benton, former U.S. Senator and now publisher of the *Encyclopaedia Britannica*, says[8] that, after his recent visit to Russia, he is "convinced that Russia's classrooms and libraries, her laboratories and teaching methods, may threaten us more than her hydrogen bombs or guided missiles to deliver them." And he went on to say that nowhere are we giving our high school students a preparation in mathematics and science comparable with that provided in Russian secondary and higher schools.[9] During the past few years, official and professional alarm has been expressed regarding the shortage of science and mathematics teachers in American classrooms, and the neglect of science and mathematics in the nation's high schools. A recent study by the U.S. Department of Health, Education and Welfare reveals that: (a) nearly one-fourth of our public high schools do not teach plane geometry, chemistry, or physics, (b) that one-third of them do not teach trigonometry, solid geometry, or advanced algebra, and (c) that one-tenth of them do not teach eleventh- or twelfth-grade mathematics.[10] Statistics are often misleading, and *The New York Times* analyst ("G.C.") reminds us that the defective schools are the small ones which enroll only a small percentage of our high-school students. The ways of Heaven and man have been mysterious, but both now seem to be pursuing the path of science. And, while we write (1955-57), the *London Times Educational*

[8] "Now the 'Cold War' of the Classrooms," *The New York Times Magazine* (April 1, 1956), pp. 15–46.

[9] See also G. K. Smith (ed.), *Current Issues in Higher Education, 1956* (Washington, D.C.: National Education Association, 1956).

[10] *The New York Times* (August 26, 1956), Sec. 4, p. E9.

Supplement reveals humanistic England turning to science and technology for salvation. *Tempora mutantur et nos mutamur in illis* (times change and we change in them). But we change fearfully and reluctantly. The new emphasis upon science does not herald the end of the humanities. Their importance no one can question, but perhaps science, one of man's greatest creations, should, with art, literature, philosophy, etc., be classified among the humanities.

The Science of Education

Until the present century, the approach to the study of educational problems was, in the main, philosophical rather than scientific. Men like Herbart, Spencer, Alexander Bain, and an array of progressive educators in Europe and America, in the nineteenth century, were either conscious of the need for exact knowledge in the field, or actually undertook experiments to test the validity of some theory, or to discover better ways of teaching. Yet, while the need for a scientific approach to education was felt earlier, little was done to realize it before 1900. Since then we have become so preoccupied with the "science" of education that we have almost forgotten the rich heritage of educational wisdom bequeathed to us by many profound thinkers since the days of Plato. The historical and philosophical approach to an understanding of educational problems has received progressively less emphasis since the turn of the century. The interest of the teaching profession has turned largely to the quantitative and measurable aspects of education. In the realm of educational values, however, there are many questions which cannot be answered through a process of quantitative analysis. The science of education, however, has brought fruitful results in the study of those aspects of education which can be tested by observation and experiment.[11]

The beginnings of the science of education might be traced back to Comenius, Basedow, Pestalozzi, and Froebel. While their schools were not education laboratories, nor their experiments conducted in a scientific way, they were testing, though with but a vaguely defined scientific curiosity, the value of certain theories and practices. In Europe and America, since about 1890, a number of progressive schools have been established, some of them, like that of Dewey at the University of Chicago, being in purpose ex-

[11] F. Bobbitt, *How to Make a Curriculum* (Boston: Houghton Mifflin Co., 1924); W. W. Charters, *Curriculum Construction* (New York: The Macmillan Co., 1929); B. H. Bode, *Modern Educational Theories* (New York: The Macmillan Co., 1927).

perimental. The movement received its first great impetus when the psychologists Alfred Binet and T. Simon published their measure of general intelligence in 1905, which Binet revised in 1908 and 1911. The Stanford Revision of the Binet Scale, by Lewis Terman, was published in 1916, and has been widely used in America. Other tests of general intelligence have since been devised.

In the measurement movement in psychology and education, Sir Francis Galton's work *Hereditary Genius* (1869) and Edward L. Thorndike's work *Theory of Mental and Social Measurements* (1904) have been historical landmarks. The substitution of fairly exact measures of general intelligence for the guesses of earlier days has brought many reforms in school practices. Different provisions for students of different abilities, as revealed by psychological tests, have been frequently made. In addition to measures of general intelligence, the psychologists have invented numerous measures of special aptitudes and abilities. Indeed, there is scarcely a single psychological phenomenon for which we have not some instrument of testing or measurement. The reliability of some of these devices has been frequently questioned. Among the many problems which such tests have thrown light upon is that of mental differences due to sex. Educational opportunities provided for women in the nineteenth century enabled them to prove that the traditional belief that women are mentally inferior to men was but a cultural prejudice. Yet all doubts were not dispelled. Psychological tests have shown that the differences, if any, are but slight and do not warrant any differentiation in education on a sex basis only. Further investigation of the influence of sex upon mind may force some revision of the views that are now current.[12] The modern educational psychologist has thus been measuring the individual differences which, since Plato's time, if not before, have been of interest to philosophers and teachers.

Some exact measure of pupils' achievement had long been desired by teachers and school administrators. It is noteworthy that, in the days of Horace Mann, written essay examinations were introduced because, it was asserted, they would furnish an exact and equal means of testing students' achievement. Educational, as distinct from psychological, measurements began when Joseph M. Rice gave a spelling test to 30,000 children in 1897. From this beginning came our standardized tests in school subjects. There are now standardized tests in nearly every subject, and they are used not only for comparing the achievement of particular grades with the

[12] C. R. Griffith, *An Introduction to Educational Psychology* (New York: Farrar & Rinehart, 1935), pp. 574–77.

standard but also for diagnosing difficulties of individual pupils so that proper remedies may be applied. Devices for detecting certain physical handicaps of children have been invented, and are used to determine the causes of certain difficulties in learning. Certain reading difficulties are due to eye defects which can now be readily detected by the use of instruments.

Experimental research of a physical and psychological nature has gone far to reveal the causes of many learning difficulties earlier unknown. We have made great progress in analyzing the mechanical processes involved in learning, and we have tested experimentally the value of different methods of teaching. Because of the difficulty of controlling certain factors in educational experiments, the validity of the findings of investigators is often open to question. The science, however, is still in its infancy and, with the refinement of procedures and techniques which are being developed, it gives promise of more certain results in the future. Intelligence and achievement tests and other diagnostic instruments are among the chief tools of the scientist in education. The science has not, however, been limited to an investigation of instructional problems. Such problems as those of school administration, school finance, school buildings, teacher training, etc., have all been subjected to scientific inquiry, with a view to finding accurate, objective measures of their efficiency. Franklin Bobbitt and Werrett W. Charters have attempted to determine even the aims of education scientifically. The measurement movement has also entered the physical education field.

The progress that has been made in the past generation has been to some observers appalling. Those aspects of education which lend themselves to statistical analysis have received nearly all the attention, while other aspects, sometimes more important, have been neglected. It has been remarked that the testing movement has mechanized instruction, and that we spend more time in perfecting an administrative machinery than we do in moulding character and building men. We have, it is said, busied ourselves in collecting facts, the meaning of which we have not taken time to learn. It should be remembered, however, that without facts, other steps are impossible. The work of interpreting them, never altogether neglected, will, when the first wave of scientific enthusiasm has passed, perhaps receive the attention it deserves.

The application of scientific method to the solution of educational problems has resulted in the rise of highly specialized fields of inquiry and learning. General and special methods of teaching, curriculum construction, educational psychology, educational sociology, character education, educational administration, educational tests and measurements, vocational education, vocational guidance, secondary education, elementary education, history of education, and comparative education are among the fields of educational specialization. In the training of teachers, supervisors, and administrators, emphasis has come to be placed upon the special knowledge and skills needed in the numerous special fields of service for which men and women are being prepared. Specialization, indeed, has been carried to the point where the future teacher or administrator may be made a very narrowly educated person from the standpoint of professional knowledge. And professional knowledge, as it grows, threatens to demand more of the time which teachers once spent in enriching their knowledge of the subjects they planned to teach.

The scientific approach to education has produced noteworthy results in our handling of mentally defective children. The first influential student of the problems of mental defectives was Edouard Séguin, a Frenchman, who came to America in 1850.[13] Manual work and sense training were made by him the basis of their instruction. He lacked, however, a scientific means of classifying such defectives. We have now many psychological tests for that purpose, and special schools and classes exist for special types of abnormal children.

In handling the problem of moral delinquency, psychological and child-guidance clinics have been established in America in the past thirty years for the chief purpose of preventing juvenile irregularities. These clinics supplement the work of the home, the school and juvenile courts in dealing with such cases, and co-operate with these agencies. In 1912, a Children's Bureau was created in the Department of Labor. Founded to promote the welfare of children, it has studied many child problems and, through its publications, has contributed many valuable factual additions to existing knowledge of the subject.

The past half-century has thus been a period of experimentation and research in education. In that movement the United States has been far ahead of the rest of the world. The volume of scientific educational literature produced in America in the past sixty years is impressive, though the value of some of it is unquestionably low, as is the value of some studies in other fields of research. To describe the movement with any degree of completeness would require a bulky volume. Here we have but sketched the movement

[13] *Supra*, p. 487.

in an incomplete outline, sufficient for a grasp of its spirit and general scope. Universal education and its steady expansion created urgent problems which, for the sake of efficiency, had to be handled with exactness and effectiveness. In gathering the information necessary for their solution, educators turned, as did investigators in other fields, to research as the only efficient approach.

Selected Readings

Adamson, J. W. *Pioneers of Modern Education, 1600–1700.* London: Cambridge University Press, 1921.

Bagley, W. C. *Determinism in Education.* Baltimore: Warwick and York, 1928.

Bain, A. *Education as a Science.* New York: Appleton-Century-Crofts, Inc., 1879.

Cajori, F. *The Teaching and History of Mathematics in the United States.* United States Bureau of Education, Circular of Information, No. 3, 1890.

Childs, J. L. *Education and the Philosophy of Experimentalism.* New York: Appleton-Century-Crofts, Inc., 1931.

Dewey, J. *Democracy and Education.* New York: The Macmillan Co., 1916.

Heck, W. H. *Mental Discipline and Educational Values.* London: John Lane, The Bodley Head, Ltd., 1911.

Huxley, T. *Science and Education.* New York: Appleton-Century-Crofts, Inc., 1896.

Kandel, I. L., ed. *Twenty-Five Years of American Education.* New York: The Macmillan Co., 1924.

Kilpatrick, W. H., *et al. The Educational Frontier.* New York: Appleton-Century-Crofts, Inc., 1933.

Knight, E. W. *Fifty Years of American Education.* New York: The Ronald Press Co., 1952.

Lynd, R. S. *Knowledge for What? The Place of Social Science in American Culture.* Princeton, N.J.: Princeton University Press, 1939.

Meriwether, C. *Our Colonial Curriculum (1607–1776).* New York: Capitol Publishing Co., 1907.

Monroe, W. S., and Engelhardt, M. *The Scientific Study of Educational Problems.* New York: The Macmillan Co., 1937.

National Education Association, Commission on the Reorganization of Secondary Education. *The Cardinal Principles of Secondary Education.* United States Bureau of Education, Bulletin 35. Washington, D.C.: U.S. Government Printing Office, 1918.

Rugg, H. *American Life and the School Curriculum.* Boston: Ginn & Co., 1936.

"Scientific Movement in Education, The." *The Thirty-seventh Yearbook of the National Society for the Study of Education,* Part II. Bloomington, Ill.: Public School Publishing Co., 1938.

Seybolt, R. F. *Source Studies in American Colonial Education. The Private School.* Urbana: University of Illinois Press, 1925.

Spencer, H. *Education: Intellectual, Moral, and Physical.* London: J. M. Dent & Sons, Ltd., n.d.

Thorndike, E. L. *Educational Psychology; Briefer Course.* New York: Teachers College, Columbia University, 1927.

Whitehead, A. N. *Science and the Modern World.* New York: The Macmillan Co., 1925.

Woody, T. *Educational Views of Benjamin Franklin.* New York: McGraw-Hill Book Co., 1931.

13 The Rise of National School Systems in Europe

Elsewhere we have examined the development of factors which brought about the disintegration of the unity of Christendom. That unity, based upon the universal ideals of the fatherhood of God and the brotherhood of men, had been imposed upon Europeans, at times by force, and was apparent rather than real. The illiterate masses and, probably, many of their ecclesiastical and civil masters did not understand its significance. Moreover, the tyranny, injustice, and greed of which the custodians of the Christian ideals had been guilty brought the ideology itself into disrepute. From the beginning of the twelfth century, the revolt against ecclesiastical authoritarianism, and against the spiritual and institutional unity imposed by such authority upon peoples differing in their own native cultural traditions, gathered momentum and culminated in the Reformation, an event which marks the end both of Catholic authoritarianism and of the Christian dream of world unity.

The Triumph of Local Cultures

The Reformation was a triumph of local ideals, local feelings and local ways of life over the universal ideal which had never become firmly rooted in the cultural soil of Europe. It was a significant victory for the national ideal. It was followed by the establishment of many Christian churches, many of them national, in the place of one universal church of the past. The change from universalism to localism, or particularism, was not a sudden one. The rise of vernacular literatures heralded its coming.

The spirit of Italian culture stirs in the vernacular writings of Dante in the thirteenth century. He would satisfy the thirst of the common native folk of Italy for knowledge by bringing it to them in their own language rather than in Latin. In the same century, the ancient folklore of Germany had been given literary expression, and German poets, writing in German, were giving voice to national feelings. Even earlier than on the Continent, the native culture of England began to find protection and nurture in the fortress of vernacular writing. This movement of the native, indigenous spirit of groups having a common and ancient cultural tradition was retarded but not stopped by the classical Renaissance. A study of the classics, indeed, tended to revive and glorify such patriotic sentiments as once prevailed in Greece and Rome, though that was not intended by the early leaders of the movement. Vernacular schools, as we have seen, had been established in later mediaeval cities, and the Bible in the vernacular was in use among some Catholics in pre-Reformation days. Yet the European masses, almost wholly illiterate prior to 1300, remained largely in that condition until the Reformation, though some improvement had been effected in the fourteenth and fifteenth centuries. Thomas More (1478-1535) reports that about one-half of the English people were unable to read English in his day.[1]

The political and religious changes of post-Reformation days accentuated the drift toward the cultural unification and exclusiveness of national groups. Vernacular schools and universal literacy, urged by Luther for religious and social ends, were eventually to be viewed as instruments for the development of national feeling, national solidarity and, among some, of national hatreds. Until the close of the eighteenth century, national Protestant churches, as we have seen, were the central agencies inculcating upon youth, through vernacular instruction, the ideals of the nations. The new Christianity, propagated through churches and schools, had the stamp of particularism on it. In the nearly three hundred years which separated the Reformation from the French Revolution considerable advance had been made, in Protestant countries, in abolishing illiteracy. Educational activity increased in Catholic countries also, though some of them, such as Italy and Spain, ran far behind their Protestant neighbors in providing instruction for the masses. National, political and commercial rivalries, and social unrest within individual nations, traceable mainly to the changing economic scene and the causes that produced it, brought, in the eighteenth and nineteenth centuries, an intensification of the em-

[1] J. W. Thompson, *The Literacy of the Laity in the Middle Ages* (Berkeley: University of California Press, 1939), p. v; F. A. Gasquet, *The Eve of the Reformation* (New York: G. P. Putnam's Sons, Inc.. 1900), p. 249.

phasis upon national ideals, and the establishment, largely under national and lay auspices, of national school systems. Elementary education, free, universal, compulsory, and, in varying degrees, secular, was the goal set and largely attained by European nations and the United States in the nineteenth century.

Development and Character of the Prussian School System

Prussia, being by far the largest German state, furnishes a good example of the development of national education in central Europe. Here the Lutheran was the state church and, until the late eighteenth century, dominated education. In 1800, Prussian economy was still largely agricultural, and a landowning nobility, enjoying many traditional feudal privileges, held a place of great eminence in society, while the bourgeois class was far less influential than was the middle class of France and England. At the head of society stood a monarch who exercised absolute authority.

For two hundred years after the Reformation, the Prussian state entrusted the execution of its education laws (1532, 1540, 1573, 1604, 1648, and 1687) to the church, although the interest of the laity in education was recognized in these laws. The law of 1648 declared that schools belong to the state rather than to the church, but the practice of church control remained. Frederick William I (1713-1740), having established earlier many elementary schools with public money and having founded two teacher-training schools (1735 and 1736), made education compulsory for children between six and twelve years of age (1736). Because of the opposition of parents, the cost of universalizing education, and the lack of an administrative machine to enforce this compulsory law, the monarch's efforts were largely abortive. Frederick the Great (1740-1786) took a long step toward the nationalization of education when, in 1763, he issued his *General School Regulation*, which required children to attend school between the ages of five and thirteen or fourteen, or until they had demonstrated their proficiency in religion, reading, writing, and other knowledge found in books approved by the school authorities of the state. The new law provided for the examination and licensing of teachers by state-approved inspectors, local pastors being named for that position. The *Regulation* fixed the amount of school fees, and provided for the payment of the fees of poor children out of a fund raised by church collections.

Only teachers of religious character and exemplary behavior were to be approved or retained. The singing of hymns, recitation of prayers and the Lutheran catechism, the memorization and interpretation of Biblical passages, reading, and writing were the studies prescribed. Religious instruction was the core of the curriculum. Memorization, drill, repetition, and attentive listening by pupils characterize the method of instruction prescribed. The assigning of school inspection to pastors left the church in a dominant position.[2] In 1787, Baron von Zedlitz, who was head of the Department of the Lutheran Church and School Affairs under Frederick the Great, prevailed upon the new king, Frederick William II (1786-1797), to place the administration of Prussian education in the hands of a central board of experts, *Oberschulcollegium*, thus separating the administration of the church from that of the schools, and placing the latter more directly under state control. The clergy, however, were given a dominant place on the new board of control. In 1794, Frederick made a general codification of Prussian basic laws. One chapter in the Code dealt with principles of educational legislation, as follows:

> Schools and universities are state institutions, charged with the instruction of youth in useful information and scientific knowledge. Such institutions may be established only with the knowledge and approval of the State. All public schools and educational institutions are under the supervision of the State and are at all times subject to its examination and inspection.[3]

The principle that education is a function of the state, not of parents or of the church, was thus clearly affirmed in 1794, and, through the nineteenth century, Prussian education approached, by a series of steps, that ideal. The defeat of the Prussians by Napoleon at Jena (1806) brought a call from the reigning monarch, Frederick William III, and from German leaders, of whom Fichte was the most influential, for a supreme effort to awaken in the bosoms of all Prussians the spirit of patriotism. Compulsory military training and the enforcement of compulsory school laws were quickly achieved. Pestalozzianism was officially approved as a means of improving the morale of the masses. Gymnastic, military, and patriotic societies were established everywhere. Individualism was denounced by Fichte and others as a national curse responsible for Prussia's humiliation. Henceforth the individual must live not for himself but for the state. In building a strong state, education was viewed as an indispensable instrument. Said Fichte: "I hope . . . that I convince some Germans, and that I shall bring them to

[2] H. Barnard, "Public Instruction in Prussia," *American Journal of Education*, XX, 338–42; XXII, 861–68.

[3] I. L. Kandel, *History of Secondary Education* (Boston: Houghton Mifflin Co., 1930), p. 239.

see that it is education alone which can save us from all the evils by which we are oppressed."[4] In 1817, the Bureau of Education, organized in the Department of the Interior (1807), was raised to the status of a national Department of Education, to which was later given the title Ministry of Religion, Education, and Public Health.[5] In 1825, provincial school boards were set up throughout Prussia to replace the local church school boards. The provinces, of which there were ten, were divided into "districts," in each of which a district school board was established, on which the clergy were permitted to hold a prominent place.

In law, and largely in practice, the control of Prussian education had thus been transferred from the church to the state. Thereafter, the schools of Germany, administered by a political hierarchy, dominated by the king, whose authority was absolute, were to have as their primary goal the fostering of a spirit of patriotic devotion to the rulers of the state. The school law compelled every district to establish a school or schools, the program of which had to conform with standards established by the national educational authority. An efficient machinery was set up to enforce the compulsory education law and, by 1840, the opposition of parents to that requirement had been generally overcome. Prussia was the first nation to have made universal education a reality. While the Prussian folk-schools were supported mainly by local taxes upon property, the pupils, until 1888, were required to pay small fees, the very poor, however, being exempted from all charges for instruction and instructional materials.

THE FOLK-SCHOOLS. (1) CLASS BASIS. The character of the folk-schools, or elementary schools, was determined mainly by the national, political purpose which they were created to serve. In the class society of Prussia, they were the schools of the laboring masses. The secondary schools, which had their own preparatory departments, beginning with the first grade, were the schools of the middle and upper classes, and were pay schools beyond the financial reach of the poor. The scheme of educational organization, whether designedly or not, was an instrument of social predestination. The folk-school was designed to stifle, rather than stimulate, the ambitions of the poor. Though public, it was under local denominational supervision.

(2) THE FOLK-SCHOOL TEACHER. To teach in a folk-school, or in a private primary school, the teacher was required to hold a cer-

[4] E. P. Cubberley, *Readings in the History of Education* (Boston: Houghton Mifflin Co., 1920), p. 480.

[5] In 1911, public health was transferred to another ministry.

tificate, obtained by examination given by state authorities. While individuals might prepare themselves privately for that examination, the usual and the most certain procedure was to attend a teachers' seminary, of which there was, in 1831, one in each county, or largest subdivision of a province. In 1840, there were thirty such seminaries in Prussia.[6] In these the future teacher was subjected to a disciplinary training similar to that of the soldier. To ensure his social orthodoxy and to guarantee the conservative character of his influence upon his pupils, the atmosphere of the seminary was profoundly religious, and its students were required to engage in a variety of religious activities. Only God-fearing teachers, it was felt, could make God-fearing and obedient citizens. Yet, the earlier seminaries, while they stressed religion and German culture, offered future folk-school teachers a fairly broad academic education. That liberalism, however, was soon attacked after the Napoleonic threat to Prussia had passed. Even Frederick William III, who, in the days of Prussia's humiliation, showed unstinted friendship toward the masses, repented for his liberalism. "We do not," he said, "confer upon the individual or upon society any benefit when we educate him beyond the bounds of his social class and vocation." [7] And Baron von Altenstein, his Minister of Education, having outlined a program for the education of common folk, remarked: "I do not think that the principles enunciated will raise the common people out of the sphere designated for them by God and human society." [8]

The revolution of 1848, created by the advocates of a democratic social order, having failed, Frederick William IV (1840-1857) and his officials subjected the teachers' seminaries to a régime of tyrannous repression. The king addressing representatives of the seminaries, in 1849, remarked: "You and you alone are to blame for all the misery which the last year has brought upon Prussia. The irreligious pseudo-education of the masses is to be blamed for it . . . by which you have eradicated religious belief and loyalty from the hearts of my subjects. . . . This sham education, strutting about like a peacock, has always been odious to me." [9] The reform of the seminaries which followed resulted in the elimination of educational theory (often dangerous) from the curriculum and restricted the program to the history of Prussian elementary schools,

[6] E. Reisner, *Nationalism in Education since 1789* (New York: The Macmillan Co., 1927), p. 137.

[7] *Ibid.*, pp. 143–44. (By permission.)

[8] *Ibid.*, p. 145. (By permission.)

[9] F. Paulsen, *German Education Past and Present* (London: Unwin, 1908), pp. 245 f.

the problems of school government, religious instruction, and practice in teaching primary school subjects. Special attention was paid in the seminaries to instruction in religion, reading, German language, history, and geography. The glorification of the Fatherland and the inculcation of patriotic devotion to it in the future teachers of the Prussian masses were the objectives aimed at. Being themselves the children of common people, these future teachers had to be purged of any class sympathy which they might have inherited.

With the establishment, in 1871, of the German empire in which the influence of Prussia was dominant, a more extensive program of studies was introduced into the teachers' seminaries. The fundamental character of the schools, however, remained unchanged. No attempt was made until the establishment of the republic, in 1918, to link these seminaries with the secondary schools and universities. Their students remained the children of the masses, and their education was so designed that, as teachers, they would not inspire unrest or ambition in those who, like themselves, could not hope for any educational or social opportunity beyond the orbit of the folk-school and its clientele.

Emperor William II, in 1889, called upon the schools to fight against the doctrines of the socialists. The school, said he, "must make a special effort to furnish even the youth with the conviction that not only are the teachings of social democracy contrary to the commandments of God and to Christian morals, but also impracticable of realization and dangerous to the individual and to society at large."[10] To that end the study of economics and economic history was introduced into the teachers' seminaries and, thereafter, anti-socialist propaganda had a prominent place in them, in the folk-schools, and also in the middle and secondary schools.

The folk-school teacher, as all other teachers, including university professors, was a state official. A large part of his salary was paid by the state, which also guaranteed him a pension out of a fund to which, after 1885, he was not required to contribute. His obligation to defend, by indoctrinating his own lower class, the existing political and social order had been impressed upon him and, in return for faithful service, the state gave him not a bountiful reward but a comfortable security, and a little social prestige.

(3) The Folk-School Student. The folk-school pupil was a child of the common people. According to the official philosophy,

[10] Reisner, *op. cit.*, p. 194. (By permission.)

God had assigned to the common man a humble but necessary rôle in the industrial and social order. It was the primary duty of the folk-school to instruct him in his social obligations and make him contented with his lot. The benevolent despots who ruled over him by divine right, fearing that he might fall a victim to the socialist heresy, not only indoctrinated him against its evils, but provided him, under Kaiser William II, with social security under a variety of forms of social insurance, which protected him and his dependents against the uncertainties of his economic life. The folk-school student was required to attend school between the ages of six and fourteen, when he usually was sufficiently prepared for church confirmation. Students who had satisfactorily completed the course at an earlier age might be excused from further attendance. After 1888, instruction in the folk-school was entirely free.

(4) THE FOLK-SCHOOL CURRICULUM. **(a) Subjects taught.** From 1872 onward, the emphasis in folk-schools was upon the following subjects: (a) religious instruction, (b) German language and literature, including reading, writing, composition and grammar, (c) arithmetic, (d) drawing, (e) history, (f) geography, (g) elementary science, (h) singing, (i) gymnastics for boys, and (j) needlework for girls.

The religion taught was that of the predominant church group in the community, Protestant, Catholic, or Jewish. Where the denominations were nearly numerically equal, each was given its own school. Where it was necessary to house all faiths in one school, ministers of the several denominations participated in providing religious instruction. The government desired its citizens to be church members.

The language used and taught was the High German, rather than various local dialects. Such a requirement had as its aim the cultural unity of Prussia. German literature, German patriotic classics, history, and geography were taught with a view to fostering national patriotism.

(b) The curriculum as nationalistic propaganda. After the establishment of the Prussian-dominated German empire, in 1871, the nationalistic and imperialistic ambitions of Prussian statesmen rose rapidly, and the schools fostered the hopes and desires of officialdom by intensifying their efforts to strengthen the faith of the people in their Fatherland and its destiny. Perhaps no religion was ever more ardently espoused than that of the love of country in the Germany of William II. Children were made to feel that the German language was the most perfect of all languages, and German literature, the most excellent of all literatures. They sang the patriotic songs of the Fatherland, an exercise with which teachers and students usually commemorated great events in German history. They committed to memory poems which inflamed them with patriotic zeal. History was not taught to transmit truth, but to instill into youths a love of country. In narrating the story of the past, the character of Germany's neighbors was frequently defamed, and their deeds maligned. In geography the children were taught that Germany was bounded on the north, south, east, and west by enemies. This teaching did not save the Hohenzollern régime from its fall in 1918 and the consequent disillusionment of its people. Looking back upon its fall and reflecting upon the rôle which intelligence ought to play in the ordering of the world, one might suggest that since we cannot foresee what the future may hold for any nation, teachers, particularly in democracies, would be well advised to abstain from prophecy, and tell their pupils the truth about the past.[11]

THE MITTELSCHULE. The caste system appears in the rise of the "middle-school," a six-year pay school, which lower middle class pupils entered at the age of ten as a path to lower positions in the civil service, commerce and industry. It was first officially proposed in the school regulations of 1872 to meet the educational needs of children of artisans and small shopkeepers who could not meet the expense of a secondary education. The chief difference between its curriculum and that of the upper grades of the folk-school was that a foreign language was taught in the last three years of the program.

PRUSSIAN SECONDARY EDUCATION. When the nineteenth century opened, Prussia had two types of secondary schools: (a) *gymnasien*, or classical schools, and (b) *realschulen* or *bürgerschulen*, which emphasized modern studies. By a regulation of the *Oberschulcollegium*, in 1788, a secondary-school leaving examination was introduced, and a certificate was granted to successful students which was accepted for admission to the universities. Only schools of the *gymnasium* type were permitted to hold this examination and issue certificates. Students from other schools who sought university education were required to pass the entrance examinations given by the universities themselves. The privilege thus officially bestowed upon the classical secondary school represents a triumph of the neo-humanistic ideal, through which leading German nationalists hoped to emancipate the individual and the Ger-

[11] J. F. Scott, *Menace of Nationalism in Education* (New York: The Macmillan Co., 1926); T. Alexander, *Prussian Elementary Schools* (New York: The Macmillan Co., 1918), pp. 305–48, 406–74.

man spirit from their domination by foreign culture, particularly the French, which had a marked influence upon German thought and expression in the eighteenth century. Neo-humanism offered not only an escape from such domination but the promise of cultural leadership for Germany.

NEO-HUMANISM AND PRUSSIAN SECONDARY EDUCATION. Neo-humanism was a cultural movement embodying a desire to restore the Greek view of life, and to attain freedom for the individual and respect for humanity. "Education for humanity" was declared by the neo-humanists to be the proper goal of education, a goal attainable through the study of literature, philosophy, history, art, and religion, if the student be permitted freedom in exploring and interpreting these fields. Individuals, thus freed from the shackles of tradition and authority, would hasten the progress of the nation and all humanity. The Greeks made their gods like men. The neo-humanists, feeling the divinity of man, dreamt of making men like God. To this end a liberal education was sought and found in the literature and art of classical antiquity, particularly the Greek, marked, as they were thought to be, by a striving for the ideal. Here, not in the traditional, barren Ciceronian Latin schools of post-Renaissance Europe, was to be found the true spirit of humanism. Through such an education Germany and the world would be provided with leaders of good taste, sound judgment and understanding who, like the Greeks, would strive to create the better world, and make Germany the cultural leader among the nations. The neo-humanistic ideal inspired the literary works of Herder, Goethe, and Schiller, names foremost in the rise to eminence of German national culture. That ideal brought also a revitalizing of classical education in secondary schools and universities, and the rise of the classical *Gymnasium* to eminence in the secondary field. The liberalism and, at times, cosmopolitanism embodied in such movements as neo-humanism and the introduction of Pestalozzian idealism into Prussian education soon gave way, because of military reverses and royal conservatism, to the spirit of narrow nationalism and militarism which came to dominate the whole school system after the revolution of 1848.

SECONDARY EDUCATION IN NINETEENTH CENTURY AND EARLY TWENTIETH. In Prussia, secondary education was supervised by the state authorities. The aim of secondary education was declared by Wilhelm von Humboldt, an ardent neo-humanist, head of the Bureau of Education (1808-1810), to be the promotion of general culture, and that purpose remained dominant until the twentieth century. In 1834, university entrance examinations were abolished, and the leaving examination of the *Gymnasium,* a state examination, was made the only gateway to universities and to all civil service positions. Schools of the *Realschule* type were thus officially dishonored. In the period of reaction against political liberalism, beginning in 1819, secondary education and all secondary school teachers and students were subjected to tyrannous state regulation and supervision. The true spirit of neo-humanism was thus destroyed by political bureaucrats. The regulations of 1834, conferring great privileges upon the *Gymnasium* and its students, among them the coveted favor of one year of voluntary military service for students who had completed six years of the course, were, among other things, a protest of officialdom against the growing social unrest of the middle class and the demands of that class for less authoritarianism in society and more realism in education. Cities were permitted, however, to organize *Realschulen,* while the central authorities withheld aid from such schools.

In 1859, the *Realschulen* were, at last, officially recognized and placed under the supervision of the Provincial School Boards. Two types of real schools were now approved: (a) the *Realgymnasium,* with a nine-year modern academic course in which Latin, but not Greek, had a place, and (b) the *Realschule,* with a shorter modern academic course, and without Latin. Students of *Realgymnasien* were given the same military privilege enjoyed by students of the *Gymnasien,* but the universities remained closed to them until 1870, when they were permitted to enter certain specified university courses. In 1878, the military privilege was bestowed upon graduates of the Latinless six-year *Realschule* and its enlargement, the nine-year *Oberrealschule.* The view had now become current that general culture (*Allgemeine Bildung*), at which von Humboldt aimed, could be attained through a study of science and mathematics, and that the classics were not essential to its attainment. Those who wished to keep the entrance to social and professional privileges restricted warred against that view, and the issue was heatedly debated.

In 1890, Kaiser William II convened an educational conference to discuss the question at issue between the advocates of the classical and of the modern emphasis in secondary education, and he delivered the opening address in which he opposed the traditionalism of the *Gymnasium.* Said he: "The national basis is lacking. We must take German as the foundation for the *Gymnasium;* we ought to educate national young Germans and not young Greeks and Romans. . . . The German exercise must be the central point about which all turns.[12] Youth, he said, must be prepared for practical pursuits and national defense. "I am looking," said he, "for soldiers; we wish to have a robust generation, who can serve the Fatherland also as intellectual leaders and as officials."[13] As a result of the deliberations and imperial pressure, German was given more time in the program of the *Gymnasium*, and the *Oberrealschule* rose in official esteem. Official regulations of 1892 recognized three six-year schools, each enjoying the one-year military privilege, the *Realschule, Progymnasium*, and the *Realprogymnasium*. In 1900, all recognized secondary studies were officially proclaimed to be of the same value from the viewpoint of "general culture." The universities, however, long continued to draw nearly all their students from *gymnasien*, which outnumbered the other nine-year schools.

THE SECONDARY SCHOOL TEACHER. The secondary school teacher received his education in universities. Indeed, the secondary schools and universities formed a single system, the former being preparatory to the latter. The *Volksschule* system was a thing apart both socially and educationally. As early as 1810 a state examination for all secondary school teachers was established, and secondary school teaching thus became a profession, from which all lacking the required preparation were excluded, whether local school authorities desired them or not. Special pedagogical seminars were created in the universities to provide professional instruction for gymnasial teachers. Herbart conducted one of these seminars at the University of Königsberg. By a regulation adopted by the Ministry in 1831, the examination standards for future teachers were raised. Henceforth, the candidates were examined in pedagogy, philosophy, theology and in all subjects taught in the *Gymnasium*. They had to demonstrate the highest proficiency especially in the subjects they proposed to teach. Prussia was thus far ahead of the world in the training and selection of secondary school teachers. Socially they came from the upper classes and carried into their classrooms a spirit of political, social and educational conservatism.

VOCATIONAL EDUCATION. The Prussian state and, then, the German empire came to realize clearly, in the second half of the nineteenth century, the importance of industry and commerce for national power. We have referred earlier to the rise of the prevocational *Mittelschule*. Somewhat earlier, part-time continuation vocational schools, each teaching a special trade or vocation, and designed chiefly for folk-school graduates, were established for in-

[12] Kandel, *op. cit.*, p. 257.
[13] *Ibid.*, p. 258.

dustrial and commercial workers. After 1820, trade and technical schools were established in the cities to serve the rapidly developing industrial and commercial state. The industrial and commercial leadership of Germany prior to World War I was due, in no small measure, to the elaborate provision made by the state for the training of a technical personnel. Higher technical schools were established to provide instruction in science as related to industry and to promote research of a practical nature.

UNIVERSITIES. The defeat of the Prussians by Napoleon was followed by the humiliating Treaty of Tilsit (1807) by which Prussia lost much of her territory and some of her leading universities, such as Halle and Göttingen. To offset this educational loss, the University of Berlin was founded in 1810, and others soon thereafter. In Berlin each professor became a specialist in a field of knowledge, and the University became a great center of research in philology, Egyptology, anatomy, zoology, chemistry, physics, history, psychology, etc. It was here that Fechner and Wundt carried on their research in psychology, and that Hegel turned philosophy to the service of the Prussian state. Berlin set the fashion for German universities in research and graduate study. The ideal of academic freedom (*Lehrfreiheit* and *Lernfreiheit*) became a mark of German universities, following the lead of Halle, founded in 1694. After 1817, Prussian universities were placed under the control of the Minister of Education who appointed all professors. Academic freedom was a privilege of the institutions rather than of individual teachers, who were expected to be orthodox in their political, social and economic theories. A teacher of sub-professorial rank could not hope for promotion if his social views were not orthodox. No restrictions, however, were placed upon freedom of research. Freedom of instruction was promoted by the substitution of lectures for the study of authoritative texts. The expanded program of studies made it imperative that the student be allowed to choose his area of specialization and, in this, he enjoyed a freedom unknown in earlier universities of Europe.

In the second half of the nineteenth century, American students and students from many lands in increasing numbers studied in German universities. It was largely through the influence of returning students that American universities came to stress graduate studies, research and specialization. Johns Hopkins University (1876) was established as a research institution. The result of German influence has been the subordination of the teaching function to that of research in our universities.

PHYSICAL EDUCATION. National interests and needs have brought everywhere an emphasis upon health and physical education. Locke and Rousseau, among many others, as we have seen, stressed its importance. Basedow and the Philanthropinists, for naturalistic ends, gave it a prominent place in the school program. The story of its rise to prominence in national schools is a long one. Among the nineteenth-century leaders in the physical education movement were the Germans, Johann Christoph Guts Muths (1759-1839), Ludwig Jahn (1778-1852) and Adolph Spiess (1810-1858). Jahn, alarmed by the defeat of the Prussians by Napoleon aimed through a system of gymnastics and physical training to build a strong Prussia, while he also aimed at the individual well-being which would result from such activities. It was Spiess, however, who finally prevailed upon the educational authorities to make physical education a part of the regular school program. We should note here that the gymnastic movement was carried from Germany and Sweden into the United States, where, in the form of calisthenics, Dio Lewis (1823-1886) became its early leading propagandist.[14] National, industrial and military demands, rather than concern for the health and development of the individual, seem to have prompted the modern emphasis upon physical education in Germany and other nations. As we shall see later, it was given a place of first importance in Nazi Germany.

EDUCATION OF GIRLS. Fichte in his proposals for a reform of Prussian education, made while Napoleon's troops held Berlin, recommended coeducation and the same general instruction for girls and boys, but this recommendation went unheeded. Except in small, rural elementary schools coeducation did not exist and, even in girls' schools, the teachers were generally men. Even under the republican régime, created after World War I by the Weimar Constitution (1919), coeducation in secondary schools was permitted only where separate schools were not available. The traditional social ideal for women was that of "*Kinder, Küche, Kirche*" (children, kitchen, church). Girls' education looked forward to the crib, the kitchen and the family laundry as God's special gifts to women. Girls had their own elementary and, later, continuation, *Mittelschulen*, and secondary schools. Conservatives would end their opportunities with the *Mittelschule*, and give it a kitchen bias.

[14] E. A. Rice, J. L. Hutchinson, and M. Lee, *A Brief History of Physical Education* (4th ed.; New York: The Ronald Press Co., 1958); N. Schwendener, *A History of Physical Education in the United States* (New York: A. S. Barnes & Co., Inc., 1942).

The girls' secondary school was called *Lyzeum*, of which there were types corresponding with schools for boys. Some of the secondary schools for girls were private but, whether public or private, they were denied the recognition and privileges accorded to boys' secondary schools. Girls, however, had educational opportunities, and the brilliant ones were admitted to the universities, beginning in 1895, when they were accepted as auditors. After 1908, when the government authorized secondary schools for them, they were admitted as regular students. Under the Weimar republic, more liberal opportunities for secondary education were provided for them, but the universities remained reluctant to enlarge the meager privileges which they already accorded them. To girls' treatment under Nazism we shall refer later.

RETROSPECT. From the opening of the present century, the nationalistic outlook made a deep impress upon Prussian secondary education. The idea of general culture became rapidly subservient to that of national culture, and the development of national character replaced the neo-humanistic aim of "education for humanity." Religion, German history, German language and literature received increasing emphasis, and the schools became shrines of national devotion, where, on frequent appropriate occasions, students sang the patriotic songs of the Fatherland and worshiped its national heroes. World War I and its aftermath intensified these nationalistic tendencies and culminated in the extreme reforms inaugurated under the Nazi régime.

The Development and Character of the French School System

At the time of the Revolution, the poorer classes of France were largely illiterate. The state had made no provision for their education. Such facilities as existed were provided by religious societies of men and women. The church dominated practically all forms and levels of education, and taught for its own glory as for that of "His most Christian Majesty," whose interests it deemed identical with its own. Schools were thus the bulwarks of the existing social, political, and ecclesiastical order and, even in the universities, everything was subordinated to that end. Traditionalism and conservatism marked education on all levels and among all classes.

THE REVOLUTION AND EDUCATION. In the revolutionary National Assembly (May, 1789-September, 1791) Talleyrand introduced an education bill which would make education exclusively a state function in the interest of the nation and its culture. He would have established a state system of free primary schools, secondary schools open to the talented poor through scholarships, and professional schools of medicine, law, military science, and religion. His bill distinguished between studies "indispensable to the individual as a man and a citizen" and preprofessional and professional studies. The primary schools would provide the first exclusively. The secondary schools would enlarge and strengthen the foundation of French culture, laid in the primary schools, and also provide preprofessional training. French language and literature and French history were to be given a foremost place in secondary schools, and secondary teachers were to be made state officials. Six State Commissioners of Education were to administer the whole system. Talleyrand's bill, however, was not acted upon.

In the Legislative Assembly (October, 1791-September, 1792) Condorcet introduced another education bill, differing in details from that of Talleyrand but having a similar national goal in view. This bill, however, was marked by a democratic idealism which was not apparent in that of Talleyrand. Condorcet desired that the natural talents of every individual be developed to their fullest extent so that there might be established "among the citizens an equality in fact, making real the political equality recognized by law." His educational philosophy is strikingly similar to that of Jefferson in America.

To attain the ideals of the French democratic state, he would have established primary schools, secondary schools, institutes, and *lycées*, and place the system, not under political officials, but under the control of a self-perpetuating, non-political, scholarly National Society of Arts and Sciences, so that the freedom of human thought and teaching might be safeguarded, and science and true enlightenment be promoted. In his plan of school organization, the institutes would correspond with the traditional secondary schools of Europe, and the *lycées* with universities. The latter, however, would not be professional in their emphasis but schools of advanced study and research in the various sciences, cultures, and art. Condorcet would give the natural and social sciences pre-eminence over the classics, and would make the development of individuality and the discovery and perpetuation of new knowledge more important than the reproduction of old sterile social and academic formulae. This bill was not acted upon by the Assembly, but it is an important record of the thought of the time.

The democratic enthusiasm of the early revolutionary years was followed by years of political and social reaction which culminated, on the educational side, in the passage of the Daunou Law, October,

1795. Unlike earlier plans, this law provided for the establishment of primary schools in only large population centers and restricted their curriculum to the rudiments. With the exception of the poorest one-fourth, all primary pupils were to pay school fees. Local authorities were to supervise and administer these schools. The law provided for the establishment of a very limited number of secondary schools, called Central Schools, free to talented poor students, and modern in their academic emphasis. "Special Schools" were authorized for advanced study in the special scientific and other fields. In the primary field, the law had no effect, but there were established ninety-seven Central Schools upon which the state spent annually 2,500,000 francs. These, however, remained unpopular, and most parents continued to patronize church and private schools.

NAPOLEON I AND EDUCATION, 1799-1815. The régime of Napoleon was despotic and reactionary. While an advocate of national education for state ends, he did little to improve the existing facilities for popular education. His ideals and purposes may be discerned in his words and his acts. Said he: "Of all political questions, that [of . . . education] is perhaps the most important. There cannot be a firmly established political state unless there is a teaching body with definitely fixed principles. Except as the child is taught from infancy whether he ought to be a republican or a monarchist, a Catholic or a free-thinker, the state will not constitute a nation."[15] He sanctioned a political catechism designed to foster in his subjects a religious worship of the emperor and his empire. A brief citation will reveal its character and purpose:

Question. What are the duties of Christians towards those who govern them, and what in particular are our duties towards Napoleon I, our emperor?

Answer. Christians owe to the princes who govern them, and we in particular owe to Napoleon I, our emperor, love, respect, obedience, fidelity, military service, and the taxes levied for the preservation and defense of the empire and of his throne. We also owe him fervent prayers for his safety and for the spiritual and temporal prosperity of the state. . . .

Question. What must we think of those who are wanting in their duties towards our emperor?

Answer. According to the Apostle Paul, they are resisting the order established by God Himself, and render themselves worthy of eternal damnation.[16]

[15] W. H. Kilpatrick, *Source Book in the Philosophy of Education* (New York: The Macmillan Co., 1934), pp. 17–18. (By permission.)

[16] C. J. Hayes, *A Political and Social History of Modern Europe* (New York: The Macmillan Co., 1921), I, 535. (By permission.)

The first end of education he thus viewed as that of political indoctrination of his subjects. He brought the secondary schools under rigid state control, even to the point of requiring students to wear a common costume. In 1808, he completed the work of organizing the Imperial University, which was in effect a national ministry of education having control of education in the empire from the universities down to the primary schools. He decreed that, in all schools, loyalty to the Catholic religion and the emperor be inculcated in students as a basis of instruction. The members of the university council were chosen directly or indirectly by the emperor. For educational administrative purposes he divided (1812) France and its possessions into subdivisions, called academies, each with its rector and educational council. National school inspectors were appointed by the grand master of the university to report on regional conditions to the central authority, and local inspectors were chosen to supervise schools in local districts. In 1808, he set up in Paris a national normal school for the training of secondary school teachers, in which the students were supported by the government.

THE EFFECTS OF NAPOLEON'S REFORMS. The highly centralized administrative system which Napoleon established has, with minor changes, survived in France to the present day. State (*lycées*) and municipal secondary schools (*collèges*) were put by him on a solid footing, although they remained unpopular with many parents who continued to patronize private and church secondary schools. As a result of imperial neglect and of social conservatism and vested church interests, but little improvement was made under Napoleon in the provision for primary education.

THE PRIMARY SCHOOL LAW OF 1833. Following the defeat of Napoleon (1815) came the restoration of the monarchy (1815-1848) and with it a policy of social and educational conservatism favorable to the church and its schools. Fearful of social unrest and determined to extend its control over the mind of the masses, and possibly also for motives of benevolence, the July Monarchy (1830-1848) organized a national system of elementary education by the law of 1833. This law required every commune (smallest political subdivision of France) to support a lower primary school; every department (larger political subdivision), a primary normal school; and cities of over 6,000 population, a higher primary school. In the lower primaries the law required instruction in reading, writing, French language, arithmetic, the French system of weights and measures, and morals and religion. In the higher primaries, there was required, in addition, instruction in practical geometry, the elements of science, history and geography, especially of France, singing, and, where feasible, a modern language. Fees were required in public schools from all students deemed by local education authorities to be able to pay, these fees supplementing school funds raised by local taxation. The appointment of teachers, under the law, rested ultimately with the minister of education, and they were required to take an oath of allegiance to the king and the laws of the nation. Minimum salaries, to be supplemented by fees, were fixed for appointees, who were also provided with dwellings, rent free.

The years of the Second Republic (1848-1852) and the Second Empire (1852-1870) were years of official repression of elementary teachers, socially and politically suspect, as they were, by conservative groups. The earlier extensive curriculum of the normal schools was limited almost to the rudimentary subjects taught in rural primary schools, and normal students were forbidden to explore the books in their school libraries. The central authority acted upon the principle that the less a primary teacher knows the less dangerous he will be. The law of 1850 restored much of the former power of the church in education. Its teachers had no longer to submit to state examination of their qualifications, and ecclesiastics and private parties might, in future, establish secondary schools without difficulty. The law, however, strengthened the educational authority of the state by giving to the Minister of Public Instruction undivided and supreme control over all schools of all grades, and by improving the machinery of administration everywhere throughout the system. When Napoleon III came to power, in 1852, he inaugurated a régime of tyranny over education. He went so far as to decree that university teachers shave off their moustaches which he viewed as evidences of rebellion, and he prohibited the reading of "dangerous books" in the Higher Normal School.

FRENCH NATIONAL EDUCATION, 1870-1918. Under the Third Republic, established in 1870 after Napoleon's defeat by the Germans, the French national system gradually assumed the basic form which has marked it until the present day. While universal male suffrage was adopted, political power, following the Napoleonic pattern, remained extremely centralized. The church opposed the liberalism of the new régime, and suffered a decisive defeat at the hands of the anti-clerical Gambetta party in the 1877 election. The anti-clericalism of the period culminated in the laws of 1901 and 1904, which were provoked by circumstances connected with the alleged treason of Alfred Dreyfus, and which seemed to show that the church was plotting against the republic. These laws placed drastic restrictions upon religious teaching societies or "orders," that of 1904 requiring their complete suppression by 1914. The struggle against clerical control of education and for public, free, lay schools was a bitter one and it has not yet entirely ceased.

Among the educational developments under the Third Republic, the following have been the most significant: (1) In 1881, primary education was made free, and, in 1882, compulsory for all children between the ages of six and thirteen. (2) In 1882, the teaching of religion in public schools was abolished, and moral and civic instruction was substituted for it, thus secularizing state education. (3) In 1886, the unification of French education into one single national system was effected, and the highly centralized state machinery of administration and supervision was given the perfected and finished form which has marked it to the present day.

Under this plan, the Minister of Public Instruction possessed very great power over education, although the schools and teachers were protected against the arbitrary exercise of that power by the central Superior Council and the Academy and Departmental councils, upon which specified duties and privileges were conferred by law. There are seventeen academies and ninety departments in France. Local boards of education, in the American sense, while they existed in the several communes, had practically no authority over schools and teachers in their area. (4) The law of 1886 called for the establishment, or further development, of post-primary courses and higher primary and other schools with a prevocational or vocational bias, local authorities being allowed much freedom in determining the curricula of the higher primaries to meet the commercial and industrial needs of their areas. (5) The spirit of nationalism and of the French concept of democracy have marked the work of the public schools of republican France, and these schools have been deemed as essential to the defense of the nation as its great military machine. (6) Private schools (mostly Catholic schools) have been permitted and left free from state requirements in methods and curriculum.

The state, until now (1958), has not prescribed qualifications for teachers in private elementary or higher schools, but private secondary school teachers must hold the usual state certificates. The diplomas and certificates granted by private schools are not recognized by the state, but private school students may get state certificates by passing the state examinations which all public school students must pass in order to be certificated. It is through state examinations that private schools have been, and are, linked to the national system.

THE FRENCH STATE AND THE INTERNAL ASPECTS OF EDUCATION. While, politically, France had been thoroughly democratic under the Third Republic, guaranteeing to its citizens freedom of thought, speech, and worship, and safeguarding individualism, its government and its control of education were the most highly centralized in the world prior to the schemes established in the totalitarian states of Russia, Italy, and Nazi Germany. Politically, such a practice had back of it the force of three centuries of tradition, and republican France accepted it because it was efficient and was believed to provide security for the nation mainly against its old enemy, Germany, and for the republic against the monarchists and the church. On the educational side of the picture, the central authorities controlled not only the *externa* (school buildings, finance, etc.) but the *interna* (curriculum and methods) of education as well. The French state, through its central educational authority, has acted as custodian of French culture, that spiritual inheritance which, emanating from the ancient fountain of Roman life and thought, and strengthened by centuries of growth, is fostered as the bond of unity and the lifeblood of the nation. Therefore the state determines, as a primary duty, what constitutes this culture, and assumes the obligation of transmitting it, though in different amounts to different groups, to the children of France.

The regionalist movement (*régionalisme*), originating in 1892 and growing in influence, especially since 1918, has advocated political decentralization and the stimulation of local cultures through the use of dialects, such as the Basque and Flemish, in the schools of regions where they are spoken.[17] Yet, French officialdom has clung rather stubbornly to the view that one cannot be truly French unless he speaks and reads the approved language of the nation. It may be noted here that the British government, in almost identical circumstances, has not opposed, in recent times, the preservation and revival of local cultures such as the Welsh and Irish. In America, where the problem has been different in some important respects, state authorities have frowned upon the use of foreign languages as a medium of instruction and have, as in the case of the Pennsylvania Germans, used the schools to wean away non-English-speaking groups from their old cultural moorings. France has adopted the policy of keeping national culture under its direct control by acting as the patron of art, science, and literature, and by fixing the content and methods in all cultural subjects of instruction such as French language, history, geography, morals, and

[17] I. Kandel, *Comparative Education* (Boston: Houghton Mifflin Co., 1933), pp. 279–80.

civics. Teacher training, school inspection, and a state system of examinations are the chief devices by which the government attains its ends in as far as the school can contribute to them. There has been much criticism by teachers and local communities of central control of education, and some concessions have been made by the Ministry to local demands, but the curriculum, methods, textbooks, examinations and teacher training still remain under central control.

CASTE AS A BASIS OF EDUCATIONAL DIFFERENTIATION. In France, democracy has existed side by side with a caste system which, of long duration, has persisted in the midst of political change. From the bottom upward, republican France has had its rather nicely marked classes of laborers, lower, middle and upper bourgeoisie, and nobility. The free elementary schools have been those attended by laborers and lower bourgeoisie, who comprise the great mass of the French people. The classes above these, desiring various degrees of social exclusiveness, sent their children to tuition schools. By a system of scholarships, the government made it possible for the talented poor to continue their studies in the higher primary schools, which trained an intermediate personnel for commerce and industry, and in the secondary schools, which were the gateway to the universities and other higher schools, and to the professions and all leading positions in the nation. World War I, as we shall note later, intensified the demand for a system free from class distinction, and for a unified system (*école unique*), in which differentiation would be based not upon wealth or social rank but upon the native ability of pupils.

SECONDARY EDUCATION PRIOR TO RECENT REFORMS. The present plan of secondary education began with the establishment of the *lycées*, or state secondary schools, in 1802, and the official recognition of the *collèges*, or municipal secondary schools, in 1808. In the latter year a higher normal school was created to train teachers for secondary schools. Since 1814, seven years have been required to complete the secondary school course. The studies prescribed at the start were Latin, Greek, French, history, geography, mythology, mathematics, optics, astronomy, natural history, physics, chemistry, logic, ethics, metaphysics, and philosophy. Controversy between the advocates of the classics and of the sciences and modern studies led, in 1852, to the adoption of a plan of a three-year common course for all students, upon which, for the remaining four years, were superimposed two courses, the literary and the scientific. The former led to the degree of Bachelor of Letters, and to university schools of arts and law; the latter, to the degree of Bachelor of Science, and to university schools of science and medicine and to special higher schools. In France, the bachelor's degree is granted on the successful completion of the secondary school course, but it is not the equivalent of the bachelor's degree of British and American universities. The plan of 1852 was abandoned in 1863, and the single-course system was re-established.

Until 1902, in spite of frequently voiced dissatisfaction with the schools, those in power upheld the classical, literary, and disciplinary tradition in education, and ignored utilitarian demands and needs. The modern course was, however, restored in 1890. The development of intellectual power was viewed as the goal of secondary education, and the classics as the surest means of attaining it. It was also urged with force and eloquence that, since French culture is rooted in that of classical antiquity, France must cling to the classics or suffer a spiritual decline. The first significant reform came, in 1902, when a single *baccalauréat,* open to students in both the modern and classical courses, was set up for secondary schools. At that time, the course was divided into two cycles of four and three years. In the first cycle, students could choose between (a) the classical and (b) the French-scientific course, either one leading to a certificate of secondary studies. During the first two years of the second cycle, the students had a choice of four courses: (a) Latin and Greek, (b) Latin-modern language, (c) Latin-scientific, and (d) modern language-scientific. In the seventh year, during which work for the *baccalauréat* was completed, students specialized in (a) philosophy or (b) mathematics. France thus recognized the place of science in modern culture but emphasized the liberal, not the applied, aspects of that study. We shall presently refer to the recent emergence of the technical secondary school.

SECONDARY EDUCATION AS A CLASS PRIVILEGE. Until 1930, tuition fees were charged in all secondary schools of France. For the talented poor a limited number of scholarships existed since the reforms of Napoleon I, but in practice few poorer people could afford to accept them because of their financial inability to meet the cost of subsequent professional training and incidental expenses of secondary schooling itself. Until 1902, there was very poor co-ordination between the work of the primary and secondary schools. They were separate systems, in which studies were so organized that it was practically impossible for one who had spent even a brief time in a primary school to transfer to a secondary one. The law of 1902 provided that the work of the first secondary school class follow directly that of the fourth primary school class. This shows an official desire to make the transition to the secondary school easier.

In practice the law had little effect, and the plan of organization remained undemocratic. It was partly to abolish the dual system of schools and caste in education that a reorganized system, resting upon a common-school foundation and called the *école unique*, was strongly advocated during World War I and realized, to a marked degree, since 1925. Secondary education, traditionally the education of a social elite, has become, in the present century, what it long aspired to be, the education of an intellectual elite for leadership in the nation.

VOCATIONAL AND TECHNICAL EDUCATION. During the régime of Napoleon III, complementary courses, supplementing the work of primary schools, became partly vocational. In 1880, manual apprenticeship schools were established by law, and recognized, in 1886, as a part of the primary system. The law of the latter year revived higher primary schools around which vocational education has been organized since 1892. In 1881 and 1882 there were established by law three "national vocational schools." Local educational authorities have been left free to choose for their higher primary schools the course best adapted to their commercial and industrial needs. In 1897, highly vocationalized higher primary schools were legally named "practical schools of commerce or industry," and placed under the control of the Minister of Commerce and Industry. With few exceptions the higher primary schools have not been narrowly vocational and, even on the practical side, have been prevocational rather than vocational. Much of the technical training they have left to be acquired on the job. In addition to such provisions as these, the state and local authorities, as well as private agencies, have established a wide variety of vocational schools of all grades and purposes. Among these are higher and lower special schools of a great variety of arts and crafts, and schools of agriculture, mining, navigation, and of the fine arts as related to industry. Official concern for the enlargement of such provisions was increased during World War I, but the only practical immediate result was the requirement by law, in 1919, that young workers in certain industries attend part-time vocational day schools up to the age of eighteen. Traditionally the vocational schools have been designed for primary school graduates, but only about one-tenth of these have availed themselves of such opportunities.

Until 1920, specialized vocational education was under other ministries than that of Public Instruction, such as the Ministry of Commerce, of Agriculture, or of Public Works. In that year all vocational and technical education was placed under the control of the Minister of Public Instruction. It has thus become an integral part of the state system.

Under the direction of the General Division for Technical Education in the Ministry much progress has been made in the development of vocational and technical education. Some of the schools which have been promoted by the Division are narrowly specialized. The whole movement has resulted in a conflict between the advocates of secondary schools providing "general culture" and the advocates of a utilitarian type of secondary education. Since World War II, technical education has been placed under the same local supervisors who direct the traditional secondary schools, with the result that technical education has been brought into the secondary-education field. A technical secondary school (*collège technique*), leading to a technical *baccalauréat* has emerged, and technical courses have been added to the program of the higher elementary schools, now called modern colleges (*collèges modernes*). Later we shall examine the Langevin proposals which attached great importance to what some Frenchmen have been calling the "technical humanities."

CHURCH SCHOOLS. There are but a few Protestant and Jewish schools in France, but there are many Catholic schools. Approximately 20 per cent of elementary- and 40 per cent of secondary-school students attend Catholic schools. Most of the teachers in these schools have received the same training as public school teachers, but the schools they conduct are even more disciplinary and conservative than the public schools which are themselves symbols of formalism and traditionalism. Until 1951 no public aid was provided for church schools. The Catholic hierarchy, fearing a state monopoly of education, has opposed the establishment of the *école unique*. Republican France has been anti-clerical but not anti-religious, and the public schools are closed on Thursdays so that parents and the churches may provide religious instruction for youth. In regard to religion the French state pursues a policy of neutrality.

EDUCATION OF GIRLS. In spite of the lay, political movement in French education, the Catholic, particularly Jesuit, tradition has remained strong. Below the universities, coeducation has been rare. Separate schools for boys and girls have been the rule wherever local conditions permit. In 1880, public secondary schools for girls were officially provided but, being only five- or, occasionally, six-year schools, they did not lead to the *baccalauréat*, and special provision had to be made in boys' schools for graduates permitted to seek the degree. In 1924, a seven-year degree course was authorized for girls' *lycées* and *collèges*, which had grown up in all cities and large towns. Prior to 1930 girls were admitted to boys' secondary schools only when no girls' school was within reach and, even then, they might not number more than one-fourth of the students nor exceed fifty in any such school. Except for the inclusion in girls' schools of domestic science, needlework, music, and translations of foreign literature, the secondary curriculum for both sexes has remained the same. Girls, however, have constituted only about one-third of the public secondary-school enrollment, chiefly because of the limited number of schools provided for them. The enlargement of opportunities for women in the last two decades has led to increased enrollment of women in the universities where, in 1949, they numbered almost one-half of the total student body, nearly one-third of those enrolled in the departments of law and medicine being women.[18] It has taken France a long time to recognize the national importance of women as, indeed, it has taken other nations also.

TEACHER TRAINING. The teachers in elementary, secondary and technical schools have, historically, been trained in separate institutions. Elementary teachers were trained, from 1879, in normal schools, one for each sex, in the many departments, or subdivisions of France, while secondary teachers were trained in universities and higher normal schools. For vocational teachers special training schools were established by the ministerial Division of Technical Education. The departmental normal schools were predominantly boarding schools, entered by competitive examination, whose graduates were required to teach for ten years following their graduation, or reimburse the government for their free education and maintenance. As teachers, these graduates received salaries and a social prestige far below that of secondary teachers. In their training, they were subjected to a rigorous mental and personal discipline reminiscent of mediaeval monastic life, and they were systematically shut off from the outside world. Their studies consisted of the usual elementary subjects, morals, educational theory, methods, observation of teaching and practice teaching.

After the fall of France to the Germans (1940), the Vichy government abolished the normal schools and prepared the way for the building, under the new government of liberated France, of a professionally and academically improved program of training for

[18] Unesco, *World Handbook of Educational Organization and Statistics,* 1951, p. 174.

elementary school teachers. The elementary teacher, sprung from the masses, and barred from secondary and university education, was a product of the elementary-school system, and was often found in the ranks of social radicals, among them the Communists of recent times. Throughout his whole period of education and training he was guided by teachers of his own social class. There are many thousand districts (*communes*) which have no secondary schools, and in them the elementary teacher was often the only person who had more than a primary school education. The cultural level thus remained low in such districts, to the detriment of the nation.

Since World War II, and in keeping with pre-existing demands, the secondary school has been made the path to the normal school, where students who have not already secured the *baccalauréat* pursue a course of professional and general education leading to it. The obnoxious distinction which had long existed between elementary and secondary school teachers, and which reflected the social prejudices of France, has thus begun to disappear.

Since 1879 there have been two national higher normal schools (Saint Cloud for men, and Fontenay-aux-Roses for women) which trained primary school inspectors and principals and teachers of normal schools but which, in recent years, have, in addition, served as training schools for secondary teachers. These have recently been raised to the status of *Grandes Écoles Normales* to be mentioned presently.

Secondary school teachers in France have been, perhaps, the most carefully selected professional group in the world. The highest standards are set for those who will teach in the *lycées*. Secondary school teachers have been, and are, usually trained in universities, and the emphasis is placed upon their scholarship in the subjects they will teach rather than upon pedagogical training. Having secured the special degree for teachers (*licence d'enseignement*), after three years of study, they, if desiring appointment in *lycées*, take a competitive examination, called the *agrégation*. Only about one candidate in ten has been able to earn the coveted title of *agrégé* at the end of his or her university course. The surest road to the title is through four *Grandes Écoles Normales*, two for men and two for women, all entered by competitive examination for which a few large *lycées* provide special post-*baccalauréat* preparation. For teaching in the *collèges*, the standards are not quite so high as they are for the *lycées*. In recent years, special higher normal schools have been established to train teachers of technical subjects and of physical education. What we have presented here is but the merest outline of what France has done to train the teachers of the nation since the rise of the Third Republic in 1870. Here, as in other nations, only the trained and chosen may teach in the public schools.

THE NATIONAL SPIRIT IN EDUCATION. Observers have described the French as the most patriotic of peoples.[19] A few brief extracts from a public school address of the educator Ernest Lavisse, in 1905, will reveal the spirit of French schools. Said he:

> The fatherland is a territory inhabited by men who obey the same laws. . . . There grew up a habit of feeling the same emotions simultaneously. France possessed a national consciousness. . . . The French nation created the French language. If today we speak a language which is one of the most beautiful in the world, it is because our fathers took a great deal of pains to make it beautiful, and their effort lasted for centuries. In our language, our fathers expressed their feelings and their ideals. . . . My children, our fatherland is then not merely a territory; it is a human structure, begun centuries ago, which we are continuing, which you will continue. . . . It is our country, the daughter of our spirit. . . . Suppose, then, you say to me: "It is an accident that brought me into the world in France. . . . First of all, I am born a man. I wish to belong only to humanity. It is humanity that I wish to serve." I will answer: "Humanity, that does not exist as yet; it is a great and beautiful idea; it is not a fact. You must have a fixed place in which to act, and I defy you to serve humanity otherwise than through the medium of a fatherland. . . . What accusation of inhumanity rises against France? . . . Have we an Ireland, a Schleswig, a Finland, a Poland? . . . Friends, feel free to take advantage of the right to love, the right to prefer France, . . . for to serve her is the most efficient means of serving humanity."[20]

Development of National Education in England

Elsewhere we have discussed the influence of the Reformation and of philanthropy upon the education of the poor in pre-nineteenth-century England. When the century opened, England was a democracy only in embryo. Society was marked by a class fixity which made it very difficult for the individual to change his social position. The masses were disfranchised. While wealth accumulated, poverty increased. There were two kinds of schools, both provided by the voluntary effort of churches and private philanthropists: (a) elementary schools for the poor, many of them deplorably bad, and (b) secondary schools, called grammar schools, for the rich, in varying degrees exclusive and aristocratic, of which

[19] C. J. Hayes, *France a Nation of Patriots* (New York: Columbia University Press, 1930).

[20] F. Buisson and F. E. Farrington, *French Educational Ideals of Today* (Yonkers, N.Y.: World Book Co., 1919), pp. 91 *passim*.

the "Great Public Schools"[21] catered to the demands of the "upper ten," not "the four hundred" as American democracy would have it. The "Great Public Schools" were feeders for the Anglican universities of Oxford and Cambridge, and they were class, not national, schools. Latin and Greek made up their curriculum almost entirely. English language, literature and history were ignored by them. Yet, from their graduates came the builders and administrators of the empire, men noted for self-control, class loyalty, and pride in the achievements of the nation. Of the poor, it is probable that the great majority attended, for at least a brief period, some elementary school. There was also the apprenticeship system, through which poor boys and girls were trained practically for their humble manual pursuits.

Against the abuses to which poor children of tender years were subjected in factories and mines, child labor laws were passed, beginning in 1802. Philanthropic educational reform movements arose partly to correct the same evils. Bills calling for state action in education were introduced in Parliament. It was an age marked by demand for social, political, and educational reform. The political Reform Act of 1832 was the first of a series of breaks in the stronghold of political and social privilege. Other acts, in 1867, 1884, and 1918, the last of which inaugurated the enfranchisement of women, continued the building of national democracy. Each of these acts was followed by another which extended the control of the state over education.

Since the opening of the nineteenth century, Englishmen, while opposed to state interference in their lives and activities, have submitted to increasing intrusion of the government into realms traditionally private, and, to remedy social evils, have frequently invited such intrusion. They have, in the present century, become reconciled to many forms of governmental interference as necessary evils. For a long time, state activity in education remained a subject of bitter controversy, both political and ecclesiastical. There were those who opposed it as a most dangerous interference with parental rights and duties, and as a step toward political domination of the human mind. There were those, too, who opposed it as a violation

[21] It should be noted that the schools which, in England, are called "Public Schools" are private. There are less than 300 such schools, of which about 130 are girls' schools. To be so classified, a school must be either completely independent financially or receive no aid from local authorities. The school and its principal must also enjoy freedom from any outside interference. Nine of the boys' schools, founded between 1387 (Winchester) and 1561 (Merchant Taylor's) are known as "Great Public Schools." Their names (*e.g.* Eton, Rugby, Harrow) are hallowed in England and their fame extends throughout the English-speaking world and beyond.

of a privilege bestowed by God upon parents and the church. The powerful Anglican church opposed it on religious grounds, and claimed the right to be recognized as the national educator of England. Nonconformists, fearing that state education would be dominated by the Anglican church, opposed it, not on grounds of principle but of expediency. These, in whose group were many influential middle-class capitalists, withdrew their opposition after the government had become representative following the Reform Act of 1867. Until 1870, when the first public school law was passed, the subject remained a storm-center of prejudices and of bitter debate. Thus political, class, and ecclesiastical prejudices, coupled with vested interests in education, long established by the churches and private agencies, thwarted the designs of those who saw the need for state support of education.

The period 1833-1870 was one when the foundation of the national system was gradually laid. In 1833, the government appropriated £20,000 as an annual grant to the Anglican National Society and the Nonconformist British and Foreign School Society. In 1839, the grant was increased to £30,000, and gradually many other sectarian and nonsectarian educational societies were permitted to share in the distribution, supervised, after 1839, by a Committee of the Privy Council. The annual grant rose gradually to about £800,000 in 1860. In 1861, the vicious practice of "payment by results" was introduced, which made the amount granted to any school depend upon the quality of the teaching as determined by annual examinations given by state inspectors. Teachers, thereafter, worked with eyes only upon formal examination questions and grants. Until 1870, England thus entrusted the education of the masses to voluntary, private agencies to which she gave limited support, and over which she exercised a modicum of supervision. Reports of state commissions revealed the inadequacy of these provisions, but reform had to wait until the need for it had been dinned into public consciousness.

ELEMENTARY EDUCATION ACT OF 1870. The Act of 1870 required the election of school boards for the purpose of providing by local taxation elementary school accommodation in districts where existing provisions were inadequate. Government grants to "voluntary" schools were continued, but these were refused any share in funds raised by local taxation. The Act continued the requirement that, in voluntary schools, no child be compelled to submit to religious instruction against his will. And, for board schools, it was provided that "no religious catechism or religious formulary which is distinctive of any particular denomination is to be taught."

Yet, "Bible reading without note or comment" was permitted in board schools. This Act left England with two systems of elementary schools: one, chiefly denominational, called the "voluntary" system; the other public and, in religious matters, "undenominational." And it took elementary education out of the realm of charity and made it a public service.

ELEMENTARY EDUCATION COMPULSORY AND FREE. In 1876, elementary education was made compulsory up to the age of ten, and, in 1891, it was made free in state-aided elementary schools, grants to such schools being thereafter so increased as to compensate them for the loss of students' fees. In 1899, school attendance was required to the age of twelve.

THE EDUCATION ACT OF 1902. This Act was passed to satisfy the persistent demands of the "voluntary" schools for a share in school money raised by local taxes, and to permit school boards to establish higher elementary and secondary schools. While the Act continued the dual system of elementary schools, it brought both of them under one authority, the elected councils of the political administrative divisions of England. It was these councils, known as L.E.A.'s (local education authority), and not the central Board of Education, created in 1899 and presided over by a President, that controlled education. The British state, unlike that of France and Germany, considered, until the passage of the Act of 1944,[22] its function to be merely that of insuring, through stimulation of local effort, that each child be provided with a minimum of instruction. Since 1902, the board schools and the "voluntary schools," have been provided for out of public funds. After thirty years of struggle for a share of local school funds raised by taxation, the churches won, but they were forced to permit L.E.A. representation on the board of six managers of each of their schools. They thus got support, but they lost much of their independence, for the agency that supports the school will, in some degree, control it.

Thus out of the charity schools of post-Reformation England there emerged the English national elementary school system, composed of denominational and board schools. In addition to these schools which form the "system" there have been thousands of purely private, proprietary schools, with which the state did not concern itself until very recently.

Before 1918, when two additional years of compulsory education were made mandatory for the nation, compulsory attendance ended at the age of twelve, although the L.E.A.'s had power to

[22] *Infra,* p. 688 *passim.* The term "board school" means an L.E.A. school.

raise the leaving age to fourteen. While the Anglican church has been retained as a national establishment, the state guarded itself fairly successfully against involvement in sectarian strife by insisting that church schools respect the rights of conscience of the pupils who attend them, and that the religious instruction authorized for board schools be undenominational in character. Yet, some Anglican and Roman Catholic divines have accused the government of subsidizing a new religion which it calls "undenominationalism." The British state, however, has not approved, as did France under the Third Republic, the secularization of education.[23]

THE ELEMENTARY CURRICULUM. The Newcastle Commission, which studied the condition of schools in the years 1858-1861, found that some of the schools whose curriculum they studied taught only religion and reading; that less than four-fifths of them taught, in addition, writing and arithmetic; and that a small fraction of better schools added such studies as geography, history, grammar, drawing, and elementary science. The Commission felt that the whole duty of the elementary school consisted in teaching youths to spell and read simple words, write legibly, to locate foreign countries on the map and to know enough about the Bible to follow "a plain Saxon sermon." After 1870, religion ceased to be the core of the curriculum and became an appendage thereto. The law of that year permitted school boards to expand the elementary school and its studies. Wealthier districts added grades above the sixth, and some of them organized "higher grade elementary schools," in which such subjects as French, mathematics, science, grammar, and history were taught. Regulations adopted in 1861 made government grants to schools depend upon results in reading, writing, and arithmetic in grades one to six. Cramming for examinations in these subjects followed, and adding grades was officially discouraged until 1882, when a seventh and an ex-seventh grade were approved.

Generally, in the nineteenth century, elementary education was limited to the 3 R's, and its aim was to master them. In the present century emphasis has been shifted from a mastery of subject matter to character formation.[24] The government has not prescribed the curriculum, as did the Prussian and French governments. It has merely indicated purposes and made "suggestions." It is the principal of each school, aided by his staff, who has determined the curriculum, but the inspector, who represents the government, has

[23] See provision of the Act of 1944 for religious instruction, *infra,* p. 688.

[24] M. Sadler, *Our Public Elementary Schools* (London: Butterworth & Co., Ltd., 1926), pp. 15–16.

had the power to disapprove it, a power seldom or never exercised. To develop the natural talents of individuals, rather than to inculcate in youth national or political ideas, has inspired the program of the schools in the present century. The studies that have come to constitute the curriculum, as an almost uniform practice, are Bible instruction, prayers and hymns, reading, writing, English, history, geography, singing, drawing, science and practical work, and physical education. Since World War I, extra-curricular activities have been increasingly stressed. Faith in the dissemination of knowledge as a cure for social ills was strong in nineteenth-century England, but the results of universal education did not justify that faith, for crime and industrial evils continued. The elementary school is no longer viewed as an informative institution, but as chiefly formative in purpose. It has become a center of varied activities designed to develop children mentally, physically, and morally for their own and the nation's well-being.

THE ELEMENTARY SCHOOL STUDENT. Sprung from the charity school system, the elementary schools of England have traditionally served only the poor and the near poor, although all except the very poor paid small fees in them until 1891. Those who could afford it received their elementary education at home from tutors, or in the elementary departments of secondary schools, where the desired degree of social exclusiveness could always be had for a price. The growth of a strong Labor Party, since 1900, has been largely responsible for a new kind of liberalism which has concerned itself with social reform in the interest of the laboring class, rather than with the protection of vested interests, long oblivious of their social obligations. Education felt the influence of that movement. By 1907, laws had been passed authorizing free meals for poor children, and recreation centers and medical examination for all public school pupils. The Act of 1902, authorizing local boards to establish secondary schools, required that 25 per cent of those admitted annually be from the public elementary schools. Since then there has been an increased mingling of the social classes in many secondary schools.

DEVELOPMENTS IN SECONDARY EDUCATION. Before 1902, England had old aristocratic and very exclusive "Great Public Schools," few in number, and other Public Schools, many endowed grammar schools and "private adventure" schools, these last having come into prominence in the nineteenth century to meet a demand of a middle class for modern and practical studies, long neglected by the other schools because of their religious, social, and educational conservatism. The "Great Public Schools" catered to the cream of the social elite and, like most of the endowed grammar schools, were Anglican in religion. All of these schools were private. After 1902, public, "undenominational" secondary schools were established by local education authorities. The Act of that year provided national grants for all secondary schools, public or private, meeting the requirements of the Board of Education. The board secondary schools were pay schools, though, as we have seen, to receive a grant, they had to provide many free places for students from public elementary schools. Under the Act of 1944, all schools maintained by the L.E.A.'s became free. The plan of providing direct government grants to private secondary schools, recognized as efficient, has continued to the present day, but it has been opposed by many on the grounds that it perpetuates the caste system in education. To maintain their freedom, very many schools did not accept a grant.

THE PRIVATE SCHOOL. National governments have pursued different policies in dealing with non-public schools, and Soviet Russia has put them out of existence entirely. The British government came late into the field of education, with the result that the private school, from the kindergarten to the Great Public Schools, had rooted itself deeply in the soil of tradition. In 1936, there were some 10,000 schools not recognized by the central Board of Education and known in most cases only to the L.E.A.'s. About three-fourths of the 400,000 students then enrolled in these schools were receiving elementary education only. A government committee appointed to investigate these schools, in 1931, found many of them excellent, the majority of them satisfactory, and a small number of them seriously defective. While the Act of 1944 requires all private schools to be registered in the Ministry of Education, they have not yet (1958) been compelled to do so, although about one-half of them have done so voluntarily. Parents who wish to pay fees for education enjoy the right to select the school, but the government wishes to protect them and the nation from inefficient educational service. In certain circumstances, the L.E.A.'s may pay the fees of students attending private secondary boarding schools in their areas.

THE SCHOLARSHIP SYSTEM IN SECONDARY SCHOOLS. The free-place system goes far back into the history of English secondary schools but, until the present century, such privileges were rarely extended to children of the masses, for secondary education was viewed as a right of the classes. Free secondary education for all is an open door to social privilege and makes for social fluidity. The rulers of English society, wishing to make the transition from one class to another difficult, kept, until 1944, secondary education a pay education. The Labor Party long demanded "free secondary education for all," but it had not the power to make its demand effective. After 1902, grant-earning secondary schools were required to provide entirely free places for at least 25 per cent of their yearly admissions, and that percentage could be increased to 50 with the approval of the Board of Education. These free places were to go to elementary-school pupils selected usually by a competitive test. By a series of steps, England advanced to the modern free secondary school of the L.E.A.'s, but the scholarship system continues in the grant-aided voluntary schools. The scholarship system, common in Western nations, has been attacked, particularly by Communists, as a bourgeois design to deprive the laboring class of its leaders. Whether it did that or not, we find no evidence that it was ever so designed. Indeed, the schools of England, through the scholarship system, have given labor some of its outstanding leaders.

AIM AND CURRICULUM IN SECONDARY EDUCATION. Character formation and the preservation or advancement of the students' social status have been the traditional basic goals of secondary education. Englishmen credit their secondary schools with the building and preservation of national character, to which they attribute the greatness of the nation. To them, also, they have entrusted the function of providing for the nation a conservative social evolution. The third goal aimed at is that of general intellectual training, but this is deemed of less importance than that of character formation and the safeguarding of one's social status. We have noted earlier that the secondary school system arose as a separate one unrelated to the elementary system. It has thus been the embodiment of a social and educational tradition peculiarly its own, with the result that efforts, in the present century, to co-ordinate it with the elementary system have encountered many difficulties, and progress toward that goal has been slow.

The classical tradition became firmly rooted in England. Chiefly after 1800, private adventure schools with a practical and modern curricular bias arose in answer to growing needs. Yet, the Great Public Schools and the endowed grammar schools clung to their classical prejudices. The Clarendon Commission (appointed 1861), which investigated nine Great Public Schools, found their chief work to be a formal study of the classics. The Commission reported that they were neglecting to teach everything which Englishmen needed to know. The Taunton Commission (appointed 1864), which studied endowed grammar schools and endowed non-classical schools, reported that the former, which were mostly Anglican, were too classical and gave but scant attention to mathematics, modern languages, and natural science. This Commission, however, while in favor of modernizing the curriculum, assumed that the purpose of education is mental discipline and that modern studies can be justified only on that basis.

Twentieth-century England thus inherited an academic and largely literary concept of secondary education which still survives in the "grammar school," one of the three types of secondary school of present-day England.[25] The old Board of Education stipulated that the curriculum of a recognized secondary school had to include English language and literature, at least one foreign language, geography, history, mathematics, science (including practical applications), drawing, organized games, physical exercises, manual instruction (for boys), domestic subjects (for girls), and singing. This interference with the secondary curriculum differs from the policy of noninterference with that of the elementary school. While, here and there, vocational studies had been introduced, they were merely an adjunct to the grammar-school curriculum.

Prior to 1917, there were eight regional examining bodies, associated with universities, which gave leaving examinations to secondary-school students. In that year, the Board of Education gave these groups recognition but, at the same time, created its own Secondary School Examinations Council whose work helped to standardize the leaving examinations of secondary-school students. These bodies granted both the School Certificate, provided for students who had completed successfully four years of secondary work, and the Higher School Certificate, provided for those who had completed two additional years of advanced, specialized academic work. In 1951, the General Certificate of Education, designed for sixteen-year-olds, was substituted for these earlier ones and was intended to represent attainments intermediate between them. The earlier ones came to bear the stamp of university matriculation or of a passport to clerical positions. To get the new General Certificate a student now needs only to pass in any five subjects on an official list of more than fifty, whereas under the old plan he was required to pass in required subjects on a small academic list. This change reflects the persistent questioning of the suitability of the traditional curriculum for students taking the earlier leaving examinations. Moreover, World War II increased the demand of the military and of industries for technical instruction. Urgent national needs have thus been transforming the

[25] *Infra*, pp. 690 f.

curriculum of the secondary schools of England. While the General Certificate of Education (G.C.E.) examination was intended for the grammar schools, not the new technical and "secondary modern schools," students in these new schools have been presenting themselves, often successfully, for it. A new examining body has been organized to bring the technical schools into the examination system, and it seems probable that a similar step will soon be taken in the case of the "secondary modern schools."

It should be noted here that the conviction is strong in England that specialization, whether it be vocational or academic, should begin only after the foundation of a broad general education has been laid. In its program leading to the first leaving examination, the secondary school, it has been felt, ought to lay the foundation of vocational training and not provide such training. While English psychologists have questioned or rejected it, the belief in formal discipline and the transfer of general training remains strong. To make men and citizens by developing the mental, moral, and physical powers during the primary and secondary stages of education has been deemed more important than to make technicians.

VOCATIONAL EDUCATION. The first evidence of direct state interest in vocational training appears in a small grant, in 1836, to aid in establishing a normal school of design in London. That indicates that the government was conscious of needs which the old apprenticeship system was not meeting. In 1852, there was created in the government the Science and Art Department, grants from which brought the establishment of science schools after 1862. There were 948 such schools with 36,783 pupils in 1872. In 1889, a law was passed authorizing larger local government councils to levy a tax for the support of technical education, among other purposes. In 1890, the government provided a national grant in aid of technical schools and classes. The Act of 1902 legalized higher elementary schools, chiefly vocational in character, which local authorities had established under the usual name of "Central Schools," and which had a vocational bias. The Act of 1902 gave the L.E.A.'s power to supply "education other than elementary." Thereafter, they established many Junior Technical, Junior Art, Junior Commercial, and Junior Housewifery schools. Under the provision of the Act of 1944, secondary technical schools have been replacing these schools in the urban centers. The continuation schools, authorized by the same law, and called "county colleges," promise to emphasize vocational training.[26] During the past several decades

[26] *Infra*, p. 690.

the L.E.A.'s have taken over evening continuation schools, which are attended usually by adults. Much of the work in these is of an advanced technical character. They have an enrollment at present of over a million students.

In addition to these, the L.E.A.'s provide part-time day, technical, and art classes, and day continuation schools. They have also absorbed, or now direct, many Technical Colleges, frequently of polytechnic character, which admit part-time and full-time students. The industrial needs of England have aroused great national concern for the training of a technical personnel.

HEALTH AND PHYSICAL EDUCATION. The physical welfare of the children of the nation has been a growing concern of the government since 1907, when medical inspection of school children was authorized by law. Since 1906, free meals have been provided for undernourished pupils and, since World War I, the L.E.A.'s, aided by national grants, have provided milk and meals at cost for all pupils. The Physical Training and Recreation Act (1937) authorized local authorities to promote programs of social and physical education and, since 1944, they are required to provide adequate facilities for the social and physical training of all students under their jurisdiction. Many of the L.E.A.'s now operate camps, recreation and play centers and, sometimes, swimming pools for students. Organized games and school teams are also supported, in part, by local funds. Of special significance in the national program of health and physical training is the "Youth Service" which, originating earlier, was taken over by the Board of Education in 1919. In 1939, the Board created a special committee to direct the program, which was limited to youth between the ages of fourteen and twenty. The L.E.A.'s established their own committees to work with the central committee, whose chief duty is to co-ordinate the work of local authorities. The Youth Service assists financially hundreds of public and private clubs, such as the Scouts, which promote social, recreational and physical activities for youth. Since 1950, the problem of training leaders for the work of the youth service has received much official attention. The Ministry of Education considers the whole program of health, social and physical training of supreme national importance.

EDUCATION OF GIRLS. Until the second half of the nineteenth century, but little public concern was shown in England for the secondary and higher education of girls. Many social reformers, both women and men, among them John Stuart Mill, had long been pleading the cause of women, and the struggle for women's emancipation was similar to that in the United States. The Charity Schools and, later, the board elementary schools admitted girls, while girls of the middle and upper classes were provided with more exclusive facilities, elementary and secondary, by private and church agencies. Until about 1880, relatively few girls attended secondary schools. In the seventies, Oxford and Cambridge began timidly to make a little provision for women. Unlike American women, English women were opposed to coeducation, and there are still few coeducational secondary schools in England. The British feel that coeducation impedes the development of manly character. While school opportunities for English girls came more slowly than in America, the present century has seen them enlarged to the point almost of sex equality. Of 1,367 grant-earning secondary schools, in 1931, 500 were for boys, 485 for girls, and 382 were coeducational. The girls constituted about 47 per cent of the total enrollment in these schools at that time. Only one-third of the students who entered universities in 1930-1931 were girls. These figures have remained almost unchanged since then.

English girls have some 130 recognized "Public Schools" similar in their academic and social aspects to those for boys. While the names of these schools for girls (*e.g.* Cheltenham, Wycombe Abbey, St. Paul's) are not as well known outside of England as are, for instance, Rugby, Eton, and Harrow, they enjoy high distinction at home. No sex discrimination appears in the selection by local authorities of students for the grammar and secondary technical schools of their areas. While English law forbids such discrimination in appointing teachers, there is still marked opposition to the teaching of older boys by women and to bestowing principalships, even of mixed schools, upon them. England has now come to accept the principle of equal pay for equal work. Though the actual differences were not great, the salaries were lower, at every point of the official scale, for women than for men. The National Union of Teachers (the N.E.A. of England) waged a very determined campaign, for over four decades, for equal pay for male and female teachers. While approximately one-third of the students in the eighteen degree-granting universities are women, the proportion of women to men is much lower in Oxford and Cambridge, where they constitute about ten per cent of the enrollment in the former and less than seven per cent in the latter. We should, however, note here that a few of our older American universities still exclude women.

TEACHER TRAINING. Teacher training originated in the demand of the churches for orthodox teachers. The first important development came in 1839 when the National and British and Foreign societies, with the aid of government grants for the purpose, began to establish training colleges. Other church education societies soon took a similar step, and the number of training schools increased rapidly. In addition to the training-college plan, there developed also the pupil-teacher plan of training, introduced from Holland in 1846, although the practice seems to have existed among English Quakers in the eighteenth century. It was an apprenticeship plan by which boys and girls, beginning at about the age of thirteen, became legal apprentices to elementary schoolmasters for five years. Then they took a competitive government examination by which the best of them were chosen for free further training in the teachers' colleges. Those who failed to earn scholarships were frequently employed as uncertificated teachers, for whom the government provided an opportunity to earn a certificate by examination and without attendance at a training college. Until 1902, when L.E.A.'s were authorized to establish public secondary schools, elementary school teachers were trained outside of the secondary system, and the universities were almost entirely closed to them though, for over twenty years, they had teacher-training departments.

After 1902, many elementary school graduates found entrance to elementary school teaching by earning free places in secondary schools and pursuing general secondary studies until the age of sixteen. These, if they met certain requirements, were given a special government grant to remain an additional year in the secondary school, part of which was to be spent in observation and practice teaching in an elementary school. That year's work being completed, the successful student was ready to pursue a two-year course in a training college, or a three-year course (raised to four years in 1911) in a university. Since 1928, the Board of Education has surrendered its traditional rôle of examining future teachers to nine regional boards formed by training colleges, universities, and other groups interested in teacher training. It should be noted that the British government leaves the training and examination of lawyers and doctors to private agencies.

The growing national interest in teacher training since 1839, coupled with the growth of professional knowledge and the demand of teachers for professional status and recognition, has culminated in many changes since 1944. Prior to 1945, there were two types of training institutions: (1) the training colleges which prepared teachers for elementary schools, and (2) the university departments of education which prepared teachers for secondary schools, although some of their graduates went into the elementary-school field. Of 133 training colleges operating in 1953, 83 were controlled by the L.E.A.'s, the rest being largely denominational. Following World War I, a series of committees of the Board of Education studied the problem of teacher training and made their recommendations for reform. Of these, the McNair Committee, whose report, *Teachers and Youth Leaders,* was submitted in 1944, had the greatest influence upon present practice. Among the recommendations were (a) that there be set up a central government agency to direct the training program, (b) that all teachers in state-maintained schools be professionally trained and their status improved, and (c) that the universities, either independently or in co-operation with other local agencies, pass upon the qualifications of all teachers, whether elementary or secondary. Implied in the numerous specific recommendations of the Committee, which cannot be listed here, was the view that teaching on all levels constitutes a single profession similar to those of law and medicine and of equal national importance.

The road to teaching in state-maintained schools is now, after decades of development, through the secondary grammar school, from which the student proceeds to the training college or, if he plans to teach in a secondary school, to the university. Seventeen "area training organizations," usually called "Institutes of Education" have been, as of this writing, established in association with universities, with the Ministry of Education having four representatives on the council of each area. The area training organizations (A.T.O.'s) of which there are two types—one directly under the Ministry and receiving direct grants, and the other indirectly and through the universities to which the grants are paid—supervise the training programs, examine students, and recommend qualified students to the Ministry for certification. The training colleges offer two-year courses for the regular students, and the studies are academic and professional, the latter including practice teaching, principles of education, history of education, health education and educational psychology. While their normal function is to train teachers for infant and primary schools, these colleges have, in recent years, been training teachers for secondary modern schools. The Ministry makes grants to students in these colleges to cover the cost of their education and maintenance.

The universities are the normal training centers of secondary-school teachers. Having acquired his degree, the student who intends to teach signs a declaration of his intention, and enters a one-year professional course, during which he receives a grant from the Ministry. This course includes the professional studies pursued by the students in the training colleges. At the completion of the course, those who have satisfied their "Institute of Education" (A.T.O.) are recommended to the Ministry for certification as "qualified teachers" (Q.T.).

A national committee, composed of representatives of the teachers, the L.E.A.'s and the Ministry, fixes the salaries which employers must pay their teachers. Since 1925, a contributory pension system has been in operation for eligible teachers. Special disability allowances and other benefits are provided under the pension plan. British and other European teachers, as servants of the state, have, after a struggle, won professional recognition and a security, still inadequate, from the nations which they serve.

BRITISH EDUCATIONAL IDEALS. The schools of a nation reflect its mind and the character of its people, both of which change with the changing world. Observers have been almost unanimous in listing respect for individuality as a mark of the Englishman. Mill, in his *Essay on Liberty*, laid a firm philosophical foundation for that attitude. While the government has restricted individual liberty in many ways, the view persists that progress is best attained through individual and local initiative. The freedom which local education authorities and teachers in their classrooms enjoy reflects that view. While the student has but little choice in the studies he pursues, he enjoys much freedom in the extra-curricular and social life of the school, in which, if he so desires, he may not participate. If he prefers the library to the cricket field, he may spend his playtime in the library without being considered an emotional misfit. With his freedom, however, go obligations which he may not shirk, for school life, as is social life, is a blend of freedom and responsibility. In the national culture the idea of "self" has been, and remains, a motivating force. Such words as self-activity, self-respect, self-control, self-help are in frequent use in the everyday language of the people. Said Tennyson:

> Self-reverence, self-knowledge, self-control,
> These three alone lead life to sovereign power.

As a reflection of respect for individuality, variety rather than uniformity is aimed at in the education of England.

Among educational ideals, we find emphasized those of religious and ethical character and healthy bodies. English educators, perhaps without convincing reasons, take credit, as once did American educators, for what they consider to be a favorable criminal record in the nation. Perhaps because of national interest in sports and games; perhaps because of wars; perhaps because of social, economic, and individual needs; but more likely because of all of these, health has come to be listed high among English educational ideals, and the health program of the schools has assumed great importance.

Lastly, citizenship as an ideal and a practice of English education needs special mention. Much has been written on the rights of Englishmen; little, on their duties. Yet the word "duty," like "self," might be said to be an idea-force in England. No thoughtful English educator disregards the need for moulding citizens loyal to British institutions, though there is much disagreement as to the method by which that end can be attained. The problem is linked to the whole structure of the empire and the British Commonwealth of Nations, upon which the island kingdom depends for many of its supplies, for its prosperity, and for its power among the nations. The English citizen, it is felt, must not only be conscious of the rôle he must play in English affairs, but he must be made empire-conscious as well. That feeling has been heightened by world events since 1914.

Foremost among the devices by which civic loyalty is created is the cult of the king-emperor or queen-empress, made all the more effective by the teaching in and out of school that the monarch is indispensable for the unity of an empire on which "the sun never sets." In the culture of England we thus find not only the fratriarchal, or brother-idea, but also the patriarchal, or father-idea, as well. Through all dignified channels of communication the people are constantly reminded of their political parent. Should he or she depart from the accepted ways of good royal life, as did Edward VIII, the office will be bestowed on one who shows proper regard for its traditions. Respect for the monarch bears many marks of a cult. The national anthem is "God Save the King." Socially the monarch is the head of the nobility, an exclusive group that the common people have, until very recently, worshiped in a way foreign to our American tradition.

In addition to the cult of the monarch, there is also fostered a cult of England—of the island, the countryside, and its historical landmarks. The schools do much to stimulate love of the land that is England through the teaching of English literature and through school excursions. Poets and novelists for centuries have been building the cult of England. There are, for instance, probably few in England who have not read Shakespeare's stirring lines:

> This royal throne of kings, this scepter'd isle,
> This earth of majesty, this seat of Mars,
> This other Eden, demi-paradise;
> This fortress built by Nature for herself

Against infection and the hand of war;
This happy breed of men, this little world,
This precious stone set in the silver sea. . . .

The green fields, the church bells, the brooks, the mountains, the valleys, the flowers, the trees, the holy wells, the schools, the army, the navy, and the people of England are among the themes that, through the sheer beauty and force of literary expression, develop in school children a devotion to their native land and its people. Historical associations and others work to preserve historical shrines and the beauty of the countryside.

The building of loyalty to the empire has been systematically carried on by empire societies and other groups which provide the schools with maps, pictures and films, and encourage the interchange of and correspondence between students and teachers of England and her dominions. "Every schoolboy knows" that imperial needs demand British naval supremacy. Yet, in moulding the national mind, there has been more of the rational and less of the cult element in the English method than in that of most of her world neighbors. For teaching domestic citizenship, English teachers depend more upon school government and the activities program than upon formal instruction. For imperial citizenship, the problem is different, and resort must be had to other devices such as those we have mentioned.

British educational leaders, generally, have little faith in the value of indoctrination, and oppose the cultist approach to the teaching of doctrines. In official and professional pronouncements, the use of the schools—which exist in the interest of the nation and all its citizens—to propagate doctrines, whether social, economic, political, theological, or military, has been frequently condemned as harmful in a nation and a world in a state of rapid change. The interests of England, it is felt, are best served by telling the truth, at times unsavory, about the past of England and her empire, and by looking realistically at her problems inherited from that past. The principle of imperialism may or may not be defended, but imperialism as an historical fact and as the source of stark necessities for modern England is defended. Jonathan F. Scott, in his *Menace of Nationalism in Education*, though his account shows some evidence of bias, found English textbooks far less offensive in their treatment of international history and relations than those of the other nations which he studied. Whether or not the schools have had much to do with it, the English mind has been marked by remarkable loyalty to the nation and the empire. England looks to education as the only means of social control which a free people will willingly accept.

Selected Readings

Adamson, J. W. *English Education 1789–1902.* London: Cambridge University Press, 1930.

Alexander, T. *The Prussian Elementary Schools.* New York: The Macmillan Co., 1918.

Archer, R. L. *Secondary Education in the Nineteenth Century.* London: Cambridge University Press, 1921.

Armfelt, R. *Our Changing Schools.* London: His Majesty's Stationery Office, 1950.

Baker, E. *British Universities.* New York: Longmans, Green & Co., Inc., 1946.

Brichenough, C. *History of Elementary Education in England.* London: University Tutorial Press, Ltd., 1939.

Buisson, F., and Farrington, F. E. *French Educational Ideals of Today.* Yonkers, N.Y.: World Book Co., 1919.

Cramer, J. F., and Browne, G. S. *Contemporary Education.* New York: Harcourt, Brace & Co., Inc., 1956.

Curtis, S. J. *History of Education in Great Britain.* London: University Tutorial Press, Ltd., 1948.

De Montmorency, J. E. G. *State Intervention in English Education.* London: Cambridge University Press, 1902.

Dent, H. C. *Education in Transition.* London: Routledge and Kegan Paul, Ltd., 1945.

———. *Growth in English Education, 1946–1952.* London: Routledge and Kegan Paul, Ltd., 1954.

Farrington, F. E. *French Secondary Schools.* New York: Longmans, Green & Co., Inc., 1910.

———. *The Public Primary School System of France.* New York: Teachers College, Columbia University, 1906.

Kandel, I. *Comparative Education.* Boston: Houghton Mifflin Co., 1933.

Knight, E. W. *Reports on European Education.* New York: McGraw-Hill Book Co., 1930.

Miles, D. W. *Recent Reforms in French Secondary Education.* New York: Teachers College, Columbia University, 1952.

Pascoe, C. F. *Two Hundred Years of the S.P.G., 1701–1900.* 2 vols.; London: Society for the Propagation of the Gospel, 1901.

Reisner, E. *Nationalism in Education since 1789.* New York: The Macmillan Co., 1927.

Smith, F. *History of English Elementary Education since 1760.* London: University of London Press, Ltd., 1931.

14 The Development of the American School System

In earlier chapters brief attention has been given to colonial and later American educational history. That picture needs to be enlarged so that the continuity of our institutional developments from colonial days until the present may not be lost sight of. Because of many unique features of our history, our educational experiences and practices show, at times, sharp contrasts with those of Europe.

Colonial Beginnings

SOME ASPECTS OF THE SOCIAL SCENE. In Chapter 7 reference has been made to colonial social life, and, in every brief account such as this one, the picture must remain very incomplete. All social institutions and ways of social life are educational, and formal schooling is but a supplement to that of the home, the farm, the workshop, the street, the church, etc. In this account of American education we must confine our attention chiefly to its formal aspects. Deserving of special mention, perhaps, is the fact that, in building our civilization, Americans have developed a rather unique respect for work of every description and a devotion to it. And we have bestowed upon manual labor a dignity largely unknown in the Old World up to the present time. Our struggle and the material rewards it has brought have made us activists and scorners of inactivity. The American heaven is not one of rest and contemplation.

Colonial America was an expansion of Europe. When the colonies were founded, Europe was seething with political, social and religious conflicts. Guiding Europe to a new way of life was the middle class who, in their own interests, strove to strengthen national governments, to build empires, to create constitutional governments as their servants, and to promote science and philosophies in harmony with their ideals.

In the New World, Europeans were confronted by a common enemy, Nature, which placed the traditional conflicts, rooted in man, in a new perspective. The wilderness gradually taught them the relative unimportance of the old conflicts. While some colonists would transplant European institutions unchanged to America, others would build here societies freed from the evils of Old-World life. The Anglicans, dominant in the South, would recreate the Old England here, but the Puritans would create a New England as an escape from the evils of the old one. Between New England and the South lay the Middle Colonies settled by Europeans of diverse national and cultural inheritances, but generally middle-class in their social outlook, and dissenters in their theologies. These Middle Colonies displayed a portentous diversity. The challenge of Nature did not, however, end all prejudices.

The problem of the relationship between church and state interested the colonists. The Anglicans (Church of England) would unite them as equal partners in an authoritarian society; the Puritans, in an unequal partnership of authority, with the church as the dominant agency. The Pilgrims and the Anabaptist groups, of humble social origin, would separate them for the sake of religious liberty. State churches were, however, the rule. Outside of Rhode Island, which had no established church, the Puritan was the legal church in New England. The Anglican was the legal church in New York, New Jersey and the South. The Dutch Reformed church of New Netherland lost its legal right with the British conquest of the Hudson-Delaware region, 1664-1674.

As we have seen in Chapter 7, common-man democracy was unknown in the colonies, but Nature and the social environment were friends of the lowly, and attempts to keep the working classes, other than slaves, "in their place" failed. Disabilities imposed upon them here, as well as memories of European oppression, placed their sympathies upon the side of the Revolution and political liberalism.

EDUCATIONAL PRACTICES. (1) MOTIVES IN ALL COLONIES. In discussing humanism and the Reformation, in Chapter 8, some attention has been given to the beginnings of American education. Sectarian, class and racial prejudices permeated the educational scene everywhere, while feelings rooted in differences in national origin were also at work, particularly in the Middle Colonies. Protestant religious motives predominated everywhere in British North America. While Jesuit and Franciscan missionaries operated schools, the former in Maryland and New York, and the latter in the Southwest from 1606 onward, Catholics played a minor rôle in education. Protestant-Catholic rivalries, however, stimulated efforts to convert and instruct Indians and Negroes, whose allegiance both groups sought to capture. Practical needs also had to be met. The colonies and their churches needed competent leaders, but they also needed followers trained in practical, commercial and manual pursuits. Although there was some degree of social fluidity, caste and racial segregation marked the education of the period. Elementary and apprenticeship education were designed for the masses; secondary and higher education, for the privileged classes.

(2) PRACTICES IN THE SOUTH. Uniform practices did not exist from Maryland to Georgia, and generalizations about the South, as about other areas, are hazardous. It is probably safe to say that, in the South, public interest in education, other than apprenticeship education of orphans and the destitute poor, was at a minimum. Where it found expression, it revealed a concern, not for the masses but for the classes, and the interest centered in the provision for secondary and higher education rather than for universal elementary education. In Chapter 8 brief reference has already been made to Southern practice. Catholic Maryland, in 1671, made legal provision for "a School or College,"[1] and Anglican Maryland, in 1696 and 1723, took steps to establish and support a system of county secondary schools, sometimes called "Free Schools" and sometimes "Public Schools," in which, by a law of 1728, some poor children should be "taught gratis."[2] Tobacco duties, fines and other public funds were provided for these schools by laws passed in the years 1727 to 1732.

In Virginia, the first settlers planned an endowed school for rich and poor, including Indians, but the plan failed and, thereafter, education was left to the undirected efforts of private agencies. With the exception of the richly-aided William and Mary College, the schools of Virginia received little or no public aid. Between 1624 and 1660, the legislature imposed stringent requirements upon parents and ministers for Anglican catechetical instruction of children.[3] Private tutors were employed by the rich planters and, outside of the plantations, a community type of school, generally elementary and known as the "old field school," became fairly common.[4] These schools were often taught by Anglican ministers. Reports of ministers to the Bishop of London, in 1724, show that the schools in that year were very few. There were three endowed schools, the

[1] *Archives of Maryland,* II, 263.

[2] *Laws of Maryland,* 1728, pp. 13–14.

[3] S. Bell, *The Church, the State and Education in Virginia* (Lancaster, Pa.: Science Press, Inc., 1930), pp. 99 ff.

[4] M. W. Jernegan, *The American Colonies, 1492–1750* (New York: Longmans, Green & Co., Inc., 1929), p. 106.

first being that founded by the will of Benjamin Symms in 1634, but their offerings were largely elementary.[5] Many parents, particularly in Virginia and South Carolina, sent their sons to schools in England and Scotland.

In North Carolina, meager public interest resulted in aid to one chartered (1764) school at Newbern, a coeducational one, which was placed under the care of the S.P.G. (Anglican Society for the Propagation of the Gospel in Foreign Parts), which was active in Southern education outside of Maryland and Virginia, where Anglicanism was probably considered safe. This society operated a number of schools in the Carolinas.

The South Carolina legislature chartered the "Charleston Free School," in 1710, and gave it public aid. It was free only to the few "charity boys" who were admitted. The teachers had to be Anglicans, as was the custom in all publicly aided schools of the South. In 1712, the state, with the S.P.G. serving as its agent, made an educational grant to each parish. Here, too, many individual bequests were made to schools. The South Carolina Society of Charleston and the Winyaw Indigo Society helped with the education of the poor, the latter supporting a school from 1756 until the Civil War.[6]

In Georgia, a Moravian school for Indians, established in 1736, closed when its founders moved to Pennsylvania. The S.P.G. was the most important provider of education here. The leading school in the colony, however, was the Bethesda Orphan House, established by the evangelist, George Whitefield, in 1737. Opened as a school for girls, it soon took all orphans. It was accused of being a "Nest for the Enemies of the Church."[7] Whitefield was a symbol of the forces of dissent from Maine to Georgia. When the colony became a royal province, in 1752, the governor required teachers seeking a license from him to take an oath of loyalty to church and state.

The publicly encouraged schools of the South served the cause of Anglicanism and of the predominantly Anglican governments of the colonies. The Bishop of London was the legal head of the church and its schools everywhere, and the S.P.G. was his special educational agent. Elementary education was largely indoctrination in the doctrines of the Church of England, but reading, writing and, sometimes, rudimentary arithmetic were supplementary studies and, with a few exceptions, the only education provided for the Anglican masses. The Dissenters provided sectarian and sometimes

[5] E. W. Knight, *A Documentary History of Education in the South before 1860* (Chapel Hill: University of North Carolina Press, 1949–53), I, 202–33.

[6] *Ibid.*, pp. 276–95.

[7] *Ibid.*, pp. 235–73.

secular education, elementary and secondary, for their own adherents. Generally, apart from provision for apprenticeship education, where public action was taken it expressed itself in providing Latin schools, or "free schools" as they were usually called, for the rich, but in which a few poor boys were "taught gratis" as a charity. A reconstruction of the social scene and its educational records forces the conclusion that the rate of illiteracy must have been high in the South.

(3) Practices in the Middle Colonies. To the brief account in Chapter 8 more should be added here to enlarge the picture of our educational beginnings. William Penn, when founding Pennsylvania, had in view a public school system,[8] but that plan was abandoned. The William Penn Charter School, still flourishing, was established by the Quaker Monthly Meeting of Philadelphia in 1689 and, under its "overseers," grew into a group of schools, crowned by a Latin school. These schools were free to choose poor students of all faiths, against the wishes of conservative Quakers who desired a "guarded education" for their children.

Pennsylvania became a haven for German immigrants, and for persecuted German sects whose indifference to everything except work and prayer,[9] coupled with their increasing numerical strength and their love of their own tongue,[10] brought alarm to the English-speaking rulers of the colony. Franklin viewed the German "foreigners" as a threat to British rule.[11] To bring them to a "correct" knowledge of God, he and others, in 1753, organized charity schools for them under the direction of the S.P.G. Twelve short-lived, unpopular schools thus resulted. It is noteworthy that these dreaded "foreigners" gave us a notable pedagogue, Christopher Dock, a Mennonite who came here around 1712.[12]

Apart from these organized efforts, a few schools of the S.P.G., one of the Presbyterian Synod of Philadelphia, and three Moravian schools, education in Pennsylvania was left to be provided by ministers, individual churches, private masters, or, as happened in a few places, by joint effort of families to support a teacher for their children. While the Philadelphia Academy, referred to in Chapter 8, had public recognition in its charter, and received gifts from the

[8] J. Mulhern, *A History of Secondary Education in Pennsylvania* (Lancaster, Pa.: Science Press, Inc., 1933), pp. 26–27.

[9] Some of them still, for religious reasons, abstain from voting.

[10] Many of their descendants do not yet speak English.

[11] J. Bigelow, *Works of Benjamin Franklin* (New York: G. P. Putnam's Sons, Inc., 1904), II, 298.

[12] M. G. Brumbaugh, *The Life and Works of Christopher Dock* (Philadelphia, Pa.: J. B. Lippincott Co., 1908).

city and the Penns, it resulted from private rather than from public effort. Education was not a matter of public concern. The churches, the Quakers in the lead, were the chief providers of it.[13] Some Presbyterian ministers established Latin schools, the most famous perhaps being William Tennent's "Log College," a forerunner of Princeton, and the Presbyterian synodical New London Academy, forerunner of the University of Delaware. The Baptists, Lutherans, Reformed, and Seventh-Day Adventists established a few Latin schools in the colony.[14] The Moravians were especially active in providing education for girls. Their Moravian Female Seminary, Linden Hall Female Seminary, and Nazareth Hall for boys were established in the seventeen forties. With the exception of apprenticeship education, soon to be examined, public interest in the education of the Pennsylvania masses is conspicuous by its absence. Philadelphia thus became a profitable field for private schoolmasters.

For New Jersey the story is similar to that for Pennsylvania. Here the Quakers, Dutch Reformed and Presbyterians were the chief sects. Before the colony became a royal province in 1702, the Quaker Assembly of West New Jersey, in 1682, granted land for a school in Burlington, while in East New Jersey, under Dutch and New England influence, laws were passed in 1693 and 1695 for the establishment of tax-supported town schools. Under the royal governors this public interest ceased, and education was left to the churches and private agencies, the Quakers being the leading providers of elementary,[15] and Presbyterian ministers, of secondary education.

In Dutch New Netherland, extending from Albany to the lower Delaware, the story was different. The schools here, while public, were adjuncts of the state-church; and the West Indian Company, village authorities and large landowners provided elementary education, while New Amsterdam had a Latin school which originated in 1652. Most of the nine incorporated Dutch towns seem to have had elementary schools in 1664, one probably being at Fort Casmier on the Delaware. Following the British occupation some of these became parochial and others continued as town schools, after the Holland fashion. Support was provided by public funds and tuition fees. Elementary teachers were chosen and supervised by church officials, and were required to perform certain church duties. The Latin master was chosen by the governor, had a public salary, and

[13] T. Woody, *Early Quaker Education in Pennsylvania* (New York: Teachers College, Columbia University, 1920).

[14] Mulhern, *op. cit.*, pp. 65 ff.

[15] T. Woody, *Quaker Education in the Colony and State of New Jersey* (Philadelphia, Pa.: The author, 1923).

had no church duties to perform. The Dutch and New England Puritans set the fashion for public education in America.[16]

Under British rule, education in New York was neglected from 1710, but the S.P.G. maintained a few charity schools in which the government, then Anglican, took an interest. In 1702 and again in 1732, the legislature approved the establishment of a "Grammar Free School," the former for seven years, and the latter for five. While these secondary schools received some public aid, they charged tuition. The school of 1732 was free to twenty students. This meager public interest centered in secondary schools and in the establishment of King's College. The Jesuits established a Latin school in British New York, but the government closed it. Private masters thus came in to fill the vacuum created by public indifference. In the Middle Colonies, as in the South, the rate of illiteracy must have been high.

(4) Practices in New England. **(a) Town elementary school.** The founders of New England, anxious to preserve Puritan orthodoxy and a class society, viewed education as a chief instrument of social control and, with the exception of Rhode Island, all the colonies adopted compulsory school laws, authorized local taxes for school support and made land grants to many town Latin schools, while Harvard College was a special object of public aid and of concern to all the colonies until Yale was founded in 1701. We have referred briefly to these developments in Chapter 8 and to the Massachusetts laws of 1642 and 1647, which set the fashion for New England in elementary and secondary education.

New Haven in 1655 and 1660 required instruction of children in reading and writing, as did Connecticut in 1650, 1690 and 1700. New England elementary schools were often officially called "writing schools," indicating the need felt by merchants for scriveners and bookkeepers. Plymouth, in 1663, asked the towns to make a similar provision[17] and, in 1671, made instruction in reading and a trade compulsory. Massachusetts laws applied here after 1691. New Hampshire and Maine, as parts of Massachusetts until 1679 and 1820 respectively, fell under the parental laws. New Hampshire, in 1693 and 1719, required towns to support elementary teachers. The compulsory school laws were hard to enforce, and many towns were lax in enforcing them. While town taxes were authorized to pay the "wages" of teachers, tuition fees were, apparently,

[16] W. H. Kilpatrick, *The Dutch Schools of New Netherland and Colonial New York* (Washington, D.C.: Government Printing Office, 1912).

[17] W. Brigham (ed.), *The Compact with the Charter and Laws of the Colony of New Plymouth* (Boston: E. P. Dutton & Co., Inc., 1836), p. 143.

everywhere required as a supplement to them. The burden of cost seems, generally, to have fallen upon parents and guardians of children, to whom the laws left the choice of schools and teachers. In 1660, the Massachusetts legislature expressed alarm over the extent of illiteracy among the people,[18] and a similar condition probably prevailed in all the colonies.

(b) The dame school. Imported from England, this was generally a private pay school conducted for a few children by women in their own homes. The "dames" generally taught only the ABC's, the rudiments of reading, and religion. These schools were often the only ones open to girls, for whom additional instruction in sewing and knitting was sometimes provided. The "dame" was evidently popular with parents, perhaps because her fees were small, and sometimes with town authorities who, at times, gave her a salary out of public funds, perhaps because she asked for so little. Her religious instruction and conduct were evidently acceptable to the ministers and town officials.

(c) Content and spirit of elementary education. Religious instruction was officially viewed as indispensable to the stability of Puritan society, as the *New England Primer* and the religious atmosphere dealt with in Chapter 8 reveal. Perhaps religion is viewed today, as it was in colonial New England, the Anglican South and in ancient Greece and Rome, as a means to social order and stability. Ability to read the Scriptures and understand the Sunday sermon and the ways of salvation were made, by law, the primary duty of parents and teachers in the upbringing of children in Puritan society. Religion, reading and writing were the principal elementary studies. Penmanship became an art of specialists who operated their own schools, or went from school to school teaching their art. Writing and arithmetic had a special value for the merchants of New England. After 1700, arithmetic and spelling got some attention. In 1740, Thomas Dilworth's reading-spelling book, *A New Guide to the English Tongue,* was published, chiefly for the charity schools of England, and it became popular here, as did his arithmetic text, *The Schoolmasters Assistant,* published in 1743. Few students had their own books. The scarcity and cost of printed texts gave rise to the use of manuscript school books in the eighteenth and first half of the nineteenth century.[19]

[18] Jernegan, *Laboring and Dependent Classes in Colonial America, 1607–1783* (Chicago: University of Chicago Press, 1931), p. 125.

[19] Mulhern, "Manuscript School-Books," *The Papers of the Bibliographical Society of America,* 33:17–37.

(d) Secondary education. The town Latin school, referred to in Chapter 8, became a unique New England institution. Church and state took a special interest in it as a nursery of leaders. However, while the bond between church and state grew weaker in Massachusetts, legislative concern for Latin schools did not decline. Land grants for these schools, usually of 1000 acres, continued to be made to some towns in Massachusetts; fines for noncompliance with laws requiring Latin schools were raised sharply after the adoption of the Charter of 1691, which enfranchised all Protestants; and the duties of towns to provide such schools was more sharply defined. Many towns, however, circumvented the laws. The Puritan ministry, no doubt, continued to be thought of as a chief branch of state service, until the church and state were separated in 1833. The laws providing land grants often called the school thus aided a "free school,"[20] thus, probably, revealing a concern for poorer youths, whom, in 1646, ministers were asked to instruct with a view to entering Harvard and the ministry. While Massachusetts Latin schools were sometimes free, or nearly so, as in Boston and Roxbury, tuition fees generally had to be paid as a supplement to town salaries paid to the masters. The Boston Latin School, authorized by the town in 1635—a year after Symms willed his property for a Latin school in Virginia—and which opened apparently in 1636, was the first active secondary school in the British colonies, and it has had a continuous existence since it opened. Other colonies followed the lead of Massachusetts.

Plymouth, in 1670, provided public funds for a "free schoole,"[21] and, in 1685, ordered every county town to provide a Latin school, in charge of an orthodox teacher, to prepare boys for college. Fees would supplement the town salary of the master, and reading, writing, and arithmetic would be taught in addition to Latin.

In New Hampshire, Portsmouth employed a Latin teacher in 1697.[22] In 1708, the legislature established the Portsmouth Latin School.[23] In 1719 and 1721, laws were passed requiring towns of 100 families to maintain tax-supported Latin schools. A plan of district Latin schools, approved by a law of 1716, evidently did not work. The towns often disregarded the laws. The literary achievements of Rome, even though they had Scriptural significance, must have seemed very unreal to men living in the shadows of the White

[20] *Records of the Governor and Company of the Massachusetts Bay in New England,* IV, Pt. I, 438, 444.

[21] *Records of the Colony of New Plymouth,* V, 107.

[22] *Portsmouth Town Records,* May 7, 1697.

[23] *Laws of New Hampshire,* II, 1702–45, 85 f.

and Green mountains, or struggling for survival in "ye wilderness north of ye Merrimack river."

For Connecticut, the story follows that of Massachusetts, but with some modifications. The law of 1690 provided for two Latin schools in the colony in which, in addition to Latin and Greek, reading, writing and arithmetic were to be taught.[24] Support would come from taxes, gifts and tuition fees. In 1700, Hartford, New Haven, New London and Fairfield were required by law to maintain Latin schools.[25]

(e) Dreams unrealized. The Latin school was not a popular institution, particularly in outlying and poorer towns. It was designed to prepare students for college. Harvard records show that its early students came almost entirely from the few coast towns. The New England Latin school was often little more than an elementary English school in which a few students studied the rudiments of Latin. Poorer towns frequently used one school to meet the requirements of all laws. The course in the Boston Latin School, a very exceptional one, came to be a seven-year course in which the students read a long list of Greek and Roman authors, as the entrance requirements of Harvard dictated.[26] How well the Latin schools met such requirements, or how rigorously Harvard and Yale insisted on them, must remain in the realm of conjecture.

(f) Rise of the district system. When, in the 1700s, New England towns began to disintegrate into autonomous districts and parishes, the town schools also disintegrated, and district schools gradually replaced them. Inaccessibility of centrally located schools and churches to distant families brought discontent and a demand by districts for exemption from taxes for town schools and for authority to establish district schools. Connecticut permitted district schools in 1715 and 1717,[27] as did New Hampshire in 1716.[28] Massachusetts followed in 1789. Before their final approval, the moving town school was tried, particularly in Massachusetts, the master dividing his time between several districts. The system, with district school boards, spread widely throughout the United States in the national period. While democratic, it is usually regarded as inefficient.

(5) SOME GENERAL ASPECTS OF COLONIAL EDUCATION. **(a) Colonial apprenticeship education.** The colonists brought from Eng-

[24] *Colonial Records*, IV, 30–31.

[25] E. W. Clews, *Educational Legislation and Administration of Colonial Governments* (New York: The Macmillan Co., 1899), pp. 97 f.

[26] E. P. Cubberley, *Readings in the History of Education* (Boston: Houghton Mifflin Co., 1920), p. 292.

[27] Clews, *op. cit.*, p. 101.

[28] *Laws of New Hampshire*, II, 1702–45, 203.

land the practice of apprenticeship education of orphans, the destitute, and illegitimate children. Anglicans and Puritans alike would have the state assume responsibility for them. The Southern colonies (except, in minor details, Georgia), with Virginia leading, made apprenticeship training compulsory, masters being required by Virginia (1727) and North Carolina (1755) to provide instruction in reading and writing for their charges.[29] Part-Negro children were covered by these laws.[30] In the Middle Colonies, apprenticeship training of orphans and the destitute became a matter of public and religious concern, beginning with the Duke of York laws (1664) for the Hudson-Delaware region. William Penn would have every youth taught a trade, and apprenticeship training of poor whites and free Negroes, much desired by the Quakers, became a practice in Pennsylvania and New Jersey.[31] Before the British came, the Dutch and Swedes approved apprenticeship training.[32] The laws of New York and Pennsylvania required masters to instruct their apprentices in reading and writing.

Apprenticeship training served well the capitalist-merchant economy of New England. The Massachusetts laws of 1642 and 1648 required the towns to compel parents and masters of apprentices to have children in their charge instructed not only in some trade or pursuit but in reading, religion and the capital laws; and, should these neglect their duty, the selectmen were made responsible for it. The Connecticut law of 1650, and the Plymouth law of 1671 follow the pattern set by Massachusetts. To regain Paradise was not the only motive back of these laws.

Apprenticeship education became associated with the class structure of colonial society and was a badge of social inferiority. It was the chief provision made for the "servant class." [33] After the Revolution, the colonial apprenticeship laws were copied in the Southwest. The mark of caste remained long on the 3 R's and trade education, and some aspects of religious education did not escape it. Obedience and respect for masters were made a religious duty of the poor.

29 Jernegan, *Laboring and Dependent Classes in Colonial America, 1607–1783*, pp. 144–48.

30 R. B. Morris, *Government and Labor in Early America* (New York: Columbia University Press, 1946).

31 Woody, *Quaker Education in the Colony and State of New Jersey*, pp. 126 *passim*, 233 ff.

32 E. M. Fee, *The Origin and Growth of Vocational Industrial Education in Philadelphia to 1917* (Philadelphia, Pa.: Westbrook Publishing Co., 1938), pp. 1 ff.

33 R. F. Seybolt, *Apprenticeship and Apprenticeship Education in Colonial New England and New York* (New York: Teachers College, Columbia University, 1916).

(b) Education of Indians. The Virginia legislature (1619) proposed to instruct some Indian children in "Religion & civile course of life," and Christianization and apprenticeship education of them continued to be generally regarded there as a "pious and charitable" work, as the laws reveal. Their Christianization was one stated purpose of William and Mary College. The Boyle Indian School of the College and the Christ Anna School (1714) were founded for them, but Indians fled from this kindness to find salvation in the wilderness to the west. Virginia's effort to educate them, the only significant Anglican attempt, antedated that of the Pennsylvania Quakers, whose efforts were more successful.[34] Dr. Bray's Associates, an S.P.G. affiliate, active in founding parish libraries in the South, educated a few Indian children, and the S.P.G. in Georgia provided funds to Christianize them.[35] In the Middle Colonies, the S.P.G., as did the Quakers,[36] showed solicitude for them, but the Indians rarely accepted their masters' charity. In New England, concern for their welfare was not entirely lacking. Some gifts were made to Harvard for their education, but few Indians seem to have sought their fruits. In 1754, the Rev. Eleazer Wheelock of Connecticut founded a school for them, the Moor's Indian School, with aid from Massachusetts and New Hampshire, which gave rise to Dartmouth College. Few Indians seem to have sought the academic blessings of this Congregationalist college. The colonists manifested no desire to enslave the Indians, although they generally considered them an "inferior people." Trading with them was more profitable than enslaving them.

(c) Education of Negroes. Unlike Indians, Negro slaves could not escape from their masters. Schoolmasters of the S.P.G. were requested, for the sake of "God and country," to spread the Anglican faith among them.[37] There was some opposition to this policy. The road to the Christianization of slaves was opened when colonial legislatures had the British law forbidding the enslavement of Christians abrogated. Liberal Puritans and Quakers, however, never respected that law. The latter were the first to provide equality of educational opportunity for all races here.

Approximately one-half of the Southern population was Negro on the eve of the Revolution. Their masters, generally, approved an

[34] Woody, *Early Quaker Education in Pennsylvania,* p. 267.

[35] Knight, *op. cit.,* I, 174, 187.

[36] Woody, *Quaker Education in the Colony and State of New Jersey,* pp. 232 ff., 283 ff.

[37] C. F. Pascoe, *Two Hundred Years of the S.P.G., 1701–1900* (London: Society for the Propagation of the Gospel, 1901).

education for them, if it made them more useful and obedient. To teach them the "principles of the true Religion," the "great and necessary Duties of Obedience and Fidelity to their Masters," as Dr. Bray's Associates did in their many Negro schools, aroused little, if any opposition.[38] Reading, writing and, sometimes, arithmetic as well as, for girls, sewing and knitting were taught in some of these schools. Presbyterian ministers, too, had Sunday schools for them. The records for the South, however, reveal a picture of neglect. Yet, it was only after the Nat Turner Insurrection (1831) that the slave-owning states forbade the education of Negroes.

In the Middle Colonies, the S.P.G. provided some instruction for them, while the Quakers made them an object of special concern. The first printed protest against slavery in America came from the Quakers. The well-known Quaker teacher, Anthony Benezet, found Negro pupils in his school as talented as whites. The Quakers considered apprenticeship training of special value for them. There were Negroes in the Delaware-Hudson area from 1648, and their numbers grew rapidly after 1700. Protestant-Catholic and inter-Protestant sectarian rivalries contributed to the growth of schooling for them.

The Puritans of New England had few slaves, but their writers who wrote about them would educate them, apparently to meet the challenge of French and Spanish Catholic missionaries. The Quakers and Anglicans in New England were beginning to provide education for them prior to the Revolution.[39]

(d) Colonial college education. Brief reference has been made in Chapter 8 to colonial higher education. Harvard, whose founding was a victory for "orthodox" Puritanism, was established by the Massachusetts legislature in 1636, and opened in 1638. Its support came from public and private sources, tuition fees being but a minor source of revenue.[40] It was to be both a theological seminary and a college of liberal learning, whose academic honors were reserved for the socially and theologically orthodox, who were to be the leaders of church and state. Admission of poor students, legally authorized in 1644, had, probably, the needs of the church in view. The colonial pulpit everywhere was, however, in the hands of the socially privileged, and served the interests of the ruling class. Prior to

[38] Knight, *op. cit.*, I, 107.

[39] C. G. Woodson, *The Education of the Negro Prior to 1861* (Washington, D.C.: Association for the Study of Negro Life and History, 1919), pp. 94, 337–39.

[40] S. E. Morrison, *Harvard College in the Seventeenth Century* (Cambridge, Mass.: Harvard University Press, 1936).

1700, about one-half of the graduates of Harvard entered the ministry. In the control of the College, the church and state were about equally represented. The studies for degrees followed the European pattern: (1) natural, moral and mental philosophy, based upon Aristotle, (2) the classics and (3) theology. Natural philosophy embraced the study of all forms of life, and included psychology. Economics and political science were in the category of moral philosophy, while mental philosophy was the academic name for metaphysics. Among the topics upon which graduates orated at the first commencement, in 1642, was "Universals do not exist outside of the mind." Early New England still lived, intellectually, in the Middle Ages. In the eighteenth century, Harvard, influenced by science and rationalism, became a center of Deism and Unitarianism.

While sectarianism was declining in Harvard, other colleges, such as Yale and Dartmouth, clung closely to religious ends. Princeton, Dartmouth, Rutgers and Brown were products of the religious revival, the Great Awakening, during which the evangelists, Jonathan Edwards and George Whitefield, preached to restore interest in religion. The colleges of the dissenting churches felt the influence of the revival most, and worked to check religious indifference attributed to science and rationalism. The Anglican colleges (Columbia and William and Mary) and the nonsectarian College of Philadelphia were, at most, but feebly influenced by the Awakening.

William and Mary College (1693), the only one in the South, was not a going concern until about 1712. It served the aristocracy and the Anglican church, although divinity students had to go to England for ordination. The Southern gentry frequently sent their sons to English and Scottish universities. Generously aided by the Virginia legislature and private benefactors, it was the richest college in the colonies.

With the exception of the College of Philadelphia (University of Pennsylvania) and, to a lesser degree, King's College (Columbia), the colleges followed a denominational pattern. While state representation on the boards of governors was the general practice, these boards represented the churches rather than the states, that of Yale being exclusively a church body until 1745. The self-perpetuating board of the College of Philadelphia represented neither church nor state. While presidents and faculties were not voiceless, these external boards were the legal rulers of the colleges. With the exception of Princeton and Rutgers, each college had exclusive educational rights in its own area, a practice which ended with the separation of church and state following the Revolution. The total colonial college enrollment was very small. President Smith of the College of Philadelphia, in 1762, placed it at about 400 students.[41]

(e) Science, rationalism, and educational change. The changing intellectual outlook of Europe made itself felt early in the congenial environment of North America. Interest in science developed in all the colonies in the eighteenth century, and notable scientists appeared on the scene, among them Franklin, a leading spokesman for the Enlightenment in the New World. Linnaeus called John Bartram "the greatest natural botanist in the world."[42] The Philadelphia Academy, described in Chapter 8, forerunner of the College, reflected the secular, scientific interests of the time. In 1753, William Smith, soon to be the first president of the College, published *The General Idea of the College of Mirania* in which he described an ideal plan of education suitable to the economic, social and political conditions of America. He would educate one group in college for the professions and another in a school of the Philadelphia Academy type for practical pursuits. His scheme represents a significant expansion of the content of a liberal education then existing in colonial schools.

In practice the Academy and College failed to achieve fully the ideals of Smith and Franklin.[43] The professional purpose of the College was advanced when the medical school, the first in the colonies, was established in 1765. In the same period, similar developments occurred in King's College whose realistic program was enlarged by the establishment of a medical school in 1767. Instruction in law was offered there in 1773, and in William and Mary College in 1779. Such changes reflect the secular outlook of the pre-Revolution decades. The eighteenth century saw Harvard drift away from sectarianism and Aristotelianism. Cartesian rationalism, Newtonian physics, and Copernican astronomy gradually replaced there the thought of Aristotle, and scientific apparatus was installed for demonstration purposes. The founding of a professorship of mathematics (1728) and the approval of specialization by teachers (1767) show Harvard's recognition of the growth of scientific knowledge. The old required college curriculum and the traditional concept of what constituted liberal studies was thus being changed before the colonial period ended.

[41] H. W. Smith, *Life and Correspondence of the Rev. William Smith, D. D.* (Philadelphia, Pa., 1879), I, 311.

[42] Mulhern, *A History of Secondary Education in Pennsylvania*, p. 171.

[43] *Ibid.*, pp. 194–97.

(f) Education of colonial girls. The colonies inherited the ancient belief that sex is reflected in mind and that women are mentally inferior to men. Educational practices were largely determined by that belief.[44] Attitudes regarding woman's social sphere differed, no doubt, among people of different national traditions, but that her place was the home had almost universal acceptance. "A good wife and a good dog," runs a Pennsylvania German proverb, "are best at home." Yet female indentured servants often "ran away," and married women sometimes deserted their husbands. A small number of women engaged in business, but their economic tie to the home was not broken until the coming of the factory system. Given educational opportunities in the nineteenth century, women destroyed the myth of their mental inferiority.

Prior to 1700, about 75 per cent of women were apparently unable to read. Girls were admitted to Dames' schools and, occasionally, to New England town schools at irregular hours. The Dutch and Quakers admitted them to elementary schools. The first permanent girls' school in the colonies was established by the Moravians in Germantown, Pennsylvania, in 1742. Moral and religious training, reading and writing were the subjects of instruction in all of these schools. After 1700, wealthier girls went to private masters for an education chiefly in the "accomplishments"—music, dancing, French, etc. These private schools prepared the way for the "female seminaries" of the early national period.

(g) Colonial private schools. In commercial centers, the private master appeared, to meet needs which town and church schools were not satisfying. There were private masters in New Netherland in 1649, and the Dames' schools were usually private. After 1700, numerous private masters began to cater to business and other secular needs. These adventurers had a keen sense of the needs of the educational market. Philadelphia, New York and Boston were profitable fields for them. Virginia saw few of them because it had no large towns. The middle class in the cities turned to them for the useful, and sometimes ornamental, education which they desired. The chief subjects which they taught were in the areas of mathematics, bookkeeping, penmanship, science and technology, in which they anticipated the demands of Franklin when he planned the Academy of Philadelphia. The list of their offerings included many modern languages, Latin, Greek, Hebrew, English, history, logic, philosophy, antiquities, dancing, fencing, music, etc. The private

[44] Woody, *A History of Women's Education in the United States* (2 vols.; Lancaster, Pa.: Science Press, Inc., 1929), I, 1–123.

master pioneered in coeducation and physical education. While our night schools seem to have originated with the Dutch,[45] the private master made them a frequent practice. Many of them were competent teachers and some were impostors.[46]

(h) The colonial teacher. With the private teacher, who was chiefly a businessman, we are not concerned here, but only with the teacher who was the officially approved servant of church or state. Following the Roman and mediaeval tradition, the colonial teacher was formally licensed, or otherwise approved, by church, state, or his employers. Religious and moral orthodoxy were his most important qualifications. New England town teachers had to be approved by ministers and, after 1712, by the selectmen of the towns. The Provincial Council of Philadelphia (1685) and the Governors of New York (1664-1686) and of New Jersey (1760) required teachers to get licenses from them. The Bishop of London, however, usually granted the licenses in Anglican colonies, but the dissenting churches did not recognize his authority, and had their own requirements for teachers. The S.P.G., generally, acted as an agent of the Bishop of London in selecting teachers for Anglican schools, and the laws of the South usually required that teachers be members of the Anglican church. Georgia required prospective teachers to take an oath of loyalty to church and state.

Usually, colonial elementary teachers were required to be able to read and write, maintain discipline and mend quill pens. Few of them had more than an elementary education. Secondary school teachers were usually well educated and often college graduates. College teachers were college graduates and often ministers. Many colonial teachers were immigrants. Although women sometimes taught children from New England to South Carolina, teaching was a male profession. Apart from apprenticeship training of some teachers, a plan not unusual with the Quakers, formal training was unknown. Franklin in his plan for the Philadelphia Academy would have it train "a number of the poorer sort" to teach English grammar and the 3R's, in order to protect children from the evil influence of vicious teachers, but he did not propose any special pedagogical training for them. Generally, colonial teachers were poorly respected and poorly paid. A very rare one earned great respect and a moderate reward. They died, almost universally, "unwept, unhonored and unsung."

[45] Kilpatrick, *op. cit.*, pp. 190–91.

[46] R. F. Seybolt, *Source Studies in American Colonial Education. The Private School* (Urbana, Ill.: University of Illinois Press, 1925); Mulhern: *A History of Secondary Education in Pennsylvania*, pp. 96 ff.

Laying the Foundations of State Education

The early national period, 1776-1860, especially the part ending about 1830, was marked by a groping for an education adapted to the economic, political and social needs of the republic in which, with the gradual acceptance of universal male suffrage, the common people eventually came to have a voice. The Revolutionary ideas of 1776 that all men are created equally free and independent and have certain natural, inalienable rights called for a social revolution which did not come immediately. It was the social conservatives who built the young republic, drafted state constitutions, and wrote the first state educational laws. The Revolution welded the colonies into a nation struggling to achieve the ideal of unity in diversity, an ideal which the present struggle for integrated schools in the South shows has not yet been fully realized. Following the Revolution, emphasis was placed by prominent statesmen and educators upon the idea that the welfare of the republic depends upon the enlightenment of the people, and that the nation owes it to itself to educate its youth. The political and educational views of French liberals who demanded national and lay education were well known to our leading statesmen and educators. A slow revolution in education followed the political revolution, but practice did not keep pace with theory in the process.[47]

EARLY NATIONAL THEORISTS. Franklin, one of the Revolutionary fathers, and our first theorist, had been laying the basis of American educational thought from the 1720s onward. His thinking reflected his own experiences as well as the realistic thought of a host of progressive European theorists. While he entertained humane sentiments for common people and opposed slavery, his outlook was that of the middle class, whose interests he would serve by a utilitarian education, as we have seen in Chapter 8. For him education should serve to create wealth and cater to realistic, national and class interests. The English School of the Philadelphia Academy, with its stress upon the mother tongue, and the attention given to mathematics and the sciences in the curriculum of the Academy reveal the outlook of Franklin. For the poor he accepted the practice of charity education, a charity school being connected with the Academy. He sought to Americanize the Germans of Pennsylvania through a scheme of charity schools. He was himself a poor boy who rose to

[47] F. de la Fontainerie, *French Liberalism and Education in the Eighteenth Century* (New York: McGraw-Hill Book Co., Inc., 1932); A. O. Hansen, *Liberalism and American Education in the Eighteenth Century* (New York: The Macmillan Co., 1926); V. L. Parrington, *Main Currents in American Thought* (2 vols.; New York: Harcourt, Brace & Co., Inc., 1927–30), Vol. II.

wealth through self-education, and he remained an advocate of self-education for poor and rich alike.

With all of his class prejudices, he was more respectful of the laboring class and more solicitous for their welfare, linked, as he saw it, to the general welfare, than were most of his contemporaries. He viewed morality and moral training as the indispensable foundation of a good society. For religious dogmas, as such, as for all dogmas, he showed little respect. The members of the Junto, an adult education club which he founded in 1727, pledged themselves to pursue truth, and to love all men and harm no one. For him, Jesus was the greatest of moral teachers. While he counted many good ministers among his friends, he was anticlerical, and subjected the dogmas of clerics to the test of reason. He was the most influential early herald of secular humanism, rationalism and science to America, where, in spite of his conservatism, he did much to create the conception of values which have become a part of our cultural heritage. Others, following the Revolution, built upon the foundation which he had laid.[48]

Following the Revolution, a succession of theorists proposed plans of education for the new republic. The American Philosophical Society, an outgrowth of Franklin's Junto, stimulated interest by giving prizes for the best essays on the subject.[49] While the proposals differed from one another in certain details, they all recognized the need for a scheme of education serving the state and the nation, the idea of compulsory education being implied or, at times, expressed in them. They viewed education as a function of the state, and some would give it a national basis. The ideal of equality of educational opportunity found expression in some of these proposals. And the principle of utility, broadly conceived, permeated the thought of the theorists. The idea of support by taxation was stressed by some of the writers, although the view generally prevailed that only elementary education should be free. Talented students should, however, be educated in secondary schools and colleges at public cost, or by a system of scholarships. While they expressed concern for the needs of the individual, and saw American republican greatness dependent upon individual leadership, the welfare of the state and the success of the political experiment seem to have been foremost in their thought. Among the proposals, that

[48] Woody, *Educational Views of Benjamin Franklin* (New York: McGraw-Hill Book Co., Inc., 1931); Woody, "Benjamin Franklin in Modern Life and Education," *School and Society,* 84:102–7; Mulhern, *A History of Secondary Education in Pennsylvania,* pp. 175 ff.

[49] Hansen, *op. cit.*

of Jefferson for Virginia deserves special mention because of the prestige which he enjoyed in the new nation.

While framer of the Declaration of Independence, with the emphasis upon equality, Jefferson showed himself more concerned with the education of leaders than of the masses. He would cultivate an aristocracy of talent to guide the nation. While he accepted, no doubt, as did most of his contemporaries, the idea of the inevitability of progress, an intellectual elite was seen by him as the instrument of that progress. His views appear in *A Bill for the More General Diffusion of Knowledge* which, as governor, he presented to the legislature of Virginia, in 1779, as a plan for a state-controlled system of education. Briefly, he would establish (1) tax-supported elementary schools of the 3R's for white boys and girls in which instruction would be free for three years, and (2) twenty state secondary schools for white males in which a few talented poor boys from the elementary schools would be taught gratis, at public expense, for varying periods up to a maximum of six years. At the end of a six-year course, the ten most promising of these scholarship students would be educated by the state in William and Mary College. The bill was rejected by a conservative legislature not yet ready to accept a scheme of universal education.

While undemocratic, Jefferson's was the most nearly democratic proposal of a statesman in the early republican years. It should be noted that girls were not accorded equal opportunities with boys, that Negroes were entirely ignored, and that compulsory attendance was not proposed, perhaps because of Jefferson's respect for individualism. Under it, the poor as a class could not rise to power in the nation, and the rich, even untalented ones, could maintain their ascendancy through education. Perhaps the most significantly democratic aspect of the plan was that it would remove the stigma of pauperism and charity from elementary education. Here he was far ahead of Franklin. As regards studies, free elementary instruction would be restricted to the 3R's; and Latin, Greek, English grammar, geography and mathematics would constitute the core of secondary education. The whole plan stressed literary training and, in this, it departed from the utilitarianism of Franklin. But it should be recalled that, traditionally, it was literary education which fostered class distinctions, and Jefferson was, no doubt, aware of that, and would see that the poor were not excluded from it. While he maintained his faith in the ideal of elementary education, his last educational effort was directed to the establishment of the University of Virginia as a nursery of an intellectual elite. The chief cause of the failure of his plan of free elementary education was, no doubt, the opposition of the rich to paying taxes for the education of the poor.[50]

FEDERAL VERSUS STATE EDUCATION. The new nation was confronted by many problems rooted in sectional and state interests, an inheritance from colonial life. It was not easy to achieve the ideal of *E pluribus unum,* as the Civil War and present-day sectional conflicts reveal. Many early nationalists stood for a national system of education, federally administered, and uniquely American in purpose and institutional forms. The idea of a national university was expressed in the Constitutional Convention, and Washington favored it, but Congress, in 1816, defeated a bill to create it. Jefferson's plan was inspired by loyalty to the Old Dominion rather than by national patriotism. The spirit of nationalism long remained weak due to surviving colonial prejudices. The Founding Fathers who drafted the Constitution were, generally, unacquainted with state education. That document does not mention education, and its silence has been interpreted, perhaps not correctly, to mean that the Fathers intended it to be a function of state governments. Yet, the federal government showed an immediate interest in it.

The Land Ordinance of 1785, dealing with the national territory between the Alleghenies and the Mississippi, provided that lot No. 16 of every township in that area be reserved "for the maintenance of public schools." And the Northwest Ordinance of 1787, which incorporated the Northwest Territory, reads: "Religion, morality and knowledge being necessary to good government and the happiness of mankind, schools and the means of education shall forever be encouraged." By later acts of Congress, most states west of the Mississippi received from two to four township sections for township schools and grants of two townships for university purposes. The land granted by the federal government to public schools is greater in area than Italy and twenty-five times the area of Connecticut.[51] The revenues derived from these lands by the states have played a most important part in building our public school system. Since 1862, when the First Morrill Act was passed, the federal government has been increasingly lavish in grants for agricultural and technical education, and for research.

STATE CONSTITUTIONS AND EARLY LAWS. Only seven state constitutions prior to 1800 mentioned education. Those of Pennsylvania (1776 and 1790), North Carolina (1776), Vermont (1777), Massachusetts (1780), and New Hampshire (1784) reflect the conflicts

[50] For other plans, see *ibid.*

[51] U.S. Department of the Interior, *School Lands,* Information Bulletin No. 1, 1939 Series (Washington, D.C.: Government Printing Office).

and official mind of the time. The Pennsylvania Constitution of 1776, similar to those of North Carolina and Vermont, called for the establishment of a school or schools in each county "with such salaries to the masters, paid by the public, as may enable them to instruct youth at low prices." The 1790 Constitution of Pennsylvania, adopted after heated debate, called for the establishment of schools throughout the state "in such manner that the poor may be taught gratis," and for the creation of one or more universities. The Constitutions of New Hampshire and Massachusetts stressed the necessity of "wisdom and knowledge" for the preservation of the people's rights and liberties, and the duty of legislatures and local officials to provide for the instruction of all the people. After 1800, the constitutions of new states gave expression to purposes and ideals similar to those of New Hampshire and Massachusetts, that of Indiana (1816), which called for a state system of education from township elementary schools to a state university in which instruction should be free to all students, being the most liberal of all the statements.[52]

Early fervor for educational reform expressed itself but slowly in law and in the creation of schools for the masses. The colonial pauper school idea proved to be tenacious. Plans of state administration of education were adopted in New York (1784), Connecticut (1810), Virginia (1815), and in Michigan (1817 and 1837). Georgia and Louisiana also made attempts, as did New York, to create a state university as an administrative device, but only New York made notable progress in administration. The problem of support of state systems was a major one. State school funds derived from a variety of sources became a general practice, and were used to supplement local school revenues. Parts of these funds were used to educate the poor, and parts went to support academies, practice varying from state to state. Progress in building a free universal school system in the old and new states was slow, and the issue became one of class and sectional conflict.

PROBLEMS AND STRUGGLE IN THE YOUNG NATION. There was a general conviction that America should be a culturally independent nation, and build its institutions in new ways. Art, literature, science and education should give expression to distinctly American ideals. Yet internal conflicts long thwarted the attainment of these ideals. Universal male suffrage came slowly; the enfranchisement of women came but yesterday; and the slavery issue almost wrecked the American dream. The privileged classes, landed and industrial, feared the common people, and some of them opposed efforts to educate

[52] Cubberley, *op. cit.*, pp. 419–25.

them at the expense of property owners. Industrialism gave rise to capitalist-labor strife, and created new problems by attracting millions of immigrants and native farmer folk into our growing cities. The interests of the industrial North clashed with those of the agrarian South, and the expanding West thought it had a destiny all its own, and should shape its life and education in its own way. Southern opposition to Northern educational and political influence, to the practice of sending Southern boys to Northern schools, and to the use of Northern textbooks in the South became increasingly marked from 1820 onward. Enthusiasm for public schools did not exist in the South because of slavery and a rigid class system. Western thought, generally, favored democratic, universal education, utilitarian in character and free from the stigma of pauperism and the conservative social and educational traditions of the older sections. The economic struggle on the frontier, coupled with the tradition in the sections from which the frontiersmen came, sometimes resulted in opposition to school "larnin" and to free schools. Western migration threatened the economic stability of the East and South through depopulation, and aroused fears of the triumph of ignorance, barbarism, anarchy and religious infidelity in the West. Easterners poured money into the West for the support of schools and churches to save religion and the republic.

To aggravate the problems, European immigrants who knew little about their adopted country came to settle in factory centers. Many of them were Catholics; and anti-Catholic mobs at times disturbed the land, as did anti-abolition ones. The republic was not safe. What happened to the French republic at the hands of Napoleon, many feared might well happen here. The story of the educational aspects of the national struggle can be told only in brief outline here, but it constitutes a most important chapter in the history of American civilization, now attracting the special attention of the Ford Foundation and of American historians.[53]

While sectional and class prejudices were reflected in the educational thought and practices of our early national period, many leading educators made the national interest their guiding light. Educators, such as George B. Emerson, joint author with Alonzo Potter of a pedagogical treatise, *School and Schoolmaster* (1842), William C. Woodbridge, editor of one of our first educational journals (1830), *American Annals of Education and Instruction,* Horace Mann, "father of common schools," and a host of others stressed the view that only education could save the nation and that its pro-

[53] P. H. Buck *et al., The Role of Education in American History* (New York: The Fund for the Advancement of Education, 1957).

vision was a primary public obligation. Some of these educators, as did Jefferson, saw intellectual education as the prime essential of national survival, while others would stress moral education as the basis of national welfare. Noah Webster, in the cause of national patriotism, pleaded for a simplified American English, and, through his textbooks, attempted to standardize the national tongue and inspire respect for American government.

Pedagogical thought in the period was concerned largely with the mode of inculcating patriotism and developing in youth a deep sense of morality. Selfishness, political corruption, anarchy and all such threats to the national welfare could be thwarted, it was believed by many, by sound moral instruction and by developing in youth patriotic devotion to the Constitution and the blessings of republican government. These ideals, widely proclaimed in textbooks and pedagogical literature, embodied a faith in the power of education to mould human nature in predetermined ways. Phrenology, a theory of psychology and ethics, which came to be widely accepted in the 1830s, and to which Horace Mann subscribed, emphasized individual differences in mental ability and moral capacity. Evil moral tendencies could be weakened and good ones strengthened by education. The phrenologists stressed the importance of health and character education as a cure for individual and social ills. Mann, as did others in his day, came to have great faith in the use of written examinations to measure exactly pupils' knowledge and the efficiency of teaching, and he strongly recommended this practice which, in America, seems to have originated in Boston in 1845. Many of his arguments for written examinations are the same as those advanced in our own day for the use of objective tests.[54] From 1805, Pestalozzianism attracted American educators and kept challenging the old methods of teaching. Mann, Henry Barnard, and reformers, generally, advocated Pestalozzian reforms. The problems of the new nation thus focused attention upon education and school reform in the interest of the nation.

BEGINNINGS OF PUBLIC OR COMMON SCHOOLS. The Massachusetts law of 1789, which legalized the district system and destroyed the administrative authority of the town, or larger unit, was a backward step. A law of 1827 made the district system mandatory. Many districts were too poor to support schools and, in them, the school committee was too often composed of men of little ability. The public school being thus weakened, many parents sent their children to private schools. A similar development occurred in Con-

[54] E. W. Knight and C. L. Hall, *Readings in American Educational History* (New York: Appleton-Century-Crofts, Inc., 1951), pp. 499–503.

necticut, where the district system became general in 1798. Here, in 1795, money received for Western lands was substituted entirely for state school taxes between 1821 and 1854, and district levies were put on a voluntary basis. As a result the once free schools became fee schools and the poor remained away from them. In the rest of New England the development was similar to that in Massachusetts and Connecticut.

In New York, where there were no public schools at the time of the Revolution, the University of the State of New York, an administrative device, was organized in 1784, and, subsequently, the state aided the counties in supporting common schools. In 1812, the legal basis of a permanent system was laid, and the office of state superintendent (the first such in America) was created. The county, the town, and the district were assigned administrative functions under this law. Notable progress was made in building the system until the state superintendency was abolished in 1820, but the schools were free only to the very poor.

The Pennsylvania Constitution of 1790 required the legislature to provide such facilities "that the poor may be taught gratis." As a result, until 1834, and with the exception, for a part of the time, of Philadelphia and Lancaster, public lists of poor children were published, and provision was made for them as "paupers" in private and church schools.

In New Jersey and Delaware, the pauper-school practice was adopted. Opposition to free schools in these states and in Pennsylvania was rooted mainly in the tradition that education was an affair of the family and the church, and in the opposition of property owners to taxation in aid of other men's children.

In the South, such public school laws as that of Virginia (1797), of South Carolina (1811), and of North Carolina (1825) were abortive attempts to establish free state schools, and little was accomplished beyond the establishment of state school funds, the income from which was used to assist the poor. Maryland pursued a similar policy. In Georgia, until 1817, all state monies were assigned to colleges and academies. In that year a very limited provision was made for aid to free elementary schools. Throughout the South, free education was generally conceived not as a public service but as a charity, although men like Jefferson and Archibald D. Murphey of North Carolina were strong advocates of the public-service principle.

In the Western states the desire to democratize education and to remove the mark of caste from the school in the interest of democratic citizenship was strong among many of the pioneers who settled there. Liberal land grants from the national government made it easier to realize their desires. Most of the state constitutions in both the Northwest and Southwest territories made provision for some scheme of public education. The first schools established were, however, proprietary, or of the academy type. Pioneer conditions and intense individualism retarded the establishment of free state schools, and the early laws indicate chiefly a striving to escape from educational burdens by finding the most profitable way to use the school lands. The district system of administration came to be generally adopted in the new territory, and the support of schools was left to small localities. Prior to 1830, little was actually accomplished in the new West except the incorporation and encouragement of many academies and the laying of the beginnings of a legal basis of state school systems.

HUMANITARIAN AND SOCIAL-REFORM EFFORTS. Between the Revolution and 1830, the masses were no better provided for than they were in colonial times. The apprenticeship system declined.[55] Class prejudices in education remained strong, and free education continued to bear the stigma of pauperism. Legislatures showed little concern for the needs of the masses. Private and church schools were often the only ones available, and illiteracy remained high even in the Eastern states.[56] To offset the effects of official neglect, philanthropists and educational reformers stepped into the gap. Infant schools, monitorial schools, and secular Sunday schools were organized to enlarge the educational opportunities of the poor. The lyceum movement, organized (1828) by Josiah Holbrook, and our first major adult-education plan, designed to spread useful knowledge and improve common schools, spread throughout the country between 1820 and 1860.[57] The monitorial system, introduced by Joseph Lancaster in 1818, in which instruction was in the hands of older pupils, thus reducing the cost of education, appealed strongly to statesmen and educators, and became a widespread practice in all sections of the land. It was introduced even into some secondary schools, such as the high school established by the New York High School Society in 1824, the Franklin High School of the Franklin Institute in Philadelphia in 1826, and into some academies.[58] With the growth of tax-supported, public schools from

[55] P. H. Douglas, *American Apprenticeship and Industrial Education* (New York: Columbia University Press, 1921), p. 54.

[56] F. C. Carlton, *Economic Influences upon Educational Progress in the United States, 1820–1850* (Madison: University of Wisconsin, Bulletin No. 221, 1908), p. 98.

[57] C. Bode, *The American Lyceum* (New York: Oxford University Press, 1956).

[58] *Report of a Committee Appointed by the High School Society of New York* (New York: J. Seymour, 1824); Knight and Hall, *op. cit.*, pp. 135–38; Mulhern, *A History of Secondary Education in Pennsylvania*, p. 458.

1830 onward, the Lancasterian plan was abandoned. Lancaster often defended it as a teacher-training device, but it was its economical aspect that appealed to most of those who advocated and used it.

The stigma of charity and class education clung to infant, monitorial and secular Sunday schools. Some looked to manual-labor schools, popularized by Fellenberg, a disciple of Pestalozzi, to reduce the cost of education and thus make it accessible to the poor. The idea of manual-labor schools was not new in America. Thomas Budd, a New Jersey Quaker, proposed such a plan in 1685,[59] and a similar plan was proposed in South Carolina, in 1787, which led to the establishment of what is thought to have been the first manual-labor school in the United States.[60] Organized labor and agricultural communities saw in the plan a means of equalizing educational opportunity and, at the same time, of providing youth with healthy, practical educational experiences.[61] Such self-supporting schools, in which students would meet their expenses by their own labor, appealed strongly to educational reformers between 1820 and 1840. The idea of manual-labor education did not, however, appeal to the rich; and for the masses, the rise of tax-supported schools made such a scheme unnecessary. The plan, however, in modified form survives in a few institutions, in pay-it-yourself schemes for students, and in agricultural and mechanical training.

Among the most significant philanthropic efforts to educate the masses were those of the "free" or "public" school societies which were organized in many of the larger cities, and which will be referred to later. Perhaps the most significant individual act of benevolence was the rich endowment, in 1830, by Stephen Girard of a school in Philadelphia, Girard College, for "poor male white orphans." This school, with an endowment of about $85,000,000, became involved in an integration dispute, but the United States Supreme Court has upheld (October, 1958) the Girard will.

Development of Universal Mass Education

The middle decades of the century were marked by a great increase in industry and wealth, greatly improved means of transportation and communication, a rapid growth of cities, and the influx of foreigners in increasing numbers. In 1860, over four million of our population were of foreign birth. Our slave population increased from about 700,000 in 1790, to nearly 4,000,000 in 1860.

59 Mulhern, *A History of Secondary Education in Pennsylvania,* p. 461.
60 Knight and Hall, *op. cit.,* pp. 196–200.
61 Mulhern, *A History of Secondary Education in Pennsylvania,* pp. 450–59.

By the close of the period male suffrage had become almost a universal practice, property qualifications for citizenship being abolished. The period ended with the abolition of slavery. Generally, it was a period of very significant and rapid economic, social and political change, when, at least in broad outline, there was moulded the form of America's destiny until the present day. Education felt the impact of all these changes. With the exception of New England and, to a degree, of New York, where it was one of "revival" of public schools, the period was one of origin of our state school systems.

Among the many influential forces operating to produce our public school system in this period were: (1) the organized labor movement and the growing consciousness among all workers of the social implications of democracy,[62] (2) foreign influence, and (3) the activities of our own social and educational reformers. Organized labor, sensing its political power and adopting the Baconian philosophy that "knowledge is power," demanded that the children of workers be admitted to all the educational advantages traditionally enjoyed by the rich. To this end labor demanded state systems of public schools in which rich and poor should meet on a basis of equality. While labor was urging its demands, American educators were studying European educational developments and publishing reports on happenings abroad, particularly in Prussia and France. John Griscom, William C. Woodbridge, Calvin Stowe, Horace Mann, and Henry Barnard were among the many who returned from Europe with important educational messages for America. The report of the French educational reformer, Victor Cousin, on public instruction in Germany (1831) was reprinted by the legislatures of Massachusetts, New York, and New Jersey, and had much influence in other states.[63] All of these reports strengthened the conviction that our states ought to provide good schools for the masses; that the curriculum ought to be enriched; that improved methods of teaching ought to be adopted; and that the children of the nation have a right to the services of teachers specially trained for their work and adequately compensated. The message of reform was published also in educational magazines which appeared from 1825 onward.

Of our numerous educational leaders of the highest rank we can mention only two here, Horace Mann and Henry Barnard, both

[62] R. V. Curoe, *Educational Attitudes and Policies of Organized Labor in the United States* (New York: Teachers College, Columbia University, 1926); Mulhern, *A History of Secondary Education in Pennsylvania,* pp. 447–50.

[63] Knight, *Reports on European Education* (New York: McGraw-Hill Book Cc., Inc., 1930).

of whom rose to national prominence. Reforms had already begun before they attained leadership from the late thirties onward. Mann, as first secretary of the Massachusetts Board of Education (1837-1848), found many of the existing school laws neglected, the public largely unconcerned about education, the amount of schooling available entirely inadequate, thousands of children growing up illiterate, teachers untrained, and the quality of instruction of a very low order. He worked indefatigably to enlighten the public regarding the importance of education and the need for reform. He went through the state, year after year, preaching the gospel of better schools. In his annual reports, his *Common School Journal*, and other publications, he continued that program of enlightenment until his message spread throughout the nation and far beyond it. His views on the reform of methods of teaching and school discipline led him into a bitter controversy with Boston schoolmasters who favored the old authoritarian practices. As a result, the reforms he proposed rose in popular favor. He was drawn, however, into a religious controversy more replete with dangers for public education. He and a majority of the State Board of Education were Unitarians and were, therefore, suspected by conservative theologians of favoring secular schools.

While property owners, opposed to taxation, were the chief obstacle to the establishment of free schools for everyone, many church leaders, fearing secular schools, stood in the first ranks of the opposition forces. Many Protestant churchmen objected to nonsectarian religious instruction on the ground that such is nonreligious, and Catholics considered it but Protestant trickery. Mann favored nonsectarian religious instruction but opposed all denominational propaganda in public schools. The Protestant churchmen asked that each school district be left free to decide the issue for itself. To that demand, Mann made a famous reply, easily accessible to students, which has contributed much to the clarity of thinking on the whole issue ever since.[64] The debate on the question throughout America brought the general acceptance of the principle that free public education in our democratic society must be secular in character, and that the family, church, or some other agency must assume responsibility for religious education. Some states and communities are now departing somewhat from that time-honored principle by providing, on public school time, for sectarian religious instruction of public school students in local churches, and by giving school credit for such instruction.

[64] R. B. Culver, *Horace Mann and Religion in the Massachusetts Public Schools* (New Haven: Yale University Press, 1929).

Our first public schools, influenced by denominational traditions, were not free from sectarianism of a Protestant flavor, offensive to Catholics, Jews, agnostics and others. The Catholics, who would make their religion central in education, adopted the practice of separatism, as have some Jews and many Protestant churches in recent decades. Synagogue schools and Protestant parochial schools have been increasing in number, but the Catholic is the most significant separatist movement. Federal aid to public schools and the reading of the Bible in them, as well as other issues related to sectarianism, have become involved in the controversy over the relation of church and state and its implications for education. There has been a growing concern for religious education, which has resulted in efforts to give the public schools a religious orientation. The Supreme Court has interpreted the Fourteenth Amendment to the Constitution to mean the erection, in Jefferson's words, of a "wall of separation between church and state" and the prohibition of state support to any or all religions. Some, particularly Catholic spokesmen, declare that this interpretation is erroneous and that, while the First Amendment prohibits the establishment of a state church, it does not mean that religion should be excluded from education, or aided by the state. This argument has been made the defense of Bible reading in public schools, of religious instruction on released time, and of the demand for tax aid to parochial schools. In some states Catholic pupils are provided with free textbooks and bus transportation. Besides, exemption of church school property from taxation—a privilege enjoyed by most schools—is a form of state subsidy. The issue of religious education has taken on some new aspects since the days of Horace Mann.[65] The view, however, has been frequently expressed that the non-public school, whatever its character, is a divisive force in the nation. The whole question has, indeed, become one of heated debate.[66]

In Connecticut, Henry Barnard, as secretary of the State Board of Education, was, with a brief intermission, the successful missionary of public education. From 1838 onward he became, like Mann, a national figure, and upon him was conferred the honor of being made first United States Commissioner of Education. In 1855 he began to publish the *American Journal of Education,* and remained its editor for thirty-one years. It was truly a national

[65] R. F. Butts, *The American Tradition in Religion and Education* (Boston: Beacon Press, Inc., 1950); J. M. O'Neill, *Religion and Education under the Constitution* (New York: Harper & Bros., 1949); P. Blanshard, *American Freedom and Catholic Power* (Boston: Beacon Press, Inc., 1949).

[66] V. T. Thayer, *The Attack upon the American Secular School* (Boston: Beacon Press, Inc., 1951).

journal. It carried information about educational developments in every state and in foreign countries. It remains today one of the priceless records of our educational past. The scholarly character of his publications, and his indefatigable labor in the cause of public education earned for Barnard the universal respect of his contemporaries. In shaping the character of our state school systems no other individual has been more influential than he.

DEVELOPMENTS IN NEW ENGLAND. Here the most important developments were: (a) the establishment in each state, between 1838 and 1846, of a state board of education as a central education authority; (b) the establishment of state normal schools, the first being created by Massachusetts in 1839; and (c) the laying of the basis of free schools by the adoption of public taxation for their support, the Massachusetts law of 1827 setting a pattern for the other states.

DEVELOPMENTS IN THE MIDDLE STATES. In New York, the office of state superintendent of schools, created in 1812 and abolished in 1820, was re-established in 1854. In 1812, local taxation for schools, previously permissive, was made compulsory. While the state added annual grants to local school funds, the money available from these sources was inadequate, and it was not until 1867 that the schools were made free through increased taxation. In educational administration, important steps were taken between 1841 and 1862 in establishing the offices of county and town superintendents and of town supervisors. These local authorities worked actively to improve the schools in their areas. State interest in teacher training appeared in 1833, when a grant was made to some academies in support of a teachers' training course. In 1837, city school systems, under local boards, were authorized by law. In 1844, the first state normal school was established at Albany. The important Union School Act of 1853 authorized adjacent districts to create a board of education. These union boards were given the power to take over academies and to establish public high schools.

In Pennsylvania, districts were permitted by the law of 1834 to establish free public schools. In 1849, that permission was made a requirement. Yet, it was not until 1886 that all districts complied with the law. Until 1857, the Secretary of State was the state superinendent of schools, but in that year a separate office of superintendent was established. In 1854, the county superintendency was authorized by law, and the township, rather than the district, was made the administrative unit. In the same year, local school boards were given power to establish schools of different grades, thus clearing the way for more efficient organization and for the establishment of high schools. Developments in the other middle states were similar to that of Pennsylvania.

DEVELOPMENTS IN VIRGINIA AND THE SOUTH. In 1829, the legislature of Virginia authorized districts to establish public schools to be supported in part by public taxation. The charity school plan of educating the poor was, however, strongly entrenched here, and only a few districts used the power given them by the law of 1829. Slavery, an aristocratic social tradition, and strong opposition to the centralization of governmental power were among the chief forces retarding the establishment of a state system of public schools. The law of 1846, however, permitted counties to vote on the question of a system of tax-supported schools if one-third of the electorate so wished. Before the Civil War, the principle of public education had been adopted in nearly one-fourth of the state, but only a few districts had resorted to taxation for the support of schools, with the result that the education of the poor remained in the realm of charities.

North Carolina passed a permissive free school law in 1839, which provided for an allotment of $60 to each district, one-third of which was to be raised by county taxes, and two-thirds to be provided by the state. The free schools thus established were popularly branded as pauper schools, and were opposed by influential and conservative social groups. In 1853, the state superintendency was created, and Caleb H. Wiley held the office until 1865. His achievements were similar to those of Horace Mann in Massachusetts, but the reforms he introduced suffered a decline after the Civil War.

Elsewhere in the South, though progress was slower, developments were similar to those described. Free school laws were usually rendered ineffective by the lack of that strong middle class which, outside of the South, was the most influential force on the side of free public schools.

DEVELOPMENTS IN THE MIDDLE WEST. Though the pioneers on the moving frontier carried the traditions of their old environments with them, some of which were antagonistic to free public schools, conditions on the frontier were hostile to old social prejudices, and demanded pioneering in the social as in the economic sphere. Our democracy is, in a significant degree, a child of the frontier. In Ohio, where New England tradition was strong, the state superintendency of schools was created in 1837, and a public tax-supported school system was established in 1838. Yet there was opposition to centralization of control, and there came some retreats from this early advanced position. In 1853, public school tuition fees were abolished legally but, often, not in practice.

In Indiana and Illinois the struggle for free schools was largely one between the settlers in the southern sections, who came mostly from below the Ohio River, and those in the northern sections, who came usually from New York and New England. Those from the South thought of public education as a charity; those from the East thought of it as a public service and a right of all children. And the settlers from the East, in revolt against privilege in education, eventually won in their struggle for democracy in education. The first Constitution of Indiana (1816) required the legislature to establish a state system of free schools ascending from the first grade up to, and including, a state university. Township schools were permitted by a law of 1816, but, proper provision for their support by local taxation being rigorously opposed, the schools did not become free until 1869, when the legislature passed a law, approved as constitutional by the courts, which permitted local taxation. Educational control was completely decentralized by the substitution of the district for the township system in 1833, and by permitting, in 1836, a family to employ its own teacher and receive a share of state funds. In Illinois, the influence of settlers from the South had results similar to those of Indiana. Here a law was passed in 1827 which provided that no citizen should be taxed for schools unless he had given his written consent. In both of these states private schools and academies flourished until public sentiment in favor of common schools had been fully aroused by leaders such as Caleb Mills, in Indiana, and Ninian W. Edwards, in Illinois.

In Michigan, where French, German, and New England influences were at work, the Territorial Legislature authorized, in 1817, the establishment of the University of Michigania to provide higher education and to control all education in the state, as had been done in New York and Georgia, in 1784. The law remained inoperative. In 1827, a township common school system to be supported by taxation was adopted, but the taxation plan was soon replaced by a tuition or rate system. In 1837, an effective law was passed which created a state superintendency and local school authorities, and provided for the support of schools by state and local taxes plus tuition. The present University of Michigan was founded in the same year. After 1850, free schools became a reality.

Public Schools Become Free

Following the Revolution, there spread generally the belief that universal education was essential to our democracy, but it took nearly three-quarters of a century to secure popular approval of taxation for schools, without which universal education is unattainable. In the meantime resort was had to various other schemes of support. Chief among these was that of charity or pauper education, generally adopted in the middle and southern states, Pennsylvania furnishing a good example of the practice. Here, the Constitution of 1790 called for the education of the poor gratis, and the laws of 1802 and 1804 gave effect to that provision by requiring all teachers of reading and writing to instruct all poor children sent them by overseers of the poor. The cost should be defrayed out of poor relief funds. The amount of free schooling was limited by state or local regulations usually to three or four years. Private and church schools thus profited at the expense of the feelings of the poor, whose poverty was made a public matter. While the rich did not want their children to sit beside paupers, the paupers were even more uncomfortable, and many of them preferred illiteracy to public scorn. Out of 350,000 children of school age in Pennsylvania in 1829, less than 10,000 were being educated as charity pupils, and apparently about one-half of them were not attending any school. Here, as elsewhere, the system was a failure.

Another method of reaching the poor appears in the work of "Public School" societies, supported by philanthropists, and conducting schools free to the poor and with low tuition rates for others. There were twelve of these in Philadelphia in 1830. The work of such societies appears at its best in that of the New York Public School Society, founded in 1805, and known as the Free School Society until 1826. Its first school was opened in 1806 on the Lancasterian monitorial plan. The city and state made grants in aid of its work. The Society established a system of graded free schools open to all classes. The churches, particularly the Catholic, attacked the Society for alleged sectarianism and protested against the grant of public funds to it. After years of controversy the Society, in 1852, turned over 115 schools and other property to the city Board of Education. While it operated, it educated over 600,000 children and trained over 1,200 teachers.[67]

Lotteries were another device frequently used for the support of schools. Churches, colleges and academies were often author-

[67] W. O. Bourne, *History of the Public School Society of the City of New York* (New York: G. P. Putnam's Sons, Inc., 1873).

ized to raise money in this way. Many states, too, conducted public lotteries, or demanded a share of monies raised in this way by colleges and academies, in order to augment state school funds. When the moral evil of the practice came to be sufficiently sensed, it was soon abandoned.

A plan of school support adopted by every state when taxation was unpopular was that of a state school fund as a form of permanent endowment of education. Land endowment of individual schools or of schools of a town was not unusual in colonial times. In 1726 and again in 1753, Connecticut set aside public land as a basis of a school fund for the whole colony. In 1795, a permanent school fund was created from the proceeds of the sale of her public lands in the Western Reserve. Other states with public land took similar steps. States without public land created a permanent school fund derived from a variety of fees, special taxes, lotteries or, sometimes, direct appropriations. At times, these funds were administered as local funds and, at times, as state funds. Ohio, by law in 1802, permitted each township to administer its sixteenth section given to it for schools. Such local administration proved to be wasteful, and the demand for state administration grew. Yet the states also, in most cases, squandered the public school endowment. It was hoped that the income from such funds, when distributed over the state, would, when supplemented by a small local tax, make tuition fees unnecessary. Where the state used the power of the purse to stimulate local effort, progress toward free education and better schools was hastened. In Connecticut between 1821 and 1854, a free school system was supported by the fund without resort to local taxation.

Lastly, there was legally authorized in New York, New England, and the northwestern states a local tuition tax on every parent who had children at school and could afford to pay. That tax was called the "rate bill." The practice was but a disguise for the charity-school practice of Pennsylvania and the South. In the rate-bill states, the schools were public, and the teacher received a small salary out of public funds which, being inadequate, had to be supplemented by rates levied upon parents. The practice was a survival of that of colonial New England towns. Many districts in the whole rate-bill area did not exempt the poor from the tax, and many parents who could afford to pay kept their children at home to avoid paying it. The result was vicious. Social reformers and educational leaders struggled against the evil, and gradually local taxation was adopted and the schools of the nation became free.

The struggle for the abolition of rate bills was long and bitter, but tax-supported free schools were authorized by law as follows: Massachusetts, 1827; Delaware, 1829; Vermont, 1850; Ohio, 1853; Iowa, 1858; New York, 1867; Rhode Island, 1868; Connecticut, 1868; Michigan, 1869; and New Jersey, 1871. Other states, such as Pennsylvania and Indiana, moved slowly from permissive to compulsory free school laws and enforced them reluctantly when they finally enacted them.

During the period, private schools in thousands existed in every state. Upon them rather than upon public schools the rich bestowed the support and patronage which, since 1870, has rapidly gone to the making of good public schools. Opposition to state interference in education, to taxation, to the principle of equality of educational opportunity and to the secular idea of education had to be overcome before our present system could be firmly established. Reformers, however, gradually convinced the public of the national need for free, universal, public and secular education, of the possibility of its support, and of its greater advantages for society. Growing world nationalism and the changing social scene at home made the adoption of state school systems a national necessity.

Secondary Education

THE ACADEMY. Although the public high school had appeared before 1830, and was actually required in Massachusetts by the law of 1827, the secondary school of the early national period, which remained the strong rival of the high school until after the Civil War, was the academy. In our treatment of humanistic and Protestant influence upon education in colonial America, we saw that our first type of secondary school was the denominational Latin grammar school. That school was required by law in the Puritan colonies of New England, and appeared under private, ecclesiastical, or state-church auspices elsewhere in the colonies. In Massachusetts, the legal requirement, long neglected by many towns, ceased in 1827. All but seven towns were exempted from that obligation in 1824.

Economic, social, political, religious, and intellectual change created gradually, in the eighteenth century, the need for a new secondary institution, and the academy arose to meet that need. Institutions bearing the name "academy," and institutions of the academy type, but bearing other names, appeared at different times and places and in such a variety of forms that generalizations about the institution are dangerous.

MARKS OF THE ACADEMY. The academy, in its more advanced form, was not a denominational school. Many shades of public, nonsectarian, and denominational character came to mark it at various times and places. It was not a town school, nor an exclusively boys' school, nor primarily a college-preparatory school, nor a school catering to the aristocratic few, nor a free school. Many of them, aspiring to national distinction, did not want to be schools of a state but schools of the nation. To state accurately in a few words what the academy was is more difficult than to state what it was not, but the following description of the academy has wide applicability: It was a semi-public, nonsectarian, boarding and (or) day secondary school, which, catering in curriculum and fees to the needs of the rapidly increasing middle class, from its upper to its lower economic stratum, met the educational demands and aspirations of that class in our period of transition from an aristocratic to a common-man republic. While a few schools of the type, notably that founded by Franklin in Philadelphia (1750), appeared prior to the Revolution, it was in the period between the Revolution and the Civil War that it became our dominant secondary school, and spread into every section of the country. While it was a pay school, state and local governments and private donors contributed to its support. States often gave it grants of land and money, and permitted it to raise money in many ways. Most academies were chartered schools governed, generally, by self-perpetuating boards of trustees. Developments in Massachusetts and Pennsylvania typify the academy movement fairly well.

In Massachusetts, Dummer Academy, opened in 1763, was given public recognition by a state charter in 1782. In 1778, the Phillips Academy at Andover was founded and, in 1780, chartered. Twelve others were chartered by the legislature before 1797. In that year the state adopted the policy regarding them that each one should serve an area with a population of between thirty and forty thousand, and land grants should be provided for properly located and endowed academies. By 1830, 68 academies had been chartered and that number had more than doubled by 1860. The annual enrollment in all of them seems not to have risen above 4,000. Some of them, such as Andover, were for boys; others, such as Leicester (1784) were for both sexes; and still others, such as Ipswich Seminary (1825), were for girls only.

In Pennsylvania, the legislature circumvented the spirit of the state constitution by encouraging the establishment of semi-public academies, in most of which provision was made, by meager state grants, for the education of a few poor children gratis. In 1838, a system of annual grants to academies and "female seminaries" chartered by the state was adopted, but that practice was abandoned in 1843. The legislature chartered approximately 70 academies between 1780 and 1830, and a total of 155 prior to 1870. It was reported to the State Superintendent of Schools in 1841 that there were 4,154 students enrolled in academies and seminaries which were receiving aid from the state. In addition to these state-chartered schools, approximately 178 others were chartered by county courts between 1840 and 1909, but these were purely local or sectarian schools which never received state aid. To these there ought to be added the female seminaries of which the state chartered 59 in the period 1829-1879, and the county courts, 26 in the period 1840-1909.[68]

In addition to grants of money, many of the earlier state-chartered academies in Pennsylvania were given grants of land. Some of these state academies were, by legislative plan, county academies, and their trustees were elected by the county electorate, and their accounts audited by the county auditors. With a few exceptions the state-chartered academies were nonsectarian in control and in spirit. With the exception of the Episcopal Academy in Philadelphia, purely denominational academies seldom or never received state grants. Because the state aid was meager, the academies depended for their support upon student fees and private gifts. When public high schools and state normal schools came into competition with them, and the state withdrew its support entirely, they closed one by one. Some of them were sold for debt, others became normal schools and colleges, and a large number were transferred to public school districts and became, in many places, the nuclei of high schools. The merging of older with newer institutions has gone on continually throughout the United States. Many old Latin schools became academies, and these have been often converted into high schools. There has been a significant continuity in our institutional development.

THE ACADEMY CURRICULUM. In keeping with our developing democracy and expanding industrial and commercial life, the academy offered instruction in such a variety of subjects that there were few, if any, whose interests and needs it did not serve. In the variety of its offerings, the academy stands in marked contrast with the Latin grammar school, which catered to an aristocratic few who were preparing themselves for college rather than for life. Yet it frequently stressed the college-preparatory purpose. The academy

[68] Mulhern, *A History of Secondary Education in Pennsylvania,* pp. 252, 416.

prepared students for anything and everything, and was not very systematic in doing so. While organized curricula appeared, students enjoyed much freedom in selecting from the conglomerate mass of offerings the studies they desired. The classical, English, teacher-training, and girls' curricula became common ones. The attention paid to mathematics, science and "the higher English branches" marks its change from the colonial Latin schools. The academy thus tried hard to meet the needs of our emerging democracy, and to give recognition to the new elements that science and economic changes had added to the culture of western nations. It is worthy of note that religious and moral instruction, without sectarian bias, was frequently provided in academies.

POPULARITY OF THE ACADEMY. Catering to a large middle class, the academy attained wide popularity. By 1850, opposition to it had become marked on the grounds (1) that it was socially exclusive and beyond the reach of the poor who could not pay fees, however small; (2) that it created class distinction; and (3) that grants to it came from everybody's pocket, while some could not afford to attend it. The demand for a secondary school, free to all, and supported by public taxes, arose, and the public high school appeared and gradually supplanted it.

THE HIGH SCHOOL. (1) BEGINNINGS. As the movement for free tax-supported elementary schools progressed, the demand for free secondary education grew. The idea of free public secondary education was not new when our first high school, probably that of Boston (1821), was established. Provision for the education of a few poor boys gratis in some colonial secondary schools which received public aid had an element of the high-school idea in it. But the first clear-cut idea of a public high school known to us comes from Portland, Maine, where, in 1795, a town committee recommended the establishment of a public school for the instruction of advanced students in "higher branches," thus providing for poor students opportunities equal to those enjoyed by the rich in academies. The school was not established because of the founding of an academy by the state in the town, which the committee felt could serve their stated purposes.[69]

We have noted the semi-public character of some academies. An occasional one, usually called a "free academy," came to be supported in part by local taxation and was free to local pupils, but it remained under the control of a board of trustees and not of a public school board. These "free academies" first appeared in some

[69] *Portland Town Records,* May 6, 1795.

of our cities in the late eighteen-forties, that of Norwich, Connecticut, probably being the first. Some preferred this type of school to the public high school which had begun to appear. Twenty years before the coming of "free academies," there appeared, first in New York and then in a few other cities, monitorial "high schools," supported mainly by philanthropists, and, while open to all classes, designed to reduce the cost of secondary education and bring it within the reach of some of the poor. Such a school for boys was opened, in 1825, by the New York High School Society, a stock company, and, a few years later, a similar school was opened in Philadelphia in connection with the Franklin Institute. Governor De Witt Clinton of New York urged the legislature to provide for the establishment of such schools throughout the state, but without effect. In the twenties and later, many stock companies were incorporated in the East, and some in the West, to establish "high schools," and some of these companies were assisted by local taxation. Providing instruction in the "higher English branches" and the sciences seems to have been among the leading aims of many organizers of such "high schools."

(2) Public High School in Massachusetts. In 1821, Boston established, as a part of the city system, the English Classical School, but changed its name, in 1824, to the English High School. It was to be for those interested in "mercantile or mechanical" pursuits what the Latin classical school was for those preparing for college. And it was designed to enlarge the free public school offerings so that parents need no longer send their children away from home to academies for instruction preparatory to "active life." It was not to be a college-preparatory school, as was the Boston Latin school of that day. It was organized as a three-year school as against the five-year plan of the Latin school. Advanced English studies, mathematics, pure and applied sciences, and some social studies constituted the first curriculum. It was, for that day, a "modern" curriculum which embodied a semi-vocational motive. As such, it was not new in America. Similar studies, prompted by a similar motive, were taught in many colonial schools and in academies from Franklin's time onward. Indeed, an organized English curriculum had been well developed in many academies before the high school appeared.

The most significant aspect of the Boston high school was that it was under public control and was supported by public taxation. It was, too, a free school. The essential features of the American high school of today were stamped upon it. However, the four-year coeducational high school preparing both for college and for life had a gradual emergence in Massachusetts and elsewhere in the United States. In 1826, Boston established a high school for girls, the popularity of which made it so costly that it was closed in 1828. Other Massachusetts towns soon followed the example of Boston. Worcester, in 1824, established a Female High School; and a high school was opened in Salem, in 1826, and in Lowell, in 1831. Of greatest import, however, was the enactment, in 1827, of the Massachusetts law requiring towns of five hundred families to establish schools of the English high school type, and towns of four thousand inhabitants to provide instruction in Latin, Greek, and other specified subjects. That was the first high school law in America, although it was often ignored until 1859 when its requirements were made more definite by a new law.

(3) THE HIGH SCHOOL MOVEMENT. The rapidity with which the movement spread through other states indicates that there was at work in the changing social scene of America a democratic spirit which created, among other things, the "poor man's college," as the high school was commonly called. In 1838, the Central High School of Philadelphia was opened. In 1839, high schools were established in Baltimore and in Charleston, South Carolina. In 1847, the New York legislature authorized the establishment of high schools in Lockport and New York City. Prior to the Civil War, high schools had appeared as far south as New Orleans (1843) and as far west as San Francisco (1858).

Many of our earliest high schools were planned in advance of their founding, but the typical high school of the American panorama just "grew up" as the top of the expanding "common" school. The way had been prepared for that development by the grading of students for the sake of school efficiency, in place of individual recitation by each student. In the graded system, the pupils were grouped according to their advancement, and each group came to have its own teacher, its own room and, later, its own floor or building. The grading movement was under way in the forties and was completed in rural areas about 1900. In the process of grading, the upper grades were frequently called "the high school grades," although they might have been the fifth and sixth grades in a district. To these, higher grades were later added, these being again called the high school grades. This upward expansion showed a general tendency to terminate with the twelfth grade, the upper four grades becoming our high school. As it evolved, the high school conformed closely with its definition as formulated by Henry

Barnard, in 1839: "A public or common school for the older and more advanced scholars of the community . . . [offering] a course of instruction adapted to their age, and intellectual and moral wants, and, to some extent, to their future pursuits in life."[70]

(4) DEVELOPMENT OF THE HIGH SCHOOL CURRICULUM. The curriculum of the Boston High School of 1821 has been described. The program of studies of early high schools was much narrower than that of academies, from which they borrowed their plan of education. The high school curriculum, however, expanded in response to public demands, as did the steadily expanding aims of the school to include preparation of youths for college and for a variety of vocations. There were occasionally forty or more subjects in the program of some city high schools by 1850. English, mathematics, history, the sciences and business subjects appeared prominently on the list. Latin, Greek, German and French were the favorite language studies until 1900, German being the most popular modern language, apparently until World War I, when German prestige suffered a marked decline in America. Beginning with the English and the classical courses in the 1820s, an array of parallel courses appeared until there were some forty, bearing different titles, in 1900.[71] As the years passed, the colleges which, traditionally, had only one course leading to one degree, began to offer parallel courses and create new degrees. This changing college plan helped the high schools to respond to public demands and to organize new curricula. America in this way was moving in the direction of equality of educational opportunity which has become its basic educational ideal. That ideal was well expressed by the superintendent of schools in Pittsburgh, Pennsylvania, in 1689: "The aim of our Public School system is to level society. There is no system of political economy in existence, nor was there ever one devised so efficient in destroying caste, and abolishing grades in the community. All systems that preceded it were artificial and perished; this one is natural and must prevail. It does not promote its aims by lowering the hills to the level of the valleys, but by filling the valleys to the height of the hill-tops, thereby producing the broad, grand plain, where the chances are equal in the great battle of life."[72]

[70] *Fifth Annual Report of the Superintendent of Common Schools of Connecticut*, 1850.

[71] I. L. Kandel, *History of Secondary Education* (Boston: Houghton Mifflin Co., 1930), pp. 450–60; Mulhern, *A History of Secondary Education in Pennsylvania*, pp. 518–51.

[72] *First Annual Report of the Superintendent*, p. 13.

Higher Education

DENOMINATIONAL FRONTIER COLLEGES. With the exception of Princeton and Rutgers, colonial colleges enjoyed a monopoly in higher education in their areas and, with the exception of the College of Philadelphia, were largely denominational in purpose and spirit. As church and state were gradually separated in the several states, the old colleges lost their exclusive rights, and the way was opened for new colleges. Washington and Lee, in Virginia; Union, in New York; Williams, in Massachusetts; Dickinson, in Pennsylvania, among many others, soon appeared. This movement, inspired largely by denominational interests, swept over the land, and hundreds of frontier colleges were founded. Alarm over the supposed threat of atheism, infidelity and, sometimes, Catholicism to American ideals gave impetus to the movement. State legislatures chartered new colleges by the score, many of which never opened. The mortality rate of those chartered before the Civil War, according to one investigator, was 81% for the nation as a whole. It ran from a low of 48% in Pennsylvania and New York to a high of 100% in Florida and Arkansas.[73] The frontier college, which still dots and lends color to the land, is uniquely an American institution. Denominational needs and rivalries stimulated its growth. There were 166 permanent Protestant colleges—the Presbyterian leading in number—and 14 permanent Catholic colleges founded before 1862. The cost of board and tuition in most of them was very low, and boarding students could often earn the A.B. degree for a total cost of much less than $1000.00, even as late as the early 1900s.

STATE UNIVERSITIES. The idea of publicly controlled universities spread widely in the Revolutionary years, and the Ordinance of 1787 provided, as we have seen, large land grants for universities in the Northwest Territory. The old colleges of the East, after a struggle, were rendered inviolate by a Supreme Court decision in 1819, which declared that the state of New Hampshire must respect the old charter of Dartmouth College. In 1789, the University of North Carolina was chartered, but it did not open until 1795, and the other southern states followed that lead one by one. Jefferson, influenced in part by French ideas which had operated earlier in New York and Georgia and later in Michigan, planned, in 1818, for Virginia a state university as the head institution in the state public school system. The University did not

[73] D. G. Tewksbury, *The Founding of American Colleges and Universities before the Civil War* (New York: Teachers College, Columbia University, 1932), p. 28.

open until 1825. In the West, one of the first activities of the legislature of each new state was to lay the plans of a state university. Thus, by 1860, a state university had come to be viewed as a part of our public school system, but only about seventeen states had one at that date.

State universities were a product of liberal, lay thought in the era of the Revolution, when French revolutionary secular ideas had found many followers. The opposition to state universities, which appeared in different degrees everywhere, and which was largely a result of the European and American religious tradition in education, checked the rise of such universities. Social prejudices, opposition to taxation for education, and uncertainty about the relation of the state to education were also factors retarding the movement. When it became apparent that the denominational colleges were not meeting effectively the needs and demands of the nation, opposition subsided, and state universities entered a period of growth and of the popularity which they now enjoy.

The great state universities of the Middle West and West have become objects of popular pride and of increasing respect and allegiance, while in the East, outside of Massachusetts, Connecticut and Rhode Island, which have neither state nor quasi-state universities, similar developments are now taking place. The great private nonsectarian universities, such as Harvard, Columbia, and Pennsylvania—independent schools dedicated to liberal learning and social service—have held their place of respect in the hearts of their alumni and of the public. While the state university bears distinctly American marks, those which enjoy independence from state control have made, and are making, a worthy contribution to our civilization, although the historian, perhaps, should shun such an evaluation. All of our schools reflect our history and social ideals, and the past still survives in the present scene. The good things in it should be preserved. The churches have entered state and nonsectarian universities through chaplaincies and other activities, while denominational universities and colleges often exclude ministers not of their own persuasion. We are still groping to achieve Jefferson's ideal of "the illimitable freedom of the human mind" on the campuses of our universities.[74]

CHANGING COLLEGE AND UNIVERSITY CURRICULUM. Colonial colleges were liberal arts colleges, with a theological bias. Courses in medicine and law, as we have seen, made their appearance in the years just preceding and following the Revolution. Jefferson pro-

[74] R. I. Glicksberg, "The Religious Motif in Higher Education," *Bulletin of the American Association of University Professors,* XLIII, 449–57.

posed a modernized curriculum for William and Mary College in 1779, which led to the introduction there of modern languages, history, political science and law; and the program of the University of Virginia, his most cherished creation, was, at its inception, broad, modern and practical, with students enjoying some freedom in the choice of their studies.

The growth of the college curriculum followed, but more slowly, the growth of the nation. Generally, not many changes occurred in it before 1825, although some colleges, by that time, had added to their old classical admission requirements a knowledge of English grammar, geography and algebra. After 1825, new studies, some of which had appeared in some colleges much earlier, were rapidly added to the curriculum. Botany, geology, chemistry, physics, history, economics, political science, and modern languages were well established liberal studies by 1860, the old colonial colleges usually leading the way in introducing them. New studies, in expanding array, demanded recognition, and the colleges found themselves confronted by a problem of disturbing dimensions which led to specialization by teachers, the emergence of parallel curricula, the elective system and new degrees.

Colonial college teachers taught a class, not special subjects. Harvard first departed from that plan in 1766, when the professors were made subject specialists. The expanding curriculum made it impossible for students to study all subjects, and new curricula and the elective system were thus forced upon the colleges. After much faculty indecision, the elective plan, which had its embryonic beginnings in William and Mary College, and was strongly advocated by President Francis Wayland of Brown University in 1842,[75] won general acceptance. When Harvard, led by President Charles W. Eliot, adopted it, after long debate, in 1870, the principle of election of studies may be said to have triumphed. It was popular with students, and with industrial and commercial interests that saw the advantages of science and practical studies in the training of their key employees. Henceforth, our higher institutions became objects of increasing financial support by industrial and commercial interests.

Reform of the college curriculum became a matter of controversy among educators. Those who stood opposed to change, as did the Yale faculty in 1827, took their stand on the doctrine that the purpose of education should be mental discipline, while the Amherst faculty, at about the same time, called for modernization

[75] F. Wayland, *Thoughts on the Present Collegiate System in the United States* (Boston: Gould, Kendall & Lincoln, 1842).

of the curriculum in keeping with public demand and advancing civilization. The rift became widespread, and the principle of election of studies, with its utilitarian overtones, became a phase of the dispute. The founding of our first engineering school, the Rensselaer Polytechnic Institute, in 1824, and of "scientific schools" at Harvard (1846), Yale (1846), and Dartmouth (1851) represent acceptance of, by the first, or concessions by the latter two, to the doctrine of utility. In 1862, the federal government in the Morrill Act, which brought our land-grant colleges, threw its influence upon the side of the utilitarians. Cornell University was founded (1867) to promote education of a "practically useful" nature. Gradually, the utilitarians triumphed over the disciplinarians, although the struggle, now little more than academic, still goes on.[76] Today there is significant agreement between the business-industrial interests and the educators regarding the values of the humanistic studies, the sciences and technology in the education of leaders for business, industry, the professions, and public service at home and abroad. But the principle that guides thought now is that of utility, not that of discipline, as formerly interpreted. After 1850, graduate schools, stressing research, slowly emerged, and research has since become a leading function of our universities.

ACADEMIC FREEDOM. Mediaeval universities, in a church-dominated educational system, were autonomous gilds and enjoyed the independence bestowed upon all gilds, but their teachers had to teach within the bounds of theological orthodoxy. They studied and taught for the "glory of God," as their ecclesiastical masters conceived it. With the Reformation and the rise of king-dominated universities in Protestant lands, having state churches, teachers were required to be politically and theologically orthodox. While the university corporation continued to enjoy an autonomy, the individual teacher had to show respect for official "truth." With the coming of rationalism and liberalism, the demand arose that the teacher pursue and teach "truth" as he himself sees it. In America, Jefferson called for "eternal hostility against every form of tyranny over the mind of man." We should not, he said, fear error as long as reason is left free to combat it. Academic freedom thus came to mean the freedom of the scholar to pursue and teach truth, as he sees it, in his own field, regardless of its social or political consequences. "Truth without preconceptions" and "truth wherever it may lead us" became principles widely accepted in the scientific and liberal world of the nineteenth century.

[76] R. F. Butts, *The College Charts Its Course* (New York: McGraw-Hill Book Co., Inc., 1939).

The laissez-faire principle of freedom in politics and in trade was considered, particularly in England, to be equally useful for mankind when applied to research and teaching. As social institutions, serving existing societies, universities have been forced, however, to be conservative, albeit in different degrees, and academic freedom has been restricted also, in varying degrees, by the demands of the time and place. Indeed universities have usually not kept pace with the changes around them. They have opposed revolutions, and revolutionary governments have robbed them and their professors of their freedom to do so. And even gradual social change has encountered their opposition. The issue of academic freedom has never appeared in a social vacuum. Our American universities and colleges have been controlled by external authorities representing political or other interests which the faculty were, therefore, expected to serve or, at least, not oppose. Their trustees, however, have seldom interfered with the freedom of the teachers, but such interference has lately increased because of the threat of Communism. Academic freedom is not a privilege claimed by irresponsible teachers in their own interest, but a means by which, they believe, they can best serve society.

While our higher schools were under church domination, Jefferson's ideal of unlimited freedom for the human mind had little effect upon them, and existing knowledge and life were seldom viewed critically in them. The issue of academic freedom was first debated here in connection with the slavery question. A few professors at Western Reserve University and one at the University of North Carolina were dismissed because of their abolitionist views. In 1870, Harvard dismissed the historian, John Fiske, because he was thought to be an "infidel." The spread of Darwinism, which conflicted with theological concepts, brought professors in church schools under close scrutiny. Attempts were made, here and there, to prohibit the teaching of evolution even in public schools, the most famous case being that of Scopes in Tennessee, in 1925. In 1897, President Andrews of Brown University resigned because of opposition to his views on bimetalism, and the faculty and alumni denounced his opponents in the name of freedom. The Constitution of Leland Stanford University gave the president power to dismiss professors at will. In 1900, President David Starr Jordan, at the behest of Mrs. Stanford, dismissed Professor Edward Ross whom she came to dislike. Many faculty members resigned in protest, to the detriment of University morale. In 1915, Scott Nearing, a teacher of economics, was denied reappointment at the University of Pennsylvania because of his "rude remarks in public" and radical views expressed in class. As at Stanford, the trustees, under criticism, declared that their relation to professors was that of employer to employee, a view which the academic fraternity has since then everywhere rejected. The introduction of the social and physical sciences into the curriculum played a part in most of the earlier disputes.

In recent years, because of the threat of Communism, some professors have been dismissed because of their actual or suspected Communist or related activities, and the academic fraternity has become divided on the question of the propriety of such dismissals. The position of the American Association of University Professors on the issue of academic freedom was formulated in 1915 in a *Report*, the principles of which are still adhered to by the Association[77] and respected by the trustees and administrators of colleges and universities, although an occasional school finds itself on the Association's list of censured institutions because of its interference with the freedom of a teacher. Academic freedom—freedom of learning and of teaching—remains one of the burning issues in higher education in America.

Developments in Girls' Education

We have seen how the academies and female seminaries enlarged the educational opportunities of girls, and how stress upon ornamental training gave way to a stress upon solid intellectual training for the female sex. For women the world had been changed by the breakdown of authoritarianism consequent upon the Reformation, by the growth of the spirit of rationalism, by the rise of political liberalism, and by the growth of economic opportunities for them resulting from the Industrial Revolution. Conscious of this new and larger world, American women began to demand for themselves "a college like a man's." The nearest approaches to the attainment of that goal before the Civil War were Mary Sharp College, Tennessee (1848), and Elmira Female College, New York (1852). Vassar College, which opened in 1865, was the first woman's college which, in endowment and solidity of its offerings, was the equal of good colleges for men. Long before, in 1833, Oberlin College had admitted women, as did coeducational Antioch College from its opening in 1853. Iowa State University opened in 1856 as a coeducational institution. The other state universities west of the Mississippi admitted girls from the start. In addition to the separate and coeducational colleges, there were established by

[77] *Bulletin of the Association,* XXIII, 431–51.

some older universities, such as Tulane (1886), Columbia (1889), and Harvard (1894) coordinate colleges for women.

While these developments were in their earliest stage, separate high schools for girls and coeducational high schools were appearing. In 1826, Boston opened its girls' high school, and other Massachusetts towns soon followed that lead. But separate high schools for the sexes were the rule until Lowell, in 1840, began the practice of coeducation. The desirability of coeducation was long debated throughout the country but for many reasons, one of which was lower cost, the coeducational high school became the almost universal practice in America. In the middle western states high schools were coeducational from the start. Only the older section of the country hesitated, but the period of hesitation was not long. State public school laws did not discriminate against girls. Only in a few large cities in the South and East do separate high schools for boys and girls still survive. The provision of coeducational high schools was one of the most significant triumphs of democracy in education in the nineteenth century. That victory was largely won by 1870. It opened to girls the same secondary educational opportunities which boys enjoyed in the public system. By 1900 there were more girls than boys in public high schools. Given the opportunity, girls demonstrated their ability to master the solid subject matter which had long been thought to be beyond their intellectual power.

General Educational Developments Since 1870

By 1870, the groundwork of our public school system had been firmly laid, but the superstructure was still very imperfect. The legal right of districts to establish high schools as part of the common-school system of states was challenged in the courts but was upheld, probably the best known decision being that of the supreme court of Michigan in the Kalamazoo Case, in 1874. Legal obstacles to the establishment of high schools were thus removed. Since 1875, when the National Education Association first undertook the task of bringing order and unity into the studies in our schools from the primary grade upward, a number of attempts have been made to standardize the work of our secondary schools. Such attempts appear in the work of regional standardizing agencies, like the New England Association of Colleges and Secondary Schools (1885), the Association of Colleges and Secondary Schools of the Middle States and Maryland (1892), and other similar organizations. In addition to these regional efforts, there were other made with a view to producing order on a national scale. Such was the work of the Committee of Ten of the N.E.A. (1892), of the Committee on College Entrance Requirements (1895), and of the Commission on the Reorganization of Secondary Education (1918). These agencies contributed much to the clarification of thinking regarding the objectives, curriculum, and organization of public secondary education. The earlier national commissions bequeathed to us the somewhat dubious principle that all subjects studied for the same length of time are of equal value, thus clearing the way for the recognition of non-academic studies in our high schools.

When the nineteenth century closed, education was compulsory in nearly all states outside of the South, and in the majority of the states the age of compulsory attendance was from eight to fourteen, no state requiring attendance below the age of seven. The minimum school year ranged from eight weeks in some states to eight months in others. In the South, the Civil War was followed by a forty-year economic depression. For education the burden was increased by the need for separate Negro schools. Yet until the close of the century, the masses were very poorly provided for. In 1900, approximately 40 per cent of the people of the South were illiterate. There were yet no compulsory education laws there. The average annual salary paid to Southern teachers was $159 in that year.

By 1900, pioneering in public education had ended. Since then its expansion has been very rapid, and private schools, numerous throughout the old century, quickly disappeared, until today less than 10 per cent of youths of compulsory school age are enrolled in private schools. In 1951, the total expenditure for public education had reached the 6½ billion dollar mark. In 1890, there were about 200,000 students enrolled in public high schools. The high school enrollment, grades 9 to 12, in 1954, was almost 6½ millions,[78] and free secondary education was within the reach of nearly every child, children living at a distance being given free transportation to their high schools. On school buildings and their equipment huge sums have been expended. From a physical standpoint many of our schools have no equal in the world. The rapid increase in school enrollment, particularly in high schools, since 1900, has created the very difficult problem of providing proper education, especially for non-academic students, who seem to be in the majority. Our earliest high schools arose to prepare youths for practical life but, in time, the high school became largely subservient to the college, and tended to revert to traditional intellectual-

[78] U.S. Office of Education, *Statistical Summary of Education, 1953–54,* p. 6.

ism. Colleges, it is true, were forced by the high school attitude of independence to broaden their entrance requirements but, becoming wedded to the college, the high school tended toward academic conservatism. Since 1900, however, the vocational ideal has gained ground in it.

THE JUNIOR HIGH SCHOOL. While dissatisfaction with the graded school system, as it took shape, appeared earlier, and attempts, foreshadowing the coming of the junior high school, had been made here and there to correct its defects, the movement proper began when Charles W. Eliot, in the eighteen-eighties, called for a shortening and enriching of the elementary school curriculum. The Committee of Ten recommended that Latin, algebra and geometry be taught in the upper elementary school grades, and the Committee on College Entrance Requirements suggested that the high school should begin with the seventh grade. To bridge the gap between the elementary and high school, as well as to meet other needs, the junior high school was organized. While schools of this type, bearing the same or other names, existed from 1880, or earlier,[79] the most influential step toward complete reorganization was taken when, in 1909, the 6-3-3 plan was adopted in Berkeley, California. The movement spread quickly to other large cities. The Commission on the Reorganization of Secondary Education, appointed in 1912, approved the view that secondary education should begin with the seventh grade, a view that has received wide acceptance in practice.

THE JUNIOR COLLEGE. The upward expansion of public education eventually brought the public junior college. The history of this school has not yet been told. Academies frequently prepared their students for admission to sophomore and higher classes in college, and were thus the first of our junior colleges. Johnstown, Pennsylvania, had what, essentially, was a public junior college in 1887.[80] In 1902, President Harper, of the University of Chicago, feeling, as did others, that the work of the first two years of college was of secondary character, recommended a six-year high school course. Almost immediately, a junior college department was added to the high school at Joliet, Illinois. In 1907, the legislature of California authorized local boards of education to establish junior colleges. The movement has spread rapidly. In 1954, there were 495 junior colleges, of which 225 were privately controlled.[81]

79 Mulhern, *A History of Secondary Education in Pennsylvania*, pp. 568 ff.
80 *Ibid.*, pp. 565, 580.
81 U.S. Office of Education, *Statistical Summary of Education, 1953–54*, p. 63.

VOCATIONAL EDUCATION. With the exception of a few private commercial schools, the apprenticeship system of vocational training was used exclusively until the nineteenth century. General education was then viewed as the work of the school. Beginning in 1820, there arose a few Mechanics' Institutes to provide secondary and technical instruction. Higher technical instruction came to be provided in such schools as the Rennselaer Polytechnic Institute (1824), the Sheffield Scientific School of Yale University (1847), and the Worcester Polytechnic Institute (1868). Such schools aimed to apply science to our industrial needs. In the meantime the manual labor schools, borrowed from Pestalozzi through Fellenberg, contributed to our growing interest in vocational training. From 1876 onward the manual training idea and practice held the center of the stage on the elementary and secondary school levels. While shopwork had a prominent place in manual training high schools, it was but a part of the whole course which continued to include basic high school subjects. The early leaders in the movement stressed the educational rather than the vocational value of such shopwork, which they considered an important part of general education. Special trades were not to be taught, but the mechanical principles underlying them all were to be. Students would not make specific articles, but they would learn how to use tools and materials. Yet, these leaders at times advocated such training so that we might not have to import our skilled workmen from abroad. The movement spread widely throughout the country, and from 1880 onward manual training gradually found a place in the program of normal schools. Teachers College, of Columbia University, had its origin in the need for teachers of manual training, and the Industrial Education Association, organized in 1884, was its founder. In 1893, it became a part of Columbia. The movement to train teachers of the manual arts spread gradually through the universities.

While these developments were taking place, special private trade schools were appearing. Of this type were the New York Trade School (1881), and the Williamson Free School of Mechanical Trades, near Philadelphia (1891). In the former were taught not only trades but the scientific principles underlying the procedures of each. In the latter, which was designed to be a substitute for the apprenticeship system, only practical work was taught. As yet, the public, which approved of public manual training schools, opposed the idea of teaching trades at public expense. The acceptance of that idea spread rapidly since 1900. The breakdown of the apprenticeship system, specialization in industry, constant change in industrial techniques, the rise of great industries, and the danger that workers might be exploited by distant employers and labor unions hastened the development.

What is known strictly as the vocational education movement dates from the appointment of a commission by Governor Douglas of Massachusetts, in 1905, to study how the schools can meet the needs of industry for trained workers. The report of this and later commissions led, within a few years, to the development of vocational education as a function of the public schools. In the meantime there was organized (1906) the National Society for the Promotion of Industrial Education, on the board of directors of which were educators, manufacturers, social workers, and representatives of labor. Labor leaders feared that the movement would create a surplus of cheap labor, but approved of public trade schools if labor were given a voice in their control. The manufacturers, however, wished to hold complete control over them. Both groups recognized the need for such schools. The Society eventually brought agreement between industrialists and labor leaders, and public support for trade education followed. The opposition of educators, influenced by the academic tradition inherited from Greece and Rome, was more difficult to overcome, and some of them in our own day continue to scorn the vocational emphasis in education. Yet, most American schoolmen today define a liberal education not in terms of subject matter but in terms of the capacity and needs of individuals.

Between 1907 and 1917, vocational schools of different types, some private and some public, made their appearance in different parts of the country. Beginning, too, with the Massachusetts law of 1906, the states, one by one, authorized local school boards to provide industrial training, and appropriated funds in aid of such local effort. Yet, the most important step in the movement was the passage, in 1917, of the federal Smith-Hughes Act, for which the National Society for the Promotion of Industrial Education long had worked. That law provided federal aid for the states by (a) paying the salaries of vocational teachers in secondary schools and (b) aiding higher institutions in training such teachers. The states were required to match the federal grant. As we have seen, the federal grants to vocational education have been greatly increased since then, particularly as a result of needs created by the Second World War.

VOCATIONAL GUIDANCE. The need of youth for scientific aid in choosing between occupations and vocational courses led to the establishment in Boston, in 1908, of the Vocation Bureau and Breadwinner's Institute. Men and women workers as well as college and high school students sought advice from the Bureau. The Boston School Committee asked the Bureau to assist in organizing a program of vocational guidance for the city schools. Soon the movement became national in scope. In 1912, the National Vocational Guidance Association was organized, and Professor Frank Leavitt, of the University of Chicago, its first president, offered, in the same year, the first graduate course in the subject of guidance. Guidance counseling has now become a prominent activity in many of our schools, and specialists are being trained for that work.

THE NON-PUBLIC SCHOOL. Private schools, under various agencies of control, of colonial origin and extending from kindergartens to universities, have developed side by side with public schools, and about 15 per cent of our students are enrolled in them. Catholic schools constitute the largest segment of this group. Many of the others are nonsectarian. The non-public higher schools still draw about 46 per cent of all students enrolled in higher institutions. During the nineteenth century, when public schools were in many ways imperfect and old social and religious prejudices still prevailed, private elementary and secondary schools flourished. Since 1900 their relative drawing power has suffered a sharp decline, and the public school has become numerically pre-eminent in the national scene.

Education of Negroes

BEFORE THE CIVIL WAR. In the South, where Negroes were about one-third of the population in 1860, the races were separated by a rigid caste barrier. Negroes were still few outside of the South. Migration from the South of free Negroes and runaway slaves increased sharply between 1815 and 1850. Life in cities, North and South, awakened them to social realities, and migration tended to elicit the sympathy of whites for their black brothers. Slavery was seen by a few in the South and by many elsewhere as a negation of the ideal of equality, the core of the American Creed, while the churches, the Quakers in the lead, saw it as a denial of Christian ideals. Many abolition societies were established in the North after the Revolution, and made the education of Negroes a basic concern.[82] While, prior to 1830, most Southern whites did not oppose their education in religion and the 3 R's, abolition of slavery, a vital economic institution on the plantations and a useful one to all those who needed menial servants, was inconceivable to the

[82] C. G. Woodson, *op. cit.*, pp. 72, 374–77.

moulders of Southern life. Farm, domestic and, generally, skilled labor passed to Negroes, and became degraded. Not only the propertied class but the "poor whites" in the South came to be more intensely anti-Negro than those in other sections, where blacks remained an insignificant minority until recent decades. Urbanization in the South and industrialization in the North have played a basic rôle in changing racial attitudes and labor prejudices.[83]

In dealing with Negroes, the North and West moved slowly toward liberalism. Vermont and Maine were the only states which did not, occasionally, restrict Negro suffrage. In thirty of the thirty-six states, in 1865, Negroes were disfranchised. The federal law of 1867, which enfranchised Negroes everywhere, was nullified in the South by a variety of legal tricks. After a struggle which almost wrecked the nation, and nearly a century of strife, the Negro is now approaching the final stage of his struggle for social and educational equality. That struggle has centered in the South, where the increase of the slave population and the rise of an insurrectionary spirit among Negroes brought the abandonment of the humane practices which existed in colonial times.

Insurrections, confined to the South, culminating in that of Nat Turner in Virginia (1831), led to the prohibition of education for slaves in all Southern and "border" states, with the exception of Maryland. These prohibitory laws date back to that of South Carolina in 1740. Insurrections came to be attributed to the awakening of the Negro mind by instruction even in the 3R's. The literacy of a few Negroes was equated with insurrection. The prohibitory laws excluded Negroes from all positions requiring literary training, and literate Negroes were forbidden to instruct others. In 1831, Mississippi expelled all free Negroes, and forbade any Negro to preach to slaves except on his own plantation. Education and slavery were thus made inconsistent with each other. The churches were forced to resort to merely oral instruction in religion, and usually taught slaves to obey their masters as a religious duty. Some Southerners felt that even such religious instruction would awaken in slaves a dangerous mental curiosity. The whole moral atmosphere of the South suffered a sharp decline as a result.[84] The intellectual life of the South also suffered from this enforced policy of Negro illiteracy. Disrespect of literacy spread among the white masses. On the eve of the Civil War, illiteracy in the North was confined mostly to immi-

[83] G. Myrdal, *An American Dilemma* (2 vols.; New York: Harper & Bros., 1944), I, 279–303.

[84] A. W. Calhoun, *A Social History of the American Family from Colonial Times to the Present* (3 vols.; Cleveland: Clark, 1917–19).

grants but, in the South, the white illiterates were native-born.[85] Data on illiteracy are not, however, very reliable.

In the industrialized North, free labor was viewed as more profitable than slave labor, and the dissenting churches, enemies of feudalized Christianity, stood opposed to slavery, although the same churches accepted it in the South. Churches obey their masters. In Northern cities, benevolent societies and churches established segregated schools for Negroes, as did free Negroes also. Generally, the demand in the ante-bellum North was for segregated schools. Until about 1830, the teachers in these schools were, by necessity, usually white. The rise of public school systems in the North brought a demand from Negroes and charitable societies for funds for education of the blacks. Here, many Negroes were taxpayers who contributed to the support of public schools. Early responses to the demand of public aid for Negro education differed from state to state, and integration and admission of Negroes to public schools came slowly and gradually. New Jersey (1844), Massachusetts (1855), Rhode Island (1866), and Connecticut (1868) legalized integration in public schools, separation being previously the official policy. Ohio authorized separate public schools for them in 1849, and Indiana provided no public aid for Negro education until after the Civil War. Illinois, Michigan and Wisconsin treated them little better than did Indiana in ante-bellum days. The benevolent societies were, thus, the chief providers of Negro education outside of the South before the Civil War. There was much opposition in the North and Middle West to efforts to educate Negroes. White workers saw Negroes threatening their jobs, and the education of Negro paupers an obstacle to the education of their own children. In 1819, the abolition societies asked Negroes not to send their children to free schools if they could pay tuition for them, since they might otherwise appear to be robbing poor white children of their opportunities.[86]

SINCE THE CIVIL WAR. In 1860, the free public school was little more than beginning in the South. After the War, many teachers were sent into the South to educate Negroes. The Freedman's Bureau, set up by Congress in 1865, organized schools for them. The Reconstruction period saw the basis of public education for both races legally established in the slave states but, when federal troops were withdrawn from the South, Negro education suffered a sharp decline there, although Northern philanthropists and churches came to its aid. The Peabody Fund (1867) was the first one created for

[85] Knight and Hall, *op. cit.*, pp. 670–72.
[86] Woodson, *op. cit.*, p. 377.

the purpose. Negro education was one of the chief concerns of this and other benevolent foundations, such as the Carnegie Foundation, the (Rockefeller) General Education Board, and the Julius Rosenwald Fund.[87]

Political freedom, demonstrated Negro ability, and race needs led to the establishment of higher schools for colored youth. The Quaker-endowed (1832-1842) Institute for Colored Youth in Philadelphia, the Presbyterian Ashmun Institute (now Lincoln University), founded in 1853, and Wilberforce University, founded by Ohio Methodists in 1855, were pioneers in secondary and higher education for Negroes. Outside of the South, many colored students were admitted to white colleges and professional schools prior to the Civil War. Some thought that such education would, through discontent, induce Negroes to return to Liberia. In the South, Hampton Institute, Virginia (1870), and Tuskegee Institute, Alabama (1881) set a fashion for Negro higher education, although many of the twenty-three Negro colleges established there between 1870 and 1890 were little better than secondary schools. In the nation, that number has risen to 106 at the present time, of which 65 are privately controlled. Many of the public ones are land-grant colleges receiving federal aid under the Morrill Act of 1862.[88] Negro colleges made teacher training and vocational education their chief functions because of the Negro's social disabilities.

The problem of studies for Negroes brought disagreement even among Negroes themselves. Booker T. Washington, founder of Tuskegee Institute, and his followers advocated vocational training for them. Other Negroes demanded an education like a white man's, and chiefly academic, so that their kinsmen might not be deprived of their share in American culture. The movement to vocationalize Negro education was checked, chiefly, by the factors of cost and the opposition of white workers to Negro competition for jobs. Southerners felt that Negro education, in any form, would wreck the caste system, which even poor whites wished to uphold. Yet, there were those whose interests would be served by the training of good cooks, servants, and commercial and industrial workers. Generalizations about attitudes and practices are, therefore, hazardous.

Outside of the South and the "border states," Negroes have been accorded, since the Civil War, equality of educational opportunity, legally and, to a large degree, in practice. In the South, the new post-war state constitutions and laws authorized "separate but

[87] E. V. Hollis, *Philanthropic Foundations and Higher Education* (New York: Columbia University Press, 1938).

[88] U.S. Office of Education, *op. cit.*, p. 80.

equal" educational provision for them. Separation, however, resulted in inequality. Guided by evidence of inequality, the United States Supreme Court, in December, 1938, ruled that the University of Missouri must admit a Negro to its law school unless it provided an equal opportunity for him elsewhere in the state. Other similar decisions of the Supreme Court followed.[89] The issue of racial segregation in public schools was legally resolved when, on May 17, 1954, the Supreme Court decided unanimously that it is unconstitutional and, on May 30, ordered the states to abolish it gradually. Massive resistance to that decree has developed, particularly in the "Deep South," as symbolized by the Little Rock conflict.

Education of Indians

The federal Ordinance of 1787 outlawed slavery in the Northwest territory and required the states there to be just to the Indians. Their education, however, was long left to missionaries. Beginning in 1819, Congress made increasingly large grants for their education, the Office of Indian Affairs being established to care for them. Until the 1870s practically all schools aided by grants were under church control. Since then, the federal government has taken over, very largely, the duty of educating Indians, although privately supported missionary schools continued. Many of the government schools have been boarding schools. Indian children have thus been provided with elementary and secondary education. The emphasis in their instruction has been placed upon the 3R's, industrial and agricultural training and, for girls, domestic science. Catholics have been far ahead of Protestants in providing missionary schools for them. Since 1924, all native-born Indians have been citizens, and may vote in their respective states, if they can meet state requirements, which some of them cannot do. They have been educated almost entirely in segregated schools as they, apparently, prefer. A recent experiment, however, in integration of Indian and white high school students in northern Utah has been reported as highly successful and acceptable to both groups.[90]

Education of Teachers

Following the Revolution, academies, female seminaries and high schools were long the chief training centers for elementary

[89] B. Fine, "Education in Review," *The New York Times* (June 11, 1950), Sec. 4, E 9.

[90] *Ibid.* (Oct. 20, 1957), p. 71.

teachers, but professional studies were seldom taught in them. Training consisted mostly of drill in elementary studies. Pedagogy, theory and practice of teaching, and "mental philosophy" were occasionally a part of the course.

From 1820, the normal school movement spread quickly here, as it did in Europe, as an expression of nationalism, humanitarianism and social idealism. Pestalozzi was a central figure in the early movement. Here, Massachusetts educators, led by James G. Carter, joined in the growing demand for teacher training. In 1823, Samuel R. Hall opened a private normal school in Concord, Vermont, and, in 1829, published his *Lectures on Schoolkeeping*. Our first state normal school was opened at Lexington, Massachusetts, in 1839, and fourteen others—three of them in the Middle West and one in California—were established before the Civil War. They did not appear in the South until Reconstruction days. Many cities, too, established their own normal schools, but only a few of these have survived.

In 1831, Washington College, Pennsylvania, originated teacher training on the college level, and, in 1832, New York University appointed a temporary professor of pedagogy. Between 1870 and 1890, many colleges and universities created teacher-training departments. The first permanent chair of "didactics" was established at the University of Iowa in 1873, and other universities soon took the same step. Graduate work in pedagogy originated in New York University in 1887. In 1889, Teachers College, Columbia University, was chartered.

Because of the growth of public high schools and the need for teachers in them, normal schools have, since about 1890, gradually been made degree-granting colleges requiring secondary-school graduation for entrance. Until recently, many states did not require high school teachers to hold degrees. The American Lyceum [91] and Lake Chautauqua Institute provided special lectures and courses for teachers. Summer schools, originating about 1872, and, soon thereafter, taken over by universities, have been an important agency of training, chiefly for in-service teachers. The universities served the profession also through extension courses, the first of which was offered by Benjamin Silliman of Yale in 1808, and which have had an impressive growth since 1890. Pedagogical courses were, however, seldom offered in extension until around 1910. Teachers Institutes, which have become a national institution, date from the offering by Henry Barnard in Hartford, Connecticut, of a six-weeks

[91] *Supra*, p. 503.

course in pedagogy and elementary subjects in 1839. Professional books and educational journals, both dating from the 1820s, have been fruitful sources of pedagogical experience.

To the professional improvement of teachers, associations have contributed significantly. New York (1811) and Boston (1812) had associations open to public school teachers. Many local and state associations, dedicated to improvement of the profession and of public schools, existed in the 1850s. Laymen were usually admitted to membership in these early associations. In 1857, the National Education Association, exclusively for teachers, was organized in Philadelphia, and has since rendered a notable service to education and the teaching profession through its journal, research and many other activities. The American Federation of Teachers and the American Education Fellowship have, also, contributed much to the improvement of teaching and to the promotion of educational causes in recent decades. Until the Civil War, which opened classrooms widely to female teachers, women members were not admitted to meetings of state associations, and, until 1866, women were admitted to the N.E.A. only as honorary members.

Professional studies in training institutions have multiplied rapidly since 1890. This growth has not occurred so much in such fundamental and theoretical areas as the history and philosophy of education, educational sociology and psychology, as in the more technical areas, such as methods, supervision, and administration. Psychology has, however, acquired an assured place in the professional curriculum, as have courses in tests and measurements of ability and achievement. New courses and subdivisions of old ones, taught by specialists, have increased rapidly with the expansion of public education and of professional knowledge; and research has come to be stressed in the graduate education of teachers and administrators.[92] "Education" is now a discipline and a science in its own right, although it still lacks the respectability of the older academic disciplines. The status of the teacher has steadily improved since the Civil War, and his remuneration has steadily increased, although his material reward still remains below that enjoyed by other professions. The recent rapid increase in the birth rate, and the financial unattractiveness of teaching, particularly to men, have created in recent years a serious shortage of teachers below the college level, and the professional requirements for certification have been relaxed in many states. Criticisms of professional training have been numerous although many of them have reflected a lack

[92] J. M. Pangburn, *The Evolution of the American Teachers College* (New York: Teachers College, Columbia University, 1932), pp. 70–95.

of understanding of the problems of mass education. We are now in a period of critical examination and evaluation of teacher education. The Cold War which has now entered the classrooms has made the nation intensely conscious of the dependence of its welfare upon the education of our and future generations.

Developments in Physical Education

Manual work has always provided physical education for those who engaged in it, and the leisure classes substituted sports, games, dancing, etc. for it as an outlet for their physical urges. The ascetic tradition surviving in most colonial religions and life brought condemnation of all physical frivolities both in school and outside of it. Quakers, Puritans and Anabaptist groups frowned upon gaiety in any form. The Anglican aristocracy, on the other hand, saw nothing essentially wicked in sports and a merry life, although such diversions as horse racing and cockfighting were forbidden to students at William and Mary College. The natural urge to play and to satisfy bodily demands could not be entirely stifled by the ascetical sects, and Quaker and Puritan schoolboys sometimes broke the rules and indulged in physical delights. Humanism and naturalism negated asceticism, and military needs in nations brought recognition of the importance of physical education. It was naturalism, as it appeared in Rousseau's *Émile*, which first inspired the gymnastic movement, in which Johann Guts Muths (1759-1839) of Germany was a pioneer. His book *Gymnastics for Youth,* translated by C. G. Salzmann, in whose school he taught, was published by William Duane of Philadelphia in 1802. German gymnastics were introduced into America in the 1820s. From Sweden flowed another wave of interest in gymnastics. Both systems made health and strength of body their objectives. Friedrich Jahn (1778-1852), a German patriot, was the leading advocate of gymnastics in Germany. Two German political refugees, Charles Beck and Charles Follen, introduced gymnastics into American education, in 1823-1824, at Round Hill School, Massachusetts. Other German refugees, later, organized *Turnvereine* and gymnasiums in American cities.[93] It was during the same period that manual labor schools were combining mental and physical training for their students.

Colonial Americans, particularly the Dutch of New York and the aristocracy of Virginia, indulged in the sports and games of the Old World. Before 1840, physical activities were poorly organized.

[93] E. A. Rice, J. L. Hutchinson, and M. Lee, *A Brief History of Physical Education* (4th ed.; New York: The Ronald Press Co., 1958), pp. 161–63.

Their rapid growth came after the Civil War, which made the nation conscious of the importance of sound bodies. Increased wealth and leisure, declining asceticism, foreign influence, plus a growing sense of national need brought an emphasis upon athletics, games and sports in both school and society. Since 1860, the Y.M.C.A. has promoted athletics and gymnastics as safeguards against vice. Athletic clubs and associations grew in number as interest increased. A normal school to train physical education instructors was established by the United Turnvereine at Rochester, New York, in 1861. In 1885, the Y.M.C.A. established Springfield College, Massachusetts, for the same purpose. State requirements for physical education in public schools brought the rise in teacher training institutions of courses designed to that end.

Baseball, football, tennis, rowing, basketball (American in origin), track and field events had a rapid development in American schools between 1850 and 1900. Leaders in the reform of girls' education stressed the promotion of the health of American women. Catherine Beecher's books on calisthenics and physiology (1832, 1856), and Dio Lewis' *New Gymnastics for Men, Women and Children* (1862) were very influential in the field of girls' education.[94]

The American Association for Health, Physical Education and Recreation, founded in 1885, has been active in promoting physical education in school and community. Ohio (1892) was the first state to make it compulsory in public schools. It is now a legal requirement in nearly all states. Medical examinations, physical exercises, supervised play, etc., are among the stated requirements for elementary and high schools. Thought on the purposes and best mode of physical education has undergone many transformations since the gymnastic movement began, and agreement as to purposes still does not exist. There are few, however, today who would deny it a place in liberal, general education.

Changing School Life and Methods

The changing spirit of democracy affected the inner life of our schools as it did also the external aspects of our education. Thus our curriculum grew in answer to popular demand, and trained teachers carried a new attitude into the school. Not the least significant of the reforms hastened by the democratic spirit, and the only one to which we can refer here, was that of the method of teaching. Imitation of the teacher, repetition and memorization of

[94] Woody, "Leisure in the Light of History," *The Annals of the American Academy of Political and Social Science,* 313:4–10.

subject matter and its rules marked colonial method. Texts were then scarce and costly. In the early national period, texts became plentiful and students were required to memorize them. Horace Mann denounced this textbook method as well as the practice of permitting different students to use different texts in the same subject. Both subject matter and method had become very formal. Ponderous rules for performing equally ponderous and often useless exercises in the several subjects taught had to be memorized. Pupils' interests and abilities were ignored. Education was viewed as an intellectual, moral, and religious discipline, and corporal punishment insured its effectiveness.

After 1820, Pestalozzianism began to change the atmosphere of the school. With it came the more sympathetic teacher who thought of education not as a discipline but as a development of child nature through interesting and useful experiences and activities. The selection of appropriate subject matter and its better organization and presentation appeared as a phase of the new education of the period. The gloomy religious outlook and discipline of earlier times gradually disappeared as we came to feel that, in a democracy, children, too, have rights. Teachers of the past would make studies difficult for the sake of discipline; the new teacher would make studies easy for the sake of the full growth and happiness of children. The hopes of "geography made easy," of "grammar made easy," and of mastering spelling "in a few easy lessons" now began to approach their realization.

Selected Readings

Arrowood, C. F. *Thomas Jefferson and Education in a Republic.* New York: McGraw-Hill Book Co., Inc., 1930.

Bell, S. *The Church, the State and Education in Virginia.* Lancaster, Pa.: Science Press, Inc., 1930.

Bond, H. M. *The Education of the Negro in the American Social Order.* Englewood Cliffs, N.J.: Prentice-Hall, Inc., 1934.

Bourne, W. O. *History of the Public School Society of the City of New York.* New York: G. P. Putnam's Sons, Inc., 1873.

Brown, E. E. *The Making of Our Middle Schools.* New York: Longmans, Green & Co., Inc., 1905.

Brubacher, J. S. *Henry Barnard on Education.* New York: McGraw-Hill Book Co., Inc., 1931.

Burr, N. R. *Education in New Jersey, 1630–1871.* Princeton, N.J.: Princeton University Press, 1942.

Cash, W. J. *The Mind of the South.* New York: Alfred A. Knopf, Inc., 1941.

Cremin, L. A. *The American Common School: An Historic Conception.* New York: Teachers College, Columbia University, 1951.

Curti, M. *The Social Ideas of American Educators.* New York: Charles Scribner's Sons, 1935.

Gallagher, B. G. *American Caste and the Negro College.* New York: Columbia University Press, 1938.

Grizzell, E. D. *Origin and Development of the High School in New England before 1865.* New York: The Macmillan Co., 1923.

Hacker, L. M. *The Shaping of the American Tradition.* New York: Columbia University Press, 1947.

Hansen, A. O. *Liberalism and American Education in the Eighteenth Century.* New York: The Macmillan Co., 1926.

Holmes, P. *A Tercentenary History of the Boston Public Latin School, 1635–1935.* Cambridge, Mass.: Harvard University Press, 1935.

Jernegan, M. W. *Laboring and Dependent Classes in Colonial America, 1607–1783.* Chicago: University of Chicago Press, 1931.

Johnson, C. *Old Time Schools and School Books.* New York: The Macmillan Co., 1904.

Kilpatrick, W. H. *The Dutch Schools of New Netherland and Colonial New York.* Washington, D.C.: Government Printing Office, 1912.

Knight, E. W. *A Documentary History of Education in the South before 1860.* 5 vols.; Chapel Hill: University of North Carolina Press, 1949–53.

———. *Public Education in the South.* Boston: Ginn & Co., 1922.

———. *Reports on European Education.* New York: McGraw-Hill Book Co., Inc., 1930.

Maddox, W. A. *The Free School Idea in Virginia before the Civil War.* New York: Teachers College, Columbia University, 1918.

Martin, G. H. *Evolution of the Massachusetts Public School System.* New York: Appleton-Century-Crofts, Inc., 1894.

Meriwether, C. *Our Colonial Curriculum, 1607–1776.* Washington, D.C.: Capitol Publishing Co., 1907.

Miller, A. S. *Racial Discrimination and Private Education.* Chapel Hill: University of North Carolina Press, 1957.

Mulhern, J. *A History of Secondary Education in Pennsylvania.* Lancaster, Pa.: Science Press, Inc., 1933.

Norton, A. O. *The First Normal School in America.* Cambridge, Mass.: Harvard University Press, 1926.

Parrington, V. L. *Main Currents in American Thought.* 3 vols.; New York: Harcourt, Brace & Co., Inc., 1927–30.

Seybolt, R. F. *Source Studies in American Colonial Education. The Private School.* Urbana, Ill.: University of Illinois Press, 1925.

Sweet, W. W. *Religion in Colonial America.* New York: Charles Scribner's Sons, 1942.

Tewksbury, D. G. *The Founding of American Colleges and Universities before the Civil War.* New York: Teachers College, Columbia University, 1932.

Turner, F. J. *The Frontier in American History.* New York: Henry Holt & Co., Inc., 1920.

Warfel, H. *Noah Webster, Schoolmaster to America.* New York: The Macmillan Co., 1936.

Woodson, C. G. *The Education of the Negro Prior to 1861.* Washington, D.C.: Association for the Study of Negro Life and History, 1919.

Woody, T. *Early Quaker Education in Pennsylvania.* New York: Teachers College, Columbia University, 1920.

———. *Educational Views of Benjamin Franklin.* New York: McGraw-Hill Book Co., Inc., 1931.

———. *A History of Women's Education in the United States.* 2 vols.; Lancaster, Pa.: Science Press, Inc., 1929.

Part V

THE DAWN OF THE NEW SOCIAL AND EDUCATIONAL ERA

15 The Crisis of the Twentieth Century

While these words are being written the Cold War between the Communist and the liberal worlds still rages, and has entered the classrooms. Man-made earth satellites of both worlds encircle the earth at tremendous rates of speed. Having explored much of the earth, man, aided by science, is now exploring outer space. However, man must continue to live on his own planet and wrestle with problems nearer home, problems that have become intensified by economic, social and political change, as well as by progress in science.

Economic Change

Economically, modern society has been in a rapid state of development, and we are entering now a "Second Industrial Revolution." Atomic power will, probably, soon replace electric power in industry and transportation. Besides, the age of automation has already begun without the aid of atomic power. Automation means the performance of work by machines without any direct use of human skill, control or intelligence. Machines in factories and business will soon be run not by men but by other machines possessing "electronic brains." The influence of automation upon human relations in the worker's world, and upon individual and social life promises to be revolutionary. We do not know what kind of personality and skill will be needed by men in the new age, nor how to educate them for their changed life. More people will have more leisure time in the years ahead, and society and schools will have to make many adjustments, sometimes probably painful, as a result.

Our modern age has been one of economic unrest within each nation as well as in the international sphere. Radio has annihilated space and time in communication, and air transport has made all men neighbors, although good neighborliness still remains to be achieved. Industrial power has become master of the world. If men cannot control it and make it their servant, humanity is entering an age of slavery. Grief and misery for the workers in factories accompanied the flowering of the machine age. Yet, men hoped, as they still hope, that somewhere ahead lay Utopia. Have we created a Frankenstein which will destroy us, or shall we make industrial power our servant in shaping a better life for humanity? We have the intelligence to meet the crisis. Sufficient knowledge of the important aspects of the problem, for which we look to our social scientists, while it may exist, is not enough. There must be the will to apply it. Perhaps the world needs a new mind. We worship machinery and the technical power it gives us. We have no desire to curb that power, even though it may destroy in a few hours, as it does in war, what it has taken years of labor to create. Into the hands of man, whose spirit is still that of our savage ancestors, we have put not a club but a deadly machine. In our greed, hatred, envy—our whole emotional nature—we are still cave-men. With the aid of applied science these traits may destroy civilization.

Social Change

POPULATION PRESSURE. The easy movement of people across national frontiers ended with World War I. Frontiers have been closed, with the result that the international struggle and the social struggle within nations have been intensified. The world's population has more than trebled since 1750, and it is now growing at the fastest rate in history—1.7 per cent per year. Sociologists estimate that, in the year 2000, if that rate continues, it will have reached the 5½ billion mark, or double the present (1957) population. The most rapid increase is occurring in areas where food is most scarce. Ruthless nature, by famine and disease, may check the increase. The problem calls for intelligent planning by governments and international agencies. Nations, like Hindustan, which are trying to eliminate illiteracy, find that the school cannot keep pace with the population increase. While we reach for the moon, there are goals nearer home still to be reached. In our generation, population pressure, real or imaginary, was made one of the bases of aggressive, nationalistic sentiment in Nazi Germany and Fascist Italy. The problem of overpopulation must be dealt with, sooner or later, by the statesmen of the world.[1]

[1] E. Huntingdon, "Agricultural Productivity and Pressure of Population," *The Annals of the American Academy of Political and Social Science*, 198: 73–92; W. S. Thompson and P. K. Whelpton, "Levels of Living and Population Pressure," *Ibid.*, pp. 93–100; F. H. Hankins, "Pressure of Population as a Cause of War," *Ibid.*, pp. 101–8; J. O. Hertzler, *The Crisis in World Population* (Lincoln: University of Nebraska Press, 1956).

COMMUNICATION AND PROPAGANDA. Men live in two worlds: the world of fact, of reality, and the world of fancy. This latter world is almost universally a very inexact copy of the real one, but it alone we know. Each of us, in a lifetime, gathers a few facts about the real world, or a small segment of it. What we accept as knowledge of the world is almost entirely but cultural prejudice, not something based upon fact. Thus, the citizens of different nations see the world in different ways. What is regarded as fact in one nation is often a lie in another. Even well-educated people accept the myths of their own different mental worlds as realities. The two worlds, in spite of efficient news-gathering agencies, are still almost as far apart as they have ever been. This is due in part to the fact that, because of technological advance and the impact of forces released by World War I, the world of the twentieth century is almost a new world, the newness of which few have yet begun to realize.

Respect for truth and the right of men to seek it have marked democratic social thought and practice. If our mental world in America, for instance, has been far removed from reality (and it has been), that was not due to obstacles to truth created by agencies of the state. Private news agencies, for motives of their own, may have at times given us distorted, or even untruthful, pictures of events, but none of these had a monopoly in the field, and the road to truth was never closed, though at times it was a tortuous one. For the totalitarian states, the story is an entirely different one. In them, governments have attempted not to change the mental world of their people, but rather to change the real world so that it might conform with their conception of it. And they have tried to shape the physical world of tomorrow by building a picture of it in the minds of their people. To these ends, academic freedom, and freedom of speech and of the press, were abolished, and all news and ideas were brought under rigid government control.

The difficulty in bringing our mental world and the real world together has been increased by official and unofficial agencies of propaganda whose aim is to mould public opinion in order to further some desired ends. One of the greatest evils of our time has been the propaganda of the totalitarian dictators by which, through schools and other very effective channels of mass impression, they have converted their youth into racial and national bigots. The almost complete control of the dictators over all instruments and agencies of communication apparently shut out very effectively the opinions of those opposed to them both at home and abroad. The views of people in democratic countries about their totalitarian neighbors have probably been distorted, but they have been crystal-clear compared with those of people living under the dictators.

Propaganda is a technique of influencing our actions, and it is a cheaper means of securing mass support for some policy than force or bribery. Its purpose is to make people think and act as we want them to do. It does that by promising them certain gains, and by appealing to some primitive instinct before real knowledge has had a chance to influence their reason. We are basically feeling or instinctive animals, as Aristotle taught. We feel first; we think afterwards. Yet we proceed from feeling to a rational justification of our behavior, and then disavow its instinctive basis. The propagandist plays upon love, hate, and fear. In peacetimes we find release for our emotion of hate in political campaigns and in some sports; in wartimes we substitute savage for civilized modes of hatred. The trained propagandist knows that. When normal, civilized outlets for men's emotions are restricted, and when the individual's life becomes regimented and largely passive, the pent-up, repressed instincts may easily result in internal revolution or war against a neighbor. A régime built upon hatreds must keep fostering those hatreds, or perish. Hatreds of neighbors, spies, races, counter-revolutionaries, and the fear of all such enemies must be constantly stimulated to keep the masses in frenzied loyalty. Today we turn our hatred not upon a Satan, but often upon our neighbors. And the motive prompting modern mass hatreds is usually the strengthening of a tyranny, or the gaining of some social or economic advantage.

International tensions are largely psychological, and are rooted in a feeling of insecurity, or some other form of dissatisfaction such as poverty, real or imaginary. Real causes of dissatisfaction, we probably can do something about. The imaginary causes, when they are the result of organized propaganda, we can remove only by controlling propaganda itself, and that presents many practical difficulties. Besides, we still know but little about the psychological enigma that is man. While propaganda goes back to our cave days, propaganda as a function of government, and operated according to official plans, has attained its perfection in the present century. The school, always an instrument of propaganda, is now but one of many agencies which governments use to influence public opinion.[2]

[2] H. L. Childs, "Public Opinion—First Line of Defense," *The Annals of the American Academy of Political and Social Science,* 198: 109–15; G. Zilboorg, "Propaganda from Within," *Ibid.,* pp. 116–23; R. D. Casey, "The Press, Propaganda, and Pressure Groups," *Ibid.,* 219: 66–75.

Political Change

NAZI-FASCIST TOTALITARIANISM. On the political side, and basically as a reflection of economic change, the present century has been marked by the rise of new political régimes, which have come to be designated as totalitarian. They represent almost a complete abandonment of the political liberalism that had been developing for a century and a half prior to World War I. While the revolt against liberalism and the liberal state has been world-wide, the totalitarian systems of Germany, Italy, and Russia present the most extreme form that the movement has assumed. All three were the results of World War I, the economic and political causes that produced it, the forces it unleashed, the problems it failed to solve, and the thirst for power of Hitler, Mussolini, Stalin, and their supporters, who took advantage of the times to attain their ends. World War I brought revolutions, of different forms and degrees of intensity, in Russia, Germany, Austria, Hungary, Turkey, and Bulgaria. It also created social unrest in Italy. The German revolution was led by more conservative men than was that of Russia, and a liberal government was established and remained in power for fourteen years. The fear on the part of the upper classes that the workers' revolutionary party might get control of the machinery of the liberal state brought the National Socialists and Hitler to power in 1933. It is worthy of note that conservatives outside of Italy and Germany welcomed the coming of Fascism, and gave it moral and sometimes financial support, because it put a curb upon labor unions and ended the threat of Communism.

In Germany, the Nazi Party, when it achieved its victory, provided the bourgeoisie with the mass support necessary to establish a Fascist dictatorship, through which capitalism would be saved and the workers' revolutionary movement suppressed. The National Socialist Germany Labor Party (Nazis) catered, as their name indicates, to many forms of prejudice, and resorted to various forms of demogoguery. Thus the Nazis diverted the workers' hatred of German capitalism into a hatred of "foreign" capitalism and "international Jewish bankers." Their bitter opposition to Marxism gained for them the support of conservative elements, while their patriotic outpourings drew still others into their camp. But it was his political acumen and ultimately his support by the bourgeoisie that brought Hitler, the Nazi leader, to power, and inaugurated the Nazi dictatorship.

The triumph of the Nazis ended the post-war liberal régime and the Weimar Constitution (1919) upon which it stood. This brief period of liberalism was one of sharp economic, social and political conflicts which raged within the government and extended even into the schools, parents and students being split into hostile groups. In the crisis, the conservatives, led by the bourgeoisie, who dreaded Communism, turned to the Fascist dictatorship of Hitler in order to save Germany from Bolshevism and their own property from confiscation, though it is very probable that the liberal government, if given a chance, would have served those same ends.

In Italy, social unrest arose upon the termination of World War I. Strikes of factory and, sometimes, professional workers occurred frequently. The cost of living kept mounting, but wages remained nearly stationary. There was, however, no violence connected with these acts. Mussolini, once a left-wing socialist, stood on the fence while the struggle was occurring, ready apparently to save the victors. When it was clear that a proletarian revolution was most improbable, he threw in his lot with the industrial and agricultural bourgeoisie, and became a violent nationalist under the reactionary banner of the Fascists, organized by himself and others during the war to foster military and civilian morale. Unlike the Italian proletariat, the Fascists resorted to violence to secure their ends. Mussolini and his Fascists came to power by force, and they remained in power by violence or the threat of violence. Fascism captured the forces of patriotism in Italian life, and created out of them the ultranationalistic strivings of Mussolini and his devotees. Like Nazism, Fascism was nationalism run to tribalism.

German Nazism and Italian Fascism were alike in all basic aspects. Both sprang from the soil of despair and social decay, and triumphed because of the weakness of the forces opposed to them. Mussolini and Hitler came as messiahs leading despairing nations out of a wilderness in the direction of a promised land of plenty and national satisfaction. As Christian leaders pointed to the evils of paganism; as monarchists, like Machiavelli, stressed the weakness of the Christian state; as liberal statesmen built strong arguments upon the defects of monarchies, so Mussolini and Hitler justified totalitarianism largely as a remedy for the evils of liberalism. It is too soon to say that their ideologies have fallen with them. Yet, we shall write of them largely in the past tense.

NEGATIVE ASPECTS OF NAZI-FASCIST SOCIETY. (1) ANTI-LIBERALISM. The creators of Nazi-Fascist society proclaimed that all the social ills of the modern world have been due to liberalism, and that civilization can be saved only by destroying liberalism forever, and by putting in its place a régime of absolute authoritarianism imposed by the totalitarian state. While the philosophy of liberalism deals with all aspects of social life, individualism is its central thought. Nazi-Fascist philosophy and practice are a complete denial of individualism, and under them the individual became the abject slave of the state. Under these systems, the leader, whether a *Duce* or a *Führer*, identified himself with the state. Different political parties with different programs were not permitted to exist. The Nazi-Fascist state was not only anti-individualistic and anti-liberal in its ideology, but in its political and, in many respects, its economic practice as well.

(2) Anti-Pluralism. Nazi-Fascist leaders opposed the breaking down of the state into groups with conflicting loyalties and interests. Capital and labor, Protestant church and Catholic church, rival political parties and other opposing groups, which diverted the citizen's loyalty from the state and dissipated its power, did not enjoy the freedom of expression and action which they did under the liberal régimes of the past. There must be no divided loyalties in such a state. Anti-pluralism means also that the dualism which had been assumed under liberalism between the state and society does not exist. For the Nazi-Fascists nothing exists but the state. There is nothing outside it; it embraces, and is, everything within it. The state is the indivisible *totality* of everything within the nation. The primary function and duty of every individual, school, church, club, scientific society, etc., is thus the political one of service to the state. The political precepts rooted in anti-pluralism applied with special force to teachers and publishers, because they were builders of Nazi-Fascist minds. Academic freedom and freedom of the press and of speech were destroyed by law.

(3) Anti-Rationalism. Emotion has always been the chief basis of social unity. Culture is predominantly an emotional thing, though philosophers have often intellectualized it. In the liberal world there has been a glorification of reason and of science. The rational, doubting, problem-solving man became the ideal man. Nazism and Fascism were revolts against the rationalism and against the "science without preconceptions" of the liberal era. They were a return to the age of myths and irrationalism. Their ideal man and citizen was not the thinking man, but the feeling, believing, doing man. Said the Nazi Goebbels: "I think with my blood." And only those of undefiled Nordic blood are, according to Hitler, capable of correct feeling and action, for such are rooted in blood and soil. Upon myths, not upon science, Nazi-Fascists leaders built their states. Their position was a negation of the Renaissance, the Reformation, rationalism, science, and every other step in the process of man's emancipation from spiritual, intellectual and social slavery.

(4) Anti-Semitism. Anti-Semitism was but one phase of the extremely racial nationalism of the Nazi-Fascist régimes. During the mediaeval period of Western society, the church enacted tyrannous laws against the Jews, and subjected them to barbarous punishments and restrictions aimed at their total destruction. The church had become anti-Christian. What the church failed to do, Hitler undertook in order to purge the Nordic state of the supposedly impure blood of the foreigner from the East, who had refused to abandon his racial and cultural exclusiveness. The myth of race and blood superiority, a product largely of long social conditioning and group conflicts, is as old as human society. When Fichte, in 1807-1808, reminded the German people of the superiority and purity of their race and their folk-culture, he stirred up feelings that were easy to arouse but difficult to still. A whole array of Germans, and many outsiders like Chamberlain, the author of *The Foundations of the Nineteenth Century*, kept adding fuel to the fire which Fichte had kindled. Alfred Rosenberg's *Myth of the Twentieth Century* was the official bible of Hitler's racial creed.

Down through human history, all societies have had their devils, or something else to hate. Among the chief things to be hated, Hitler gave his people the Jews, with their non-national religious culture, and whose alleged vices he described in his *Mein Kampf*. Under the Nazi régime, they were brutally persecuted and deprived of practically all political and civil rights. They could not be citizens, nor peasants, nor civil servants. Intermarriage between them and "Aryan" Germans was forbidden. Much of their property was confiscated. Those of them who could escape fled into exile. All "non-Aryans," Christian or not, were legally subjected to the same disabilities as the Jews, though the latter were the chief sufferers. While Mussolini, in early days of Fascism, denounced racial prejudice, he, under the influence of Hitler, launched a program of anti-Semitism. He forbade (1938), as did Hitler earlier, intermarriage between Italians and non-Aryans, most of whom he subjected to a wide variety of disabilities. In enforcing German and Italian laws against the Jews, a Jew was defined in terms of blood alone. Here again we have a return to the primitive feeling of tribal blood unity.

(5) Anti-Feminism. In the liberal world men slowly and reluctantly emancipated women from an age-old bondage. The enfranchisement of women in England and America since World War I was a last step in a long struggle for freedom. The Weimar Constitution gave German women equal civil rights with men, and the earlier German concept of women's duty—*Kinder, Kirche, Küche* (children, church, kitchen)—was officially rejected. Hitler imme-

diately denounced the idea of woman's equality as "a product of decadent Jewish intellectualism." Her one duty, said he, is to bear strong children for the state. It is a man's duty to die for the nation; a woman's, to furnish another soldier-son to take his place. In the official Nazi view, a woman's nature is different from a man's, and in creative ability she is his inferior. The home was declared to be her natural sphere of activity. In political and social affairs she, with the rest of the "anonymous masses," both male and female, had no voice. Mussolini's views on woman's nature, ability and sphere were similar to those of the Nazis. After his rise to power, Mussolini called upon women to perform their "natural female function" of childbearing, in the military interest of Italy and "Christian civilization."

In practice, Nazism excluded women from political offices, and those under the age of thirty-five, or the wives of employed men who were over thirty-five, from government employment. A law of June 3, 1933, required all private employers to dismiss all married women whose husbands could support them, and all single women whose parents, brothers, or sisters could support them. Military needs resulted in the neglect of that law. Not more than 10 per cent of the officially limited enrollment in German universities might be women, and women who graduated found the professions for which they prepared hard to enter. Only 75 women might enter the medical profession yearly. Said the Nazi medical journal: "The woman doctor is a hermaphrodite who offends the natural and healthy instinct of the people." Women teachers might hold only subordinate positions. Said a Nazi educational journal: "The men teachers' aversion to women superiors is in keeping with the healthy instinct of men." [3] A state program of training girls for their future duties was thoroughly organized. All girls between ten and eighteen years years of age had to belong to the League of German Girls, the activities of which were chiefly physical. Those between eighteen and twenty had to perform compulsory labor service. Labor camps were provided for these. Among their duties were draining swamps, farming, and domestic service in homes where there were more than three children.

In Italy the drift was also backward. The minimum age for marriage of girls was lowered from fifteen to fourteen. A husband might inflict physical correction on his wife, provided it was not so violent as to injure her health. Should she die as a result, the penalty was but eight years' imprisonment. A wife was severely punished for leaving her husband, but a husband might abandon his

[3] S. Parkhurst, "Women in Totalitaria," *Living Age* (June, 1939).

wife with impunity. Sex irregularities of men were legally approved, condoned, or but mildly punished; those of women and girls, severely punished. Fascism in Italy was a return to the double standard of morality at its worst.[4]

POSITIVE ASPECTS OF NAZI-FASCIST SOCIETY. Thus far we have seen these régimes as a negation of beliefs and practices of the liberal world. They had also their positive aspects which were officially stressed. The rights and will of the all-powerful state were opposed in theory and practice to individualism, and the state was put at the top in the list of values. Irrationalism, emotionalism, and subjectivity of truth were substituted for intellectualism and the objectivity of truth. The feeling and active man replaced the man of thought as the ideal of Nazi-Fascist manhood. Truth was viewed not as an objective, scientific thing, but only that, be it myth or fact, which serves the ends of the state. Truth is essentially a subjective thing, said the Nazis, and Nordic feeling, not science, is the only reliable testimony to it. Among the important positive aspects of the régimes are the following:

(1) Rule by Elite. It was asserted that only the leader and a select few have the right to rule. Society, and not nature, determines who are fit to be leaders. There are no "natural" and "inalienable" rights. Society gave each one even his life, and can take it away from him. Yet, while the doctrine of "natural" right was rejected, the dictators and their spokesmen justified the rule of their governments on the ground of the natural gifts and demonstrated ability of those in power. The ruling elite were not of Plato's philosopher type, but they were, in theory, heroic, ambitious, strong men of indomitable will. The courageous despot who demonstrates his awe-inspiring hold upon the masses is the one fit to rule. The benevolent, humanitarian ruler who is beloved, rather than feared, by his subjects is unfit to rule. Young men possessed of the desired traits were prepared through Nazi and Fascist youth organizations and special schools for positions of political and military leadership.

(2) Collectivism. Nazi-Fascists stressed the idea of the collectivity of the *Volk*-state. It is a unity in which the fratricidal struggle between individuals and groups is no longer to be countenanced. The Marxian doctrines of economic determinism and the class struggle were denied by the Nazi-Fascists. The Nazi-Fascist man is not, it was said, an economic animal thirsting for the property, or blood, of his fellows. He does not live by bread alone. He is nourished more by the common spirit, or culture, of the national

[4] *Ibid.*

Volk than by bread. In Italy and Germany collectivism did not mean, as it does in Russia, collective ownership of property or unity of the laboring class, but the political and spiritual collectivity of the national community (*Gemeinschaft*). Property was not collectivized, and labor unions were abolished as detrimental to the common interests of the *Gemeinschaft*. Individual and class interests were subordinated to the interests of the state, and the laboring class was forced to make the chief sacrifice in the building of the new collectivized society.

(3) ACTIVISM. While they have been given a philosophical basis, Nazism and Fascism were activistic movements, and it is the movements that were stressed rather than the philosophies. The Nazi-Fascist man was a doer rather than a thinker; he demanded action rather than talk from his leaders. All social systems, either explicitly or implicitly, rest upon some conception of the nature of man. Activism, whether we find it in America or in *Totalitaria*, rests upon a monistic view of man's nature which negates the old idea of a dualism between mind and body. While the Nazi-Fascist régimes embodied the Hegelian idealistic conception of the state, which was viewed as a spiritual and moral reality, they operated on the pragmatic basis that what is useful for them is reality and truth. Man, for them, is an active, unitary organism, and it is the collective activity of all individuals that produces the strong state. Intellectualism was accordingly rejected in favor of activism both in school and society.

COMMUNIST TOTALITARIANISM. Humanism, the Reformation, the scientific movement, political liberalism, the spread of common-man democracy, and the Industrial Revolution, which brought the modern world of Europe and America into being, left Russia almost untouched. She stood, in 1914, as a mediaeval society in a modern world. While the upper classes were educated, and some Russians stood in the ranks of world intellectuals, about 70 per cent of Russians were illiterate. Intellectually and culturally the teeming masses were still in the Dark Ages, while even many of them led a pre-literate, tribal existence. They lived by superstition, not by science. The state church helped to make them obedient to the will of the Tzars. Revolutionary ideas had been spreading for about a century before the Revolution of 1917, and many revolutionists were exiled or executed. The reactionary measures of Tzar Nicholas brought the Revolution of 1917 and the execution of the royal family in 1918. It was a violent reaction against political and social tyranny and economic injustice. The policy of the Tzars throughout the nineteenth century and early twentieth was generally opposed to all liberal demands, and their rule was marked by autocratic repression of the masses and reformers alike. The overthrow of autocracy and all its approved orthodoxies in 1917 is proof of the instability of such a régime and the futility of the methods used to preserve it.

(1) Laying the Bases of the Soviet State. Some elements of Communism may be found in many societies from primitive times onward, and the theory can be traced far back through the stream of distant thought. Marx, Engels, and Lenin crystallized the idea and brought it into touch with modern conditions. In the Communist Manifesto (1848), Marx and Engels issued the call: "Workers of the world, unite." The workers were told by them that they had nothing to lose in the struggle but their chains. It was a call to international revolution by the working class against their employers, and against an economic system in which they were presumed to have no stake. The international and class character of the movement thus took shape. Communism embodies the ideas that the economic force determines human actions and social institutions, that there is a class struggle, that revolt of the workers against their bourgeois masters is inevitable, and that capitalism is doomed. Contrary to the theory that the revolution would occur first in the most advanced industrial nation, it came first in Russia, one of the most backward of the industrial nations. And capitalism, again contrary to theory, has proved its adaptability to new social conditions, theories and practices.

Marxist-Leninists, while indebted to Hegelian idealism, make historical materialism their basic philosophy. For them, the mode of production, in each historical period, determined the economic basis of society, and that basis, then, shaped everything above it—religion, philosophy, law, art, science, etc. They reject the philosophy of idealism as an expression of aristocratic-bourgeois institutions and interests. History is but a reflection of the operation of materialistic forces in societies. The social goals which Marxist-Leninists profess to strive for will be, they assert, attained by applying the philosophy of dialectical materialism to social problems. This philosophy teaches that all life and institutions are in a state of continuous change, and that every social institution carries the germ of its own decay. In all society, and in all its parts, there exists a continuous struggle between the conflicting forces of conservatism and destruction. Eventually the struggle leads to a new stage in social evolution. Man, who is both a creator and a creature of his environment, participates in the struggle. Properly educated, or conditioned, he can shape his environment and direct the struggle toward desired ends. The Russian revolutionists changed the old environment, and hoped to produce a new man with a new mind, one who would be social and co-operative rather than individualistic and acquisitive. Economic and educational planning, they held, would provide the material and psychological conditions necessary to that end. In the practical work of building the new society, the leaders themselves have been in sharp disagreement on important points of policy. Under Lenin's New Economic Policy (1921), peasant proprietorship of small farms was provided for, and the international idea in Communism was kept to the fore.

Stalin, who succeeded Lenin in 1924, gave more attention to internal developments than to promoting an international revolution of workers. The Soviet régime, as it has developed, has been nationalistic, and Stalin placed love of the Fatherland first among civic virtues, but he wished workers everywhere to look to the Soviet state as their friend and worthy of their love. And Russians should revere not only the Russia of the present but the Russia of the past, whose past glories and achievements should be, he said, an object of pride to every Soviet citizen. He tried, by ruthless methods, to destroy the last vestiges of capitalism, and to perpetuate his own power by destroying those opposed to his policies or whose influence he feared. On his death, March 6, 1953, the political officials who had worked under him proceeded to desanctify their allegedly long-cherished idol, but their reasons for renouncing him have not yet become clear. Contradictions and disagreements are not unknown in the Soviet state. Since the French Revolution, nothing has happened in the world of such significance as the Russian Revolution. The spin which the Bolsheviks gave to the wheel of history has been changing the ways of the world, and people everywhere have felt its influence.

Since the rise of Stalin, Russia has been transformed from a feudal-peasant society into a technological power equal, perhaps, to the United States. The rapidity of that change almost surpasses the imagination. Central planning, and harnessing of natural resources, talent and man power explain this rapid change. In the process, labor was exploited as inhumanly as it was in the early stages of industrialism in capitalist countries. If the goals were humane (and the Communists say they were), the methods were not. The system, however, appeals strongly to backward people who desire to leap from semi-primitive ways into modern technological life. Mao-Tse-tung, following Marxist-Leninist theory, is now transforming the Chinese peasant society into an industrialized and agricultural one by a process similar to that of Russia. Whether he can succeed in collectivizing farming remains to be seen. All people do not react to coercion in the same way.

(2) THE SOVIET STATE AND ITS PEOPLE. The Soviet state covers about one-sixth of the earth. While most inhabitants are European, Asiatic cultural influence upon Russian ways of life has been strong. The population now (1958) is approximately 210 millions. It is a motley patchwork of about two hundred peoples, some of them mountain tribes who were pre-literate in 1917. The Russians comprise more than one-half, and the Ukranians, about one-fifth of the total population. Some 75 per cent of the population are Slavs. Each group has its own language. Under the Tzars, Russian was the official language, and those who did not speak it were deprived of many privileges. The Communists rejected the coercive Russification policy of the Tzars, and proclaimed the equality of all racial and linguistic groups. The Soviet state is a multi-national one, called the Union of Socialist Soviet Republics, a federal state of equal nations, of which the Russians are the dominant national group. The larger groups are organized into "Union Republics," and smaller ones, into "Autonomous Republics" within the Union Republics, while still other smaller groups are assigned "Autonomous Regions" and districts. The powers of these local governments is sharply limited by the enormous constitutional powers conferred upon the central government. The government of the Soviet state is highly centralized, although the several republics are, by plan, always represented in it.[5] The Communist Party controls the whole governmental machinery through the decisions of its Central Committee, which are binding upon all the republics. The secretary of that committee, whether a Stalin or a Khrushchev, plays the rôle of dictator.

Power resides in the Party and its rulers, and is exercised in complicated ways which cannot be described here. The Party, which now consists of about 7,000,000 members, is the source of all power, and the only political party in the USSR. Membership in it opens the door to every office and privilege in the state. Theoretically, it is the instrument of the dictatorship of the proletariat. The chief duty of its members is to keep all state institutions—army, navy, schools, etc.—in harmony with "the Party line." These members are, in theory, the elite of the working class who accept devoutly the Party program, and live and act under rigid Party discipline. An elaborate educational program has been set up to teach them the doctrines of Marxism-Leninism and the history of the Party, special

[5] W. W. Kulski, *The Soviet Regime* (Syracuse, N.Y.: Syracuse University Press, 1954), pp. 131–217.

stress being laid upon the philosophy of dialectical and historical materialism as the theoretical basis of the Party and the state.[6] While workers and peasants, often with little education, were once numerically dominant in the Party and the government, those with higher education have, recently, largely outnumbered those with only secondary and elementary education. The Party charter of 1952 declares that "The Communist Party of the Soviet Union is a voluntary and militant union of one-minded Communists recruited from among the working class people, the toiling peasants and the working intelligentsia." [7] One-mindedness does not preclude criticism within the Party, but criticism must not be such as to interfere with the raising of the "cultural level of the working class," or such as to undermine the Party. Free discussion and criticism must keep within the bounds of orthodoxy—an old and respected principle of ecclesiastical and political systems. Those proposed for Party membership are subjected to the closest scrutiny during a probationary period and, after admission, may be expelled, which is a matter most serious in its consequences. Only those of strong faith and the spirit of sacrifice would dare to seek Party membership. The duties of the members are most arduous, and few there are who are desirous of undertaking them.

Throughout the USSR, safeguards of the rights of minorities have been established. The government created new alphabets for illiterate tribes, and books are published in the approximately one hundred and thirty languages of the major groups. Because, presumably, no Soviet citizen may have foreign political interests, such as Zionism, Jews have occasionally been attacked in the Soviet press, but there is no evidence of racial anti-Semitism in these attacks. While Jews are not recognized as a nationality, there is one "autonomous region" (not "republic") which is theirs.[8] Jewish religion is treated with official hostility as are all religions.

(3) Soviet Collectivism. The state is the owner of nearly all property, land, factories, industrial and farming machinery, etc., and operates, through various departments and agencies, nearly all businesses, farms, etc. Private business has almost entirely vanished. A central State Planning Commission directs the economic life of the nation and integrates education with it. With Stalin's first Five Year Plan (1928-1933), collectivization of farms and livestock began, and grasping peasants (*kulaks*) who opposed the program were either brutally "liquidated," or compelled by taxation and other devices to

6 *Ibid.*, p. 165.
7 *Ibid.*, p. 172.
8 *Ibid.*, p. 191.

support it.[9] Collective farms are now the almost universal practice. All land has been nationalized. Individual peasants on the collective farms may own some livestock and have the use of a plot for gardening. While Nazi-Fascist collectivism was basically political, that of Russia is basically economic and social, designed, said Lenin, to protect the weak against the strong.[10]

(4) THE STATUS OF WORKERS. Theoretically, the Soviet state is a workers' state, a proletarian dictatorship, but actually the industrial worker and the peasant have not yet fared well. Everyone, no matter how employed, is a worker, and the "idle rich" have no recognized place in the new society. In towns, the compulsory working age begins at sixteen; in rural districts, at twelve. Town youths may begin work at fourteen, under certain conditions. Youths under eighteen are exempted from certain heavier tasks. The working hours of everyone are minutely regulated by the Code of Labor Legislation. Generally, the work week is one of forty-eight hours. For teachers and physicians it is shorter. With some minor exceptions, women workers are subjected to the rules governing males. All workers are frozen to their jobs, and may not quit them, or seek employment elsewhere, without permission of the managers of the enterprise on which they work; and these managers represent the state and the Party. While the worker is a member of a union, he is subject to the command of one man. And he does not have complete freedom in choosing his first job. Most workers in mines and factories have been assigned to their jobs by the state. Graduates of many types of vocational schools have to accept, for a compulsory period of four years, whatever job the state offers them. Those without special vocational training are given some freedom in choosing their first jobs. Workers are employed under formal contract, and carry "labor books," which are a requirement for employment in the Soviet workers' world. The "labor book" is held by the management during the worker's period of employment, and no new manager can sign a contract with a man who has no "labor book." Workers on collective farms are given "passports," which betray them as runaways when they seek employment elsewhere. By a strict rule, peasants must remain peasants, although the state sometimes recruits them for industrial work. They are not deemed state employees, and are not covered by state insurance, as are factory and other workers. Absenteeism, etc., and some violations, such as willful absence, are considered criminal offenses, punishable by im-

[9] *Ibid.*, p. 550.

[10] T. Woody, *New Minds: New Men?* (New York: The Macmillan Co., 1932), p. 297.

prisonment for up to four months. Managers, too, are subjected to severe discipline if they fail to enforce the Code. The courts handling the cases have not been lenient in punishing offenders against the law. Employees who have access to military, scientific or state secrets, and who divulge them, are guilty of treason and subject to capital punishment.

Wages and salaries are fixed by the central government, and are so calculated as to insure to the state most of the gross income from each enterprise. The average employee gets about one-third of the value of his output which, for white-collar and manual workers, amounts to about 700 roubles per month. There is no guaranteed minimum wage, and a worker's take-home pay depends largely upon his output, which is closely measured. Wives and children are thus forced into labor by the low incomes of men, as they are in other countries, too. While workers, generally, are provided with generous social security, their living standard is still low, because the cost of living is very high.[11] Competition among enterprises and workers is encouraged by special rewards for increased output and better quality of products, and the cash prizes and bonuses are often high. The capitalist incentive has not vanished in this socialist state. Here, again, we see life as education.

(5) Status of Women. The Soviet Constitution (Article 122) reads: "Women in the USSR are accorded equal rights with men in all spheres of economic, state, cultural, political, and other public activities." The principle of "equal pay for equal work" is embodied in practice. Women, however, are not permitted to engage in a few very heavy occupations, and pregnant women may not engage in night work or overtime work. Some women work as miners, as railroad engineers and as stokers on ships—positions rarely, if ever, held by women in capitalist countries. Since we do not have the result of a Gallup poll, it is impossible to say whether or not Russian women enjoy their equality. Generally, the rules of the Labor Code apply to men and women alike. Trade unions are required to do whatever they can to attract women into the labor field. Maternity leave is provided for working women, and mothers of large families are honored with medals and titles. Thus, mothers of seven children are enrolled in the order of "Maternal Glory," and those who have raised ten children receive the title of "Mother-Heroine." The Russian 1955 beauty queen was a television announcer who was learning to speak six languages.[12] In the field of government the

[11] H. Schwartz, "A Worker's Life in a Workers' State," *The New York Times Magazine* (Oct. 19, 1952), pp. 16 *passim.*

[12] E. M. Kirkpatrick, *Target: The World* (New York: The Macmillan Co., 1956).

principle of equal rights has not yet been achieved in practice. Theoretically, the Supreme Soviet is the highest organ of state power, but only twenty-five per cent of its members, in 1954, were women. It is the Party that really rules the state, and the evidence available to us indicates that relatively few women have been admitted to membership in it. There is at present (1958) one woman in the top echelon of power, but the apex of the pyramid, where she sits, is still controlled by men. In school, or out, the minds of Soviet women are thus being formed.

(6) THE FAMILY IN THE USSR. The family, which in the early years of the régime, was weakened, apparently deliberately, by official policy has become sacrosanct. Soviet law deems its purpose to be the rearing of minor (under age 18) children for patriotic service to the state. When it neglects that duty, the state will rear the children. Parents must support minor and incapacitated children, and adult children must support incapacitated parents. Where parents cannot do so, adult brothers and sisters must support their minor brothers and sisters. Unmarried mothers, or their parents, must support illegitimate children. The state frowns upon illegitimacy, but unmarried mothers are assisted by the state in supporting their offspring. Birth and monthly state family allowances are provided for the support of all children beyond the first two born into the family. A similar practice exists, for instance, in France, England, and Canada. The family has become very important in Russia, and children inherit family property. The state wants large families. For children, however, loyalty to the state must precede loyalty to the family. Should parents act disloyally, children are expected to reveal their crimes. The recently (1955) announced policy of the state to establish boarding schools for children of working parents may embody a distrust of the family as an educational agency.

(7) THE STATE AND RELIGION. While liberal states, whatever their motives, have, in minor respects, been modifying their policies regarding religious education and church schools, the Soviet state has espoused atheism, and has viewed religion, whether institutionalized or not, as an enemy of the working class and of the proletarian state. Youth newspapers attack youths who attend church services, and teachers' journals urge the teaching of atheism and the guarding of children from the religious superstitions of their parents.[13] Teachers are urged by the government to spread "militant materialism and atheism," but in ways that do not offend believers. The Constitution of 1936 declares: "The church . . .

13 "A Student of Eastern Europe," *London Times Educational Supplement* (Feb. 18, 1955), p. 165.

is separated from the state and the school from the church. Freedom of religious worship and freedom of anti-religious propaganda are recognized for all citizens." Freedom of religious propaganda is thus not countenanced. The state is militantly atheistic. Separation does not mean noninterference by the state with churches. The churches remain open, and may train their clergy, but they are subjected to many disabilities. Two state Councils—one for the Orthodox church and the other for some forty minor denominations—regulate religious activities. Churches, unlike all other associations, may not own property (though they may use it), may not make legally valid contracts, may hold services only with permission of local state authorities, may not build new churches (an unfriendly state owns the materials), may not teach religion to youths under eighteen years of age, and then only privately, and may not establish funds for religious purposes, nor have in their reading rooms any but religious books. These are but some of the disabilities to which the churches are subjected. Mrs. Eleanor Roosevelt, on her recent visit to Russia (October 1957), found the churches poorly attended and young people noticeably absent from the services.[14] During the war with Nazi Germany, the churches preached loyalty to the Soviet state, for which they were officially praised, but the government continued to espouse atheism. The anti-religious policy is in keeping with the philosophy of materialism embodied in the régime. Religion is viewed as being capitalistic superstition, and as providing an untrue explanation of life and the world. Viewed historically, it is seen as being aristocratic and an opiate, robbing the workers of their power to revolt against social injustice. Science is made the foundation of social life, and religious dogmas are rejected in the name of science. Museum exhibits, scientific experiments, art, literature, etc. are often designed to show the fallacies of religion.

(8) THE STATE AND SCIENCE. The emphasis of the government upon the sciences, and Soviet progress in science, particularly the physical sciences, is well known. Objectivity in science, however, ends where official dogmas begin. No scientist may expound a philosophy or history of science opposed to Marxist-Leninist doctrines. While the research worker in the physical and natural sciences works in freedom, if he preaches no unorthodox scientific philosophy, the social scientists enjoy no such freedom. Interference with the former might check technological progress. Like the Nazi-Fascists, the Communists subscribe to the principle of

[14] *The Evening Bulletin* (Philadelphia, Oct. 17, 1957), p. 13.

anti-intellectualism where reason becomes a threat to their faith. Yet, the 1958 Nobel prize in literature went to a nonconformist. Objectivity in the social sciences has been an aim of scientists in the liberal world, but it has been, in practice, little more than an ideal. Even liberal scientists have found Bacon's principle of discarding prejudices difficult to achieve, but there were no infallible social dogmas to which they were compelled to adhere.

Marxism-Leninism has its infallible dogmas of social science, revolution and the ultimate triumph of Communism, which no Russian may weaken or destroy, except at grave personal risk. Western "bourgeois" sociologists, philosophers, historians, artists, literary men, etc., are denounced as enemies of the proletariat, and their works are labelled "decadent." The awakening spirit of Russian nationalism probably has had much to do with these attitudes to Western cultural achievements. The Soviet state rates its scholars, scientists and professors highly, and rewards them munificently. President Pusey, of Harvard, reports that university professors' salaries run from a minimum of $18,000 to a maximum of $50,000, as compared with the average annual salary of $5,400 paid to American college teachers.[15] Soviet intellectuals, however, are not men with free minds. The Soviet Union's Council of Ministers, in 1949, laying down rules to guide the editors of the "Great Encyclopedia" of Russia, said that "it must show the superiority of Socialist culture over the culture of the capitalist world," and should present a "party criticism" of "reactionary bourgeois tendencies in various provinces of science and technics."[16] The editors of the French *Encyclopedia,* or of the *Encyclopaedia Britannica* were not thus restricted. The Soviet *Encyclopedia* aims to make Marxism-Leninism the intellectual foundation of the state. Historical and dialectical materialism are the approved faith of the Soviet citizen, and no scientist or scholar is free to weaken that faith. Sovietism displays many of the marks of traditional religions. And the theologians of the new faith would reconcile it with official reason. That practice is not new.

(9) Early Dreams Unfulfilled. In practice, Sovietism has departed far from Marxism. Upon that the authorities agree, although in regard to some particulars of Marx's teaching there is disagreement. Early Bolsheviks sought the Epicurean ideal of a stateless state, and the "withering away" of the political instrument of oppression. That proved to be an unrealistic dream, and the

[15] *The Philadelphia Inquirer* (Nov. 3, 1957), p. 3.

[16] W. Benton, "The Party Line from A to Z," *The New York Times Magazine* (Jan. 22, 1956), pp. 13 *passim.*

Soviet state has shown no desire to wither away. As opposed to the Communist ideal of peace, the Soviet state has accepted war as a means of settling international disputes. The classless society, which was a goal of Communism, has not been realized. In practice, it would be a proletarian-class society. But, in the new proletarian state, there are many classes, and economic and social inequalities are everywhere apparent. Brain workers, with their greater pecuniary rewards, stand upon a much higher social level than those who work with their hands. Differences in mental ability and in educational opportunities create class differences in Russia, as everywhere else. While the Soviet state accepts the principle of equality of educational opportunity, it has not yet achieved it in practice, and peasant youths are deliberately treated unequally. Ideals, no doubt, had often to be abandoned as the state faced realities. Facts are stubborn things, and politics is the science of the possible.

TOTALITARIANISM IN ESSENCE. The totalitarian man believes that there is some absolute theory and practice that will answer all man's needs and which all individuals must accept, if the good life is to be achieved. Totalitarianism covers all areas of life—economic, political, religious, etc. It is not something new. The mediaeval religious system was totalitarian, and was dominated by an all-powerful church. In any form, totalitarianism demands complete conformity from the individual. Authoritarianism and intolerance of nonconformists are of its essence. Every totalitarian man must stand against sin. Any thought or practice which cannot be reconciled with the dogmas is evil. The particular must conform with the total, the absolute. Infallibility is of the essence of totalitarianism. Since all things are but parts of the total, knowledge is viewed as basically unitary and indivisible—a whole. All totalitarian knowledge must conform with the absolute pattern. The deductive method of inquiry, discarded by Francis Bacon and all inductive scientists, is again approved by totalitarian states, whose political and social absolutes stand as the major premises, the "first principles" of all inquiry. Here, fragmentation of knowledge, a mark of science in the liberal world, is condemned. Personal experience and discovery must fit into the pattern of the totality, sense experience to the opposite notwithstanding.

The true scientist realizes that facts are facts (*e.g.* that the earth is round) regardless of men's dogmas, and that the meaning of life and things cannot be established infallibly by a dictum of church or state. The dogmas, too, of science, philosophy or of any men should not ignore human feelings and the dictates of human hearts.

Rousseau stressed that principle. Man's knowledge will always be incomplete, and the perfect world will always lie in the future.

The theological and political absolutes of yesterday and today are of questionable value, if not grave obstacles to man as he struggles for the better world. Theories and ideas, if not imposed upon us as absolutes, serve a desirable end—a challenge to further inquiry. Humanism and individualism come to mind here. Today, as in many societies of the past, words and "logic" continue to deceive men. The free mind is critical of absolutes and of all authority. Totalitarianism can be but a passing stage in social evolution. There is always a heaven beyond, and the schools of tomorrow may trace the path to it. UNESCO may now be pointing the way. Perhaps we, too, should cling to our scientific principle of "objectivity," and avoid interpretations, philosophizing and moralizing, but even historians have, as men, if not as scientists, a right to interpret. It may be good to be wrong. It often was, and no one should be ashamed to be honestly wrong, nor to admit his proven errors. No thought or institution is good enough to be above criticism. Free men and institutions should welcome it.

THE CHANGING LIBERAL STATE. Side by side with the complete rejection of liberalism by the totalitarian states, there have occurred in liberal states themselves some important changes in the traditional principles and practices of liberalism. Pure democracy, which leaves the individual completely free from social control, is anarchy, and would destroy the state. In practice it has never existed in any organized society. We have had only degrees of democracy.

The present century saw a great increase in government activity for the protection of workers and the common good of all citizens. In the United States and in England, laissez faire was never entirely adopted. A program of steadily increasing state interference in America checked, almost from the start, the individualistic tendencies of the Revolutionary period. A tariff act was passed in 1789; the Embargo Act in 1807; the Interstate Commerce Act in 1887; the Sherman Anti-Trust Act in 1890; and many similar acts since then, culminating in many measures of the New Deal legislation of the Roosevelt administration. In addition to federal regulatory laws, many states have enacted labor and factory laws, more recent ones covering such matters as workmen's compensation, minimum wages, and hours of labor. The amount of social legislation adopted in America, particularly since 1932, means that we have become, in a large degree, socialists. And the welfare state in England has gone further than any other modern state in making life secure for all citizens.

SOCIAL DEMOCRACY VERSUS LIBERALISM. Two tendencies appear in the cultural development of Western civilization: the democratic and the socialist. Christianity was an embodiment of both. They are logically contradictory tendencies, for the essence of democracy is freedom; of socialism, equality. Freedom and equality are mutually exclusive. Give men freedom, and they will destroy equality. Freedom is an individual need; equality, a social need. We cannot have social equality unless we restrict individual freedom. Viewed logically, then, the problem presents irreconcilable contrasts. But democracy, in practice, has been founded not upon logic but upon human feelings. Viewed from the standpoint of the human heart, rather than the intellect, freedom and equality have not been, and are not, contradictory. The Christian has accepted both, though he may not have attempted to reconcile them logically. In the "human rights" which liberal philosophers and statesmen have long advocated, the principles of freedom and equality have been combined. Though equality was often assigned a subordinate place, it was accorded wide recognition. The socialists stressed the principle of equality, but as a means to a higher and wider freedom. The difference, in this regard, between the liberal and the socialist was not one of fundamental principles but of emphasis; not one of ends but of means. The feeling, then, generally prevailed that a just and workable synthesis between freedom and equality, and between the rights of the individual and those of society, is possible. The alternatives to that synthesis are anarchy and social chaos, on the one hand, or the destruction of personality by social tyranny, on the other.

Liberalism, as a theory and practice of noninterference with men by society, may perish, and it has long been perishing, but freedom need not perish with it. Liberalism is a way of life which triumphed in the republican revolutions of the eighteenth century. It had its economic, social, political and intellectual aspects. It was suited to the age in which it arose, and was an expression of the spirit of the times. The striving of men for freedom found expression in our political democracies of the past century and a half. As they evolved, there emerged the problem of reconciling freedom with equality, and of individual with social rights. In the process of solving it we have found it necessary to emphasize more and more the principles of equality and social justice. What we have now is not democracy but *social democracy,* in which freedom, while restricted, has strong institutional safeguards, and more individuals enjoy it in greater quantities because of the concessions we have made to equality. Political freedom, moreover, has tended to increase. The restrictions have been placed mainly upon our economic activities.

INTELLECTUAL DEVELOPMENTS

PHYSICAL AND NATURAL SCIENCES. The present century has witnessed extraordinary progress in physics, astrophysics, chemistry, biology and medicine. In physics, research has brought a greater understanding of the atom and the harnessing of atomic energy. In astrophysics, Einstein's deductions from his principle of relativity negate, or demand modification of, Newtonian doctrines regarding space, time and motion.[17] We have discovered a universe so extended that the human mind is apparently unable to comprehend it. Hoyle's theory that space is infinite and that the universe is ever expanding in it is a significant inference from the limited, established data which astrophysicists have thus far gathered.[18] Exploration of outer space in the years ahead will provide further data on the nature of still uncharted seas. Science now promises to solve the riddle of the universe and of man's place in it. In chemistry, our century has seen the creation of many synthetic products. More important, perhaps, chemical research has provided a fuller understanding of the chemical nature of life itself and of the relationship between the secretions of the endocrine glands and bodily growth and human behavior. In biology, perhaps the discovery most important for education has been that hereditary traits are controlled by a biological element called the *gene,* which cannot be changed by environmental influence. This means that we cannot mould human nature at will. It should be noted here that the Machurin-Lysenko biology of Soviet Russia rejects the findings and conclusions of Western biologists, and takes the position that nature can be transformed by the influence of a controlled environment.[19] Where science must conform with political and social dogmas it ceases to be science. Such an occurrence even in the liberal world is not inconceivable.

[17] D. Dietz, *The Story of Science* (New York: Holston House, Sears Publishing Co., 1931), pp. 265–66.

[18] F. Hoyle, *The Nature of the Universe* (Oxford: Basil Blackwell & Mott, Ltd., 1951).

[19] Kulski, *op. cit.,* pp. 56–59; C. Zirkle (ed.), *Death of a Science in Russia* (Philadelphia: University of Pennsylvania Press, 1949).

SOCIAL SCIENCES. Here a significant advance has occurred in the refinement of the methods of research. Where social scientists have been free from political, social and ecclesiastical domination they have made discovery of facts their goal without regard to the effect the facts might have upon traditional social practices. History, political science, economics, sociology and anthropology have become areas of increasing research interest, with the result that we have now much more definite knowledge of social phenomena and the forces that affect them than ever before in history. Under the leadership of such men as Bertrand Russell and John Dewey, ethics has been studied scientifically. Its goal is no longer outside of this world. While modified as a result of new findings, Darwin's basic evolutionary principle has been confirmed by recent research.

PSYCHOLOGY. Since the turn of the present century, there has been a significant growth of interest in man's mental and emotional behavior and in the scientific testing and measuring of human traits. Psychology has now become a full-fledged experimental science, sometimes classified with the natural and sometimes with the social sciences, and occasionally with both. It is as important to know the nature of man as the nature of the universe, and, no doubt, more important for education. While some have continued to reject the doctrines of the unity of mind and body and of the evolution of mind, most psychologists accept the evolutionary hypothesis, and see mind as a complex behavioral product of the physiological mechanism and of man's use of his physical organism. Wilhelm Wundt established, in 1879, at the University of Leipzig, the first experimental laboratory of psychology, dedicated to the view that we should study the human mind as we do other natural phenomena. Soon psychologists were busy investigating the measurable aspects of human behavior, such as memory span, responses to stimuli, intelligence, and a lengthy array of other behavioral phenomena such as moral attitudes, introversion-extroversion, social adjustment, mechanical and musical abilities, appreciation of art and literature, etc.

The new psychologists have been sharply divided in their interpretations of man's psychic life. Such early ones among them as Hall, James, Dewey and Thorndike are known as "functionalists" who, while they viewed psychology as a study of the functions, or responses, of the organism, seen as a unitary, indivisible thing, considered mind and consciousness as something more than physical. These were followed by the "behaviorists" who discarded the concepts of "mind" and "consciousness" completely, and developed a psychology in which thought and emotion were viewed as purely physical functions of the nerves, glands and muscles. For the behaviorists, psychology should concern itself only with behavioral phenomena which could be clearly observed. Against the views of the functionalists and behaviorists, both of whom view behavior as specific response to specific stimuli, Gestalt psychologists, protesting against an overanalysis of behavior, advance the theory, which they say is supported by scientific evidence, that there is in the organism a unifying element, "insight," which produces a generalized response to stimuli. They assert that by "insight" one perceives an object or a situation as a whole, not as an accumulation of separate parts, and that whole things, as they are perceived, are more than the sum of their parts. It is through "insight" into the "whole" situation, they hold, not through a perception of its parts, that problems are solved. Growing out of Gestalt psychology is the "field theory." In this view, the organism lives in a psychological field, "life space," where growth and learning are a matter of action and interaction between the organism and its total environment, not just a result of stimulus and response nor yet of "insight." The field theory is an attempt to bring psychology into harmony with the recent theory of physics which sees matter and energy as one and the same thing.

While it is a theory of psychology as well as a mental therapy, the psychoanalysis of Freud lacks entirely any experimental basis. It is nothing more than hypotheses, none of which has been tested experimentally. Yet it has been widely used in the treatment of abnormal behavior by progressive schools, psychiatrists, and social workers.

PSYCHOLOGY AND LEARNING. Early in the century, Thorndike and his followers studied experimentally the learning process, with a view to discovering the laws of learning. Thorndike, on the basis of insufficient experimental evidence, formulated laws embodying the view that learning is a process of establishing connections between neurons by a method based upon these laws. The child, in this view, learns by his own responses to stimuli—by doing—under the guidance of a teacher who supplies the stimuli. The functionalists and behaviorists saw all responses as basically physical, and thus rejected the traditional view of learning as a purely mental process. The principle of learning by doing took the emphasis off book learning and mental discipline, and focused it upon "activity." The problem-project method, widely acclaimed by American educators, was an attempt to reduce the theory to practice.[20] Teachers

[20] W. H. Kilpatrick, *The Foundations of Method* (New York: The Macmillan Co., 1925).

who followed "behaviorism" considered the total response of the child to a problem more important than specific responses to its parts, and modified Thorndike's doctrine of neural connections in their practices.

Progressive educators turned from these earlier positions to Gestalt psychology and psychoanalysis. The doctrine of "wholeness" of the former has much in common with Herbartian "apperception."[21] Teachers, following the Gestalt theory, presented objects of instruction to students in wholes not in parts. Words, for instance, were taught as wholes, not as separate letters or syllables. And learning of specific things by drill and memorization, apparently implied in the S-R psychology, were avoided, since they tended to interfere with the operation of "insight."

Psychoanalysis ignores the physical basis of behavior and sees mind and personality as a result of intangible, somewhat mysterious, influences in one's early experience. It has had little influence upon education beyond that of providing a theory and a method of treating abnormal behavior of pupils.

These various conflicting theories of human nature and of behavior and learning have left modern teachers in a state of confusion. Foreign educators, until very recently, have paid little attention to psychology. It has been otherwise in the United States. Here psychology has received a unique recognition in the military, business and educational fields, and educational psychology has received universal recognition in our teacher-training programs. Until the psychologists find a scientific basis for the settlement of their differences, educators will have to be satisfied with their state of confusion.[22]

PROGRESS IN PHILOSOPHY. While the older philosophies have survived, and continue to be ably defended, the most significant development in philosophy has come from the expansion of science and the use of the scientific method in exploring the physical and the social worlds. The philosophy of Dewey, Russell, and Morris Cohen embodies the conviction that science and the scientific method are the necessary and only acceptable bases of philosophy. Among the philosophers of this school, Dewey stands pre-eminent. Said he: "The method we term 'scientific' forms for the modern man (and man is not modern merely because he lives in 1931) the

[21] *Supra*, p. 469.

[22] E. L. Thorndike, *The Elements of Psychology* (New York: A. G. Seiler, 1907); B. F. Skinner, *The Behavior of Organisms* (New York: Appleton-Century-Crofts, Inc., 1953); L. Shaffer and E. Shoben, *The Psychology of Adjustment* (2d ed.; Boston: Houghton Mifflin Co., 1956); *Educational Outlook*, XXXI (Nov. 1956).

sole dependable means of disclosing the realities of existence. It is the sole authentic mode of revelation."[23] A critical examination of the philosophy of Dewey, as representing this modern outlook and as compared with other schools of thought, together with a similar study of his educational theory, might well be included in all teacher-training programs. He views man as a psychophysical organism struggling to preserve itself against its environment. What counts is success in that struggle, not futile speculation about the traditional questions of philosophy. The related philosophies of pragmatism and instrumentalism have built upon foundations laid by empiricism, positivism and Darwinism. Where accepted by educators, as frequently happened in the United States, they brought a rejection of the dogmas of "eternal verities" and an acceptance of the dogma of "uncertainty." The pragmatic principle that that idea only is true which works successfully in solving a problem was a denial of the doctrine of traditional philosophies that there are truths which are independent of time, place and circumstances. The new philosophies lent support to the growing tendencies to stress in the curriculum those studies of undoubted functional value in everyday life of individuals and societies.

Developments in Art

Upton Sinclair, in his *Mammonart*, advanced and elaborated the thesis that all art is propaganda and that the artist, because he must sell his products and his service, must cater to the needs and tastes of the ruling, conservative elements in society. Various interpretations, no doubt, of art might be, and have been, advanced, and there is some element of truth in them all. Art is one proof of man's superiority to the animals, and one evidence of his striving to lift himself above the level of creatures that seek merely physical comforts. That it has reflected the needs, ideals and tastes of societies, or the rulers of societies, is more than an assumption. It could not have been otherwise. There probably never has been, strictly speaking, a free, creative art. The freedom of the artist, as of us all, is limited by culture and by those who control culture.

The architectural progress of this century has been the result largely of commercial and industrial needs, and has appeared mainly in factories and business buildings, particularly the latter. Population pressure in urban areas created the need for architectural change, and the perfection of structural steel made that change possible. American cities have been the chief centers of

[23] A. Einstein, *et al.*, *Living Philosophies* (New York: Simon and Schuster, 1931), p. 24.

the development. We have become the land of skyscrapers, the Empire State Building in New York towering above a city of skyscrapers to the height of 1,248 feet. Louis Sullivan and Frank Lloyd Wright, whose influences have been felt in Europe as well as America, have been the creators in this field. The motive of utility has permeated their work. The form of a building must, they held, follow its function, or purpose.

In painting, Cubism, Expressionism, Dadaism, Surrealism, and Futurism have been departures from traditionalism, and have been attempts to create an art reflecting a purely aesthetic motive. They represent an embodiment of individualism, of the free creative spirit, in art. Subjectivism is their chief general characteristic. These artists strove to express their own conceptions and feelings rather than to depict their themes objectively. Subject matter is of secondary importance for them. It is the mode of artistic expression which is the measure of the value of art. The subject very often has been an unreal, sometimes weird, creation of the artist's imagination, and the mode of depicting it has accentuated its unreality. Men, however, have always created realities, and these modern artists exercised a right to create theirs. They were not working aimlessly. The Futurist, for instance, aimed to give to his creations a sense of motion, thus recognizing the fact that everything is in a state of change. Theirs we might call dynamic art. The Surrealists were influenced by Freudian psychology, and dream worlds became their realities. Traditional art aimed to be true to objective reality. These new forms of art aimed to be true to the artists' emotionalized conception of life.

INDUSTRIALISM, SOCIALISM, COMMUNISM, AND ART. Recent forms of painting and, indeed, much of the older painting, have been either beyond the comprehension of the masses or far removed from their lives. Whether the masses could, or could not, appreciate it, traditional art in general was not intended primarily for their enjoyment and enlightenment. The architectural art of cathedrals and churches, their images of saints, their mural ornamentation and stained-glass windows that decorated them were once the literature of the illiterate masses. Only religious art can be said to have really reached them, until the moving picture, with its various forms of propaganda, developed in the present century.

The Communists have taught that art is the people's own creation, that it ought to be comprehensible to them, and that its purpose is to stimulate them to artistic effort, and to unite them in one great cultural brotherhood. Holding that all art in the past has been class art, they have been creating a proletarian art, which they frankly admit is propaganda and justify on the ground that it is in the interest of the laboring masses. They further claim that only in a classless society can the artist attain the maximum degree of freedom possible to man living in organized society. The whole Soviet experiment, in its largest aspect, is an attempt to build a culture different from that of their western neighbors, and to universalize it throughout the entire Union of Socialist Republics. The creators of literature, music, and painting are among the most honored and highly rewarded workers in the socialist state. Here we have art with the single purpose of building a socialist society.

A somewhat similar development, but limited largely to painting, has occurred in Mexico where artists such as Rivera and Orozco have created murals depicting events in Mexican history, and modern social conditions. They have told their story in a way intelligible to the Mexican masses. Some of Rivera's murals in public buildings in the United States gave offense to some who thought they saw in them socialistic and anti-ecclesiastical propaganda.

In the United States, the economic depression stimulated certain artists to depict the evils of our social system. Their interest turned upon such subjects as the lives of strikers, of the unemployed and hungry, and of corrupt politicians. There was also organized the American Artists' Congress, the members of which pledged themselves to work against the spread of Fascist propaganda. The federal government, through the Works Progress Administration, aided many unemployed artists. American art has tended to break away from European patterns and to become national in its content and forms.

We have but touched upon a small part of the changing cultural scene in our review of the art of the century, and we have looked at but a few forms of art. Any complete account would require an examination of all forms of art, including music, and of the literary output of the period. In all of these fields, each nation has made its contribution. While the spirit of internationalism has not disappeared from literature and art, the local and national stamp marks most of it. Local color has always given charm and significance to men's cultural creations, and the world has grown richer through its cultural exchange. Science, art, literature, religion, and philosophy have not been national. To them all the nations have contributed. We all have given, and we all have borrowed. To examine all things and hold fast to the things that are good is a principle the wisdom of which has been attested by experience.

The Age of Uncertainty

Dewey and his school tell us that the only certainty is uncertainty; that everything is subject to the law of change. The scientists, philosophers, and theologians are bewildered in proportion to their knowledge. Only the uninformed man knows no doubts. From the certainties of mediaeval theology and scholastic philosophy we went on, in the nineteenth century, to supposed certainties of science. While the scientific "laws" still furnish a usable working basis of human behavior, even the once most certain of them, such as that of causality and the conservation of energy, are now of doubtful validity. Science, and rightly so, does not propose to give us meanings, but it keeps searching for facts without which there can be no sound meanings. The uncertainties of our time and alarm over their possible social consequences have been, among other considerations, responsible for such educational demands as have come from Professor Mortimer J. Adler and Robert M. Hutchins, former President of the University of Chicago. Regretting the disunity in intellectual life in the modern age, which they attribute largely to the development of the sciences and to specialization in education, they would restore a oneness of purpose to university education and a unity of higher studies based upon a study of metaphysics. They have singled out the philosophy of Dewey and the functionalists for special attack. Their views may be examined in Hutchins' *The Higher Learning in America* and *No Friendly Voice*.

An attempt has been made by Stringfellow Barr and Scott Buchanan at St. John's College, Annapolis, to reduce the Hutchins philosophy to practice. It has been, however, subjected to telling criticism by Dewey and many others. It has, for instance, among other reasons, been criticized on the grounds that metaphysics is but another name for theology; that there is no one metaphysics but many metaphysics, just as there are many theologies; that the intellectual unity it aims at can be achieved only by coercion and indoctrination, as was mediaeval cultural unity; that the so-called "chaos" which it rails against is more desirable than the "order" which it aims to create; that, for all essential purposes, the grounds upon which unity is needed can be reduced to a few ethical principles embodied in fundamental laws which our people have accepted; and that unity of belief in the dogmas of theology and metaphysics is not necessary for peaceful social life.[24] In periods

[24] F. H. Knight, "Theology and Education," *American Journal of Sociology*, XLIV (March 1939), 649–83.

of unrest and rapid change, there is always a hankering on the part of some to restore some "golden age" that has passed. That desire seldom accords with realities that change has brought and which men must face realistically.

Science, Social Change, and Religion

There has been a rapid decline of supernaturalism and of public interest in church activities during the past fifty years. While progress in the sciences has weakened the hold of supernatural religion upon the masses, city life and the rise of secular interests, due largely to industrialism, have been more potent factors back of that change. Many have found modern books, magazines and Sunday newspapers more interesting than sermons. Radio and newspaper moralists and practical ethical experts have gained in popularity at the expense of ministers and priests. Social work, recreation, and charity, formerly prominent church activities, have passed largely into the hands of lay, secular agencies, of which the state is the leading one. However, nothing has weakened the influence of the church as much as has the secularization of education which, in varying degrees, has accompanied the development of national school systems. Once the church was responsible for the building of character and the inculcation of morals. The lay, public teacher now carries that responsibility, and our secular teacher-training institutions offer courses in "character education."

The doctrine of evolution and the views of the "higher critics" of the Bible have been reaching the masses through such channels as textbooks in biology and cultural history, popular scientific and historical books, and popular magazines. Many psychologists have interpreted the rise and acceptance of basic theological dogmas as well as men's religious experiences and behavior, both normal and abnormal, in a natural, psychological way, and they have acquired a considerable following. The theologian has not profited by the admitted inability of the scientist to unravel the mysteries of the universe and of life, for it is not easy for him to convince the world that he has succeeded where the scientist has failed. The belief that, if an answer to these mysteries is possible, science, not theology, will provide it seems to have been gaining wider acceptance. The quest of the scientist, like that of the theologian, is a quest for God, or the first cause of things, but scientists generally hold to the view that that discovery is dependent upon the completion of man's exploration of the physical universe. Says Professor James H. Leuba: "The claims of the religions and of philosophers that they have given an adequate answer to the problem of God are made in an adolescent conceit. An adequate solution would demand a complete knowledge of all things in heaven and earth; it will, therefore, be long delayed!"[25] Some scientists, such as Eddington and Millikan, bewildered by scientific discoveries and uncertainties, have found in theology the consolation they sought, but other scientists, such as Russell and Dingle, have condemned that stand as unjustifiable.

In theological circles and churches, the fundamentalist-modernist controversy came to a head as a result of advancing science. The most radical of the modernists, found chiefly among the Unitarians and Universalists, but also among other Protestants, have either rejected the basic Christian theological dogmas as untrue or hold that we can have no certainty about them. Against all of these the fundamentalists have stood for the continued belief in all the old-time "fundamentals" of the Christian religion. This group has been unrelenting in the war against science at every point where it clashed with the traditional dogmas of formal Christianity. Their leaders attacked modernist ministers and teachers, and organized many societies to carry on their work. They succeeded in having anti-evolution laws passed in a few states, one of them being Tennessee, where a teacher, J. T. Scopes, was tried in 1925 for teaching evolution. William Jennings Bryan, the chief prosecuting attorney and prominent fundamentalist, urged the view that the schools exist to teach not what is true but what the people want them to teach. Scopes was convicted in spite of his able defense by Clarence Darrow, a leading modernist.

The Catholic church, fearful of modernist thought, which a few prominent Catholics would have the church accept, has consistently refused to make any concession to modernism. Such Catholic modernists as George Tyrell, Alfred Loisy, and Louis Duchesne, and their writings have been pronounced heretical. In 1907, Pope Pius X placed the official anathema of the church upon modernism. One cannot be a modernist and remain within the Catholic fold.

The Growing Distrust of Science

Fear of knowledge, particularly of new knowledge, is as old probably as human society. In the Hebrew-Christian epic, knowledge is represented as having brought the curse of heaven upon the

[25] J. H. Leuba, *God or Man* (New York: Henry Holt & Co., Inc., 1933), pp. 320–21.

human race. Christian ecclesiastics, in varying degrees since early Christian days, have opposed the free spirit of inquiry. They viewed reason and the intellect as dangerous aspects of man's nature.[26] Distrust of science by theologians is thus an old phenomenon. They have been joined, in our own day, by some eminent scientists who have become bewildered by the magnitude of the mysteries which scientific research has revealed. A popular form of distrust of science has been based upon the belief that progress in science has dehumanized man and is responsible for many of our economic and social dislocations and the more horrible aspects of modern warfare. Science and scientists are thus blamed for our failure to keep our spiritual culture in step with our advancing material culture, for our failure to control the machine, and for our abuse of scientific discoveries and inventions.

Perhaps the worst aspect of the revolt against science appears in the anti-rationalism and the worship of myths which characterized the totalitarian régimes, particularly those of the Nazi-Fascists. Hitler and Mussolini rejected science when it conflicted with their socio-political programs. Alfred Rosenberg, the high-priest of the Nazi cult, would, however, destroy the scientific foundation of human certainty, even in the physical realm, by making feeling rather than observation and reason its basis. Said he, in his *Blut und Ehre:* "We believe that the three possibilities of understanding the universe through perception, will and reason, originate from a single faith, from a single myth, the myth of the blood, the myth of the people."[27] Professor P. Lenard, of Heidelberg University, a prominent Nazi physicist, rejects the international character of science and scientific truth. Said he: "Science, like every other human product, is racial and conditioned by the blood."[28] To make nation and race the test and measure of scientific truth destroys objectivity which is the essence of science.

Back of most of this distrust of science are prejudices, both old and new, and the failure of educational agencies to keep pace with advancing knowledge and to interpret it to the public. The scientific method of discovery is itself known only to specialists in scientific fields, to technologists, to businessmen, who reap profit from its use, and to an almost negligible fraction of the general public. That it is a way of discovering and dealing with facts in every

[26] J. B. Bury, *A History of Freedom of Thought* (New York: Henry Holt & Co., Inc., 1913); A. D. White, *History of the Warfare of Science with Theology in Christendom* (New York: Appleton-Century-Crofts, Inc., 1896).

[27] Cited in M. Rader, *No Compromise* (New York: The Macmillan Co., 1939), p. 25. (By permission.)

[28] *Ibid.*, p. 31. (By permission.)

field of reality, including that of human life and activity, is still largely unknown. The modern politician and preacher generally approach their problems through rhetoric and ancient logic rather than through scientific thinking. Perhaps the teacher, too, fails often to use the tool of scientific method where it applies to problems that confront him. One of the big tasks of educators in the future is to teach men to substitute science for prejudice in the world of social as well as of physical phenomena.

Selected Readings

Abel, T. F. *Why Hitler Came to Power.* Englewood Cliffs, N.J.: Prentice-Hall, Inc., 1938.

Baur, J. I. H., ed. *New Art in America.* New York: Graphic, 1957.

Chandler, A. R. *The Clash of Political Ideals.* New York: Appleton-Century-Crofts, Inc., 1940.

Cheney, S. *The New World Architecture.* New York: Tudor Publishing Co., 1935.

Demiashkevich, M. J. *The National Mind.* New York: American Book Co., 1938.

Hitler, A. *Mein Kampf.* Harrisburg, Pa.: Stackpole, 1939.

Hocking, W. E. *The Lasting Elements of Individualism.* New Haven: Yale University Press, 1937.

Hook, S. *Toward the Understanding of Karl Marx.* New York: John Day Co., Inc., 1933.

Huxley, J. *Religion without Revelation.* New York: Harper & Bros., 1957.

Kirkpatrick, E. M. *Target: The World.* New York: The Macmillan Co., 1956.

Kulski, W. W. *The Soviet Regime.* Syracuse, N.Y.: Syracuse University Press, 1954.

Marx, K. *Capital.* (Trans. S. Moore and E. B. Aveling). London: Sonnenschein, 1889.

Mason, F. B. *Creation by Evolution.* New York: The Macmillan Co., 1928.

Mecklin, J. M. *The Passing of the Saint.* Chicago: University of Chicago Press, 1941.

Mumford, L. *Technics and Civilization.* New York: Harcourt, Brace & Co., Inc., 1934.

Mussolini, B. *My Autobiography.* New York: Charles Scribner's Sons, 1928.

Planck, M. *The Universe in the Light of Modern Physics.* (Trans. W. J. Johnston). New York: W. W. Norton & Co., Inc., 1931.

Rader, M. *No Compromise.* New York: The Macmillan Co., 1939.

Ragsdale, C. E. *Modern Psychologies and Education.* New York: The Macmillan Co., 1932.

Salvemini, G. *The Fascist Dictatorship in Italy.* New York: Henry Holt & Co., Inc., 1927.

Tawney, R. H. *Religion and the Rise of Capitalism.* New York: Harcourt, Brace & Co., Inc., 1926.

Tillich, P. *The Protestant Era.* Chicago: University of Chicago Press, 1948.

Trachtenberg, J. *The Devil and the Jews.* New Haven: Yale University Press, 1943.

Webb, S. and B. *Soviet Communism: A New Civilization.* New York: Charles Scribner's Sons, 1936.

Whitehead, A. N. *Science and the Modern World.* New York: The Macmillan Co., 1925.

Woody, T. *New Minds: New Men?* New York: The Macmillan Co., 1932.

16 Education and the World Crisis

In the preceding chapter we have examined the changes in the economic, social, political, and cultural scene—chiefly of the Western world—in the present century. Education in the great nations has been profoundly influenced by these changes. In the United States and England, and in France until its temporary defeat by Germany, the most significant changes appear in the increasing democratization of education. In Nazi Germany and Fascist Italy, educational change was a phase of the revolt against liberalism and the democratic way of life. The Communist social experiment in Russia has been accompanied by an educational experiment of equal magnitude and import. The internal social struggle within nations as well as the international tensions of the period have affected, in greater or less degree in different countries, the educational practices of the world.

Educational Developments in Germany Since World War I

In Chapter 13, we saw how the school system of Prussia, the German state dominant in area, population and influence, developed. Germany, however, is divided into separate states, eleven of which, since 1949, constitute the Federal Republic of Germany. About education in the Russian zone, which includes East Berlin, little reliable information was available in 1958. Under the Empire (1871) and under the Weimar Republic (1919), each state controlled its own school system. During the latter, the Prussian Ministry of the Interior was given the duty to consider educational issues of concern to the whole nation, but control remained in the states. Under Hitler, in 1934, a central "Ministry of Science, Education and Popular Development" was established for the whole nation, and the states lost their independence. Details of financing and administering education, differing slightly from state to state, have been arranged in the present Republic between central and local authorities, while the right of each central state authority to inspect schools goes unquestioned.[1]

DEVELOPMENTS IN THE WEIMAR REPUBLIC. Following World War I, demands for reform of education came from many groups. In answer to these demands and to the provisions of the Weimar Constitution of 1919, the following were among the changes effected in the Weimar Republic: (a) The preparatory departments (*Vorschulen*) of secondary schools were legally (1920) closed, and a common four-year foundation school (*Grundschule*) was made compulsory for all German children. Its purpose was to provide the basic training necessary to pursue the work of the upper four grades (*Oberstufe*) of the elementary school, and to enter the traditional middle and secondary schools. The studies in the *Oberstufe* of Prussia, which may be considered typical, were religion, German, civics, history, geography, natural science, arithmetic, geometry, drawing, music, physical education, and sewing and home economics for girls and manual training for boys. In keeping with the tradition, free education ended here in all states. (b) New secondary schools were established—the rural 6-year *Aufbauschule,* open to able elementary school students at the end of the seventh grade, and the German High School (*Deutsche Oberschule*), which stressed national culture. From both of these, students might enter universities. (c) To abolish caste in education, and to unite elementary with secondary education, future teachers were required to be graduates of secondary schools, and the traditional teachers' seminaries were officially given university status, under the name "pedagogical academies." Secondary teachers, still to be trained in universities, were required to have professional training under state supervision. The salaries of elementary teachers were raised; and, to free elementary teachers from church domination, supervision of teaching was transferred from ministers and priests to professional supervisors. (d) A liberal system of scholarships was established to enable poor students to enter universities. (e) Vocational education, traditionally separated rigidly from general education and bearing the stigma of caste, was raised in dignity. (f) The path of girls to universities was made easier by new regulations for their secondary schools.[2]

[1] A. M. Lindegren, *Germany Revisited: Education in the Federal Republic* (Washington, D.C.: United States Department of Health, Education, and Welfare, Bulletin No. 12, 1957), pp. 6–16.

[2] *Ibid.,* pp. 23–25.

While the Weimar Republic knew the meaning of equality of educational opportunity, it failed to achieve it. The scholarship system in secondary schools and universities, while enlarged, was inadequate to insure its attainment. Germany had begun, however, to see more clearly the vision of democracy in education.

DEVELOPMENTS UNDER THE NAZIS. In the Weimar Republic, the schools became centers of political strife and social unrest. Furthermore, Catholics, Protestants, Communists, the Youth Movement, and other groups established adult schools to propagate their particular ideals. The schools of the Republic lacked a common unifying ideal, and the demand that a common goal be set for them arose and was frequently urged, particularly by teachers. In its nationalistic emphasis, Nazi education built upon the German heritage of the eighteenth and nineteenth centuries, as did, in many ways, the Republican régime which preceded it.

(1) EDUCATIONAL AIMS. The Nazis rejected, as inimical to national interests, the Republic's acceptance of experimentation in education and of the view that schools should aim to develop personalities. They demanded that all schools and other educational agencies should aim to bring every individual into complete harmony with the will of the nation. The "common goal" of all education, said the Minister in 1938, is that "of forming the National Socialist Man."[3]

(2) EDUCATIONAL VALUES. First in value the Nazis placed physical training, and after this, in order of importance, character building and intellectual training. Back of this evaluation, as indeed of all aspects of Nazi educational theory and practice, lay the social and political struggle. Said Reich Minister Rust: "The National Socialist system of education is not the outcome of a pedagogical planning but of political struggle and of the laws which govern such a struggle. . . . The National Socialist historical epoch will build a school which will be its true image."[4] To this end it must develop the body and then the soul. Ernst Krieck, *Rektor* of the University of Frankfurt am Main, saw the Prussian soldier as the embodiment of the finest traits of German character.[5] In intellectual training, the pupil should be taught only the things essential to his own needs and the needs of the national community. All education should be rooted in devotion to blood and soil, for these are the sources of race and character.

[3] *Educational Yearbook*, 1939, p. 183. All citations from the *Yearbooks* by permission of Teachers College, Columbia University.

[4] *Ibid.*, pp. 185–86.

[5] *Ibid.*, 1934, pp. 460–61.

(3) Volk as the Basis of Science and Teaching. The theorists denounced the "scholar" of the old schools who stood aloof from the *Volk* and their life and struggles. They denounced the old universities with their ideals of academic freedom, pure intellectualism, and science without preconceptions. All teaching and research must be rooted in the spirit of the people and must promote National Socialist truth, for that truth springs from the spirit of the people, the soul of the nation. Emphasis upon the *Volk* and the idea of the *Volk*-state did not imply an official respect for common people, in whose judgment and capacity for government Nazi leaders had little faith. The rôle assigned them, as a group, was that of meek and obedient followers of leaders, headed by the "great personality" (Hitler) himself. And great stress was placed upon the special training of leaders imbued with the ideals of blood, race, soil, and race-folk nationality, and possessed of the necessary physical and emotional traits. Some such leaders might, however, be sprung from the common people.

(4) Views on Women's Education. "The goal of feminine education," said Hitler, "must be fixed as the education of the future mother." On that principle the theorists agreed. They viewed women as beings different from men in nature, and destined by nature and the needs of the Nazi state for their own peculiar social sphere and activities.[6] State officials and other Nazi writers declared coeducation to be opposed to the interests and spirit of National Socialism.

(5) Theory of Activism. In keeping with the anti-intellectualism and activism of the state and its philosophy, the theorists stressed activism in education. Said Rust: "Action and action only, not indolent pondering of the past, is the soul of education."[7] Because the state imposed its philosophy upon the schools, the entire ideology of Nazi education was activistic, pragmatic, and opposed to the problem-solving philosophy of the Republican years. The Nazi theorists stressed the training of the will as the source of action. All this does not mean that intellectual training and knowledge were to be ignored in the educational process.

(6) Anti-pluralism and Its Implications. For education, the principle of anti-pluralism, discussed in the preceding chapter, implies that (1) youths must be educated in the ideals of the Nazi state, to which alone they owe loyalty, and (2) that the state is

[6] *Ibid.*, 1939, p. 191.

[7] G. Ziemer, *Education for Death* (New York: Oxford University Press, 1941), p. 18.

the only legal educational agency, and that other agencies, such as the family and church, may educate only by authority delegated to them by the state. Education for citizenship under the Republic was said to have been impossible because the schools then had to stress loyalty to the family, church, and other groups which often differed in their political beliefs.

(7) Reform of the Spirit of Education. On gaining control of the state, Hitler and the Nazis proceeded immediately to bring the school, the Youth Movement, and all other educational agencies into harmony with the new political ideology. All teachers from the elementary to the university level were required to renounce all liberal educational ideals and practices, such as individualism and intellectualism, and to accept the new philosophy. Jewish teachers were dismissed. Fear of dismissal or the concentration camp brought German teachers of wavering faith into submission.

In the classroom the teacher was expected to assume the rôle of a *Führer*, and obedience to his authority and respectful listening were declared by officialdom to be the duties of students. Education was made again a physical, moral, and mental discipline. The lecture method was given high official praise, as was also directed student activity. Freedom of the student to question and discuss was declared by Minister Rust to be harmful.

Religion was retained in the curriculum, but there seems to have developed an official fear of instruction in it. The Reich Minister said in 1938: "I refrain from issuing a new program for religious instruction. All matters conducive to the disruption of the educational unity of the school shall be carefully guarded against in religious instruction."[8] Fear of some aspects of denominationalism resulted in the taking over by the Reich of the Catholic schools of Württemberg and of Bavaria in 1937.[9]

The military ideal permeated the physical training program in and outside of the schools. History was taught to inflame the will and to develop national pride, and without regard for objective truth. The Teachers' Journal (*Allgemeine Deutsch Lehrerzeitung*), August 19, 1933, declared: "We care nothing about an insipid enumeration of 'objective' facts; we want a historical science for Germans."[10] Later in 1933, the *Lehrerzeitung* said: "The taste for militarism must be inculcated in children. . . . Germans will

[8] *Educational Yearbook,* 1939, p. 182.
[9] *The New York Times* (June 5 and 22, 1937).
[10] *Educational Yearbook,* 1934, pp. 487–88.

be victorious in the next war; it is the will and the way of God. . . . No one can resist our health within and our young strength." [11]

(8) ADMINISTRATION AND CONTROL. The leadership principle (*Führerprinzip*) determined all administrative and supervisory practices. Instead of many teachers' associations of the past there was now but the National Socialist Teachers *Bund,* with its own *Führer.* Each principal, *Führer* of his school, explained to teachers and pupils their duties. There were local school committees, appointed by the local Nazi leader, a majority of whom had to be approved by the Nazi Party. Each committee *Führer* might decide issues without taking a vote. At the top of the administrative hierarchy stood the Reich Minister, whose authority extended over all aspects of the school system. The press, radio, cinema, theater, music, art, and all other cultural activities fell under the supervision of the Chamber of Culture, of which Goebbels was the *Führer.* What state control of education meant for the individual can be gathered from the following words of Dr. Ley, the *Führer* of the Labor Front: "We begin with the child when he is three years old. As soon as he begins to think, he gets a little flag put in his hand; then follows the school, the Hitler Youth, the S.A., and military training. We don't let him go; and when adolescence is past, then comes the *Arbeitsfront,* which takes him again and does not let him go till he dies, whether he likes it or not." [12]

(9) ORGANIZATION. **(a) The general system.** The Nazis introduced a few changes into the plan of school organization which they inherited. Nazi education began with the selection of parents of pure Nordic blood. For children of working mothers many day nurseries were established, where children began to practise the cult of the *Führer.* In addition there was a growing number of pre-schools, supervised by the state, in which the cult of the *Führer* was also stressed. One additional year of compulsory education was instituted for city children. That year (*Landjahr*) they spent, under leaders, among farmers and peasants for the purpose of physical training and indoctrination in Nazi ideology.

To provide more time for compulsory labor and for political and military training, the secondary school courses were reduced from nine to eight years, and the many traditional school types were reduced to three for boys and two for girls. Under this plan there remained the *Gymnasium,* which was for boys only, and the

[11] *Ibid.,* p. 489.
[12] *Ibid.,* 1941, pp. 200–01.

Deutsche Oberschule and *Aufbauschule*, of which there were types for both sexes, special schools and courses for each sex being the rule.

(b) Schools for leaders. For political, social, and military leaders new types of schools were created: (a) local leadership schools, of which there were about 150; (b) the National Political Educational Institutions, of which there were about 20; (c) the Adolf-Hitler Schools, of which there were about 10; and (d) four higher schools for leaders of leaders called *Ordensburgen*. It was from these special schools, not from secondary schools and universities, that Nazi leaders were to be chosen.

(10) STUDENTS AND THEIR SELECTION. The selective process began at the end of the *Grundschule*. Those deemed unable to profit by a transfer at this point to middle or secondary schools, which were pay schools, or who could not bear the financial burden involved, remained in the free *Volksschule* for the four remaining compulsory school years. Said Minister Rust: "There is no place in a secondary school for incapable pupils nor for pupils showing clear signs of weakness of will power and character."[13] There were, however, many free places available in the pay schools for deserving poor students. Character, physical fitness, intelligence, and "national fitness" were the chief bases of selection for these schools. "National fitness" meant the acceptance of Nazi ideology. Selected graduates of middle schools (*Mittelschulen*) might enter the seventh grade of a secondary school, but had to make up work in Latin and Greek if they entered a *Gymnasium*. In order to prevent overcrowding in the universities and other higher schools and in the professions, and to divert secondary school graduates into non-professional careers, the Nazi government, in 1934, instituted a *numerus-clausus* (closed number) procedure to control enrollment. Before being admitted to higher institutions all males had to have completed six months of labor service (*Arbeitsdienst*), which was compulsory between the ages of eighteen and twenty-five. Military training for two years was also compulsory for males under the age of twenty-five, and many secondary school graduates were diverted by that requirement from higher institutions. Women might not constitute more than 10 per cent of the enrollment in any university, and Jews not more than 2 per cent.

(11) CURRICULUM. (a) Elementary. In the *Grundschule* the curriculum drew its inspiration from the local environment and Nazi ideology. The subjects studied were: the environment, Ger-

[13] *Ibid.*, 1939, p. 180.

man, arithmetic, gymnastics, music, drawing and manual training, and needlework. The environment and German were given nearly three times more hours weekly than the other subjects. In the upper four classes of the *Volksschule,* stress was placed upon the study of German, history, geography, biology and race study, and physical education. Nazi bias colored the work of these years. Students studied such topics as the status of labor in Germany, Germans abroad, population problems, German autarchy, airplanes, flying and air defense, cost of defectives, Nazi race theory, German military needs, etc. Beyond the *Grundschule,* National Socialist needs and ideology were the basic influence determining the curriculum; education of the body and will, leading to action, predominated. Eugenics and home economics had a prominent place in the elementary education of girls.[14]

(b) Secondary. In the *Deutsche Oberschule* the curriculum included: physical education; German subjects—German, history, geography, art, and music; science—biology, physics, chemistry—and mathematics; foreign languages—English, Latin; and religion. In the *Aufbauschule* the subjects were the same as in the *Deutsche Oberschule* but, being a six-year school, less time was given to them. Here, however, there was no choice between two lines, or majors. In the *Gymnasium,* the subjects were the same as in these other schools, except that Greek was included, that Latin was given more time, and English less.

The general plan of the Minister for eight-year schools called for two courses in the last three years, one emphasizing science and mathematics, and the other, foreign languages. To safeguard the unity of education for all the students, he ordered that "all will receive instruction in common in the other subjects of the program, that is in the subjects bearing upon German civilization (German, history, geography, art, music), in biology, and in physical education."[15]

The spirit that pervaded the elementary school pervaded the secondary school as well. In 1935, the Minister ordered that instruction in heredity, race science, and Nazi family and birth policies be given in the fifth year of the *Volksschule,* and be fully studied in all middle and secondary schools.[16] Biology, history, geography and German, as well as the study of "race science," were used to develop a feeling of Germany's need for pure blood. Gen-

14 Ziemer, *op. cit.,* p. 64.
15 *Educational Yearbook,* 1939, p. 181.
16 A. M. Lindegren, *Education in Germany,* United States Office of Education, 1938, Bulletin No. 15, p. 9.

eral culture was relegated to the scrap-heap of traditional fallacies and of liberal stupidity or hypocrisy. Knowledge was not viewed as power but the root of weak character unless, in acquiring it and through it, there was developed a passionate devotion to National Socialism and a strong will to realize its objectives.[17]

(12) Education of Girls. "The absence," said Alfred Rosenberg, "of all-round abilities in women is directly to be attributed to the fact that woman is vegetative."[18] There seems to have been agreement among Nazi leaders regarding woman's peculiar sphere and destiny in the social order, and for her they established an education in keeping with their views. Coeducation was forbidden for children above the age of four,[19] unless conditions in the local community made separation of the sexes impossible. Boys were taught by men; girls, by women and men. In exceptional cases, and under special provisions, girls were admitted to secondary schools for boys. Boys were never admitted into secondary schools for girls.

Girls had their own *Landjahr* training, and their own labor service for those between the ages of eighteen and twenty, although the latter was compulsory only for those entering the universities. Assigned their own special place and activities in the social system, their studies and instruction were especially designed to prepare them for the life that had been decreed for them, that of being the mothers of pure-blooded soldiers.

On the elementary level, studies were the same for both sexes, except that eugenics, and home economics, with the stress on needlework, had a prominent place in the training of girls. On the secondary level, girls might, in the *Deutsche Oberschule,* elect, during the last three years of the course, the language line or the home economics line. English was the only foreign language they studied, except that language majors in the last three years of the *Oberschule* might substitute Latin or another foreign language for it. There were no choices for them in the *Aufbauschule.* German subjects, home economics, and physical education were the subjects stressed throughout the middle- and secondary-school courses. Since Latin had been almost eliminated from the curriculum for girls, their admission to universities became very difficult.

(13) Education of Jews. Under a state regulation of 1937, Jews had to comply with the compulsory education law, and attend

[17] *Educational Yearbook,* 1941, p. 282.
[18] *The Nation,* Feb. 6, 1935.
[19] Ziemer, *op. cit.,* p. 50.

public schools where there were no private or special public schools for them. The *Landjahr* was for Aryans only. One-fourth Jews were admitted without restriction to middle, secondary, and technical schools but, in these, students of more than one-fourth Jewish blood might not number more than 1.5 per cent of the total among new admissions. Only the academic activities of schools were open to pure Jews. The teachers in Jewish schools had to be Jews or part-Jews. German children might never be taught by Jews or part-Jews.

(14) VOCATIONAL EDUCATION. Elementary school graduates not enrolled in other schools had to attend a part-time vocational continuation school, having a three-year course in cities and a two-year course in rural areas. These schools were free. There was also the full-time, pay, trade school (*Fachschule*), open to graduates of *Mittelschulen* and often of *Volksschulen,* and designed to train an intermediate personnel for industry, commerce and agriculture. Above these, but open only to graduates of secondary schools, were many special higher technical schools, such as mining academies, technical high schools (*Hochschulen*), higher schools of agriculture, forestry, commerce, physical education, political science, art, etc., all of them being of university rank.

Apprenticeship held an important place in vocational training, and the Labor Front, which was the Nazi substitute for the old labor unions, encouraged and guided youths in their vocational education. As much attention was given in vocational schools to German culture, Nazi ideology, and the sciences as to technical training for jobs. That the state might be served, an elaborate system of vocational guidance and placement was organized.

(15) ADULT EDUCATION. In the totalitarian nations adult education has aimed at the political re-education of the masses. In Germany, a branch of the Labor Front, called the Strength through Joy Association, acting with the Minister of Education and local committees, directed the program for adults. Except in sparsely settled rural areas, every Nazi community had its Popular Education Group or its better organized Popular Education Centre (*Volksbildungsstätte*). The program was built around the needs of the home, the local community, and the nation, with stress upon Nazi ideology.

(16) THE TRAINING OF NAZI TEACHERS. The Republican two-year *Hochschulen für Lehrerbildung,* of university rank and operating until 1941, was replaced by new institutions of lower rank. The

aim of the new training schools was to mould heralds of "the community spirit in education."[20] Just as Christian ecclesiastics, kings, and emperors, among them those of old Germany, had thought that too much learning in teachers is dangerous, so a similar fear probably lay back of this Nazi reform. The Nazis admitted no one to the training schools whose political orthodoxy had not been proved by his activities in the Youth Movement. The curriculum included educational theory, race science, sociology (*Volkskunde*), practice teaching, physical education, German and political activities, and arts and crafts. The students were expected to participate in the activities of such groups as the League for Germans Abroad and other political and social agencies.

The Nazis introduced the practice of requiring secondary teachers to spend a year in a teachers' *Hochschule* with future elementary teachers. An approved one then entered a university, or one of the special technical *Hochschulen,* where he completed his academic and professional preparation, folk-culture and race science receiving all possible attention. Having passed his final examination, he was appointed to a position as practice teacher for one year, during which he was enrolled in a seminar in education. At the end of this year he took an examination in professional subject matter, which included training of youth in Nazi ideals. A permanent appointment was the reward of success. The whole program of teacher training was under the supervision of the Party and the Labor Front.

(17) The Landjahr. Introduced in 1934, the *Landjahr* was a striking innovation of the Nazis. It brought city elementary school graduates into contact with the peasantry and rural life for nine months, in order to strengthen their health and character and make them realize the importance of the peasant in the life of the nation. Small groups of boys or girls were housed in hostels or farmhouses and, in addition to physical training through athletics, military training, and hikes, were instructed by their teachers in (a) the German environment, (b) race science, (c) history, (d) geography, and (e) singing, music, and folk-dancing. Through the *Landjahr,* the Youth Movement, and the labor service, the transition of youth from family to community life was effected.

(18) The Youth Movement. By a decree of 1936, all German boys and girls at the age of ten had to join the youth organizations. Those for boys, in the order of age, were (a) *Pimpf,* (b) *Jungvolk,* and (c) *Hitlerjugend.* These were the official road to membership

[20] *Educational Yearbook,* 1941, p. 319.

in the Storm Troops (S.A.), the Elite Guard (S.S.), and the Party. The organization for girls between ten and fourteen years of age was the *Jungmädel;* for those between fourteen and twenty-one, the *Bund Deutscher Mädel.* Only pure Aryans, or those of less than one-fourth "defilement" in blood, were admitted to these groups. All groups had their officer-leaders, uniforms and emblems, elaborate ceremonies, titles and degrees, and physical and ideological activities. They assisted the formal schools, which in turn acted in close unison with them.[21]

(19) Leadership Training. From these organizations were selected the students of the schools for leaders, already mentioned, in which the future political and military leaders of Nazi Germany were trained. The physical stamina, character, race purity, and ideological orthodoxy of those selected were thoroughly tested, and selection was deemed, apparently by most boys, the greatest honor and privilege. From the graduates of the lower leadership schools were chosen physically perfect students who, between the ages of twenty-five and thirty, entered the *Ordensburgen.* During their three-year course they were given complete financial support and, if needed, a family allowance. The course was two-thirds physical and one-third ideological in character. Leaders of leaders were formed here.

(20) Girls' Youth Activities. Girls of the *Jungmädel* wore uniforms and engaged in many forms of physical activity. Even in these earlier years they were taught the duties of women to the state, particularly the duty of motherhood. They had but little leisure. When not in school they were with their youth group or attending girls' meetings, through which they were imbued with Nazi ideology. Later, as members of the *Bund Deutscher Mädel,* they were instructed further in their duties as future mothers and housewives. Many of them, at the age of eighteen, went to camps for labor service. The *Bund* established leadership schools for girls, in which teachers of home economics and eugenics were trained for duties in schools and camps.

Thus, briefly, did the totalitarian Nazi state of Germany mould its citizens. The story of education in Fascist Italy was similar to that of the Nazis. Here, too, education sank to the level of indoctrination. Mussolini's *Autobiography* will ever remain as evidence of the fitful fever from which Italy and its schools suffered during the Fascist régime. And it is yet too soon to say that Nazism and

[21] For a significant account of the work of these groups see Ziemer, *op. cit.*

Fascism have been laid to rest, for they were but manifestations of nationalism run to tribalism.

SOME CHARACTERISTICS OF TRADITIONAL PRACTICE. The system as it existed at the end of World War II was, as described earlier, still essentially a three-track system, social gulfs, in spite of the *Grundschule*, separating the elementary, middle, and secondary schools. The Nazis had done much to abolish cleavages based upon religion. The free *Volksschule* was the school of nearly 95 per cent of the children. Above this were vocational schools (*Berufsschulen*) and apprenticeship training. The *Berufsschule* provided, generally, the theory of vocational work, while practical training was left, generally, to the master craftsmen, who trained five apprentices for every two trained in big industry. Devotion to family life and their *Beruf* (calling) was stressed for all workmen. Their skills were the foundation of German industry, which was the envy of the industrial world. German workmen took pride in their vocations, and they never became slum-dwellers. Indeed, there is no German word for slum. But society did not honor their work as they themselves did, and they had little chance to climb the social ladder. The professions and officerships in the army and navy were closed to graduates of the *Volksschule*.[22]

The road to the universities was through the secondary schools, which bore the marks of wealth and caste. Intermarriage between students of the three types of schools seldom, if ever, occurred. Coeducation, except in the lowest grades, did not exist. Teachers, generally, were pedantic and academic-minded specialists, who sat on platforms and lectured, and who frowned upon free discussion and students' questions, since such procedure might reveal their own ignorance or create embarrassing situations. There were 103 state elementary textbooks in use under Hitler, and they were Nazi in spirit through and through. Traditionally, the universities were nurseries of nationalism and class conservatism, and they had accepted Nazism readily. On all educational levels, the teachers and school administrators were predominantly Nazi in allegiance and spirit.[23]

RE-EDUCATING THE GERMANS. The victors in World War II decentralized Germany. Each of the areas (*Länder*) which they set up was controlled by occupying authorities from the victorious nations and had its own ministry of education. For some years the

[22] "Shaping by Vocational Training," *London Times Educational Supplement* (May 28, 1954), p. 525.

[23] S. K. Padover, "The Failure of the Re-education of Germany," *Schoolmen's Week Proceedings,* 1947. Publication of the University of Pennsylvania.

conquerors attempted to re-educate the Germans and impose their own educational traditions upon them. "Denazification" and "democratization" were among the five "de's" of the policy adopted in Potsdam in 1945.[24] Extreme nationalism, imperialism, militarism, and authoritarianism were marked for destruction, and the schools were to be used, in the words of the Potsdam agreement, to eliminate "Nazi and militaristic doctrines and to make possible the successful development of democratic ideas." Nazism, however, was but an intensification of traditional Prussianism, which always stood opposed to popular government and embodied a belief in German racial and cultural superiority. It was, no doubt, juvenile on the part of the victors to think that they could change, in a few years, the mind and folkways of a great nation whose roots extended far back into the past. Besides, the victors themselves had been guilty, in varying degrees, of the evils which they saw in German life, and the vanquished were conscious of that fact. Nationalism and militarism, for instance, were not peculiar to Germany.

How all of the occupying powers attempted to reconstruct education cannot be described here. America played a leading rôle in the effort. The United States Education Mission to Germany tried to set up in the American zone a unified system (*Einheitsschule*) up to the university level, with free secondary schools superimposed upon the elementary schools. The Mission recommended that, for the first six years, children should not be divided "according to sex, social class, or vocational intentions," and that an enlarged scheme of university scholarships be provided. The Mission was silent on the issue of division of students on sectarian grounds, apparently because the American zone was largely Catholic. The Germans listened to our proposals, but not always sympathetically. It was difficult to purge the school system of Nazi teachers and administrators, but we tried to do that. Hitler's textbooks had to be replaced by books free from the ideologies we wished to destroy. Nor were the pre-Hitler textbooks free from sin. We asked the Germans to abandon their traditional authoritarian method of drill and memorization and to transform their listening schools, especially in matters of social and political issues, into schools of student questioning and free discussion. We discovered that authoritarian patterns of education rooted in social traditions are hard to destroy.

DEVELOPMENTS IN THE FEDERAL REPUBLIC. (1) CONTROL AND SUPPORT. The present Federal Republic of West Germany is a

[24] J. Mulhern, "Re-educating the Germans," *World Affairs Interpreter* (Autumn 1948), pp. 260–75; T. Woody, "The Re-education of Germans," *Education* (Sept. 1945).

federation of independent states, which send to the central Bonn government their freely elected representatives. The educational rights and duties of the states are dealt with, loosely, by the Bonn Constitution, which states, among other things, that (a) each state possesses supreme supervisory authority, (b) that religious instruction, as demanded by the separate churches concerned, be provided in state schools, the rights of parents in the matter always to be respected, (c) that private schools may be permitted if, in aims and the quality of their work, they meet state standards and do not cater to an economic elite, and (d) that preparatory departments of secondary schools be abolished. Generally, the cost of education is defrayed by arrangement between the state and its local subdivisions on about an equal basis. The abolition of fees in all schools below the universities, while not yet (1958) completely achieved, has been rapidly adopted by the states since 1948. Free textbooks and instructional material are now, too, the general practice. One state, Hesse, has made higher education free.

(2) ORGANIZATION. The practices of the states in organizing their systems are marked by variety. Generalizations about these practices are hazardous. Generally, the states have established a foundation school (*Grundschule*) of four or six grades leading to *Mittelschulen*, and a variety of secondary schools, most of which lead to the "maturity examination" and to universities. Admission to secondary schools is, generally, by examination and most students remain in the *Volksschule* to enter the continuation and vocational schools above it, or, in some cases, the *Aufbauschule*, through which they can secure the certificate of "maturity," the diploma of secondary education. The plan provides a great variety of opportunities for students, based upon their abilities and interests. The *Einheitsschule*, in the sense of a uniform, free system resting upon a common school for all children to the age of twelve, followed by secondary schools of three types—academic, technical and multi-curricular—has been adopted in West Berlin and in the states (*Länder*) of Bremen and Hamburg. The other states in the Western sector, while they have established a *Grundschule* for children to the age of ten, divide pupils at that point into two groups: (a) those who remain to complete their education in the upper elementary grades and continuation schools, and (b) those who are transferred to secondary schools. Only about 25 per cent of students entering secondary schools secure the coveted distinction of matriculation.

The traditional caste system of school organization has thus been largely retained in spite of the efforts of the victors in war to change it. Some experiments in secondary education are being tried in the Western states, *e.g.* commercial and agricultural high schools and coeducational secondary schools. Coeducational schools are still almost entirely rejected. The predominantly Catholic states of Bavaria and North Rhine-Westphalia demand denominational schools, while the other Western states, almost entirely, want secular community schools (*Gemeinschaftsschulen*). Catholics demand that teacher-training schools be denominational, and they have won their point where they are the majority.[25]

(3) THE SECONDARY CURRICULUM AND METHOD. Foreign languages, ancient and modern, stand high in prestige, and the Federal Republic has returned to an emphasis upon intellectualism in secondary and higher education.[26] The *Gymnasium* still remains an honored school, although the *Real* or modern schools outnumber it by four to one.[27] Most teachers consider the study of German, modern languages, history, science, mathematics, and art of greater value than the study of Latin and Greek, the traditional core of the *gymnasium* program. Today, the classics are accorded only about one-third of the time of *gymnasien* students. A liberal education, however, is now defined chiefly in terms of modern content, and the humanistic *Gymnasium* of the nineteenth century has been significantly modernized in its curriculum, although in its student body it is still largely a school of the social elite.[28] While core and optional studies mark the German secondary curriculum, the secondary schools are schools of general education, not specialization. With the exception of history, geography, and German politics, all presented in a coloring of nationalism, the social studies were given almost no attention in the traditional schools.

American educators who went to Germany after 1945 recommended to German ministers of education that study of the social sciences be given a leading place in the curriculum of elementary and secondary schools, and that students be instructed regarding the nature and solution of important social problems. The American concept of the social studies was clarified for German educators in an International Workshop on the Social Studies held in Heidelberg, in 1950. As a result of the proposals of foreign educators and the discussions, the states of West Germany have introduced new social

[25] E. Wiskemann, "Coordination in Germany," *London Times Educational Supplement* (April 2, 1954), p. 321.

[26] G. W. Prange and A. M. Lindegren, *Education in the German Federal Republic* (Washington, D.C.: U.S. Department of Health, Education and Welfare, 1954), pp. 7–19.

[27] A. M. Lindegren, *Germany Revisited,* p. 25.

[28] G. Goldschmidt, "The German Gymnasium To-Day," *London Times Educational Supplement* (Nov. 27, 1953), p. 1005.

content into the framework of the old curriculum, have come to relate history and geography to the problems of the present, have abandoned their traditional formal, bookish treatment of social problems, and substituted for it that of free discussion, stimulated by audio-visual aids and other realistic portrayals of actual social conditions. It is yet too soon to say that chauvinism, political indoctrination and anti-liberalism have been eradicated from German education. The nation, rightly proud of its past, is now divided and humiliated.

(4) Vocational Education. Vocational education is provided by all the states in part-time schools for working youths between the ages of fifteen and eighteen. Full-time vocational training is provided in lower technical schools open to students at the age of eighteen, in technical high schools, and in a variety of higher technical and scientific schools of veterinary medicine, agriculture, mining, etc. German youths who are not destined for universities and the professions are given extensive opportunity for training in specific trades in continuation schools and in an organized apprenticeship system.

(5) Physical Education. Physical education is provided in the program of all elementary, middle and secondary schools. A back-to-nature sports movement began to bloom in the nineteenth century, side by side with gymnastics, and came to full blossom under the Weimar Republic. The Nazis captured this movement for war purposes, and their emphasis upon physical education resulted in a reaction against it after 1945. The stigma has now been largely removed. In spring and summer, the emphasis is on athletics and outdoor games; in winter, on gymnastics. Folk dancing is especially popular. Athletics receive as much time in girls' as in boys' schools.[29] The educational authorities in West Germany attach great importance to the health and physical development of youth.

(6) Universities. The Federal Republic has over one hundred higher schools of university rank, seventeen of which are the old classical universities, while the rest are schools specializing in a variety of technical and professional pursuits, such as theology, economics, politics, gymnastics, medicine, mining, etc. Since 1945, the universities have faced many problems in their efforts at restoration of freedom. Many Nazi professors, expelled in 1945-46, found their way back to their chairs later. It was difficult to check the resur-

[29] J. G. Dixon, "German Physical Education," *ibid.* (Dec. 4, 1953), p. 1021; Prange and Lindegren, *op. cit.*, pp. 7 ff.

gence of nationalism and social snobbery in the universities which had long been nurseries of patriotism and national pride. Observers report, however, the rapid return to pre-Nazi standards of scholarship which long placed German universities in a position of leadership in the Western world.[30]

Three new universities were opened in the Federal Republic between 1945 and 1949. One in West Berlin was founded by financial aid from the Ford Foundation and the United States Military Government. The French gave financial aid to a new university in the Saar. The West Berlin University was dedicated to the principle of academic freedom and, therein, stands in sharp contrast to Humboldt University in Russian-controlled East Berlin.

The basic faculties in the universities are law, medicine, philosophy, and theology, to which are added, under different schemes of organizations, other faculties such as those of political science, economics, agriculture, etc.[31] While the universities have their own requirements for degrees and diplomas, there are state examinations for those entering such professions as law, medicine, dentistry, pharmacy, secondary-school teaching, etc. But few changes have been made in the traditional practices. The student enters the professional school of the university or his chosen field of specialization directly from the secondary school, and attempts to extend general education into the universities have not been very successful. Narrow specialization marks German higher education.

The university students of today are more representative of the total population than under the earlier régimes, the majority of them coming from the middle and low income groups. The enrollment has increased since 1945, but the greatest increase has occurred in the technological schools (*Hochschulen*). In all types of higher institutions the enrollment in West Germany in 1953 was approximately 82,000, of whom about 18,000 were women.[32]

(7) Adult Education. Adult education, long a well organized practice, is provided in community centers, evening high schools which prepare for university matriculation, evening technical classes, continuation vocational schools, and university extension courses. West Germany is well supplied with public libraries, city theaters and concert halls, and students and adults make extensive use of such cultural opportunities.

30 "Reaction in German Universities," *London Times Educational Supplement* (May 23, 1952), p. 447.

31 Lindegren, *Germany Revisited*, p. 76.

32 J. F. Cramer and G. S. Browne, *Contemporary Education* (New York: Harcourt, Brace & Co., Inc., 1956), p. 462.

(8) Teachers and Their Training. Until the years of the Weimar Republic, elementary and secondary school teachers were rigidly separated, only the latter entering the profession through secondary schools and universities. In 1945, the gap between elementary and secondary teachers still remained. In the present Federal Republic, the gap has been largely closed. Elementary teachers are now required to be secondary school graduates. They then enter a teachers' college, now elevated in dignity, or a university, where they pursue academic studies for two or three years, and take the first of two state examinations for certification. After an additional two years of actual teaching and practical school work, they take the second state examination for permanent certification. In the theoretical training of all teachers, elementary and secondary, emphasis is placed upon such studies as history of education, comparative education, educational anthropology, educational psychology, and educational sociology. Variations, however, exist between the practices of the schools. Secondary teachers, after four years of university study, are appointed for two years as probationers before being given a permanent appointment. The present American tendency to reduce the professional course requirements for future teachers has not yet appeared in West Germany.[33] The annual salaries of teachers in elementary and middle schools (*Volksschulen* and *Mittelschulen*) range from $3000 to $5500 plus a living allowance. In secondary schools the salaries range from $5500 to $9000, to which a living allowance is also added. Headmasters receive much larger salaries. After thirty years of service, a teacher may retire on a pension equal to 75 per cent of his salary at the time of his retirement. Women teachers, generally, are paid 10 per cent less than men.

Recent Developments in British Education

REORGANIZING THE SYSTEM. (1) Before 1944. In Chapter 13, we have examined briefly the development of the national school system of England, and have dealt with some recent changes introduced since 1944. The most important developments since World War I have been the gradual reorganization of the system following the Education Act (Fisher Act) of 1918, the increasing public interest in education, the persistent demand, particularly of the Labor Party, for secondary education for all, and the efforts of the Board of Education and the L.E.A.'s (local education authorities) to improve the system.

[33] Lindegren, *Germany Revisited*, pp. 49–65.

The Fisher Act raised the school leaving age from twelve to fourteen. Other important laws were (1) the Act of 1921, a general school Code, which, among other provisions, permitted L.E.A.'s, with official permission, to keep children in school to the age of sixteen, and placed all "provided" and "non-provided" schools in their areas under their supervision; (2) the Act of 1936, which raised the school leaving age for those not "beneficially employed" to fifteen; and (3) the Act of 1944, which created a national Ministry of Education, and provided for many changes it was not possible to make under earlier acts.

The Fisher Act (1918) created the problem of what to do with children compelled to stay in school for two additional years, and it led, following the recommendation of a committee of the board of education, in 1926, to the rise of the nonselective, "senior school" for elementary school pupils who failed to qualify in an examination at the age of eleven plus for admission into a secondary school, or any selective school. At the age of thirteen, selected students could transfer from the senior school to junior vocational schools, classified as secondary. The new school was a terminal one into which were channeled 90 per cent of elementary school graduates, but it was the forerunner of the secondary modern school of today.

Reorganization efforts did not stop with the creation of the senior school. In 1931, the Consultative Committee of the Board published its report, *The Primary School;* in 1933, its report, *Infant and Nursery Schools;* and, in 1938, its report, *Secondary Education with Special Reference to Grammar Schools and Technical High Schools,* known as the Spens Report. Some progress has been made in realizing the various recommendations of the Committee. Of particular difficulty, due to a variety of conditions, has been the attempt to bring all secondary schools into one unified national system. The proposal of the Fleming Committee (1944), which suggested a plan to open the Public Schools to graduates of state elementary schools has not resulted in any important change in practice, and these schools still remain socially apart from the national system.

The Spens Report urged that senior, central, secondary, and technical high schools (a new type of school) be recognized as equal in status as regards their administration, size of classes, etc., and that fees should be abolished as soon as national finances warranted. The Committee rejected the idea of an all-purpose secondary school, such as the American high school. The growing popularity and success of the new secondary modern school and of the comprehensive secondary school indicates that the Spens' one-purpose school plan was not acceptable to many in England.

(2) THE ACT OF 1944. In the midst of war, England laid the legal basis for plans of progressive reorganization of education. We can mention here only a few of the many provisions of the Act of 1944.

Earlier laws divorced county elementary from county secondary education by creating 169 L.E.A.'s whose responsibilities were restricted to elementary education. These sent their pupils to secondary schools provided by other local authorities. The Act of 1944 overcame the evils of that old plan by merging many of the non-county authorities with those of the counties, by reducing the number of the L.E.A.'s and by enlarging the function of the county authority.

The new law defines compulsory school age as that between five and fifteen years, and it authorizes the Minister of Education to raise the upper limit to sixteen when that has "become practicable."

Religious education, with which the Board was previously only negatively concerned, has by the new Act been made compulsory in every county and voluntary school, though parents may secure the exemption of their children from school worship and religious instruction. Religious instruction in county schools must not "be distinctive of any religious denomination." However, if students who have been exempted from it by parental request cannot conveniently find the sectarian instruction of their choice, provision may be made for such instruction in the school, provided the education authority concerned does not have to bear the cost. Religious instruction in schools classified as "aided" comes under the control of the managers of such schools. Teachers of religion in the aided schools are to be appointed by the L.E.A.'s, but they may be dismissed for incompetence in teaching that subject by the managers of these schools.

The law classifies schools in the state system into the categories of (a) county, (b) controlled and (c) aided schools. The second and third categories are called "voluntary schools," nearly all of them of denominational origin, and one of whose chief characteristics is that their buildings have not been provided by the L.E.A.'s. Whether "controlled" or "aided," such a school is maintained by the L.E.A.'s, the difference in status being determined by the amount of money which the local authority has to contribute to it. The "controlled" school, as the term implies, has lost almost completely its independence, while the "aided" school still enjoys independence in the matter of religious instruction. Many Church of England schools have been forced, for financial reasons, into the "controlled" category, but Catholic schools have remained in the category of "aided" schools, and have thus far preserved their independence. The Catholics of England are a minority of some 3½ millions out of a total population of some 42 millions, and they have been aggressive opponents of state control of their schools. The Act embodied the principle that children should be educated according to their "parents' wishes," but the parents' clause of the law, by court decisions, is virtually dead, and state interests have been given precedence over sectarian ones.[34]

England has still a dual system of schools, the state nonsectarian system and the sectarian system. The Protestant churches, Anglican and non-Anglican, have generally accepted the plan of nonsectarian religious instruction embodied in an "agreed syllabus," but the Catholic church has not accepted that plan.[35]

The Act brings the purely independent, proprietary schools under close government supervision. It requires them, with certain exceptions, to register with the Ministry, and imposes fairly heavy penalties for noncompliance with the law.

There are, under the law, three recognized stages of education: (1) *primary*, for pupils under twelve; (2) *secondary*, for pupils over twelve who are of compulsory school age; and (3) *further education*, which is that for all pupils who have passed the compulsory age, whether it be the education provided by schools, or that provided by organized cultural, vocational, or recreational agencies outside of schools.

SCHOOLS IN OPERATION. (1) PRIMARY. The primary school has two divisions: Infant School (5 to 7) and Junior School (7 to 11+). There is practically no difference between the primary curriculum and that of the American elementary school. Except in a few areas where reorganization has not yet been completed, the pupil goes from the primary to one of three types of secondary school: secondary modern, technical, or grammar school. The first of these is for the great mass of students who fail to meet the entrance requirements of the second two schools. The fitness of students for these schools is determined chiefly by an examination taken by primary school students at the age of 11+. While students may transfer from the secondary modern to a technical or grammar school at the age of 13, the decision made at 11+ is almost final. There has been growing opposition to sealing a child's fate at the age of 11, and making his destiny depend almost entirely

[34] "Comment in Brief," *London Times Educational Supplement* (Feb. 11, 1955), p. 133.

[35] R. Barker (ed.), *The Education Act, 1944* (London: Chas. Knight and Co., 1944), pp. 44, 57–59, 74–83.

upon his performance in an examination and his score on an intelligence test. The Labor Party would abolish the examination, and some L.E.A.'s have already done so. The Conservatives, however, have favored the policy of selection at 11+.[36]

(2) SECONDARY MODERN SCHOOLS. The secondary modern school is generally nonselective. It is taking the shape of the multicurricular American high school. It has no specific educational objective, and offers a variety of courses, mostly of a prevocational character, based upon a two-year foundation of general education. The variety of curricular practices which mark the school, as it has thus far developed, defies generalization. The studies include, among others, English, foreign languages, physical education, mathematics, general science, commercial studies, arts and crafts, biology, history, geography, etc. Preparation for life rather than for college, through a realistic curriculum and activity methods, is, generally, the guiding philosophy of the school, but a few of these schools have begun to invade the realm of the grammar schools.[37] The teachers in these modern schools have until now been educated in the training colleges, not the universities, and are not as well prepared in some academic areas as are the products of the universities. The great majority of the students leave at the end of the compulsory period (age 15), after which they continue as part-time students in the "county colleges," chiefly vocational, until the age of 18.

(3) THE GRAMMAR SCHOOLS. Students not assigned by the L.E.A.'s to modern secondary schools at 11+ are assigned to a grammar school or a technical high school. Grammar school students go on to the universities, to better positions in business, and to positions in the civil and military service. Abler students remain in the school until the age of 18, the last two years of the course being a period of specialization, called the "sixth-form," which prepares students for the highest form of the General Certificate Examination. There are three levels of this examination: ordinary, advanced, and university-scholarship. Ancient and modern languages and literatures, science, mathematics, history and geography, music and art—all taught in academic fashion—are the chief studies in grammar schools. The Public Schools, famed for academic greatness and distinguished graduates, have given these grammar schools a glory and prestige all their own, and a grammar school diploma is a badge of character and social distinction. There seems to be a general

36 R. Pedley, "New Labor Policy for Secondary Schools," *London Times Educational Supplement* (June 26, 1953), p. 582.

37 "Modern Schools To-day," *ibid.* (Sept. 19, 1952), p. 763.

conviction that a student with an I.Q. of less than 120 should not be assigned to a grammar school.

(4) THE TECHNICAL HIGH SCHOOL. The technical high school is an outgrowth of junior technical schools which date back to 1905. By 1958 there were about 300 of them, and they enroll about 80,000 students, as compared with about 520,000 in the grammar schools. They prepare students for such fields of service as engineering, navigation, aeronautics, building trades, etc., the technical training being based upon a foundation of general education in the first years of the five-year program. Many of the graduates go on to higher technical schools (Technical Colleges). The Labor Party has become a strong advocate of technical education, and industrial leaders are alarmed by England's backwardness in technical education as compared with Germany, the United States, Russia, and other countries.[38] In 1953, the government authorized the expansion of the London University Imperial College of Science and Technology into an institution of university rank. Only universities hold the privilege of granting degrees. Of about 85,000 university students in 1951, some 10,000 were students of technology.[39]

(5) THE COMPREHENSIVE SECONDARY SCHOOL. English secondary school pupils are segregated in schools, each with its own purpose, or purposes, mental ability being the chief basis of segregation. The Labor Party, generally, opposes such a plan as an obstacle to the attainment of equality of educational opportunity and as a negation of the doctrine of social equality. Some Laborites, however, argue, on the grounds of national need, for the training of an aristocracy of brains based upon ability, not social privilege, and favor selective education on the secondary and higher levels.[40] The Conservative Party, as such, defends segregation on educational grounds. The equalitarians would not have three types of secondary school but a single type, the comprehensive school, into which all students, regardless of their ability, destination in life, or social origin, would be brought together under one roof and one principal. The Labor Party made such a plan their policy in 1950 and 1953, and asked the government to aid the L.E.A.'s in promoting it. The London County Council, elected in part on that issue, has since adopted the comprehensive school plan, as have other L.E.A.'s. Conservative politicians have everywhere opposed the plan, although Conservative Ministers of Education have approved it as an

[38] M. W. Perin, "The Case for the Technical University," *ibid.* (Jan. 20, 1950), p. 40.

[39] "Returns from Universities," *ibid.* (Sept. 5, 1952), p. 733.

[40] "Fabian Tactics," *ibid.* (Oct. 12, 1951), p. 785.

experiment. Some see in it the danger of the lowering of educational standards, leading to defects which they see in American high schools.[41] The issue has become both a political and educational one.

(6) Secondary School Support. Secondary education in schools completely maintained by the L.E.A.'s, whether "voluntary" or state schools, is free. The L.E.A.'s also provide maintenance grants for students remaining in school beyond the age of 15, the amount depending upon parental income. There are, in addition, many grammar schools, not so maintained, but which receive grants from the Ministry of Education. The L.E.A.'s are represented on the governing boards of all such "Direct Grant" schools, and the grants to them are made with the condition that they admit 25 per cent of their pupils as free-place students. Some of the "Public Schools" are on the "Direct Grant" list. Others are placed by inspectors on the list of "efficient" schools, which receive no grants. The fees in the Public Schools run from about $500 to $900 per year for board and tuition. In addition to these, there are many proprietary secondary schools that subsist by the tuition of their students. The desire of some parents for social and religious exclusiveness for their children explains, in large degree, this variety of schools in England. The "Public Schools," however, have established an outstanding place in the competition of students for scholarships in Oxford and Cambridge.[42]

(7) The Preparatory Schools. There are nearly 500 expensive boarding schools, mostly proprietary, which prepare youths between the ages of 8 and 14 for admission into the "Public Schools" and for the disciplined, corporate life of these schools. The boarding school has always been popular with English parents, and the Public Schools and many voluntary secondary schools are boarding schools, where character is formed in a disciplinary atmosphere.

(8) The Ministry of Education. The Act of 1944 created a national Ministry of Education, endowed with great power, and decreased the powers of the L.E.A.'s. The ministers thus far have not used their powers autocratically, and have respected the wishes of the L.E.A.'s. Many educational matters have not been brought under the minister's jurisdiction. The universities, some forms of agricultural education, and military training are under the supervision of other ministries. The Act of 1944 created two Central Ad-

[41] I. L. Kandel, *The New Era in Education* (Boston: Houghton Mifflin Co., 1955), p. 263.

[42] G. D. N. Worswick, "Schools and Firsts," *London Times Educational Supplement* (Sept. 7, 1956), p. 1093.

visory Councils—one for England, one for Wales—whose duty it is to advise the minister as they see fit. The members are appointed by the minister, and must include persons experienced in British education. To see that the law is complied with and to improve instruction, over 500 inspectors, who represent the Ministry, are employed.

(9) THE UNIVERSITIES. The universities are self-governing institutions with power to grant degrees. The University Grants Committee, appointed by the Ministry of the Treasury, makes large grants to them for general and specific purposes. These grants are supplemented by aid from the Ministry of Education for their program of adult education. Some L.E.A.'s also make substantial grants to universities in their areas. Well over 50 per cent of university income comes now from the state. While their freedom is being threatened, they stand as the best example of laissez-faire control in the educational world. Various ministries have called upon them for an increased supply of specialists, and the government has even threatened to create new professorships, such as that of industrial design, if the universities do not take the initiative.[43] Universities can no longer ignore the demand of the state for service.

University enrollment in England is, in proportion to population, the lowest in Western nations. About 75 per cent of the students have whole or partial scholarships granted by the state, the L.E.A.'s, and the universities themselves. Over 70 per cent of Oxford students are "assisted." Substantial maintenance grants are added to free tuition of needy students.[44] The universities set their standards for admission, academic achievement and promise being the chief consideration.

Of the approximately 85,000 students in British universities in 1952, some 9,000 were "overseas" students, of whom about 6,000 came from Commonwealth countries.[45] Male students numbered about 66,000 and women about 19,000. The liberal arts, pure science, medicine and technology—in that order—were the leading academic choices of students. Fifteen per cent of the women were medical students.

The ancient universities of Oxford and Cambridge, with some 15,000 full-time students, are the most famous, while the University

[43] "Questions to Universities," *ibid.* (Dec. 9, 1949), p. 860; J. H. Goldthorpe, "British Universities and the Government," *American Association of University Professors Bulletin* (Autumn 1947), pp. 474 ff.

[44] S. D. Simon, "How Many Poor Scholars," *London Times Educational Supplement* (Oct. 16, 1953), p. 879; "Grants to Students," *ibid.* (May 6, 1955), p. 446.

[45] "Returns from Universities," *ibid.* (Sept. 5, 1952), p. 783; *cf.* Kandel, *op. cit.*, p. 273.

of London, with its 36 colleges and an enrollment of over 18,000, is the largest. Oxford and Cambridge are each a federation of many separately incorporated, independent resident colleges, in which students are registered, live a community life, and are instructed individually by tutors who usually require them to attend lectures given by university professors, attached not to individual colleges but to the central administration. Each college student is a specialist working for an Honor's Degree.

In the cities of England there arose in the nineteenth century municipal universities, sometimes called "red-brick universities," which are more local in their student body and services than the ancient universities. The University of London is a distinctly unique institution in the scope of its activities. Among its many colleges are twelve medical schools, the Imperial College of Science and Technology, the famous London School of Economics, and some denominational liberal arts colleges. It has examination centers throughout the empire and grants degrees to students who pass, even though they have never attended university classes.

All universities require a qualification in mathematics and science for admission, while Oxford and Cambridge, in addition, require a knowledge of a classical language. The student enters the professional as well as academic courses directly from the secondary school. Unlike American practice, no four-year college course separates the secondary school graduate from the professional schools. Here it should be noted that the "sixth form" of the English grammar school is the equivalent of at least the first two years of the American college. University students represent the intellectual elite of England, and a cross-section of English society, many of them coming from the lower-middle and working classes.[46]

(10) Adult Education. English adult education is liberal, or academic. It has grown up since the early nineteenth century when literacy training was given adults to enable them to read the Bible, and Mechanics Institutes taught workingmen the sciences and politics mostly for liberal ends. University extension non-credit courses were first offered to working adults in 1873. Since 1909, university tutorial credit courses have been offered chiefly to skilled workers, and in this activity the Workers' Educational Association, organized in 1903 and pursuing a broad social purpose, has participated with the universities. With the rise of the welfare state that purpose has been achieved. Many agencies, public and private, provide and help to support the courses, students' interests determining the

[46] "Undergraduate Families," *London Times Educational Supplement* (April 2, 1954), p. 318.

courses to be offered. The L.E.A.'s, in 1952, provided evening schools in which well over 1,000,000 students, most of them over the age of 21, were enrolled.[47] Public funds meet 80 per cent of the cost, while students pay small fees.

Recent Developments in French Education

THE EDUCATIONAL HERITAGE. As we have seen in Chapter 13, France has a state and a church school system. The ideal of lay education finally triumphed under the Third Republic, but there remain those who place the religious above the political purpose of education. Jesuit and Napoleonic practices of centralization of educational control, and of the education of an elite for leadership, took firm root as did the view that "general culture," always rather loosely defined but essentially humanistic, is the best content of such an education. To secondary education was assigned the task of providing this *"Culture Générale."* While theoretical science, mathematics and modern languages were among studies recognized as of general cultural value, Latin and Greek languages and literature were viewed as the best instruments of that culture.

From participation in the higher culture of the nation the masses were excluded, as we have seen, as they were also from civil and professional careers, to which intellectual attainments led. They received in their own primary schools only the knowledge of rudimentary subject matter of which no Frenchman could afford to be ignorant. Above this came training for various trades and practical pursuits, but vocational education lacked respectability. Secondary and higher education had as their purpose the training of state officials, army officers and members of the liberal professions of law, medicine, etc. The clientele of secondary schools and higher schools came from an upper social group, and were sifted by competitive examination for each advanced stage of their training. Until recently, few secondary or university students contemplated a business career. More important, in French thought, than any technical proficiency is an individual's interest in art, literature, philosophy, etc., and one's ability to enjoy leisure with taste and pleasure. Crises, however, have forced French leaders to examine this educational heritage critically.

THE REFORM MOVEMENTS. During World War I, there arose a demand for a common school (*l'école unique*) which led to the official approval of a foundation curriculum common to both primary and secondary schools, and of the recognition of abilities and inter-

[47] *Ibid.* (May 29, 1953), p. 488.

ests, not wealth and caste, as the basis of educational differentiation. This demand led to the abolition of fees in state secondary schools in the years 1930-1937, and the official acceptance of the view that secondary is a continuation of primary education. The reform movement between 1917 and 1940 made the *l'école unique* its central goal.

When France fell to the Nazis in 1940 and with it the ideals of the French Revolution—liberty, equality and fraternity—the French Fascist statesmen, Pétain and Laval, denounced the reformers, and sponsored a reactionary educational policy in keeping with Fascist ideology.

In 1944, while France was still occupied by the Germans, a commission appointed by the Free French government in Algiers recommended a number of educational reforms, among them a modified *école unique* and greater stress upon scientific and technical studies. With the liberation of France, a new commission, headed by professors Paul Langevin and Henri Wallon, after a two-year study, submitted (1947) their report on educational reform known as the Langevin Plan. The Delbos Act of 1949 and André Marie Act of 1953 were legislative attempts to implement the Plan, but these efforts have resulted in little change beyond (1) experimentation with new methods of instruction in special classes (*classes nouvelles*) in secondary schools, (2) greater public and official respect and concern for technical education, and (3) a growing recognition of the importance of psychology and vocational guidance in education.

The Langevin Plan, among other basic proposals, called for the organization of education on three levels: (a) the primary-secondary (ages 7 to 18), (b) the pre-professional higher level (ages 18 to 21) leading to the degree of *Licence*, and (c) the university level proper, leading to the Ph.D. and various professional diplomas granted by universities and *Grandes Écoles*. The foundation of the structure would be the common school (ages 7 to 11). On it would be erected a seven-year secondary school whose work would be adapted to the vocational and academic interests and abilities of students who, in the last three years of the course, would be placed in sections on these bases. At the age of 18, all students would be examined and given certificates, if their performance warranted, the *baccalauréat*, or university matriculation, being reserved for those in the academic section. The Plan called for the abolition of all examinations before the age of eighteen, and would make all courses and certificates of equal worth and dignity. There would be two classes of teachers: (a) those teaching many subjects and (b) specialists, and all would be required to hold the university degree of *Licence*.

The Plan would open the life of culture to the French masses, and make the school an institution of national unity in a nation which, in spite of its great cultural achievements, had failed to create socially unifying institutions. The proposals were sharply criticized by traditionalists and enthusiastically defended by modernists.[48]

VOCATIONAL EDUCATION. The crisis in France and the demands of reformers have resulted in an increased emphasis upon vocational training for factory workers, farmers, etc. Free factory apprenticeship training courses have been widely established for boys and girls who have completed their years of compulsory education. Cities and private business houses have long provided vocational courses also. In addition to these locally sponsored efforts there are a few national apprenticeship centers which grant a variety of trade and commercial certificates to successful students. Among vocational schools are the public technical colleges (see Chapter 13), craft schools mostly privately supported, and many national vocational schools. The last, as do the technical colleges, prepare students for admission to national engineering schools. The industrial cities provide a great variety of highly specialized trade schools as, indeed, they have done for a long time. Since the Minister of Education now administers the program, vocational education is being more closely integrated with general education.

CLASSES NOUVELLES. Perhaps the most significant actual reform of education has appeared in the organization in secondary schools of "new classes," embodying a progressive philosophy of education and modern methods of instruction. Even before the war, activity methods had been tried in some elementary and lower grades of a few secondary schools. The first of the "new classes" were established with the approval of the Ministry in 1945. The old secondary education was extremely bookish, and the school a listening school. Character development and physical education were scarcely thought of. Discipline was severe and was enforced by a paid disciplinarian, sometimes a student, who behaved like an army sergeant. The teacher (*professeur*) evaluated his work by the success of his students in the state *baccalauréat* examination, in which generally less than 50 per cent of students passed. This method of educating the elite was sharply criticized by reformers.

The students of the "new classes" are recruited voluntarily from those who had passed the entrance examination of the secondary school, but only 25 are accepted for each class. The principles gov-

[48] P. Boyancé, "French Proposals for Reform," *ibid.* (Feb. 6, March 5, and 12, 1949); G. Roger, "The Langevin Plan," *ibid.* (April 23, 1949).

erning the instruction are (1) that the student is more important than subject matter and that teachers and school psychologists should learn more about him, (2) that doing is more important for learning than listening and repeating, (3) that different subjects of instruction should be correlated by using "centers of interest"—somewhat similar to the American "unit plan" and Herbartian "correlation"—as a method of learning, (4) that the local and national environment be studied whenever possible with the center of interest, and (5) that marks (grades) be abolished.

Some 900 new classes were organized in the secondary schools, but the number has not grown. Fear of failure in the state examinations retarded their development. The experiment, although it seems to have lost some of its earlier popularity, will probably lead to a modification of the academic formalism which has traditionally marked the practice of French schools.

THE STATE AND PRIVATE EDUCATION. Since the establishment of the Third Republic, there has been a bitter struggle between the advocates of secular and of Catholic education. While the population of France is predominantly Catholic, there are Protestants, Jews, and Muslims scattered over the country. Many Catholics, particularly men, are Freethinkers or, perhaps not infrequently, atheists.[49] Rationalists at heart, and advocates of the rights of the state as against the claims of the church to mould the minds and loyalties of youth, French secularists have stood for "a lay school for a lay society" in the interest of the state and its ideals. Until the Revolution and, indeed, until 1904, when church and state were legally separated, the church played an influential rôle in education, although the ideal of secularism continued to gain ground under the Third Republic.

Political conservatives, representing Catholic and anti-Republican interests, continued to oppose public, secular compulsory education, and Catholic churchmen kept denouncing the doctrine of "secular morality" and insisting that Catholicism alone provided a true basis of morality. Catholic Freethinkers and non-Catholics stood opposed to the official Catholic position and supported the state, secular schools. Said Victor Hugo to the priests:

> I would not have you entrusted with . . . the development of young minds just awakening to life. . . . Against whom are your shafts directed? . . . They are against human reason. Why? Because it reveals the truth. Shall I tell you the cause of your alarm? It is the flood of freely flowing light that has emanated from France for the last three centuries; a light whose substance is reason.[50]

[49] F. Sieburg, *Who Are These French* (New York: The Macmillan Co., 1932).

[50] J. Debiesse, *Compulsory Education in France* (Paris: Unesco, 1951), pp. 21 f.

The view of the opposition was well expressed by a political conservative, Chesnelong, who remarked:

> Your real aim [in demanding compulsory education is] to give the whole population an anti-Christian education. . . . A demand for compulsory education is to be expected from a secularist, just as tyranny is to be expected from a usurper. . . . If the rising generations in France are subjected for any length of time to the educational system you intend to impose on them, there will be an end to social stability and moral dignity in this country.[51]

With the views of Chesnelong, a political Rightist, the Catholic hierarchy would agree. The battle for free, secular, compulsory education was won by the secularists, and the state was accepted by the majority of French citizens as the essential moulder of minds and guardian of the interests of the state. Secularity was ably defended by its advocates. It does not, said the historian, Lavisse,

> limit human thought to the visible horizon, nor forbid man to aspire after God; . . . it will not allow religions, which are ephemeral, the right to govern humanity, which is enduring; . . . it is out to fight the spirit of hatred with which all religions are imbued. . . . Secularity holds that life is worth living; enjoys life; declines to regard this world as a "vale of tears"; . . . fights against evil in the name of justice.[52]

The church, as we have seen, has its own school system. While the state has almost a monopoly of elementary education in the nation as a whole, there are areas where church schools are the only ones operating. These latter have everywhere been relatively poor in equipment and the quality of instruction. Pétain, during his Vichy régime, provided some financial aid for them, and the issue of such support became a matter of political debate in the Chamber of Deputies after the establishment of the Fourth Republic. The long and bitter debate ended in September, 1951, when a law was passed providing a state allowance of about $3.00 a term for each child attending a private or public elementary school. The Socialists in the Chamber were loud in denouncing such aid to church schools as an infringement of the principle of the lay state upon which the Republic was founded. And the secular state schools are still being attacked by members of the clergy as "godless."[53]

The private schools grant their own certificates, which the state does not recognize, and their graduates, to secure state certificates, must take the state examinations. It is chiefly through control of degrees, diplomas and certificates that the state tries to keep private

[51] *Ibid.*, p. 22.
[52] *Ibid.*, p. 26.
[53] "The French School Debate," *London Times Educational Supplement* (Sept. 7, 1951), p. 700; "French Debate Ends," *ibid.* (Sept. 14, 1951), p. 716; P. Blanshard, "The Vatican versus the Public Schools," *The Nation* (March 3, 1951), pp. 201–04.

schools up to the educational standards of the national system. Respect for intellectualism and high academic standards have, however, resulted from the educational leadership of the French Ministry of Education.

The Making of Communists in the Soviet Union

New minds, if not new men, were needed for the success of the Communist social experiment in the Soviet Union. An educational revolution was needed for the success of the social revolution. To industrialize the backward nation, and to train workers to serve it, called also for large-scale reforms in education. Some changes in official policy have occurred as the régime developed, and the official policy has always been reflected in education.

EDUCATIONAL IDEALS AND PURPOSE. The social principles of the Communist state, discussed earlier, find educational expression in an emphasis throughout schools and other agencies of education upon anti-liberalism, militarism, activism, atheism, materialism, sex equality, social equality, the dignity of work, and the duty of everyone to be a worker.[54]

Education, officially viewed as extending from birth to death, must be closely integrated with the changing ideals, practices and needs of the régime. The aims of the government and the school must always be the same. The secular, political morality approved by the state must be inculcated in youth by teachers who are instructed in the content and method of moral education.[55] The whole system of state-approved economic, social, political, ethical, philosophical and other forms of ideology must be promoted by the school.

Marx and his followers viewed mass education in capitalist countries as an instrument of social predestination, designed to keep the laboring masses the servants of the bourgeoisie. Marx himself stressed the importance of technical education for an industrial, proletarian society, but noted that capitalist societies linked it to elementary education, designed for the masses, and thus put the mark of caste upon it. Marxists would confer upon technical training the same dignity and importance which they would give to mental and physical education. The theory of education for technical

[54] A. P. Pinkevitch, *The New Education in the Soviet Republic* (New York: John Day Company, Inc., 1929); T. Woody, *New Minds: New Men?* (New York: The Macmillan Co., 1932).

[55] G. S. Counts, *I Want to Be Like Stalin* (New York: John Day Company, Inc., 1947).

efficiency in a workers' state was a part of the educational philosophy of the Communists who came to power in Russia.[56]

SOVIET SCIENCE OF EDUCATION. Marx, Engels, and Lenin laid the theoretical basis of Communist educational "science." Philosophically it finds its justification in dialectical materialism. The "science of education" must conform with changing political ideals and needs. Utility is the test of truth in the Soviet world. The freedom of the earlier schools has been replaced by planned discipline, and by formal courses, methods and examinations, which are rigidly adhered to.

LIQUIDATING ILLITERACY. Considering the diversity in language and culture in Russia, and the prejudices that had to be overcome in building the new society, the magnitude of the Soviet educational problem was stupendous. Tzarist Russia had state schools for the few, modeled after German secondary schools, and designed to train a social elite for government service and the professions. The peasants and city laborers had little opportunity to share in the culture of the privileged class. Philanthropists and reformers had long provided some opportunities for them, and the Parliament (Duma), just before the Revolution, was taking steps to provide universal primary schooling for them.[57] When the Communists came to power, approximately 70 per cent of the population was illiterate. Not only the government, but the army, youth organizations and other agencies attacked the problem.[58] In 1935, the government ordered the publication of 30,000,000 textbooks in various languages for use in literacy schools and schools for semi-literates.[59] In 1947, it was officially announced that the percentage of literacy among workers had risen to 99.7 per cent, but literacy seems to be defined in the Soviet Union as an ability merely to read and write.[60]

EDUCATIONAL CONTROL AND SUPPORT. Educational policies are determined by the Central Executive Committee, the Council of Peoples' Commissars, and the General Committee of the Communist Party, while educational planning is done by the State Planning Commission. Legally, control of general education and libraries is vested in the Commissariat of Education in each of the republics,

[56] U.S. Office of Education, *Education in the USSR* (Washington, D.C.: Government Printing Office, 1957), pp. 11–12.

[57] G. Vernadsky, *A History of Russia* (3d ed.; Yale University Press, 1951), p. 195.

[58] *Educational Yearbook*, 1937, p. 527.

[59] *Ibid.*

[60] *World Handbook of Educational Organization and Statistics* (Paris: Unesco, 1951), p. 391; *Year Book of Education* (London: Evans Bros., Ltd., 1949), pp. 383, 411.

but Party officials insure their concordance with central powers. Vocational education is controlled for the whole Union by an array of industrial Commissariats, each one in charge of a special industry, or a subdivision of it, though each of these takes suggestions from the Council of Peoples' Commissars. That Council, the Red Army, and other appropriate groups control adult education. Special Union committees have control of physical and art education, the press, etc. The support of the system comes from the Central Government, the Republics, local communities and from funds of industrial, agricultural and other organizations. About 12.5 per cent of the total state budget goes to educational and cultural activities.[61] Parents, however, bear directly about 30 per cent of the cost of nurseries and kindergartens. In 1940, the government abandoned the practice of free education on all levels, and inaugurated a fee system in universities, *technicums* and the last three grades of the 10-year, or "complete secondary" school. Instruction in the Labor Reserve vocational schools, established in 1940 for those who did not remain in school beyond the compulsory age of 14, is free. Parents have to pay for textbooks and uniforms worn by students. In the new boarding schools, first opened in 1956 and by 1958 numbering about 300, boarding and tuition costs are distributed between the state and parents on the basis of the parents' ability to pay.[62]

SCHOOLS AND THEIR ORGANIZATION. (1) REGULAR SCHOOLS FOR THE MASSES. Nurseries (*crèches*) and kindergartens, controlled by industries or the Republics, exist for children under the age of seven, when compulsory education begins. These schools are supervised by state health and educational authorities. General education is provided in the 10-year school organized on a 4-3-3 basis—primary, incomplete secondary and complete secondary levels. Until now compulsory education has ended with grade seven. The content and standards of instruction are identical at each grade level throughout the country, and transfer from one school to another is easy. An examination, however, is required for transfer from the incomplete to the complete secondary level and, like all other Russian examinations, it is a grim ordeal, upon the results of which much in one's life depends. Psychological and objective tests, which the Communists brand as bourgeois devices to justify predetermined decisions, are not used in the selection of youths for further opportunities.

[61] U.S. Office of Education, *Education in the USSR*, pp. 23–27.

[62] A. G. Korol, *Soviet Education for Science and Technology* (New York: John Wiley & Sons, Inc., 1957), pp. 33, 41–42.

The 10-year school is the basic plan of general education. There are, however, important qualitative differences between city and rural schools in the general, mass system, and many children do not yet attend the full-time schools. For such so-called "working youth," part-time day schools (urban) and part-time evening schools (rural) were established in 1943, and are now (1958) apparently a part of the permanent system.[63]

Education for work, and the ideal of respect for work, are stressed by the state. In 1940, the "State Labor Reserve" was created chiefly for non-academic youths, male and female, between the ages of fourteen and nineteen. Into it, such youths are drafted for a course of training, varying in length from six months to two years, in the various manual occupations in industry, agriculture, transportation, etc., actual work in jobs and trades being the chief part of the process. In the 2-year courses, mathematics, physics, the Russian language, political doctrines and physical education are taught, in addition to job training. When trained, these youths constitute a cheap, mobile labor force to be drafted into service in any part of the country where there is need for them.

Since 1954, to relieve labor shortage as well as, apparently, to limit admissions to higher institutions, there have been established, within the Labor Reserve system, some 450 technical trade schools, with short-term courses in about 280 trades, for graduates of complete secondary schools. These students are thus denied an opportunity for higher education and the social privileges identified with it. Since 1950, the total enrollment in the tenth grade has increased from 300,000 to 1,300,000, thus creating a serious problem of selection for higher schools and social privilege.

(2) BOARDING SCHOOLS FOR THE MASSES. The Twentieth Party Congress (1956) recommended boarding schools for all children from the cradle to the age of seventeen and, in 1956, the first boarding schools within the compulsory, mass system were opened. In 1957, it was reported that there were 1000 such schools in operation and with an enrollment of 300,000 pupils.[64] The basic idea, as revealed in official and semiofficial pronouncements, seems to be to bring the whole life of the child under directed Communist influence for the realization and safeguarding of Marxist-Leninist ideals.[65]

63 *Ibid.*, pp. 4–7.

64 A Correspondent, "Russian Boarding Schools," *London Times Educational Supplement* (Nov. 22, 1957), p. 1491.

65 *Ibid.*

(3) Technicums. Outside of the schools in the regular system of mass education, but overlapping in part the complete secondary school, are technical schools, called *Technicums.* They are subprofessional, specialized secondary schools, usually with a 4-year course, which require at least seven years of general education for admission. About one-half of their students enter them at the end of the 10-year school. Many others come to them after some years of practical experience in several vocational pursuits. Each *Technicum* specializes in one area, and there were 23 such areas provided for in 1948.[66] Only a fraction of these schools prepared students for engineering. Many of them specialize in such areas as physical culture, art, public health, and teacher training. In 1956, the enrollment in all of them was 843,000.

(4) Higher Education. The main road to higher schools, which include some 34 universities and over 700 institutes, is through the complete secondary school. The universities build their program around a major academic subject, while the institutes stress the applied sciences. Very superior students are admitted to these schools without examination. Russian language and literature, mathematics, physics, chemistry and foreign languages are the chief subjects on which students are examined for admission. In some instances the examinations are competitive, in others, noncompetitive. Veterans of World War II, children of officials and industrial administrators are among those who are admitted by noncompetitive examination. The merit system is not always practised.[67] Admissions are limited by a state-planned quota system.

Since 1940, tuition of from 300 to 500 roubles per year has been charged in higher schools. The state has, however, provided an elaborate scheme of scholarships and maintenance grants, the amount granted to holders depending to a large extent upon their grades.

The courses in higher schools run from two to six years in length, a 5-year one being standard for universities and engineering schools. Some 835 fields of specialization are provided for, each in its own special way. In 1954, there were 57 special faculties in 25 engineering schools offering 171 different engineering courses.[68] What stands out in the picture is the elaborate, functional plan of training professional technical and political leaders for Soviet society. Nothing, however, of intellectual importance is neglected in Soviet education. To think that the state merely aims to train monkeys to run

66 Korol, *op. cit.*, p. 103.
67 *Ibid.*, p. 190.
68 *Ibid.;* U.S. Department of Health, Education, and Welfare, *op. cit.*

machines would be a serious delusion. All curricula in all higher schools include instruction in physical education, foreign languages, and the social sciences, these last studies being viewed and taught with a Marxist-Leninist bias.

(5) WOMEN'S EDUCATION. Coeducation, checked officially in 1943, was restored in 1954.[69] The doctrine of equality of the sexes, not entirely practised in social life, is a practice in the schools. Women have demonstrated their competence as engineers, technicians, physicians, teachers, etc. There are reported to be now (1958) 500,000 female engineers and technicians and 1,164,000 female teachers in Russia. More than half the specialists trained in higher schools are women.[70]

(6) CURRICULUM. **(a) Crèches and kindergartens.** Health training is the chief activity of the *crèches.* To it are added rhythmic movement, singing, and Communist propaganda. In kindergartens, which aim at all-round development of the child, there is added to the activities of the *crèche* the rudiments of knowledge and some formal social and ideological instruction. The program includes free play, dressing, bathing, meals, and sleep. Teaching love for "the Soviet Fatherland," the Soviet army, and the Soviet people and their rulers is a stated aim of kindergartens.

(b) Elementary and secondary. Being the schools of general education, and united into one unbroken organization, the curriculum is an unbroken unity of general studies. These studies are Russian language and literature, mathematics, USSR Constitution, history, geography, biology, physics, astronomy, chemistry, psychology, logic, foreign languages (English, German, or French), physical education, drawing, drafting, singing and shop work. Thirteen of these subjects are taught in grades one to seven, and nine of them are constant throughout the ten grades.[71] State textbooks are the basis of instruction. Laboratory work and visualized instruction are everywhere in use. Promotion from grade to grade is based upon examination results. Planned by the state, the grading system is uniform throughout the whole country.

For children in their out-of-school hours, a well-organized extracurricular program of cultural activities related to the regular curriculum and their individual interests and talents has been developed. Much of the program is under the direction of the Party and

69 "Back to Co-Education," *London Times Educational Supplement* (Aug. 27, 1954), p. 801; Y. N. Medinsky, *Public Education in the U.S.S.R.* (Moscow: Foreign Language Publishing House, 1953), pp. 57–60.

70 *The New York Times* (Feb. 16, 1958), Sec. 1, p. 29.

71 Korol, *op. cit.*, p. 58.

the trade unions. Children's theaters, television programs, science, arts and athletic clubs, etc. are included in the program. For pupils with inventive or technical interests there are many clubs which help them to develop and apply their talents. Athletics and sports are now receiving large official approval, and the state is providing athletic directors for this phase of the program.

(c) Technicums and higher schools. Enough has already been presented to indicate the studies in *Technicums* and higher schools. For more detailed information we refer the student to the accounts found in readily available publications, some of which are listed at the end of this chapter.

(7) State Control of Curriculum and Method. Unlike, particularly, England and the United States, Soviet Russia extends state control over the internal aspects of education, especially in the 10-year school, although the program of *Technicums* and higher schools is planned by the central state authority. As the system operates for the 10-year school, there are official state syllabi in all subjects, which all schools must follow. Common to them all, even in those of mathematics and the physical sciences, is a requirement in the teaching of patriotism and loyalty to Russia and Soviet ideals, although the texts in such fields are largely free from ideological bias.[72] For each subject, there is a state textbook, which each student is expected to purchase at a low official price. A numerical grading system has been adopted, and the highest mark, 5, is reserved for a pupil who "exhaustively knows, excellently understands, and has firmly mastered all the material."[73]

In 1944, the central authority prescribed formal, final examinations for graduation from primary, incomplete secondary, and complete secondary schools, and a certificate was decreed in 1945 for successful graduates of the last of these schools. Gold medals, in addition to certificates, were then authorized for students having a final grade of "5" in all subjects, and silver medals for those just below this perfect record.

While promotion examinations from grade to grade in the 10-year school system are left largely to individual schools, the final-examinations questions are set by the central Ministry of Education, although the teachers are given a modicum of freedom in reformulating specific questions. To get the certificate of maturity, granted to graduates of the tenth grade, the student must have at least a grade of "3" (the equivalent of our "C") in all subjects and a grade

[72] *Ibid.*, p. 70.
[73] *Ibid.*, p. 77.

of "5" (our "A") in conduct. Having this certificate he may apply for admission to higher schools. The examination questions show that the Soviet state demands a thorough coverage of the content of the various subjects, and academic standards are high.

(8) POLYTECHNIZATION. The aim of training youth for technical, industrial efficiency has been a part of the Marxist tradition. Marx preordained polytechnization when he said that one purpose of education is to "impart the general principles of all processes of production and simultaneously initiate the child and young person in the practical use and handling of the elementary instruments of all trades." [74] Soviet authorities, while they have stressed specific training for trades for non-academic youths would have all youths in the general, mass school system instructed in the fundamentals of production and distribution of goods, and trained for a life of labor, raised to a status of dignity by official policy. While the state respects the life of the mind and intellectual pursuits, it discourages contempt for manual labor in any form. It would seem that the ideal of polytechnization implies the application of science to technical practice if not the vocationalizing of all schools in the 10-year system.[75]

(9) EDUCATION OF EXCEPTIONAL CHILDREN. For the deaf, blind, crippled, orphaned, retarded, mentally and artistically gifted, the state provides special schools whose teachers are paid higher salaries than are those in the regular schools. Soviet cultivation of exceptional talent is a notable practice.[76]

(10) ADULT EDUCATION. Schools for adults have been a part of the Soviet program from its inception. The fourth 5-year plan (1946-1950) aimed to abolish the last remnants of illiteracy, and schools and ministries of education of the several republics were called upon to participate in the campaign. In each ministry there is a department of adult education which supervises the schooling of adults. The schools for adults are usually in large industrial cities, and are organized on the 10-grade plan of the regular schools. Many of the students in the schools of the Labor Reserve and of part-time systems fall into the adult category. Supplementing such formal schooling is an extensive system of state libraries, stationary and traveling, and there are many hundreds of museums devoted to art, industry, health, science, technology, the Revolution, etc. Theaters attended annually by hundreds of millions, who pay a

[74] *Educational Yearbook*, 1937, p. 504.

[75] Korol, *op. cit.*, pp. 27–32.

[76] U.S. Office of Education, *Education in the USSR*, pp. 105–10.

small admission charge, are an important agency of Soviet propaganda and adult education.

(11) HEALTH, PHYSICAL, AND MILITARY EDUCATION. A department in the central government has, since 1923, had charge of the health of the nation. Doctors are state, salaried employees, and medical service is free. There are thousands of state athletic fields in the Union, and Russia has been carrying off many honors in recent Olympic games. About seven per cent of the time allotment in the 10-year regular school program is assigned to physical education. Sports and athletics are emphasized, also, in the extracurricular program. Physical culture has a prominent place in the activities of the Youth Movement. In 1929, physical culture was introduced into higher schools, and has since been a compulsory practice for two hours weekly during the first four semesters. The stated purpose of the physical education program in higher schools is to prepare youths for work and for national defense.

For all Soviet citizens military service of from two to five years, depending on the type of service, becomes compulsory at the age of eighteen or nineteen.[77] Normally, students in higher schools are exempted from military draft until the end of their course, and special exemptions are extended to engineering students. The Constitution states that national defense is the duty of every citizen. Outside of the general scheme of military training there are formal military schools, some of them on the secondary and others on the higher level of education. The regular 10-year curriculum supplemented by special physical and military training marks the former type. The higher schools of military training specialize in various military specializations, and offer both undergraduate and graduate studies.[78]

(12) LEADERSHIP SCHOOLS. There is a wide network of Party schools and educational circles designed for the special training of leaders for the Party and the state. Party officials and leading state bureaucrats are trained in these schools. Ability is now the chief basis of selection of Party leaders. In 1952, it was stated in *Pravda* that 400,000 Party leaders had been graduated in the preceding five years from the various leadership schools and courses.[79]

(13) TEACHERS AND TEACHER TRAINING. The Soviet state holds teachers in high respect, and the supply of teachers is adequate. There are approximately 2,000,000 in the Union of whom about

[77] W. W. Kulski, *The Soviet Regime* (Syracuse, N.Y.: Syracuse University Press, 1954), p. 308.

[78] Korol, *op. cit.*, p. 141.

[79] Kulski, *op. cit.*, p. 166.

eighty per cent are women. The teachers in secondary grades are mostly men. Appointed usually for life, teachers may retire on pension after twenty-five years of service. Salaries are paid by the state and vary for the several officially classified categories of teachers. As compared with other servants of the state, they are well rewarded.

The reorganization of teachers' seminaries has gone on progressively since the Soviet régime began, and standards for teachers have been steadily raised. Primary school teachers are trained in Teachers' Institutes, which require for admission graduation from an incomplete secondary school. The course of training now requires four years, and the curriculum emphasizes methods of teaching, mathematics, physics, chemistry, botany, zoology, anatomy, physiology, Darwinism, and the subjects usually taught in primary schools. Russian language, Constitution of the U.S.S.R., history of the Communist Party, history of education, psychology, and physical education are among the many studies of these training schools.[80] To teach in a secondary school, one has to be a graduate of the complete secondary school and of a two-year Teachers' Institute, now disappearing, a four-year Pedagogical Institute, now on the increase, or a university department of education. The central, state authority for teacher training drafts the syllabi and dictates the textbooks to be used in training the teachers of secondary school subjects. In the Pedagogical Institute the studies are the same as in the Teachers' Institute.[81] Instruction in Marxism-Leninism is a universal requirement. The program in universities is a five-year one, has less education courses in it, and provides some training in research techniques.

Admission to the Institutes is by a competitive examination, and the personal qualifications of applicants are closely scrutinized. The abolition of fees was announced in 1955. Maintenance grants, the amount depending upon the quality of the students' work from year to year, are provided for nearly all students. To graduate one must pass a rigid state examination.

Crowning the teacher training edifice is the RSFSR Academy of Pedagogical Sciences in Moscow, founded in 1943 to guide the educational forces of the nation. Educational research is its chief function. It maintains the State Library of Education, with over 700,000 volumes, the National Education Museum in Leningrad, research archives, etc. It supervises the writing of school text-

[80] Korol, *op. cit.*, p. 47.
[81] U.S. Office of Education, *Education in the USSR*, p. 206.

books, arranges school programs, sponsors lectures on education, chooses teachers and administrators for awards, etc.

YOUTH ORGANIZATIONS. In the moulding of citizens, youth organizations supplement the work of the family and the school. Children between the ages of eight and eleven may join the *Octobrists*. Above this group stands the *Pioneers*, for children between the ages of nine and thirteen. Some twenty million children are Pioneers, who at initiation take an oath to defend Communism and be good citizens of their "Socialist Fatherland." The training of citizens and the raising of educational standards are goals of the Pioneer organization. The Pioneers have their clubs, playgrounds, courses of training in crafts, summer camps, etc. From their ranks are selected, on the basis of ability and loyalty to Communist ideals, the members of the All Union Leninist Communist Youth League (*Komsomols*) for youths between the ages of fourteen and twenty-six. The Komsomols were reported to number about 16,000,000 in 1958. The purposes of the Komsomols are to train the cream of youth for Party membership and to help the Party achieve its goals. They are the active auxiliary of the Party in all of its various activities. Among their duties are the guidance of youth and the prevention of juvenile delinquency, which plagues the Soviet state as it does others today. They spread the political, anti-religious, and other official doctrines of the Party among youths and adults.[82]

SUMMARY AND EVALUATION. The Communist dictatorship exercises complete control over all aspects of life, and the schools must serve the Party, which dictates what they must do at any time. The state, the tool of the Party, fixes quotas for admission to all types of higher schools and the professions. The masses are predestined to remain hewers of wood and drawers of water. While practices of education have changed, the goal of building an efficient socialist state has remained as the basic objective of education. The liquidation of illiteracy, and universal, general, mass education have been largely achieved in the brief forty years of the régime. The percentage of Soviet youths admitted to higher institutions is less than one-half of that of the United States, but engineering students in higher schools outnumber ours by two to one.

The Soviet state is as much concerned with the education of leaders in every professional and cultural field as in that of engineer-

[82] "Communism for the Young," *London Times Educational Supplement* (Nov. 12, 1954), p. 1057.

ing. Higher education is the path to eminence and social prestige in Soviet society, and a realization of that fact stimulates students to their maximum effort. Since research and teaching in the area of the physical sciences are largely safe from charges of political heresy, many students are attracted to these fields of specialization. Centralized state control of curriculum, methods, examinations, awards, etc. has resulted in the maintenance of minimum standards and the raising of the academic level of the nation, but individual and local initiative has suffered as a result. The Party sets the moral, social and political standards for the nation, and individual students and citizens are thus relieved of the heavy responsibility of thinking for themselves. Political indoctrination and technical training, both efficiently achieved, have marked Soviet education since its inception. Therein lies its challenge to the liberal world.[83]

A Further Look at American Education

CRITICISMS OF PUBLIC EDUCATION. During the past few decades the public school practices of the nation have been subjected to criticism by educators and the laity. School study programs, contents of textbooks, and loyalty of teachers were among the first matters of attack following the termination of World War II. Colleges and universities were attacked as centers of radicalism, and academic freedom was threatened by an emotionalism rooted in the fear of Communism. The period since 1945 has been generally one of unrest in American education.[84] The attack upon the schools brought a counterattack, but the wave of criticism has not yet subsided. The "National Commission for the Defense of Democracy through Education" of the National Education Association published, in 1951, a list of 179 articles and books representing the attack and counterattack. Since then the basis of attack upon public education has shifted to the issue of the quality of the educational program and of its product.

This later aspect of the attack has found its best-known expression in Arthur E. Bestor's *Educational Wastelands,*[85] and in Albert Lynd's *Quackery in the Public Schools.*[86] In their opposition to pragmatism, functionalism, vocationalism, and "progressive educa-

[83] G. S. Counts, *The Challenge of Soviet Education* (New York: McGraw-Hill Book Co., Inc., 1957).

[84] F. H. Horn, "An Intellectual Iron Curtain," *N.E.A. Journal* (March 1953), pp. 152–55; J. H. Haefner, "The Battle of the Books," *ibid.* (April 1953), pp. 227–28; *Loyalty in a Democracy* (Public Affairs Pamphlet, No. 179, 1952).

[85] Urbana, Ill.: University of Illinois Press, 1953.

[86] Boston: Little, Brown & Co., 1950.

tion" the views of such writers are not new.[87] The philosophy of Dewey and the pragmatists lent support to the advocates of change and modernization, but the opposition to functionalism would not be silenced. In recent years their most influential voice has been Robert M. Hutchins, former Chancellor of the University of Chicago. Although Bestor is critical of colleges and professors who merely pass out information without stressing meanings and methods of inquiry and thinking, his attack, as is Lynd's, is directed chiefly at the high school program and educational administrators and professors of education, whom he holds responsible for the defects which he sees in our secondary schools. In a nutshell, our schools are accused by Bestor, Lynd and others of being anti-intellectual and of neglecting to develop the talents of superior students to whom the nation must look for leadership. Such sweeping generalizations are not based upon an adequate knowledge of the total scene, nor of the problems that the public school, as a social servant, must contend with. What effect this conflict is going to have upon education in the future remains in doubt. Public sentiment will, no doubt, determine the outcome.

PROGRESSIVES VERSUS TRADITIONALISTS. World War I and the national and international uncertainties which followed it brought doubt and unrest into educational thought in the liberal nations. Unlike the totalitarian states, liberals did not settle the issues. The struggle among liberal theorists, which has centered in the United States, is largely a reflection of the struggles of the world and of the anxieties created by change in our rapidly changing civilization. The "good old days" are gone. Men's conceptions of educational values are colored by some philosophy, such as idealism or pragmatism, each of which has its social implications. The educational theorist cannot reasonably ignore the suitability of his theory of knowledge, and its underlying assumptions regarding reality and truth, to the needs of his society.

How can the school serve our society best? The answers of the theorists to that question are colored by a variety of philosophical and social preconceptions and, at times, by differences in psychological conceptions.

Among the many educational issues upon which contradictory or divergent views have been urged are those of (1) the nature and meaning of education, (2) educational aims, (3) curriculum and (4) method and discipline. The views expressed run from marked conservatism to a progressivism which is less extreme now

[87] R. F. Butts, *The College Charts Its Course* (New York: McGraw-Hill Book Co., Inc., 1939).

than it was twenty years ago. Few, no doubt, would have us return to the extreme authoritarianism of our distant ancestors, but there are still many who question the position of those who stress the need for educational change in a civilization viewed as ever-changing. These conservatives defend the doctrine of the existence of "eternal verities," and of the need for fixed ways of thought and behavior, which must be imposed upon the child by a method perhaps more effective than that of the rod. Others oppose indoctrination and ask that we teach youth not what to think but how to think intelligently about the changing world so that they may participate sanely in directing change and in adjusting themselves to it.

The problem of the curriculum loomed large in the debate. The progressives would make the realities of the present and the interests and experiences of pupils the chief guides to its content. Dewey's principle of "education of, by and for experience" was misinterpreted by some, and in his *Experience and Education* he clarified his position. There he stated that some experiences are mis-educative. Yet he would not have the child's education follow the path of traditional subject matter.

Opposing the moderate progressives, such as Dewey and Boyd Bode, and the ultra-progressives, who would break with the past entirely and make child interests and impulses the guide to content and method, were the "essentialists," led by Professors Bagley and Kandel of Teachers College, Columbia University. These latter rejected the "progressive" doctrines of "freedom," "interest," "personal experience," "immediate needs," etc. as proper guides to educational procedures. They looked upon "effort," "discipline" and "remote goals" as among the "essentials" of a sound education, and advocated vigorously the need for a curriculum of organized subject matter in which solid studies and "race experience" would be taught not incidentally in connection with pupil experience but systematically. And they condemned the increasing emphasis upon the social studies and modern social problems. The theorists were thus themselves divided. The moderate progressives, however, seem to have had the greater influence upon the practices of the schools.

That our public secondary schools, the chief object of adverse criticism, have been often imperfect in many respects no well-informed person would deny. Nor could any reasonable person deny that we have built a civilization which, by comparison with others, is a credit to the ingenuity and democratic spirit of its architects. However, our schools deserve some credit for the good things in our civilization even though we do not entirely exonerate them from responsibility for its defects.

EFFORTS TO IMPROVE THE SYSTEM. Nowhere in the world, past or present, has any nation engaged in an educational enterprise of such magnitude as ours. Today, high school education has become almost universal, and the compulsory school age has in some states been raised above the average of sixteen to seventeen or even eighteen. How the system should be organized to serve the nation best has been a problem of major gravity. In 1945 about one-half of our local school systems were organized on the 6-3-3 plan, only smaller districts retaining the older 8-4 plan. The value of the junior high school is now being questioned by apparently many school officials.[88] It was established, among other purposes, to make the transition from the elementary to the high school easy. As we built our system there emerged the junior college, which President Tappan of the University of Michigan, as early as 1852, recommended as necessary to raise college standards. Secondary education has thus grown downward and upward.[89]

As the system expanded in answer to public demand and needs, it became difficult to maintain standards. Accrediting agencies were set up, as we have seen, to establish standards for high schools and raise the quality of their work. Yet, in our democratic effort to serve all youths well, time for the gifted ones was probably often wasted. Grouping by ability and enrichment of studies for superior students were frequently practised, although they were deemed by some undemocratic. It was felt by these that to make special provisions for the gifted ran counter to the ideal of equality of educational opportunity.

THE ISSUE OF RELIGIOUS EDUCATION. Among the issues that have been forced upon public attention in recent years have been those of religious education and of public aid for sectarian schools. The secularization of public education has its legal roots in the separation of church and state required by the Constitution. The young nation inherited from colonial times a parochial plan of education. Church control of education disappeared gradually as public school systems were established. Religious instruction, with a Protestant flavor, was often provided in our early public schools, and Catholics opposed the use of public funds for such a purpose. Controversy between Catholics and Protestants broke out also over

[88] B. Fine, "Education in Review," *The New York Times* (April 21, 1957), Sec. 4, p. E9.

[89] W. C. Eels (ed.), *American Junior Colleges,* Washington, D.C.: American Council on Education, 1940, p. 11.

the question of Bible reading in public schools on the ground that the Bible is a sectarian document.[90] Clarification of the political and education implications of the separation of church and state and of sectarian disputes brought the adoption of the policy of leaving religious instruction to the family, the church and private schools.[91] While most Protestant groups turned the secular education of their children over to the public elementary and high schools, there were few of them who did not continue to maintain colleges, theological seminaries, and, sometimes, secondary schools to safeguard their beliefs. Catholics, many Lutherans, and Quakers, however, have adhered closely to the tradition of church schools, and the Jews have a well-organized system of schools, most of them week-end ones, which their children attend.

The enrollment in Catholic schools, the largest church system, is now approaching 5,000,000, and is growing more rapidly than that of the public schools.[92] In 1952, the Catholic bishops expressed alarm over "the efforts to create a monopoly of education for a secularized public school," and declared that the state has a duty to assist parents in providing religious education, said to be important for good citizenship. That "duty," they said, could be discharged by providing "auxiliary services" for children attending parochial schools. The bishops rejected the view that church schools are divisive and, thus, detrimental to the state.[93]

There have been many court decisions, state and federal, in recent years involving issues connected with the problem of religious instruction.[94] Generally, the state courts have permitted Bible reading in public schools, and some states require it. The wearing of religious garb by teachers in public schools has been legally forbidden. The legality, under the Constitution, of many practices involving religion awaits future court decisions.

In 1948, in the McCollum Case, the United States Supreme Court declared as unconstitutional a released-time plan of excusing children from public school classes so that they could attend religious education classes in the public school building. In 1952, that Court further ruled that the practice of releasing students, during public school hours, for religious instruction of their choice

[90] W. E. Drake, *The American School in Transition* (Englewood Cliffs, N.J.: Prentice-Hall, 1955), pp. 256 ff.

[91] *Ibid.*, pp. 485 ff.

[92] B. Fine, "Education in Review," *The New York Times* (April 8, 1956), Sec. 4, p. E9.

[93] "Text of Statement of Bishops on Secularism and Schools," *ibid.* (Nov. 16, 1952), p. 80.

[94] Drake, *op. cit.*, pp. 491 ff.; L. O. Garber, *The Yearbook of School Law*, 1950–1958 (Danville, Ill.: Interstate Printers and Publishers).

outside of public schools is constitutional.[95] Local boards of education are thus free to release or not to release, as they see fit.

THE TEACHER-TRAINING ISSUE. Within the past decade, the issue of teacher training has become one of heated debate. The value of many professional courses in teacher-training programs has come to be questioned both by educators and laymen. As a result of criticisms, the amount of time given to professional courses in education is being sharply lessened, and more time is being assigned to the liberal education of future teachers and, for secondary school teachers, to the study of the subjects they are preparing to teach. In the professional area itself, there has been an increasing recognition of the value of such basic studies as philosophy of education, history of education, educational sociology, and educational psychology. The problem of what we should teach the future teachers of the nation is now being re-examined, and the requirements for certification are being changed in the light of experience and modern national and professional needs.

In some of the selected readings suggested at the end of this chapter the student will find information on various aspects of the problems of American education and on the divergent views of our educators regarding the rôle which the school must play in preserving and improving our civilization.

SOME CONTRASTS BETWEEN AMERICAN AND FOREIGN EDUCATION. The educational practices of different nations are a result of historical factors and social conditions, which differ from nation to nation. While America has, at times, borrowed from Europe, and Europe, from America, the borrowing has, and must continue to be, of very moderate proportions. Education has its roots in its own social soil.

Europe and Russia have no four-year liberal arts colleges separating their secondary schools from the professional education of universities. We have far more students between the ages of sixteen and twenty in school than any other nation, but the proportion of students of university age in professional schools here and abroad is about the same. While the foreign nations which we have examined have been struggling to achieve equality of educational opportunity, the United States has come closer to realizing it than has any of its neighbors. Foreign nations have concerned themselves with the problem of selection of students for vocations and the professions much more seriously than we have done. They

[95] "Religious Ruling Settles Old Issue," *The New York Times* (May 4, 1952), Sec. 4, p. E9.

select early; we postpone selection as long as possible. Stiff competitive examinations are used abroad to close the doors of the professions to the less fit. That practice is now being challenged by many parents and reformers both on educational and social grounds, and educational issues have become political ones.

The American plan keeps all children below the college in one all-purpose school. The European general practice is to separate them in one-purpose schools at the secondary level. Training for the professions in all the nations is much the same. American students enjoy far more freedom and initiative than do European and Russian students. Our educational aims demand that students below the university level be accorded opportunity for critical, independent thinking and free expression far beyond anything known abroad. Recent demands in France, England and Germany for the reform of methods and the whole life of the school promise the coming of more freedom for their youths.

While American educators struggle, against obstacles of serious proportions, to raise the educational standards of the nation, European social conditions and demands tend to lower the standards which, until now, educational authorities have been able to maintain there. Perhaps even high ideals must yield in liberal states to the voice of the people. To make that voice an enlightened one remains perhaps the greatest challenge to education in democratic societies.

Unesco and Its Activities

Confronted by the tragedies of war and their causes, architects of men's future destiny undertook, during World War II, to plan a better world. The United Nations Educational, Scientific and Cultural Organization (Unesco), a specialized agency of the United Nations which the United States joined officially in 1946, had its roots in earlier developments dating from 1919, although it actually had its beginning in London in 1943. Back of its founding lay the conviction that "wars begin in the minds of men" and that free exchange of ideas and educational reform in backward countries can produce international harmony.

Among Unesco's objectives are (a) the elimination of illiteracy everywhere, (b) education for everyone in keeping with each one's abilities and social needs, (c) promotion of science for the benefit of mankind, (d) an understanding by everyone of the interdependence of nations and of the causes of international strife, (e) the promotion of the free flow of persons and ideas between nations,

(f) the cultivation of loyalty to the United Nations, and (g) the promotion of respect for "human rights."

In December, 1948, the United Nations General Assembly approved "The Universal Declaration of Human Rights," with eight countries, including the U.S.S.R., abstaining from voting. Article 26 of the Declaration reads:

1. Everyone has a right to education. Education shall be free at least in the elementary . . . stages. Elementary education shall be compulsory. Technical and professional education shall be made generally available and higher education shall be equally accessible to all on the basis of merit.
2. Education shall . . . promote understanding, tolerance and friendship among all nations, racial or religious groups. . . .
3. Parents have a prior right to choose the kind of education that shall be given to their children.[96]

Since about half of the world's people are illiterate, still live in filth, poverty and ignorance, die prematurely, and are ready tools of would-be disturbers of peace, the plans of Unesco and of the framers of the Declaration of Human Rights conform with the realities of the modern world. Historical evidence, however, lends little, if any, support to the view that education alone can save the world. Economic, political and social conflicts must first be eradicated if the goals of Unesco are to be achieved. Wars do not begin in the minds of men but in conditions which shape their minds.

The various activities of Unesco, conducted through branches scattered over the world, are too many to be enumerated here. Its many publications are a fruitful source of information about educational affairs everywhere and about progress made in promoting international understanding.

The world's response to the proposals of the United Nations has often been one of apathy or skepticism. The articles on labor and social security of the Declaration of Human Rights aroused opposition from some quarters, as did its principles of educational rights. The Veterans of Foreign Wars, meeting in Los Angeles in 1952, adopted a resolution denouncing Unesco, and demanded that "its study program" be abolished in American schools, since it advocated world citizenship and was a threat to national sovereignty.[97] The Daughters of the American Revolution have opposed both Unesco and the United Nations. Some local school authorities (*e.g.* Houston, Texas, and Los Angeles authorities), under pressure from local

[96] Washington, D.C.: U.S. Government Printing Office, 1949, p. 39.

[97] "Unesco Plan Hit by VFW," *The Evening Bulletin* [Philadelphia] (Aug. 8, 1952), p. 3.

groups, banned participation by their schools in Unesco educational activities on the grounds that it was an atheistic, communistic and subversive agency.[98] The Archbishop of Philadelphia described the United Nations' doctrine of human rights as "godless" since it did not recognize the divine origin of human rights.[99]

The attacks upon Unesco and, indirectly, upon the United Nations organization led President Eisenhower to appoint a committee to investigate the charges. In 1953, that committee reported its findings which exonerated Unesco from all charges directed against it, and listed the many advantages accruing to the United States from participation in its activities.[100] By 1958 the storm against the United Nations and Unesco seemed to have somewhat subsided. It has survived the criticisms, and the United States continues to contribute some $3,000,000 annually to Unesco's support.

Abolishing illiteracy, the primary goal of Unesco, is an almost impossible undertaking. There are still primitive tribes which consider literacy an evil, and resist the "benefits" of civilization. In countries such as India, the school cannot keep pace with the rise in population, and the percentage of illiterates has not been decreasing. In itself, illiteracy is no great evil where it is the rule, and highly literate societies have often been the most beastly ones. Illiteracy, however, has usually been accompanied by disease, hunger, superstition, primitive modes of housing and agriculture and, often, by brutish indifference to human suffering. Unesco is an expression of the belief that the advanced, technological nations should not isolate themselves from less fortunate peoples, and should be generous in their efforts to aid them. Its motives are not purely humanitarian. Prosperity is becoming indivisible, and the welfare of advanced nations depends to a large degree upon the prosperity of all peoples. In an interdependent world of nations, the elevation of one means the elevation of all.

The free flow of ideas between different cultures cannot quickly produce the desired result, since ideas are interpreted in terms of existing cultural assumptions. Where, for instance, forced labor is a normal social condition, the idea of its immorality cannot be understood. Primitives may accept the scientific explanation of rain, but they continue to give the magician credit for deciding when and where it should fall. Indeed, the educational problem of

98 B. Fine, "Pressure Groups Prodding Schools to End Study of U.N.," *The New York Times* (June 29, 1952), p. 27.

99 "Archbishop Assails 'Human Rights' UN Plan," *The Evening Bulletin* [Philadelphia], Feb. 14, 1952.

100 *N.E.A. Journal* (Nov. 1953), pp. 467–68; K. McLaughlin, "Women Answering Anti-U.N. Campaign," *The New York Times* (April 5, 1953), p. 14.

Unesco often involves a complete reconstruction of knowledge and a substitution of science for superstition. The triumph of its aims in many areas of the world lies in a distant future. It will take the "lost tribes" of New Guinea a long time to complete the journey from primitive ways to "high civilization."

Socrates' faith in education, shared by many since his time, finds expression today in the aims and work of Unesco.

Selected Readings

American Council on Education. *American Junior Colleges.* Washington, D.C.: American Council on Education, 1948.

———. *Universities of the World outside U.S.A.* Washington, D.C.: American Council on Education, 1950.

Barker, R., ed. *The Education Act, 1944.* London: Chas. Knight and Co., 1944.

Bestor, A. E. *Educational Wastelands.* Urbana, Ill.: University of Illinois Press, 1953.

Brogan, D. W. *French Personalities and Problems.* New York: Alfred A. Knopf, Inc., 1947.

Brown, F. J., ed. *Selected Issues in Education.* Washington, D.C.: American Council on Education, 1947.

Childs, J. L. *Education and Morals.* New York: Appleton-Century-Crofts, Inc., 1950.

———. *Education and the Philosophy of Experimentalism.* New York: Appleton-Century-Crofts, Inc., 1931.

Committee on Religion and Education. *The Relation of Religion to Public Education.* Washington, D.C.: American Council on Education, 1947.

Conant, J. B. *The American High School.* New York: McGraw-Hill Book Co., Inc., 1959.

Counts, G. S. *I Want to Be Like Stalin.* New York: John Day Company, Inc., 1947.

Counts, G. S., and Lodge, N. *The Country of the Blind.* Boston: Houghton Mifflin Co., 1949.

Curtis, S. J. *Education in Great Britain since 1900.* London: A. Dakers, 1952.

Debiesse, J. *Compulsory Education in France.* Paris: Unesco, 1951.

Floud, J. E., Halsey, A. H., and Martin, F. M. *Social Class and Educational Opportunity.* London: William Heinemann, Ltd., 1957.

Henry, N. R., ed. *American Education in the Postwar Period.* 44th Yearbook, Part I, of National Society for the Study of Education. Chicago: University of Chicago Press, 1945.

———. *Modern Philosophies and Education.* 54th Yearbook of National Society for the Study of Education. Chicago: University of Chicago Press, 1955.

Johnson, W. H. E. *Russia's Educational Heritage.* Pittsburgh: Carnegie Press, 1950.

Kilpatrick, W. H., *et al. The Educational Frontier.* New York: Appleton-Century-Crofts, Inc., 1933.

Kline, G. L., ed. *Soviet Education.* New York: Columbia University Press, 1957.

Kneller, G. F. *The Educational Philosophy of National Socialism.* New Haven: Yale University Press, 1941.

Korol, A. G. *Soviet Education for Science and Technology.* New York: John Wiley & Sons, Inc., 1957.

Kulski, W. W. *The Soviet Regime.* Syracuse, N.Y.: Syracuse University Press, 1954.

LOWNDES, G. A. N. *The British Educational System.* New York: Rinehart and Company, Inc., 1955.
MCWILLIAMS, C. *Witch Hunt: The Revival of Heresy.* Boston: Little, Brown and Co., 1951.
MANN, E. *School for Barbarians.* London: Lindsay Drummond, Ltd., 1939.
MOEHLMAN, C. H. *School and Church: The American Way.* New York: Harper & Bros., 1944.
———. *The Wall of Separation between Church and State.* Boston: Beacon Press, Inc., 1951.
OGILVIE, V. *The English Public School.* New York: The Macmillan Co., 1957.
PRESIDENT'S, THE, COMMITTEE ON EDUCATION BEYOND THE HIGH SCHOOL. *Second Report to the President.* Washington, D.C.: Government Printing Office, 1957.
SCOTT, J. F. *Menace of Nationalism in Education.* New York: The Macmillan Co., 1926.
SHANNON, G. P., ed. *Academic Freedom and Tenure.* American Association of University Professors, Bulletin 44, March 1958. Washington, D.C.: The Association.
SMITH, W. O. L. *Education in Great Britain.* 2d ed.; London: Oxford University Press, 1956.
UNESCO. *Compulsory Education and Its Prolongation.* Geneva: International Bureau of Education, 1951.
U.S. OFFICE OF EDUCATION. *Education in the USSR.* Washington, D.C.: Government Printing Office, 1957.
WENKE, H. *Education in Western Germany.* Washington, D.C.: Library of Congress, 1953.
WOODRING, P. *A Fourth of a Nation.* New York: McGraw-Hill Book Co., Inc., 1957.
WOODY, T. *New Minds: New Men?* New York: The Macmillan Co., 1932.
WYLIE, L. *Village in the Vaucluse.* Cambridge, Mass.: Harvard University Press, 1957.
ZIRKLE, C., ed. *Death of a Science in Russia.* Philadelphia: University of Pennsylvania Press, 1949.

Index